AMERICA'S BEST RESTAURANTS

Bon Appétit Magazine's Guide to

AMERICA'S BEST RESTAURANTS

A Readers' Choice selection of where to eat in the nation's 25 most visited cities.

Edited by
Susan Fisher

Wilshire Marketing Corporation
Raymond E. Hebert, *President and Publisher*

647.9573
B697

Designer Karen McBride
Production Coordinator Karen Hebert
Cover Design Philip Kaplan,
Executive Graphics Director, Bon Appétit Magazine

Copyright © 1981 by WILSHIRE MARKETING CORPORATION
a subsidiary of Knapp Communications Corporation
5900 Wilshire Blvd., Los Angeles, CA 90036

BON APPETIT® IS THE REGISTERED TRADEMARK OF
BON APPETIT PUBLISHING CORPORATION

ISBN #0-89535-016-5

CONTENTS

Introduction .... *vii*
How to Use The Guide .... *ix*
Restaurant Listings:
    Atlanta *1*
    Baltimore *15*
    Boston *29*
    Chicago *47*
    Cleveland *69*
    Dallas/Fort Worth *83*
    Denver *97*
    Detroit *109*
    Honolulu *123*
    Houston *137*
    Kansas City *149*
    Las Vegas *163*
    Los Angeles *173*
        Palm Springs *214*
    Miami *217*
    Minneapolis/St. Paul *229*
    New Orleans *243*
    New York *259*
    Philadelphia *301*
    Phoenix *315*
    Pittsburgh *327*
    St. Louis *339*
    San Diego *351*
    San Francisco *367*
    Seattle *393*
    Washington, D.C. *407*
Diner's Dictionary *423*
Wine *443*
Index *449*
Best of the Best *450*

INTRODUCTION

Our readers inspired us to develop this guide. They've always taken such an active interest in the recipes and articles we feature, often submitting ideas and suggestions of their own.

Their interest, information and enthusiasm for great food, both in and out of the home, gave us the idea for a new kind of restaurant guide, one that our readers would help us create. They would rate some of the outstanding restaurants in the nation's 25 most visited cities.

We know that BON APPETIT readers are people who have traveled, seen and sampled the best this country has to offer in the way of wonderful food in marvelous restaurants. Their informed body of opinion is valuable and is what makes this book unique.

We asked readers in each of the 25 cities (more than 5,000 people in all) to fill out questionnaires in which they rated a wide variety of restaurants for quality of food, service, ambience, wine selection and value.

The results were tabulated, and restaurants with high ratings in all categories were selected for this guide. We then went to work refining, editing and verifying information with the restaurateurs, until we arrived at the present listing — alphabetized by city, with easy-to-spot reader ratings and type of cuisine noted for each entry. The information you really need to know about each restaurant is there, including hours open, credit cards accepted, parking facilities, whether or not reservations are needed and dress restrictions. We also include a detailed description of some of the house specialties and give you a general idea of what each restaurant has to offer in terms of atmosphere and decor.

We think you'll find BON APPETIT'S GUIDE TO AMERICA'S BEST RESTAURANTS to be an ideal traveling companion. It's easy to use, informative and selective in its choice of some of the very finest restaurants in each city (though not always the most expensive). We've also included convenient city maps, with approximate restaurant locations noted by number, to help you find your way to the restaurant of your choice.

We hope you'll find this guide not only practical for business and pleasure travel, but also fun for rediscovering the dining pleasures in your own hometown.

We have tried to create a guide that is as accurate as possible. However, the restaurant business is always changing. New restaurants may open while others may close, with some coming under new ownership at any time. Restaurants that were closed on Sunday may now be open then and closed on Monday, while that special menu item you were looking for may no longer be available. It is also possible that we may have unintentionally overlooked some very worthy restaurants, notably those that have opened only recently.

As we go to press, these and a number of similar developments may have just occurred or may be about to occur. Unfortunately, we cannot accept responsibility for these sudden changes after publication. However, if they happen, we apologize and pledge to catch up with them in future editions.

We would like to hear from you regarding any comments or omissions that we may have overlooked. Please send your additions and suggestions to Raymond E. Hebert, Publisher, Wilshire Marketing Corporation, 5900 Wilshire Boulevard, Los Angeles, California 90036.

Now more than 900 restaurants from Boston to San Diego, Minneapolis to New Orleans, Miami to Seattle, await your visit. BON APPETIT!

Raymond E. Hebert — Publisher
Susan Fisher — Book Editor

HOW TO USE THE GUIDE

BON APPETIT'S GUIDE TO AMERICA'S BEST RESTAURANTS is easy to use. Here's how it works. Our readers rated each restaurant in five areas: quality of food, service, ambience, wine list and average price per entrée.

They then rated the first four areas as either excellent, good, fair or poor. Average price per entrée was broken down into very expensive, expensive, moderate and inexpensive. By tabulating reader response to each area in each category, we were able to come up with ratings for each restaurant.

Thus, four symbols stand for excellent; three, good; two, fair; and one, poor. As for price, four dollar symbols mean very expensive; three, expensive; two, moderate; and one, inexpensive.

RATINGS

⚓ Indicates ambience — the design, style, "atmosphere" of a restaurant.

🎩 Indicates overall quality of service.

🍽 Indicates quality of food.

🍷 Indicates wine selection — its quantity, quality and availability.

$ Indicates price of an average entrée, excluding tax, tips and wine or spirits. An individual entrée under $5 would be considered "inexpensive," under $10 "moderate," over $10 "expensive," and over $20 "very expensive."

MAP LOCATION

The circled number following the name of each restaurant corresponds to the number circled on the city map. The maps are divided roughly into quadrants with restaurants numbered consecutively by location.

CREDIT CARDS
AE American Express
D Diners Club
MC MasterCard
V Visa
CB Carte Blanche

ATLANTA

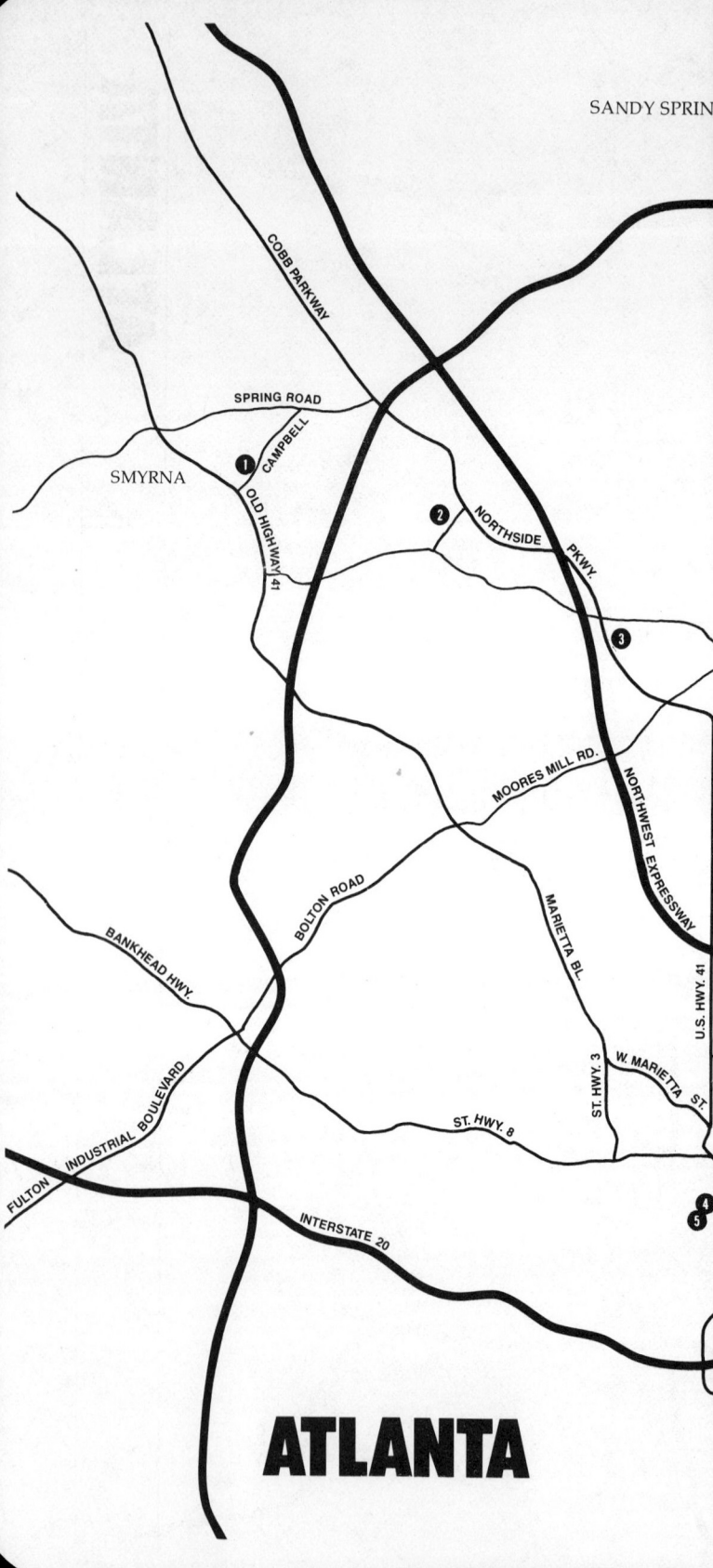

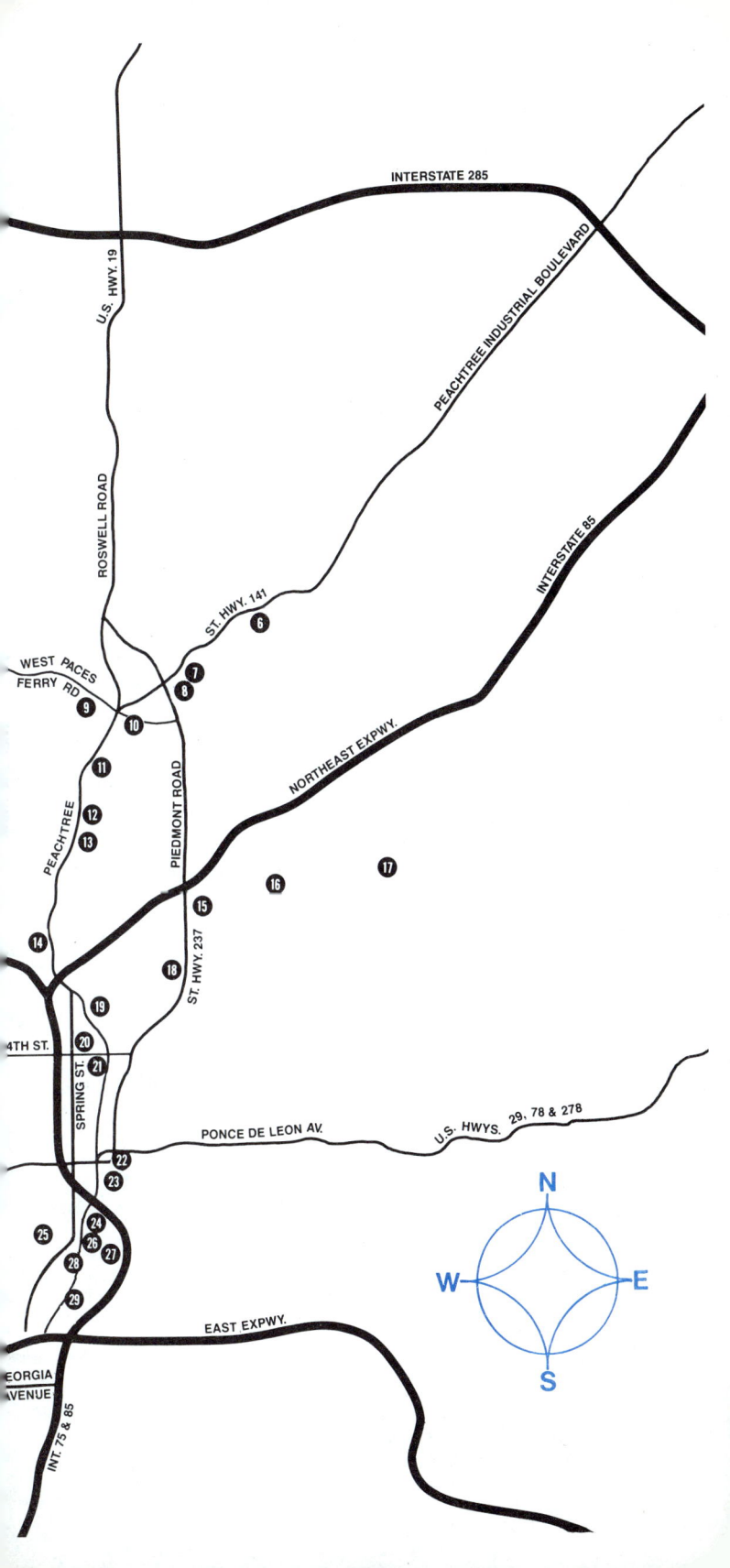

THE ABBEY ㉒   *Continental*

163 Ponce de Leon Ave.
Atlanta
(404) 876-8831
Maître d': George A. Gore (manager)
Full Bar/Valet Parking
AE, D, MC, V, CB
Jacket for men
No jeans

The Abbey, appropriately enough, is located in a former Methodist church. And, in an ecumenical gesture, waiters are dressed in monks' robes. The menu offers such out-of-the-ordinary entrées as roast goose, venison and pheasant. You may dine either in the Wine Cellar or, if you feel pure enough of heart, in The Sanctuary.

Reservations suggested
Dinner: Daily, 6 P.M. – 11 P.M.

ANTHONY'S ⑧   *Continental*

3109 Piedmont Rd. N.E.
Atlanta
(404) 262-7379
Maître d': Jerry Bures
Full Bar/Valet Parking
AE, D, MC, V, CB
Jacket for men

It seems that more and more enterprising restaurateurs are turning historic homes into historic restaurants. Such is the case with Anthony's, a 1797 plantation home, carefully restored and decorated. The plantation fare ranges from Maine lobster to quail to frogs' legs to prime steaks. Private party rooms accommodate groups of 20 to 500.

Reservations required
Dinner: Mon. – Fri., 5 P.M. – 11 P.M.
*   Sat., 5 P.M. – Midnight*
*   Closed Sunday*

AUNT FANNY'S CABIN ❶   *Southern*

2155 Campbell Rd.
Smyrna, Ga.
(404) 436-5218
Full Bar/Valet Parking
AE, D, MC, V, CB
No dress restrictions

You might expect to find traditional Southern fried chicken at a place called Aunt Fanny's Cabin and you needn't be disappointed. You'll also find Smithfield Country Ham, fresh rainbow trout, home-cooked vegetables—such as baked squash and turnip greens—rice and gravy, cornbread and, if you're *still* hungry, peach cobbler for dessert.

No reservations required
Dinner: Mon. – Fri., 6 P.M. – 10 P.M.
*   Sat., 6 P.M. – 10:30 P.M.*
*   Sun., 1 P.M. – 10 P.M.*

THE BRASS KEY ⑫   *International*

2355 Peachtree Rd. N.E.
Atlanta
(404) 233-3202
Maître d': Penny Dolan
Full Bar/Lot Parking
AE, D, MC, V, CB
No dress restrictions

The Brass Key offers a varied selection of international cuisine. The aim is to appeal to "those of sophisticated dining taste who genuinely appreciate superior food and atmosphere." Specialties include rack of lamb, Mongolian style, with apricot-teriyaki sauce and Honey-Glazed Peking Duck, flamed at your table.

Reservations requested
Lunch: Mon.–Fri., 11:30 A.M.–2:30 P.M.
Dinner: Mon.–Sat., 6 P.M.–11 P.M.
      Closed Sunday

BRENNAN'S OF BUCKHEAD ⑨   *Creole*

103 W. Paces Ferry Rd. N.W.
Atlanta
(404) 261-7913
Maître d': Frank Antunovich
Full Bar/Valet Parking
AE, D, MC, V, CB
Jacket for men preferred

You'll find all the Brennan favorites here—the New Orleans Creole specialties, interesting egg dishes, fresh fish and prime beef. Flourishes include flaming desserts prepared at your table and one-of-a-kind breakfasts that have long been associated with the name Brennan's. "Come let us splurge you," is their motto.

Reservations suggested
Breakfast/Lunch: Mon.–Fri., 9 A.M.–2 P.M.
                  Sat.–Sun., 9 A.M.–3 P.M.
Dinner: *Daily, 6:30 P.M.–10 P.M.*

BUGATTI ④   *Northern Italian*

Omni International Hotel
Marietta and Techwood Drive
Atlanta
(404) 659-0000, Ext. 7209
Maître d': Tino Venturi (manager)
Full Bar/Valet Parking
AE, D, MC, V, CB
Jacket for men

Here is a haven for traditional Northern Italian cuisine right in the heart of the South. Look for such specialties as Zuppa di Pesce (seafood casserole) and Vitello con Funghi (veal cooked in a delicate lemon butter sauce and topped with fresh sauteed mushrooms) Bugatti also features prime rib and a selection of fresh fish.

Reservations required
Lunch: Daily, Noon–2:30 P.M.
Dinner: Daily, 6 P.M.–11 P.M.

COACH & SIX ⑭   *American*

1776 Peachtree Rd.
Atlanta
(404) 872-6666
Maître d': John Wadsworth
Full Bar/Valet Parking
AE, D, MC, V, CB
Jacket for men

An "Old English" atmosphere pervades Coach & Six, enriched by fine oil paintings and enhanced by candlelight. It is a place for "thick and juicy" steaks, triple-cut loin lamb chops, Maine lobster and Florida stone crabs. All baking is done on the premises.

Reservations required
Lunch: Mon.-Fri., 11:30 A.M.-2:30 P.M.
Dinner: Sun.-Fri., 6 P.M.-11 P.M.
       Sat., 6 P.M.-Midnight

THE COUNTRY PLACE ⑳   *French*

Colony Square
1197 Peachtree St.
Atlanta
(404) 881-0144
Maître d': Bob Amick (manager)
Full Bar/Lot Parking
AE, D, MC, V
No dress restrictions

The Country Place, located on the mall at Colony Square, is a "visual delight" according to the management. A Mediterranean feeling pervades this spacious restaurant. The house specialty is The Country Place Steak, a 12-ounce New York strip steak marinated in soy sauce and rolled in a blend of herbs. It is broiled to order.

No reservations required
Lunch: Sun.-Fri., 11 A.M.-2:30 P.M.
Dinner: Sun.-Fri., 5:30 P.M.-Midnight
       Sat., 5:30 P.M.-1:30 A.M.

DIPLOMAT ㉕   *Continental*

230 Spring St. N.W.
Atlanta
(404) 525-6375
Maître d': Arturo Santos
Full Bar/Valet Parking
AE, D, MC, V, CB
No dress restrictions

The Diplomat boasts a 62-item menu that includes prime steaks, prime rib, lamb chops, shellfish, red snapper and veal specialties. There is an orchestra in the lounge for evening dancing.

Reservations required
Lunch/Dinner: Mon.-Sat.
              Closed Sunday

THE FRENCH RESTAURANT ❺   *French*

Omni International Hotel
Marietta and Techwood Drive
Atlanta
(404) 659-0000, Ext. 7222
Maître d': Francis Labaillif
Full Bar/Valet Parking
AE, D, MC, V, CB
Jacket, tie for men
No jeans

Imagine yourself on the Riviera dining amid lush foliage on a secluded garden terrace. That is The French Restaurant's message to its patrons. Classic French cuisine is the basis for an ever-changing menu of one-of-a-kind specialties.

Reservations required
Dinner: Mon. – Sat., 6 P.M. – 11 P.M.
    Closed Sunday

GENE & GABE'S ⓲   *Northern Italian*

1578 Piedmont Ave. N.E.
Atlanta
(404) 874-6145
Maître d': Gene Dale (owner)
Full Bar/Lot and Street Parking
AE, D, MC, V, CB
Good taste in dress required

Gene & Gabe's specializes in milk-fed veal and fresh seafood dishes. Pasta is prepared on the premises. A different special is featured every day. The surroundings are cozy and comfortable.

Reservations required
Dinner: Daily, 6 P.M. – 2 A.M.

HAL'S MID-MEDITERRANEAN ⓳   *Hungarian*

375 Pharr Rd.
Atlanta
(404) 262-2811
Full Bar/Lot Parking
AE, MC, V
No dress restrictions

"This tiny, mirror-walled white-linened room is the home of some of Georgia's most inventive food," states co-owner Barry Donovan. The person responsible for all this inventiveness in the kitchen is Donovan's partner, Ron Cohn. Hungarian ingredients and recipes predominate, but there are also Greek and French selections.

Reservations required
Dinner: Tues. – Thurs., 6 P.M. – 10 P.M.
    Fri. – Sat., 6 P.M. – 11 P.M.
    Closed Sunday

HUGO'S ㉙   *Continental*

Hyatt Regency Atlanta
265 Peachtree St. N.E.
Atlanta
(404) 577-1234
Full Bar/Lot Parking
AE, D, MC, V, CB
Jacket for men; no jeans

Hugo's promises — and delivers — an atmosphere of elegance. Candlelight and harp music add to the dining experience. Specialties include Sweetbreads Financière, medallions of veal, Veal Oskar and a very complete wine list.

Reservations suggested
Dinner: Sun.-Thurs., 6 P.M.-10:30 P.M.
        Fri.-Sat., 6 P.M.-11:30 P.M.

JOE DALE'S CAJUN HOUSE ⑦   *Cajun*

3209 Maple Dr. N.E.
Atlanta
(404) 621-2741
Full Bar/Lot Parking
AE, D, MC, V, CB
No dress restrictions

Joe Dale's means informal, casual dining in a setting of antique toys, part of the owner's personal collection. The New Orleans-style menu emphasizes fresh oysters, shrimp and fish, all prepared to order. The foods are all well seasoned in that unique Cajun way.

No reservations required
Lunch/Dinner: Mon.-Fri., 11:30 A.M.-11 P.M.
                Sat., 5:30 P.M.-11 P.M.
                Closed Sunday

LA GROTTA ⑪   *Northern Italian*

2637 Peachtree Rd. N.E.
Atlanta
(404) 231-1368
Maître d': Sergio Favalli (owner)
Full Bar/Valet Parking
AE, D, MC, V, CB
Jacket, tie for men requested

Owner Sergio Favalli presents the classic cuisine of Northern Italy amid a rustic, candlelit setting. There is a terrace garden for outdoor dining. House specialties include homemade pastas, Veal Scaloppine, Filet of Beef Michelangelo, carpaccio, Zuppa Inglese and zabaglione.

Reservations required
Dinner: Tues.-Sat., 6 P.M.-10 P.M.
        Closed Sunday, Monday

McKINNON'S LOUISIANE ⓰ Creole

2100 Cheshire Bridge Rd.
Atlanta
(404) 325-4141
Maître d': Billy McKinnon (owner)
Full Bar/Lot Parking
AE, MC, V
No dress restrictions

Owner Wiliam B. "Billy" McKinnon serves up fresh seafood prepared New Orleans Creole style. He also promises to personally assist first-timers in menu selection. Tuxedoed waiters will serve you creations starring fresh fish, crab meat and oysters.

Reservations suggested
Dinner: Mon. – Sat., 6 P.M. – 10 P.M.
Closed Sunday

THE MIDNIGHT SUN ㉖ Scandinavian

Peachtree Center
225 Peachtree St. N.E.
Atlanta
(404) 577-5050
Maître d': Georg Schwedler
Full Bar/Lot Parking
AE, D, MC, V, CB
Jacket for men

Scandinavian specialties are served to the strains of strolling violinists. There is a prix fixe menu that includes wine, and features such specialties as a smörgåsbord for two and classic Continental dishes. The decor in this downtown area restaurant is contemporary Scandinavian, of course.

Reservations requested
Lunch: Mon. – Fri., 11:30 A.M. – 2:30 P.M.
Dinner: Daily, 6 P.M. – 11 P.M.
Brunch: Sun., 11:30 A.M. – 2:30 P.M.

NAKATO ⓯ Japanese

1893 Piedmont Rd.
Atlanta
(404) 873-6582
Maître d': Shotaro Yano
Full Bar/Valet Parking
AE, D, MC, V, CB
No dress restrictions

Most of the traditional dishes of Japan are offered at Nakato. The list includes tempura, sukiyaki, shabu-shabu, sushi, sashimi, teppanyaki and special full course dinners. There is a separate Sushi Bar apart from the main Tatami Room.

No reservations required
Dinner: Mon. – Thurs., 5:30 P.M. – 10:30 P.M.
Fri. – Sat., 5:30 P.M. – 11:30 P.M.
Sun., 5 P.M. – 10 P.M.

NIKOLAI'S ROOF ㉔   French/Russian

Atlanta Hilton Hotel
Courtland & Harris Sts. N.E.
Atlanta
(404) 659-2000
Full Bar/Valet and Lot Parking
AE, D, MC, V, CB
Jacket, tie for men

The Russian czars delighted in affecting the ways of the French court and then doing them one better. Such is the case with Nikolai's and its classical French cuisine served amid czarist trappings. There are five-course prix fixe dinners that may include fresh poached salmon in pastry, Tournedos Esterhazy, Veal Marengo or Canard au Muscadet.

Reservations required
Dinner: Daily, 7:15 P.M.–11:15 P.M.

OLD VININGS INN ❷   Continental

3020 Paces Mill Rd.
Vinings, Ga.
(404) 434-5270
Maître d': Yvette Greune (owner)
Full Bar/Lot Parking
No credit cards
Good taste in dress required

This 90-year-old country inn has been cheerfully refurbished and now offers dining on the plant-filled enclosed porch or outside in the summer months. There is a choice of six appetizers and six main courses every night. Desserts are all homemade.

Reservations required
Lunch: Tues.–Sat., 11:30 A.M.–3 P.M.
Dinner: Tues.–Sat., 6 P.M.–10 P.M.
    Closed Sunday, Monday

PANO'S & PAUL'S ❸   Continental

1232 W. Paces Ferry Rd.
Atlanta
(404) 261-4739
Maître d': Daniel Senne
Full Bar/Lot Parking
AE, D, MC, V, CB
Jacket for men

Pano's & Paul's lets you dine in Victorian splendor. The standards have traditionally been high at this Atlanta restaurant and the service friendly.

Reservations required
Dinner: Mon.–Sat., 6 P.M.–10:30 P.M.
    Closed Sunday

THE PEASANT UPTOWN ❻   *French*

Phipps Plaza
3500 Peachtree Rd.
Atlanta
(404) 261-6341
Maître d': Barbara Van (manager)
Full Bar/Lot Parking
AE, D, MC, V
No dress restrictions

You'll sit in an elegant garden that may remind you of old New Orleans. The center of attention is a 100-foot-high greenhouse filled with antiques. The house specialty is Steak au Poivre, a 12-ounce New York strip steak marinated in a mustard sauce, with cracked peppercorns.

No reservations required
Lunch: Sun.-Fri., 11 A.M.-3 P.M.
      Sat., 11 A.M.-3:30 P.M.
Dinner: Sun.-Thurs., 5:30 P.M.-11 P.M.
      Fri.-Sat., 5:30 P.M.-Midnight

PETITE AUBERGE ⓱   *French*

2935 N. Druid Hills Rd.
Atlanta
(404) 634-6268
Full Bar/Lot Parking
AE, D, MC, V, CB
Jacket for men

"The European chefs of the Petite Auberge prepare classic French dishes, served with flair, in the comfortable elegance of quietly understated dining rooms." Such is owner Helmut Bittl's assessment of Petite Auberge. Specialties include Fillet of Trout Admiral, Beef Wellington, Strawberries Romanoff, Baked Alaska and various soufflés.

Reservations suggested
Lunch: Mon.-Fri., 11:30 A.M.-2:30 P.M.
Dinner: Mon.-Sat., 6 P.M.-11 P.M.
      Closed Sunday

PITTYPAT'S PORCH ㉗   *Southern*

25 International Blvd. N.W.
Atlanta
(404) 262-7379
Maître d': Gallo Moya
Full Bar/Lot Parking
AE, D, MC, V, CB
No dress restrictions

Remember dear, sweet, old Aunt Pittypat from *Gone With The Wind?* Well she would feel right at home in this re-creation of an antebellum plantation home. Sip a cool mint julep before feasting on traditional Southern specialties. There is also an appetizer buffet and salad bar featuring 30 different items, including fresh shrimp and oysters.

No reservations required
Dinner: Mon.-Sat., 4 P.M.-Midnight
      Closed Sunday

PLEASANT PEASANT ㉓ — *French*

555 Peachtree St. N.E.
Atlanta
(404) 874-3223
Maître d': David Douglass (manager)
Full Bar/Lot Parking
AE, D, MC, V
No dress restrictions

Located in a building which first housed a Victorian ice cream parlor, The Pleasant Peasant now bills itself as a country French cafe. Embellishments include lots of plants, antiques and brassware. They play supporting roles to such specialties as oyster gumbo, pâtés, Scallops Parisienne and Steak au Poivre.

No reservations required
Dinner: Sun.-Thurs., 5:30 P.M.-Midnight
  Fri.-Sat., 5:30 P.M.-1 A.M.

RUE DE PARIS ⑩ — *French*

315 E. Paces Ferry Rd. N.E.
Atlanta
(404) 261-9600
Maître d': Yves Durand (owner)
Full Bar/Lot Parking
AE, D, MC, V, CB
Jacket for men

Despite its name, a country inn theme prevails at Rue de Paris. Special care is taken with table settings and presentation, and owner Yves Durand points to his wine list with considerable pride. Entrées include selections of beef, veal, lamb, fish and poultry. Many meals are prepared tableside.

Reservations required
Dinner: Mon.-Sat., 6 P.M.-Midnight
  Sun., 6 P.M.-11 P.M.

SUN DIAL ㉘ — *Continental*

Peachtree Plaza Hotel
Peachtree at International Blvd. N.W.
Atlanta
(404) 659-1400
Maître d': Elio Espinal
Full Bar/Valet Parking
AE, D, MC, V, CBX
Good taste in dress required

This revolving tri-level restaurant atop the world's tallest hotel offers a variety of dinner specialties. There are such items as Shrimp Provençale, Veal Cordon Bleu, filet mignon and lobster. Freshly baked desserts include Key Lime Pie and strawberry cheesecake.

Reservations required
Lunch: Mon.-Fri., 11:30 A.M.-2:30 P.M.
Dinner: Daily, 6 P.M.-11:30 P.M.
Brunch: Sat.-Sun., 10:30 A.M.-3:30 P.M.

TOULOUSE ㉑ French

14th & Peachtree Rd. N.E.
Atlanta
(404) 892-7911
Maître d': George Pic (manager)
Full Bar/Valet and Lot Parking
AE, D, MC, V, CB
Jacket, tie for men

Located in the downtown area, Toulouse offers French cuisine in richly elegant surroundings. A prix fixe menu is complemented by a substantial wine list and meticulous service and presentation.

Reservations required
Dinner: Mon.–Sat., 6:30 P.M.–11 P.M.
 Closed Sunday

VITTORIO'S ⓭ Italian/American

2263 Peachtree Rd. N.E.
Atlanta
(404) 355-0874
Maître d': Georgia Hill
Full Bar/Valet Parking
AE, D, MC, V, CB
Jacket for men preferred

"Vittorio's is a friendly restaurant that maintains a high quality of food and service," maintains its owner Victor J. Impeciato. The wide-ranging menu includes veal, pasta, chicken, seafood and a selection of steaks.

No reservations required
Dinner: Mon.–Sat., 5 P.M.–1 A.M.
 Closed Sunday

BALTIMORE

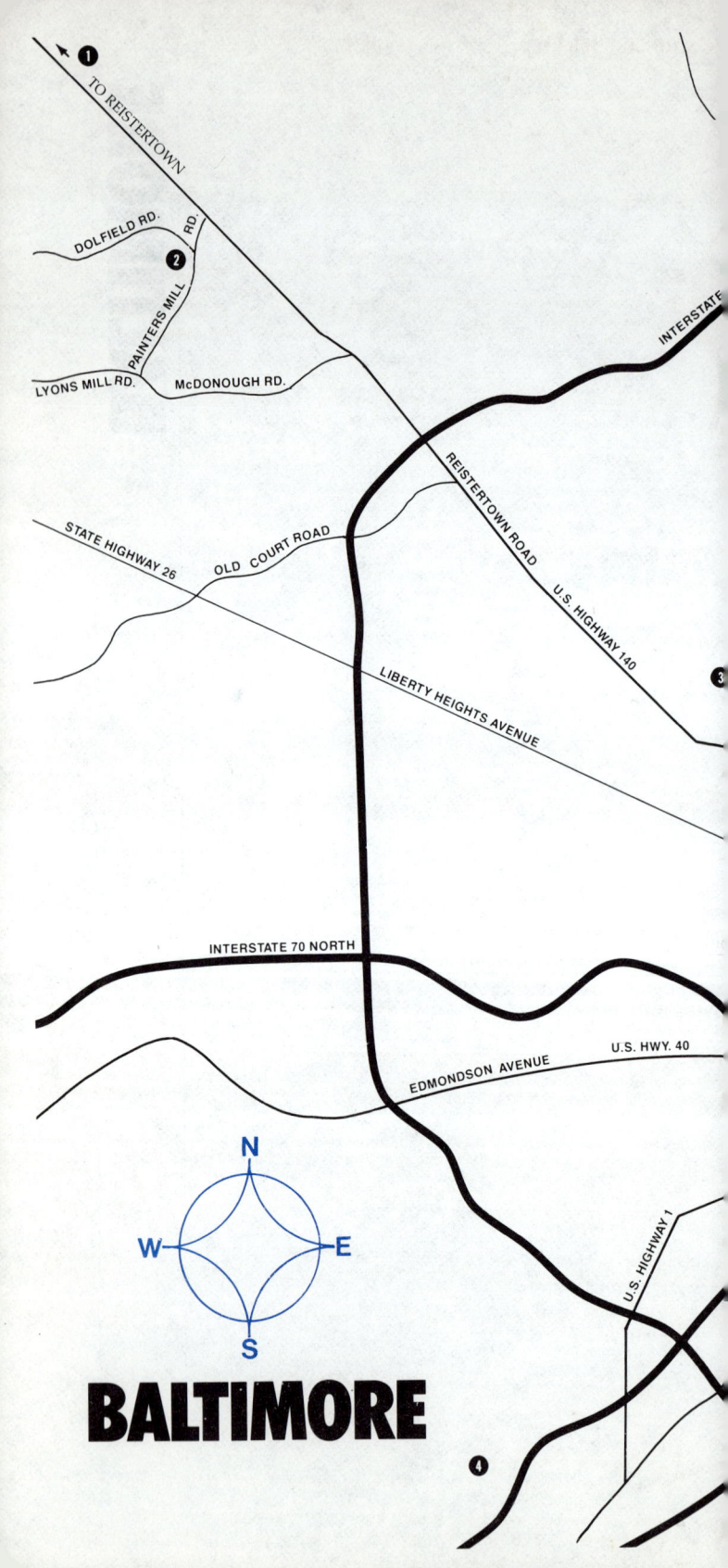

THE ATHENIAN ㉗   *Greek*

4700 Eastern Ave.
Baltimore
(301) 732-7881
Maître d': Spyros M. Stavrakas (owner)
Full Bar/Lot and Street Parking
MC, V
No dress restrictions

Owner Spyros M. Stavrakas says he serves "typical Greek cuisine of the Athenian variety." This doesn't mean there aren't special touches such as his unique shrimp entrée, roast lamb wrapped in a pastry leaf and homemade Greek bread. A good city for this type of cuisine.

Reservations required
Lunch/Dinner: Tues.–Sun., Noon–10:30 P.M.
Closed Monday

BAMBOO HOUSE ❻   *Chinese*

26 Yorktown Plaza Shopping Center
Cockeysville, Md.
(301) 666-9550
Maître d': Joey Chiu
Full Bar/Lot Parking
AE, MC, V
Jacket for men

Of Oriental design and filled with bamboo, the Bamboo House focuses on hot and spicy food — Szechuan style. A menu highlight is Peking Duck.

Reservations required
Lunch: Sun.–Fri., 11:30 A.M.–3 P.M.
Dinner: Sun.–Thurs., 5 P.M.–11 P.M.
Fri.–Sat., 5 P.M.–1 A.M.

THE BRASS ELEPHANT ⓱   *Northern Italian*

924 N. Charles St.
Baltimore
(301) 547-8480
Maître d': Jon Ritter (manager), Richard Davis
Full Bar/Lot Parking
MC, V
Good taste in dress required

The present Brass Elephant dining rooms were created from the small rooms used to display furniture when the restaurant building served as home and showroom for a family who made furniture. You'll still see a considerable amount of handcarved woodwork and other handcrafted items. Northern Italian cuisine, complemented by a variety of white sauces, is the specialty.

Reservations recommended
Lunch: Mon.–Fri., 11:30 A.M.–2 P.M.
Dinner: Mon.–Thurs., 5:30 P.M.–9 P.M.
Fri., 5:30 P.M.–10 P.M.
Sat., 5:30 P.M.–10:30 P.M.
Sun., 5 P.M.–8:30 P.M.

CAFE DES ARTISTES ㉑ French

9 Hopkins Plaza
Baltimore
(301) 837-6600
Maître d': Dominique and Kathy
Full Bar/Valet and Lot Parking
AE, MC, V
Jacket, tie for men requested

Range and variety are the order here with a menu featuring more than 25 entrées, plus daily specials and a wine cellar of 150 labels. There is duck pâté with hazelnuts and trout with a salmon mousse stuffing served with lobster sauce. There's also nightly entertainment in the Brasserie lounge.

Reservations required
Lunch: Mon.-Fri., 11:30 A.M.-2:30 P.M.
Dinner: Mon.-Thurs., 5:30 P.M.-10 P.M.
  Fri.-Sat., 5:30 P.M.-11: P.M.
  Closed Sunday

CAPRICCIO ㉔ Northern Italian

242 S. High St.
Baltimore
(301) 685-2710
Maître d': Bruno Vigo (owner)
Full Bar/Street Parking
AE, D, MC, V
No dress restrictions

Capriccio chef and co-owner Giovanni Rigato claims his is the only Northern Italian restaurant in the area. Nestled in downtown Baltimore's "Little Italy" section, Capriccio features Rigatoni Vodka, Veal Chop Valdostana, Chicken Gismonda, Steak "Cafe de Paris" and homemade pasta. Co-owner Bruno Vigo keeps a watchful eye on service.

Reservations required
Lunch: Mon.-Fri., 11:30 A.M.-2:30 P.M.
Dinner: Mon.-Thurs., 5 P.M.-11 P.M.
  Fri.-Sat., 5 P.M.-1 A.M.
  Sun., 3 P.M.-11 P.M.

THE CHESAPEAKE ⑫ American

1701 N. Charles St.
Baltimore
(301) 837-7711
Maître d': Isadore Friedman
Full Bar/Valet Parking
AE, D, MC, V, CB
Jacket for men preferred

The Chesapeake has been serving thick steaks, prime rib and the best of Maryland's seafood since 1904. These specialties, plus a distinctive Caesar salad, are served in an atmosphere that is "handsome, but unpretentious," according to owner Richard Friedman. There is a private dining room as well as a courtesy bus for transport to evening events.

Reservations required
Lunch/Dinner: Mon.-Fri., Noon-10 P.M.
  Sat., 5 P.M.-Midnight
  Sun., 5 P.M.-10 P.M.

CHIAPPARELLI'S ㉒ *Italian*

237 S. High St.
Baltimore
(301) 837-0309
Maître d': Buddy Chiapparelli
Full Bar/Street Parking
AE, D, MC, V, CB
No dress restrictions

The look is solid red brick both inside and out. The food is creative Italian, including Veal Leo (sautéed veal cutlet topped with fresh tomatoes, proscuitto, provolone and whole fresh mushrooms), Shrimp Pasquale and lobster and clams Italian-style.

Reservations required
Lunch/Dinner: Sun. – Thurs., 11 A.M. – 11 P.M.
     Fri., 11 A.M. – 1 A.M.
     Sat., 11 A.M. – 2 A.M.

THE COUNTRY FARE INN ❷ *Continental*

100 Painters Mill Rd.
Owings Mills, Md.
(301) 363-3131
Maître d': Owners: Stuart A. Teper, Richard
     M. Pirone and Roland Jeannier (chef)
Full Bar/Lot Parking
MC
No dress restrictions

Housed in a carefully restored historic (circa 1767) brick building, The Country Fare Inn offers fresh clams and oysters, pâté maison, escargots, French onion soup, fresh fish, Veal Française and freshly baked pastries. The stone Wine Cellar features a special lunch and supper menu and live music.

Reservations suggested
Lunch: Mon. – Fri., 11:30 A.M. – 2 P.M.
Dinner: Mon. – Thurs., 5:30 P.M. – 9:30 P.M.
   Fri. – Sat., 5:30 P.M. – 10 P.M.
   Sun., 4 P.M. – 8:30 P.M.

CRABTREE'S ⓲ *Continental*

413 N. Charles St.
Baltimore
(301) 539-5473
Maître d': Reid M. Vogelhut (owner)
Full Bar/Lot and Street Parking
AE, MC, V, CB
Good taste in dress required

Intimate and cheerful, housed in an old brownstone, Crabtree's boasts an intensely creative chef who prepares such innovations as Cream Baltimore — vichyssoise made with sweet potatoes, mild curry seasoning and crab meat. The Queen Mother Torte is a chocolate cake made without flour, but with crushed almonds!

Reservations required
Dinner: Tues. – Sat., 5 P.M. – 11 P.M.
   Closed Sunday, Monday

DANNY'S ⑭   *Continental*

1201 N. Charles St.
Baltimore
(301) 539-1393
Maître d': Stuart Dickman
Full Bar/Lot Parking
AE, D, MC, V, CB
Good taste in dress required

Owner/chef Danny Dickman arrives at his restaurant early in the morning to begin baking his pies, stirring his soups and sauces, finessing his Steak Diane, Dover Sole, Beef Wellington and crab cakes. He's also there in the evening to prepare a Caesar salad or flaming steak at your table, or to recommend a wine from his stock of rare French vintages.

Reservations suggested
Lunch/Dinner: Mon.–Fri., 11:30 A.M.–11 P.M.
              Sat., 5 P.M.–Midnight
              Closed Sunday

FIORI ❶   *Northern Italian/Continental*

808 Westminster Rd.
Reisterstown, Md.
(301) 833-6300
Full Bar/Lot Parking
MC
No dress restrictions

Housed in a 225-year-old stagecoach stop, Fiori presents a menu featuring milk-fed veal entrées, fresh seafood and an array of Northern Italian specialties.

No reservations required
Lunch: Mon.–Fri., Noon–2 P.M.
Dinner: Mon.–Thurs., 5 P.M.–9:30 P.M.
        Fri.–Sat., 5 P.M.–10 P.M.
        Sun., 4 P.M.–9 P.M.

HARVEY HOUSE ⑮   *American*

920 N. Charles St.
Baltimore
(301) 539-3110
Full Bar/Lot and Street Parking
AE, D, MC, V, CB
No dress restrictions

Located in the historic Mt. Vernon section of Baltimore, Harvey House is close to theaters, art galleries, boutiques and sporting events. A lengthy menu offers selections of local seafood, prime rib and vintage wines. Nightly entertainment is centered around a "mini" piano bar.

Reservations suggested (weekends)
Lunch/Dinner: Mon.–Sat., 11 A.M.–2 A.M.
              Closed Sunday

HAUSSNER'S ㉖   *German/Seafood*

3242 Eastern Ave.
Baltimore
(301) 327-8365
Maître d': Jerome Zavas
Full Bar/Street Parking
MC, V
No dress restrictions

A restaurant which boasts a collection of paintings, bronzes, china, wood carvings, clocks and etchings, Haussner's can also claim an enormous seating capacity (500) and one of the longest menus in Baltimore. It lists more than 50 seafood items and better than 40 meat selections. There are also dozens of appetizers and desserts.

No reservations required
Lunch/Dinner: Tues.-Sat., 11 A.M.-11 P.M.
    Closed Sunday, Monday

HERSH'S ORCHARD INN ⑩   *Continental*

1528 E. Joppa Rd.
Baltimore
(301) 823-0384
Maître d': Valerie Talucci
Full Bar/Lot Parking
AE, MC, V
Good taste in dress required

Owner Hersh Pachino says he serves the finest prime beef, seafood, veal and poultry to the finest clientele. Fresh Maine lobster and Florida stone crabs are flown in twice each week. As Pachino tells it, he's been called "the Toots Shor of Baltimore."

Reservations suggested
Lunch/Dinner: Daily, 11:30 A.M.-Midnight

JEAN CLAUDE'S CAFE ㉓   *French*

Harbor Place
The Promenade
Baltimore
(301) 332-0950
Maître d': Jean Claude and Sanford (owners)
Full Bar/Lot Parking
AE, D, MC, V, CB
Good taste in dress required

This warm and friendly bistro facing Chesapeake Bay (with a view of the *Constellation*) features traditional Burgundian cuisine. Specialties include Chicken Dijon, veal liver, homemade pâtés and homemade fudge sauce with walnuts.

No reservations required
Lunch: Mon.-Sat., 11:30 A.M.-2:30 P.M.
Dinner: Mon.-Thurs., 5:30 P.M.-10 P.M.
        Fri.-Sat., 5:30 P.M.-11 P.M.
Brunch: Sun., 11:30 A.M.-3 P.M.

JOHN EAGER HOWARD ROOM ⑯ — American

Belvedere Hotel
1 E. Chase St.
Baltimore
(301) 539-7110
Maître d': Jean Wisniewski, Ben Terehan
Full Bar/Valet Parking (evenings)
AE, MC, V
Jacket, tie for men (evenings)

The John Eager Howard Room is done in rich burgundy and gray-blue hues, with thick oak walls and grand chandeliers. Lobster and steak are the menu stars, along with weekend chef's specials. There is carrot cake and pecan pie for dessert.

Reservations required
Lunch: Mon.–Fri., 11:30 A.M.–2 P.M.
Dinner: Sun.–Thurs., 5:30 P.M.–10:30 P.M.
Fri.–Sat., 5:30 P.M.–11:30 P.M.

KARSON'S INN ㉙ — American

5100 Holabird Ave.
Baltimore
(301) 675-1600
Full Bar/Lot Parking
AE, MC, V, CB
No dress restrictions

Karson's Inn is renowned for its ample portions of beef and seafood. There are such dishes as Shrimp Roberto, stuffed soft crab, Breast of Capon Valentino, Calves' Liver Viennese and extra-thick slabs of prime rib. The crab cakes are shipped throughout the country.

No reservations required (except weekends)
Lunch/Dinner: Mon.–Fri., 11:30 A.M.–1 A.M.
Sat., 4:30 P.M.–1 A.M.
Sun., 11:30 A.M.–9 P.M.

THE KING'S CONTRIVANCE ❹ — French

8341 Route 32
Columbia, Md.
(301) 995-0500 (301-596-3455 from
    Washington area phones)
Maître d': Paul Bukovsky (owner)
Full Bar/Valet and Lot Parking
MC
Jacket, tie for men preferred

Housed in a 19th-century country mansion in Howard County, The King's Contrivance is now a restaurant specializing in French-style sophistication and Chesapeake Bay-style seafood.

Reservations recommended
Lunch: Mon.–Fri., 11:30 A.M.–2 P.M.
Dinner: Mon.–Fri., 5:30 P.M.–9:30 P.M.
Sat., 5:30 P.M.–10 P.M.
Sun., 4 P.M.–9 P.M.

MAISON MARCONI ❷⓪   *Italian*

106 W. Saratoga St.
Baltimore
(301) 752-9286
Full Bar/Street Parking
MC, V
Jacket for men

Chesapeake Bay food, Baltimore style, is what to expect from Maison Marconi, as well as many French and Italian specialties. This means oysters sauteed with ham, soft-shelled crabs, Lobster Cardinal and Chicken Tetrazzini. The city's VIPs and VIP-watchers have been finding their way to this former row house for the past 60 years or so.

No reservations required
Lunch: Tues.–Sat., Noon–3:30 P.M.
Dinner: Tues.–Sat., 5 P.M.–8 P.M.
    Closed Sunday, Monday

MILTON INN ❺   *Continental*

14833 York Rd.
Sparks, Md.
(301) 771-4366
Maître d': Eleanora E. Allori (owner)
Full Bar/Lot Parking
AE, MC, V
Jacket, tie for men

A very traditional family-run restaurant with a formal main dining room, the Milton Inn is housed in a building dating back to 1740. Fresh Maryland seafood is featured. There is a spacious cocktail area around an inviting fireplace. Guests are welcome to explore the wine cellar.

Reservations required
Lunch: Tues.–Fri., Noon–2:30 P.M.
Dinner: Tues.–Fri., 6 P.M.–10 P.M.
    Sat., 6 P.M.–11 P.M.
    Sun., 4 P.M.–10 P.M.
    Closed Monday

OLDE OBRYCKI'S CRAB HOUSE ❷❺   *Seafood*

1729 E. Pratt St.
Baltimore
(301) 732-6399
Maître d': Richard Cernak and Rose M. Cernak (owners)
Full Bar/Street Parking
AE, MC, V
Good taste in dress required

"We specialize in serving steamed crabs the 'Obrycki' way," says owner Richard Cernak. The crab cakes are famous, he claims, and the Colonial atmosphere is warm and congenial. Olde Obrycki's is housed in buildings that date back 140 years and features a bar (one of Baltimore's oldest) that is about 115 years old. Tradition reigns supreme here.

No reservations required
Lunch: Tues.–Fri., 11:30 A.M.–2:30 P.M.
Dinner: Tues.–Sat., 5 P.M.–11 P.M.
    Sun., 2 P.M.–8:30 P.M.
    Closed between early November and late April
    Closed Monday

PEERCE'S DOWNTOWN   ❽   *Continental*

225 N. Liberty St.
Baltimore
(301) 727-0910
Maître d': Rudi Paul (manager/co-owner)
Full Bar/Lot Parking
AE, MC, V
Jacket, tie for men

Pink linen and pink roses are on every table. The European-trained staff will serve you such delights as Veal Rostoff (scallopini with cucumbers and herbs), Chicken Narcissus (breast of chicken with honey and Mandarin liqueur) and Bananas Copacabana (vanilla ice cream, bananas, chocolate sauce and almonds).

Reservations required
Lunch: Mon. – Thurs., 11:30 A.M. – 2:30 P.M.
Dinner: Mon. – Thurs., 5 P.M. – 10 P.M.
        Fri. – Sat., 5 P.M. – 11 P.M.
        Sun., 4 P.M. – 9 P.M.

PEERCE'S PLANTATION   ❼   *Continental*

Dulaney Valley Road
Phoenix, Md.
(301) 252-3100
Maître d': Harry Blank
Full Bar/Valet and Lot Parking
AE, MC, V
Jacket for men

Peerce's features a large, comfortable dining room with white brick fireplaces and wrought iron accoutrements. There's a view of the surrounding countryside from the glass-enclosed porch. Featured are generous portions of such items as Filet Stephanie and stuffed grouper.

Reservations required
Lunch/Dinner: Mon. – Thurs., 11:30 A.M. – 10 P.M.
              Fri. – Sat., 11:30 A.M. – 11 P.M.
              Sun., 1 P.M. – 9 P.M.

THE PIMLICO HOTEL   ❸   *International*

5301 Park Heights Ave.
Baltimore
(301) 664-8014/15/16
Maître d': Alfred Davis (owner)
Full Bar/Valet and Lot Parking
AE, MC, V
Good taste in dress required

Alfred Davis, owner of The Pimlico, is another to point to his lengthy menu with loving pride. It is also extremely "diversified" and inordinately "palatable," he says. Some eclectic offerings from this marathon listing include fresh lobster, Veal Parmesan, pizza, Chinese selections, steaks, etc., etc. Portions are generous, to say the least.

Reservations required
Lunch/Dinner: Daily, 11:30 A.M. – 1 A.M.

BALTIMORE 25

THE PRIME RIB ⓭   *American*

1101 N. Calvert St.
Baltimore
(301) 539-1804
Maître d': Captain Harry
Full Bar/Lot Parking
AE, D, MC, V, CB
Jacket for men

Be prepared for a world of gold-trimmed black walls, *art deco* prints and Oriental carpeting when you enter The Prime Rib. There's also a lucite-topped grand piano. "One very sexy steak house," comments owner C. P. Beler. He features Midwestern prime aged beef and Maryland seafood.

No reservations required
Dinner: Daily, 5 P.M. – 2 A.M.

STALL 1043 ㉘   *French*

1043 Marshall St.
Baltimore
(301) 547-0919
Maître d': Christopher Bergen (manager)
Full Bar/Street Parking
AE, D, MC, V
No dress restrictions

A "fresh and appealing atmosphere" says the management of Stall 1043. In addition to ground-floor seating, there is a mezzanine where you can dine beneath a skylight. The menu is handwritten and changes according to which items can be purchased at the local markets. Desserts are baked on the premises.

Reservations required
Dinner: Tues. – Sat., 6 P.M. – 10 P.M.
       Closed Sunday, Monday

THOMPSON'S SEA GIRT HOUSE ⓫   *Seafood*

5919 York Rd.
Baltimore
(301) 435-1800
Maître d': Pierre Zaguary
Full Bar/Lot and Street Parking
AE, MC, V
Jacket for men (dinner)

Thompson's specializes in fresh regional seafood, as well as Colorado beef and veal. Their crab cakes are star attractions as are their sauteed soft crabs. (They claim to be "the restaurant that made a Maryland crab cake famous.") A Baltimore staple, Thompson's has been in continuous operation since 1885.

Reservations required
Lunch: Mon. – Sat., 11 A.M. – 4 P.M.
Dinner: Mon. – Sat., 4 P.M. – Midnight
      Sun., 11 A.M. – 11 P.M.

TIO PEPE ⑲ *Spanish*

10 E. Franklin St.
Baltimore
(301) 539-4675
Full Bar/Valet Parking
AE, MC, V
Good taste in dress required

Here you'll find the haute cuisine of Spain served in a converted townhouse basement that has been transformed with the help of authentic Spanish decor. Look for specialties such as suckling pig, pheasant, tournedos, rack of lamb, filet of sole sauteed with bananas and finished with Hollandaise and, of course, the traditional paella.

Reservations required
Lunch: Mon.–Fri., 11 A.M.–2:30 P.M.
Dinner: Mon.–Thurs., 5 P.M.–10:30 P.M.
  Fri.–Sat., 5 P.M.–11:30 P.M.
  Sun., 4 P.M.–10:30 P.M.

TOM JONES ⑨ *Continental*

6920 Donachie Rd.
Baltimore
(301) 828-1187
Full Bar/Lot Parking
AE, MC, V
Jacket for men (evenings)

Tom Jones himself might feel at home in this English-style pub. Antiques and pewter make their mark throughout. A special menu feature is Steak Diane, flamed at your table. As an added treat, the Irish Coffee is flamed as well.

Reservations suggested
Lunch/Dinner: Mon.–Sat., 11:30 A.M.–2 A.M.
  Sun., 11:30 A.M.–Midnight

BOSTON

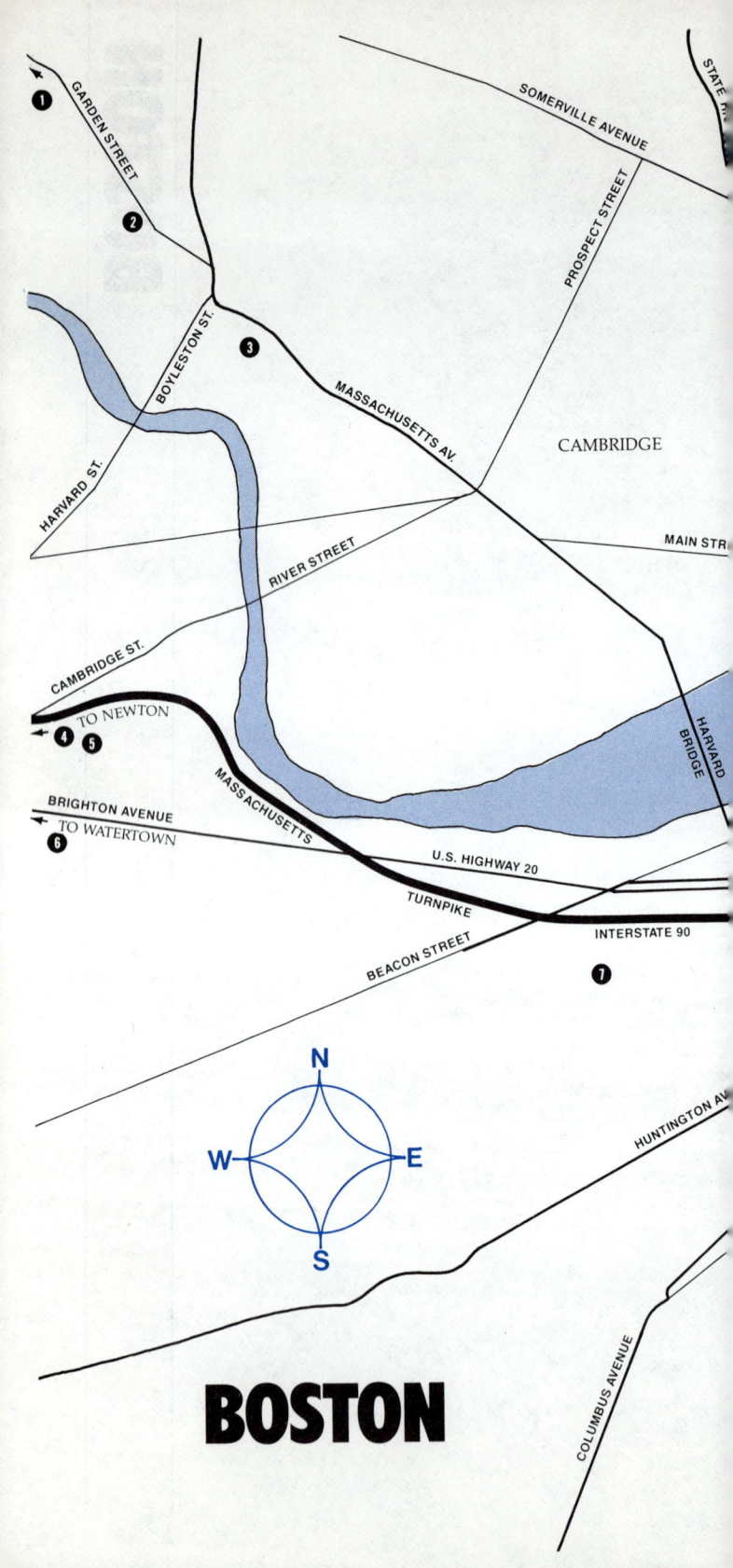

ANOTHER SEASON ⑭   *Continental*

97 Mount Vernon St.
Boston
(617) 367-0880
Beer and Wine/Street Parking
AE, MC
Good taste in dress required

Here you'll find elegant dining among murals depicting the Champs Elysées. Menu selections change weekly to reflect the changing seasons. There is "a full range of dishes to delight any palate," assures owner Odette Bery.

Reservations suggested
Dinner: Mon.–Thurs., 5:30 P.M.–10:30 P.M.
        Fri.–Sat., 5:30 P.M.–11 P.M.
        Closed Sunday

ANTHONY'S PIER 4 ㉒   *Seafood*

140 Northern Ave.
Boston
(617) 423-6363
Full Bar/Valet and Lot Parking
AE, D, MC, V, CB
Jacket for men

Anthony's offers much of what you'd expect from a Boston restaurant: a location at the end of a pier jutting into the harbor, memorabilia of America's early sailing days adorning various nooks and crannies and, most importantly, lobster and other fresh seafood, plus steaks and chops. This is a large establishment with portions to match.

No reservations required
Lunch/Dinner: Mon.–Fri., 11:30 A.M.–11 P.M.
              Sat., Noon–11 P.M.
              Sun., Holidays, 12:30 P.M.–10:30 P.M.

ATHENS OLYMPIA ㊱   *Greek*

51 Stuart St.
Boston
(617) 426-6236
Maître d': William Cocoris (manager)
Full Bar/Street Parking
AE, MC, V
No dress restrictions

You may be reminded of an Old World taverna as you step across the threshold. The feeling is warm and congenial. There are highbacked booths complemented by Greek embellishments in decor.

No reservations required
Lunch/Dinner: Mon.–Sat., 11 A.M.–11:30 P.M.
              Sun., 11 A.M.–10 P.M.
              Closed Sunday, July and August

THE BAY TOWER ROOM ⓭   *Continental*

60 State St.
Boston
(617) 723-1666
Maître d': Francisco Di Rey
Full Bar/Lot Parking
AE, MC, V, CB
Jacket, tie for men

The Bay Tower Room offers five tiers of dining 33 stories above the Boston Harbor. The menu is continental, with a French flair and includes an abundance of fresh seafood. One specialty is Veal Marsala.

Reservations required
Dinner: Mon.-Thurs., 5:30 P.M.-10 P.M.
        Fri.-Sat., 5:30 P.M.-11 P.M.
        Closed Sunday

CAFE BUDAPEST ㉕   *Hungarian*

90 Exeter St.
Boston
(617) 734-3388
Maître d': Mario Labadini
Full Bar/Street Parking
AE, D, MC, V, CB
Jacket, tie for men

The "Old World" ambience of guess-what-city is featured here. Owner Edith Ban offers Beef Stroganoff, Chicken Paprikash, wiener schnitzel, plus plenty of homemade soups, salads and desserts — strudels, dobos torte, raspberry-chocolate torte — to name a few. A violinist is on hand to serenade you with waltz music. "A very romantic setting," says Mrs. Ban.

Reservations recommended
Lunch: Mon.-Sat., Noon-3 P.M.
Dinner: Sun.-Thurs., 5 P.M.-10:30 P.M.
        Fri.-Sat., 5 P.M.-Midnight

CAFE PLAZA ㉜   *Continental*

Copley Plaza Hotel
136 St. James Ave.
Boston
(617) 267-5300, Ext. 1638
Maître d': Heinz U. Bunger (manager)
Full Bar/Valet Parking
AE, D, MC, V, CB
Jacket, tie for men

There is an emphasis here on opulence in surroundings and elegance in presentation. You'll find Waterford crystal chandeliers, oak panelled walls, a sculptured ceiling, silver serving plates and pink carnations. Classical music is heard playing in the background while breast of pheasant, broiled swordfish and sweetbreads play in the foreground.

Reservations required
Breakfast: Daily, 7 A.M.-10 A.M.
Lunch: Daily, Noon-2 P.M.
Dinner: Daily, 5:30 P.M.-10:30 P.M.

CAFE PROMENADE ㊴   *Continental*

Colonnade Hotel
120 Huntington Ave.
Boston
(617) 261-2800
Full Bar/Street Parking
AE, D, MC, CB
Good taste in dress required

The Colonnade Hotel's Cafe Promenade treats you to a view of the Prudential Center, frequent fashion shows and nightly musical entertainment. The casual menu fits in with after theater suppers or early morning breakfasts.

Reservations suggested
Breakfast/Lunch/Dinner: Daily, 7 A.M.–11:30 P.M.

CASA ROMERO ㉗   *Mexican*

30 Gloucester St.
Boston
(617) 261-2146
Maître d': José L. Romero (owner)
Full Bar/Street Parking
AE, MC, V
No dress restrictions

If you yearn for the specialties of Mexico City while in Back Bay Boston, Casa Romero may be the answer. A quiet, intimate place decorated with painted terra cotta tiles, Casa Romero features Camarones al Cilantro, Puerco Adobado, flaming bananas and strawberries sauteed with Cointreau.

No reservations required
Dinner: Mon.–Thurs., 6 P.M.–10 P.M.
       Fri.–Sat., 6 P.M.–11 P.M.
       Closed Sunday

CHARLEY'S EATING & DRINKING SALOON ㉛   *American*

344 Newbury St.
Boston
(617) 266-3000
Full Bar/Valet Parking
AE, D, MC, V, CB
Good taste in dress required

Charley's is a colorful Victorian-era saloon complete with authentic artifacts and architectural antiques of the late 19th century. Mustachioed waiters in bright red vests serve house specialties consisting of prime rib, New York sirloin, Boston scrod, Cape scallops and "immense" sandwiches.

No reservations required
Lunch/Dinner: Daily, 11:30 A.M.–Midnight

COPLEY'S ㉝　　　　　　　　　　*Continental*

Copley Plaza Hotel
136 St. James Ave.
Boston
(617) 267-5300, Ext. 542
Maître d': James Landry (manager)
Full Bar/Valet and Street Parking
AE, D, MC, V, CB
Good taste in dress required

The Edwardian era is born again at Copley's. There's a brass-railed bar, Old English memorabilia and, of course, roast beef with Yorkshire pudding. Also offered are fresh fish from local waters, carpetbagger steaks and samples of *nouvelle cuisine*. "Save room for the dessert," the management cautions. "Everything is homemade including the ice cream."

Reservations suggested
Lunch: Mon.–Sat., 11:30 A.M.–3 P.M.
Dinner: Daily, 5:30 P.M.–Midnight
Brunch: Sun., Noon–4 P.M.

DAVIO'S ㉚　　　　　　　　　　　*Italian*

269 Newbury St.
Boston
(617) 262-4810
Beer and Wine/Valet Parking
AE, D, MC, V, CB
Jacket for men

"Davio's Ristorante e deliziosamente Italiano," comments manager Iolanda Di Censo Dolpe, and somehow you know what she means. Elegant decor and attentive service are strong suits. So is the Linguine Fra Diavolo, fettuccine and veal "of unequaled tenderness."

Reservations required
Lunch/Dinner: Mon.–Thurs., Noon–11 P.M.
　　　　　　　Fri.–Sat., Noon–Midnight
　　　　　　　Sun., 5:30 P.M.–11 P.M.

DERTAD'S ❷　　　　　　　　　　*Continental*

16 Garden St.
Cambridge, Mass.
(617) 354-1234
Maître d': Enrico Donati
Full Bar/Valet Parking
AE, D, MC, V, CB
Jacket for men

Manager Edward Guleserian describes Dertad's as "a posh hideaway — intimate and relaxed." Service, he says, is "correct and unobtrusive." Such is the setting for specialties like Crab Edward, escalopes de veau, rack of lamb and sweetbreads. A pianist provides the undoubtedly unobtrusive background music.

Reservations required
Dinner: Daily, 6 P.M.–11 P.M.

DINI'S SEA GRILL ⑱   *Seafood*

94 Tremont St.
Boston
(617) 227-0380
Full Bar/Street Parking
AE, MC, V
No dress restrictions

Dini's is famous for its broiled fresh native scrod. The atmosphere is casual and the service friendly and courteous, contends co-owner Nancy Dini. "We make the diner feel welcome," she adds.

No reservations required
Lunch/Dinner: Mon.–Sat., 10 A.M.–10:30 P.M.
               Sun., Noon–10:30 P.M.

DURGIN PARK ⑪   *American*

340 N. Market St.
Boston
(617) 227-2038
Full Bar/Street Parking
AE
No dress restrictions

If you like your prime rib to overlap your plate, this is the place to visit. The "Yankee cooking" includes a large selection of seafood, homemade pies and Indian pudding. Admittedly not the spot for an intimate rendezvous, Durgin Park is instead a place for hearty food in abundant quantity.

No reservations required
Lunch/Dinner: Mon.–Sat., 11:30 A.M.–10 P.M.
               Sun., Noon–9 P.M.

THE 57 RESTAURANT ㉞   *American/Continental*

200 Stuart St.
Boston
(617) 423-5700
Full Bar/Lot Parking
AE, MC, V
Jacket for men

"A warm, friendly ambience pervades The 57," according to the management. They are famous for their prime rib, steaks and Greek and seafood specialties.

No reservations required (except Saturday dinner)
Lunch/Dinner: Daily, 11:30 A.M.–11:30 P.M.

FRANCESCA'S ❾   *Italian*

147 Richmond St.
Boston
(617) 523-8826
Full Bar/Street Parking
Major credit cards
Good taste in dress required

A small, intimate restaurant that neatly covers the field of traditional Italian cooking. You'll find such items as fettuccine, veal, seafood and homemade desserts such as cannoli on the menu.

Reservations suggested
Lunch/Dinner: Mon.–Sat.
            Closed Sunday

GALLAGHER ⓴   *French/American*

55 Congress St.
Boston
(617) 523-6080
Full Bar/Valet Parking
AE, D, MC, V, CB
No dress restrictions

The dining room is done in blue and white with table settings of antique silver. Featured are salmon soufflé, Scallops in Parchment, rack of lamb and scrod.

Reservations required
Lunch: Mon.–Fri., 11:45 A.M.–2:30 P.M.
Dinner: Mon.–Wed., 5:30 P.M.–9:30 P.M.
          Thurs.–Sat., 5:30 P.M.–10:30 P.M.
          Closed Sunday (except bar)

THE HERMITAGE ❼   *Continental*

Institute of Contemporary Art
955 Boylston St.
Boston
(617) 267-3652
Maître d': Rafael Pons (manager)
Full Bar/Street Parking
AE, MC, V
No dress restrictions

Catherine the Great might have found happiness at The Hermitage. Located in The Institute of Contemporary Art in Back Bay, The Hermitage gives Russian cuisine a French twist. Specialties include duck stuffed with truffled foie gras, Russian eggs, borscht and smoked salmon.

No reservations required (except Saturdays)
Lunch: Tues.–Sat., Noon–2:30 P.M.
Dinner: Tues.–Sun., 6 P.M.–10 P.M.
Brunch: Sun., Noon–3 P.M.
          Closed Monday

THE HOUNDSTOOTH ㉙ *Continental*

150 Boylston St.
Boston
(617) 482-0722
Full Bar/Street Parking
AE
No dress restrictions

Located across from the Boston Common, The Houndstooth offers entrées ranging from Steak au Poivre to baked fillet of sole to seasonal game dishes. There is also a pub where salads, stews, sandwiches and soups are served.

Reservations required
Lunch: Mon.–Fri., 11:30 A.M.–2:30 P.M.
Dinner: Daily, 5:30 P.M.–11 P.M.
    Closed Sunday in summer

JIMMY'S HARBORSIDE ㉓ *Seafood*

242 Northern Ave.
Boston
(617) 423-1000
Maître d': Constantine Rockas (manager)
Full Bar/Valet and Street Parking
AE, D, MC, V, CB
Jacket for men (dinner)
No jeans

Jimmy's has been at the Boston waterfront for more than 55 years. Patrons get a fine view of the Fish Pier and historic harbor, as well as just-caught fish and seafood. Specialties include creamy fish chowder, poached finnan haddie and baked stuffed filet of sole.

Reservations suggested
Lunch/Dinner: Mon.–Sat., 11:30 A.M.–9:30 P.M.
    Closed Sunday

JOYCE CHEN RESTAURANT ❶ *Chinese*

390 Rindge Ave.
Cambridge, Mass.
(617) 492-7373
Maître d': Stephen Chen (manager)
Full Bar/Lot Parking
AE, MC, V
No dress restrictions

Manager Stephen Chen calls eating at Joyce Chen's "an educational dining experience." The varied menu offers specialties from all regions of China, served in a setting accented by plants and Chinese objets d'art. A buffet is featured where you can sample Peking Duck, Szechwan Chicken and spicy fish soup.

Reservations suggested
Lunch/Dinner: Sun.–Thurs., Noon–10:30 P.M.
    Fri.–Sat., Noon–11:30 P.M.

LE BOCAGE ❻   *French*

72 Bigelow Ave.
Watertown, Mass.
(617) 923-1210
Maître d': Enzo Danesi
Full Bar/Lot and Street Parking
MC, V
Good taste in dress required

Le Bocage is small and casual with white tableclothes, red napkins and paintings done by local artists. You dine overlooking an outdoor garden. The menu changes frequently to keep all the selections as fresh as possible. There are such items as Homard Buerre Blanc, Roulade de Boeuf and Gâteau au Chocolat et Praline.

No reservations required
Dinner: Mon.–Thurs., 6 P.M.–11 P.M.
Fri.–Sat., 5:30 P.M.–11 P.M.
Closed Sunday

LECHNER'S GOURMET RESTAURANT ⓰ *German*

21 Broad St.
Boston
(617) 523-1016
Maître d': Larry Catalani
Full Bar/Lot Parking
AE, D, MC, V, CB
Jacket, tie for men

"A quiet and properly European establishment," is how owner Vincent Traietti sees Lechner's. He serves his guests such specialties as Veal Cordon Bleu, rack of lamb, scrod and a variety of special soups and appetizers. An executive lunch with changing entrées is offered on weekdays.

Reservations required
Lunch: Mon.–Fri., 11:30 A.M.–3 P.M.
Dinner: Mon.–Fri., 5:30 P.M.–10 P.M.
Sat., 5:30 P.M.–11 P.M.
Closed Sunday

LEGAL SEAFOODS ㉟   *Seafood*

Park Plaza Hotel
Arlington and Columbus Sts.
Boston
(617) 426-4444
Maître d': Roger
Full Bar/Lot Parking
AE
Good taste in dress required

"We serve the largest variety of fresh seafood anywhere—practically every species of fish caught in the North Atlantic," claims George Berkowitz, president of Legal Seafoods. And, if you're still not satisfied, he even flies salmon in from the West Coast, rainbow trout from Idaho and red snapper in from Florida.

No reservations required
Lunch/Dinner: Sun.–Thurs., 11 A.M.–9:30 P.M.
Fri.–Sat., 11 A.M.–10 P.M.

L'ESPALIER ㉘   *French*

384 Boylston St.
Boston
(617) 247-7406
Maître d': Donna Doll (co-owner)
Wine/Lot and Street Parking
AE, MC, V
Good taste in dress required

High ceilings and oversized chairs set the stage for classic and *nouvelle* French cuisine. Specialties include duck sautéed in red wine and duck liver sauce and a dessert combination of chocolate mousse and chocolate buttercream pastry.

Reservations required
Dinner: Mon.–Sat., 6 P.M.–10:30 P.M.
     Closed Sunday and month of August

LILY'S OF BOSTON ⑫   *French*

29 Quincy Market Building
Faneuil Hall Marketplace
Boston
(617) 227-4242
Full Bar/Lot and Street Parking
AE, MC, V
Jacket for men

Lily's offerings cover the field of French cuisine: *nouvelle*, provincial and classic. Some entrées include Beef Wellington, Veal Oskar and Duckling Montmorency.

Reservations suggested
Lunch: Mon.–Fri., Noon–2 P.M.
Dinner: Daily, 5:30 P.M.–10:30 P.M.

LOCKE-OBER CAFE ㉑   *Continental*

3 and 4 Winter Place
Boston
(617) 542-1340
Full Bar/Lot Parking
AE, D, MC, V
Jacket, tie for men

Locke-Ober first opened its doors in 1875. Then the downstairs dining area was a "man's cafe" with tables encircling a large bar. Now this and two second-floor dining rooms serve such specialties as baked oysters, Lobster Savannah, Filet of Beef Mirabeau and roast duckling, to men and women alike.

Reservations required
Lunch/Dinner: Mon.–Sat., 11 A.M.–10 P.M.
        Closed Sunday

MAISON ROBERT ⓳   *French*

45 School St.
Boston
(617) 227-3370/71/77
Maître d': Hugo Biasizzo and Dette Davin
Full Bar/Lot Parking
AE, D, MC, V, CB
Jacket, tie for men (upstairs)

Maison Robert, located in the renovated Old City Hall, is owned and managed by chef Lucien Robert. He offers you a choice of two restaurants: the formal Bonhomme Richard and the more casual Ben's Cafe (previously the city vault). Some menu features are striped bass, Veal Prince Orloff and rack of lamb.

Reservations required
Lunch: Mon.–Fri., 11:30 A.M.–2:30 P.M.
Dinner: Mon.–Fri., 5:30 P.M.–10 P.M.
     Sat., 6 P.M.–10:30 P.M.
     Sun., 6 P.M.–10 P.M. *(downstairs)*

MODERN GOURMET ❹   *French*

81 R Union St.
Newton Centre, Mass.
(617) 969-1320
Beer and Wine/Lot and Street Parking
No credit cards
Good taste in dress required

This small, intimate restaurant specializes in French cuisine prepared and presented in the *nouvelle* manner. Only the freshest seasonal ingredients are used. There are homemade pâtés, cold pasta salad and a salad of smoked trout.

Reservations required
Lunch/Snacks: Tues.–Sun., 10 A.M.–6 P.M.
     Closed Monday

9 KNOX STREET ㊲   *English*

9 Knox St.
Boston
(617) 482-3494
Maître d': Jeffrey Wayne Davies (owner)
Beer and Wine/Street Parking
No credit cards
No dress restrictions

Housed in a unique old building in downtown Boston, 9 Knox Street features a limited menu and occasional entertainment. Specialties include Beef Wellington and rack of lamb.

Reservations required
Dinner: Tues–Sat., 6:30 P.M.–9:30 P.M.
     Closed Sunday, Monday

NINO'S PLACE AT MAITRE JACQUES ❽ *Continental*

10 Emerson Pl.
Boston
(617) 742-5676/5480
Maître d': Nino Todesco (owner)
Full Bar/Lot Parking
AE, D, MC, V, CB
Good taste in dress required

Dine on the likes of Veal Oskar, rack of lamb or Lobster Graziella as you look out upon Boston's Charles River. Nino prides himself on setting a tone of elegance and warmth.

Reservations required
Lunch: Mon.–Fri., Noon–3 P.M.
Dinner: Mon.–Thurs., 6 P.M.–10 P.M.
      Fri.–Sat., 6 P.M.–11 P.M.
      Closed Sunday

NO NAME RESTAURANT ㉔ *Seafood*

15½ Fish Pier
Boston
(617) 338-7539
No Wine or Spirits/Street Parking
No credit cards
No dress restrictions

No Name is the kind of no-nonsense restaurant you look for when you're just plain hungry. In this case, the object of your hunger should be Boston seafood. There are chunky chowders, broiled scallops, broiled scrod and various seafood plates, among other selections.

No reservations required
Lunch/Dinner: Mon.–Sat.
            Closed Sunday

PARKER'S DINING ROOM ⑮ *Continental*

The Parker House
60 School St.
Boston
(617) 227-8600
Maître d': Walter Wagner
Full Bar/Valet and Lot Parking
AE, D, MC, V, CB
Jacket for men

"Formal, elegant, Bostonian." Such is Parker's, located on the Freedom Trail in one of the city's most historic hotels. Special dishes include snapper in pastry, veal with watercress sauce, scrod, Chateaubriand and roast rack of lamb. You'll hear a piano playing in the background every night and a harp at brunch on Sunday.

Reservations required
Breakfast: Mon.–Fri., 7:30 A.M.–9:30 A.M.
Lunch: Mon.–Fri., 11:30 A.M.–2:30 P.M.
Dinner: Daily, 5 P.M.–10 P.M.
Brunch: Sun., 11:30 A.M. and 1:30 P.M. seatings

PILLAR HOUSE ❺   *American*

26 Quinobequin Rd.
Newton Lower Falls, Mass.
(617) 969-6500
Maître d': Thomas H. Larsen (owner)
Full Bar/Lot Parking
AE, D, MC, V, CB
Jacket for men
No jeans

Housed in an elegant old Colonial homestead, The Pillar House features à la carte menu selections of steaks and seafood. The suburban location will allow you to see some of the interesting surrounding area.

Reservations required
Lunch/Dinner: Mon.–Thurs., 11:30 A.M.– 9 P.M.
              Fri., 11:30 A.M.– 10 P.M.
              Closed Saturday, Sunday

THE RITZ-CARLTON DINING ROOM ㉖ *Continental*

The Ritz-Carlton Hotel
15 Arlington St.
Boston
(617) 536-5700
Maître d': Joseph Lucherini
Full Bar/Valet Parking
AE, MC, V
Jacket, tie for men
No jeans

Overlooking the city's Public Garden, the Dining Room at The Ritz-Carlton is strong on elegance and formality. Featured are Lobster au Whiskey, braised sweetbreads and Dover Sole Meunière. Some menu entrées change daily. A string quartet helps to create the right mood.

Reservations required
Lunch: Mon.–Sat., Noon–2:30 P.M.
       Sun., Noon–4:30 P.M.
Dinner: Sun.–Thurs., 6 P.M.–10 P.M.
        Fri.–Sat., 6 P.M.–11 P.M.

ST. BOTOLPH ㊳   *Continental*

99 St. Botolph St.
Boston
(617) 266-3030
Full Bar/Street Parking
AE, MC, V
No dress restrictions

Housed in a carefully restored 19th-century townhouse, St. Botolph serves "first quality" food in a "casually elegant" environment. They're noted for daily fresh fish specials, as well as Lamb Chops Moutarde, veal chops with orange butter, and Cornish hen.

Reservations recommended
Lunch: Mon.–Fri., Noon–2:30 P.M.
Dinner: Daily, 6 P.M.–10:30 P.M.
Brunch: Sun., Noon–4 P.M.

STELLA OF BOSTON   ⓱   *Italian*

74 E. India Row
Boston
(617) 227-3559
Maître d': Henry
Full Bar/Lot Parking
AE, D, MC, V
Jacket for men

If you crave a combination of harbor view and Florentine decor, this is the place for you. Located near the new Faneuil Hall Marketplace, Stella's offers you the likes of Chicken Valdostana, Veal Sçallopini al Marsala, Braciolettine di Manzo al Ferri and Gamberi alla Stella.

Reservations recommended
Lunch/Dinner: Mon.–Thurs., 11:30 A.M.–11:30 P.M.
               Fri., 11:30 A.M.–Midnight
               Sat., 4 P.M.–Midnight
               Sun., Noon–11 P.M.

THE UNION OYSTER HOUSE   ⑩   *Seafood*

41 Union St.
Boston
(617) 227-2750
Full Bar/Sreet Parking
AE, D, MC, V
No dress restrictions

Staking its claim as Boston's oldest restaurant, The Union Oyster House is located on the Freedom Trail in a building that's over 300 years old. Freshly shucked oysters are the specialty. Try them at the same oyster bar frequented by that famous oyster lover, Daniel Webster. Also featured is Yankee-style seafood and char-broiled meats.

No reservations required
Lunch/Dinner: Sun.–Thurs., 11 A.M.–9:30 P.M.
               Fri.–Sat., 11 A.M.–10 P.M.

THE VOYAGERS   ③   *Continental*

45½ Mt. Auburn St.
Cambridge, Mass.
(617) 354-1718
Maître d': Paul Lolax
Full Bar/Lot Parking
AE, MC, V
Good taste in dress required

The chef at The Voyagers places emphasis on a personal cuisine which closely follows the changing seasons. Herbs and vegetables are grown in the restaurant's own gardens and there is a "greenhouse" dining room where varieties of flowers thrive all winter long. As with so many Boston restaurants, there is music to accompany dinner — a harp or harpsichord in this case.

No reservations required
Dinner: Tues.–Sun., 6 P.M.–10 P.M.
       Closed Monday

ZACHARY'S ⓴   *Continental*

Colonnade Hotel
120 Huntington Ave.
Boston
(617) 424-7000
Maître d': Paolo
Full Bar/Valet Parking
AE, D, MC, V, CB
Jacket, tie for men

Lobster cocktail with Salignac brandy, Escargots à la Suisse, steak flamed with a sauce of whisky and oysters — all are examples of the chef's wizardry at Zachary's. The restaurant also features "European" service, *art deco* surroundings, breads and pastries baked on the premises and more than 200 wines. Wild game is offered in season.

Reservations required
Lunch: Fri. buffet, 11:30 A.M. – 2:30 P.M.
Dinner: Mon. – Sat., 5:30 P.M. – 11:30 P.M.
      Closed Sunday

CHICAGO

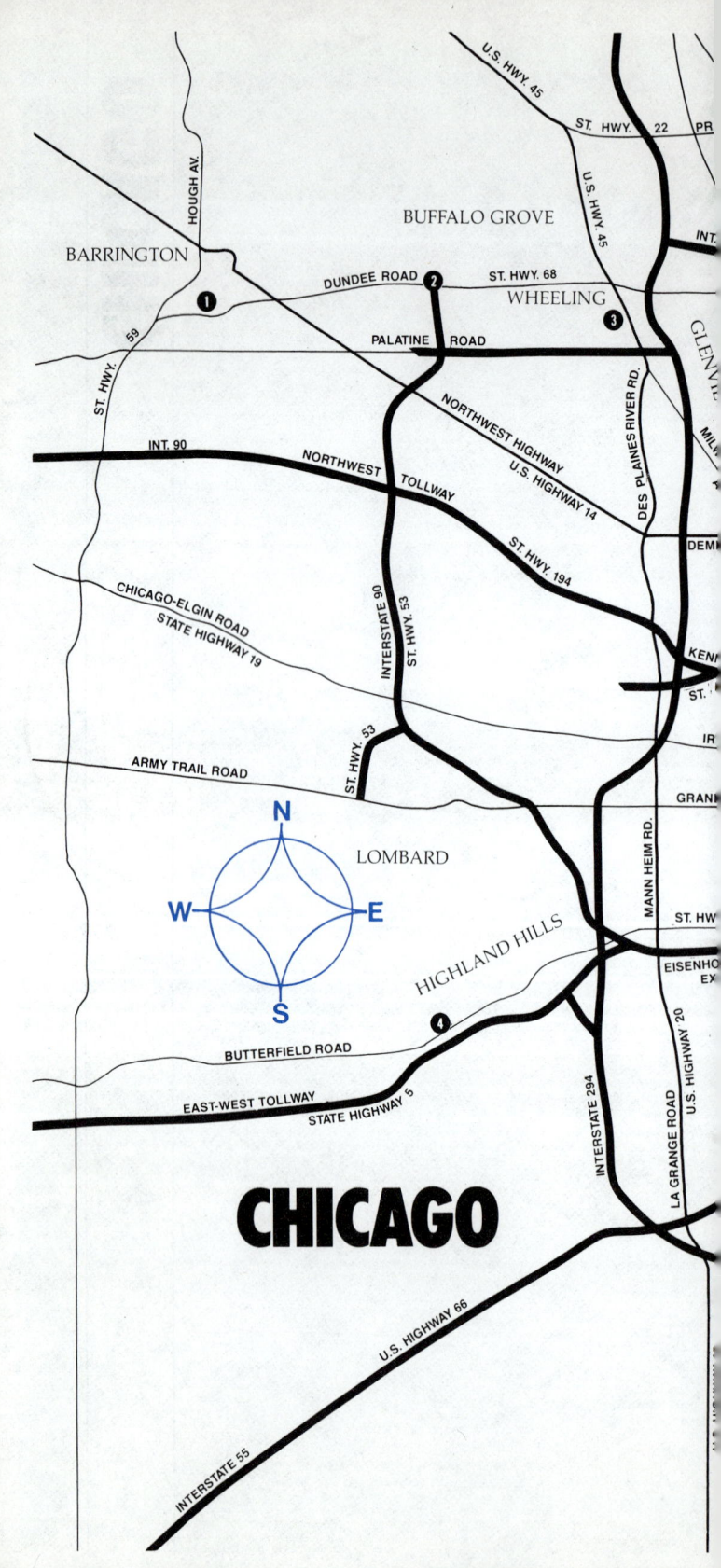

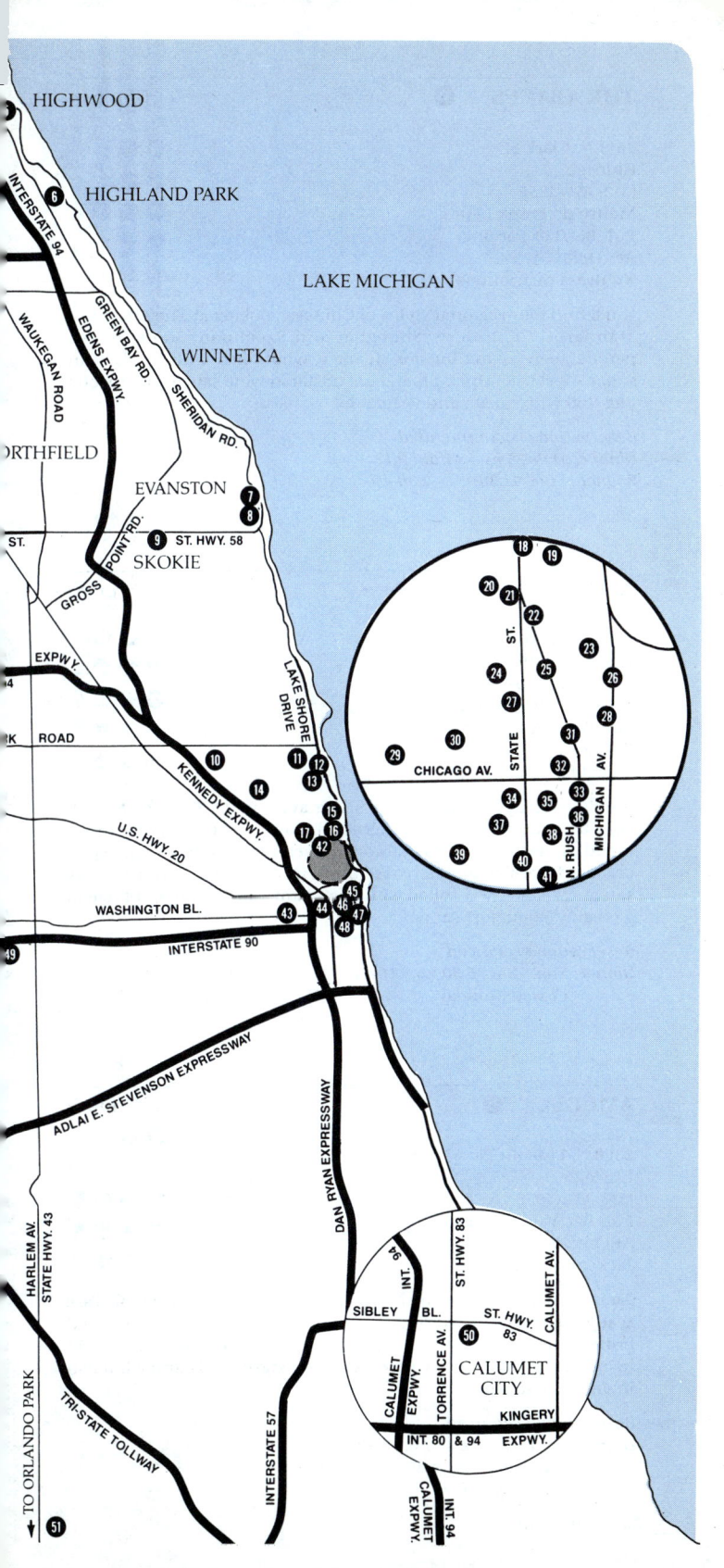

THE ABACUS ⓱   *Chinese*

2619 N. Clark St.
Chicago
(312) 477-5251
Maître d': Frank Leung
Full Bar/Lot Parking
AE, D, MC, V
No dress restrictions

You'll find four regional styles of Chinese cooking at The Abacus — Mandarin, Cantonese, Shanghai and Szechuan. Some dishes people keep asking for are steamed whole fish with black bean sauce, West Lake Duck, Shanghai Lobster in wine sauce and Abacus Egg Roll with meats and vegetables.

Reservations recommended
Dinner: Daily, 5 P.M. – Midnight
Brunch: Sun., 11:30 A.M. – 2:30 P.M.

ALOUETTE ❺   *French*

440 N. Green Bay Rd.
Highwood, Ill.
(312) 433-5600
Maître d': Paul Christian
Full Bar/Lot Parking
MC, V
Jacket for men

Ambience plays a big part in dining at Alouette. It oozes French country charm. Baroque background music also contributes to the mood. House specialties include tiny sea snails with bay shrimp in creamed parsley sauce, roast duck in a raspberry and brandy sauce, rack of lamb broiled with fresh mint and tournedos of veal in a creamy Roquefort sauce.

Reservations required
Dinner: Sun. – Sat., 5:30 P.M. – 11 P.M.
  Closed Monday

AMBRIA ⓯   *French*

2300 N. Lincoln Park West
Chicago
(312) 472-5959
Full Bar/Valet Parking
AE, MC, V
Jacket for men

Ambria offers *nouvelle cuisine* in an Art Déco setting. Vegetables are really a specialty here — from the vegetable mousses in flavored butter sauces to those accompanying such entrées as swordfish in beurre rouge, veal liver with cracked mustard seeds and whitefish in anchovy sauce.

Reservations required
Dinner: Mon. – Thurs., 6 P.M. – 9:30 P.M.
  Fri. – Sat., 6 P.M. – 10:30 P.M.
  Closed Sunday

ARNIE'S ㉗   *Continental*

1030 N. State St.
Chicago
(312) 266-4800
Full Bar/Street Parking
AE, D, MC, V
Jacket for men

You'll be at the center of sophisticated Chicago as you sip wine, dine on Dover Sole, Veal Piccata or Strip Steak Arnie's and listen to the music playing discreetly in the background. There's also a plant-filled atrium at Arnie's, dancing, and a brunch on Sundays.

Reservations required
Lunch: Mon.–Fri., 11:30 A.M.–2:30 P.M.
Dinner: Mon.–Sat., 5:30 P.M.–11 P.M.
      Sun., 11 A.M.–2:30 P.M.

ARNIE'S NORTH ❻   *Continental*

1876 First St.
Highland Park, Ill.
(312) 432-1200
Maître d': Michael Sternberg
Full Bar/Lot and Street Parking
AE, D, MC, V
No dress restrictions

A Grand Buffet featuring an array of salads, meats, fish and two hot entrées is the star attraction at Arnie's North, followed close behind by the Hamburger Bar with no fewer than 50 toppings. The setting is full Art Déco, complemented by stained glass windows. Party facilities are available.

No reservations required
Lunch/Dinner: Tues.–Sat., 11:30 A.M.–Midnight
               Sun., 10:30 A.M.–Midnight
               Closed Monday

AVENUE ONE ㉔   *American*

The Drake Hotel
140 E. Walton St.
Chicago
(312) 787-2200
Maître d': Gene Graves
Full Bar/Valet Parking
AE, D, MC, V
Jacket for men

What was once The Drake's famous Camellia House is now Avenue One. The idea here is to feature regional specialties from across the country. This means you'll find Veal Oskar, Red Snapper Bayou, Bourbon Beef, Florida pompano in parchment and Bookbinder Red Snapper Soup.

Reservations preferred
Dinner: Daily, 5 P.M.–Midnight
Brunch: Sun., Noon–3 P.M.

THE BAKERY ⓰   *Continental*

2218 N. Lincoln Ave.
Chicago
(312) 472-6942
Maître d': Geza Szathmary
Full Bar/Street Parking
AE, MC, V, CB
No dress restrictions

Owner/chef Louis Szathmary and his family have operated this very personal restaurant for nearly 20 years. The five-course prix fixe dinner focuses on entrées such as Beef Wellington and roast duck, or at least five other seasonal specialties. True to its name, The Bakery features desserts that are baked on the premises.

Reservations required
Dinner: Tues.–Sat., 5 P.M.–11 P.M.
   Closed Sunday, Monday

THE BARN OF BARRINGTON ❶   *Continental*

1415 S. Barrington Rd.
Barrington, Ill.
(312) 381-8585
Maître d': Jerry Swartz, Ron Lasocki
Full Bar/Lot Parking
AE, D, MC, V
Good taste in dress required

The Barn is really two different restaurants — each with its own distinctive antique collection — in one 120-year-old structure that was once actually a barn. French cuisine is featured in The Carvery and Continental selections can be ordered in the more casual Great Hall.

Reservations required
Lunch: Mon.–Fri., 11 A.M.–2:30 P.M.
Dinner: Mon.–Fri., 5 P.M.–10:30 P.M.
        Sat., 5 P.M.–11:30 P.M.
        Sun., 5 P.M.–10 P.M.
Brunch: Sun., 11 A.M.–2:30 P.M.

THE BERGHOFF ㊼   *German*

17 W. Adams
Chicago
(312) 427-3170
Full Bar/Street Parking
No credit cards
No dress restrictions

You should have no trouble satisfying a really big appetite at The Berghoff. The substantial German fare includes sauerbraten, wiener schnitzel, trout and other seafoods, plus several kinds of roasts and stews. People say the rye bread is something special. There's plenty of German beer on draft to wash it all down.

No reservations required (except for four or more)
Lunch/Dinner: Daily, Noon–Midnight

BINYON'S (48)   American

327 S. Plymouth Ct.
Chicago
(312) 341-1155
Maître d': Hal and Jack Binyon (owners)
Full Bar/Lot Parking
MC, V
No dress restrictions

Run by the Binyon family for over 50 years, Binyon's features an extensive menu starring prime steaks and chops. There is also fresh fish and seafood along with several German specialties. They are famous for their turtle soup, ox tails, lamb shanks, corned beef, Irish lamb stew and American pot roast.

Reservations required
Lunch/Dinner: Mon. – Sat., 11 A.M. – 10 P.M.
              Closed Sunday

THE BLACKHAWK (35)   American

139 N. Wabash Ave.
Chicago
(312) 726-0100
Maître d': Don Roth (owner)
Full Bar/Lot Parking
AE, D, MC, V, CB
No dress restrictions

Something of a landmark in downtown Chicago, The Blackhawk presents a spinning salad bowl, roast prime ribs of beef, fresh Boston scrod and charbroiled prime steaks. They provide a courtesy shuttle service back to your hotel or to nearby theaters.

Reservations required
Lunch/Dinner: Mon. – Fri., 11 A.M. – 10:00 P.M.
              Sat., 11 A.M. – 11 P.M.
              Sun., 5 P.M. – 10:00 P.M.

CAFE BOHEMIA (44)   American

Adams and Clinton Sts.
Chicago
(312) 782-1826
Maître d': Jim Janek, Ann Rowe
Full Bar/Valet, Lot and Street Parking
AE, D, MC, V, CB
No dress restrictions

If you're *really, really* hungry and only an eight-course dinner will do, then Cafe Bohemia is the place to turn to. Wild game is served year 'round. There are also aged prime steaks (up to 60 ounces for the King Kong appetite) and fresh seafood, including 2½-pound Maine lobsters. There is complimentary limousine service to and from your hotel.

No reservations required
Lunch/Dinner: Mon. – Fri., 11:30 A.M. – 11:30 P.M.
              Sat., 5 P.M. – Midnight
              Closed Sunday, Holidays

CHICAGO   53

CAFE PROVENCAL ❽   *Country French*

1625 Hinman
Evanston, Ill.
(312) 475-2233
Full Bar/Street Parking
MC
Good taste in dress required

Owner/chef Leslie Reis likes to use the freshest possible ingredients in her special dishes. That means that entrées change with the seasons. There is heavy emphasis on fresh fish and vegetables *and* on imagination and originality in preparation. You can sip a before-dinner drink in the adjoining salon.

Reservations requested
Dinner: Mon.–Thurs., 6 P.M.–9:30 P.M.
*   Fri.–Sat., 6 P.M.–10:30 P.M.*
*   Closed Sunday*

CAPE COD ROOM ㉔   *Seafood*

The Drake Hotel
140 E. Walton St.
Chicago
(312) 787-2200
Maître d': Patrick Bredin
Full Bar/Valet, Lot and Street Parking
AE, D, MC, V, CB
Jacket for men

Checkered tablecloths, captain's chairs, copper pots and chowder kettles comprise the setting for this seafood restaurant of long standing. They count among their specialties Bookbinder Red Snapper Soup, cherrystone clams on the half shell, scallops, sole, turbot and pompano.

Reservations required
Lunch/Dinner: Daily, Noon–11 P.M.

CARSON'S — THE PLACE FOR RIBS ㉙ *Barbecue*

612 N. Wells (2 other locations)
Chicago
(312) 280-9200
Full Bar/Street Parking
AE, D, MC, V
No dress restrictions

Reportedly moist and meaty ribs come with hot rolls, a big salad with anchovy dressing or cole slaw, and a heaping helping of potatoes. Steaks are also available, such as a mammoth double sirloin, weighing in at more than 24 ounces. There are goldbrick sundaes and cheesecake for dessert.

No reservations required
Lunch/Dinner: Mon.–Thurs., 11 A.M.–Midnight
*   Fri.–Sat., 11 A.M.–1 A.M.*
*   Sun., 2 P.M.–11 P.M.*

CHEZ PAUL ㊱ — *French*

660 N. Rush St.
Chicago
(312) 944-6680
Maître d': Jean Pierre Sire
Full Bar/Valet Parking
AE, D, MC, V, CB
Jacket for men

Chez Paul's home is in the 19th-century Robert Hall McCormick mansion, another of Chicago's many landmarks. The several lovingly restored dining rooms are settings for such specialties as Salmon en Croûte, Duck à l'Orange, Beef Wellington and rack of lamb.

Reservations required
Lunch: Mon.–Fri., 11:30 A.M.–2:30 P.M.
Dinner: Daily, 6 P.M.–10:30 P.M.

THE CONSORT ㉓ — *Continental*

Continental Plaza Hotel
909 N. Michigan Ave.
Chicago
(312) 943-7200
Maître d': Roy Mariani
Full Bar/Valet Parking
AE, D, MC, V, CB
Jacket for men, no jeans

A place to visit if you fancy haute cuisine served to the strains of violins — seven of them — in concert nightly. The rooftop restaurant is described as "regal" by the management. Selections from the extensive menu include Steak Diane, Tournedos Consort and Beef Wellington.

Reservations required
Lunch: Mon.–Fri., Noon–2:30 P.M.
Dinner: Sun.–Thurs., 6 P.M.–Midnight
Fri.–Sat., 6 P.M.–1 A.M.
Brunch: Sun., 11 A.M.–3 P.M.

THE COTTAGE ㊿ — *Continental*

525 Torrence Ave.
Calumet City, Ill.
(312) 891-3900
Maître d': Gerald J. Buster (owner)
Full Bar/Lot Parking
MC, V
Jacket for men

With its beamed ceilings and artifacts relating to food and wine lining the walls, The Cottage may remind you of a European country inn. There is "proper" service, a congenial atmosphere and a host of unusual specialties. For example, you'll find Steak Madagascar, Cottage Schnitzel, homemade soups and freshly baked desserts on the menu.

No reservations required (except Saturday)
Dinner: Tues.–Thurs., 5 P.M.–10 P.M.
Fri.–Sat., 5 P.M.–11 P.M.
Closed Sunday, Monday

CRICKET'S ㉚ *Continental*

100 E. Chestnut St.
Chicago
(312) 280-2100
Maître d': Jean Pierre Lutz
Full Bar/Valet Parking
AE, D, MC, V, CB
Jacket, tie for men

A club-type atmosphere prevails at Cricket's. There are corporate logos and interesting memorabilia hanging from ceilings and walls. Special items include Veal Cricket, double sirloin steaks, Dover Sole and nightly entertainment in the bar area.

Reservations required
Lunch: Mon.–Sat., Noon–2:30 P.M.
Dinner: Mon.–Sat., 6 P.M.–9:30 P.M.
Brunch: Sun., 11 A.M.–2:30 P.M.

DORO'S ㉛ *Northern Italian*

871 N. Rush St.
Chicago
(312) 266-1414
Maître d': Emilio Manconi
Full Bar/Valet Parking
AE, D, MC, V, CB
Jacket for men

Old World elegance is invoked at Doro's, in terms of crystal chandeliers, gold service plates, gleaming sterling and a staff in black tie. Diners are encouraged to take their time with each course. House specialties include a variety of veal dishes, from Piccata Lombarda to Costoletta Valdostana. The zabaglione is prepared at your table.

Reservations required
Lunch: Mon.–Fri., 11:30 A.M.–2:30 P.M.
Dinner: Mon.–Sat., 6 P.M.–11 P.M.
   Closed Sunday

ELI'S THE PLACE FOR STEAK ㉜ *American*

215 E. Chicago Ave.
Chicago
(312) 642-1393
Maître d': Henry or Bob
Full Bar/Valet Parking
AE
Jacket for men

Intimate and comfortably plush, Eli's is known for its celebrity clientele as much as for its hearty specialties. Steaks, prime rib, barbecued back ribs and Liver Eli are well-known standbys. The piano bar is in full swing seven nights a week.

Reservations required
Lunch: Mon.–Fri., 11 A.M.–2:30 P.M.
Dinner: Daily, 4 P.M.–11:30 P.M.

ENZIO'S ㊷

Northern Italian

21 W. Goethe
Chicago
(312) 280-1010
Maître d': Vito Lantz
Full Bar/Valet and Street Parking
AE, MC, V
No dress restrictions

Family-style service lives at Enzio's. It is a main ingredient in more than 30 entrées, including the house specialty, Veal Sardianoloa with avocado, shrimp and Fontina cheese. Enzio's also offers eight specially blended coffees and home-baked bread and desserts.

Reservations recommended
Dinner: Daily, from 5 P.M.

EUGENE'S ⑱

Continental

1255 N. State Parkway
Chicago
(312) 944-1445
Maître d': Alain Sitbon
Full Bar/Valet Parking
AE, D, MC, V, CB
Jacket for men

"Opulent yet understated elegance," is owner Gene Sage's description of Eugene's. "Convivial and sophisticated," he adds. The special features here are escargots, prime aged steaks, Red Snapper Arlésienne, seafood and veal. Vegetables are prepared fresh to your order.

Reservations required
Dinner: Daily, 4:30 P.M.–2 A.M.

FANNY'S ❼
WORLD FAMOUS RESTAURANT

American/Italian

1601 Simpson St.
Evanston, Ill.
(312) 475-8686
Full Bar/Lot Parking
AE, D, MC, V, CB
Jacket for men (first floor)

What is Fanny famous for, you ask? Why, it's her spaghetti, her southern fried chicken, her fresh fish and her fettucini, for starters. Owner Fanny Lazzar permits nothing synthetic to enter her kitchen — no artificial colorings or flavorings. She has collected a large number of original oil paintings to place on her walls and roses to place on her tables.

No reservations required
Dinner: Mon.–Sat., 5 P.M.–10 P.M.
    Sun., Noon–8 P.M.

FARMER'S DAUGHTER   **51**   *International*

14455 La Grange Rd.
Orland Park, Ill.
(312) 349-2330
Maître d': Kathi A. Henely
Full Bar/Lot Parking
AE, D, CB
Good taste in dress required

Reminiscent of San Francisco in the 1930s is the way owner Kandy Norton-Henely sees her restaurant, and it's no wonder. There are Casablanca fans, ferns, rattan furnishings, lighted prism glass windows and an oak and brass bar at the Farmer's Daughter. As for food, there is milk-fed veal, a pickle cart to go with sandwiches and a cracker cart for soups.

Reservations suggested
Lunch/Dinner: Mon.–Fri., 11:30 A.M.–2 A.M.
*   Sat., 5 P.M.–2 A.M.*
*   Sun., 2 P.M.–Midnight*

FLORENTINE ROOM   **46**   *Northern Italian*

Italian Village
71 W. Monroe
Chicago
(312) 332-7005
Maître d': Tony
Full Bar/Valet and Lot Parking
AE
Jacket for men, no jeans

The Florentine Room focuses on elegance in atmosphere and service. The setting is one of soft lights and mirrors, with Florentine family crests on the walls to remind you where you are. Specialties include Veal Piccata, Beef Scaloppini Pitti and Chicken Strozzi.

Reservations required
Lunch: Mon.–Fri., 11:30 A.M.–2:30 P.M.
Dinner: Mon.–Fri., 5 P.M.–10 P.M.
*   Sat., 5 P.M.–1 A.M.*
*   Closed Sunday*

FOND DE LA TOUR   **4**   *French*

Oak Brook Towers
40 N. Tower Rd.
Oak Brook, Ill.
(312) 620-1500
Maître d': Hans Lautenbacher
Full Bar/Valet and Lot Parking
AE, D, MC, V, CB
Jacket, tie for men

Imagine yourself on the Left Bank as you dine in this intimate outdoor French cafe. Specialties are Tournedos Rossini, rack of lamb, Sole Meunière, Steak au Poivre and Beef Wellington. There is also an extensive wine list.

Reservations required
Lunch: Mon.–Fri., 11:30 A.M.–2:30 P.M.
Dinner: Mon.–Fri., 6 P.M.–11 P.M.
*   Sat., 6 P.M.–Midnight*
*   Closed Sunday*

GIANNOTTI'S ㊾ *Italian*

7711 W. Roosevelt
Forest Park, Ill.
(312) 366-1199
Full Bar/Valet Parking
AE, D, MC, V, CB
No dress restrictions

A "homey" atmosphere prevails at Giannotti's says the management. Seven-course dinners are featured. There is also a Fiesta Dinner for three or more, served family style and including soup, salad, fettuccine, ravioli and chicken entrées.

Reservations required (three or more)
Lunch: Mon.-Fri., 11 A.M.-3 P.M.
Dinner: Tues.-Thurs., 4 P.M.-12:30 A.M.
        Fri.-Sat., 4 P.M.-1 A.M.
        Sun., 2 P.M.-11 P.M.

GORDON ㊴ *Continental*

512 N. Clark
Chicago
(312) 467-9780
Full Bar/Street Parking
AE, MC, V
Good taste in dress required

The emphasis at Gordon is on fresh fish, delicately prepared. It somehow seems to fit the lean and subtle setting of tile floors and just a few appropriate embellishments. Specialties include mahi mahi in cognac sauce, poached salmon, cream of lettuce soup and several well-prepared desserts.

Reservations required
Lunch: Tues.-Fri., 11:30 A.M.-2:30 P.M.
Dinner: Sun., Tues.-Thurs., 5:30 P.M.-10:30 P.M.
        Fri.-Sat., 5:30 P.M.-Midnight
Supper: Sun., Tues-Thurs., 10:30 P.M.-Midnight

GREEK ISLANDS ㊸ *Greek*

766 W. Jackson St.
Chicago
(312) 782-9855
Maître d': John Karantonis
Full Bar/Lot Parking
AE, D, MC, V, CB
No dress restrictions

A restaurant so named conjures up images of white, gleaming buildings scattered across green, fertile hillsides overlooking a sparkling blue sea. But if you're in Chicago and not Mykonos, this restaurant may well suffice. All the Greek staples are featured here — lamb, squid, octopus, cheese pie — as well as seafood selections such as red snapper and sea bass.

No reservations required
Lunch/Dinner: Sun.-Thurs., 11 A.M.-Midnight
              Fri.-Sat., 11 A.M.-1 A.M.

JIMMY'S PLACE ❿   *Continental*

3420 N. Elston
Chicago
(312) 539-2999
Maître d': Jimmy (owner)
Full Bar/Street Parking
MC, V
Good taste in dress required

Nouvelle cuisine is the basis for such specialties as sautéed veal served on a bed of spinach, fluffy liver mousse, marinated raw salmon (Japanese style) and fresh vegetables. Tiny long-stemmed mushrooms are *the* spotlighted feature.

Reservations required
Dinner: Mon., Wed.–Sat., 5:30 P.M.–10 P.M.
  Sun., 4 P.M.–9 P.M.
  Closed Tuesday

JOVAN ㊲   *French*

16 E. Huron St.
Chicago
(312) 944-7766
Maître d': Jean-Marie Vandenbulcke
Full Bar/Valet Parking
AE, D, CB
Jacket for men

"Cuisine bourgeoise in elegant surroundings" is the management's whimsical way of describing Jovan. The prix fixe menu, which changes daily, offers a choice of three soups, six appetizers and eight entrées. There are such specialties as salmon mousse, duck pâté in green peppercorn sauce, Sweetbreads Calvados and Grand Marnier Soufflé.

Reservations required
Lunch: Mon.–Fri., Noon–2:30 P.M.
Dinner: Mon.–Sat., 6 P.M.–10 P.M.
  Closed Sunday

LA CHEMINEE ⑳   *French*

1161 N. Dearborn St.
Chicago
(312) 642-6654
Full Bar/Valet Parking
AE, D, MC, V, CB
No dress restrictions

If you're in the mood for loads of "ambience" in the form of candlelight dining and tucked-away alcove seating, turn to La Cheminée. To satisfy other appetites, there is Beef Wellington and Veal Florentine among many other selections, including a nightly chef's special.

Reservations required
Dinner: Daily, 5 P.M.–Midnight

LA FONTAINE ⓴   *French*

2442 N. Clark
Chicago
(312) 525-1800
Maître d': Jean Claude Poilevey
Full Bar/Lot Parking
AE, D, MC, V, CB
Jacket, tie for men

A sturdy Lincoln Park townhouse has become an elegantly remodeled French restaurant. The classic cuisine covers some 17 different entrées, ranging from Veal Normande to Paupiette du Saumon. The appetizers and desserts are just as varied.

Reservations required
Lunch: Tues.-Fri., 11:30 A.M.-2 P.M.
Dinner: Mon.-Sat., 5:30 P.M.-11 P.M.
          Closed Sunday

LAWRY'S THE PRIME RIB ㊶   *American*

100 E. Ontario St.
Chicago
(312) 787-5000
Full Bar/Valet Parking
AE, MC, V
No dress restrictions

Lawry's is housed in an old mansion that once belonged to the McCormick family of Chicago. The bill of fare is prime rib, and only prime rib, but that's usually enough for most people. There are three cuts available, plus all the trimmings. Dessert includes homemade English trifle and chocolate pecan pie.

Reservations suggested
Lunch: Mon.-Fri., 11:30 A.M.-2 P.M.
Dinner: Mon.-Thurs., 5 P.M.-11 P.M.
          Fri.-Sat., 5 P.M.-Midnight
          Sun., 3 P.M.-10 P.M.

LE BASTILLE ㉞   *French*

21 W. Superior
Chicago
(312) 787-2050
Maître d': Elliot Baron (manager)
Full Bar/Street Parking
AE, MC, V, CB
No dress restrictions

Le Bastille is an informal Parisian-style grill, specializing in grilled seafood and meats and featuring one of the city's most complete wine bars. Selections include steak with *pommes frites* (french fries), mixed seafood grill, grilled sea bass and duck in a variety of sauces.

Reservations required
Lunch/Dinner: Daily

LE FESTIVAL ㉑ *French*

28 W. Elm
Chicago
(312) 944-7090
Maître d': Robert Garzan
Full Bar/Street Parking
AE, MC, V
Jacket for men (dinner)

Housed in a restored Victorian townhouse, Le Festival provides a good measure of quiet elegance as befits its aristocratic heritage. The chef turns out such specialties as Sole Bonne Femme, Veal Normande, Pigeon Poêle and Beef Wellington.

Reservations required (dinner)
Lunch: Mon.–Fri., 11:30 A.M.–2:30 P.M.
Dinner: Mon.–Sat., 5:30 P.M.–10:30 P.M.
    Closed Sunday

LE FRANCAIS ❸ *French*

269 S. Milwaukee Ave.
Wheeling, Ill.
(312) 541-7470
Maître d': Doris Banchet
Full Bar/Valet Parking
AE, MC, V
Jacket for men

This is a restaurant that has received a good deal of national attention lately, most of it due to the efforts of its exacting owner/chef Jean Banchet. Imagination and innovation, without fussiness or pretention, are combined to produce such specialties as partridge pâté, boneless squab with squab mousse stuffing, sole with lobster mousse stuffing, pheasant with cream sauce and on and on.

Reservations required
Dinner: Tues.–Sun., 5:30 P.M.–10 P.M.
    Closed Monday

LE MIGNON ㉝ *Continental*

712 N. Rush St.
Chicago
(312) 664-1033
Maître d': Toni Tontini
Full Bar/Valet Parking
AE, D, MC, V
Jacket, tie for men

Located in a restored mansion, Le Mignon features Dover Sole, imported turbot, Long Island pearl scallops, frogs' legs, roast duckling with wild rice, rack of lamb and steaks in many and wondrous variety.

No reservations required
Lunch: Mon.–Fri., 11:30 A.M.–2:30 P.M.
Dinner: Mon.–Sat., 5:30 P.M.–10:30 P.M.
    Closed Sunday

LE PERROQUET ㉕ French

70 E. Walton Place
Chicago
(312) 944-7990
Full Bar/Street Parking
AE, D
Jacket, tie for men

A "cheerful modern room with fresh flowers" (so described by owner Jovan Trboyevic) is the scene for "innovative, modern French cuisine." Le Perroquet's third-floor private-elevator entrance allows you to believe you're dining in a private club. There is a choice of at least six different soufflés every night, as well as many other creative entrées.

Reservations required
Lunch: Mon.–Fri., Noon–3 P.M.
Dinner: Mon.–Sat., 6 P.M.–Midnight
   Closed Sunday

L'ESCARGOT ㉘ French

701 N. Michigan Ave.
Chicago
(312) 337-1717
Maître d': Alan C. Tutzer
Full Bar/Lot Parking
AE, D, MC, V, CB
No dress restrictions

Chef and co-owner Lucien Veige likes his French Provincial food "honest," his service "gracious" and the setting "warm and comfortable." Such are the standards at L'Escargot. Here you'll choose from among fresh fish entrées, roasted lamb, cassoulet, Burgundy-style escargots and an array of homemade desserts.

Reservations required
Breakfast: Daily, 7 A.M.–10 A.M.
Lunch: Daily, 11:30 A.M.–2:30 P.M.
Dinner: Daily, 5:30 A.M.–10:30 P.M.

LE TITI DE PARIS ❷ French

2275 Rand Rd.
Palatine, Ill.
(312) 359-4434
Maître d': Dominique
Full Bar/Lot Parking
AE, D, MC, V, CB
Jacket for men

This small country French restaurant is the scene for chef/owner Pierre Pollin's personal specialties. He features fresh scallops, filet of beef baked in puff pastry and stuffed with veal mousse and avocado purée, homemade fruit sorbets and gossamer-light soufflés that contain no milk or flour.

Reservations required
Lunch: Tues.–Fri., 11:30 A.M.–2:30 P.M.
Dinner: Tues.–Sat., 5:30 P.M.–Midnight
   Sun., 4 P.M.–Midnight
   Closed Monday

MAXIM'S DE PARIS ⓳ *French*

1300 Astor St.
Chicago
(312) 943-1111
Maître d': Guy Schulz
Full Bar/Valet Parking
AE, D, MC, V, CB
Jacket, tie for men

Maxim's is a replica of its Paris ancestor, says owner Nancy Goldberg. Its Art Nouveau design, classical French menu and extensive wine list do mirror the original Maxim's. Specialties include Sole Albert, Veal Orloff and Crêpes Veuve Joyeuse (filled with lemon souffle).

No reservations required
Lunch: Mon.-Sat., Noon-3 P.M.
Dinner: Daily, 6 P.M.-Midnight

NICK'S FISHMARKET ㊺ *Seafood*

1 First National Plaza
Chicago
(312) 621-0200
Maître d': John Hogan, Aaron Placourakis
Full Bar/Valet Parking
AE, D, MC, V, CB
Jacket for men preferred

Nick's 60-item menu highlights fresh seafood, including specialties such as mahi-mahi, catfish, opakapaka and abalone. There is also veal, chicken and beef for those who prefer the delights of the land. The setting is one of oversized leather booths, each equipped with a handy telephone jack and lighting dimmer switch!

Reservations required
Lunch: Mon.-Fri., 11:30 A.M.-3 P.M.
Dinner: Mon.-Fri., 5:30 P.M.-11:30 P.M.
        Sat., 5:30 P.M.-Midnight
        Closed Sunday

THE NINETY-FIFTH ㉖ *Continental*

John Hancock Center
875 N. Michigan Ave.
Chicago
(312) 787-9596
Full Bar/Valet Parking
AE, D, MC, V, CB
Jacket for men, no jeans

Wouldn't you know it, The Ninety-Fifth is 95 floors above Chicago. Along with the magnificent view, there is "heavenly" food. Look for such specialties as poached trout, Beef Wellington and Tournedos Rossini. There's also a wine list strong on both quantity and quality.

Reservations preferred
Lunch: Mon.-Sat., Noon-3 P.M.
Dinner: Daily, 6 P.M.-11:30 P.M.
Brunch: Sun., 11:30 A.M.-3 P.M.

THE PARADISE CAFE ⓫　　　*Continental*

3352 N. Broadway
Chicago
(312) 348-8454
Full Bar/Street Parking
AE, D, MC, V, CB
Good taste in dress required

There are two ways of dining at The Paradise Cafe. You can take advantage of the "Cafe Menu" offering a choice of three soups, salads, burgers and fried chicken, or you can select from the dinner menu that lists several appetizers and entrées. There are pasta starters, fillet of sole, Veal Marsala, roast duck and lamb and beef dishes.

Reservations required
Dinner: Mon.-Thurs., 6 P.M.-10 P.M.
　　　　Fri.-Sat., 6 P.M.-11 P.M.
　　　　Sun., 6 P.M.-9:30 P.M.
Brunch: Sun., 11:30 A.M.-2:30 P.M.

THE PUMP ROOM ⓬　　　*Continental*

Ambassador East Hotel
1301 N. State Parkway
Chicago
(312) 266-0360
Full Bar/Valet Parking
AE, MC, V
Jacket for men

The large and varied menu at The Pump Room features at least seven selections not included on the regular listing. Fine, formal dining is the attraction, along with the "celebrity entrance" lined with photos of the famous. There is a separate "cafe" area overlooking that great street, State.

Reservations required
Breakfast: Daily, 6:30 A.M.-11:30 A.M.
Lunch:　　Daily, 11:30 A.M.-3 P.M.
Dinner:　　Sun.-Thurs., 6 P.M.-10 P.M.
　　　　　Fri.-Sat., 6 P.M.-1 A.M.
Brunch:　　Sun., 10:30 A.M.-2:30 P.M.

SAGE'S ON STATE ⓭　　　*Seafood*

1255 N. State Parkway
Chicago
(312) 944-1383
Maître d': Alain Sitbon
Full Bar/Valet Parking
AE, D, MC, V, CB
Jacket for men

You'll dine in a plush red velvet dining room, Victorian in style. Specialties include Oysters Rockefeller, Steak Tartare, Clams Casino, seafood crêpes with mornay sauce, Cherries Jubilee and New York-style cheesecake.

Reservations required
Dinner: Mon.-Thurs., 5 P.M.-Midnight
　　　　Fri.-Sat., 5 P.M.-1 A.M.
　　　　Closed Sunday

SU CASA ⓸   *Mexican*

49 E. Ontario St.
Chicago
(312) 943-4041
Maître d': Hugo Aranda
Full Bar/Street Parking
AE, D, MC, V, CB
Jacket for men

There was, no doubt, some daring involved in bringing authentic Mexican food to the Midwest back in 1962. But the people at Su Casa prevailed. Subtly spiced offerings such as Steak Ranchero, Shrimp à la Vera Cruz and Carne Asada are served in the converted stables of a 19th-century townhouse.

Reservations required
Lunch/Dinner: Mon.–Sat., 11:30 A.M.–1 A.M.
           Closed Sunday

SWEETWATER ㉒   *American*

1028 N. Rush St.
Chicago
(312) 787-5552
Maître d': Dorothy Francisco
Full Bar/Valet Parking
AE, MC, V
No dress restrictions

Sweetwater consists of several dining areas. The "forever-summer" peach-toned Gourmet Room, the intimate paneled Walnut Room, the indoor sidewalk cafe and the skylight bar. Specialties are steaks, prime rib, scallops in wine and cream sauce, ribs, chicken, multiple salads and four kinds of homemade bread. A place to watch the city's political elite come and go.

Reservations suggested
Lunch/Dinner: Mon.–Sat., 11:30 A.M.–2 A.M.
           Sun., 10:30 A.M.–2 A.M.

TANGO ⓭   *Seafood*

Hotel Belmont
3172 N. Sheridan Rd.
Chicago
(312) 935-0350
Full Bar/Valet Parking
AE, MC, V
Good taste in dress required

Seafood selections prepared in a subtly French manner are the specialty here. There is fresh sea bass en croûte, Sea Scallops Tango, bouillabaisse, brook trout stuffed with shrimp and crab meat and broiled walleye pike. There are also steak and chop alternatives.

Reservations required
Lunch: Tues.–Sat., 11:30 A.M.–2 P.M.
Dinner: Sun.–Thurs., 5 P.M.–11 P.M.
       Fri.–Sat., 5 P.M.–Midnight

TOWER GARDEN & RESTAURANT ❾   *French*

9925 Grosse Point Rd.
Skokie, Ill.
(312) 673-4450
Maître d': Marc Jaggi
Full Bar/Lot Parking
AE, D, MC, V, CB
Jacket for men

Skylights, flowers and fountains join forces to create the Tower Garden's unmistakable floral atmosphere. As for the food, there are crêpes filled with crab meat in lobster sauce or filled with spinach soufflé, along with many other European specialties. The new Wine Bibliothèque is a showcase for the restaurant's substantial and varied selection.

Reservations required
Lunch: Mon. – Sat., 11:30 A.M. – 3 P.M.
Dinner: Mon. – Thurs., 4:30 P.M. – 11 P.M.
       Fri. – Sat., 4:30 P.M. – Midnight
       Closed Sunday

TRUFFLES ㊳   *Continental*

Hyatt-Regency Chicago
151 E. Wacker Dr.
Chicago
(312) 565-1000
Maître d': Dieter H. Schafer
Full Bar/Valet Parking
AE, D, MC, V, CB
Jacket for men

Here you can dine on all the things you dreamed of eating as a child (if elegantly prepared food was what you dreamed of then). Such items as foie gras, fresh pâtés, medallions of veal, lobster, rack of lamb and crisp roast duckling are offered at Truffles. Desserts come flambéed and soufflés come hoveringly high.

Reservations required
Lunch: Mon. – Fri., 11:30 A.M. – 2:30 P.M.
Dinner: Daily, 6 P.M. – 11 P.M.

CLEVELAND

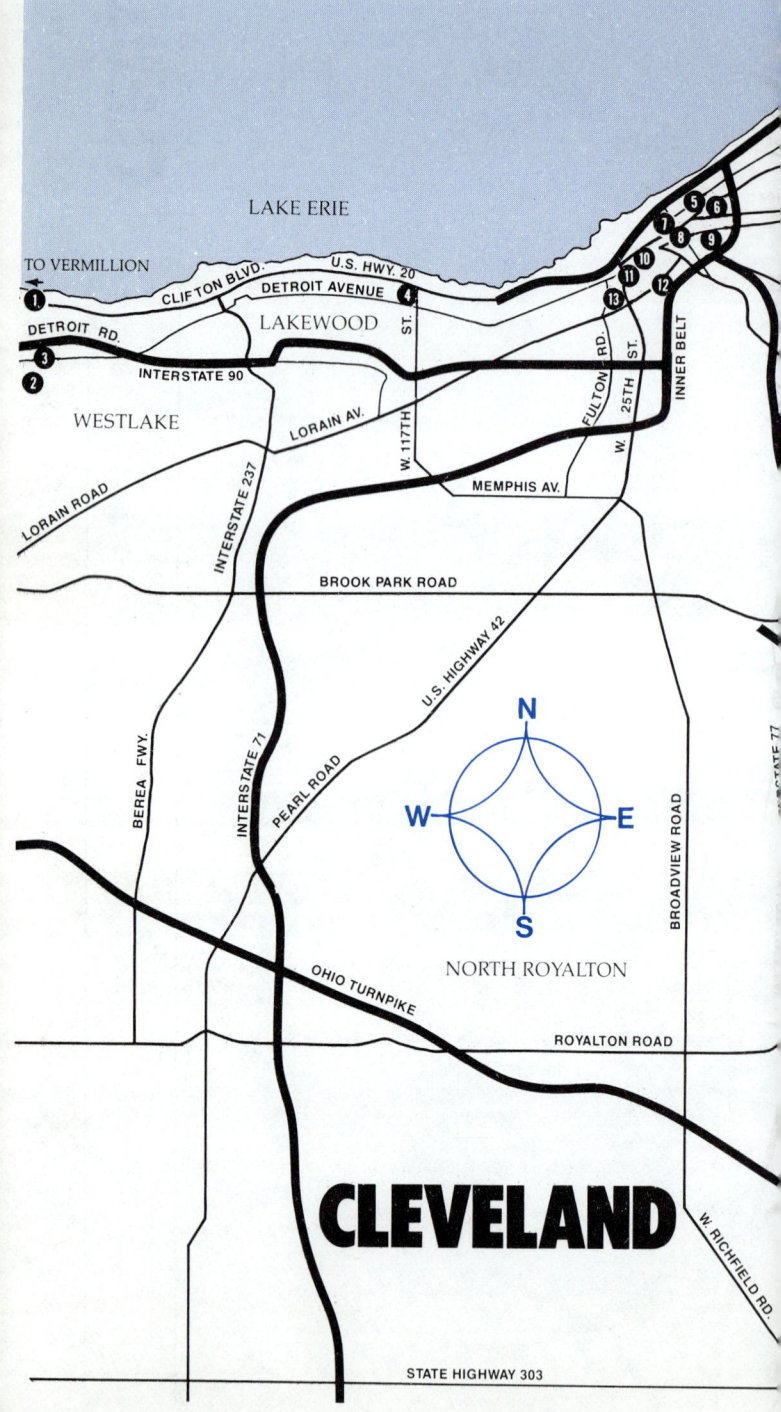

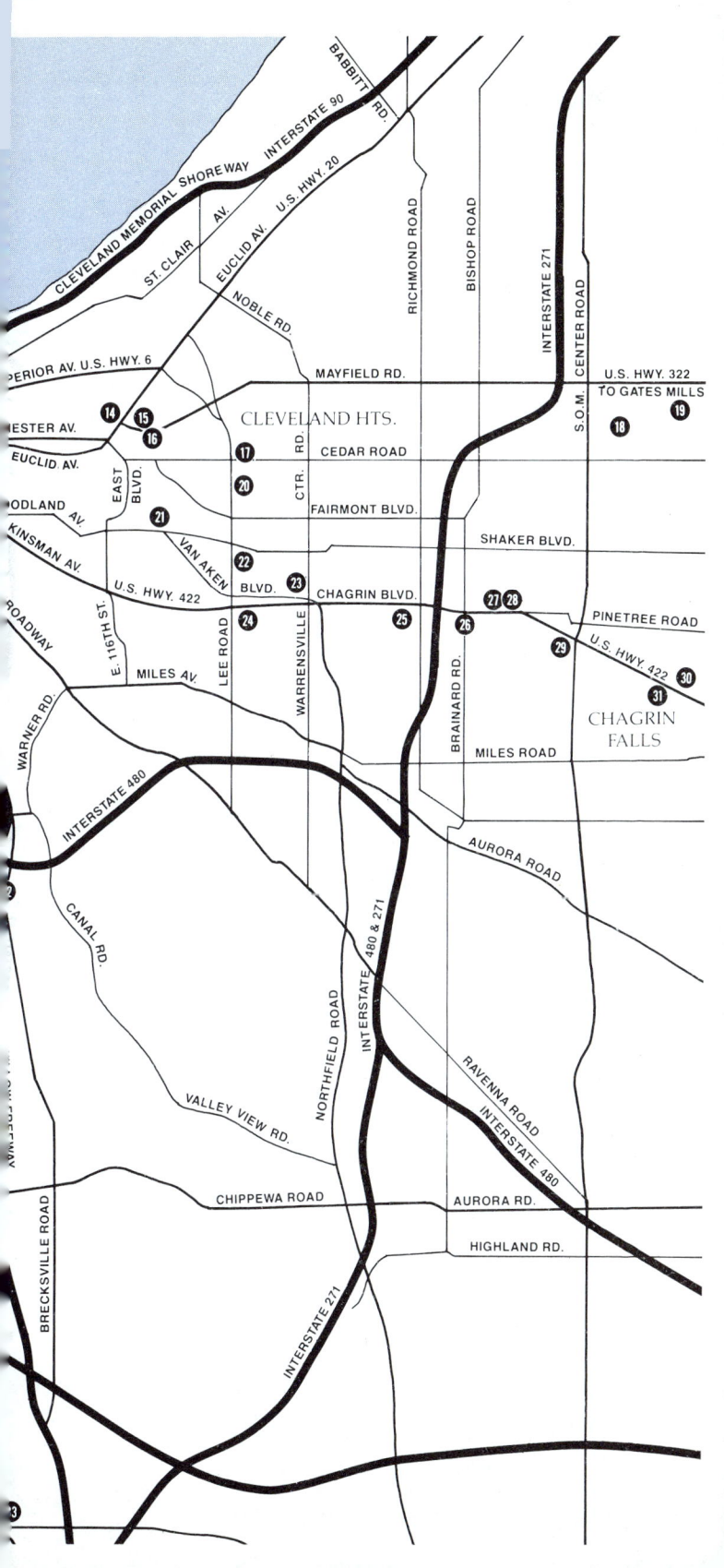

AU PERE JACQUES ㉙ *French*

34105 Chagrin Blvd.
Chagrin Falls, Ohio
(216) 831-8558
Maître d': Alvin Sapp
Full Bar/Lot Parking
MC, V
Jacket, tie suggested for men

A small French Provincial-style restaurant owned by its chef, J. F. Schindler. The menu offers you 34 ways with Dover Sole and turbot, eight variations on the humble chicken, 10 on veal, 19 on prime beef and even five on sweetbreads, for goodness sake! An extensive wine selection includes some labels from Australia and South Africa.

Reservations suggested
Dinner: Mon.–Sat., 6 P.M.–10 P.M.
 Closed Sunday

AU PROVENCE ⓴ *French/Creole*

2195 Lee Rd.
Cleveland Heights, Ohio
(216) 321-9511
Maître d': Robin Keating
Full Bar/Lot and Street Parking
AE, V, CB
No dress restrictions

Another small French Provincial dining spot noted also for its Creole cuisine, including Trout-in-Parchment and marinated shrimp. A very personal place with a menu created by chef and co-owner Richard Taylor and wines produced by partner Dr. Thomas Wykoff in his winery next door.

Reservations required on Saturday
Dinner: Mon.–Thurs., 6 P.M.–10 P.M.
 Fri., 6 P.M.–11 P.M.
 Sat., 6:30 P.M. and 9:15 P.M. seatings
 Closed Sunday

BALATON ㉒ *Hungarian*

12521 Buckeye Rd.
Cleveland
(216) 921-9691
No Wine or Spirits/Street Parking
No credit cards
No dress restrictions

A good city for this type of cuisine (there's a large Hungarian population). Balaton's menu changes daily, but can include any of 20 to 25 house specialties such as gulyas (goulash) soup, wiener schnitzel served with applesauce, homemade dumplings, Chicken Paprikash and stuffed cabbage. Dobos torte awaits for dessert.

No reservations required
Lunch/Dinner: Tues.–Wed., 11:30 A.M.–8 P.M.
 Thurs.–Sat., 11:30 A.M.–9 P.M.
 Closed Sunday, Monday

EARTH BY APRIL ⓱   *Seafood/Vegetarian*

2151 Lee Rd.
Cleveland Heights, Ohio
(216) 371-1438
Maître d': Mary Ellen Sullivan
Full Bar/Lot Parking
AE, D, MC, V
No dress restrictions

A vegetarian restaurant lately come to seafood, Earth by April specialties include scampi, Eggplant Parmesan, Salmon Hollandaise and Vegetable Tempura, plus a substantial salad buffet. All this is served in an informal atmosphere set to soft background music with entertainment on weekends.

Reservations requested (dinner, parties of six or more)
Lunch: Tues. – Sat., 11:30 A.M. – 3 P.M.
Dinner: Tues. – Thurs., 5 P.M. – 11 P.M.
       Fri. – Sat., 5 P.M. – Midnight
       Sun., 5 P.M. – 9 P.M.
Brunch: Sun., 11 A.M. – 3 P.M.
       Closed Monday, major holidays

FRENCH CONNECTION ⓬   *French*

24 Public Square
Cleveland
(216) 696-5600
Maître d': Robert A. Fishman (manager)
Full Bar/Lot Parking
AE, D, MC, V
Jacket, tie for men

International specialties with French names — Medaillons de Veau (veal), Carré d'Agneau (lamb) and Canard Rôti aux Olives (duck) — are featured in this "top-of-the-line" member of the Stouffer chain. The furnishings are "antique" French and the Public Square location is convenient to shops and offices.

Reservations required
Lunch: Mon. – Fri., 11:30 A.M. – 1:30 P.M.
Dinner: Mon. – Sat., 6 P.M. – 10 P.M.
       Closed Sunday

THE GARLAND ❷   *French/Italian*

25651 Detroit Rd.
Westlake, Ohio
(216) 835-9372
Full Bar/Valet Parking
AE, MC, V
No dress restrictions

A soft and rosy Art Nouveau atmosphere prevails at The Garland. Entrées are mostly cooked to order and "plate presentation" is taken seriously. The emphasis is on comfort and innovative cuisine according to the dictates of chef Pamela Grosscup's imagination.

Reservations requested
Lunch: Mon. – Fri., 11:30 A.M. – 2:30 P.M.
Dinner: Tues. – Sat., 6 P.M. – 11 P.M.
       Closed Sunday, and Monday dinner

GIOVANNI'S ㉕ *Continental*

25550 Chagrin Blvd.
Beachwood, Ohio
(216) 831-8625
Maître d': Ernesto DeGiorgis
Full Bar/Lot Parking
AE, D, MC, V, CB
Jacket for men

Located along suburban Cleveland's "Restaurant Row," Giovanni's offers lots of atmosphere — Italian-style. That means crystal chandeliers, paintings and a marble fireplace. Specialties include "exquisite" veal and freshly prepared fish entrées. A popular zabaglione is featured for dessert.

Reservations required
Lunch/Dinner: Mon.–Fri., 11:30 A.M.–10:30 P.M.
             Sat., 4:30 P.M.–10:30 P.M.
             Closed Sunday

THE GOLDEN BOWL ⑯ *Italian*

12312 Mayfield Rd.
Cleveland
(216) 721-1650
Maître d': Rico Sciulli (manager)
Full Bar/Valet and Lot Parking
AE, D, MC, V, CB
No dress restrictions

Located in the heart of Cleveland's "Little Italy," The Golden Bowl has been serving all manner of Italian specialties plus seafood, steaks and chops for more than 35 years. Family owned and operated, its specialties include Eggplant Caponatina, Fettucine Alfredo and Beef Funghettos.

Reservations required
Lunch/Dinner: Mon.–Fri., 11:30 A.M.–11 P.M.
             Sat., 11:30 A.M.–Midnight
             Closed Sunday

GUARINO'S ⑮ *Italian*

12309 Mayfield Rd.
Cleveland
(216) 231-3100
Maître d': Salvatore (Sam) Guarino (owner)
Full Bar/Valet and Lot Parking
AE, D, MC, V, CB
Jacket for men preferred

Another family-owned "Little Italy" standby featuring Old World decor and a large wine list. Sam Guarino numbers among his specialties Snails Marinara, a dense minestrone, Veal Parmigiana and a rolled stuffed steak. He is also extremely proud of his cappucino as a grand finale.

Reservations suggested on weekends
Lunch/Dinner: Mon.–Sat., 11 A.M.–Midnight
             Closed Sunday

HECK'S CAFE ⓫ ㉗   *Continental*

2927 Bridge Ave.   Eton Square Mall
Cleveland   28699 Chagrin Blvd.
(216) 861-5464   Woodmere Village, Ohio
                       (216) 292-2545
Beer and Wine (Cleveland)/Street and Lot Parking
AE, MC
No dress restrictions

Hamburger in all its many moods is Heck's specialty. They call it "the ultimate in ground beef cuisine." There's the Burger au Poivre, for instance, and Burger Basque and Burger Champignon. Plus, there are several soups, salads and non-hamburger entrées.

No reservations required
Lunch/Dinner: Mon.–Thurs., 11:30 A.M.–Midnight
                 Fri.–Sat., 11:30 A.M.–4 A.M.
                 Sun., 3 P.M.–Midnight
Brunch: Sun., 11 A.M.–3 P.M.

HOLLENDEN TAVERN ❺   *American*

610 Superior Ave. N.E.
Cleveland
(216) 621-0700
Maître d': Duncan Stewart
Full Bar/Lot Parking
AE, D, MC, V
Jacket for men preferred

A popular steak and chop house in this city, the Hollenden also features an ample variety of seafood, including scrod and scallops. A "regular" clientele of business types and politicians mixes with convention visitors in an elegantly appointed dining room

No reservations required
Lunch: Mon.–Fri., 11:30 A.M.–2:30 P.M.
Dinner: Mon.–Thurs., 5 P.M.–10 P.M.
        Closed Saturday, Sunday

HUNTER'S HOLLOW TAVERNE ㉚   *Continental*

100 N. Main St.
Chagrin Falls, Ohio
(216) 247-5222
Maître d': Pablo Poklepovic
Full Bar/Valet, Lot and Street Parking
AE, MC, V, CB
Jacket for men

A rustic atmosphere befitting a country squire describes Hunter's Hollow. You dine on such specialties as Florida stone crab, Veal Thomas, beef tenderloin and she-crab soup, amidst lots of antique furniture and somebody's memorabilia. There's live entertainment nightly.

Reservations required
Lunch: Mon.–Sat., 11:30 A.M.–4 P.M.
Dinner: Mon.–Sat., 4 P.M.–1 A.M.
        Closed Sunday

THE INN AT FOWLER'S MILL ⓲ *Continental*

10700 Mayfield Rd.
Chardon, Ohio
(216) 729-1313
Full Bar (Sunday, beer only)/Lot Parking
AE, D, MC, V
No dress restrictions

Fashioned after an old roadside tavern, The Inn at Fowler's Mill (there really was a mill) is filled with gleaming copper and original old wood. Specialties include roast duck, prime rib, steaks, chops and fresh fish.

Reservations required
Lunch: Tues.-Sat., 11:30 A.M.-2:30 P.M.
Dinner: Tues.-Thurs., 5:30 P.M.-10 P.M.
        Fri.-Sat., 5:30 P.M.-11 P.M.
        Sun., 5:30 P.M.-10 P.M.

IRON GATE ③ *Continental*

24481 Detroit Rd.
Westlake, Ohio
(216) 871-7880
Maître d': Bill Wilson
Full Bar/Valet and Lot Parking
AE, MC, V
Jacket for men preferred

A New Orleans-style restaurant comes to Cleveland's West Side in the form of Iron Gate. The main room was designed with alcoves for privacy. A Garden Room features patio furnishings and plants. A specialty is baked pompano stuffed with crab and shrimp and topped with grapefruit sections.

Reservations recommended
Lunch: Mon.-Fri., 11:30 A.M.-3 P.M.
Dinner: Mon.-Thurs., 5:30 P.M.-11:30 P.M.
        Fri.-Sat., 5:30 P.M.-12:30 A.M.
        Closed Sunday

JAMES TAVERN ㉖ *American*

28699 Chagrin Blvd.
Beachwood, Ohio
(216) 464-4660
Full Bar/Lot Parking
AE, D, MC, V
No dress restrictions

If you fancy your prime rib accompanied by Yorkshire pudding and if you revel in the tradition of an American Colonial setting, the James Tavern should be your cup of tea. There are wood-burning fireplaces to warm you and strolling folk singers to entertain you.

Reservations suggested
Lunch: Mon.-Thurs., 11:30 A.M.-3 P.M.
        Fri.-Sat., 11:30 A.M.-4 P.M.
Dinner: Mon.-Thurs., 5:30 P.M.-10 P.M.
        Fri.-Sat., 5:30 P.M.-Midnight
        Sun., 4 P.M.-8 P.M.
Brunch: Sun., 11 A.M.-3 P.M.

JIM'S STEAK HOUSE ⑩   *American*

1800 Scranton Rd.
Cleveland
(216) 241-6343
Full Bar/Lot Parking
AE, MC, V
No dress restrictions

Prime, aged steaks are stars at Jim's, nicely foiled by the hash browns accompanying them. Located in the city's industrial "flats" area, Jim's also features a somewhat funky, fun atmosphere. You'll enjoy a scenic view of the city as you dine facing the collision bend of the Cuyahoga River.

Reservations required
Lunch/Dinner: Mon.-Fri., 11 A.M.-11 P.M.
                Sat., 11 A.M.-Midnight
                Closed Sunday

KEG & QUARTER ❽   *Continental*

Swingos Celebrity Hotel
1800 Swingos Court
Cleveland
(216) 861-1810
Maître d': Hanna El-Bayeh
Full Bar/Valet Parking
AE, D, MC, V, CB
Formal dress preferred

A formal downtown restaurant with tableside preparation, stained glass windows and a full hierarchy of serving personnel. There are house specialties such as Tenderloin El Greco, Veal Oskar and Milanese, fettucine in various forms and the fresh catch of the day. Where many people tend to go after the theater or the big game.

Reservations required
Lunch: Mon.-Fri., 11 A.M.-3 P.M.
Dinner: Sun.-Thurs., 5 P.M.-11 P.M.
       Fri.-Sat., 5 P.M.-1 A.M.

L'AUBERGE DU PORT ❶   *French*

255 Main St.
Vermilion, Ohio
(216) 967-5333
Maître d': Gerard Humilier (owner)
Full Bar/Street Parking
MC, V
Jacket for men

L'Auberge du Port is located in a small lakeside town some miles west of Cleveland. The setting is a building dating back to the 1840's, with exposed brick walls and the original building beams intact. Specialties include fish pâté, fresh rabbit served with white wine and mustard sauce, and trout stuffed with a scallop mousse.

Reservations advised
Dinner: Mon.-Sat., 5 P.M.-10:30 P.M.
        Sun., 3 P.M.-9 P.M.
        Closed December to March 17

LEONELLO'S ㉔ Continental

16713 Chagrin Blvd.
Shaker Heights, Ohio
(216) 752-6464
Maître d': Jacques Laumier
Full Bar/Valet Parking
AE, MC, V
Jacket, tie for men

Elegant yet intimate is how co-owner Diane Armington describes her restaurant. She also calls it "Cleveland's best kept secret for 22 years." Favorite entrées include Duckling Cointreau à l'Orange and Veal Piccata. Tableside preparation is featured.

Reservations required
Dinner: Tues.-Sat., 6 P.M.-Midnight
  Closed Sunday, Monday

MARKET STREET EXCHANGE ⓭ International

2516 Market Ave.
Cleveland
(216) 579-0520
Full Bar/Lot and Street Parking
AE, MC, V
Good taste in dress required

A restaurant that bills itself as "eclectic," the Market Street Exchange has the most changeable of menus. On any given day you might be offered anything from crawfish and bay scallops sautéed in bananas to unusual concoctions of vegetables and fish. Located in historic Ohio City and housed in two structures that date back to the 1830s.

Reservations recommended
Lunch/Dinner: Mon.-Sat., 11:30 A.M.-1 A.M.
  Sun., Noon-8 P.M.

McNALLY-DOYLE RED FOX INN ⓲ Continental

River Road
Gates Mills, Ohio
(216) 423-4408
Full Bar/Valet, Lot and Street Parking
No credit cards
Jacket, tie for men

Here you'll find a gracious New England-style setting that is intimate yet elegant. The extensive menu (at least three dozen entrées at all times) includes selections of veal, beef, seafood, "strictly" fresh vegetables and fruits. The wine list dates from the 1920's.

Reservations required
Lunch: Mon.-Sat., Noon-3 P.M.
Dinner: Mon.-Thurs., 6 P.M.-10 P.M.
  Fri.-Sat., 6 P.M.-11:30 P.M.
  Closed Sunday

NEW YORK SPAGHETTI HOUSE ❼ *Italian*

2173 E. 9th St.
Cleveland
(216) 241-9541
Full Bar/Street Parking
AE, V
Good taste in dress required

The Brigotti family has been serving their downtown patrons dishes such as Veal Parmigiana, a multitude of pastas, homemade soups, steaks, chops and chicken for over 50 years. The wine list is lengthy; the atmosphere is New York-influenced European; the feeling is clubby.

Reservations suggested
Lunch: Mon.–Sat., 11 A.M.–2 P.M.
Dinner: Mon.–Sat., 2 P.M.–10:30 P.M.
      Closed Sunday

PAN ASIA ㉜ *Chinese*

6080 Brecksville Rd.
Independence, Ohio
(216) 524-6830
Maître d': Robert Hong (owner)
Full Bar/Lot Parking
AE, MC, V
Good taste in dress required

A small restaurant with less emphasis on decor (which is simple) and presentation (which isn't elaborate) than on a wide variety of Chinese foods. Specialties are offered from the five cuisine capitals of the Mainland — Szechuan, Hunan, Shanghai, Cantonese and Mandarin. Also offered are dishes from Korea, Japan and India.

Reservations required
Lunch/Dinner: Tues.–Thurs., 11:30 A.M.–9:30 P.M.
        Fri., 11:30 A.M.–11:30 P.M.
        Sat., 4:30 P.M.–11:30 P.M.
        Sun., Noon–8 P.M.

PARTHENON ❾ *Greek*

1518 Euclid Ave.
Cleveland
(216) 241-7119
Maître d': Peter Shinohoritis (owner)
Full Bar/Street Parking
MC, V
No dress restrictions

Located in the heart of the downtown theater district, the Parthenon provides Clevelanders with an answer to the Athenian taverna. Owner Peter Shinohoritis not only tries to provide customers with the camaraderie of such a place, but also with food the likes of gyros, moussaka, shish kabob and five different kinds of lamb.

No reservations required
Lunch/Dinner: Mon.–Thurs., 11 A.M.–Midnight
        Fri.–Sat., 11 A.M.–1 A.M.
        Sun., 11 A.M.–11 P.M.

PEARL OF THE ORIENT ㉓ *Chinese*

20121 Van Aken Blvd.
Shaker Heights, Ohio
(216) 751-8181
Maître d': Rose Wong (co-owner)
Full Bar/Lot Parking
AE, D, MC, V, CB
Good taste in dress required

Specialists in Northern Chinese and Szechuan cooking, the folks at Pearl of the Orient try to combine authenticity, variety and elegance. There is Peking Duck in three courses, Moo Shu dishes and filet mignon Chinese style, to name just a few items on the menu. They want you to know there's more to Chinese cooking than choices from columns A, B and C.

Reservations required
Lunch: Mon.-Sat., 11:30 A.M.-3 P.M.
Dinner: Sun.-Thurs., 5 P.M.-10 P.M.
Fri.-Sat., 5 P.M.-11:30 P.M.

PIER W ❹ *Seafood*

12700 Lake Ave.
Lakewood, Ohio
(216) 228-2250
Maître d': G. A. Logue (manager)
Full Bar/Valet and Lot Parking
AE, D, MC, V
No dress restrictions

Pier W is a "drop in" kind of seafood restaurant on the shores of Lake Erie. Bouillabaisse is a specialty, as are the "fresh catches," which could include a variety of local freshwater fish. There is also fresh lobster, if you like.

Reservations recommended
Lunch: Mon.-Fri., 11:30 A.M.-3 P.M.
Dinner: Mon.-Thurs., 5:30 P.M.-10 P.M.
Fri.-Sat., 5:30 P.M.-Midnight
Sun., 3 P.M.-9 P.M.
Brunch: Sat., 11:30 A.M.-3 P.M.
Sun., 10 A.M.-2:30 P.M.

RAINTREE ㉛ *Continental*

25 Pleasant Dr.
Chagrin Falls, Ohio
(216) 247-4800
Full Bar/Lot Parking
AE, MC, V
No dress restrictions

Located in an ideally picturesque small town southeast of Cleveland, Raintree is a "rare mix of honest elegance and rustic warmth," according to its manager, Richard Tonelli. Specialties include Chicken Breast Oscar, king crab, buffalo strip steak and Veal Henry. There are wild-game entrées on Thursday nights.

Reservations required
Lunch: Mon.-Sat., 11:30 A.M.-2:30 P.M.
Dinner: Mon.-Sat., 5:30 P.M.-10 P.M.
Sun., 4 P.M.-9 P.M.

STEFFON'S GOURMET WIZARDRY ㉘ *Continental*

29425 Chagrin Blvd.
Pepper Pike, Ohio
(216) 464-2980
Maître d': Steffon Rieger (owner)
Full Bar/Lot Parking
AE, D, MC, V
Jacket for men

It's understandable if you take a while to decide on your order at Steffon's, as there are about 350 entrées to choose from. (Availability on some items varies from day to day.)

Reservations required
Lunch: Mon.-Fri., 11:30 A.M.-2:30 P.M.
Dinner: Mon.-Sat., 5:30 P.M.-11 P.M.
   Closed Sunday

THE TAVERNE OF RICHFIELD ㉝ *American*

Front Street
Richfield Township, Ohio
(216) 659-3155
Maître d': Mel Rose (owner)
Full Bar/Valet, Lot and Street Parking
AE, MC, V
No dress restrictions

The Richfield Taverne, built in 1886, is one of the several surviving coach-stop inns that dot the Midwest. Dining here is not unlike dining in a friendly family's comfortable eating parlor. There is Duck à l'Orange, rack of lamb, lots of prime beef and a full selection of vintage wines. Sunday brunch features waffles prepared tableside.

Reservations required
Lunch: Mon.-Sat., 11 A.M.-3 P.M.
Dinner: Mon.-Thurs., 6 P.M.-11 P.M.
   Fri.-Sat., 6 P.M.-Midnight
   Sun., 6 P.M.-9 P.M.
Brunch: Sun., 10 A.M.-3 P.M.

THAT PLACE ON BELLFLOWER ⑭ *French*

11401 Bellflower Rd.
Cleveland
(216) 231-4469
Maître d': Hiroshi Tsuji
Full Bar/Valet Parking
AE, MC, V
No dress restrictions

An intimate bistro in a century-old carriage house and stable is how owner Isabella Chesler describes That Place. Add to that original contemporary paintings, track lights and Oriental rugs, plus specialties that include Veal Oskar and Salmon en Croûte, and you have a very complete restaurant adjacent to the home of the Cleveland Orchestra and the Art Museum.

No reservations required
Lunch: Mon.-Sat., 11:30 A.M.-3 P.M.
Dinner: Mon.-Sat., 6 P.M.-12:30 A.M.
   Closed Sunday

THEATRICAL RESTAURANT ❻ *American*

711 Vincent Ave.
Cleveland
(216) 241-6166
Maître d': Morris Fisher
Full Bar/Valet Parking
AE, D, MC, V, CB
Good taste in dress required

The Theatrical has been serving a variety of prime meats and seafood in the downtown area for the past 45 years. A bakery on the premises turns out hot rolls, breads and desserts. Some specialties include fresh stone crab, prime rib, stuffed pompano and Lobster Tail Romano.

Reservations required
Lunch/Dinner: Mon.–Sat., 11 A.M.–1:30 A.M.
         Closed Sunday

WAGON WHEEL ㉑ *French*

13114 Woodland Ave.
Cleveland
(216) 561-6900
Maître d': Alfred Voisin (owner)
Full Bar/Lot Parking
No credit cards
No dress restrictions

A thoroughly French feeling pervades this restaurant, from owner Alfred Voisin, to his staff, to his house specialties. You can choose from Duck à l'Orange, Cuisses de Grenouille (frogs' legs), Veal Parisienne and Trout Amandine. Each meal is prepared to order and homemade mints are the final accompaniments.

Reservations required
Dinner: Mon.–Thurs., 5:30 P.M.–11 P.M.
       Fri.–Sat., 5:30 P.M.–Midnight
       Closed Sunday

DALLAS/FORT WORTH

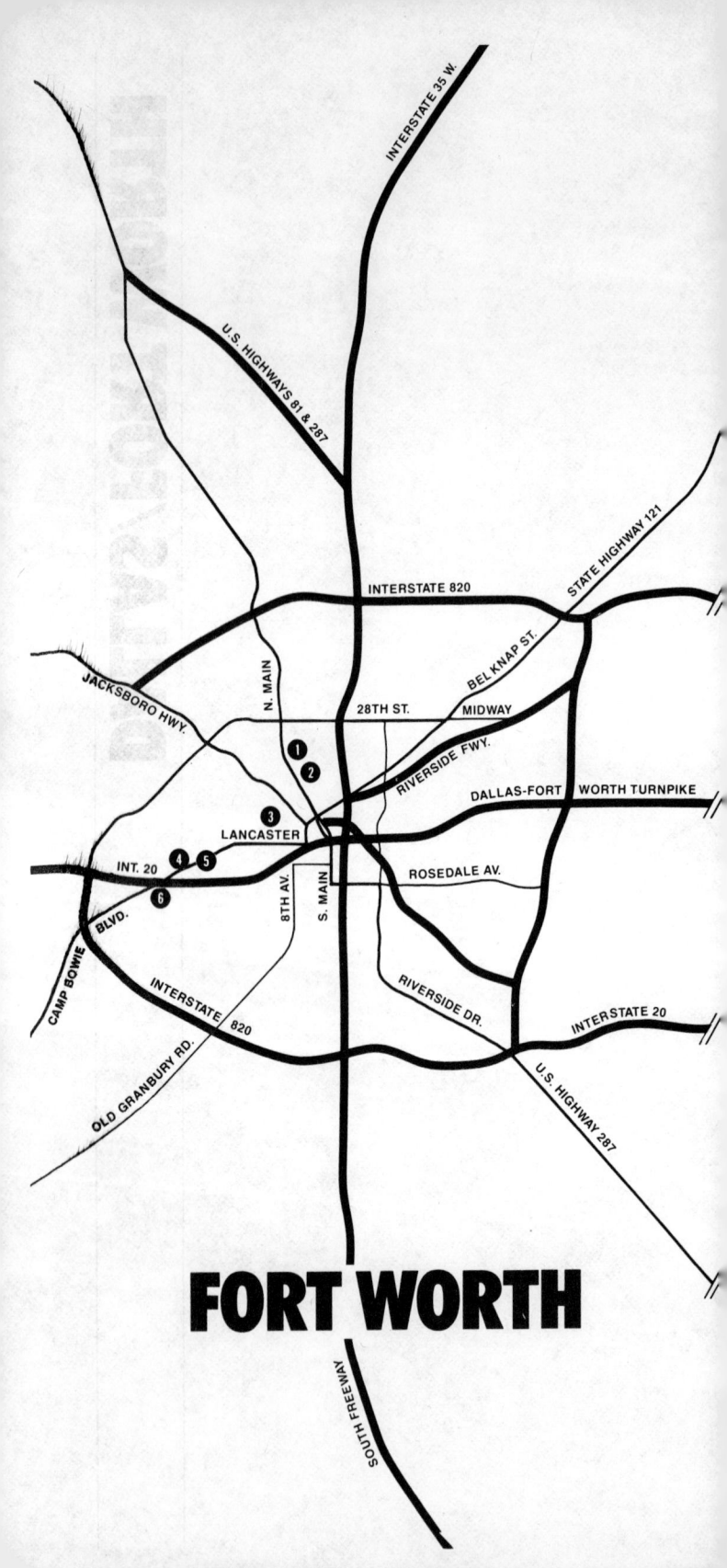

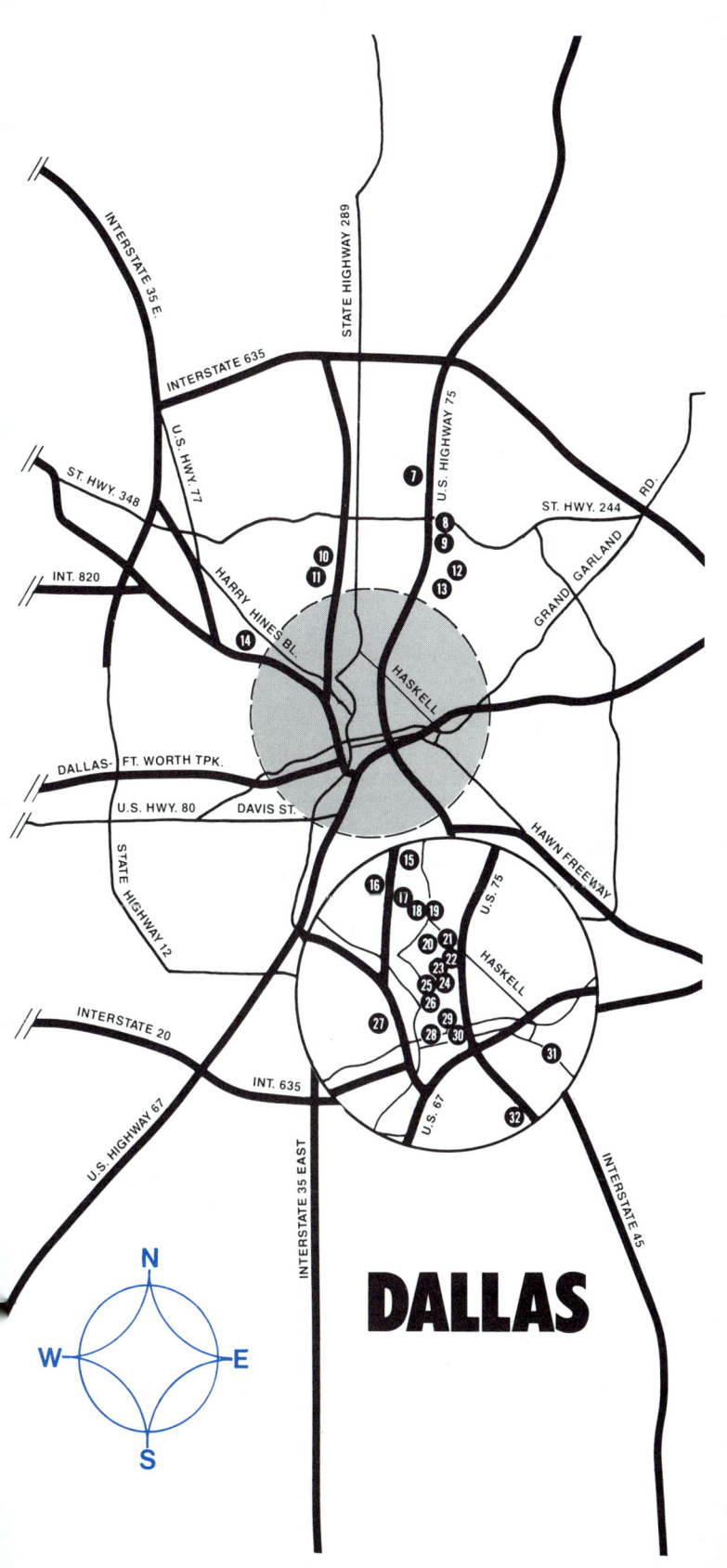

ANGELO'S ❸   *Barbecue*

2533 White Settlement Rd.
Fort Worth
(817) 332-0357
Beer/Street Parking
No credit cards
No dress restrictions

Many claim this is the best barbecue spot in Texas. Those, of course, may be fighting words. If you don't mind waiting in a fast-moving line or sawdust on the floor or a less than fashionable exterior, Angelo's can offer you well-seasoned spareribs and all varieties of tender beef.

No reservations required
Lunch/Dinner: Mon.-Sat., 11 A.M.-10 P.M.
           Closed Sunday

ARTHUR'S ❽   *American*

1000 Campbell Centre
Dallas
(214) 361-8833
Maître d': Danny Russo
Full Bar/Valet Parking
AE, D, MC, V, CB
No jeans

What's innovative and different in American cooking is the news here. Pheasant, roast duckling and numerous beef and seafood dishes are served against a hunting lodge background. The bar is jumping at Happy Hour and at other hours both before and after.

Reservations required
Lunch/Dinner: Mon.-Fri., 11 A.M.-11 P.M. (Bar until 1 A.M.)
Dinner: Sat.-Sun., 6 P.M.-11 P.M.

BAGATELLE ❾   *Continental*

4925 Greenville Ave.
Dallas
(214) 692-8224
Maître d': Joseph Melito
Full Bar/Lot Parking
AE, D, MC, V, CB
Jacket for men; no jeans

Chef/owner Leodegar Meier keeps a watchful eye over cuisine and service at Bagatelle. The atmosphere may remind you of a French country inn. The specialties include roast pheasant, quail, bouillabaisse, tournedos, roast duckling and pepper steak.

Reservations required
Lunch: Mon.-Fri.
Dinner: Daily, 6 P.M.-11 P.M.
Brunch: Sun.

BRASSERIE ㉙   *Continental*

Fairmont Hotel
Ross and Akard
Dallas
(214) 748-5454
Maître d': Gerrit de Goederen
Full Bar/Valet Parking
AE, D, MC, V
No dress restrictions

At the Brasserie you can satisfy every whim — well, almost. Everything from a toasted English muffin to Eggs Benedict to a full-course dinner is available at all hours. The setting is casual, reminiscent of a European sidewalk cafe.

No reservations required
Breakfast/Lunch/Dinner: Daily, 24 hours

BRENNAN'S ㉛   *Creole*

One Main Place
Dallas
(214) 742-1911
Maître d': Jim Williams
Full Bar/Lot Parking
AE, D, MC, V, CB
Jacket for men (evenings)

All the Creole originals — the famous New Orleans drinks, the notable breakfast specialties, the turtle soup, the flaming desserts — are available at this particular Brennan's. Sample all the poached egg variations, for starters. Brennan's also offers a Jazz Brunch on weekends.

Reservations suggested
Breakfast: Daily, 9 A.M.-11:30 A.M.
Lunch: Daily, 11:30 A.M.-2:30 P.M.
Dinner: Daily, 6 P.M.-9 P.M.
            Closed Christmas Eve, Christmas
Brunch: Sat.-Sun., 9 A.M.-2:30 P.M.

CAFE PACIFIC ⑮   *Seafood*

24 Highland Park Village
Dallas
(214) 526-1170
Maître d': Mel Hollen
Full Bar/Lot Parking
AE, MC, V
Jacket for men

A "San Francisco-style" restaurant, Cafe Pacific sports a casual atmosphere, yet has an interior consisting of marble floors, chandeliers and cut glass accoutrements. Specialties include bouillabaisse, lemon veal and fresh fruit crêpes.

Reservations required
Lunch: Daily, 11:30 A.M.-2:30 P.M.
Dinner: Sun.-Thurs., 5:30 P.M.-10:30 P.M.
          Fri.-Sat., 5:30 P.M.-11 P.M.

CAFE ROYAL ③⓪   *French*

Plaza of the America's Hotel
650 N. Pearl St.
Dallas
(214) 747-7222
Maître d': Jean Loubat (Food and Beverage Director)
Full Bar/Valet Parking
AE, D, MC, V, CB
Jacket, tie for men

Duckling enhanced by a light mustard sauce, bass wrapped in lettuce leaves, veal basted with Grand Marnier, saddle of lamb embellished by a handful of herbs. If such delicate and subtle dishes tempt you, then Cafe Royal is for you. They also feature a lobster soup with basil that is said to be quite different from the "run-of-the-mill" bisque.

Reservations required
Lunch: Mon.-Fri., 11:30 A.M.-3 P.M.
Dinner: Mon.-Thurs., 6:30 P.M.-10:30 P.M.
Fri.-Sat., 6:30 P.M.-11 P.M.
Closed Sunday

CALLUAD RESTAURANT ②④   *French*

2619 McKinney Ave.
Dallas
(214) 823-5380
Maître d': Mrs. Calluad
Full Bar/Valet Parking
AE, D, MC, V
Jacket, tie for men

Enter through Martine and Guy Calluad's large French doors and begin fantasizing. You're in the Loire Valley once again (or for the first time) and you're dining on Sole Bourguignonne, Noisettes d'Agneau en Croûte, Entrecôte au Poivre Rose, Ris de Veau "Calluaud," etc. etc. The elegant decor offers ample proof that fantasies *can* come true.

Reservations required
Dinner: Mon.-Thurs., 6 P.M.-10:30 P.M.
Fri.-Sat., 6 P.M.-11 P.M.
Closed Sunday

THE CARRIAGE HOUSE ④   *Continental*

5136 Camp Bowie Blvd.
Fort Worth
(817) 732-2873
Full Bar/Valet Parking
AE, MC, V
Good taste in dress required

"The Carriage House offers what every discerning diner looks for," notes owner Willis McIntosh, to wit: "superb cuisine, continental service and a wine list for the connoisseur." The atmosphere is one of mirrored walls, Old English furnishings, Scottish plaid carpeting. The food is a selection of broiled beef, seafood, lamb and veal.

Reservations required
Lunch: Daily (except Saturday), 11:30 A.M.-2 P.M.
Dinner: Mon.-Sat., 6 P.M.-11 P.M.
Sun., 6 P.M.-10 P.M.

CATTLEMEN'S STEAK HOUSE ❶   *American*

2458 N. Main St.
Fort Worth
(817) 624-3945
Maître d': Rex Brewer (manager)
Full Bar/Lot Parking
AE, D, MC, V, CB
No dress restrictions

It seems fitting and proper to enjoy huge, sizzling steaks in the heart of Texas. That's what you can do at this original Cattlemen's, located, as it is, in the stockyards area of Fort Worth. There are plenty of steaks to suit anyone's taste here, as well as calf fries, chicken and seafood.

No reservations required
Lunch/Dinner: Mon. – Fri., 11 A.M. – 10:30 P.M.
  Sat., 4:30 P.M. – 10:30 P.M.
  Closed Sunday

CHATEAUBRIAND ㉕   *Continental*

2515 McKinney Ave.
Dallas
(214) 741-1223
Full Bar/Valet Parking
AE, D, MC, V, CB
Jacket for men preferred

A very established Dallas meeting place and watering hole, Chateaubriand is strong on charbroiled steaks, prime rib and some French and Greek specialties. There are several daily specials and two separate dining areas.

Reservations required
Lunch: Mon. – Sat., 11:30 A.M. – 2:30 P.M.
Dinner: Mon. – Sat., 5 P.M. – 1 A.M.
  Closed Sunday

THE CHIMNEY ❼   *Austrian/Swiss*

9739 N. Central Expressway
Dallas
(214) 369-6466
Full Bar/Lot Parking
AE, D, MC, V, CB
Jacket for men

Filled with Old World warmth and charm, The Chimney features several different veal dishes, all exquisitely prepared, according to owner and chef Heinz Prast. He also offers Calf's Liver Tyrolienne and Rehsteak Chimney (Montana venison) — a Dallas exclusive.

Reservations required
Lunch: Tues. – Sat., 11:30 A.M. – 2 P.M.
Dinner: Tues. – Sat., 6 P.M. – 10:30 P.M.
  Closed Sunday, Monday

CHIQUITA'S ⓱   *Mexican*

3810 Congress
Dallas
(214) 521-0721
Maître d': Salvador Herrera
Beer/Lot Parking
AE, MC, V
No dress restrictions

"The cheeriest dining room in town," is owner Mario Leal's opinion of his place. Its white walls *are* covered with colorful Mexican paper flowers. The special dishes include tortilla soup, Carne Asada, Carnitas Tampiquenas, Chicken Parrilla, Chiles Rellenos, Drunken Shrimp, Pollo en Crema and seafood entrées.

No reservations required
Lunch/Dinner: Mon.–Sat., 11:30 A.M.–11 P.M.
       Closed Sunday

THE COURTYARD ⓺   *Continental*

5718 Locke
Fort Worth
(817) 738-6670
Full Bar/Lot Parking
MC, V
No dress restrictions

The Courtyard is a small restaurant, with a seating capacity of 44. Its special guests are surrounded by lattice work, indoor trees and flowering plants. At night, the restaurant is aglitter with candles, according to owner Peggy Hatchell. She considers her chocolate nut pudding a particular specialty.

Reservations requested
Lunch: Mon.–Sat., 11:30 A.M.–2 P.M.
Dinner: Mon.–Sat., 6:30 P.M.–10 P.M.
       Closed Sunday

EWALD'S ⓫   *Continental*

5415 W. Lovers Lane
Dallas
(214) 357-1622
Maître d': Ewald Scholz (chef and owner)
Full Bar/Lot Parking
AE, MC, V
Good taste in dress required

Chef and owner Ewald Scholz has bathed his restaurant in a warm, comfortable glow. Both the candlelight atmosphere and the European-style menu reflect his very personal efforts. His specialties include Shrimp du Chef, Snapper Alphonso, Veal Papagallo, Entrecôte Café de Paris and Steak au Poivre.

Reservations required
Dinner: Mon.–Fri., 6 P.M.–10:30 P.M.
       Sat., 6 P.M.–11 P.M.
       Closed Sunday

THE GRAPE ⓭   *Continental*

2808 Greenville Ave.
Dallas
(214) 823-0133
Maître d': Diane Casebeer (manager)
Full Bar/Lot and Street Parking
MC, V
No dress restrictions

"The Grape is Dallas' original bistro," according to manager Diane Casebeer. The atmosphere is one of casual charm. A constantly changing menu is listed on the blackboard and a printed menu offers sandwiches, salads, soups, desserts and 30 cheeses. Ms. Casebeer says her wine list is one of the most respected in the city.

No reservations required
Lunch: Mon.–Fri., 11:30 A.M.–2 P.M.
Dinner: Daily, 6 P.M.–11 P.M.

GUADALAJARA ㉘   *Mexican*

3308 Ross Ave.
Dallas
(214) 823-9340
Beer and Wine/Street Parking
No credit cards
No dress restrictions

Most of the "Tex-Mex" specialties are offered here, plus piñatas, Mexican comic books and lots of local flavor. Look for tamales, enchiladas, Chicken Mole, Chiles Rellenos, Huevos con Nopalitos (eggs with cactus), Carne Asada, and sopapilla for dessert.

No reservations required
Lunch/Dinner: Daily, 11 A.M.–3:30 A.M.

JAVIER'S ㉗   *Mexican*

4912 Cole Ave.
Dallas
(214) 521-4211
Maître d': Eduardo Pria (chef and co-owner)
Full Bar/Lot Parking
AE, D, MC, V
No dress restrictions

Javier Gutierrez and his partner Eduardo Pria say they have gone to great lengths to present a "high form" of Mexican cuisine to their customers. Based more upon European than native tradition, Javier's specialties focus on beef, chicken, shrimp and red snapper. All are seasoned with freshly prepared sauces.

No reservations required
Dinner: Mon.–Thurs., 5:30 P.M.–10:30 P.M.
        Fri.–Sat., 5:30 P.M.–11:30 P.M.
        Sun., 5:30 P.M.–10 P.M.

JEAN-CLAUDE ⓰   *French*

2404 Cedar Springs Rd.
Dallas
(214) 653-1823
Maître d': Michel Baudouin
Full Bar/Lot Parking
AE, MC, V
Jacket, tie for men

Very small and very intimate, with a "verbal" menu that changes daily, Jean-Claude's features several variations on fresh fish, veal, lamb and quail. Owner Jean-Claude Prevot also presents an impressive array of appetizers and showpiece desserts.

Reservations required
Dinner: Tues.–Sat., 6 P.M. and 9 P.M. seatings
    Closed Sunday, Monday

JOE T. GARCIA'S ❷   *Mexican*

2210 N. Commerce St.
Fort Worth
(817) 626-4356
Full Bar/Street Parking
No credit cards
No dress restrictions

Something of a celebrity hangout, Joe T's also is a place to try Tex-Mex specialties. There's family-style cooking, a *very* casual and comfortable atmosphere, margaritas and mariachis.

No reservations required.
Lunch: Mon.–Fri., 11 A.M.–2 P.M.
Dinner: Daily, 5 P.M.–10:30 P.M.

JOZEF'S ㉒   *Seafood*

2719 McKinney Ave.
Dallas
(214) 826-5560
Maître d': Jozef Juck, Peter Polakovic (owners)
Full Bar/Lot Parking
AE, D, MC, V, CB
Good taste in dress required

Simple but elegant is Jozef's style. Hanging plants, solid wood walls, large picture windows. Specialties include shrimp in beer batter, Crab Meat Imperial, Maine lobster, bouillabaisse and sea scallops sautéed with garlic, tomatoes and parsley.

Reservations recommended
Lunch: Mon.–Fri., 11 A.M.–2:30 P.M.
Dinner: Sun.–Thurs., 6 P.M.–10 P.M.
        Fri.–Sat., 6 P.M.–11 P.M.

KIRBY'S CHARCOAL STEAKS ⑫   *American*

3715 Greenville Ave.
Dallas
(214) 823-7296
Maître d': B. J. Kirby (owner)
Full Bar/Lot Parking
AE, D, MC, V, CB
Good taste in dress required

Kirby's stakes its claim as the oldest steak house in Dallas. They serve high-quality steaks and the "most fabulous baked potato." There's also "all the crisp salad you can eat." Basic but substantial is the rule here.

No reservations required
Dinner: Sun., Tues.-Thurs., 5:30 P.M.-10 P.M.
       Fri.-Sat., 5:30 P.M.-Midnight
       Closed Monday

LES SAISONS ⑲   *French*

165 Turtle Creek Village
Dallas
(214) 528-1102
Maître d': Jack Konko, Joelle Ramsey, Paul Pinnell
Full Bar/Lot Parking
AE, D, MC, V, CB
Good taste in dress required

Country French in feeling and cuisine, Les Saisons features a setting of antiques, greenery and murals. The chef's specialties include pâté maison, duckling in saffron sauce and Poulet Supreme — chicken breast stuffed with shrimp in a rich and savory sauce.

Reservations required
Lunch/Dinner: Sun.-Thurs., 11:30 A.M.-11 P.M.
       Fri.-Sat., 11:30 A.M.-Midnight

MANSION ON TURTLE CREEK ⑳   *American*

2821 Turtle Creek Blvd.
Dallas
(214) 526-2121
Full Bar/Valet Parking
AE, D, MC, V
Jacket, tie for men

They renovated the lovely old Sheppard King mansion on Turtle Creek, hired a management team from New York's 21 restaurant to supervise operations and then waited for the beautiful people of Dallas to find the place. It didn't take long. Many of the 21 specialties are offered at The Mansion, including chicken with wild rice, Scottish salmon, beluga caviar and oysters in season.

Reservations required
Lunch: Mon.-Fri., 11:30 A.M.-2 P.M.
Dinner: Sun.-Fri., 6 P.M.-10:30 P.M.
       Sat., 6 P.M.-11 P.M.
Supper: Mon.-Fri., 10:30 P.M.-Midnight
       Sat., 11 P.M.-Midnight
Brunch: Sun., 11 A.M.-3 P.M.

MARIO'S ⓲ *Italian*

135 Turtle Creek Village
Dallas
(214) 521-1135
Maître d': Tom Ruggeri, Nick Foukas
Full Bar/Lot Parking
AE, D, MC, V, CB
Jacket for men

Northern Italian specialties are served in an atmosphere "steeped in Old World charm." Look for items such as Shrimp Mario, Pollo alla Christine and a variety of fish, veal and pasta dishes.

Reservations required
Dinner: Sun.-Fri., 6 P.M.-11 P.M.
Sat., 6 P.M.-Midnight

MR. PEPPE ⓾ *French*

5617 W. Lovers Lane
Dallas
(214) 352-5976
Full Bar/Lot Parking
AE, D, MC, V
Jacket, tie for men preferred

This intimate neighborhood restaurant has been serving traditional French cuisine since 1958. Appetizers include Crab Meat Peggy and Artichoke Elizabeth, and entrées include Pepper Steak Mr. Peppe, Shrimp Provençale, Fillet of Sole San Francisco. And for dessert, there's Black Forest Cake and Torte Grand Marnier.

Reservations required
Dinner: Daily, 6 P.M.-10 P.M.

OLD SWISS HOUSE ⓹ *Continental*

5412 Camp Bowie Blvd.
Fort Worth
(817) 738-8091
Maître d': Bradley C. Speck
Full Bar/Valet and Lot Parking
AE, D, MC, V
Jacket for men

You know you're "out to dinner" at the Old Swiss House. Tables are set with sparkling crystal, fresh flowers and snow-white linen. Specialties include Veal Oskar, Filet Mignon King Henry IV (topped with mushrooms, artichokes and Béarnaise) and salmon — either poached or broiled.

Reservations required
Dinner: Mon.-Thurs., 6 P.M.-10 P.M.
Fri.-Sat., 6 P.M.-10:30 P.M.
Closed Sunday

THE OLD WARSAW (La Vieille Varsovie) ㉑ *French*

2610 Maple Ave.
Dallas
(214) 528-0032
Maître d': Horst Pohl, Tom Tarjan
Full Bar/Valet Parking
AE, D, MC, V, CB
Jacket for men

Dine on such delicacies as brie soup, Salade Vieille Varsovie, Medaillons de Veau Chanterelles and Steak au Poivre at this family-owned Dallas restaurant of long standing. The wine list is of special interest. A pianist and violinist provide background music.

Reservations required
Dinner: Sun.-Fri., 6 P.M.-11 P.M.
Sat., 6 P.M.-Midnight

PAPILLON ㉜ *Continental*

7940 N. Central Expressway
Dallas
(214) 691-7455
Maître d': Ali Tabatabai
Full Bar/Street Parking
AE, D, MC, V, CB
Jacket for men

You'll get a country French feeling at Papillon. (You might even imagine the butterflies cavorting through the air.) You'll be surrounded by stained glass and chandeliers. Specialties are variations on veal, steak, fowl and seafood.

No reservations required
Lunch: Mon.-Fri.
Dinner. Daily

PATRY'S ㉖ *French*

2504 McKinney Ave.
Dallas
(214) 748-3754
Full Bar/Lot and Street Parking
AE, D, MC, V, CB
No jeans

Patry's is home for such French-Continental specialties as Coq au Vin, Steak au Poivre, rack of lamb and Duck à l'Orange. The management takes pride in offering the freshest vegetables to accompany the main courses. An extensive wine list encompasses both French and American selections.

Reservations required
Dinner: Sun.-Thurs., 6 P.M.-10:30 P.M.
Fri.-Sat., 6 P.M.-11 P.M.

PYRAMID ROOM ㉚ *French*

Fairmont Hotel
Ross and Akard Streets
Dallas
(214) 748-5454
Maître d': Franco Lorenzotti
Full Bar/Valet Parking
AE, D, MC, V
Jacket, tie for men

The Pyramid is named for the focal point of the room — a startling floor-to-ceiling lighting fixture in the shape of an inverted pyramid. Such is the setting for specialties like Coquelet au Homard (Cornish hen and lobster), Filet of Sole en Croûte, Crevettes Flambées (large shrimp cooked in Pernod) and lemon soufflé.

Reservations required
Lunch: Mon.–Fri., 11:30 A.M.–2 P.M.
Dinner: Daily, 7 P.M.–9:45 P.M.

S & D OYSTER COMPANY ㉓ *Seafood*

2701 McKinney Ave.
Dallas
(214) 741-2644
Beer and Wine/Lot Parking
MC, V
No dress restrictions

This oyster bar and seafood restaurant is housed in a 100-year-old warehouse that looks as if it might belong on the New Orleans waterfront. The typically Southern Gulf Coast menu includes fresh oysters on the half shell, boiled shrimp, seafood gumbo, fried shrimp and oysters, red fish, broiled red snapper, trout and flounder.

No reservations required
Lunch/Dinner: Mon.–Thurs., 11 A.M.–10 P.M.
              Fri.–Sat., 11 A.M.–11 P.M.
              Closed Sunday

SONNY BRYAN'S SMOKEHOUSE ⑭ *Barbecue*

2202 Inwood Rd.
Dallas
(214) 357-7120
Beer/Lot Parking
No credit cards
No dress restrictions

Hickory-smoked barbecued beef is the specialty at Sonny Bryan's. You'll also find barbecued ham and pork ribs, lots of cole slaw, plenty of barbecued beans, onion rings and french fries. They've been dishing out hundreds of pounds of barbecued meat every day since 1910!

No reservations required
Lunch: Mon.–Fri., 11 A.M.–5 P.M.
       Sat.–Sun., 11 A.M.–2 P.M.

DENVER

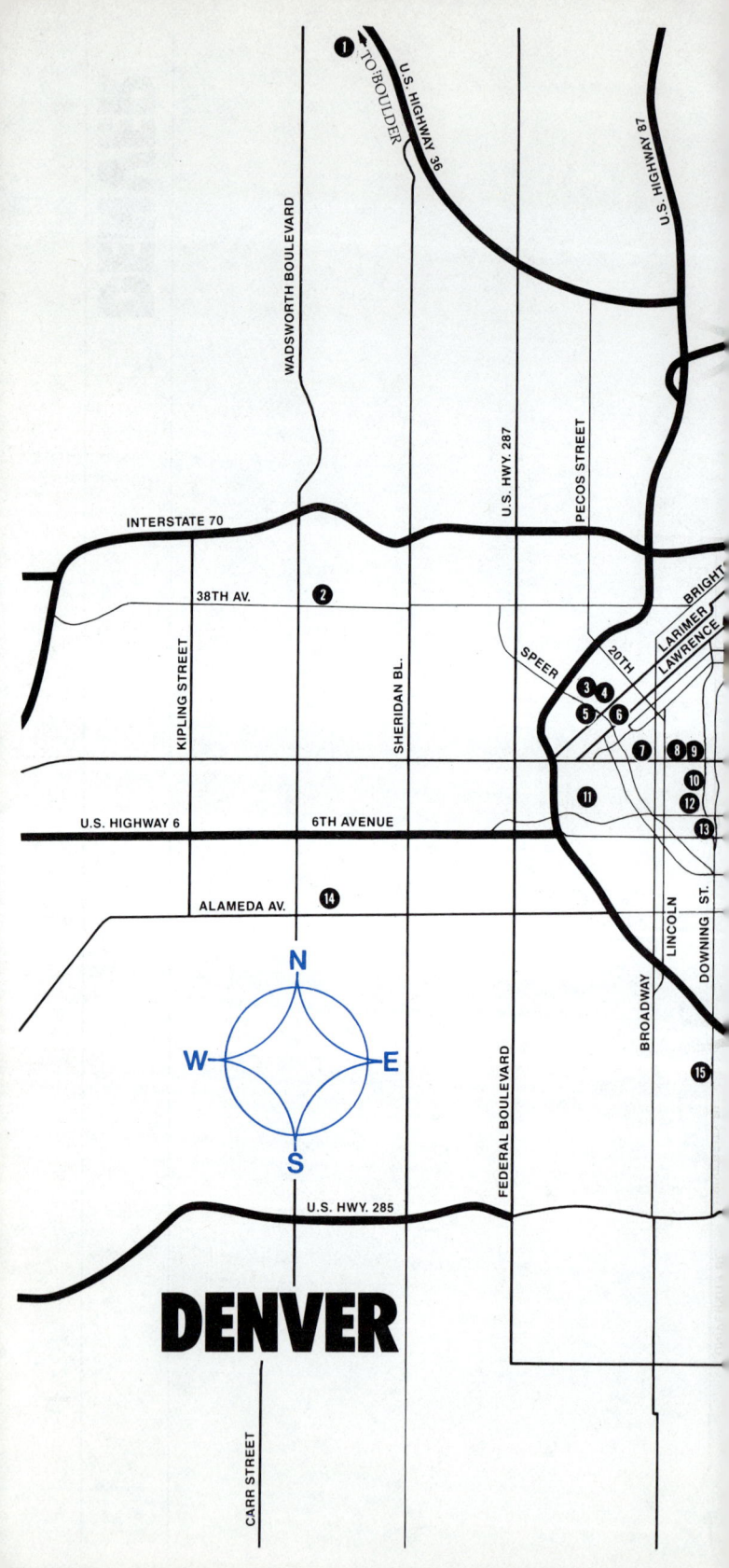

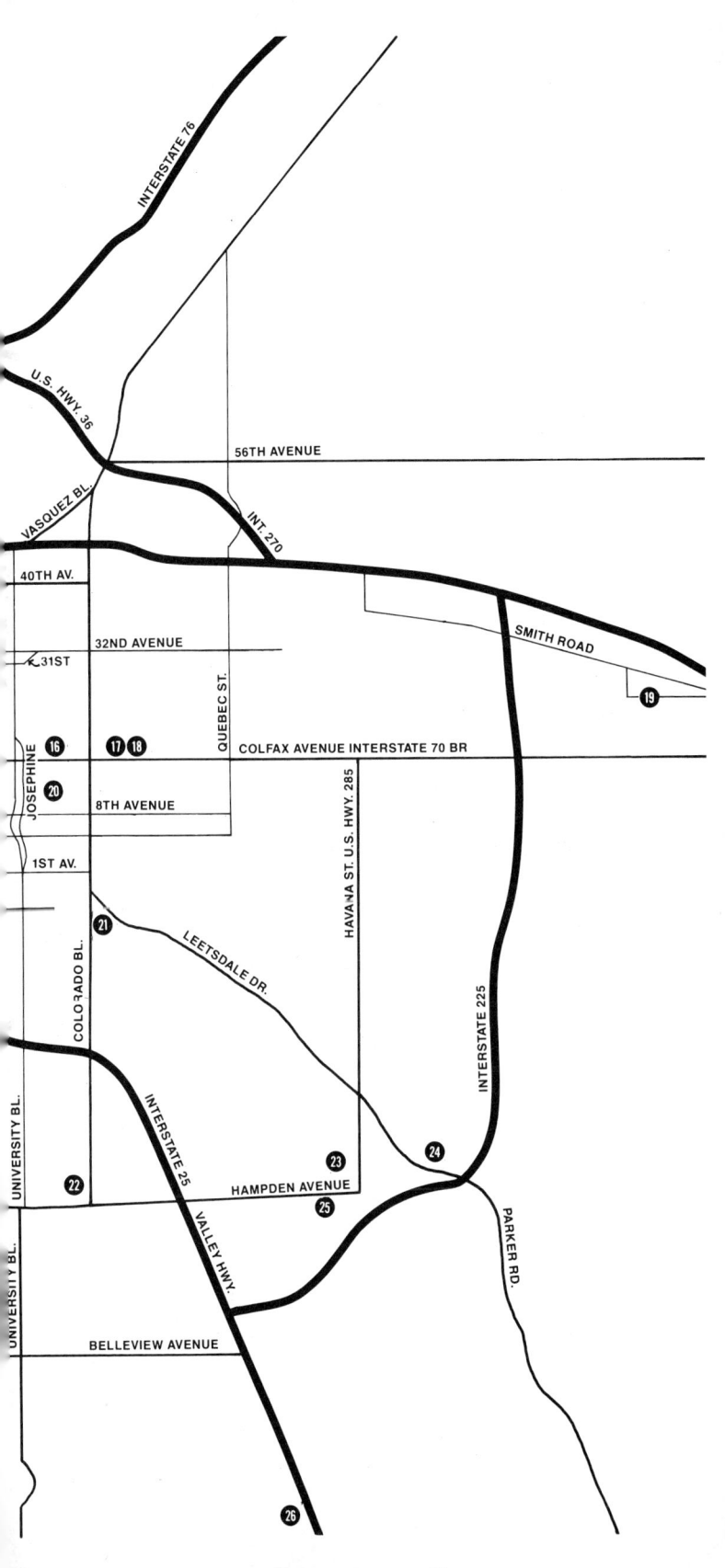

BERARDI & SONS ❻ *Italian*

1525 Blake
Denver
(303) 623-7648
Maître d': Dick Berardi
Full Bar/Lot and Street Parking
AE, D, MC, V
No dress restrictions

It's a milieu of red tile, lace tablecloths and candlelight that awaits you at Berardi's. You'll also find veal selections, rabbit, chicken and steak, as well as Fettucine Alfredo and Carbonara. The antipasto is substantial and the wine list is "the most extensive in Colorado," according to the management.

No reservations required
Lunch: Mon.–Fri., 11:30 A.M.–2:30 P.M.
Dinner: Sun.–Thurs., 5:30 P.M.–10 P.M.
     Fri.–Sat., 5:30 P.M.–11 P.M.

THE BROKER RESTAURANT ❼ *Continental*

821 17th St.
Denver
(303) 893-5065
Full Bar/Valet Parking
AE, MC, V
Jacket, tie for men

You'll dine in the old Denver National Bank's "Coupon Room," complete with its original vault and 33-ton door. Your meal will be enlivened (or not) by the quote tape from the New York Stock Exchange, which you can read from your table. You can enjoy Beef Wellington, gulf shrimp, chicken or fresh fish.

Reservations recommended
Lunch: Mon.–Fri., 11 A.M.–3 P.M.
Dinner: Daily, 5 P.M.–11 P.M.

BUCKHORN EXCHANGE ⓫ *American*

1000 Osage St.
Denver
(303) 534-9505
Maître d': Dick Williams (manager)
Full Bar/Lot Parking
AE, D, MC, V
No dress restrictions

Legend has it that this was the favorite watering hole of Buffalo Bill. Founded in 1893, the Buckhorn Exchange specializes in T-bone steaks, quail, trout *and* buffalo. There are sandwiches, salads and pot roast for lunch. Awarded the state's first liquor license, the Buckhorn also boasts an oak bar brought from Germany to the United States in 1857.

Reservations required
Lunch: Mon.–Fri., 11:15 A.M.–3 P.M.
Dinner: Daily, 5:30 P.M.–10 P.M.

CAFE GIOVANNI ❸   *Italian/French*

1515 Market St.
Denver
(303) 825-6555
Maître d': Patrick and Sandy
Full Bar/Street Parking
AE, D, MC, V
No dress restrictions

This restaurant, patterned after a turn-of-the-century San Francisco-style cafe, features pasta items and some French specialties such as Escargots de la Maison (in light cream sauce with shallots, garlic and cognac). There are two working oak fireplaces in the dining room and lots of natural brick, oak and brass.

Reservations required
Lunch: Mon.–Fri., 11 A.M.–3 P.M.
Dinner: Mon.–Thurs., 5:30 P.M.–11 P.M.
         Fri.-Sat., 5:30 P.M.–Midnight
         Closed Sunday

CAFE PROMENADE ❹   *Continental*

1430 Larimer Square
Denver
(303) 893-2692
Maître d': Fred Thomas, Luciano Giomo
Full Bar/Lot and Street Parking
AE, D, MC, V, CB
No dress restrictions

Cafe Promenade's Austrian master chef presides over a kitchen that turns out Continental and Northern Italian specialties. There are such selections as oxtail soup, leg or rack of lamb, cannelloni, Beef Stroganoff, Oysters Florentine and wiener schnitzel. The homemade desserts are the work of the Swiss pastry chef.

Reservations required
Breakfast/Lunch/Dinner: Mon.–Sat., 9 A.M.–11:30 P.M.
                    Closed Sunday

CHATEAU PYRENEES ㉖   *Continental*

6548 S. Yosemite Circle
Englewood, Colo.
(303) 770-6660
Maître d': Angelo
Full Bar/Valet Parking
AE, D, MC, V, CB
Jacket for men

Fresh flowers, original artwork and live background music help you enjoy dining at Chateau Pyrenées. Specialties include Dover Sole, veal in sweet butter and white wine, Duck à l'Orange, Beef Wellington and Rocky Mountain trout.

Reservations required
Lunch: Mon.–Fri., 11:30 A.M.–2 P.M.
Dinner: Daily, 6 P.M.–10 P.M.

THE COACH HOUSE ㉓ *Continental*

10607 E. Dartmouth
Aurora, Colo.
(303) 751-5790
Maître d': John Lawrence (manager)
Full Bar/Valet and Lot Parking
AE, MC, V
No dress restrictions

The Coach House features comfortable booths, cut glass chandeliers, paintings lining the walls and antiques lining the shelves. Also featured are traditional Continental entrées as well as examples of *la nouvelle cuisine*. They say the beef has been aged for three weeks and they're particularly proud of their Veal Piccata.

Reservations required
Lunch: Mon.-Fri., 11:30 A.M.-2 P.M.
Dinner: Mon.-Sat., 6 P.M.-10:30 P.M.
　　　　Sun., 5:30 P.M.-9 P.M.

COLORADO MINE COMPANY ㉑ *American*

4490 E. Virginia Ave.
Denver
(303) 321-6555
Full Bar/Valet Parking
AE, MC, V
No dress restrictions

"Chivas Regal is our only Scotch — that should tell you something about our food," says manager Patty Clark. A faithful reproduction of an 1880's mine tipple, the Colorado Mine Company serves Colorado beef, plus seafood selections. A roaring fire blazes in the open hearth on cold Rocky Mountain nights.

No reservations required
Dinner: Mon.-Sat., 4:30 P.M.-2 A.M.
　　　　Sun., 4:30 P.M.-Midnight

DUDLEY'S ⓭ *French*

1120 E. 6th Ave.
Denver
(303) 744-8634
Full Bar/Lot Parking
AE, D, MC, V, CB
No dress restrictions

A Parisian bistro in downtown Denver. That is Dudley's raison d'être. The *nouvelle cuisine* covers such items as Veal Tournedos, fresh salmon and Normandy duck stew. The wine list is regarded by many as outstanding. The setting is informal.

Reservations required
Lunch: Tues.-Sat., 11:30 A.M.-2 P.M.
Dinner: Tues.-Sat., 6 P.M.-10:30 P.M.
　　　　Closed Sunday, Monday

EMERSON ST. EAST ❾ American

900 E. Colfax Ave.
Denver
(303) 832-1349
Full Bar/Valet Parking
AE, D, MC, V
No dress restrictions

If the hearty fare of Emerson St. East (steaks, prime rib, seafood) is too much for you, you can sample a selection from the "light" dinner menu. The atmosphere is comfortably cozy, warmed by brick walls and sports memorabilia.

No reservations required
Lunch/Dinner: Mon.-Thurs., 11 A.M.-10:45 P.M.
            Fri.-Sat., 11 A.M.-11:45 P.M.
            Sun., 5 P.M.-9:45 P.M.

EMIL-LENE'S SIRLOIN HOUSE ⓴ American

16000 Smith Rd.
Aurora, Colo.
(303) 366-6674
Maître d': Emil Kuchar (owner)
Full Bar/Lot Parking
MC, V
Good taste in dress required

The Sirloin House features prime steaks cooked over charcoal fires. There are varying daily specialties as well.

No reservations required
Lunch/Dinner: Daily, 11:30 A.M.-11 P.M.

FLAGSTAFF HOUSE ❶ Continental

Flagstaff Road
Boulder, Colo.
(303) 442-4640
Maître d': Don Monette (owner)
Full Bar/Valet and Lot Parking
AE, MC, V
No dress restrictions

The Flagstaff House is nestled on the secluded side of Flagstaff Mountain, just a little over a mile west of Boulder. Terrace dining here is really something. An extensive menu includes such entrées as Tournedos Oscar, Colorado buffalo, quail and fresh seafood. Owner Don Monette terms his wine list "exceptional."

Reservations recommended
Dinner: Daily, 5 P.M.-Midnight

FOOTERS ❿ *Northern Italian*

1076 Ogden St.
Denver
(303) 832-3304
Maître d': Todd Disner, James Lambatos (co-owner)
Beer and Wine/Street Parking
MC, V
No dress restrictions

The management terms Footers a "New York-style" restaurant, with semi-formal atmosphere and ultra modern feeling. Specialties include veal stuffed with prosciutto and cheese, shrimp sautéed in butter, lemon and wine, and pasta dishes.

No reservations required
Dinner: Daily, 5:30 P.M.–11:30 P.M.

THE HUNGRY FARMER ⓮ *American*

6925 W. Alameda Ave.
Lakewood, Colo.
(303) 238-4321
Maître d': Ronald Evers (manager)
Full Bar/Lot Parking
AE, D, MC, V
No dress restrictions

"This is one folksy farmhouse that really delivers — and for 17 years!" comments Hungry Farmer manager Ronald Evers. Along with the usual steaks and chicken, there are original versions of pot roast, duckling and soups. "Aimed at the farmer who knows his Beaujolais," says Evers of his wine selection.

No reservations required
Dinner: Mon.–Thurs., 5 P.M.–10 P.M.
         Fri.–Sat., 5 P.M.–10:30 P.M.
         Sun., Noon–9 P.M.

LA FONTANELLA ⓯ *Italian*

1700 E. Evans Ave.
Denver
(303) 778-8598
Maître d': Ron Wegmann
Full Bar/Lot Parking
AE, D, MC, V
No dress restrictions

"A very fresh atmosphere" prevails at La Fontanella, according to owner Ennio Bonifazi. The setting of stucco walls, exposed brick and leafy foliage plays host to such special dishes as tortellini, gnocchi, spinach ravioli, Veal Capri, Shrimp Marinara and cannelloni.

No reservations required
Lunch: Mon.–Fri., 11:30 A.M.–2:30 P.M.
Dinner: Mon.–Thurs., 5:30 P.M.–10:30 P.M.
         Fri.–Sun. 5:30 P.M.–11:30 P.M.

T. Michael's ❽   *French*
LE PROFIL

1560 Sherman St.
Denver
(303) 839-1704
Maître d': Clifford
Full Bar/Valet and Street Parking
AE, D, MC, V, CB
No dress restrictions

Le Profil has been serving French-Continental food for more than 25 years. The large, varied menu features such items as Escalope de Veau Verona, Beef Wellington and red snapper. Patrons are welcome to try their luck at backgammon, chess and other games at T. Michael's Club adjoining the dining area.

Reservations recommended
Lunch: Mon.–Fri., 11:30 A.M.–2 P.M.
Dinner: Mon.–Sat., 6 P.M.–11 P.M.
    Closed Sunday

MATAAM FEZ ⓱   *Moroccan*

4609 E. Colfax Ave.
Denver
(303) 399-9282
Maître d': Abderafih Benjelloun
Full Bar/Street Parking
AE, MC, V
No dress restrictions

You'll be seated at a low Moroccan table under a tented ceiling. You'll lounge on plush pillows and dine on authentic Moroccan cuisine. Dinner begins with a rich soup and three different salads. Next is B'stilla, a tissue-thin baked pastry. Main entrées include Cornish game hen, lamb, hare and couscous. Mint tea and pastries are served at the finale.

Reservations advised
Dinner: Daily, from 6 P.M.

MON PETIT ❷   *French*

7000 W. 38th Ave.
Wheat Ridge, Colo.
(303) 424-4700
Maître d': Frank Pourdad (manager)
Full Bar/Lot Parking
AE, D, MC, V, CB
Jacket for men (evenings)

Created from a 19th-century home, Mon Petit is filled with Persian rugs, antiques and crystal chandeliers. Waiters in tuxedos serve an assortment of appetizers, plus entrées of seafood, veal, lamb, beef, chicken and duckling. Desserts are plentiful.

Reservations required
Lunch: Mon.–Fri., 11:30 A.M.–2:30 P.M.
Dinner: Mon.–Sat., 6 P.M.–10 P.M.
    Closed Sunday

NORMANDY FRENCH RESTAURANT ⓰   *French*

1515 Madison St.
Denver
(303) 321-3311
Maître d': Heinz Gerstle (owner/manager)
Full Bar/Valet and Lot Parking
AE, D, MC, V, CB
No dress restrictions

Here you'll find the "rustic atmosphere of an elegant French country inn," insists Normandy owner Heinz E. Gerstle. His specialties include Escalope de Veau "Marie Antoinette," Coq au Beaujolais and Escargots Bourguignonne. The Normandy also has one of the area's largest wine cellars.

Reservations suggested
Lunch: Tues.–Sat., 11:30 A.M.–2 P.M.
Dinner: Tues.–Sun., 5 P.M.–10:30 P.M.
      Closed Monday

PALACE ARMS ⓴   *American*

Brown Palace Hotel
321 17th St.
Denver
(303) 825-3111
Maître d': John Rousso
Full Bar/Valet Parking
AE, D, MC, V, CB
Good taste in dress required
(Jacket, tie for men)

Memories of the French Empire period are rekindled in this restaurant filled with old French prints and objets d'art. To add a local touch, the stained glass windows were salvaged from the old Denver Court House. Specialties are Rocky Mountain rainbow trout, prime rib and Steak Diane "Brown Palace."

Reservations suggested
Lunch: Mon.–Fri., Noon–2:30 P.M.
Dinner: Mon.–Sat., 6 P.M.–10 P.M.
      Sun. 4 P.M.–9 P.M.

PASQUINEL'S ㉔   *Continental*

3005 S. Parker Rd.
Aurora, Colo.
(303) 755-9111
Maître d': Tom Walls (manager)
Full Bar/Lot Parking
AE, D, MC, V
No dress restrictions

This airy French-style cafe specializes in fresh seafood and veal. Fresh salmon is poached and served with a light cream and white wine sauce. There is patio dining when weather permits.

Reservations recommended
Lunch: Mon.–Fri., 11:30 A.M.–2 P.M.
Dinner: Daily, 6 P.M.–10:30 P.M.

PIERRE'S QUORUM ⑫ *French*

East Colfax at Grant
Denver
(303) 861-8686
Maître d': Pierre Wolfe (owner/manager/chef)
Full Bar/Valet Parking
AE, D, MC, V, CB
Good taste in dress required

Tableside preparation is a special feature at the Quorum. You can order such entrées as Veal Ritz Carlton, Veal Scallopini Jerusalem, Steak Diane and Filet of Beef Marengo. Alsacian owner/chef Pierre Wolfe has been offering a very personal brand of food and service for over 20 years.

Reservations required
Lunch: Mon.–Fri., 11:30 A.M.–2 P.M.
Dinner: Mon.–Sat., 5:30 P.M.–10 P.M.
    Closed Sunday

SPERTE'S LAFFITE ⑤ *Seafood*

1400 Larimer St.
Denver
(303) 629-6657
Maître d': Jeffrey Dutter
Full Bar/Valet Parking
AE, D, MC, V, CB
Good taste in dress required

Sperte's Laffite, located in the center of downtown Denver, specializes in New Orleans-style seafood entrées. The cooking staff likes to take particular care with stocks and sauces, using only the best, freshest ingredients. There is live entertainment nightly in the lower-level Rogue Room.

Reservations recommended
Lunch/Dinner: Mon.–Fri., 11 A.M.–2 A.M.
           Sat., 5 P.M.–2 A.M.
           Closed Sunday

TANTE LOUISE ⑱ *Continental*

4900 E. Colfax
Denver
(303) 355-4488
Maître d': Corbin Douglass III (owner-manager)
Full Bar/Lot and Street Parking
AE, D, MC, V, CB
No dress restrictions

Owner Corbin Douglass III wants you to "step into the warm and friendly atmosphere of a European country inn." Once inside, he'll offer you Veal Rossini, braised lamb shanks, sweetbreads, Canadian hare and Beef Wellington. The floors are hardwood, the fireplaces are brick and earth tones and candlelight predominate.

Reservations recommended
Lunch: Mon.–Fri., 11:30 A.M.–2 P.M.
Dinner: Mon.–Sat., 5:50 P.M.–10:30 P.M.
    Closed Sunday

TURN OF THE CENTURY ㉕   *American*

7300 E. Hampden Ave.
Denver
(303) 758-7300
Maître d': Mel Day (manager)
Full Bar/Valet Parking
AE, D, MC, V, CB
No dress restrictions

Turn of the Century offers you Tiffany lighting, intimate seating and lush tropical greenery. It also provides a 40-item salad bar and such entrées as prime rib, steaks and a variety of seafood. Comedy and musical entertainment are featured in the restaurant's "Las Vegas-style" showroom.

Reservations suggested
Lunch: Mon.–Fri., 11:30 A.M.–2:30 P.M.
Dinner: Mon.–Thurs., 6 P.M.–11 P.M.
          Fri., 6 P.M.–11:30 P.M.
          Sat., 5 P.M.–11:30 P.M.
          Sun., 5 P.M.–10 P.M.
Brunch: Sun., 10:30 A.M.–2:30 P.M.

WELLSHIRE INN ㉒   *International*

3333 S. Colorado Blvd.
Denver
(303) 759-3333
Maître d': Bill Brokaw
Full Bar/Lot Parking
AE, D, MC, V, CB
No dress restrictions

Built in 1926 as a private country club, the Wellshire Inn now shares its baronial splendor with one and all. Proprietor Leo Goto will tell you that dinner at the Wellshire Inn "speaks to you of another time and place." The menu reflects an interesting melange of various cultures. There seems to be something for everyone.

No reservations required
Lunch/Dinner: Mon.–Sat., 11:30 A.M.–10:30 P.M.
                 Sun., 10 A.M.–4 P.M.

DETROIT

AH WOK ❼   *Chinese*

41563 W. 10 Mile Rd.
Novi, Mich.
(313) 349-9260
Maître d': David Ng
Full Bar/Lot Parking
AE, D, V
Good taste in dress required

Ah Wok is a mellifluous blend of watercolors, Oriental objets d'art and subtle Chinese decor. Owner Peter Moy serves mainly Cantonese and Mandarin dishes. Two of his well-known specialties are Peking Duck and Rice Paper Shrimp.

Reservations required on weekends
Lunch/Dinner: Tues.-Thurs., 11 A.M.-10 P.M.
Fri.-Sat., 11 A.M.-Midnight
Sun., Noon-10 P.M.
Closed Monday

ALDO'S ⓴   *Italian*

19143 Kelly Rd.
Detroit
(313) 839-2180
Full Bar/Lot and Street Parking
No credit cards
No jeans or shorts

Italian food of a traditional nature is featured here. Every dish is cooked to order; the pasta is homemade; the meat is all cut to order. There just isn't any pre-cooked food at Aldo's, insists owner/chef Aldo Ottaviani. "No frozen meats or vegetables. Everything is fresh."

Reservations required
Dinner: Tues.-Thurs., 5 P.M.-10 P.M.
Fri.-Sat., 5 P.M.-11 P.M.
Sun., 4 P.M.-10 P.M.
Closed Monday

ALIETTE'S BAKERY ⓯   *French*

Porter at 24th
Detroit
(313) 554-0907
Maître d': C. Benson (owner)
Wine/Street Parking
No credit cards
No dress restrictions

Presided over by Aliette Lannaluc-Sanson of Bordeaux, this 36-seat French provincial restaurant and bakery offers an à la carte menu specializing in veal. Other selections include cream of garlic soup, duck with oysters, Steak Niçoise and Tournedos Rossini.

Reservations required
Lunch: Tues.-Sat., 11:30 A.M.-1:30 P.M.
Dinner: Tues.-Sat., 6 P.M.-9:30 P.M.
Closed Sunday, Monday

BENNO'S ㉒   *Continental*

8027 Agnes
Detroit
(313) 499-0040
Full Bar/Street Parking
No credit cards
Good taste in dress required

There is a feeling of exclusivity at Benno's. It is tiny, naturally intimate and filled with the kind of period furnishings and fine china you might want for your dream home. There are such specialties as Beef Wellington, quail in Burgundy and mushroom sauce, Omelet Stephanie, and goose, which must be ordered in advance.

Reservations required
Dinner: Tues.-Thurs., 6 P.M.- 9 P.M.
Fri.-Sat., 6 P.M.-11 P.M.
Closed Sunday, Monday

THE BIJOU ❸   *Continental*

30855 Southfield Rd.
Southfield, Mich.
(313) 644-5522
Maître d': Walter Maeder (manager)
Full Bar/Valet Parking
AE, MC, V
Good taste in dress required

"The stunning decor brings back the glamour of Hollywood, where each customer is the star," says owner James Thompson, Jr., of The Bijou. Playing vital supporting roles are the rack of lamb with peanut butter sauce, the abalone sautéed to your order, the Veal Zurich and several flaming desserts.

Reservations required
Lunch: Fri.-Sat., 5 P.M.-11 P.M.
Dinner: Sun., 4 P.M.-10 P.M.
Closed Monday

CARL'S CHOP HOUSE ⓳   *American*

3020 Grand River
Detroit
(313) 833-0700
Maître d': Kogy Aronsson
Full Bar/Valet Parking
AE, D, MC, V, CB
No shorts, T-shirts

Carl Rosenfield's Chop House has been in its present location for more than 50 years. The number of 4-H Blue Ribbon Steaks and cuts of prime rib served in that time must be staggering. There is ample seating capacity (room for 750) and private dining rooms for banquets and such.

Reservations advised
Lunch/Dinner: Mon.-Sat., 11:30 A.M.-1 A.M.
Sun., Noon-1 A.M.

CAUCUS CLUB ㉓ American

150 W. Congress
Detroit
(313) 965-4970
Maître d': Jose Acevedo
Full Bar/Valet Parking (evenings)
AE, D, MC, V, CB
Jacket, tie for men (evenings)

Sister establishment to the London Chop House across the street, the Caucus Club, says owner Lester Gruber, shares the same high standards of quality and service. Dover Sole and baby back ribs are top draws among a varied selection of house specialties. The Toby Room bar is supposedly the site where the Bullshot and other notable potables were "invented."

Reservations recommended
Lunch/Dinner: Tues.–Fri., 11:30 A.M.–2 A.M.
Mon., 11:30 A.M.–8 P.M.
Sat., 5 P.M.–2 A.M.
Closed Sunday, holidays

CHARLEY'S CRAB ⑬ Seafood

Northfield Hilton Inn
5498 Crooks Rd.
Troy, Mich.
(313) 879-2060
Maître d': Michael Stevens (manager)
Full Bar/Valet Parking
AE, D, MC, V, CB
No dress restrictions

The fresh fish express just in from the East stops first at Charley's Crab, it seems. The catch of Canada, Florida and the Great Lakes also makes its way here. Located in an impressively reconstructed room of a Grosse Pointe mansion, Charley's dispenses Chatham oysters, Cherrystone and Little Neck clams and loads of shrimp.

Reservations suggested
Dinner: Mon.–Thurs., 5 P.M.–11 P.M.
Fri.–Sat., 5 P.M.–Midnight
Sun., 3 P.M.–10 P.M.

THE EARLY AMERICAN ROOM ⑩ American

The Dearborn Inn
20301 Oakwood Blvd.
Dearborn, Mich.
(313) 271-2700
Maître d': Gary Cunningham
Full Bar/Lot Parking
AE, D, MC, V
No dress restrictions

The management terms the fare at The Early American Room "traditional American cuisine served in the grand style of a bygone era." The dining room features crystal chandeliers and high arched windows. Menu selections include prime rib, planked lake trout, veal and steaks.

Reservations suggested
Lunch: Mon.–Fri., 11:30 A.M.–2:30 P.M.
Dinner: Sun.–Thurs., 6 P.M.–10 P.M.
Fri.–Sat., 6 P.M.–11 P.M.

FOX & HOUNDS ❶   *American*

1560 N. Woodward
Bloomfield Hills, Mich.
(313) 644-4800
Maître d': Charles Negohosian
Full Bar/Valet Parking
AE, D, MC, V
Good taste in dress required

Fox & Hounds features *Old* English decor but *New* England cuisine, among other things. Specialties include New England-style seafood and a variety of steaks.

No reservations required
Lunch/Dinner: Mon.–Fri., 11 A.M.–2 A.M.
 Sat., 5 P.M.–2 A.M.
 Sun., 3 P.M.–8 P.M.

THE GANDY DANCER ⓬   *Seafood*

401 Depot St.
Ann Arbor, Mich.
(313) 769-0592
Maître d': Sara Coe, Pat French
Full Bar/Lot and Street Parking
AE, D, MC, V, CB
No dress restrictions

Housed in the historic old Ann Arbor train depot, built in 1886, The Gandy Dancer could easily be located along the Eastern seaboard. Its seafood specialties include "The Chesapeake Bucket for 2," which features two Maine lobsters, one-half Dungeness crab, steamed clams, mussels, corn on the cob and red-skinned potatoes.

Reservations recommended
Lunch: Mon.–Fri., 11:30 A.M.–4 P.M.
Dinner: Mon.–Thurs., 5 P.M.–11 P.M.
 Fri.-Sat., 5:30 P.M.–Midnight
 Sun., 3 P.M.–9 P.M.

THE GOLDEN MUSHROOM ❽   *Continental*

18100 W. Ten Mile Rd.
Southfield, Mich.
(313) 559-4230
Maître d': Christian Hubert
Full Bar/Valet Parking
AE, D, MC, V
Jacket, tie for men preferred

If romantic privacy is a priority, The Golden Mushroom may have all the answers. Its setting of natural woods, subdued lighting and warm earth tones seems to help hand-holding along. House specialties include rack of lamb, Michigan rainbow trout, beef tenderloin en croûte and Veal Cutlet Golden Mushroom.

Reservations suggested
Lunch/Dinner: Mon.–Thurs., 11:30 A.M.–11 P.M.
 Fri.–Sat., 11:30 A.M.–Midnight
 Closed Sunday, holidays

JACQUES SEAFOOD ❹   *Seafood/Continental*

30100 Telegraph Rd.
Bingham Farms, Mich.
(313) 642-1373
Maître d': Vicki Hann, Mark Fraker (manager)
Full Bar/Valet Parking
AE, D, MC, V
No dress restrictions

Manager Mark Fraker describes Jacques Seafood as an elegant contemporary restaurant with a mirrored dining room that faces a landscaped atrium and patio. Specialties include Pampano en Papillote Marguery and homemade European-style pastries.

Reservations required
Lunch: Mon.–Fri., 11 A.M.–2:30 P.M.
Dinner: Mon.–Sat., 6 P.M.–Midnight
  Closed Sunday

JIM'S GARAGE ㉖   *Continental*

300 W. Larned
Detroit
(313) 961-5175
Maître d': Jack Mulhall
Full Bar/Valet Parking
AE, MC, V
Jacket for men

Jim's Garage makes maximum use of what this city is famous for. Early automotive memorabilia is on display on the lower level of this converted parking garage opposite Cobo Hall and the Joe Louis Arena. Specialties are Swiss Onion Soup and daily chef's specials.

Reservations suggested
Lunch/Dinner: Mon.–Fri., 11:30 A.M.–10 P.M.
  Sat., 5:30 P.M.–10 P.M.
  Closed Sunday, Holidays

JOE MUER'S ⓲   *Seafood*

2000 Gratiot Ave.
Detroit
(313) 567-1088
Full Bar/Valet and Lot Parking
AE, MC, V
Jacket for men (evenings)

Joe Muer's, a 50-year Detroit institution, serves a complete catalog of fresh and saltwater fish and a wide assortment of seafood. The brick and oak interior is divided into five dining areas. The wine list features a good variety of select domestic wines.

No reservations required
Lunch/Dinner: Mon.–Thurs., 11:30 A.M.–10 P.M.
  Fri., 11:30 A.M.–11 P.M.
  Sat., 5 P.M.–11 P.M.
  Closed Sunday, holidays

LA ROTISSERIE ❾ *International*

Hyatt Regency Hotel
Fairlane Town Center
Dearborn, Mich.
(313) 593-1234
Maître d': Bernard Viola (manager)
Full Bar/Valet and Lot Parking
AE, D, MC, V, CB
Jacket for men, no jeans

Despite its French name, this is a place for such Chinese specialties as Peking Duck and Shrimp Cantonese, as well as international/eclectic offerings such as Duck Madagascar, Rack of Lamb Reforma and Amaretto Soufflé. Duck is a really special attraction.

Reservations suggested
Dinner: Mon.-Sat., 6 P.M.-10:30 P.M. (winter)
            Mon.-Sat., 6:30 P.M.-11 P.M. (summer)
Brunch: Sun. 10 A.M.-2 P.M.

LELLI'S INN ⓰ *Northern Italian*

7618 Woodward Ave.
Detroit
(313) 871-1590
Maître d': Victor Dazbaz (manager), Del Ah Leong
Full Bar/Valet Parking
AE, MC, V
No dress restrictions

In the family for 42 years, Lelli's features prime meats and special sauces. The pasta is all homemade and the substantial Porterhouse steak is carved tableside. The setting is an old home converted into a Mediterranean-style restaurant with many alcoves for intimate dining.

Reservations advised
Lunch/Dinner: Tues.-Fri., 11 A.M.-10 P.M.
                Sat., 11 A.M.-11 P.M.
                Sun., Noon-9 P.M.

LONDON CHOP HOUSE ⓴ *American*

155 W. Congress
Detroit
(313) 962-0278
Maître d': Ray Hansen
Full Bar/Valet Parking (evenings)
AE, D, MC, V, CB
Jacket, tie for men

It seems almost everyone who has ever eaten out in Detroit has eaten here. The London Chop House exudes clubbiness and conviviality. You get the feeling important decisions could be made at just about any table. Some decisions are easy: look for lake perch, Dover Sole or veal on the menu.

Reservations required
Lunch/Dinner: Mon.-Sat., 11:30 A.M.-2 A.M.
                Closed Sunday, holidays

DETROIT   117

MARIO'S ⓘ   *Italian*

4222 Second Ave.
Detroit
(313) 833-9425
Full Bar/Valet Parking
AE, D, MC, V, CB
No dress restrictions

Mario Lelli keeps a watchful eye on his 30-year-old establishment. A Bolognese-style cuisine "veers to the French occasionally." Such items as the antipasto, the veal and the tournedos have received raves. Several of the desserts are flamed before your eyes.

No reservations required
Lunch/Dinner: Tues.–Fri., 11:30 A.M.–1 A.M.
             Sat., 4 P.M.–1 A.M.
             Sun., 2 P.M.–1 A.M.
             Closed Monday

THE MONEY TREE ⓘ   *Continental*

333 W. Fort St.
Detroit
(313) 961-2445
Maître d': Byron Thompson
Full Bar/Garage Parking
AE, D, MC, V
No jeans (evenings)

A restaurant done in appropriately copper and bronze tones, The Money Tree features a selection of quiche, crêpes and salads for lunch. Dinner entrées include items such as Veal Boursin, sweetbreads, charcuterie and fresh seafood. You may be able to detect the aroma of fresh bread baking.

Reservations required
Lunch: Mon.–Fri., 11:30 A.M.–2:30 P.M.
Dinner: Mon.–Thurs., 6 P.M.–9 P.M.
        Fri., 6 P.M.–10 P.M.
        Sat., 5:30 P.M.–10 P.M.

NEW HELLAS CAFE ⓘ   *Greek*

583 Monroe St.
Detroit
(313) 961-5544
Maître d': Gus Anton,
          Demetrious Papatriantafyllou (owners)
Full Bar/Lot Parking
D, MC, V
No dress restrictions

The New Hellas Cafe claims to be the oldest existing restaurant in Detroit's Greek Town. It was established in 1901 by the Antonopulos family and is still going strong. The menu features Greek favorites such as Saganaki (flaming cheese), lamb and rice entrées, spinach pie, moussaka, octopus, squid and broiled split lamb chops.

No reservations required
Lunch/Dinner: Sun.–Thurs., 11 A.M.–2 A.M.
             Fri.–Sat., 11 A.M.–4 A.M.

PONTCHARTRAIN WINE CELLARS ㉗ *Continental*

234 W. Larned
Detroit
(313) 963-1785
Maître d': Heinz Steinbrink
Beer and Wine/Valet Parking
AE, D, MC, V
Jacket for men (evenings)

If tonight's the night for romance — or whatever — this may be the place to seal the deal. Dim lighting, natural brick and dark paneling combine to produce the proper effect. The menu does its part with such things as escargots, gazpacho, noisettes of lamb and Ratatouille de Provence. There are also 85 selections of French, German and California wines.

Reservations required
Lunch: Mon.–Fri., 11:30 A.M.–2:30 P.M.
Dinner: Mon.–Sat., 5:30 P.M.–10 P.M.
    Closed Sunday

RESTAURANT DUGLASS ❻ *French*

29269 Southfield Rd.
Southfield, Mich.
(313) 424-9144
Maître d': Maureen Byrne (manager), Manuel Chavez
Full Bar/Valet and Lot Parking
AE, D, MC, V
Good taste in dress required

Restaurant Duglass features dining in the grand style, even though the feeling is intimate and personal. There is nightly entertainment and dancing on Friday and Saturday nights. The menu is a series of innovative chef's specials, and changes daily.

Reservations required
Lunch: Mon.–Fri., 11:30 A.M.–2:30 P.M.
Dinner: Mon.–Sat., 6 P.M.–10 P.M.
    Closed Sunday

THE ROYAL EAGLE ㉕ *Polish*

1415 Parker
Detroit
(313) 331-8088
Maître d': Thomas Verwest
Full Bar/Lot Parking
MC, V
No dress restrictions

Detroit is a great place to enjoy Polish-Eastern European cuisine. At the Royal Eagle, with its fine china and crystal, its original oil paintings and its waiters in traditional garb, the Polish culinary accent is strong. You'll find Veal Paprikas, Beef Polonaise, mushrooms in sour cream sauce, walnut torte and Cheesecake Polonaise.

Reservations required
Dinner: Wed.–Sat., 6 P.M.–10 P.M.
    Sun., 4 P.M.–8 P.M.
    Closed Monday, Tuesday

SHEIK RESTAURANT ㉑ *Lebanese*

316 E. Lafayette
Detroit
(313) 964-8441
Maître d': Esther Michael (owner)
Full Bar/Lot and Street Parking
MC, V
No dress restrictions

As Esther Michael tells it, "Father started the business 59 years ago in the same location bearing the same name." Since then Sheik has served Lebanese specialties, including lamb cooked 20 different ways. Ms. Michael adds that "atmosphere and ambience are second to our lamb."

Reservations suggested
Lunch/Dinner: Tues.-Fri., 11 A.M.-10 P.M.
Sat., 4 P.M.-11 P.M.
Sun., 3 P.M.-10 P.M.

TWEENY'S CAFE ❷ *International*

280 N. Woodward
Birmingham, Mich.
(313) 644-0050
Maître d': Yvonne Gill-Davis (owner)
Full Bar/Valet Parking
MC, V
No dress restrictions

"The heart of Tweeny's Cafe is its extraordinary cuisine," comments owner Yvonne Gill-Davis. The ever-changing menu stresses creativity and may include sweetbreads with spinach and bacon nestled in an egg wrapper and finished with Pernod. Music is an integral part of life at Tweeny's.

Reservations required (weekends)
Lunch: Tues.-Sat., 11:30 A.M.-3:30 P.M.
Dinner: Tues.-Sat., 5:30 P.M.-11 P.M.
Supper: Tues.-Sat., 11 P.M.-2 A.M.
Closed Sunday, Monday

VINEYARDS ❺ *Continental/Seafood*

29230 Franklin Rd.
Southfield, Mich.
(313) 357-3430
Maître d': Rhonda
Full Bar/Valet Parking
AE, D, MC, V
Jacket for men

The Vineyards is actually three restaurants: the quietly elegant Vineyards, specializing in roast pork with sweet and sour sauce and Chicken à la Chantilly; Cocos, a New York-style bistro featuring Cape Cod seafood served under the soft gleam of gaslights; Benny's, a good-time restaurant and disco.

Reservations required
Dinner: Mon.-Thurs., 5 P.M.-10:30 P.M.
Fri.-Sat., 5 P.M.-Midnight
Closed Sunday

WIN SCHULER'S ⓫ *American*

3600 Plymouth Rd.
Ann Arbor, Mich.
(313) 769-9400
Maître d': Leon Varney
Full Bar/Lot Parking
AE, D, MC, V
Good taste in dress required

It's a bit of a hike to get to this lovely college town from downtown Detroit, but many people have found Win Schuler's well worth it. Homey hospitality is as much a specialty here as the generous slabs of prime rib, steaks, seafood, caldrons of homemade soup and freshly baked breads and pies.

Reservations required
Breakfast/Lunch/Dinner: Mon.–Sat. 6:45 A.M.–11 P.M.
           Sunday, 8 A.M.–10 P.M.

HONOLULU

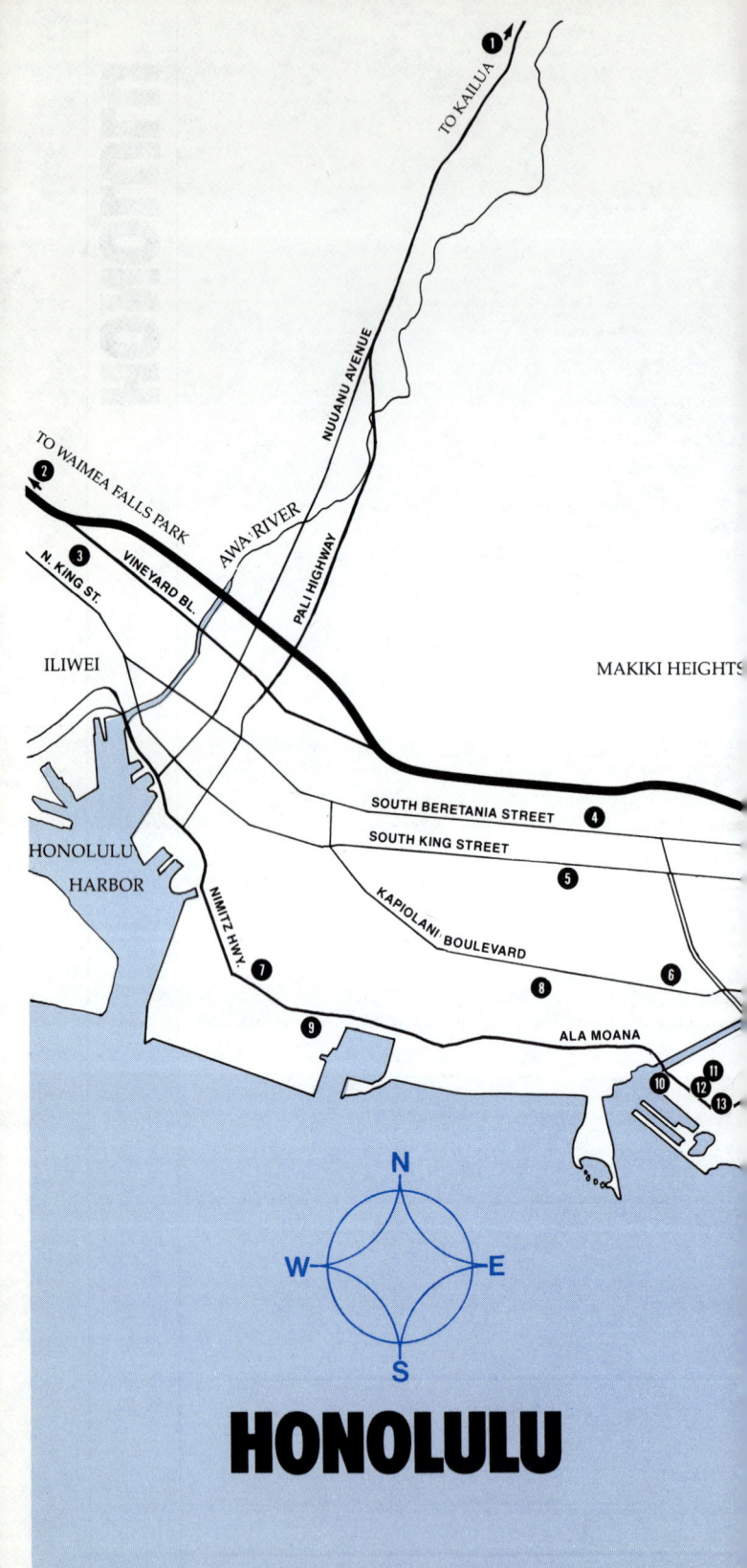

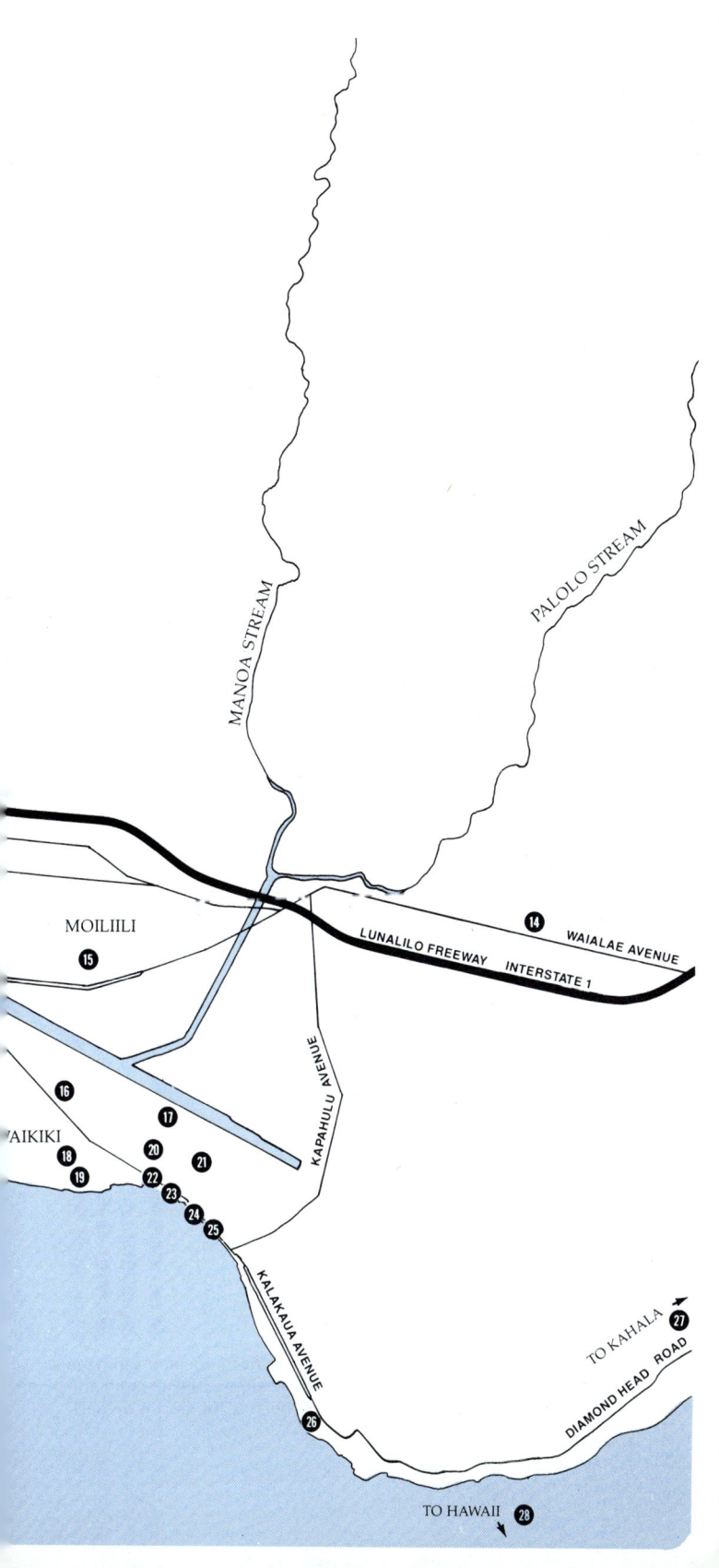

ALFRED'S EUROPEAN RESTAURANT ❼ *Continental*

677 Ala Moana Blvd.
Honolulu
(808) 523-1602
Maître d': Alfred Vollenweider (chef and owner)
Full Bar/Valet and Lot Parking
AE, D, MC, V
No dress restrictions

Alfred's presents a menu with an international flair. There are such specialties as wiener schnitzel, sauerbraten, duckling with lingonberry sauce, Red Snapper Georgia, Opakapaka in Champagne Sauce and Entrecôte Cafe de Paris. And for dessert, there's apple strudel, soufflés and Strawberries Romanoff.

Reservations required
Lunch: Mon.-Fri., 11 A.M.-2 P.M.
Dinner: Tues.-Sun.

BAGWELLS 2424 ㉔ *Continental*

Hyatt Regency Waikiki
2424 Kalakaua Ave.
Honolulu
(808) 922-9292
Maître d': Noel Trainor
Full Bar/Valet and Lot Parking
AE, D, MC, V, CB
Good taste in dress required

Here you'll find the Seafood Potpourri, a shellfish bar starring fresh crustaceans from all parts of the world. Some of the main courses or "roasts" include breast of chicken with lobster and crayfish and fillet of lamb. Also known for its selective list of wines and cordials, Bagwells offers rare vintages as part of the Sommelier's Selection.

Reservations required
Dinner: Daily, 6:30 P.M.-10:30 P.M.

BLUE HAWAII ❺ *Continental*

1150 S. King St.
Honolulu
(808) 523-1388
Maître d': Frank Daniel
Full Bar/Valet Parking
MC, V
No dress restrictions

A glamorous water fountain is the focal point for elegant dining at Blue Hawaii. The menu focuses on fresh seafood, rack of lamb and chateaubriand. There are soufflés and Cherries Jubilee for dessert.

Reservations required
Lunch: Mon.-Fri., 11 A.M.-2 P.M.
Dinner: Daily, 4 P.M.-11 P.M.

CANLIS ⓰ American

2100 Kalakaua Ave.
Honolulu
(808) 923-2324
Maître d': David J. Hill (manager)
Full Bar/Valet Parking
AE, D, MC, V, CB
Jacket for men (upper dining room)

Located in the heart of Waikiki, Canlis is one of the few restaurants in the area not connected to a hotel. The interior decor is Polynesian. Kimono-clad waitresses serve such American specialties as fried jumbo shrimp, Dungeness crab, scallops, steaks and Canlis Special Salad with its dressing of lemon juice, olive oil, coddled eggs and herbs.

No reservations required
Dinner: Daily, 6 P.M.-11:15 P.M.
Closed major holidays

CAVALIER ⓺ Continental

1630 Kapiolani Blvd.
Honolulu
(808) 949-4134
Maître d': Martin Kelly
Full Bar/Valet and Lot Parking
AE, D, MC, V, CB
No dress restrictions

Located just blocks from Waikiki and now in its 12th year of operation, Cavalier offers such specialties as Escargots Bourguignonne, Bouillabaisse Rosato, Veal Cordon Bleu Cavalier, Paella Valenciana and Roast Duckling à l'Orange. There is an extensive selection of imported and domestic wines.

Reservations required
Lunch: Mon.-Fri., 11:30 A.M.-2 P.M.
Dinner: Sun.-Thurs., 6 P.M.-10 P.M.
Fri.-Sat., 6 P.M.-10:30 P.M.

CHAMPEAUX'S TOP OF THE "I" ⓾ French

Ilikai Hotel
Honolulu
(808) 949-3811
Maître d': Patric Crichton (manager)
Full Bar/Lot Parking
AE, D, MC, V, CB
Good taste in dress required

Sky-high views of Waikiki and Diamond Head can be enjoyed at this French restaurant on the 30th floor of the Ilikai. The *nouvelle cuisine* specialties include Carré d'Agneau aux Aromates, Poisson Neapolitan and Faison Perigourdine. Many dishes are prepared tableside, including the flambé desserts.

Reservations required
Dinner: Daily, 6 P.M.-10 P.M.
Brunch: Sun., 10:30 A.M.-2 P.M.

CHEZ MICHEL ⓫   *French*

444 Hobron Lane
Honolulu
(808) 955-7866
Maître d': Michel F. Martin (owner)
Full Bar/Valet Parking
AE, D, MC, V, CB
Good taste in dress required

If such delights as Carré d'Agneau Jardinière, King Crab Dieppoise, Ris de Veau des Gourmets and Canard à l'Orange sound appealing, then Chez Michel is for you. Michel Martin's "south of France garden setting" is also the place for such sweet treats as chilled orange soufflé, Crêpes Suzette and chocolate soufflé.

Reservations required
Lunch: Mon.–Fri., 11:30 A.M.–2:30 P.M.
Dinner: Daily, 6 P.M.–11 P.M.
Brunch: Sun., 11 A.M.–2 P.M.

DINING PAVILLION ㉘   *International*

Mauna Kea Beach Hotel
Kamuela, Hawaii
(808) 882-7222
Full Bar/Lot Parking
No credit cards
Jacket for men

Formal and elegant, the Dining Pavillion is of Oriental design, with red lacquered service plates, red and white table settings and brass table lamps. You may choose selections from countries around the world. (A different country is featured each night.)

Reservations required
Dinner: Daily, 6:30 P.M.–9 P.M.

HALA TERRACE ㉗   *International*

Kahala Hilton Hotel
5000 Kahala Ave.
Honolulu
(808) 734-2211
Maître d': Adam Suapaia (night) and Lucy White (day)
Full Bar/Valet and Lot Parking
AE, D, MC, V, CB
Good taste in dress required

Adding "the flavor of Hawaii" to everything they do is important to the Hala Terrace staff. Breakfast, for instance, means Macadamia nut pancakes or banana muffins; for lunch, it's a pineapple boat with Macadamia rum cream dressing; and for dinner, mahi mahi is served sautéed with lemon butter and capers. Even Shrimp Madras is prepared with pineapple to give it an island touch.

Reservations required
Breakfast/Lunch/Dinner: Daily, 7 A.M.–11 P.M.

HANOHANO ROOM   *Continental*

Sheraton Waikiki Hotel
2255 Kalakaua Ave.
Honolulu
(808) 922-4422
Maître d': J. P. Germain
Full Bar/Lot Parking
AE, D, MC, V, CB
Good taste in dress required

Another 30-floor-high place to dine, the Hanohano Room provides a dramatic view from Diamond Head to Pearl Harbor. It also provides various Continental entrées and dancing to Trummy Young's Orchestra.

Reservations required (dinner)
Breakfast: Daily, 7 A.M.-10:30 A.M.
Dinner: Daily, 6:30 P.M.-1 A.M.
Brunch: Sun., 8:30 A.M.-2 P.M.

HY'S STEAK HOUSE   *Continental*

2440 Kuhio Ave.
Honolulu
(808) 922-5555
Maître d': Wes Zane
Full Bar/Valet Parking
AE, D, MC, V, CB
Good taste in dress required

Hy's offers you a choice of three elegant dining rooms. One is an old Victorian-style library. Another spotlights the chef behind a glass partition. Still another is of Greek design with green velvet embellishments. The specialty entrée is steak, of course. In this case, it's either a nine-ounce or 13-ounce New York strip.

Reservations suggested
Dinner: Daily, 6 P.M.-11 P.M.

JOHN DOMINIS   *Seafood*

43 Ahui St.
Honolulu
(808) 523-0955
Full Bar/Valet Parking
AE, D, MC, V, CB
Good taste in dress required

At John Dominis', you'll dine overlooking the channel entrance to Ala Moana Harbor. That means a double treat for you: a wide variety of fresh seafood and a constant parade of boats cruising in and out of the harbor. A special feature is the John Domino Platter, which includes a tempting taste of all kinds of seafood.

Reservations recommended
Dinner: Daily, 5:30 P.M.-10:30 P.M.

HONOLULU   129

KOBE JAPANESE STEAK HOUSE ⓬   *Japanese*

1841 Ala Moana Blvd.
Honolulu
(808) 941-4444
Full Bar/Valet Parking
AE, D, MC, V, CB
Good taste in dress required

The emphasis at Kobe is on dramatic meal preparation and presentation (often one and the same). Dexterous chefs grill specialties such as teppanyaki (a combination of shrimp, steak and vegetables) and seafood on hot slabs while you sit and wait and enjoy the show.

Reservations required
Dinner: Sun.–Thurs., 5 P.M.–10 P.M.
       Fri.–Sat., 5:30 P.M.–10:30 P.M.

L'AUBERGE ❶   *French*

117 Hekili St.
Kailua, Oahu
(808) 262-4835
Maître d': Marcel Baltzer (owner)
Beer and Wine/Lot Parking
MC, V
No dress restrictions

Owners Marcel and Elvi Baltzer have created a restaurant with a "charming country inn atmosphere." The country-Continental dishes include escargots, blinis, celery remoulade, Coq au Vin, Beef Bourguignon, Strawberries Romanoff and Crêpes Suzette.

Reservations required
Dinner: Wed.–Sun., 6 P.M.–10 P.M.
       Closed Monday, Tuesday

LE BON ❽   *French*

1376 Kapiolani Ave.
Honolulu
(808) 941-5051
Maître d': John Nicholas
Full Bar/Valet Parking
AE, D, MC, V, CB
Good taste in dress required

Le Bon features French country elegance in the tropics. Specialties include pepper steak, Beef Wellington, pheasant and duck. For dessert, there is homemade cheesecake with a macadamia nut crust.

Reservations advised
Dinner: Tues.–Sat., 6 P.M.–Midnight
       Sun.–Mon., 6 P.M.–11 P.M.

LE CAFE DE PARIS ⑬ French

Discovery Bay
1778 Ala Moana Blvd.
Honolulu
(808) 947-6467
Full Bar/Street Parking
AE, MC, V
Good taste in dress required

The traditions of Parisian dining are upheld at Le Café de Paris as proprietor Claude Leruitte sees to it that high standards are maintained. He presents such specialties as Coquilles St. Jacques, Coq au Vin, Frogs' Legs Provençal and Confit de Canard. Several French wines are available, by the glass or bottle.

Reservations accepted before 7:30 P.M.
Dinner: Mon.–Thurs., 6 P.M.–11 P.M.
 Fri.–Sat., 6 P.M.–2 A.M.
 Closed Sunday

MAILE ㉗ Continental

Kahala Hilton Hotel
5000 Kahala Ave.
Honolulu
(808) 734-2211
Maître d': Charlie Goodness
Full Bar/Valet and Lot Parking
AE, D, MC, V, CB
Jacket for men

Maile's menu is a harmonious blend of European cuisine with Hawaiian flair and flavor. A specialty is Roast Duckling Waialae, served with bananas, lichees, Mandarin oranges and a spiced peach half. It is flamed at the table with Grand Marnier. Fountains, pools and a vivid variety of orchids turn this public restaurant into a private garden.

Reservations required
Dinner: Daily, 6:30 P.M.–9:30 P.M.

MANDARIN PALACE ⑳ Chinese

Hotel Miramar
2345 Kuhio Ave.
Honolulu
(808) 922-1666
Maître d': Maurice Lau (manager)
Full Bar/Lot Parking
AE, D, MC, V
No dress restrictions

Impeccable service and distinctive decor enhance the experience of the Mandarin Palace, according to manager Maurice Lau. His special dishes include Peking Duck, minced squab on lettuce, sizzling prawns and deep fried stuffed tofu.

Reservations recommended
Lunch: Daily, 11 A.M.–2 P.M.
Dinner: Daily, 5:30 P.M.–10 P.M.

MATTEO'S ⑰   *Italian*

Marine Surf Hotel
364 Seaside Ave.
Honolulu
(808) 922-5551
Maître d': Robert
Full Bar/Valet Parking
AE, D, MC, V, CB
Good taste in dress required

Veal is king at this Southern Italian restaurant. It stars in such preparations as Piccata di Vitella, Saltimbocca, Scaloppine ala Marsala and Osso Bucco. Also featured are made-from-scratch fettucine, ravioli and manicotti, plus entrées of chicken and shellfish.

Reservations required
Dinner: Daily, 6 P.M.–2 A.M.

MEKONG ❹   *Thai*

1295 S. Beretania St.
Honolulu
(808) 521-2025
Maître d': Keo Sananikone (owner)
No Wine or Spirits/Lot and Street Parking
AE, MC, V
No dress restrictions

"A meal at Mekong is a cultural experience," states owner Keo Sananikone. The Thai cuisine is "exotic and delicious" and the Thai atmosphere is "charming," he adds. Dishes range from blindingly hot to blissfully mild. Many dishes are prepared with vegetarian tastes in mind.

No reservations required
Lunch: Mon.–Fri., 11 A.M.–2 P.M.
Dinner: Daily, 5:30 P.M.–9 P.M.

MICHEL'S AT THE COLONY SURF ㉖   *French*

2895 Kalakaua Ave.
Honolulu
(808) 923-6552
Maître d': Horst Beneke
Full Bar/Valet Parking
AE, D, MC, V, CB
Jacket for men

French cuisine is presented before a backdrop of beach, sea and sky. Look for such selections as palm hearts vinaigrette, lobster bisque flamed with cognac, crab crêpes, scampi, Tournedos Bordelaise and Grand Marnier Soufflé.

Reservations required
Breakfast: Daily, 7 A.M.–10 A.M.
Lunch: Mon.–Fri., 11:30 A.M.–2:30 P.M.
Dinner: Daily, 6 P.M.–11 P.M.
Brunch: Sun., 11 A.M.–2:30 P.M.

NICK'S FISHMARKET ㉒   *Seafood*

Waikiki Gateway Hotel
412 Lewers St.
Honolulu
(808) 955-6333
Maître d': Bill Vogler
Full Bar/Valet Parking
AE, D, MC, V, CB
Good taste in dress required

The flagship of a growing chain, this Nick's features over 50 entrées, ranging from local fish (mahi mahi, swordfish and Maui catfish) to East Coast and Caribbean shellfish to Louisiana prawns, frogs' legs and oysters. There are also steaks and Mediterranean-style salads. Homemade desserts and a good selection of wines in all price ranges complete the experience.

Reservations required
Dinner: Daily, 5 P.M. - 2 A.M.

THE POTTERY STEAKHOUSE ⓮   *American*

3574 Waialae Ave.
Honolulu
(808) 737-0633
Full Bar/Valet Parking
MC, V
No dress restrictions

The Pottery Steakhouse is a colorful, if unusual, blend of the world of ceramics and the world of fine aged prime beef. If you've always wanted to cut into a juicy steak while surrounded by ceramic murals and pottery, here's your chance. In addition to steak, you can choose prawns, fish and Cornish hen cooked in a clay pot.

Reservations suggested
Dinner: Daily, 5:30 P.M. - 10 P.M.

PROUD PEACOCK ❷   *Continental*

Waimea Falls Park
59-864 Kamehameha Hwy.
Haleiwa, Oahu
(808) 683-8668
Full Bar/Lot Parking
AE, D, MC, V, CB
No dress restrictions

You dine at the Proud Peacock surrounded by lush tropical gardens, filled with peacocks and the other exotic birds that inhabit this lovely park on Oahu's North Shore. A salad bar complements every entrée. There are selections of the island's fresh fish, seafood and steaks.

No reservations required
Lunch/Dinner: Daily, 10 A.M. - 2 A.M.

SHIP'S TAVERN ㉓   *Seafood*

Surfrider Hotel
2353 Kalakaua Ave.
Honolulu
(808) 922-3111
Maître d': Jimmy Liu
Full Bar/Valet and Lot Parking
AE, D, MC, V, CB
Good taste in dress required

As you might expect, a nautical atmosphere prevails at this restaurant overlooking Waikiki Beach. There are specialties such as clam chowder, Maui prawns, turtle steak, Maine lobster and homemade Molokai bread, as well as a selection of steaks, chops and fowl.

Reservations requested
Dinner: Daily, 6 P.M. – 11 P.M.

THIRD FLOOR ㉕   *Continental*

Hawaiian Regent Hotel
2552 Kalakaua Ave.
Honolulu
(808) 922-6611
Maître d': Siegfried Poesch
Full Bar/Valet Parking
AE, D, MC, V, CB
Jacket for men

Naan bread with liver pâté begins the dining experience at The Third Floor. It is followed by a tray of assorted relishes, a salad and then a main course featuring fresh seafood, game, beef, poultry, lamb or veal. Assorted desserts may be selected from the pastry cart, and then for the finale — a tray of ice cream bonbons misted with a flourish of dry ice.

Reservations required
Dinner: Daily, 6:30 P.M. – 11 P.M.

TRATTORIA ⓳   *Italian*

Edgewater Hotel
2168 Kalia Rd.
Honolulu
(808) 923-8415
Full Bar/Valet Parking
AE, MC, V, CB
Good taste in dress required

Italy comes to the islands at this restaurant resembling a Roman villa, with its Florentine furnishings and Byzantine frescoes. The Northern Italian specialties include Veal Piccata, Chicken Spiritoso, linguine, scampi and cannelloni.

Reservations recommended
Dinner: Daily, 5:30 P.M. – 11:30 P.M.

THE WILLOWS ⑮ — *International*

901 Hausten St.
Honolulu
(808) 946-4808
Full Bar/Valet Parking
AE, D, MC, V, CB
No dress restrictions

Set in a two-acre flower-filled garden with thatched hales and open air pavilions, The Willows is an island dream come true. Complete with pond, waterfall, coconut trees and weeping willows, it is an ideal setting for a luau. Featured is "Spice of the Islands" cuisine. This means, for instance, Hawaiian curries, poi suppers and coconut cream pie.

Reservations required
Lunch: Mon. - Sat., 11:30 A.M. - 3 P.M.
Dinner: Daily, 5:30 P.M. - 9:30 P.M.
Brunch: Sun., 9:30 A.M. - 2 P.M.

WO FAT ❸ — *Chinese*

115 N. Hotel St.
Honolulu
(808) 533-6393
Maître d': Ella Tan
Full Bar/Lot Parking
AE, D, MC, V, CB
No dress restrictions

Wo Fat is proud of its distinction as one of the oldest Chinese restaurants in Hawaii. It will soon celebrate its centennial year! Featured is a wide selection of traditional Cantonese food.

No reservations required
Lunch/Dinner: Daily, 10:30 A.M. - 9 P.M.

HOUSTON

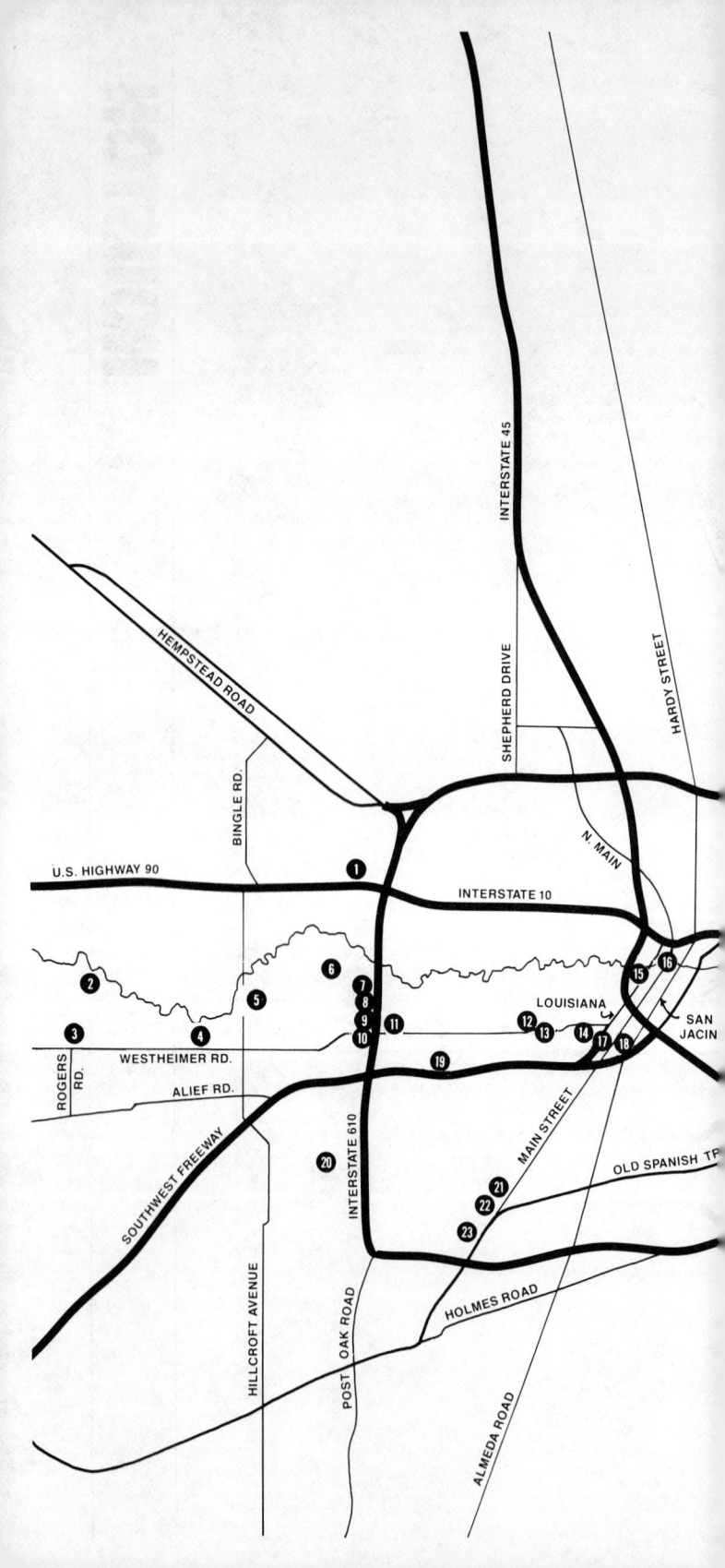

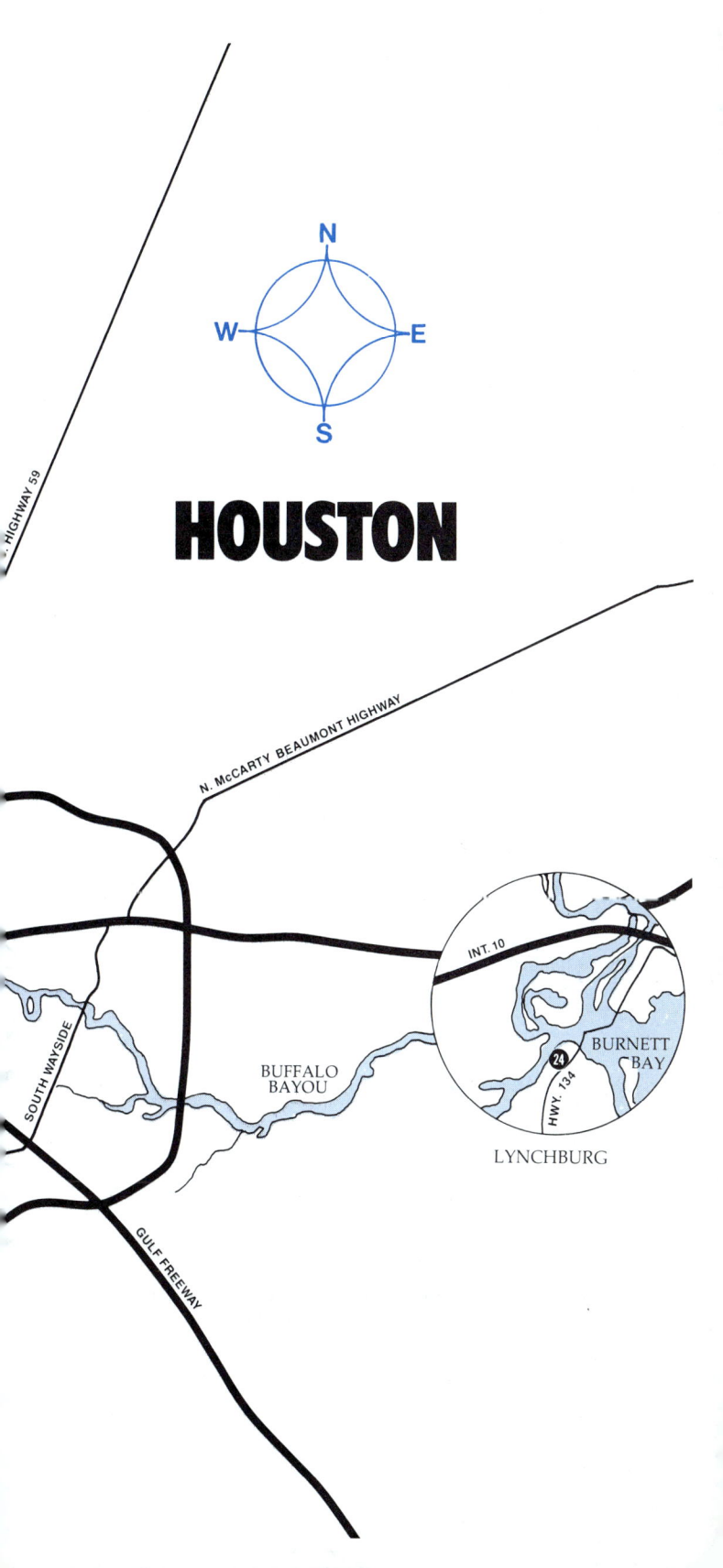

ARNO'S ⓴   *Northern Italian*

5213 Cedar St.
Bellaire, Texas
(713) 668-4299
Beer and Wine/Lot Parking
MC, V
No dress restrictions

Although Arno's specializes in Northern Italian cuisine, the menu also includes dishes from other countries. Half the menu changes daily so that only the freshest seafood items can be offered. There are mussels, clams, baby squid, shrimp and sea scallops. The veal is also the freshest and is cut by a "resident butcher." Pastas are homemade.

No reservations required
Lunch: Tues.–Fri., 11:30 A.M.–2:30 P.M.
Dinner: Mon.–Thurs., 6 P.M.–10 P.M.
   Fri.–Sat., 6 P.M.–11 P.M.
   Closed Sunday

BRENNAN'S ⓱   *Creole*

3300 Smith St.
Houston
(713) 522-9711
Maître d': Ricardo Sanchez
Full Bar/Valet Parking
AE, D, MC, V, CB
Jacket for men

Located in one of the city's oldest buildings (and in such a young city, that counts for a lot), Brennan's strives for just the right mixture of Texas luxury and Creole charm. People usually rave about their breakfasts, which can be ordered every day but Saturday, when a Jazz Brunch is the main attraction. A Dixieland band accompanies the brunch.

Reservations requested
Breakfast/Lunch: Daily, 9 A.M.–2:30 P.M.
Dinner: Daily, 6 P.M.–11 P.M.

BRENNER'S ❶   *American*

10911 Katy Freeway
Houston
(713) 465-2901
Maître d': Dean Edwards, Carl Brenner (owner)
Full Bar/Lot Parking
AE, D, MC, V
Good taste in dress required

Brenner's features a rustic atmosphere, with cypress paneling. You dine by candlelight, overlooking a mill and waterfall. The concentration is on beef — eight-ounce filets, 14- or 16-ounce rib eyes, 16-ounce sirloin strips — all broiled to perfection. The salad dressings are homemade and Mrs. Brenner bakes the apple strudel herself.

Reservations recommended
Lunch: Tues.–Fri., 11:30 A.M.–2 P.M.
Dinner: Tues.–Sun., 5:30 P.M.–11 P.M.
   Closed Monday

BUD BIGELOW'S ❹   *American*

7939 Westheimer
Houston
(713) 782-0430
Full Bar/Valet Parking
AE, D, MC, V
No dress restrictions

Bud Bigelow's offers "fine dining in a comfortable setting," says manager Klaus Elfeldt. There's everything from prime rib to veal to local seafood selections to chicken.

Reservations suggested
Lunch: Mon.–Fri.
Dinner: Daily, from 5:30 P.M.

CHARLEY'S 517 ⓰   *Continental*

517 Louisiana
Houston
(713) 224-4438
Maître d': Karl Goedereis
Full Bar/Valet Parking
AE, MC, V
Jacket, tie for men

At least two artists exist at Charley's — the one who worked on the Impressionist paintings that line the walls and the one in the kitchen, turning out such masterworks as Snapper Pontchartrain, Poached Dover Sole with lemon/cucumber sauce and chocolate soufflé. Not only can you enjoy the products of the Wine Cellar, but you can also be seated there for lunch or dinner.

No reservations required
Lunch: Mon.–Fri., 11:30 A.M.–2:30 P.M.
Dinner: Mon.–Fri., 6 P.M.–11 P.M.
        Sat., 6 P.M.–Midnight
        Closed Sunday

COURTLANDT'S ⓲   *Continental*

3200 Louisiana (enter on Stuart)
Houston
(713) 526-3247
Maître d': Chris Eichman
Full Bar/Valet Parking
AE, D, MC, V
Jacket, tie for men (evenings)

If you find yourself in Houston, but yearn for old New Orleans, many might suggest you head for Courtlandt's. Here you can satisfy your cravings with the likes of Singing Shrimp (flamed at the table in lemon butter) and Courtlandt's Meat Masterpiece (filet mignon on a bed of wild rice with a special sauce). The dining rooms are replicas of those found in the Crescent City.

Reservations required
Lunch: Mon.–Fri., 11:30 A.M.–2 P.M.
Dinner: Mon.–Sat., 6 P.M.–11 P.M.
        Closed Sunday (except special occasions)

DON'S SEAFOOD RESTAURANT & STEAKHOUSE ❼   *Seafood/Cajun*

307 E. North Belt
Houston
(713) 931-7654
Maître d': Joseph Larriverre
Full Bar/Lot Parking
AE, D, MC, V
No dress restrictions

It looks like Don's has got it all covered — both seafood specialties like crayfish, stuffed crabs, oysters on the half shell and gumbo, and landlocked entrées like steaks and chops. They take no chances with the fresh seafood. It is controlled by Don's from ocean to table.

No reservations required
Lunch/Dinner: Sun. - Thurs., 11 A.M. - 10 P.M.
              Fri., 11 A.M. - 11 P.M.
              Sat., 5 P.M. - 11 P.M.

FOULARD'S ❸   *French*

10001 Westheimer Rd.
Houston
(713) 789-1661
Maître d': Martin A. Robert
Full Bar/Lot Parking
AE, D, MC, V, CB
Good taste in dress required

Foulard's is all smooth service, sleek decor and impeccable presentation. Chef/owner Edmond Foulard creates dishes such as Duckling Normande (with apples and brandy), Escargots Bourguignonne, Beef Wellington and Rack of Lamb Persille (with spices and parsley). Style — from kitchen to table — is important here.

Reservations suggested
Lunch/Dinner: Mon. - Sat., 11 A.M. - 11 P.M.
              Sun., Noon - 10 P.M.

GAIDO'S ㉓   *Seafood*

9200 S. Main
Houston
(713) 668-4444
Maître d': F. J. "Rick" Gaido (owner)
Full Bar/Valet and Lot Parking
AE, D, MC, V
No dress restrictions

Family owned and family operated (it's now the third generation's turn) since 1911, Gaido's features fresh local seafood in season. You can call ahead to find out the fresh selections of the day. Steaks and chicken are also available. Your meal begins with Gaido's Italian Salad or spicy Louisiana-style seafood gumbo.

No reservations required
Dinner: Tues. - Sat., 5 P.M. - 10:30 P.M.
       Sun., 11:30 A.M. - 9 P.M.
       Closed Monday

HOBBIT HOLE   ❸ ⓬   *Vegetarian*

1715 S. Shepherd   10001 Westheimer
Houston   and   Houston
(713) 528-3418   (713) 783-9170
Maître d': Forrest and Raymond Edmonds (owners)
Beer and Wine/Lot Parking
MC, V
No dress restrictions

The Hobbit Hole is a natural foods restaurant specializing in vegetarian quiches, sandwiches, salads and fruit drinks.

No reservations required
Lunch/Dinner: Tues.-Thurs., 11:30 A.M.-10:30 P.M.
Fri.-Sat., 11:30 A.M.-11 P.M.
Sun., 3 P.M.-8:30 P.M.
Closed Monday

HUGO'S WINDOW BOX   ⓯   *Continental*

Hyatt Regency Houston
1200 Louisiana
Houston
(713) 654-1234
Maître d': Henry Newman
Full Bar/Lot Parking
AE, D, MC, V, CB
Jacket for men

You get the feeling they might have had heaven in mind when they designed this restaurant. Dim twinkling lights and ethereal harp music are background for soufflés described as "airy." The more down-to-earth main courses include Lobster Thermidor, Steak Diane and Veal Marsala.

Reservations required
Lunch: Mon.-Fri., 11:30 A.M.-2 P.M.
Dinner: Daily, 6:30 P.M.-11:30 P.M.

KAPHAN'S   ㉒   *American*

7900 S. Main
Houston
(713) 668-0491
Maître d': Mike Contreras
Full Bar/Valet Parking
AE, D, MC, V, CB
No dress restrictions

You might think Houston is even closer to the Gulf after visiting Kaphan's. The A to Z seafood selection includes myriad crab and oyster dishes (Crab Imperial, Dichotomy of Oysters appetizer), plus Trout Amandine and lots of entrées starring prime quality northern beef.

No reservations required
Lunch/Dinner: Daily (except Wednesday), 11:30 A.M.-11 P.M.

LA HACIENDA DE LOS MORALES ❷   *Continental*

10440 Deerwood
Houston
(713) 780-0933
Full Bar/Valet and Lot Parking
AE, D, MC, V, CB
Jacket, tie for men

"The lush grounds surrounding the Spanish-style mansion and the lavishly furnished interior announce that lunch and dinner here are special events," says Luis DeCastilla of La Hacienda. The mansion is a detailed replica of Mexico City's 16th-century Plantation of the White Mulberry. The cuisine is European with certain Mexican influences.

Reservations required
Lunch: Tues. – Fri., 11:30 A.M. – 2 P.M.
Dinner: Tues. – Fri., 7 P.M. – 10:30 P.M.
        Sat., 6 P.M. – 10:30 P.M.
        Sun., 6 P.M. – 9:30 P.M.
Brunch: Sun., 11:30 A.M. – 2:30 P.M.

MAXIM'S ⓳   *French*

3755 Richmond Ave.
Houston
(713) 877-8899
Full Bar/Valet and Street Parking
AE, D, MC, V, CB
Jacket, tie for men

Ah, remember the Paris of Toulouse-Lautrec? Well, if you don't, Maxim's, with its plush red interior, may remind you. The menu offers choices of capon with wild rice and black cherries, Trout Mousseline, Red Snapper Meunière and Gulf crab meat with either remoulade, spicy red sauce or lemon juice accompaniment.

Reservations advised
Lunch: Mon. – Sat., 11 A.M. – 2 P.M.
Dinner: Mon. – Fri., 5 P.M. – 10:30 P.M.
        Sat., 5 P.M. – 11 P.M.
        Closed Sunday

THE RED LION ㉑   *British*

7315 S. Main
Houston
(713) 795-5000
Maître d': Rusty Andrews (manager)
Full Bar/Valet Parking
AE, D, MC, V, CB
Good taste in dress required

Romance is definitely alive and presumably well at The Red Lion. It is amour of the cozy convivial pub variety. If you're hungry as well as in love, you can try the prime rib, the steak and kidney pie, the Welsh Rarebit, London Grill, deviled grilled beef bones or the sherry trifle. "Our staff strives to make each customer's evening a special occasion," says banquet manager Teresa Andrews.

No reservations required
Dinner: Daily, 5 P.M. – 11:30 P.M.

THE RIVOLI ⓭ *Continental*

5636 Richmond Ave.
Houston
(713) 789-1900
Maître d': Jeff McNeil
Full Bar/Valet Parking
AE, D, MC, V
Jacket for men, no jeans

"Sophisticated" is how most people begin to describe this "New York-style" restaurant. That description extends to the kitchen, which presents selections such as Dover Sole stuffed with shrimp and crab meat, rack of lamb and Red Snapper Zielinsky, sautéed with cucumber sauce.

Reservations required
Lunch: Mon.-Fri., 11:30 A.M.-2 P.M.
Dinner: Mon.-Sat., 6:15 P.M.-11 P.M.
   Closed Sunday

RUDI'S ⓾ *Continental*

1728 S. Post Oak Rd.
Houston
(713) 622-4100
Full Bar/Valet Parking
AE, MC, V
Jacket for men

Owner Joe Lucia calls Rudi's atmosphere "majestic, but comfortable." The house specialties include Snapper à la Pontchartrain and a lemon veal.

Reservations required
Lunch/Dinner: Mon.-Thurs., 11:30 A.M.-1 A.M.
              Fri.-Sat., 11:30 A.M.-2 A.M.
              Closed Sunday

RUGGLES ❺ ⓮ *Continental*

903 Westheimer   6540 San Felipe
Houston   and   Houston
(713) 524-3839   (713) 977-4949
Maître d': Joel Oppenheim, Dieter Lehman
Full Bar/Valet Parking
AE, D, MC, V
No dress restrictions

Ruggles' reputation rests with its food, says owner Manfred Jachmich, and that seems like a supremely logical decision. There are fresh fish entrées, veal, fowl and steak. The setting of stained glass windows, antiques and hanging plants creates a relaxed and casual atmosphere.

Reservations recommended
Lunch: Mon.-Fri., 11:30 A.M.-2:30 P.M.
Dinner: Mon.-Thurs., 6 P.M.-1 A.M.
        Fri.-Sat., 6 P.M.-3 A.M.
        Sun., 6 P.M.-10:30 P.M.
Brunch: Sun., 11 A.M.-2 P.M.

SAN JACINTO INN ㉔   *Seafood*

Route 1 (Battleground Road)
La Porte, Texas
(713) 479-2828
No Wine or Spirits/Lot Parking
AE, D, MC, V, CB
No dress restrictions

Located in the historic San Jacinto Battleground, overlooking the battleship *Texas* and the Ship Channel, this family-style, all-you-can-eat inn has been serving lots of fresh Gulf seafood for more than 60 years. Look for fried catfish, oysters on the half shell, broiled shrimp and crab, plus plenty of biscuits with strawberry jam.

Reservations suggested
Dinner: Tues. – Fri., 6 P.M.-10 P.M.
Sat., 5:30 P.M. – 10 P.M.
Sun., 1 P.M. – 9 P.M.
Closed Monday

SWISS CHALET ❻   *Swiss/German*

511 S. Post Oak Lane
Houston
(713) 621-3333
Full Bar/Valet Parking
AE, D, MC, V
No dress restrictions

Antiques and oil paintings surround you as you dine on Albert Martin's Swiss German specialties. He also offers lots of warmth and hospitality.

Reservations required
Lunch/Dinner: Mon. – Fri., 11 A.M. – 1 A.M.
Sat., 5 P.M. – 2 A.M.
Closed Sunday

TOKYO GARDENS ⓫   *Japanese*

4701 Westheimer
Houston
(713) 622-7886
Full Bar/Valet Parking
AE, D, MC, V, CB
Good taste in dress required

The quiet elegance of a Japanese teahouse comes to Houston. Tokyo Gardens' kimono-clad waitresses serve authentic sukiyaki, teriyaki and tempura. There is also a sushi bar, performances of classical Japanese dances and a choice of either Oriental or Western seating.

No reservations required
Lunch: Mon. – Fri., 11:30 A.M. – 2 A.M.
Dinner: Mon. – Fri., 6 P.M. – 11 P.M.
Sat., 5:30 P.M. – Midnight
Sun., 5:30 P.M. – 10:30 P.M.

TONY'S ❾   *Continental*

1801 S. Post Oak Rd.
Houston
(713) 622-6778
Maître d': Tino or Aldo
Full Bar/Valet Parking
AE, MC, V
Jacket, tie for men

"To step into Tony Vallone's Houston restaurant is instant transport to the atmosphere of uptown Manhattan." That's none other than Tony Vallone talking. His restaurant is one of wine-colored walls, antique Chinese screens, crystal, starched linen, tuxedoed waiters and fresh flowers everywhere. Specialties include Veal Oskar, capon with black cherries and Grand Marnier Soufflé.

No reservations required
Lunch: Mon.-Fri., 11:30 A.M.-2:30 P.M.
Dinner: Mon.-Fri., 5:30 P.M.-11:30 P.M.
         Sat., 5:30 P.M.-12:30 A.M.
         Closed Sunday

UNCLE TAI'S HUNAN YUAN ❽   *Chinese*

1980 S. Post Oak Rd.
Houston
(713) 960-8000
Maître d': Horace Ng, Howard Tai
Full Bar/Lot Parking
AE, D
Jacket for men

This traditional-style Chinese restaurant spotlights the Hunan school of cooking. There are many spicy specialties, including Uncle Tai's Beef sautéed with black peppers and orange peel. It is crisp on the outside and tender and juicy on the inside!

Reservations recommended
Lunch/Dinner: Mon.-Thurs., 11:30 A.M.-10 P.M.
               Fri., 11:30 A.M.-10:30 P.M.
               Sat.-Sun., Noon-10:30 P.M.

KANSAS CITY

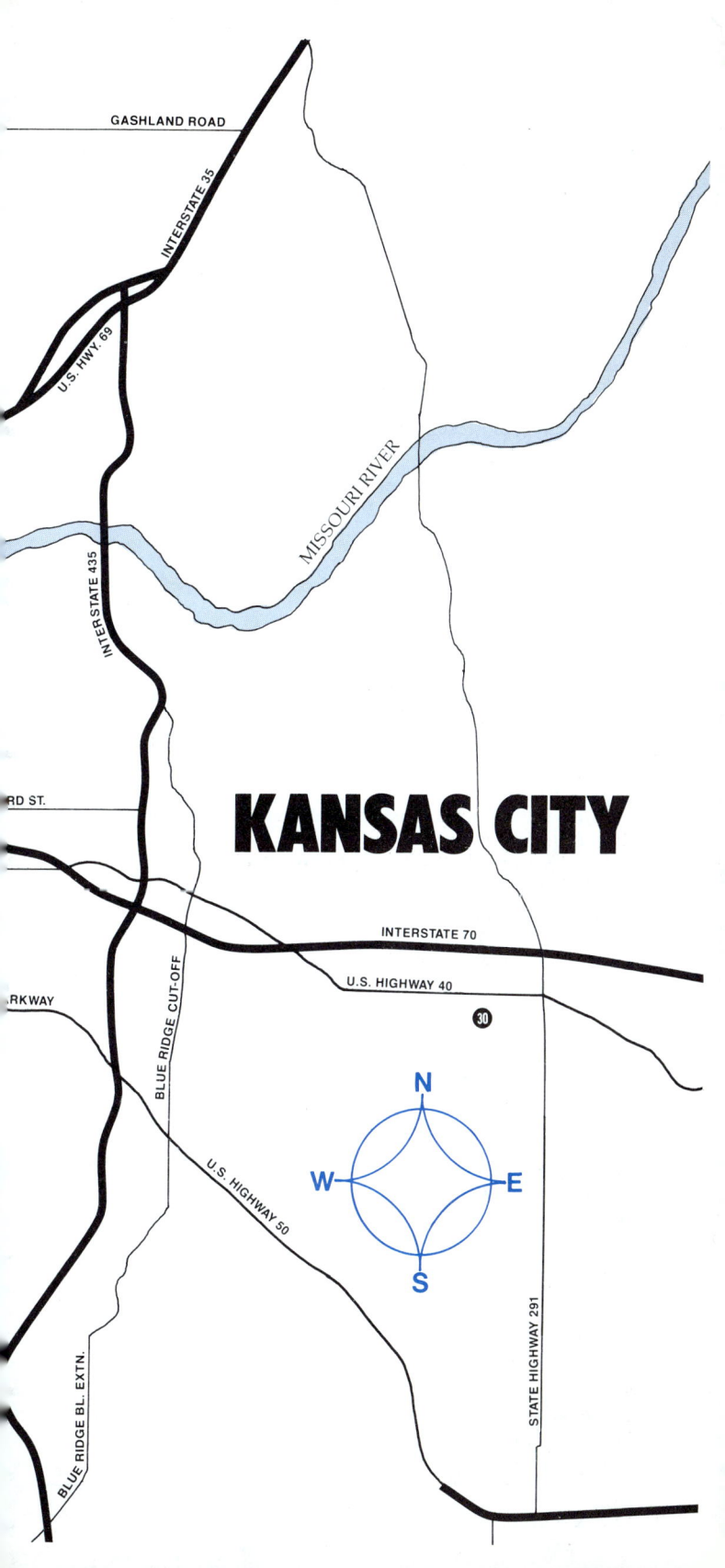

ALAMEDA PLAZA ROOF ⑯   *Continental*

Alameda Plaza Hotel
Wornall Rd. at Ward Parkway
Kansas City
(816) 756-1500
Maître d': Robert Mendoza (manager)
Full Bar/Lot Parking
AE, D, MC, V
Jacket for men (dining room)

The Alameda offers intriguing contrasts: a Moorish interior accented by autumn hues *and* an impressive view of Kansas City's Country Club Plaza, a pioneer among suburban shopping centers. House specialties are rack of lamb, Veal Française and fresh seafood. Strolling musicians are on hand as "mood-enhancers."

Reservations suggested
Lunch: Mon.–Sat., 11:30 A.M.–2 P.M.
Dinner: Mon.–Sat., 5:30 P.M.–11 P.M.
        Sun., 5:30 P.M.–10 P.M.

THE AMERICAN ⑧   *American*

2450 Grand
Kansas City
(816) 471-8050
Full Bar/Valet and Lot Parking
AE, D, MC, V
Jacket for men preferred

The American is just that — a restaurant featuring the best this country has to offer in the way of regional specialties. Some examples: Florida pompano baked in parchment, Montana elk with lingonberries, K.C. strip steaks, Arkansas roast chicken and New Orleans Carpetbagger steak. The interior has recently been refurbished.

Reservations required
Lunch: Mon.–Fri., 11:30 A.M.–2:30 P.M.
Dinner: Mon.–Fri., 6 P.M.–9:30 P.M.
        Sat., 6 P.M.–11 P.M.
        Closed Sunday

ANDRE'S SWISS CANDIES, ㉒   *Swiss*
PASTRIES & TEA ROOM

5018 Main St.
Kansas City
(816) 561-3440
No Wine or Spirits/Lot and Street Parking
No credit cards
Good taste in dress required

André's is operated in the typical Swiss tradition of Confiserie-Tea Rooms, according to co-owner Marcel Bollier. The two-item luncheon menu changes daily and Quiche Lorraine and cheese pie are available at all times. There is also a multitude of chocolate candies, tortes and pastries.

No reservations required
Breakfast: Mon.–Sat., 8:30 A.M.–11 A.M.
Lunch: Mon.–Sat., 11 A.M.–2:30 P.M.
Tea: Mon.–Sat., 2:30 P.M.–5:30 P.M.
            Closed Sunday

ANNIE'S SANTA FE ㉑   *Mexican*

Country Club Plaza
100 W. Ward Parkway
Kansas City
(816) 753-1621
Maître d': Bill Taylor (manager)
Full Bar/Lot and Street Parking
AE, D, MC, V
No dress restrictions

Annie's eight-page menu offers a wide variety of Mexican dishes, from tacos, enchiladas and burritos to such house specialties as chimichangas, tortilla pizza and The Conquistador. The "Magnificent Margaritas" are by the glass or pitcher. The setting is one of handcrafted artifacts and lush greenery.

No reservations required
Lunch: Mon.–Sat., 11 A.M.–4:30 P.M.
Dinner: Mon.–Thurs., 4:30 P.M.–11 P.M.
      Fri.–Sat., 4:30 P.M.–1 A.M.
      Sun., 1 P.M.–10 P.M.

BRISTOL BAR & GRILL ㉓   *Seafood*

Country Club Plaza
4740 Jefferson
Kansas City
(816) 756-0606
Maître d': Tom Hart (manager)
Full Bar/Lot Parking
AE, D, MC, V, CB
No dress restrictions

A "club-style" atmosphere and menu selection prevails at the Bristol Bar & Grill. The fresh grilled seafood is specially prepared on mesquite broilers. Daily dessert specials are all made in house.

No reservations required
Lunch: Mon.–Sat., 11 A.M.–2:30 P.M.
Dinner: Mon.–Thurs., 5:30 P.M.–11 P.M.
      Fri., 5:30 P.M.–Midnight
      Sat., 5 P.M.–Midnight
      Sun., 5 P.M.–10 P.M.

BUTTONWOOD TREE INN & PUB ⑰   *Continental*

4800 Main St.
Kansas City
(816) 753-0500
Maître d': André N. Barrero
Full Bar/Lot and Street Parking
AE, D, MC, V, CB
No dress restrictions

Expect to find prime rib, steaks, seafood and duckling all served in the Buttonwood's authentic Old World atmosphere. Fresh-cut flowers grace the tables and table settings are all old pewter.

Reservations suggested
Lunch: Mon.–Fri., 11 A.M.–2:30 P.M.
Dinner: Mon.–Sat., 5 P.M.–10 P.M.
Brunch: Sun., 10 A.M.–2 P.M.

COLONY STEAK HOUSE ⑫   American

3560 Broadway
Kansas City
(816) 842-5007
Full Bar/Street Parking
AE, D, MC, V
No dress restrictions

Here they bring top aged beef to your table on charcoal brazier carts so they can be sure to broil the steaks to your order. The Colony also offers a "bottomless" salad bar and an atmosphere that is "pure Kansas City." Steaks are revered in this town, and justly so.

No reservations required
Lunch: Mon.–Sat., 11:30 A.M.–2 P.M.
Dinner: Mon.–Sat., 5 P.M.–11 P.M.
    Closed Sunday

THE DINNER HORN COUNTRY INN ❶   American

2820 N.W. Barry Rd.
Kansas City
(816) 436-8700
Full Bar/Lot Parking
AE, D, MC, V, CB
No dress restrictions

The hale and hearty home cooking of the Pennsylvania Dutch folk is the order here. And the setting is a Dutch mansion, located atop a hill on 15 acres of woodland. The five-course meal begins with old-fashioned relishes and finishes with Dutch Chocolate Coffee. Two specialties are baked stuffed pork chops and buttermilk fried chicken.

Reservations requested
Lunch: Tues.–Fri., 11 A.M.–2 P.M.
Dinner: Tues.–Sat., 5 P.M.–10 P.M.
        Sun., 4 P.M.–8 P.M.
Brunch: Sun., 10:30 A.M.–3 P.M.
        Closed Monday

THE GOLDEN OX ❺   American

1600 Genessee
Kansas City
(816) 842-2866
Full Bar/Street Parking
AE, D, MC
No dress restrictions

A steak house in the heart of the city's old stockyards, The Golden Ox is noted for its beautiful cuts of beef rather than for its decor. A 13-ounce K.C. strip is served with potato, salad and garlic toast. There's also seafood and chicken, if you feel like cheating.

No reservations required (except for eight or more)
Lunch/Dinner: Mon.–Fri., 11:30 A.M.–10 P.M.
              Sat., 5 P.M.–10:30 P.M.
              Sun., Noon–9 P.M.

HARRY STARKER'S ⓳   *American*

4708 Wyandotte
Kansas City
(816) 753-3565
Full Bar/Street Parking
AE, D, MC, V, CB
No dress restrictions

Harry Starker's combines the styles of English pub and contemporary Californian. Stained glass, brick and plants meet warmth and intimacy. Specialties include rack of lamb, Chicken Kiev, King Crab, prime rib and Bananas Foster.

No reservations required
Lunch: Mon.-Sat., 11 A.M.-5 P.M.
Dinner: Mon.-Fri., 5 P.M.-11 P.M.
       Sat., 5 P.M.-Midnight
       Sun., 5 P.M.-10:30 P.M.

HEREFORD HOUSE ❼   *American*

Main at 20th
Kansas City
(816) 842-1080
Full Bar/Valet, Lot and Street Parking
AE, D, MC, V, CB
No dress restrictions

One of the city's several places for steaks, the Hereford House serves them charcoal-broiled and "superbly done," according to the management. The Old West decor seems appropriate for fare that includes prime rib, chicken and ribs, and steaks and more steaks.

No reservations required
Lunch/Dinner: Mon., 11 A.M.-10 P.M.
                 Tues.-Fri., 11 A.M.-11 P.M.
                 Sat., 4 P.M.-11 P.M.
                 Closed Sunday

IMPERIAL PALACE ㉗   *Chinese*

1215 W. 103rd St.
Kansas City
(816) 942-5500
Maître d': Chi Wang (owner)
Full Bar/Lot Parking
AE, MC, V
No dress restrictions

Here you'll discover the traditional Mandarin style of cooking. The house specialty is a Da Ken dinner — a seven-course banquet that includes appetizer, soup, four entrées and dessert. Background artifacts include replicas of the classic architectural ornaments which embellished the original Imperial Palace in Peking.

Reservations required
Lunch: Daily, 11:30 A.M.-2 P.M.
Dinner: Sun.-Thurs., 5 P.M.-10 P.M.
        Fri.-Sat., 5 P.M.-11 P.M.

ITALIAN GARDENS ⑥   *Italian*

1110 Baltimore
Kansas City
(816) 221-9311
Full Bar/Street Parking
AE, MC, V
No dress restrictions

A Kansas City institution, founded in 1925 and still in operation under the guidance of the Bondon, Lipari and DiCapo families, Italian Gardens is tradition all the way. Recipes are prepared by Italian women chefs who "take great pride in the wide selection of excellent food served in a warm and friendly atmosphere."

No reservations required
Lunch/Dinner: Mon.–Thurs., 10:30 A.M.–11 P.M.
               Fri.–Sat., 10:30 A.M.–Midnight
               Closed Sunday

JASPER'S ㉔   *Continental*

405 W. 75th St.
Kansas City
(816) 363-3003
Maître d': Leonard Mirabile
Full Bar/Lot Parking
D, MC, V
Jacket for men

"Bere, Mangiare, Bene" is Italian for "good eating and drinking." It's the motto of Jasper's, a restaurant of red and gold velvet plushness, brocaded walls, chandeliers and sconces everywhere. Pasta and veal dishes seem to be favorites. Dine in either of three rooms: La Scala, La Medici or La Borghese.

No reservations required
Lunch: Mon.–Fri., 11:30 A.M.–2 P.M.
Dinner: Mon.–Thurs., 6 P.M.–11 P.M.
        Fri.–Sat., 6 P.M.–Midnight
        Closed Sunday

JESS & JIM'S ㉙   *American*

135th and Locust
Martin City, Mo.
(816) 942-9909
Full Bar/Street Parking
No credit cards
No dress restrictions

Kansas City people say it's worth the 30-minute drive out to Jess & Jim's. The steaks uphold K.C.'s reputation. They serve a K.C. Playboy Strip that weighs in at 25 ounces. Accompaniments include cottage fries, pickled beets and cole slaw. Chicken and seafood are also available, if you insist.

No reservations required
Lunch/Dinner: Mon.–Sat., 11 A.M.–11 P.M.
               Closed Sunday

LA BONNE AUBERGE ❸   *French*

Ramada Inn
610 Washington (may move to 800 Main St.)
Kansas City
(816) 474-7025
Full Bar/Lot Parking
MC, V
Jackets for men, no jeans

The cuisine is *nouvelle;* the decor is *ancien.* Chef and owner Augustin Riedi features a daily variety of fresh fish, bisques, quenelles and pâtés, plus a regular menu selection of milk-fed veal, beef, lamb and duck, all complimented by subtle sauces. More than 250 different wines are available, as are a number of European brandies.

Reservations required
Dinner: Tues.–Sat., 5:30 P.M.–11 P.M.
    Closed Sunday, Monday

LA MEDITERRANEE ⓮   *French*

4742 Pennsylvania
Kansas City
(816) 561-2916
Maître d': Gilbert (owner)
Full Bar/Lot and Street Parking
AE, MC, V
Good taste in dress required

As its name suggests, La Méditerranée spotlights the classic cuisine of southern France. This translates into tournedos, Terrine de Saumon, Coquilles St. Jacques, Sole Vermouth and Veal Monsigneur. Strawberry soufflé and Crêpes Monaco are two of several desserts.

Reservations required
Lunch: Mon.–Sat., 11:30 A.M.–2 P.M.
Dinner: Mon.–Sat., 6 P.M.–10 P.M.
    Closed Sunday

LE CARROUSEL ❹   *Continental*

Radisson Muehlebach Hotel
12th and Baltimore
Kansas City
(816) 471-1400
Maître d': Bob Kearney (asst. manager)
Full Bar/Valet Parking
AE, D, MC, V, CB
Jacket for men (evenings)

Located in one of the city's grand old hotels, Le Carrousel, with its rich mahogany furnishings, etched glass and brass trimmings, blends easily into its surroundings. The dinner menu features Duckling à l'Orange, Steak Diane, boneless trout, prime rib and Veal Oskar. There is music to accompany dinner, and dancing on weekends.

Reservations required
Lunch: Tues.–Fri., 11:30 A.M.–2 P.M.
Dinner: Tues.–Sat., 6 P.M.–10 P.M.
Brunch: Sun., 10:30 A.M.–2 P.M.
    Closed Monday

LOBSTER POT   ❾   *Seafood*

30 W. Pershing Rd.
Kansas City
(816) 842-5090
Maître d': Mike Elam
Full Bar/Lot Parking
AE, D, MC, V
No dress restrictions

Located in Kansas City's historic Union Station, the Lobster Pot features an ample seafood buffet which includes salads, oysters on the half-shell, crabs' legs, clams, scallops, spicy shrimp scampi and baked fish. After all that, you still have a choice of five entrées. *Then you can make your own strawberry shortcake for dessert — if you dare!*

No reservations required
Dinner: Mon.–Thurs., 5 P.M.–10 P.M.
       Fri., 5 P.M.–11 P.M.
       Sat., 5 P.M.–Midnight
       Sun., 5 P.M.–9 P.M.

THE OLIVE TREE   ⓲   *Mediterranean*

4916 Main St.
Kansas City
(816) 753-1332
Full Bar/Street Parking
MC, V
Good taste in dress required

If any Moors should ever come to Kansas City, they would feel right at home here. The Olive Tree is a place of Moroccan design and Mediterranean plants. Look for Greek salad, couscous, rack of lamb and papillon, a pastry stuffed with red snapper, shrimp and lobster. Belly dancers perform on Wednesday through Saturday evenings.

Reservations required
Lunch: Mon.–Fri., 11 A.M.–2:30 P.M.
Dinner: Mon.–Thurs., 6 P.M.–10 P.M.
        Fri.–Sat., 6 P.M.–11 P.M.
        Closed Sunday

PATRICIO'S   ㉘   *Mexican*

9849 Holmes
Kansas City
(816) 942-4443
Full Bar/Lot Parking
MC, V
No dress restrictions

"Patricio's opens the door to the complete Mexican fiesta," states co-owner Ruth Moran. The fiesta includes whipped and creamy bean dip, bubbly, cheesey burritos and enchiladas, and the special blend of spices that go into all the house specialties.

No reservations required
Lunch/Dinner: Mon.–Thurs., 11 A.M.–10 P.M.
              Fri.–Sat., 11 A.M.–11 P.M.
              Sun., 1 P.M.–10 P.M.

PEPPERCORN DUCK CLUB ⓫   Continental

Hyatt Regency
2345 Magee St.
Kansas City
(816) 421-1234
Maître d': John Platt, Al Otten
Full Bar/Valet and Lot Parking
AE, D, MC, V, CB
Jacket for men; no jeans

Fresh lavender orchids, flown in twice weekly from Hawaii, grace the tables. A "Market Island" is the dining room's center of attention, piled high as it is with plenty of salad fixings and every chocolate dessert imaginable. Specials include duck with brandy and orange, duck with peppercorns and kumquats and duck perfectly plucked and plain.

Reservations recommended
Lunch: Mon.-Fri., 11 A.M.-2:30 P.M.
Dinner: Sun.-Thurs., 5:30 P.M.-10:30 P.M.
       Fri.-Sat., 5:30 P.M.-11 P.M.

PLAZA III   American

4749 Pennsylvania
Kansas City
(816) 753-0000
Full Bar/Valet Parking
AE, D, MC, V
Good taste in dress required

An environment of dark wood, bricks, brass and hanging plants greets you at Plaza III. It is a restaurant bent on being stylish *and* on being noted for such special items as steak soup, giant oyster crackers, fresh fish, prime rib, rack of lamb and, per usual, Kansas City steaks.

Reservations suggested
Lunch: Mon.-Fri., 11:30 A.M.-2 P.M.
Dinner: Mon.-Thurs., 5 P.M.-11 P.M.
       Fri.-Sat., 5 P.M.-Midnight
       Sun., 5 P.M.-10 P.M.

PRINCESS GARDEN ㉕   Chinese

8906 Wornall Rd.
Kansas City
(816) 444-3709
Maître d': Robert Chang
Full Bar/Valet Parking
AE, D, MC, V
No dress restrictions

Authentic Mandarin and Szechuan cooking that is "exquisite to the taste, as well as to the eye," is the order here. House specialties are spiced duck, Peking Duck, Mongolian Pork, lobster or shrimp sautéed with ginger, wine and garlic, and Moo Shi Pork.

No reservations required (except for six or more)
Lunch: Daily, 11:30 A.M.-2 P.M.
Dinner: Daily, 5 P.M.-10 P.M.

THE RAPHAEL ⑳   *American/Seafood*

Raphael Hotel
325 Ward Parkway
Kansas City
(816) 756-3800
Full Bar/Street Parking
AE, D, MC, V
Good taste in dress required

You're supposed to feel like you're dining at an English inn when you're at The Raphael. The house specialty, though, is very American — a skewer of Boston scallops and jumbo shrimp on a bed of rice. Other entrées focus on prime rib, steaks and more seafood.

Reservations required
Lunch/Dinner: Mon.–Thurs., 11 A.M.–10:30 P.M.
            Fri.–Sat., 11 A.M.–11 P.M.
            Closed Sunday

SAM WILSON'S ㉖   *American*

1029 W. 103rd St.
Kansas City
(816) 942-9119
Maître d': Jack Garlach (manager)
Full Bar/Lot Parking
AE, D, MC, V
No dress restrictions

The decor is turn-of-the-century cozy with various artifacts from that era covering the walls. Featured are Alaskan King Crab, prime rib, steaks, Southern pan-fried chicken and Chicago-style ribs.

No reservations required
Lunch: Mon.–Sat., 11:30 A.M.–2:30 P.M.
Dinner: Mon.–Thurs., 5:30 P.M.–10 P.M.
         Fri.–Sat., 5 P.M.–11 P.M.
         Sun., 11:30 A.M.–9 P.M.

SAVOY GRILL ❷   *Seafood*

9th and Central
Kansas City
(816) 842-3890
Maître d': Joe Duran, Bob Chandler
Full Bar/Lot and Street Parking
AE, D, MC, V, CB
No dress restrictions

The Savoy, with its original 1903 decor — the high ceilings, the large Victorian mirrored bar, the stained glass windows — is a throwback to simpler, perhaps happier days. Lobster is the big thing here (literally so) along with steamed clams, New England clam chowder and Kansas City steaks. They are famous for their cinnamon rolls.

No reservations required
Lunch/Dinner: Mon.–Thurs., 11 A.M.–11 P.M.
            Fri.–Sat., 11 A.M.–Midnight
            Sun., 4 P.M.–10 P.M.

STANFORD & SONS ❸ *American*

504 Westport Rd.
Kansas City
(816) 756-1450
Maître d': Craig Glazer, Ronald Madd
Full Bar/Lot Parking
AE, D, MC, V, CB
Good taste in dress required

You are meant to be reminded of turn-of-the-century San Francisco at Kansas City's Stanford & Sons. Specialties include the bread baked in clay flower pots, quiche, Cornish game hen, pan-fried catfish and omelets.

No reservations required
Lunch/Dinner: Daily, 11 A.M.–1:30 A.M.
Brunch: Sun., 10 A.M.–3 P.M.

STEPHENSON'S OLD APPLE FARM ❸⓿ *American*

Lee Summit Rd. and Highway 40
Kansas City
(816) 373-5400
Maître d': Rick Stephenson, Mike May, Jerry Vick
Full Bar/Lot Parking
AE, D, MC, V, CB
No dress restrictions

"Quiet, warm, unhurried, relaxed, casual, country." If that sounds the way you like to live your life, you should probably head on out to Stephenson's. You'll find lots of wholesome American food: wood-cooked chicken, K.C. steaks, home-baked muffins and fritters, plus apple dumplings, apple butter and apple cider. (There really is an orchard next door.)

Reservations advised
Lunch/Dinner: Mon.–Fri., 11:30 A.M.–10 P.M.
*   Sat., 11:30 A.M.–11 P.M.*
*   Sun., 11:30 A.M.–9 P.M.*

TOP OF THE CROWN ❿ *Continental*

Crown Center Hotel
1 Pershing Rd.
Kansas City
(816) 474-4400, Ext. 451
Maître d': Victor Hugo Berndt, Jr. (manager)
Full Bar/Valet and Lot Parking
AE, D, MC, V, CB
Jacket for men, no shorts

You know you're in for a view when a restaurant mentions "top" in its name. Well, the Top of the Crown, as they say, won't let you down. They serve rack of lamb, Scampi du Provence, chateaubriand, Veal Oskar, Steak Diane and a variety of salads and appetizers.

Reservations required (except for brunch)
Lunch: Mon.–Fri., 11:30 A.M.–2:30 P.M.
Dinner: Daily, 6 P.M.–11 P.M.
Brunch: Sun., 10 A.M.–2:30 P.M.

LAS VEGAS

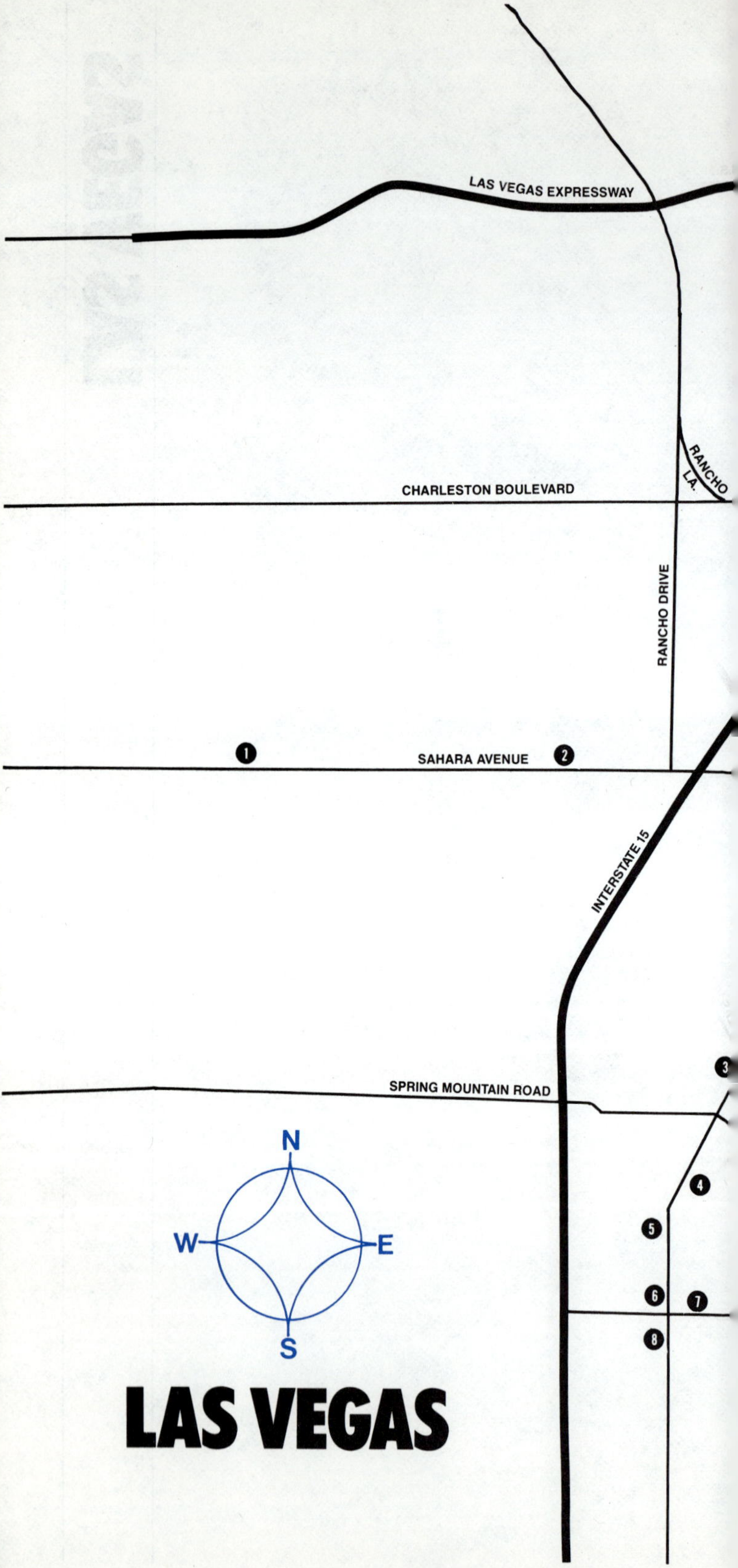

LAS VEGAS

LAS VEGAS EXPRESSWAY

RANCHO LA.

CHARLESTON BOULEVARD

RANCHO DRIVE

❶ SAHARA AVENUE ❷

INTERSTATE 15

SPRING MOUNTAIN ROAD ❸

❹
❺
❻ ❼
❽

N / W / E / S

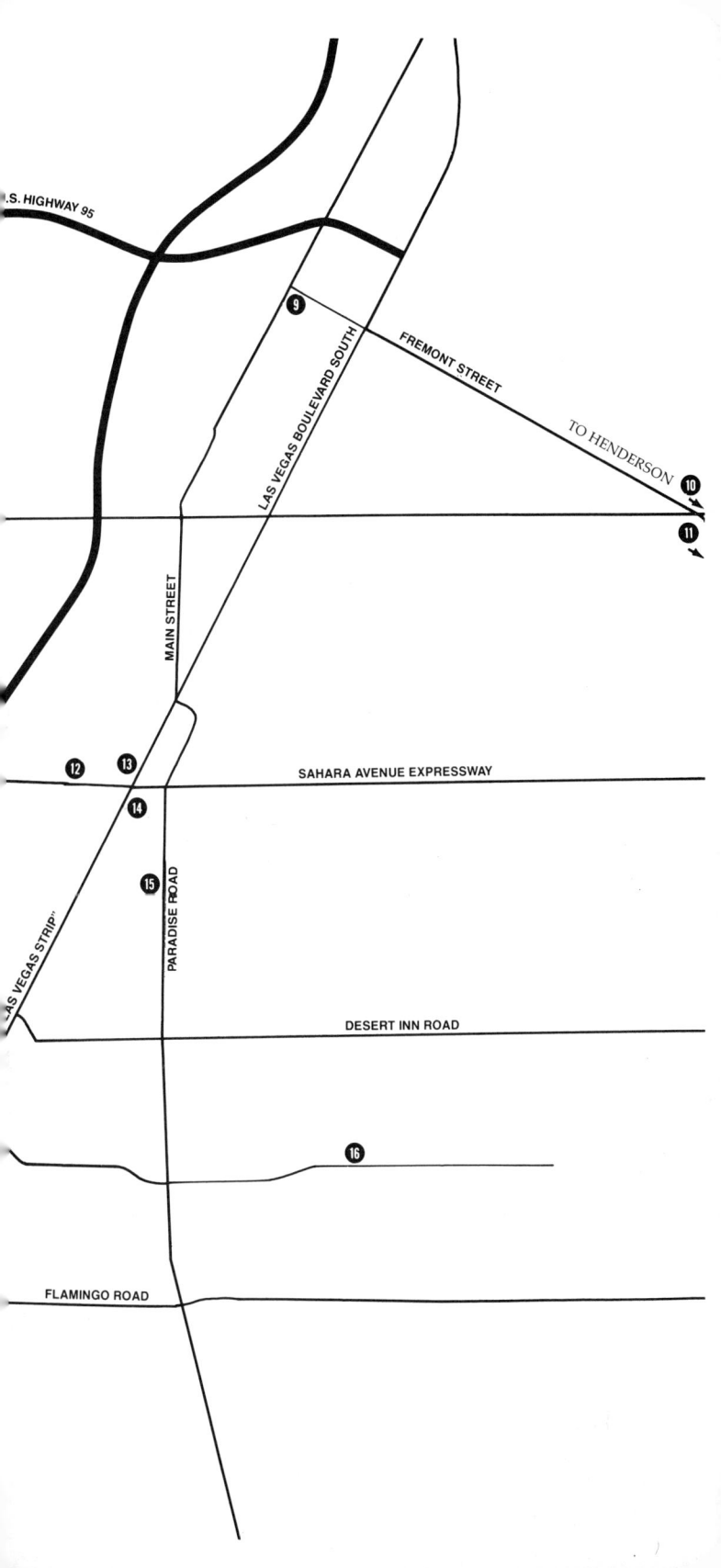

ALPINE VILLAGE INN ⓯   *Swiss/German*

3003 Paradise Rd.
Las Vegas
(702) 734-6888
Maître d': Edvard Zochert
Full Bar/Valet and Lot Parking
AE, D, MC, V, CB
Good taste in dress required

This happy Swiss chalet is a natural setting for hearty Swiss-German specialties. You'll find wiener schnitzel, sausages, smoked pork chops, sauerkraut and spiced apples on the menu. The downstairs Rathskeller is reportedly even more jovial. There is entertainment nightly.

Reservations required
Dinner: Daily, 5 P.M.–Midnight

BACCHANAL ROOM ❻   *Continental*

Caesar's Palace Hotel
3570 Las Vegas Blvd. South
Las Vegas
(702) 731-7525
Maître d': Salvadore Domenech
Full Bar/Valet Parking
AE, D, MC, V, CB
Good taste in dress required

The Bacchanal is named for Bacchus, the mythological god of wine and revel. That should tell you something about this restaurant patterned after the private garden of an ancient Roman villa. For one thing, "vestal virgins" stand behind your chair and gently massage you in preparation for the feast to come. That could include pheasant, seafood, soufflés, etc., etc.

Reservations required
Dinner: Daily, 6 P.M.–11:30 P.M.

BATTISTA'S HOLE IN THE WALL ❼   *Italian*

4041 Audrie
Las Vegas
(702) 732-1424
Maître d': Battista Locatelli (owner)
Full Bar/Street Parking
AE, D, MC, V
Good taste in dress required

"The finest Italian cuisine in the West," says the less than impartial Battista Locatelli of Battista's. But, with dinners that include salad, soup, garlic bread, cappuccino *and* all the house wine you can drink, who's to argue? The pasta is homemade. Other entrées include veal, scampi and eggplant specialties. A place for people-watching and celebrity-spotting.

Reservations recommended
Dinner: Daily, 5 P.M.–10:30 P.M.

DIAMOND LIL'S ⓫   American

5111 Boulder Highway
Las Vegas
(702) 456-7777, Ext. 1138
Maître d': Pat Macias, Millie Arangio
Full Bar/Valet and Lot Parking
AE, D, MC, V
No dress restrictions

The ambience is early Victorian, with a western flair. You ease into comfortable red and pink booths and dine on a variety of broiled steaks, scampi, trout, salmon, crab and a daily chef's special.

Reservations suggested
Lunch: Sat.–Sun., 11 A.M.–3 P.M.
Dinner: Sun.–Thurs., 5:30 P.M.–11 P.M.
      Fri.–Sat., 5:30 P.M.–Midnight

DOME OF THE SEA ❺   Seafood

Dunes Hotel
3650 Las Vegas Blvd. South
Las Vegas
(702) 737-4255
Maître d': Fred J. Schilling
Full Bar/Valet and Lot Parking
AE, D, MC, V, CB
Jacket for men

The setting is one of fantasy — an imaginary underwater seascape. The seafare is very real — Maine lobster, bouillabaisse, and Dover Sole.

Reservations required
Dinner: Daily, 6 P.M.–Midnight

GOLDEN STEER STEAKHOUSE ⓬   American

308 W. Sahara
Las Vegas
(702) 384-4470
Maître d': Frank Musso
Full Bar/Valet Parking
AE, D, MC, V, CB
No dress restrictions

Italian specialties and prime steaks are served in a setting reminiscent of the early West. Look for such entrées as Chicken of the Angels, Veal Française, prime rib, quail and fresh seafood. The accompanying baked potatoes are reportedly huge. The atmosphere is casual.

Reservations required
Dinner: Daily, 5 P.M.–Midnight

HOUSE OF LORDS   ⓮   *Continental*

Sahara Hotel
2535 Las Vegas Blvd. South
Las Vegas
(702) 737-2111
Maître d': Johnny Larson
Full Bar/Valet and Lot Parking
AE, D, MC, V, CB
No dress restrictions

The House of Lords is all Old English decor, booth seating and "proper" service. Opened in 1962, it is considered one of Las Vegas's oldest formal dining rooms. The principal focus is on steak and lobster, but there's also a variety of fish and chicken entrées. Hot apple fritters and petits fours are dessert specialties.

Reservations required
Dinner: Daily, 6 P.M. – 10:30 P.M.

LIBRARY, BUTTERY & PUB   ⓭   *Continental*

200 W. Sahara
Las Vegas
(702) 384-5200
Maître d': David A. Facciani, Ronald Fortner (owners)
Full Bar/Valet Parking
AE, D, MC, V, CB
No dress restrictions

"At the Library, the excellence of the dining is surpassed only by the warmth and friendliness of the service." That is manager Virginia Fortner's description of this restaurant just off The Strip. Along with the books lining the walls, there is also a collection of special entrées such as suckling pig, rack of lamb, Dover Sole Brittany and Veal Française.

Reservations requested
Lunch: Mon. – Fri., 11:30 A.M. – 5 P.M.
Dinner: Daily, 5 P.M. – 1 A.M.

LILLIE LANGTRY   ⑨   *Chinese*

Golden Nugget Hotel
129 E. Fremont St.
Las Vegas
(702) 385-7111
Maître d': Alfred Yue
Full Bar/Valet Parking
AE, D, MC, V
No dress restrictions

"There is no restaurant in the world quite like the fabulous Lillie Langtry's," boasts the management. They call the decor of crystal and mahogany "breathtaking"; they term the service "impeccable." It may come as a small surprise that the cuisine is Cantonese, but that too they describe as "incomparably delicious."

Reservations suggested
Dinner: Daily, 5 P.M. – 11 P.M.

NICK'S SUPPER CLUB ⑩　　　　　　　*Continental*

15 E. Lake Mead Dr.
Henderson, Nev.
(702) 565-0122
Maître d': Lasca Lathuris
Full Bar/Valet and Lot Parking
MC, V
No dress restrictions

Nick's offers formal dining — by a fireplace in winter and by a waterfall in summer. The 40 entrées include King Crab, prime rib, lobster tails, rack of lamb and shrimp and chicken kabobs. The Greek salad is popular, and so is the homemade baklava.

Reservations recommended
Lunch: Mon.–Fri., 11 A.M.–2 P.M.
Dinner: Daily, 5 P.M.–Midnight

PALACE COURT ⑥　　　　　　　　*French*

Caesar's Palace Hotel
3570 Las Vegas Blvd.
Las Vegas
(702) 731-7547
Maître d': Jacques Achiardi
Full Bar/Valet, Lot and Street Parking
AE, D, MC, V, CB
Jacket for men

At the Palace Court, waiters don tuxedos and white gloves to serve such specialties as Tournedos Gastrôme, Sole Anglaise, Steak Diane, lobster flamed in cognac and a variety of dessert soufflés. The tables are set with lace tablecloths, Lennox china, gold flatware and hand-blown stemware.

Reservations required
Dinner: Daily, 6:30 P.M.–11 P.M.

PHILIPS SUPPER HOUSE ❶　　　　　*Continental*

4545 W. Sahara
Las Vegas
(702) 873-5222
Maître d': Walter J. Slaughter
Full Bar/Lot Parking
AE, D, MC, V, CB
Good taste in dress required

New England and the Edwardian era come to the desert in the form of Philips Supper House. There is alcove seating in antique-filled rooms done up in soft earth tones. Specialties include the New England Shore Dinner, lobster, steamed clams, corn-on-the-cob, plus some Italian-style entrées.

Reservations required on weekends
Dinner: Daily, 5 P.M.–Midnight

PORT TACK ❷   *Seafood*

3190 W. Sahara
Las Vegas
(702) 873-3345
Full Bar/Street Parking
Major Credit Cards
No dress restrictions

In an all-night town, there's an obvious need for comfortable all-night restaurants. Port Tack is such a place. Everything from hamburgers to sautéed prawns to prime rib to steamed lobster is offered here. The nautical atmosphere is enhanced by brick archways, intimate booth seating, two fireplaces and plush red carpeting.

No reservations required
Lunch/Dinner: Daily, 24 hours

REGENCY ROOM ❹   *French*

Sands Hotel
3355 Las Vegas Blvd. South
Las Vegas
(702) 733-5000
Full Bar/Valet Parking
AE, D, MC, V, CB
Jacket for men

Elegant, quiet and tasteful is how many people describe the Regency Room. There are both table d'hôte and à la carte menu selections. Specialties include Beef Wellington, Chateaubriand Bouquetière, Chicken Kiev, Tournedos Rossini and Steak au Poivre.

Reservations required
Dinner: Daily, 7 P.M.– Midnight

THE SPANISH STEPS ❸   *American/Spanish*

Caesar's Palace Hotel
3570 Las Vegas Blvd. South
Las Vegas
(702) 731-7560
Maître d': Giovanni Vancheri
Full Bar/Valet and Lot Parking
AE, D, MC, V, CB
No dress restrictions

Borrowing its name from the famous steps in Rome, this Caesar's Palace restaurant features a variety of steaks along with some Spanish-accented dishes. The steaks are "gaucho size." The Spanish classics include Arroz con Pollo, Paella Valenciana and Gambas al Ajillo.

Reservations required
Dinner: Daily, 6 P.M.–11:30 P.M.

THE SULTAN'S TABLE ❽ *Continental*

Dunes Hotel
3650 Las Vegas Blvd. South
Las Vegas
(702) 737-4681/82
Maître d': Pietro Musetto
Full Bar/Valet Parking
AE, D, MC, V, CB
Jacket for men

As the name suggests, The Sultan's Table is formal dining fit for a potentate. You'll dine on such specialties as rack of lamb, Chicken Grand Mere and Pietro Fettuccine. The "Magic Violins" play accompaniment to the cuisine.

Reservations required
Dinner: Daily, 6 P.M.–11 P.M.

VINEYARD ⓰ *Italian*

3630 S. Maryland Parkway
Las Vegas
(702) 731-1606
Maître d': John Sheridan (manager)
Full Bar/Lot Parking
MC, V
No dress restrictions

The Vineyard promises you all your favorites — from lasagne, cannelloni and manicotti to scampi, Veal Parmigiana and Italian meatballs. An antipasto buffet features more than 30 items including marinated mushrooms, Fontana cheese, artichoke hearts and pepperoni.

No reservations required
Lunch/Dinner: Sun.–Thurs., 11:30 A.M.–11 P.M.
Fri.–Sat., 11:30 A.M.–Midnight

LOS ANGELES

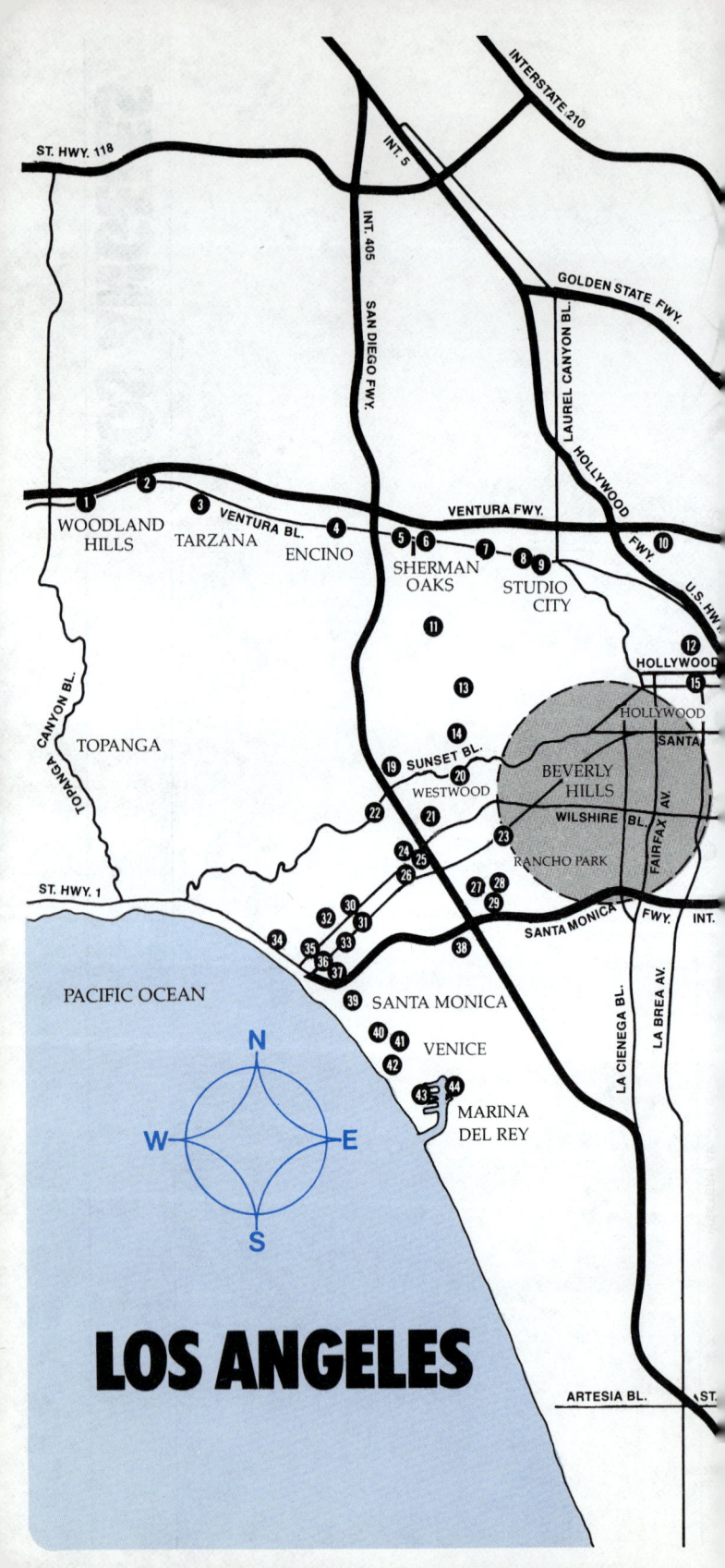

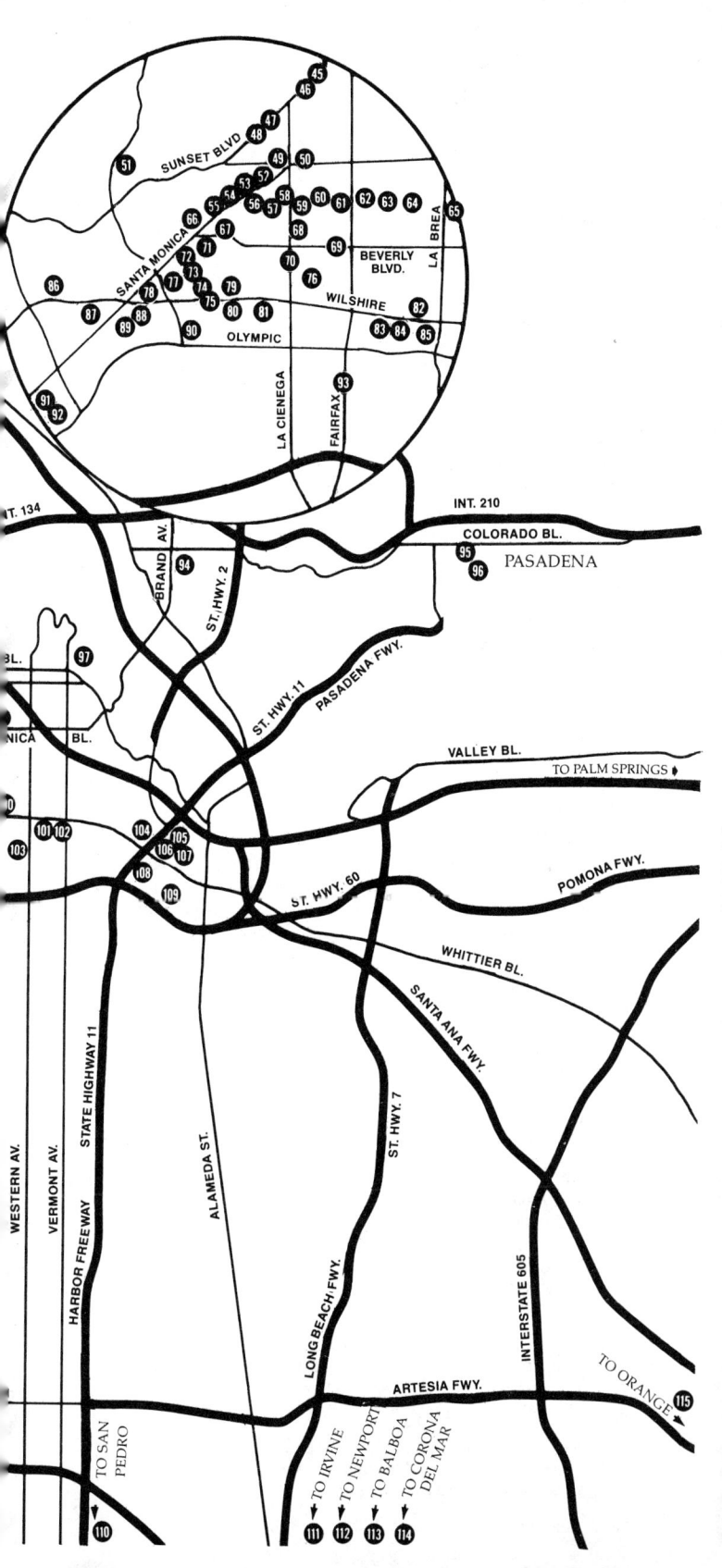

ADRIANO'S ⑪   *Northern Italian*

2930 Beverly Glen Circle
Los Angeles
(213) 457-9807
Maître d': Adriano Reborn (owner)
Full Bar/Lot Parking
AE, MC, V
Jacket for men

At Adriano's, the focal point of the dining room is the brass-trimmed center pavilion where foods and wines are displayed. Walls are washed in pastel peach and surrounding banquettes are sand colored. The menu features such items as Quaglie con Uva, Risotto con Funghi and Gran Grigliata Mista di Mare.

Reservations required
Lunch: Tues.–Sat., 11:30 A.M.–2:30 P.M.
Dinner: Tues.–Thurs., 6 P.M.–10:30 P.M.
        Fri.–Sat., 6 P.M.–11 P.M.
        Sun., 5:30 P.M.–10:30 P.M.
Brunch: Sun., 11 A.M.–3 P.M.
        Closed Monday

ALBION'S ⑦   *French*

13422 Ventura Blvd.
Sherman Oaks, Calif.
(213) 981-6650
Maître d': Claude and Gloria
Full Bar/Valet Parking
AE, D, MC, V, CB
No dress restrictions

Edwardian decor, an authentic 60-year-old San Francisco bar, a French bronze statue dated 1874, crystal chandeliers and polished wood are all things you'll find in this San Fernando Valley restaurant. You'll also find salmon pâté, roasted duck in green peppercorn sauce, Filet Mignon Maturini and scallop mousse with chives.

Reservations suggested
Lunch: Mon.–Sat., 11:30 A.M.–2:30 P.M.
Dinner: Mon.–Sat., 6 P.M.–10:30 P.M.
        Closed Sunday

AMBROSIA ⑫   *Continental*

501 30th St.
Newport Beach, Calif.
(714) 673-0200
Maître d': James Conway
Full Bar/Valet Parking
AE, D, MC, V, CB
Jacket, tie for men

"Uncompromising" is how Ambrosia owner Geril Muller describes his Orange County restaurant. One of the few grandly formal places in the area, Ambrosia offers prime beef, snow white veal, fresh fish and a wine list of 700 labels.

Reservations required
Dinner: Mon.–Fri., 6 P.M.–Midnight
        Sat.–Sun., 5:30 P.M.–Midnight

AMELIA'S ⓫   *Italian*

311 Marine Ave.
Balboa Island
Newport Beach, Calif.
(714) 673-6580
Maître d': John Robinson (owner)
Beer and Wine/Street Parking
MC, V
No dress restrictions

Although it is only 20 years old, Amelia's is one of Newport's original restaurants. A small place that stresses warmth and intimacy, Amelia's provides diners with such cooked-to-order specialties as bouillabaisse, abalone stuffed with Alaskan king crab, milk-fed veal, tortellini and, for dessert, amaretto mousse pie.

Reservations required
Dinner: Tues.–Sun., 6 P.M.–10 P.M.
  Closed Monday

ANTONIO'S ⓫   *Mexican*

7472 Melrose Ave.
Los Angeles
(213) 655-0480
Full Bar/Valet Parking
AE, MC, V
No dress restrictions

Host Antonio Gutierrez uses a wide assortment of seasonings to create imaginative Mexican food. Some of his specialties include peppers stuffed with beef, apples, bananas and coriander, Beef en Mole Oaxaca style, stuffed zucchini and jicama salad.

Reservations advised
Lunch: Tues.–Fri., Noon–2:30 P.M.
Dinner: Tues.–Fri., 5 P.M.–11 P.M.
  Sat.–Sun., 3 P.M.–11 P.M.

AU PETIT CAFE ⓫   *French*

1230 N. Vine St.
Los Angeles
(213) 469-7176
Full Bar/Lot Parking
AE, MC, V
No dress restrictions

Called "the granddaddy of French restaurants in L.A.," Au Petit Cafe has been in business for a good number of years. You can choose to dine provincial style on the first and second floor or cafe style in a downstairs cellar lined with antique mirrors. Specialties include rack of lamb, Abalone Meunière, Veal Forestière and pepper steak.

Reservations required
Lunch: Mon.–Fri., 11:30 A.M.–2:30 P.M.
Dinner: Mon.–Sat., 6 P.M.–10:30 P.M.
  Closed Sunday

AUX DELICES ❺ — French

15466 Ventura Blvd.
Sherman Oaks, Calif.
(213) 783-3007
Maître d': Roger E. Martini (co-owner)
Beer and Wine/Street Parking
AE, D, MC, V
Good taste in dress required

Bouquets of fresh flowers on each table and lights dimmed to a romantic glow signify a restaurant of considerable intimacy and warmth. This is what Aux Délices is all about. Special dishes include French-cut lamb chops Arlésienne and the best veal, tenderloin, fresh fish and fresh vegetables on the market. The French food has a Parisian bent.

Reservations required
Dinner: Tues.–Sun., 5:30 P.M.–10 P.M.
    Closed Monday

BAGATELLE ⑳ — French

8690 Wilshire Blvd.
Beverly Hills, Calif.
(213) 659-0782
Maître d': Lucia Pister (co-owner)
Beer and Wine/Lot Parking
MC, V, CB
No dress restrictions

A small French restaurant that began life as a small French delicatessen. The uptown take-out section is still there as well as a dining atmosphere that co-owner (with husband and chef André) Lucia Pister labels "peaceful and unhurried." You'll find charcuterie, cold poached salmon, ham and cheese soufflé, and napoleon for dessert.

Reservations required
Lunch: Mon.–Fri., 11:30 A.M.–2:30 P.M.
Dinner: Mon.–Sat., 6 P.M.–10 P.M.
    Closed Sunday

BEAUDRY'S ⑯ — Continental

Los Angeles Bonaventure Hotel
Fifth and Figueroa Sts.
Los Angeles
(213) 624-1000
Maître d': Joseph Nagy
Full Bar/Valet Parking
AE, D, MC, V, CB
Jacket for men

Located in the new Los Angeles Bonaventure Hotel, not far from the city's Convention Center and Music Center, Beaudry's features Sea Bass Nantua and Escalope of Veal Parisienne for lunch and Chateaubriand, Petrale Sole Chez Marie and roast duckling for dinner. There is nightly entertainment in the lounge.

Reservations requested
Lunch: Mon.–Fri., 11:30 A.M.–2 P.M.
Dinner: Daily, 6 P.M.–Midnight

BEL-AIR HOTEL ⓮   *Continental*

701 Stone Canyon Rd.
Los Angeles
(213) 472-1211
Full Bar/Valet Parking
AE, D, CB
Jacket, tie for men preferred

The hotel dining room is small and intimate, with an open fireplace at one end and large picture windows overlooking the bougainvillea on the terrace at the other. Carefully prepared European and American specialties are featured.

Reservations required
Breakfast/Lunch/Dinner: Daily, 7:30 A.M.–11 P.M.
Brunch: *Sun, 11 A.M.–2:30 P.M.*

BELMONT PIER ㉔   *Seafood/Mediterranean*

11954 Wilshire Blvd.
Los Angeles
(213) 477-1281
Beer and Wine/Street Parking
AE, MC, V
No dress restrictions

Your entrées will be shown to you and thoroughly explained before you order. The seafood preparations are given a Mediterranean twist. Several different cooking methods are available for each dish.

Reservations required
Dinner: Mon.–Sat., 5:30 P.M.–11 P.M.
      Closed Sunday

BERNARD'S ⑩⑤   *French*

Biltmore Hotel
515 S. Olive St.
Los Angeles
(213) 624-1011
Full Bar/Valet Parking
AE, D, MC, V, CB
Jacket for men

Bernard's, in the refurbished Biltmore Hotel, specializes in French *haute cuisine* with a New World accent, such as filet of red snapper braised with rhubarb and kiwi. Offerings from the extensive menu and wine list are enhanced by Mies van der Rohe furniture, hand-decorated beamed ceilings, lush plants and even a few trees.

Reservations required
Lunch: Mon.–Fri., 11:30 A.M.–2 P.M.
Dinner: Mon.–Thurs., 6 P.M.–10 P.M.
      Fri.–Sat., 6 P.M.–10:45 P.M.
      Closed Sunday

THE BISTRO　㊼　　　　　　　　　　　　*Continental*

246 N. Canon Dr.
Beverly Hills, Calif.
(213) 273-5633
Maître d': Casper Morselli
Full Bar/Valet Parking
AE, D, MC, V, CB
Jacket, tie for men

Located in the heart of Beverly Hills, The Bistro serves all the "right people" all the right things, including fresh fish, oysters, Beef Flamande, osso buco, bouillabaisse and chocolate soufflé. There are party facilities for groups of 10 to 200. Decor is Old World elaborate.

Reservations required
Lunch: Mon.-Fri., 11:30 A.M.-3 P.M.
Dinner: Mon.-Fri., 6 P.M.-11 P.M.
　　　　Sat., 6:30 P.M.-11 P.M.
　　　　Closed Sunday

BISTRO GARDEN　㊕　　　　　　　　*Continental*

176 N. Canon Dr.
Beverly Hills, Calif.
(213) 550-3900
Maître d': Horst
Full Bar/Lot Parking
AE, D, MC, V, CB
No dress restrictions

Just as the name suggests, this is The Bistro's "garden" restaurant — more sunshine, more casual, more emphasis on lighter fare. Featured are such international items as Mexican quesadilla, bratwurst with hot potato salad, and German apple pancakes.

Reservations required
Lunch/Dinner: Mon.-Sat., 11:30 A.M.-Midnight
　　　　　　　Closed Sunday

CAFE FOUR OAKS　⑬　　　　　　　　*American*

2181 N. Beverly Glen
Los Angeles
(213) 474-9317
Beer and Wine/Lot Parking
No credit cards
No dress restrictions

Located in a breathtakingly beautiful part of the Santa Monica Mountains, Cafe Four Oaks serves California-influenced American cuisine. Sunday brunch is a specialty.

Reservations required
Dinner: Tues.-Sat., 6 P.M.-9:30 P.M.
Brunch: Sun., 11 A.M.-3 P.M.
　　　　Closed Monday

CHAMBORD ⑲   *French*

8689 Wilshire Blvd.
Beverly Hills, Calif.
(213) 652-6590
Full Bar/Valet Parking
AE, MC, V
Jacket for men

A quiet, rather serene place on a busy thoroughfare, Chambord seems to make an effort to do everything right. Featured are such specialties as Alaskan King Crab aux Petits Legumes, New York steak with gooseberry vinegar, cassoulet of fresh fish and filet mignon with Roquefort sauce. Co-owner Raoul Jouglet has tried to evoke the style of the Château Chambord in France.

Reservations required
Lunch: Mon.–Fri., 11:30 A.M.–2:30 P.M.
Dinner: Mon.–Sat., 6 P.M.–10:30 P.M.
      Closed Sunday

CHANTECLAIR ⑪⑪   *Continental*

18912 MacArthur Blvd.
Irvine, Calif.
(714) 752-8001
Maître d': Cornelius Van De Grahff
Full Bar/Lot Parking
AE, D, MC, V, CB
Jacket, tie for men optional

A French country inn in inland Orange County, you say? Well, yes, if you're referring to Chanteclair, with its stuffed boneless chicken Alsace, its numerous imported wines and its profusion of country flowers and shrubbery. You may soon forget you're not breaking bread somewhere in the Loire Valley.

Reservations required
Lunch: Daily, 11 A.M.–2:30 P.M.
Dinner: Daily, 6 P.M.–10 P.M.

CHARLEY BROWN'S ㊹   *American*

4445 Admiralty Way (various locations)
Marina del Rey, Calif.
(213) 823-4534
Full Bar/Lot Parking
AE, MC, V
No dress restrictions

Featuring a view of the Marina channel, Charley Brown's has a large dining room and equally large bar area. There is a heavy emphasis on prime steaks and fresh seafood. A special dessert is the Fantasy Strawberry Fondant — vanilla ice cream, a secret sauce, strawberries and whipped cream.

Reservations suggested
Lunch: Mon.–Fri., 11 A.M.–3 P.M.
Dinner: Mon.–Fri., 5 P.M.–10 P.M.
      Sat., 5 P.M.–11 P.M.
      Sun., 4:30 P.M.–9:30 P.M.
Brunch: Sun., 9 A.M.–3 P.M.

CHASEN'S ⓺⓻ *Continental*

9039 Beverly Blvd.
Los Angeles
(213) 271-2168
Maître d': Julius
Full Bar/Valet Parking
No credit cards
Jacket, tie for men

Arguably one of L.A.'s most heard-of restaurants, Chasen's has been serving its famous chili to the notable and the starstruck for a good number of years. Maude Chasen calls it a "clublike" atmosphere with paneled walls, red carpeting and generous circular booths. Chasen's is also noted for its Hobo Steak, Maryland Fish Chowder and banana shortcake.

Reservations required
Dinner: Tues.–Sun., 6 P.M.–Midnight
Closed Monday

CHEZ CARY ⓊⒸ *Continental*

571 S. Main St.
Orange, Calif.
(714) 542-3595
Maître d': Alex Carral
Full Bar/Valet Parking
AE, D, MC, V, CB
Jacket, tie for men

Manager Sean Lewis calls Chez Cary "opulent," and with its interior emphasis on velvet and crystal, plus elaborate table settings, one can easily see why. Strolling violinists accompany a meal which may include Jambon de Parme, Scampi Glacé Comtesse or Médaillon de Veau au Calvados, along with banana flambé for dessert.

Reservations required
Dinner: Sun.–Fri., 6:30 P.M.–10:30 P.M.
Sat., 5:30 P.M.–10:30 P.M.

CHEZ HELENE ⓐ *French Canadian*

1029 W. Washington Blvd.
Venice, Calif.
(213) 392-6833
Beer and Wine/Street Parking
No credit cards
No dress restrictions

A tiny restaurant that's big on warmth and charm, Chez Hélène features the French country cooking of Quebec.

Reservations required
Lunch: Tues.–Sat., Noon–3 P.M.
Dinner: Tues.–Sun., 7 P.M.–10 P.M.
Closed Monday

CHEZ JAY ③⑨ *French*

1657 Ocean Ave.
Santa Monica, Calif.
(213) 395-1741
Full Bar/Lot Parking
AE, D, MC, V, CB
No dress restrictions

Chez Jay sports an extremely casual atmosphere, which is in interesting contrast to its elegantly prepared food. There are peanut shells and sawdust on the floor (you're invited to add to the collection) and a menu that includes La Jolla Potatoes (au gratin with bananas), shrimp curry, Sand Dabs Amandine, Steak au Poivre and whole broiled lobster tail.

Reservations advised
Lunch: Mon.-Fri., Noon-2 P.M.
Dinner: Sun.-Thurs., 6 P.M.-10:30 P.M.
 Fri.-Sat., 6 P.M.-11:30 P.M.

CHIANTI ⑥④ *Northern Italian*

7383 Melrose Ave.
Los Angeles
(213) 653-8333
Maître d': Luciano Bardinelli
Full Bar/Valet Parking
AE, MC, V
No dress restrictions

An Italian restaurant of long standing in this area, Chianti prides itself on serving the "Alta Cucina" of Northern Italy. An ornate last-century decor is the setting for such specialties as saltimbocca, osso buco, Chicken Cacciatore and Eggplant Parmigiana. The wine list is substantial.

Reservations required
Dinner: Daily, 5:30 P.M.-11:30 P.M.

THE CHRONICLE ④⓪ ⑨⑥ *American*

897 Granite Dr.   2640 Main St.
Pasadena, Calif. and   Santa Monica, Calif.
(213) 792-1179   (213) 392-4956
Maître d': Arturo Chardon
Full Bar/Valet Parking
AE, MC, V
No dress restrictions

In the last 10 years or so, a growing number of restaurateurs have chosen a vividly re-created turn-of-the-century look for their establishments. The Chronicle is no exception. A premium is placed on freshness, simplicity and natural ingredients. Look for a variety of fresh fish, veal, lamb, crêpes and homemade pastries.

Reservations required
Lunch: Mon.-Sat., 11:30 A.M.-2:30 P.M.
Dinner: Mon.-Thurs., 5 P.M.-10:30 P.M.
 Fri.-Sat., 5:30 P.M.-11 P.M.
 Sun., 5 P.M.-10 P.M.

THE COVE ⓘ02   *Continental*

3191 W. 7th St.
Los Angeles
(213) 388-0361
Maître d': Kadar
Full Bar/Valet Parking
AE, D, MC, V, CB
Jacket for men (evenings)

A New York-style restaurant in downtown L.A., The Cove features comfortable leather booths, a large menu with daily chef's specials and a strolling violinist. There are a number of German dishes, including weiner schnitzel and sauerbraten. A Caesar salad accompanies each entrée.

Reservations recommended
Lunch: Mon.–Fri., 11:30 A.M.–3 P.M.
Dinner: Mon.–Sat., 4:30 P.M.–Midnight
   Sun., 4:30 P.M.–10 P.M.

DAN TANA'S ⓘ52   *Northern Italian*

9071 Santa Monica Blvd.
Los Angeles
(213) 275-9444
Full Bar/Valet Parking
AE, D, MC, V, CB
Good taste in dress required

The Northern Italian specialties include Veal Rollatini, Chicken Florentine, sautéed whitefish, linguini with clam sauce and cannelloni.

Reservations required
Dinner: Mon.–Sat., 5 P.M.–1 A.M.
   Sun., 5 P.M.–12:30 A.M.

DANTE ⓘ25   *Northern Italian*

11917 Wilshire Blvd.
Los Angeles
(213) 479-3991
Maître d': Angelo Sambeat, Raphael (owners)
Beer and Wine/Lot Parking
AE, MC, V
No dress restrictions

Dante's management prides itself on dependable, courteous service and on consistency of food preparation. The Northern Italian specialties consist of homemade pastas, veal dishes and fresh fish.

Reservations required
Lunch: Tues.–Fri., 11:30 A.M.–2:30 P.M.
Dinner: Tues.–Sun., 5:30 P.M.–10:30 P.M.
   Closed Monday

DAR MAGHREB ⓯   Moroccan

7651 Sunset Blvd.
Los Angeles
(213) 876-7651
Full Bar/Valet Parking
MC, V
No dress restrictions

Dar Maghreb presents traditional Moroccan cuisine in traditional Moroccan surroundings. They take you from the ritual handwashing before dinner to the Mint Tea Ceremony at the conclusion, with full explanations along the way. You eat with your fingers from a single serving dish and feast on such items as B'stilla, Lemon Chicken, pigeon with almonds, and couscous.

Reservations required
Dinner: Mon.-Fri., 6 P.M.-11 P.M.
Sat., 5:30 P.M.-11 P.M.
Sun., 5:30 P.M.-10:30 P.M.

THE EGG AND THE EYE ⓼⓸   Continental

5814 Wilshire Blvd.
Los Angeles
(213) 933-5596
Maître d': Louis Ledesma (manager)
Full Bar/Lot Parking
AE, MC, V
No dress restrictions

Omelets, omelets and more omelets is the rule here. Located atop a small craft and folk art museum, The Egg and the Eye features 55 different omelets, from caviar and sour cream to zucchini and parmesan cheese to cinnamon and apple. There are also salads, chicken entrées and crêpes.

Reservations required
Lunch/Dinner: Tues.-Sat., 11 A.M.-8:30 P.M.
Sun., 10 A.M.- 6 P.M.
Closed Monday

EL CHOLO ⓵⓪⓷   Mexican

1121 S. Western Ave.
Los Angeles
(213) 734-2773
Full Bar/Lot and Street Parking
MC, V, CB
No dress restrictions

A near-downtown restaurant and gathering place that is reminiscent of a traditional Mexican hacienda. When you've gotten through the mammoth Margaritas, there are still chili rellenos, green corn tamales, crab enchiladas and chicken tacos to sample.

No reservations required
Lunch/Dinner: Daily, 11 A.M.-10 P.M.

EL PADRINO [78]   Continental

Beverly Wilshire Hotel
9500 Wilshire Blvd.
Beverly Hills, Calif.
(213) 275-4282
Full Bar/Valet Parking
AE, D, MC, V, CB
No dress restrictions

A relaxed atmosphere prevails at El Padrino. Featured are Catalina sand dabs, Eastern milk-fed veal and a variety of steaks and chops. Piano music accompanies cocktails, dinner and late supper.

Reservations preferred
Lunch/Dinner/Supper: Daily, 11:30 A.M. – 2 A.M.
Brunch: Sun., 11 A.M. – 3 P.M.

EMILIO'S [65]   Italian

6602 Melrose Ave.
Los Angeles
(213) 935-4922
Full Bar/Valet Parking
AE, D, MC, V, CB
Jacket for men

Emilio's serves white veal, cioppino, cannelloni, gnocchi, calamari and various fish entrées in a very traditional, elegant "Italian restaurant" atmosphere. Service and preparation are closely scrutinized by owner Emilio Baglioni.

Reservations required
Dinner: Sun. – Thurs., 5 P.M. – Midnight
        Fri. – Sat., 5 P.M. – 12:30 A.M.

EN BROCHETTE [90]   International

9018 Burton Way
Beverly Hills, Calif.
(213) 276-9990
Maître d': Richard Spencer (co-owner)
Beer and Wine/Valet and Street Parking
AE, D, MC, V, CB
No dress restrictions

Featuring an idyllic garden setting, neatly separated from a busy thoroughfare, En Brochette concentrates on just what its name implies. There are brochettes of beef, ham, lamb, seafood and chicken. They are served with homemade soups and salads, fresh seasonal vegetables and a variety of desserts.

Reservations required
Lunch/Dinner: Tues. – Sun., 11:30 A.M. – 10 P.M.
            Closed Monday

ENTOURAGE 76   *French*

8450 W. 3rd St.
Los Angeles
(213) 653-1079
Maître d': Robert Lachkar
Full Bar/Valet Parking
AE, MC, V
Good taste in dress required

Considered by many to be one of the prettier restaurants in the area, Entourage is big on intimacy and quiet elegance. Specialties include Tuna à la Niçoise, Duck Mirabelle, Filet Mignon Mathurini and fresh fish.

Reservations required
Lunch: Mon.–Fri., 11:30 A.M.–3 P.M.
Dinner: Daily, 6 P.M.–11 P.M.

FIASCO 43   *Continental*

4451 Admiralty Way
Marina del Rey, Calif.
(213) 823-6395
Full Bar/Lot Parking
AE, MC, V
No dress restrictions

Cedarwood and glass are the main ingredients in the setting. You dine overlooking the Marina Main Channel. A glass-enclosed outdoor deck is open year 'round. Specialties include Scampi del Rey, Veal Piccata, fettuccine and, for brunch, Eggs Benedict.

No reservations required
Lunch: Mon.–Fri., 11:30 A.M.–2:30 P.M.
Dinner: Mon.–Thurs., 5:30 P.M.–10 P.M.
           Fri.–Sat., 5:30 P.M.–11 P.M.
           Sun., 4:30 P.M.–10 P.M.
Brunch: Sat.–Sun., 10 A.M.–3 P.M.

THE FINE AFFAIR 19   *Continental*

666 N. Sepulveda Blvd.
Bel Air, Calif.
(213) 476-2848/472-5555
Maître d': Sinisha "Sam" Zivic (owner)
Full Bar/Valet Parking
AE, MC, V
No dress restrictions

The Fine Affair is composed of three dining rooms filled with plants and fresh flowers. Tables are set with hand painted china and elegant crystal. There are several daily chef's specials, along with such entrées as rack of lamb, bouillabaisse and veal.

Reservations required
Lunch: Tues.–Fri., 11 A.M.–2:30 P.M.
Dinner: Tues.–Sun., 6 P.M.–11 P.M.
Brunch: Sun., 11 A.M.–2:30 P.M.
            Closed Monday

FIVE CROWNS ⑭   *Continental*

3801 E. Pacific Coast Highway
Corona del Mar, Calif.
(714) 760-0331
Full Bar/Valet Parking
AE, MC, V
No dress restrictions

Five Crowns is a faithful reproduction of "Ye Old El," reputed to be the oldest inn in England. The timbered walls and ceilings and multiple fireplaces help put you in the proper mood. Offerings include prime rib, rack of lamb and English Beef Chop, plus English trifle for dessert.

Reservations required
Dinner: Mon. – Thurs., 5 P.M. – 10 P.M.
         Fri. – Sat., 5 P.M. – 11 P.M.
         Sun., 4 P.M. – 10 P.M.
Brunch: Sun., 10:30 A.M. – 2:30 P.M.

FRANCOIS ⑱   *Continental*

Arco Plaza
555 S. Flower St.
Los Angeles
(213) 680-2727
Maître d': Horst Habeler
Full Bar/Valet and Lot Parking
AE, D, MC, V, CB
Jacket for men

You may discover "Old World France" right in downtown L.A. if you head for François. They feature personal service, fine wines and a full complement of European specialties such as Roast Duckling Flambé au Calvados, calf's sweetbreads in a puffed pastry and pan-fried salmon steak.

Reservations required
Lunch: Mon. – Fri., 11:30 A.M. – 2:30 P.M.
Dinner: Mon. – Fri., 6 P.M. – 10:30 P.M.
         Sat., 5:30 P.M. – 10:30 P.M.
         Closed Sunday

THE GINGER MAN ⑧⑧   *American*

369 N. Bedford Dr.
Beverly Hills, Calif.
(213) 273-7585
Full Bar/Valet Parking
AE, MC, V
No dress restrictions

"A fun gathering place for eating and drinking for all types of people from celebrities to unknowns," says manager Richard Liss of The Ginger Man. If you fit into one of the above categories, this is probably your place. Specialties include hamburgers, omelets, Beef Wellington, bouillabaisse and fresh fish.

No reservations required
Lunch/Dinner: Mon. – Sat., 11:30 A.M. – 2 A.M.
                  Sun., 11 A.M. – 11:30 P.M.

GIUSEPPE! ⓖ9   *Italian*

8256 Beverly Blvd.
Los Angeles
(213) 653-8025
Full Bar/Valet Parking
AE, MC, V
Good taste in dress required

Giuseppe Bellisario used to work at Scandia and now puts his training to work in his own restaurant. He has created a garden environment for Giuseppe! along with such specialties as fettucine, medallions of veal, and Zabaglione alla Barbara.

Reservations required
Lunch: Mon.–Fri., 11:30 A.M.–3 P.M.
Dinner: Mon.–Thurs., 6 P.M.–11 P.M.
   Fri.–Sat., 6 P.M.–Midnight
   Closed Sunday

GLADSTONE'S 4 FISH ③4   *Seafood*

17300 Pacific Coast Highway
Pacific Palisades, Calif.
(213) GL4-FISH
Full Bar/Valet Parking
MC, V
No dress restrictions

Gladstone's presents casual oceanfront dining. There are peanut shells and sawdust on the floor and a large peanut barrel to encourage you to contribute to the collection. Specialties include Maine lobster, cioppino, oysters and a variety of fresh fish.

Reservations recommended
Dinner: Daily, 7 P.M.–Midnight

THE GREENHOUSE ⑧3   *Continental*

5900 Wilshire Blvd.
Los Angeles
(213) 933-8333
Maître d': Casey Goeller
Full Bar/Lot Parking
AE, D, MC, V
No dress restrictions

Sporting an airy greenhouse setting, The Greenhouse offers such entrées as prime rib, Veal Piccata, Seafood Newburg, Cobb Salad and daily fresh fish selections. The management describes the wine list as underpriced and interesting.

Reservations suggested
Lunch/Dinner: Mon.–Fri., 11:30 A.M.–9 P.M.
    Closed Saturday, Sunday

GUIDO'S ❷⓺   *Northern Italian*

11980 Santa Monica Blvd.
Los Angeles
(213) 820-6649
Full Bar/Valet Parking
AE, D, MC, V
No dress restrictions

Guido's is an Italian restaurant big on *brio*, charm and a different sort of ambience. The place resembles an Italian hunting lodge with its blazing hearth, hand-carved wood statues and rustic brick patio. Guido Perry offers such specialties as Pollo Arrosto al Arancio and Brocconcini alla Romana.

Reservations recommended
Lunch: Mon.–Fri., 11:30 A.M.–3 P.M.
Dinner: Daily, 5:30 P.M.–Midnight

HAMPTON'S ⓾ ⓱   *American*

1342 N. Highland Ave.   4301 Riverside Dr
Los Angeles   and   Burbank, Calif.
(213) 469-1090   (213) 845-3009
Beer and Wine/Valet and Street Parking
MC, V
No dress restrictions

Hampton's bills itself as a "gourmet hamburger restaurant." It serves 24 different kinds of hamburgers (at last count), as well as foot-long sandwiches and a build-it-yourself salad bar. The hamburger meat is ground twice daily on the premises. There are also some vegetarian dishes.

No reservations required
Lunch/Dinner: Sun.–Thurs., 11:30 A.M.–10 P.M.
*   Fri.–Sat., 11:30 A.M.–11 P.M.*
Brunch: Sun., 11 A.M.–2 P.M.

HARRY'S BAR & ⓽⓵   *Northern Italian/American*
AMERICAN GRILL

2020 Avenue of the Stars
Los Angeles
(213) 277-2333
Maître d': William Moyles
Full Bar/Valet Parking
AE, MC, V
No dress restrictions

The venerable "Harry" did a lot of good for hungry expatriates all over the world when he started opening Italian/American restaurants for travelers and literary types far away from home. This one in L.A.'s Century City continues the tradition with specialties that include prime steaks, many varieties of pasta and fresh fish.

Reservations required
Lunch: Mon.–Sat., 11:30 A.M.–2:30 P.M.
Dinner: Daily, 5:30 P.M.–10:30 P.M.
Late Supper: Daily, 10:30 P.M.–Midnight

JIMMY'S (89)   *French*

201 Moreno Dr.
Beverly Hills, Calif.
(213) 879-2394
Full Bar/Valet Parking
AE, D, MC, V, CB
Jacket for men (lunch)
Jacket, tie for men (dinner)

"Jimmy's is perfectly lovely in every detail," says its biased but proud owner, Jimmy Murphy. The fabrics used are Fortuny, the crystal chandeliers are Baccarat and the table settings are Limoges. Specialties include pheasant pâté with truffles and pistachios, fresh smoked salmon with avocado, sour cream and caviar, and filet mignon with foie gras.

Reservations required
Lunch: Mon. – Fri., 11:30 A.M. – 3 P.M.
Dinner: Mon. – Sat., 6 P.M. – Midnight
  Closed Sunday

KNOLL'S BLACK FOREST INN (37)   *German*

124 Santa Monica Blvd.
Santa Monica, Calif.
(213) 395-2212
Maître d': Hildegard J. Knoll (owner)
Full Bar/Street Parking
AE, MC, V
No dress restrictions

Patterned after an Alpine chalet, Knoll's Black Forest Inn offers authentic German fare in the form of Geschnetzeltes Kalbfleisch (veal with German wild mushrooms), Kalbshaxe (roast veal for two) and roast goose (served from November through February).

Reservations required
Dinner: Tues. – Sat., 5:30 P.M. – 10:30 P.M.
  Closed Sunday, Monday

LA BELLA FONTANA (45)   *Continental*

Beverly Wilshire Hotel
9500 Wilshire Blvd.
Beverly Hills, Calif.
(213) 275-4282
Full Bar/Valet Parking
AE, D, MC, V, CB
Jacket for men (evenings)

You dine near the fountain that gave the restaurant its name. Belgian lace curtains, velvet walls and sparkling chandeliers add to the effect. Serenity and elegance are specialties here, along with such entrées as pheasant, salmon and veal with truffles.

Reservations preferred
Lunch: Mon. – Fri., Noon – 3 P.M.
Dinner: Mon. – Sat., 6 P.M. – 11 P.M.
  Closed Sunday

LA DOLCE VITA ⓼⓻   *Italian*

9785 Santa Monica Blvd.
Beverly Hills, Calif.
(213) 278-1845
Maître d': George A. Smith, James Ullo (owners)
Full Bar/Valet Parking
AE, D, MC, V
Jacket for men

An intimate restaurant with mostly booth seating, La Dolce Vita lives up to its name in terms of the Italian specialties its chefs prepare. There are several different kinds of pasta, veal and seafood dishes.

Reservations required
Dinner: Mon.–Sat., 5 P.M.–11:30 P.M.
    Closed Sunday

LA FAMIGLIA ⓻⓶   *Northern Italian*

453 N. Canon Dr.
Beverly Hills, Calif.
(213) 276-6208
Full Bar/Valet Parking
AE, D, MC, V, CB
No dress restrictions

La Famiglia is home for the "succulent foods of Northern Italy," comments the management. The atmosphere is decidedly warm and inviting, with lush plants scattered here and there. It is "subtly unpretentious," says owner Joe Patti. His specialties include scampi, Veal Piccata, tagliarini and Vitello Tonnato.

Reservations required
Lunch: Mon.–Fri., 11:30 A.M.–2:30 P.M.
Dinner: Mon.–Thurs., 5 P.M.–11 P.M.
       Fri.–Sat., 5 P.M.–1 A.M.
       Closed Sunday

LA GRANGE ㉗   *French*

2005 Westwood Blvd.
Los Angeles
(213) 279-1060
Maître d': Raymond Fouquet (co-owner)
Full Bar/Lot and Street Parking
AE, D, MC, V, CB
No dress restrictions

La Grange's French provincial barn decor is in interesting counterpoint to its elegant food. Surrounded by farm implements and stuffed birds, you dine on Bouillabaisse Marseillaise, Veal Arboisienne, stuffed quails, Trout Cancalaise, Eggplant à la Hongroise and Tarte Normande.

Reservations required
Dinner: Mon.–Fri., 6 P.M.–10:30 P.M.
     Sat., 6 P.M.–11 P.M.
     Closed Sunday, Holidays

LA MASIA (53) *Spanish*

9077 Santa Monica Blvd.
Los Angeles
(213) 273-7066
Maître d': Juan Jose (owner), Josie (manager)
Full Bar/Valet Parking
AE, D, MC, V
No dress restrictions

Modeled after an old Spanish country house, La Masia offers Castilian and Continental specialties such as paella, Polla à la Gitana (Gypsy chicken), Beef Andaluza, and mariscada, a hearty seafood casserole. There's also a strolling guitarist who "sings for your pleasure."

Reservations suggested
Dinner: Tues.-Sun., 6 P.M.-11:30 P.M.
Closed Monday

LAND'S END (42) *Seafood/French*

321 Ocean Front Walk
Venice, Calif.
(213) 392-3997
Maître d': Enrique Cabrera (owner), Pierre Denerome
Beer and Wine/Lot Parking
MC, V
No dress restrictions

You might expect a restaurant located on "Ocean Front Walk" to offer you fish and that's just what Land's End does, with a French accent. There is salmon in mustard sauce, Lake Superior whitefish, and scampi in paprika sauce, among other offerings. The Sunday brunch features quiche and Eggs Benedict.

Reservations required
Dinner: Daily, 5:30 P.M.-10 P.M.
Brunch: Sunday

LA POLONAISE (77) *Basque/French*

225 S. Beverly Dr.
Beverly Hills, Calif.
(213) 274-7246
Maître d': France Rouard (co-owner)
Full Bar/Valet Parking
AE, D, MC, V, CB
Good taste in dress required

Small and cozy, with fresh-cut flowers on the tables and muted mood music in the background, Rouard's Polonaise presents such creations as Basque fish soup, Entrecôte Poelée Basquaise and Petit Poisson Frais aux Laitues. The interior of brick, brass, beams and mirrors provides a picturesque setting.

Reservations required
Dinner: Tues.-Sat., 6 P.M.-11 P.M.
Sun., 5 P.M.-10 P.M.
Closed Monday

LA SCALA 66   *Italian*

9455 Santa Monica Blvd.
Beverly Hills, Calif.
(213) 275-0579
Maître d': Antonio Vazquez
Full Bar/Valet Parking
AE, D, MC, V, CB
Jacket for men

La Scala is known for special ways with fresh fish, chicken, beef and pasta that translate into dishes such as Veal Piccata, three versions of cannelloni and steak and peppers sautéed in cognac. A large selection of wines provides accompaniment. La Scala Boutique is next door, featuring some simpler dishes served in a less formal atmosphere.

Reservations required
Lunch: Mon. - Fri., 11:30 A.M. - 2:30 P.M.
Dinner: Mon. - Sat., 5:30 P.M. - Midnight
    Closed Sunday

LA SERRE 8   *French*

12969 Ventura Blvd.
Studio City, Calif.
(213) 990-0500
Full Bar/Valet Parking
AE, MC, V
Jacket for men

La Serre is a lush French garden in the midst of the monotonous glass and concrete that is Ventura Boulevard. Most guests remark about the physical beauty of the restaurant *and* about the beautiful presentation of such dishes as Tournedos Grillé Béarnaise, Cuisses de Grenouilles Provençale, Truite Amandine and Poulet à l'Estragon.

Reservations required
Lunch: Mon. - Fri., Noon - 10 P.M.
Dinner: Mon. - Sat., 6 P.M. - 10 P.M.
    Closed Sunday

LA TOQUE 45   *French*

8171 Sunset Blvd.
Los Angeles
(213) 656-7515
Maître d': Henri Fiser (co-owner)
Full Bar/Valet Parking
AE, MC, V
No dress restrictions

"We are a small, select restaurant dedicated to the best quality only," says co-owner/chef Ken Frank. The menu changes daily, reflecting the best available market produce. There is a covered garden lounge for cocktails or dining.

Reservations required
Dinner: Mon. - Sat., 6:30 P.M. - 10:30 P.M.
    Closed Sunday

LAWRY'S THE PRIME RIB ⓺⓼   *American*

55 N. La Cienega Blvd.
Beverly Hills, Calif.
(213) 652-2827
Maître d': Tim Hart
Full Bar/Valet Parking
AE, MC, V
Good taste in dress required

The home of the famed one-entrée specialty — roast prime ribs of beef individually carved and served tableside. Joining it are mashed potatoes, Yorkshire pudding, selections from a "spinning salad bowl" and, of course, Lawry's horseradish sauce. They often take the boys from the Rose Bowl teams here, so you might guess there's plenty to eat.

No reservations required
Dinner: Daily, 5 P.M. – Midnight

LE CELLIER ⓷⓪   *French*

2628 Wilshire Blvd.
Santa Monica, Calif.
(213) 828-1585
Maître d': Jacques Don Salat (co-owner)
Full Bar/Valet Parking
AE, D, MC, V, CB
No dress restrictions

Le Cellier owners Jacques and Madeleine Don Salat serve their classic French cuisine in an atmosphere they term "subdued and elegant." Their specialties include rack of lamb, Dover Sole, bouillabaisse, Duckling au Citron and Veal Forestière. The quality of the service is carefully monitored by the owners.

Reservations required
Dinner: Tues. – Thurs., 5:30 P.M. – 10:30 P.M.
Fri. – Sat., 5:30 P.M. – 11 P.M.
Sun., 5 P.M. – 10 P.M.
Closed Monday

LE DOME ⓸⓺   *French*

8720 Sunset Blvd.
Los Angeles
(213) 659-6919
Maître d': Henri Labadie
Full Bar/Valet Parking
AE, MC, V, CB
Jacket for men

Welcome to the deep greens and gleaming chrome of the 1920's and 30's. Once past Le Dôme's large circular bar, reminiscent of those aboard transatlantic luxury liners of years ago, you can dine on such specialties as fresh tuna steak, boudine noir (blood sausage) with apple sauce, and charcuterie. There are five daily specials.

Reservations required
Lunch/Dinner: Mon. – Fri., Noon – 1 A.M.
Sat., 6 P.M. – 1 A.M.
Closed Sunday

LE PETIT MOULIN ㊱ *French*

714 Montana Ave.
Santa Monica, Calif.
(213) 395-6619
Maître d': Marcel Bourque (owner)
Beer and Wine/Street Parking
MC, V
No dress restrictions

This small, carefully run restaurant specializes in only the freshest fish, plus rabbit in wine sauce, Sole Bonne Femme, duckling adorned with peaches, chocolate mousse and café filtre.

Reservations required
Dinner: Mon.–Sat., 5:30 P.M.–10 P.M.
   Closed Sunday

LE RESTAURANT ㊿ *French*

8475 Melrose Pl.
Los Angeles
(213) 651-5553
Maître d': Mark
Full Bar/Valet Parking
AE, D, MC, V
Jacket for men

A converted bungalow that is divided into several small dining areas, Le Restaurant pursues a romantic image with lots of fresh flowers on each well-appointed table. Some examples of its classic French cuisine include sautéed duck, veal with apple cider and Steak Tartare.

Reservations required
Lunch: Mon.–Fri., Noon–3:30 P.M.
Dinner: Mon.–Sat., 5:30 P.M.–11 P.M.
   Closed Sunday

L'ERMITAGE ㊾ *French*

730 N. La Cienega Blvd.
Los Angeles
(213) 652-5840
Maître d': Jean-Claude
Full Bar/Valet Parking
AE, MC, V
Jacket for men

As its name implies, L'Ermitage has an air of elegant seclusion. Blue damask walls, fine china, classic *haute cuisine* are the basic ingredients. The kitchen offers such specialties as breast of duckling basted with Bordeaux, saddle of lamb with eggplant, and fresh fruit sorbet.

Reservations required
Dinner: Mon.–Sat., 6:30 P.M.–10:30 P.M.
   Closed Sunday

LE ST. GERMAIN ⑱　　　　　　　　　　　　*French*

5955 Melrose Ave.
Los Angeles
(213) 467-1108/9
Maître d': Jacques Dassise
Full Bar/Street Parking
AE, D, MC, V
No dress restrictions

A grand old home located on a busy Hollywood thoroughfare, Le St. Germain features velvet walls, dark wood paneling, lots of paintings and tapestries, and fresh flowers arranged by the owners. Food is not forgotten amid all this atmosphere. There is, for example, poached salmon, rack of lamb and Whitefish Hollandaise.

Reservations required
Lunch: Mon.–Fri., Noon–2 P.M.
Dinner: Mon.–Sat., 6 P.M.–10:30 P.M.
　　Closed Sunday

LE SAINT-MICHEL ㉛　　　　　　　　　　　　*French*

3218 Santa Monica Blvd.
Santa Monica, Calif.
(213) 829-3173
Beer and Wine/Street Parking
AE, V
Good taste in dress required

A French country-style restaurant, Le Saint-Michel makes a small dining room perform maximum duty — without crowding its customers. The kitchen concentrates on roast duck, prepared in a variety of different ways. There are also seafood items and a popular bouillabaisse.

Reservations required
Dinner: Tues.–Sun., 6 P.M.–10:30 P.M.
　　Closed Monday

LE SANGLIER ❸　　　　　　　　　　　　*French*

5522 Crebs Ave.
Tarzana, Calif.
(213) 345-0470
Full Bar/Lot and Street Parking
AE, D, MC, V
No dress restrictions

If you revel in restaurants with hunting lodge atmospheres, this is the place for you. It seems fitting that Le Sanglier should serve wild boar in season. For the less adventurous there is a variety of fresh fish, veal selections and duck and beef entrées. Appetizers include escargots, onion soup and, of course, their own wild boar pâté.

Reservations required
Dinner: Tues.–Sun., 5:30 P.M.–10:30 P.M.
　　Closed Monday

L'ESCOFFIER ⑧⑥   *French*

Beverly Hilton Hotel
9876 Wilshire Blvd.
Beverly Hills, Calif.
(213) 274-7777
Maître d': Leo Waters
Full Bar/Valet, Lot and Street Parking
AE, D, MC, V, CB
Jacket, tie for men
Dresses for women

The penthouse of the Beverly Hilton has been given over to the likes of fresh Maine lobster, a series of flambé dishes, soufflés and gala desserts. L'Escoffier also features an extensive wine selection, as well as dancing nightly to the strains of a live orchestra.

Reservations required
Lunch: Mon.-Fri., Noon-3 P.M.
Dinner: Mon.-Sat., 6:30 P.M.-Midnight
    Closed Sunday

LES PYRENEES ㉝   *French*

2455 Santa Monica Blvd.
Santa Monica, Calif.
(213) 828-7503
Maître d': Jacques Toulet (owner)
Full Bar/Street Parking
AE, MC, V
Good taste in dress required

"Excellent French cuisine with the most delightful atmosphere," comments owner Dr. Jacques Toulet of Les Pyrénées. His daily specialties include quails in the nest, variations on the duckling and rabbit, baby salmon in sorrel sauce and seafood selections. Presentations and service are given particular emphasis.

Reservations required
Lunch: Mon.-Fri., Noon-2 P.M.
Dinner: Daily, 6 P.M.-11 P.M.

L'ETOILE ㊿   *French*

8941½ Santa Monica Blvd.
Los Angeles
(213) 278-1011
Maître d': Giancarlo Zaretti (owner)
Full Bar/Street Parking
AE, MC, V
No dress restrictions

L'Etoile is the ultimate in intimacy, according to owner Zaretti. He boasts plates signed by famous celebrities as well as specialties such as Veal Maltese, Chicken l'Etoile, White Fish Alice, Trout Walewska, chestnut mousse and chocolate fondue.

Reservations required
Dinner: Tues.-Sun., 5:30 P.M.-11 P.M.
    Closed Monday

LEW MITCHELL'S ORIENT EXPRESS ⓈⒺ

Chinese/American

5400 Wilshire Blvd.
Los Angeles
(213) 935-6000
Maître d': Lew Mitchell (owner)
Full Bar/Lot Parking
AE, MC, V
Good taste in dress required

Mandarin and Szechuan dishes are served in a stylish interior done in soft mauve tones. Special items include Beggar's Chicken, minced pigeon in lettuce leaves, Kung Pao seafood, steaks and chops.

Reservations suggested
Lunch: Mon.-Fri., 11:30 A.M.-3 P.M.
Dinner: Sun.-Thurs., 6 P.M.-11 P.M.
          Fri.-Sat., 6 P.M.-1 A.M.

L'ORANGERIE ⓈⒺ

French

903 N. La Cienega Blvd.
Los Angeles
(213) 652-9770
Maître d': Sam Van Hoeve
Full Bar/Valet Parking
AE, D, MC, V
Jacket for men

L'Orangerie owner Gerard Ferry takes pride in his restaurant's stunning, spacious interior. He also takes pride in such specialties as turbot soufflé, filet of beef in red wine, carré de veau, seafood salad with raspberry-vinegar dressing, eggs with caviar, and breast of duckling in green pepper sauce.

Reservations required
Dinner: Daily, 6:30 P.M.-2 A.M.

LOS FELIZ INN ⓈⒺ

Continental

2138 N. Hillhurst
Los Angeles
(213) 663-8001
Maître d': Ron Erickson (owner)
Full Bar/Valet Parking
AE, D, MC, V, CB
Jacket for men

Los Feliz Inn presents a large collection of original Millard Sheets watercolor paintings, as well as leisurely dining. Offered are such specialties as fresh fish from around the country, several veal dishes and seasonal cooking that includes game dishes in the fall and fowl in the winter.

Reservations required
Lunch: Mon.-Fri., 11:30 A.M.-4 P.M.
Dinner: Sun.-Thurs., 4 P.M.-11 P.M.
          Fri.-Sat., 4 P.M.-Midnight

MADAME WU'S GARDEN (32) *Chinese*

2201 Wilshire Blvd.
Santa Monica, Calif.
(213) 828-5656
Maître d': Madame Sylvia Wu (owner)
Full Bar/Valet Parking
AE, D, MC, V, CB
Jacket, tie for men (Imperial Room)

Madame Sylvia Wu's four dining rooms are all done in the classic Chinese style, complete with private jade collection. Among the specialties served are Peking Duck, Sizzling Go Ba and Madame's Shredded Chicken Salad. A six-entrée "Long Life" menu that follows the Pritikin Diet guidelines has also been introduced.

Reservations required
Lunch/Dinner: Mon.-Thurs., 11:30 A.M.-10 P.M.
Fri., 11:30 A.M.-11 P.M.
Sat., 5 P.M.-11:30 P.M.
Sun., Noon-10 P.M.

MALDONADO'S (95) *Continental*

1202 E. Green St.
Pasadena, Calif.
(213) 796-1126
Maître d': Albert Richards
Full Bar/Lot and Street Parking
AE, D, MC, V, CB
Jacket for men

A popular favorite with Maldonado's guests is Shrimp and Scallops Romana with fettucine. That is according to owner Bill Maldonado, who also takes a turn at the piano, Wednesday through Sunday, accompanying "artists from the Broadway and opera stages."

Reservations required
Lunch: Mon.-Fri., 11 A.M.-2:30 P.M.
Dinner: Tues.-Sun., 6 P.M. and 9 P.M. seatings
Closed Monday night

MA MAISON (61) *French*

8368 Melrose Ave.
Los Angeles
(213) 655-1991
Maître d': Claude Gourdal (manager)
Full Bar/Valet and Lot Parking
AE, MC, V, CB
Jacket for men

A restaurant that is small on interior seatings and big on outdoor dining under a tentlike awning, Ma Maison has developed a "super-chic" reputation over the years. In addition to the star-gazing, they feature innovative fish dishes, a duck entrée in two stages and their own private version of house wine. "A little of Paris on Melrose Avenue," say the owners.

Reservations required
Lunch: Mon.-Sat., Noon-2:30 P.M.
Dinner: Mon.-Sat., 6:30 P.M.-10 P.M.
Closed Sunday

THE MANDARIN ⑦¹   *Chinese*

430 N. Camden Dr.
Beverly Hills, Calif.
(213) 272-0267
Maître d': Bill Chow
Full Bar/Valet Parking
AE, D, MC, V, CB
No dress restrictions

Following in the footsteps of its sister in San Francisco, The Mandarin in Beverly Hills spotlights Peking Duck, Minced Squab and Beggar's Chicken. Owner Cecilia Chiang is interested in an elegant atmosphere as well as elegantly presented food.

Reservations required
Lunch: Mon.-Sat., Noon-4 P.M.
Dinner: Daily, 5 P.M.-10:30 P.M.

MARRAKESH ⑪²   *Moroccan*

1100 W. Coast Highway
Newport Beach, Calif.
(714) 645-8384
Maître d': Mohamed Zahoui (manager)
Full Bar/Valet Parking
AE, D, MC, V, CB
Good taste in dress required

Here you are speeding down Pacific Coast Highway, gazing at surfers and suntans, when you notice something quite different. It may well be Marrakesh, a Moroccan restaurant featuring bastilla and chicken, lamb, fish and rabbit dishes. "As you step in, you will have flown over to the Sahara desert," says manager Mohamed Zahoui.

Reservations required
Dinner: Mon.-Thurs., 6 P.M.-10 P.M.
        Fri.-Sun., 5:30 P.M.-11 P.M.

MAURO'S ⑨⁴   *Italian*

514 S. Brand Blvd.
Glendale, Calif.
(213) 243-6908
Maître d': Giovanni Tromba (owner)
Full Bar/Valet and Lot Parking
AE, MC, V
Jacket for men

Roman specialties are the order here, including 10 types of freshly made pasta, from Pesto Carbonara to ravioli and gnocchi. There's also a variety of veal, chicken and fish dishes (Saltimbocca alla Romana, Chicken Cacciatora) and homemade gelatin for dessert.

Reservations required
Dinner: Tues.-Sun., 5:30 P.M.-10:30 P.M.
        Closed Monday

MICHAEL'S ㉟   *French*

1147 Third St.
Santa Monica, Calif.
(213) 451-0843
Maître d': Michael McCarty (owner)
Full Bar/Lot and Street Parking
AE, D, MC, V
Jacket for men

Young owner Michael McCarty has taken some pains to make his Santa Monica restaurant special. He serves such specialties as Coquilles au Cresson and Chicken Sauté au Foie Gras de Canard on signature dishes in impeccably designed dining rooms. Some of the food arrives via Air France.

Reservations required
Lunch: Tues.–Sun., Noon–2 P.M.
Dinner: Tues.–Sun., 6:30 P.M.–10 P.M.
       Closed Monday

MICHEL RICHARD ㉛   *French*

310 S. Robertson Blvd.
Los Angeles
(213) 275-5707
Beer and Wine/Street Parking
MC, V
Good taste in dress required

Michel Richard features a European breakfast of fresh orange juice, croissants, brioches and espresso. Later on, you can select from a menu of crêpes, omelets, quiche, salads and pâtés. The pastries are very special.

No reservations required
Breakfast/Lunch/Snacks: Mon.–Sat., 9 A.M.–7 P.M.
       Closed Sunday

MR. CHOW ㉝   *Chinese/Continental*

344 N. Camden Dr.
Beverly Hills, Calif.
(213) 278-9911
Full Bar/Valet Parking
AE, D, MC, V, CB
Good taste in dress required

Chinese food, served and prepared in a Continental fashion, best describes the eclectic Mr. Chow. Specialties include Peking Duck, Peking Chicken and deep-fried seaweed. The main attraction is the nightly noodle show where the chef comes out and makes noodles from scratch.

Reservations required
Lunch: Mon.–Fri., Noon–2:30 P.M.
Dinner: Mon.–Thurs., 6 P.M.–11:30 P.M.
       Fri.–Sat., 6 P.M.–Midnight
       Sun., 5:30 P.M.–11 P.M.

MON GRENIER ❹   *French*

18040 Ventura Blvd.
Encino, Calif.
(213) 344-8060
Maître d': André Lion (owner)
Full Bar/Lot Parking
MC, V
Good taste in dress required

An "antique look" predominates at Mon Grenier (My Attic), along with "a very French atmosphere," according to owner André Lion. There are different specialties daily, including Salmon in Crust, Lamb Wellington, Quails Beajolais and Veal Loin Sorrel. Chocolate-coated strawberries injected with Grand Marnier are featured for dessert.

Reservations required
Lunch: Mon.–Fri., 11:30 A.M.–2 P.M.
Dinner: Mon.–Sat., 6 P.M.–10 P.M.
    Closed Sunday

MORTON'S ❺❻   *Continental*

8800 Melrose Ave.
Los Angeles
(213) 276-5205
Full Bar/Valet Parking
AE, MC, V
Good taste in dress required

A place for making contacts, arranging deals and being seen, Morton's also is a place for a wide range of entrées, including smoked salmon, grilled chicken, prime New York steaks and several fresh fish selections.

Reservations required
Dinner: Mon.–Sat., 6 P.M.–Midnight
    Closed Sunday

MOUSTACHE CAFE ❻❷   *Continental*

8155 Melrose Ave.
Los Angeles
(213) 651-2111
Beer and Wine/Valet Parking
MC, V
No dress restrictions

Unpretentious, charming and upbeat are apt adjectives for Moustache Cafe, according to most patrons. It is modeled after a typical French sidewalk cafe with outdoor patio. The 70-item menu includes a full range of hors d'oeuvre, salads, crêpes, omelets, veal entrées and fresh fish.

Reservations required
Lunch/Dinner: Daily, 11:30 A.M.–1 A.M.

MUSSO AND FRANK GRILL ⓰   *Continental*

6667 Hollywood Blvd.
Los Angeles
(213) 467-7788/5123
Maître d': Philip Cano
Full Bar/Lot Parking
AE, D, MC, V, CB
No dress restrictions

A Hollywood landmark for over 60 years, Musso and Frank's is known for such stick-to-the-ribs fare as homemade chicken pot pie, corned beef and cabbage, bouillabaisse and rack of lamb. The numerous homemade pastries and puddings are also special features.

Reservations advised
Lunch/Dinner: Mon.–Sat., 11 A.M.–11 P.M.
Closed Sunday

NICK'S FISHMARKET ㊽   *Seafood*

9229 Sunset Blvd.
Los Angeles
(213) 550-1544
Maître d': Dennis Daley
Full Bar/Valet Parking
AE, D, MC, V, CB
Good taste in dress required

This elegantly appointed seafood restaurant features individually controlled lighting over each booth. Specialties include fresh opakapaka and sashimi from Hawaii, swordfish, salmon, scallops and catfish. Of particular note is the abalone from California and the lobster from Maine.

Reservations required
Dinner: Sun.–Thurs., 6 P.M.–11:30 P.M.
Fri.–Sat., 6 P.M.–Midnight

ORLANDO-ORSINI ㉘   *Italian*

9575 W. Pico Blvd.
Los Angeles
(213) 277-6050
Full Bar/Valet Parking
AE, D, MC, V, CB
Jacket for men

Three Romans — two Orlandos and one Orsini — recently joined forces to open this restaurant specializing in "authentic Italian cuisine." Some examples of their handiwork include Fettucine in Salsa Rosa, Spaghetti Pascatora and Calamari alla Caprese.

Reservations required
Lunch: Mon.–Fri., Noon–2:30 P.M.
Dinner: Mon.–Sat., 6 P.M.–11 P.M.
Closed Sunday

PACIFIC DINING CAR ⓘ   *American*

1310 W. Sixth St.
Los Angeles
(213) 483-6000
Maître d': Michael Green
Full Bar/Valet Parking
MC, V
Good taste in dress required

Said to be the oldest steak house in downtown L.A., Pacific Dining Car features Eastern prime beef that is aged and cut in the restaurant's own cooling box. It is then cooked to your order over a charcoal broiler. There are also fresh seafood items and a wine list of over 200 labels.

Reservations suggested
Breakfast/Lunch/Dinner: Mon.-Fri., 6 A.M.-2 A.M.
                        Sat., 8 A.M.-2 A.M.
                        Sun., 10 A.M.-Midnight

THE PALM ⓘ   *American*

9001 Santa Monica Blvd.
Los Angeles
(213) 550-8811
Full Bar/Valet Parking
AE, D, MC, V, CB
No dress restrictions

Steaks so large they demand bigger plates, giant Nova Scotia lobsters, sawdust on the floor. This combination, plus lots of people waiting to get in, adds up to The Palm. Like its New York cousin (and others around the nation), this Palm offers large portions of simple food. There are also hamburgers and daily specials.

Reservations advised
Lunch: Mon.-Fri., Noon-3 P.M.
Dinner: Daily, 5 P.M.-10:45 P.M.

PAPADAKIS TAVERNA ⓘ   *Greek*

301 W. Sixth St.
San Pedro, Calif.
(213) 548-1186
Maitre d': John Papadakis (owner)
Beer and Wine/Lot Parking
MC, V
Good taste in dress required

"An eatery in love with its customers, its food, itself and its way of pleasing" is how owner/chef John Papadakis describes his restaurant. All that love translates into such dishes as roast lamb, spiced fish, pastitsio, moussaka, octopus and shish kabob.

Reservations required
Dinner: Tues.-Sat., 5 P.M.-Midnight
        Sun., 4 P.M.-10 P.M.
        Closed Monday

PAUL BHALLA'S CUISINE OF INDIA ⓴   *Indian*

10853 Lindbrook Dr.
Los Angeles
(213) 478-8535
Full Bar/Street Parking
MC, V
No dress restrictions

Authentic Indian cuisine has found a home at Paul Bhalla's. He features a variety of curried preparations, plus Tandoori Chicken, Lamb, Beef and Lobster. Look for other special dishes such as Tikka, Saag Lela and Tandoori Naan.

Reservations required
Dinner: Sun.–Thurs., 5:30 P.M.–10 P.M.
Fri.–Sat., 5:30 P.M.–11 P.M.
Closed Monday

PEPPONE ㉒   *Italian*

11628 Barrington Ct.
Los Angeles
(213) 476-7379
Maître d': Maria
Full Bar/Lot and Street Parking
AE, D, MC, V
No dress restrictions

Peppone's Gianni Paoletti wants to make his restaurant an extension of your home. Such tender loving care means he will prepare any dish you like. Or, you can choose from such specialties as Sole Filets Florentine, Sweetbreads Pompeii, Chicken Parmigiana, Veal Piccata and a healthy variety of pasta dishes.

Reservations required
Lunch: Tues.–Fri., 11:30 A.M.–2:30 P.M.
Dinner: Tues.–Sun., 5:30 P.M.–11:30 P.M.
Closed Monday

PERINO'S ⓼   *Continental*

4101 Wilshire Blvd.
Los Angeles
(213) 383-1221
Full Bar/Lot Parking
AE, D, MC, V, CB
Jacket for men

Long a Los Angeles tradition, Perino's has set a standard of luxury for Southern California restaurants. Specialties include saddle of lamb, Fritto Piccata, fresh seafood and pasta.

Reservations required
Lunch/Dinner: Mon.–Fri., Noon–11 P.M.
Sat., 5:30 P.M.–Midnight
Closed Sunday

POLO LOUNGE ⑤¹   *Continental*

Beverly Hills Hotel
9641 Sunset Blvd.
Beverly Hills, Calif.
(213) 276-2251
Maître d': Nino Osti
Full Bar/Valet Parking
AE, D, MC, V, CB
Jacket for men (dinner)

If you wanted to observe this city's ever-changing scene, you could take all your meals here, beginning with a dainty breakfast or sumptuous brunch and ending with a late-night snack. Complete dinners are served in The Coterie adjoining the Lounge.

Reservations required
Breakfast/Lunch/Dinner: Daily, 7 A.M. – 2 A.M.

RANGOON RACQUET CLUB ⑤⁵   *Continental*

9474 Santa Monica Blvd.
Beverly Hills, Calif.
(213) 274-8926
Full Bar/Valet Parking (evenings)
AE, D, MC, V, CB
No dress restrictions

Intended to put you in mind of the English Officers' Club in Burma, the Rangoon Racquet Club is a throwback to the days of Victorian colonialism. There are steaks and chops, numerous curries, fresh fish and award-winning chili. Dessert specialties include English trifle and chocolate-coated strawberries.

Reservations required
Lunch/Dinner: Mon. – Fri., 11:30 A.M. – 2 A.M.
             Sat., 6 P.M. – 2 A.M.
             Closed Sunday

SAIGON FLAVOR ⑨³   *Vietnamese*

1044 S. Fairfax Ave.
Los Angeles
(213) 935-1564
Maître d': Lehoang Duc (owner)
Beer and Wine/Street Parking
MC, V
No dress restrictions

Vietnamese food, a cuisine apart from other Oriental foods, is featured here. Owner Lehoang Duc offers specialties such as crab claws wrapped in shrimp and deep fried, charbroiled meatballs on a skewer and Imperial Rolls, a marriage of pork, crab and shrimp rolled in thin rice paper and deep fried.

Reservations required
Lunch: Wed. – Mon., 11:30 A.M. – 3 P.M.
Dinner: Wed. – Mon., 4:30 P.M. – 10 P.M.
        Closed Tuesday

ST. MORITZ ❾   *Continental*

11720 Ventura Blvd.
Studio City, Calif.
(213) 980-1122
Maître d': Irwin Hoffberg (owner)
Full Bar/Valet Parking
MC, V
No dress restrictions

A Swiss chalet in the midst of the San Fernando Valley, St. Moritz is big on warmth, charm and ambience. German-born owner/chef Wolfgang Braun creates such specialties as Schnitzel à la Holstein and Tarragon Chicken.

Reservations required
Lunch: Tues.-Fri., 11 A.M.-2 P.M.
Dinner: Tues.-Thurs., Sun., 5 P.M.-10 P.M.
         Fri.-Sat., 5 P.M.-11 P.M.
         Closed Monday

THE SALOON ㊹   *American*

9390 Santa Monica Blvd.
Beverly Hills, Calif.
(213) 273-7155
Maître d': Rafael Menchaca
Full Bar/Valet and Street Parking
AE, D, MC, V, CB
No dress restrictions

If a hunting lodge had a pub, it might take after The Saloon. A good people-watching spot with a convivial bar and lounge, The Saloon features hearty sandwiches, Scotch salmon, a luncheon buffet and meaty hamburgers.

Reservations recommended
Lunch/Dinner: Mon.-Sat., 11:30 A.M.-2 A.M.
              Sun., 6 P.M.-11:30 P.M.

SCANDIA ㊼   *Scandinavian*

9040 Sunset Blvd.
Los Angeles
(213) 278-3555/272-9521
Maître d': Michel
Full Bar/Valet Parking
AE, D, MC, V, CB
Jacket for men

The pride of the late Ken Hansen, its original owner, Scandia features the specialties of Scandinavia such as Veal Oskar, smoked Baltic salmon, plaice and turbot, and a smörgåsbord. There are also menu selections from other parts of Europe, not to mention goose soup at Christmas and even chili con carne.

Reservations required
Lunch: Tues.-Sat., 11:30 A.M.-3 P.M.
       Sun., 11 A.M.-3 P.M.
Dinner: Tues.-Sat., 6 P.M.-1 A.M.
        Sun., 5 P.M.-Midnight
        Closed Monday

THE SEASHELL   *French/Seafood*

19723 Ventura Blvd.
Woodland Hills, Calif
(213) 884-6500
Full Bar/Lot and Street Parking
AE, D, MC, V, CB
Good taste in dress required

A seafood house with a decidedly French flavor, The Seashell turns out such preparations as Snapper Belle Meunière (sautéed with lemon butter and mushrooms), Sand Dabs Véronique (sautéed with grapes) and Salmon Sorrel. They also serve bouillabaisse, filet mignon, veal and poultry selections.

Reservations required
Lunch: Mon.–Fri., 11:30 A.M.–2 P.M.
Dinner: Mon.–Thurs., 5:30 P.M.–10 P.M.
       Fri.–Sat., 5:30 P.M.–10:30 P.M.
       Sun., 5 P.M.–9 P.M.

SHANGHAI WINTER GARDEN   *Chinese*

5651 Wilshire Blvd.
Los Angeles
(213) 934-0505
Full Bar/Lot Parking
AE, MC, V, CB
No dress restrictions

Just down the street from the L.A. County Art Museum, the Shanghai Winter Garden offers both Mandarin and Shanghai specialties. Featured are such items as Peking Duck, Kung-Pao Shrimp, sizzling rice soups and Soong-tse Chicken.

Reservations advised (four or more)
Lunch: Mon.–Sat., 11 A.M.–3 P.M.
Dinner: Daily, 4 P.M.–10:30 P.M.

SILVANA'S   *Continental/Northern Italian*

268 S. La Cienega Blvd.
Beverly Hills, Calif.
(213) 659-8422
Maître d': Edward Colon (owner)
Beer and Wine/Lot and Street Parking
AE, MC, V, CB
No dress restrictions

Silvana's features intimate dining and dishes cooked to order. "Silvana has integrity and respect for the original recipe," states owner Colon. You'll find an infinite variety of pasta dishes, including fettuccine, lasagne and cannelloni. Other entrées follow the dictates of Bologna, Rome, Milan or Sicily.

Reservations required
Dinner: Mon.–Thurs., 6 P.M.–11 P.M.
       Fri.–Sat., 6 P.M.–Midnight
       Closed Sunday

STRATTON'S ㉑   *Continental*

10886 Le Conte Ave.
Los Angeles
(213) 208-8880
Maître d': Gene Stratton (owner)
Full Bar/Lot Parking
MC, V
No dress restrictions

Housed in a 50-year-old building of Moorish design, Stratton's features Veal Normande, Beef Wellington, Poached Salmon Printanière and Yellow Fin Belle Meunière. You dine in the hushed atmosphere of an intimate dining room with a large fireplace and high timbered ceiling. There is also an outdoor patio.

Reservations required
Lunch: Tues.-Sat., 11:30 A.M.-3 P.M.
Dinner: Tues.-Thurs., 6 P.M.-10 P.M.
          Fri., 6 P.M.-Midnight
          Sat., 5 P.M.-Midnight
          Sun., 5 P.M.-10 P.M.
Brunch: Sun., 11:30 A.M.-3 P.M.
          Closed Monday

THE STUDIO GRILL ㊹   *Continental*

7321 Santa Monica Blvd.
Los Angeles
(213) 874-9202
Maître d': Ron Braun
Beer and Wine/Valet Parking
AE, D, MC, V, CB
Good taste in dress required

The Studio Grill exists for those who crave privacy (it's located near many of the Hollywood studios) and fine food, suggests owner Ardison Phillips. He offers shrimp in lime-ginger sauce, linguine with shellfish, tournedos and fresh fruit tarts. There are some 350 wines to choose from.

Reservations required
Lunch: Mon.-Fri., Noon-2:30 P.M.
Dinner: Mon.-Thurs., 6 P.M.-10:30 P.M.
          Fri.-Sat., 6 P.M.-11:30 P.M.
          Closed Sunday

SWISS ECHO ㉙   *Swiss*

10769 W. Pico Blvd.
Los Angeles
(213) 279-1142
No Wine or Spirits/Street Parking
No credit cards
No dress restrictions

Swiss food with a German accent is served at Swiss Echo. There is sauerbraten with potato pancakes, wiener schnitzel, Veal Piccata and home-baked desserts, prepared on the premises.

Reservations required
Lunch/Dinner: Tues.-Sat., 11:30 A.M.-10 P.M.
                Closed Sunday, Monday

A THOUSAND CRANES 🔴107   *Japanese*

New Otani Hotel
120 S. Los Angeles St.
Los Angeles
(213) 629-1200
Maître d': T. Abe
Full Bar/Valet and Garage Parking
AE, D, MC, V, CB
No dress restrictions

A Thousand Cranes offers you authentic Japanese food in its main dining room and has a tempura bar and a sushi bar as well as private tatami rooms. You dine overlooking a traditional Japanese garden. There is tableside preparation of such items as shabu-shabu, sukiyaki, yose-nabe and ishikari-nabe.

Reservations recommended
Lunch: Daily, 11:30 A.M. – 2 P.M.
Dinner: Daily, 6 P.M. – 10 P.M.

THE TOWER 🔴109   *French*

Occidental Center
1150 S. Olive St.
Los Angeles
(213) 746-1554/1825
Maître d': Francis
Full Bar/Valet Parking
AE, D, MC, V, CB
Jacket for men (dining room)

On a lucky clear day, you can see for miles around as you partake of classical French cuisine. The Tower, 32 stories up, features fresh seafood and fish flown in daily (brook trout, lobster, shrimp, salmon, for instance), prime lamb and milk-fed veal. The wine cellar is well stocked with a diverse sampling of French and domestic wines.

Reservations required
Lunch: Mon. – Fri., 11:30 A.M. – 2:30 P.M.
Dinner: Mon – Fri., 6 P.M. – 10 P.M.
Sat., 6 P.M. – 10:30 P.M.
Closed Sunday, Holidays

TRADER VIC'S 🔴86   *Polynesian*

Beverly Hilton Hotel
9876 Wilshire Blvd.
Beverly Hills, Calif.
(213) 274-7777
Maître d': Oswaldo Llorens (manager)
Full Bar/Valet Parking
AE, D, MC, V, CB
Jacket for men

Enter another time and another place as you step across the threshold onto a South Sea island, complete with tropical garden, carved tiki gods and seashell decorations. Trader Vic's is known for its exotic tropical drinks and meats from the Chinese Ovens. Special dishes include Bongo Bongo Soup, Indonesian Lamb Roast and Crab Crêpe Bengal.

Reservations required
Dinner: Sun. – Thurs., 4:30 P.M. – 1 A.M.
Fri. – Sat., 4:30 P.M. – 2 A.M.

TRUMPS ㉗ International/Eclectic

8764 Melrose Ave.
Los Angeles
(213) 855-1480
Full Bar/Valet Parking
MC, V
Good taste in dress required

A recent addition to what is fast becoming a "Restaurant Row" on Melrose Avenue, Trumps is a triumph of understatement. It is all muted "non-colors" and no frills — just clean lines and geometric shapes. Featured are such dishes as Chesapeake Bay oysters with cheese and caviar, fettucine and other pastas, and lamb chops with tarragon.

Reservations required
Lunch: Mon.–Fri., Noon–2:30 P.M.
Dinner: Mon.–Sat., 6:30 P.M.–11:30 P.M.
Tea: Mon.–Fri., 4 P.M.–6 P.M.
    Closed Sunday

VALENTINO ㊳ Italian

3115 Pico Blvd.
Santa Monica, Calif.
(213) 829-4313
Maître d': Antonio Battaglia
Full Bar/Valet Parking
AE, D, MC, V, CB
Good taste in dress required

The unusual in Italian cooking is Valentino's specialty. The chef likes to be creative with quail, rabbit and pheasant, for example. As for pasta, he complements tortellini with walnut sauce and gnocchetti with artichoke sauce. One can't forget to mention the Buffalo Mozzarella. The wine list numbers over 1,000 different labels.

Reservations required
Lunch: Fri., Noon–2:30 P.M.
Dinner: Mon.–Sat., 5 P.M.–11:30 P.M.
    Closed Sunday

VERITA'S LA CANTINA ㉓ Mexican

10323 Santa Monica Blvd.
Los Angeles
(213) 277-3362
Maître d': Milo Korac
Full Bar/Valet and Lot Parking
AE, D, MC, V, CB
Jacket for men

Mexican food you may never have tried before is offered at Verita's. Owner Verita Thompson terms her cooking "gourmet Mexican" — and it is unusual. There is game hen stuffed with cactus dressing, for instance, and sea bass baked in a corn husk along with corn peppers and chiles. Mariachis play in the background.

Reservations required
Lunch: Mon.–Sat., 11 A.M.–3 P.M.
Dinner: Mon.–Sat., 5 P.M.–11 P.M.
    Closed Sunday

THE WINDSOR 🔟   *Continental*

3198 W. Seventh St.
Los Angeles
(213) 382-1261
Full Bar/Valet Parking
AE, D, MC, V, CB (and House Accts.)
Jacket for men

The Windsor has been serving diners in the downtown area for the past 30 years. Special features include beef tournedos and tenderloin of beef piqué as well as several chicken and seafood entrées.

Reservations required
Lunch/Dinner: Mon–Fri., 11:30 A.M.–Midnight
             Sat., 4:30 P.M.–Midnight
             Closed Sunday

YAMASHIRO 🔟   *Japanese*

1999 N. Sycamore
Los Angeles
(213) 466-5125
Maître d': Ben
Full Bar/Valet Parking
MC, V
Good taste in dress required

"Japanese Continental" is how the management describes Yamashiro. That means the menu offers Tournedos Imperiale and filet mignon with crabs' legs, along with more traditional Japanese dishes such as tempura. Yamashiro is located in the Hollywood Hills, and on a clear day or night you are treated to a 30-mile panoramic view.

Reservations required
Lunch: Mon.–Fri., 11:30 A.M.–2:30 P.M.
Dinner: Mon.–Sat., 5 P.M.–11:30 P.M.
         Sun., 4:30 P.M.–11 P.M.
Brunch: Sun., 10:30 A.M.–2:30 P.M.

YAMATO 🔟   *Japanese*

Century Plaza Hotel
2025 Avenue of the Stars
Los Angeles
(213) 277-1840
Full Bar/Valet and Lot Parking
AE, D, MC, V, CB
Good taste in dress required

Yamato offers three different dining areas: a Western-style room (meaning chairs are included); the same menu served Japanese style in tatami tea rooms; and a room where chicken, steaks and vegetables are cooked before your eyes on teppans, or steak tables. There is also a sushi bar.

Reservations required
Lunch: Mon.–Fri., 11:30 A.M.–2:30 P.M.
Dinner: Mon.–Sat., 5 P.M.–11:30 P.M.
         Sun., 4:30 P.M.–11 P.M.

YELLOWFINGER'S CAFE ❷ ❻   *French*

15013 Ventura Blvd.   22616 Ventura Blvd.
Sherman Oaks, Calif. and   Woodland Hills, Calif.
(213) 990-1791   (213) 347-6711
Full Bar/Lot and Street Parking
MC, V
No dress restrictions

The salads are huge (enough for two) and filled with fresh ingredients. There is also onion soup, escargots and 20 different types of crêpes. The atmosphere is casual.

Reservations required
Lunch/Dinner: Mon.–Thurs., 11:30 A.M.–11:30 P.M.
              Fri.–Sat., 11:30 A.M.–1:30 A.M.
              Closed Sunday)

PALM SPRINGS
(no map locations indicated)

LA CAVE   *French*

70-064 Highway 111
Rancho Mirage, Calif.
(714) 324-4673
Full Bar/Valet Parking
AE, MC, V
Jacket, tie for men

An exclusive and refined enclave, La Cave presents different specialties daily depending upon the availability of fresh ingredients. Fresh fish is flown in daily. It is located along "Restaurant Row" in Rancho Mirage

Reservations required
Dinner: Daily, 6–7:30 P.M. and 9:30–10:30 P.M. seatings

LAS CASUELAS NEUVAS   *Mexican*

70-050 Highway 111
Rancho Mirage, Calif.
(714) 328-8844
Full Bar/Valet and Lot Parking
AE, MC, V
No dress restrictions

The management invites you to step into an authentic re-creation of colonial Mexico *and* to enjoy equally authentic Mexican cuisine in the Delgado family tradition. House specialties include Lobster Ensenada, Shrimp Guaymas, Burrito Ranchero and giant Margaritas.

No reservations required
Lunch/Dinner: Daily, 11:30 A.M.–Midnight
Brunch: Sun., 10 A.M.–3 P.M.

LE VALLAURIS *French*

385 W. Tahquitz McCallum
Palm Springs
(714) 325-5059
Full Bar/Valet Parking
MC, V
Good taste in dress required

It is an interesting contrast: feasting on French *haute cuisine* in the middle of the desert. At Club Le Vallauris you'll find such delicacies as quenelles, salmon in sorrel sauce, rabbit in red wine and a full selection of East Coast fish, flown in daily.

Reservations suggested
Lunch: Tues.-Sun., Noon-3 P.M.
Dinner: Tues.-Sun., 6 P.M.-11 P.M.
   Closed Monday

LORD FLETCHER INN *English*

70-385 Highway 111
Rancho Mirage, Calif.
(714) 328-1161
Maître d': Jim Condon
Full Bar/Valet Parking
MC, V
No shorts

Patterned after an "Olde English" inn, Lord Fletcher's (the owner is W. H. Fletcher) features chicken dumplings, beef stew, pot roast, prime rib, prime steaks and roast pork. There are varying nightly specials.

Reservations required
Dinner: Mon.-Sat., 5 P.M.-10:30 P.M.
   Closed Sunday

MEDIUM RARE *American*

70-064 Highway 111
Rancho Mirage, Calif.
(714) 328-6563
Full Bar/Valet Parking
AE, MC, V
Good taste in dress required

As the name implies, this is a place for steaks and prime rib (you can order them any way you want), as well as seafood and Florida stone crab. It is also located along the restaurant strip portion of Highway 111.

Reservations suggested
Dinner: Daily, 5 P.M.-11 P.M.

MELVYN'S — Continental

Ingleside Inn
200 W. Ramon Rd.
Palm Springs
(714) 325-2323
Full Bar/Valet Parking
Major credit cards
Good taste in dress required

Melvyn's is an oasis in an oasis. It is a haven for Old World ambience and service. There are such dinner entrées as Escalope of Veal Ingleside, Steak Diane, Alaskan King Crab Melvyn and Poached Turbot Margery. Save room for French pastries for dessert. Champagne flows at brunch time.

Reservations suggested
Lunch: Mon.–Fri., Noon–3 P.M.
Dinner: Daily, 6 P.M.–Midnight
Brunch: Sat.–Sun., 9 A.M.–3 P.M.

WALLY'S DESERT TURTLE — Continental

71775 Highway 111
Rancho Mirage, Calif.
(714) 568-9321
Full Bar/Valet Parking
AE, MC, V
Jacket for men

Wally's presents dining in the main room and on the terrace. The à la carte menu includes medallions of veal, Veal Marsala, frogs' legs, bay scallops, Sole Amandine and rack of lamb. For dessert, there is Grand Marnier Soufflé and chocolate or strawberry crêpes.

Reservations required
Dinner: Tues.–Sun., 6 P.M.–11 P.M.
Closed Monday
Closed July and August

MIAMI

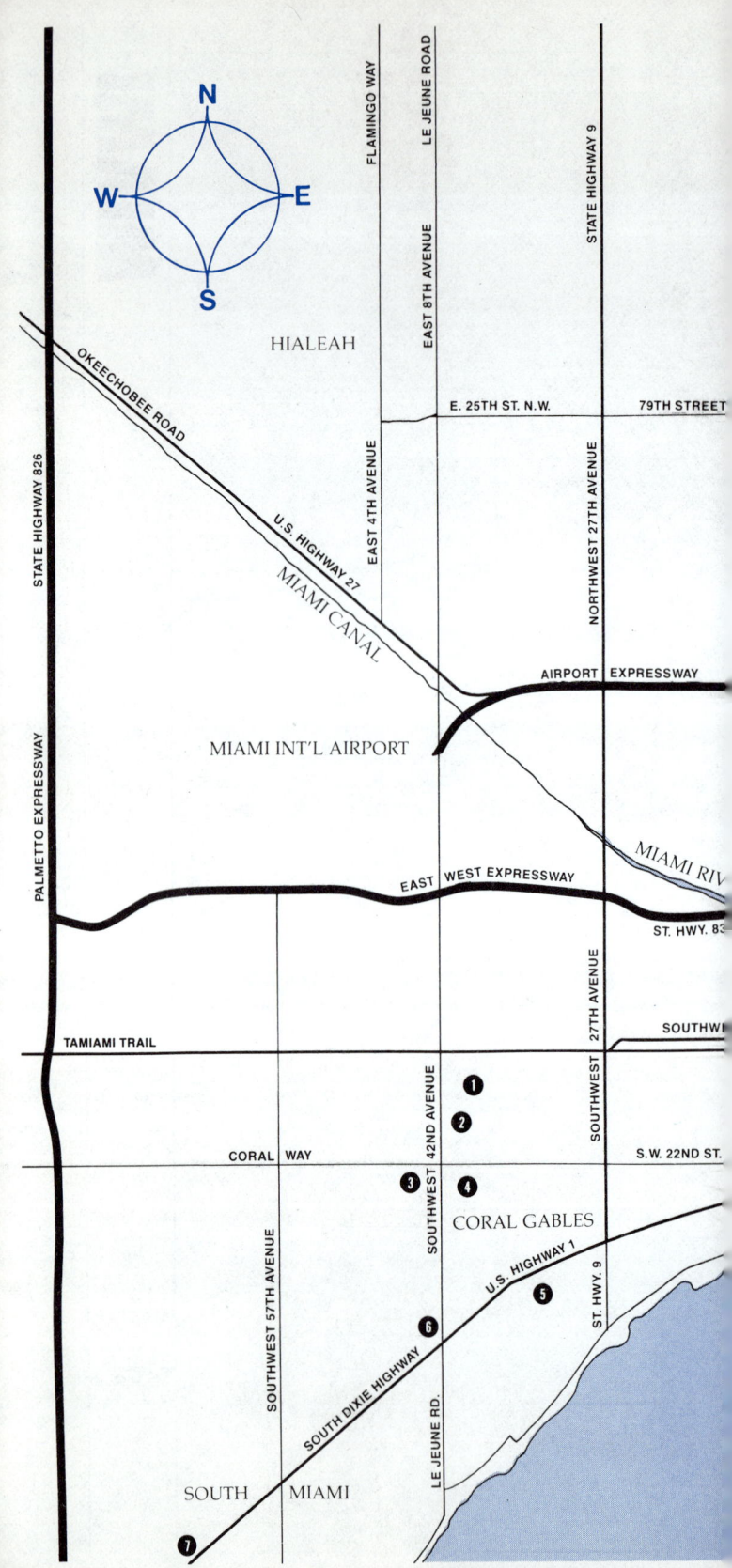

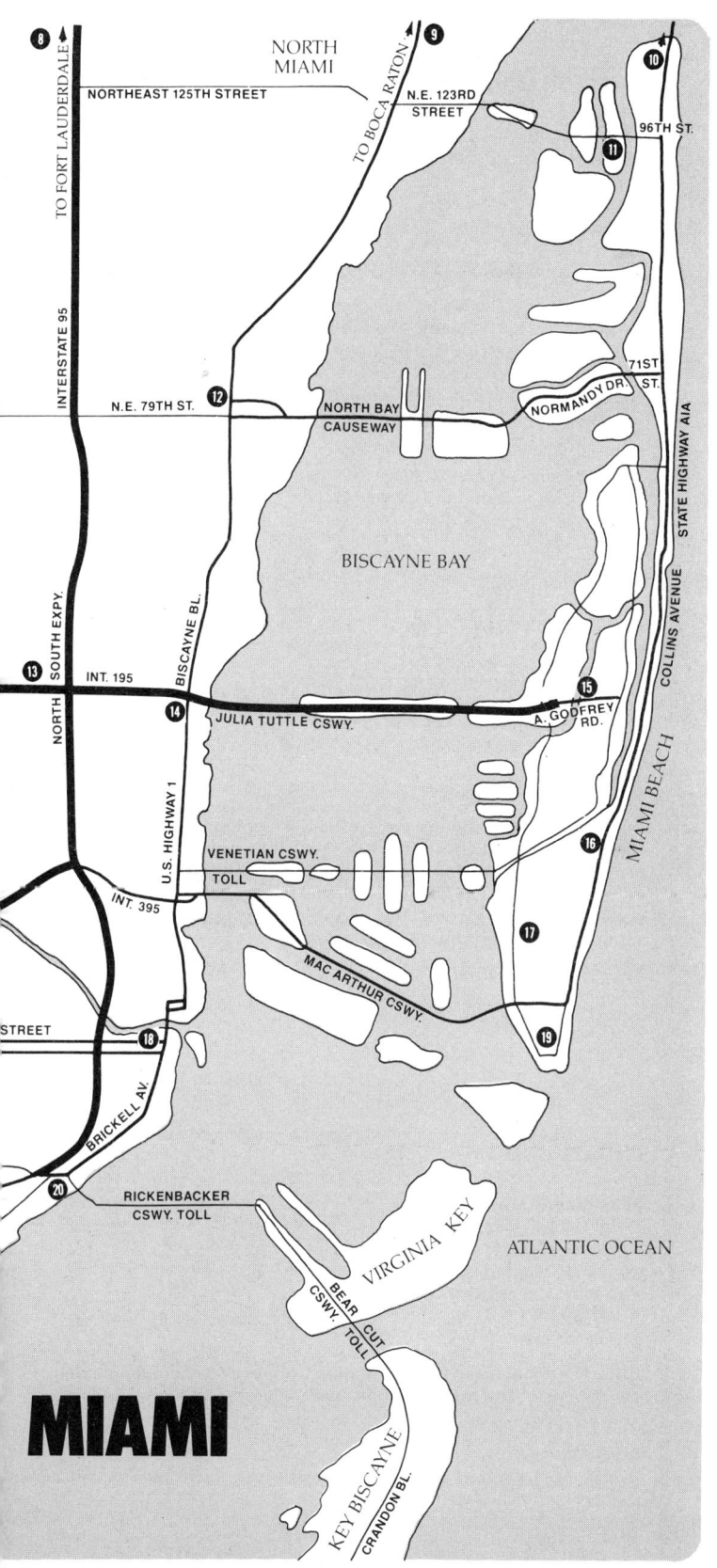

CAFE CHAUVERON ⓫   *French*

9561 E. Bay Harbor Dr.
Bay Harbor Islands, Fla.
(305) 866-8779
Maître d': Jean Machon
Full Bar/Valet Parking
AE, D, MC, V, CB
Jacket, tie for men

Haute cuisine Escoffier would deem "merveilleuse" is the aim of restaurateur Curtis Blank. Nestled in a quiet inlet of Biscayne Bay, Cafe Chauveron is a place of "impeccable service and elegant but subdued surroundings." There are such cooked-to-order specialties as veal kidneys in white wine, Dover Sole, Carré d'Agneau and Bouillabaisse à la Marseillaise.

Reservations required
Dinner: Daily, 5:30 P.M. – 10:30 P.M.
      Closed June 1 to October 15

CASA VECCHIA ❽   *Northern Italian*

209 N. Birch Rd.
Fort Lauderdale, Fla.
(305) 463-7575 (947-8944 Dade County)
Full Bar/Valet Parking
AE, D, MC, V
Jacket for men preferred

"All our menu selections are specialties," comments the staff at Casa Vecchia. "The chef puts a lot of time into everything he makes." That includes several intriguing veal dishes and pasta made fresh every evening. The subtle seasonings are from herbs grown in the restaurant's own garden. You dine overlooking the intercoastal waterway and surrounded by gardens.

Reservations required
Dinner: Sun. – Thurs., 6 P.M. – 10 P.M.
      Fri. – Sat., 6 P.M. – 10:30 P.M.

CHEZ VENDOME ❸   *French*

700 Biltmore Way
Coral Gables, Fla.
(305) 443-4646
Maître d': Flemming
Full Bar/Valet and Street Parking
AE, D, MC, V, CB
Jacket for men

Chez Vendôme means formal dining in red velvet Napoleonic decor. The extensive menu includes rack of lamb, Veal Françoise and Sole Véronique.

Reservations required
Lunch: Mon. – Sat., 11:30 A.M. – 3 P.M.
Dinner: Daily, 5:30 P.M. – 11 P.M.

CHRISTINE LEE'S GASLIGHT ❽ ❿   *Chinese*

18401 Collins Ave.
Miami Beach, Fla. and
(305) 931-7700
Full Bar/ Valet Parking
AE, D, MC, V
Jacket for men preferred

6191 Rock Island Rd.
Fort Lauderdale, Fla.
(305) 726-0430

The interior of Christine Lee's is filled with Chinese artifacts and the kitchens are filled with the simmering specialties of the Cantonese, Mandarin and Szechuan cuisines. Lobster, chicken, shrimp, pork, duck and Chinese vegetables are prepared at your table on a sizzling cooking cart.

Reservations suggested
Dinner: Daily, 5 P.M.–11 P.M.

CLUB 41 ⓯   *French*

432 Arthur Godfrey Rd.
Miami Beach
(Unlisted number)
Full Bar/Valet Parking
AE, D, MC, V
Jacket for men

Nouvelle cuisine for the very *haute* is Club 41's mission. Under the supervision of food expert Marina Polvay, this exclusive enclave, done up in velvet and earth tones, boasts an outstanding menu and extensive wine list. Definitely for those who crave privacy and intimacy while in Miami Beach.

Reservations required
Dinner: Mon.–Sat.
    Closed June 1 to October 15

CYE'S RIVERGATE ⓲   *American*

444 Brickell Ave.
Miami
(305) 358-9100
Maître d': James
Full Bar/Valet and Lot Parking
AE, D, MC, V
Good taste in dress required

Cyé's offerings are simple yet direct: Maine lobsters, prime steaks, local fresh fish and specially prepared duck and chicken.

Reservations required
Lunch: Mon.–Sat., 11:30 A.M.–4 P.M.
Dinner: Mon.–Fri., 6 P.M.–1 A.M.
    Sat., 6 P.M.–2 A.M.
    Closed Sunday

THE DEPOT ❼   *American*

5830 S. Dixie Highway
Miami
(305) 665-6261
Maître d': Catherine Myers
Full Bar/Valet Parking
AE, D, MC, V
No dress restrictions

The Depot is a meticulous re-creation of Miami's historic Larkin Train Station. Dinner is served "aboard" an 85-year-old dining coach or at glass-topped tables encasing fully operating model trains. Train fare includes prime aged beef, veal, baby back ribs, giant prawns, stone crab and three- to five-pound Maine lobsters.

Reservations required
Dinner: Daily, 5 P.M.-2 A.M.
       Closed Monday during summer

THE DOWN UNDER ❽   *Continental*

3000 Oakland Park Blvd. East
Fort Lauderdale, Fla.
(305) 563-4123
Maître d': Lee Handley (lunch),
         Alfred Deutch (dinner)
Full Bar/Valet Parking
AE, V
No dress restrictions

The Down Under has variously been described as a rustic waterfront tavern, a bit of Old New York, a French bistro and a California cafe. "To us," says owner Leonce Picot, "it is a little of all these, reflecting our travel experiences and observations." The extensive menu is basically French, but has borrowed the best from other countries, other cuisines.

No reservations required
Lunch: Mon.-Fri., 11:30 A.M.-2 P.M.
Dinner: Daily, 6 P.M.-10:30 P.M.

EMBERS ⓰   *American*

245 22nd St.
Miami Beach
(305) 538-4345
Maître d': Louis Fabry
Full Bar/Valet Parking
AE, D, MC, V
Good taste in dress required

As Embers owner Walter Kaplan tells it, "Wisps of hickory smoke waft through the air as one approaches the open brick ovens and spits turning ribs, duck and chicken over open fires." Specialties include prime sirloin, red snapper, lobster tails and fresh stone crabs, among other things.

Reservations required
Dinner: Daily, 5:30 P.M.-11 P.M.

FOOD AMONG THE FLOWERS ⓴ *Continental*

21 N.E. 36th St.
Miami
(305) 576-0000
Full Bar/Valet Parking
AE, V, MC
No dress restrictions

There *are* flowers just about everywhere...and native plants...and fountains...and statues...and a feeling of Old Florida, of Southern tropical elegance. Somehow the chefs are Danish, but it all seems to fit. Look for international specialties emphasizing veal, lamb and fish.

Reservations required
Lunch: Mon.–Sat., 11:30 A.M.–4 P.M.
Dinner: Mon.–Sat., 6:30 P.M.–10:30 P.M.
      Closed Sunday

THE FORGE ⓯ *American*

432 Arthur Godfrey Rd.
Miami Beach
(305) 538-8533
Maître d': Philip
Full Bar/Valet Parking
AE, D, MC, V, CB
Good taste in dress required

A night spot that stays open long enough to become an early-morning spot, The Forge features prime rib, steaks, stone crabs and a wine list of more than 1,000 labels. The Art Nouveau interior is filled with authentic antiques, paintings and murals.

Reservations required
Dinner: Daily, 6 P.M.–2:30 A.M.

GATTI ⓱ *Northern Italian/Continental*

1427 West Ave.
Miami Beach, Fla.
(305) 673-1717
Maître d': Joseph Gatti (owner)
Full Bar/Valet Parking
AE, D, MC, V
Jacket for men

Under the same family management for a number of years, Gatti concentrates on the cuisine of Northern Italy, but also presents interesting preparations of local seafood, steaks, chops and stone crabs.

No reservations required
Dinner: Tues.–Sun., 5:30 P.M.–10:30 P.M.
      Closed Monday

MIAMI 223

JOE'S STONE CRAB ⑲   *Seafood*

227 Biscayne St.
Miami Beach
(305) 673-0365
Maître d': Roy Garret
Full Bar/Valet Parking
AE, D, MC, V
Good taste in dress required

Something of a legend in Miami Beach, Joe's is the area's oldest established "eating house." Their specialties are famous: stone crabs, of course, plus clam chowder, pompano, mackerel, cole slaw, hash browns, cottage-fried sweet potatoes and the quintessential key lime pie.

No reservations required
Lunch: Mon.–Fri., 11:30 A.M.–2 P.M.
Dinner: Daily, 5 P.M.–10 P.M.
    Closed May 15 to October 15

KALEIDOSCOPE ⑤   *Continental*

3112 Commodore Plaza
Coconut Grove, Fla.
(305) 446-5010
Beer and Wine/Lot and Street Parking
MC, V
No dress restrictions

Located in an older section of Coconut Grove, Kaleidoscope is situated among a modern complex of stores and galleries. Dining is intimate, both indoors and out. There are specialties such as Crêpe Mallorca, Pork Tenderloin, Tournedos Marchand de Vin and Duckling Bigarade.

Reservations required (dinner)
Lunch: Mon.–Sat., 11:30 A.M.–3 P.M.
Dinner: Sun.–Thurs., 6 P.M.–11 P.M.
    Fri.–Sat., 6 P.M.–Midnight

LA VIEILLE MAISON ⑨   *French*

770 E. Palmetto Park Rd.
Boca Raton, Fla.
(305) 391-6701
Full Bar/Valet Parking
AE, MC, V
Jacket for men

This "old house" of the 1920's is now home to a restaurant featuring both classic and *nouvelle* French cuisine. There are several dining areas, including a Spanish-style courtyard. The prix fixe dinners feature such items as Ris de Veau aux Trois Champignons, Caille aux Raisins and Terrine de Truite Trufée.

Reservations required
Dinner: Dinner, 6 P.M.–10 P.M.

LE CORDON BLEU ⓴   *French*

1201 N. Federal Highway
Dania, Fla.
(305) 922-3519
Full Bar/Valet Parking
AE, D, MC, V
Jacket for men

Located on one of the nation's busiest thoroughfares, Le Cordon Bleu might as well be in the French provinces. Items such as Sole Albert, boneless chicken breast with raspberry sauce, cheese soufflé and chocolate mousse are served in a rambling white frame home filled with flowers, mirrors and knickknacks, and illuminated by candlelight.

Reservations required
Dinner: Daily, 5:30 P.M.-11 P.M.
      Closed May 1 to November 1

LE DOME OF THE FOUR SEASONS ⑧   *Continental*

333 Sunset Dr.
Fort Lauderdale, Fla.
(305) 463-3303
Maître d': Chris Donnelly (asst. manager)
Full Bar/ Valet Parking
AE, D, MC, V
Jacket for men

Le Dôme offers picturesque dining and tableside cooking. You can enjoy a variety of fresh fish, plus veal, rack of lamb and chateaubriand as you gaze across the Intercoastal Waterway to the ocean.

Reservations required
Dinner: Daily, October-May, 5 P.M.-10 P.M.
      Closed Sunday, June-September

LE FESTIVAL ②   *French*

2120 Salzedo St.
Coral Gables, Fla.
(305) 442-8545
Maître d': Jacques Baudean (owner)
Beer and Wine/Street Parking
AE, MC, V
No dress restrictions

Typically French, with a simple decor of striped walls, banquettes, white tablecloths and fresh flowers on every table, Le Festival presents fresh red snapper prepared differently every night. There is also Chicken Normande served with wine sauce, mushrooms and apples. Owner Baudean says the desserts "are enough to break anyone's diet."

No reservations required
Lunch: Mon.-Fri., 11:45 A.M.-2:30 P.M.
Dinner: Mon.-Sat., 6 P.M.-10:30 P.M.
      Closed Sunday

LE PARISIEN ⑬ *French*

474 41st St.
Miami Beach
(305) 534-2770
Beer and Wine/Street Parking
AE, D, MC, V
Jacket for men

Away from the glitter that is Miami Beach is the quiet intimacy that is Le Parisien. Here you'll also find Dover Sole Marguery, Duckling Montmorency, Sweetbreads Florentine and Shrimp Remoulade. For dessert, there is Coupe de Marrons — vanilla ice cream topped with candied chestnuts and real whipped cream.

Reservations required
Dinner: Daily, 6 P.M. – 10:30 P.M.
Closed Sunday during summer months

LES TROIS MOUSQUETAIRES ⑧ *French*

2447 E. Sunrise Blvd.
Fort Lauderdale, Fla.
(305) 564-7513
Maître d': Louis Rubeau, André Laborie (co-owners)
Beer and Wine/Valet Parking
AE, D, MC, V
No dress restrictions

"This unpretentious but comfortably charming restaurant is limited in capacity so as to best individualize preparation and service," says chef Jacky Samain. The chef calls the salmon mousse, Duckling and Chicken des Mosquetaires, Veal Normande and several desserts "fastidious and thoroughly beguiling."

Reservations required
Lunch: Mon. – Sat., Noon – 2:30 P.M.
Dinner: Mon. – Sat., 6 P.M. – 10:30 P.M.
Closed Sunday

NEW RIVER STOREHOUSE ⑧ *Caribbean*

Marina Bay Club
2175 State Road 84
Fort Lauderdale, Fla.
(305) 791-7600
Maître d': Jean Philip (co-owner)
Full Bar/Valet and Lot Parking
AE, D, MC, V
Good taste in dress required

A restaurant that bills itself as "friendly Floridian" and "excitingly tropical," the New River Storehouse overlooks a floating hotel and a luxury marina. Alligator (cooked) is listed among the entrées, as are prime ribs, Bahamian Chicken and lots of fresh fish. Hot homemade breads, including the special coconut bread, are also featured.

No reservations required
Dinner: Daily, 5:30 P.M. – 11 P.M.

THE PLUM ROOM ❽   *French*

3001 E. Oakland Park Blvd.
Fort Lauderdale, Fla.
(305) 561-4400
Maître d': Michael d'Agnese
Full Bar/Valet Parking
AE, MC, V
Jacket for men

Cooking in the classic French style is the goal of The Plum Room. The chef uses his imagination and his talents in the preparation of pheasant, quail, partridge, elk and buffalo. There is also a standard French menu for the tamer appetite.

Reservations required
Dinner: Mon.–Sat., 7 P.M.–Midnight
       Closed Sunday

PRINCE HAMLET ⓬   *Danish*

8301 Biscayne Blvd.
Miami
(305) 754-4400
Maître d': Robert Kyrimes,
       Michael Williams, Victor Zepka
Full Bar/Valet Parking
AE
No dress restrictions

There are two worlds of dining at Prince Hamlet: an outdoor gazebo in a garden and a rustic antique-filled interior. The traditional Danish fare includes a *koldtbord* of caviar, herring and a variety of smoked fish. There are entrées such as Veal Oskar, Danish Lobster Tails and Duck Danolse.

Reservations required
Lunch: Mon.–Fri., 11:30 A.M.–2:30 P.M.
Dinner: Daily, 5:30 P.M.–10 P.M.
Brunch: Sun., 11:30 A.M.–2 P.M.

RAIMONDO'S ❻   *Italian*

4612 Le Jeune Rd.
Coral Gables, Fla.
(305) 666-9919
Beer and Wine/Valet Parking
No credit cards
No dress restrictions

Creativity and flair are two of Raimondo's principle attributes. They are put to work in such specialties as Pompano en Papillote, veal chops with cepes and morrels, Zuppa di Pesce alla Peppino, Spaghetti Carbonara, Fettucine Alfredo and Veal Dante, plus several blackboard specials. Advance notice is required for very special dishes.

Reeervations required
Dinner: Daily, 6 P.M.–11 P.M.

VINTON'S ❶   *Continental*

La Palma Hotel
116 Alhambra Circle
Coral Gables, Fla.
(305) 445-2511
Beer and Wine/Lot and Street Parking
AE, MC, V
No dress restrictions

Vinton's is a family affair with owners Hans and Susan Eichmann seeing to the comfort and well-being of their loyal and mostly local patrons. Their brothers Rene and Jim are in the kitchen preparing the likes of Filet Wellington, Steak au Poivre, Veal Casimir, Lobster à la Vinton and Duck à l'Orange.

Reservations required
Lunch/Dinner: Mon.–Thurs., 11 A.M.–Midnight
                    Fri.–Sat., 11:30 A.M.–1 A.M.
                    Closed Sunday

WHIFFENPOOF ❹   *Continental*

2728 Ponce de Leon Blvd.
Coral Gables, Fla.
(305) 445-6603
Maître d': Robert Guerin (owner)
Full Bar/Street Parking
AE, MC, V
No dress restrictions

"Whiffenpoof radiates a high Victorian luxury," claims the management. They refer to the high-backed red velvet chairs, the stained glass arches and muted lighting. Appetizers include marinated salmon and Crêpe Whiffenpoof, and there are such entrées as Snapper Caprice (with thin banana slices), Veal Scallops Suissesse and Filet Napoleon.

Reservations suggested
Lunch: Tues.–Fri., 11:30 A.M.–2:30 P.M.
Dinner: Daily, 6 P.M.–11 P.M.
            Closed August 15 to September 15

MINNEAPOLIS/ST. PAUL

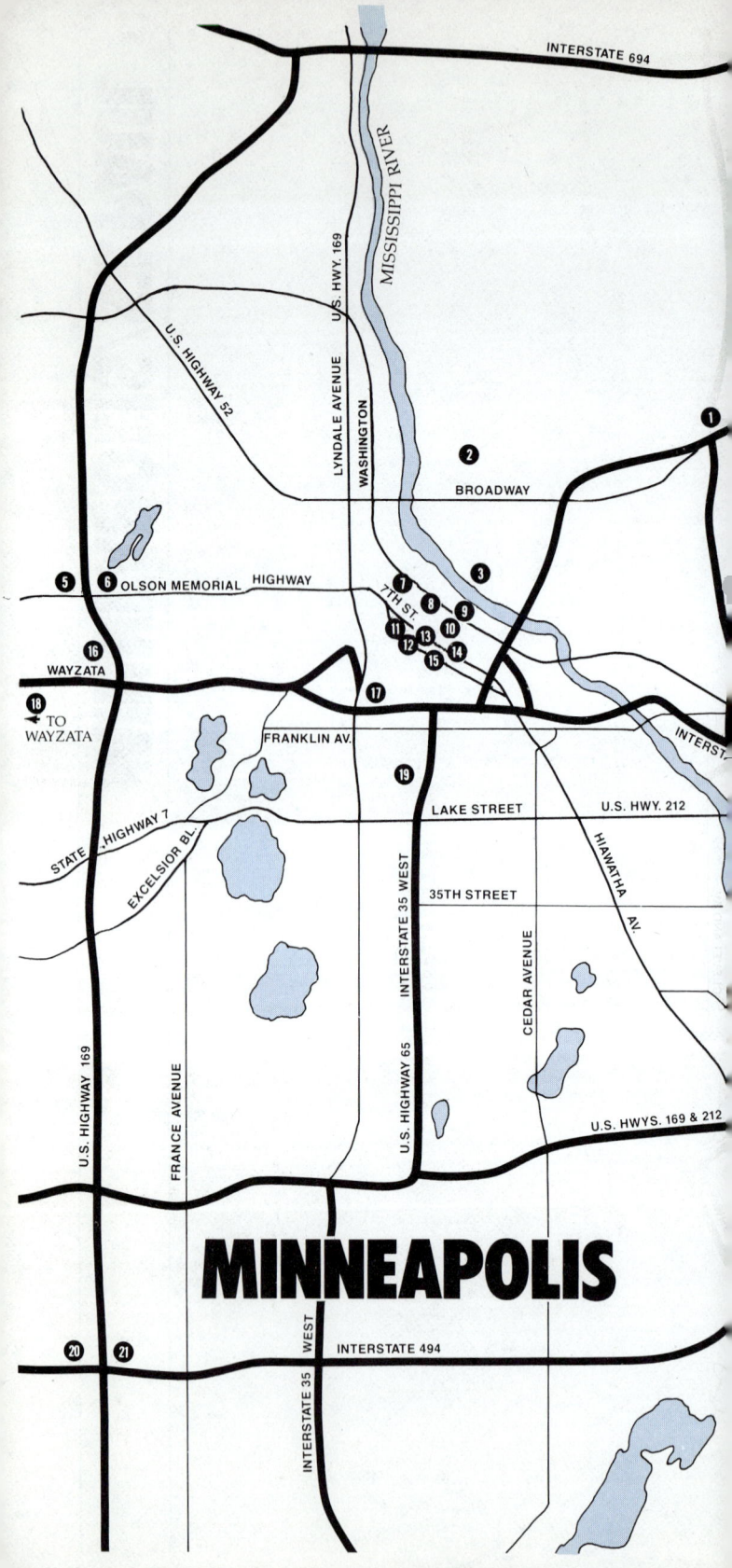

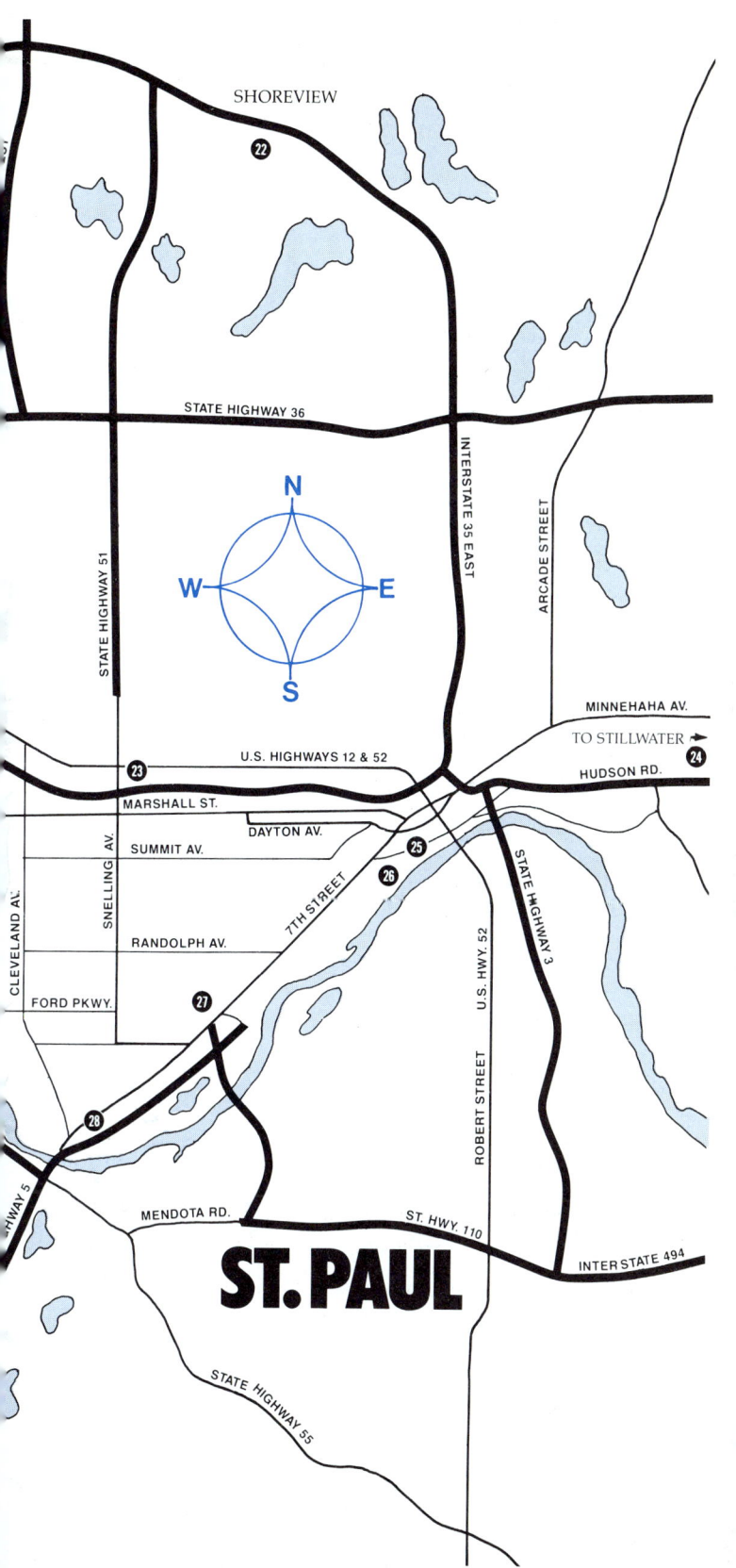

THE ANCHORAGE ❶ *Seafood*

1330 Industrial Blvd.
Minneapolis
(612) 379-4444
Full Bar/Lot Parking
AE, D, MC, V, CP
No dress restrictions

As you might expect, The Anchorage features a nautical decor with an emphasis on gleaming brass. Daily seafood specials are flown in from their place of origin. Menu selections include abalone from California and lobster from Maine. Desserts include Mocha Kahlua Pie and Amaretto Cream Pie.

Reservations required (lunch and dinner)
Breakfast: Daily, 6:30 A.M.–11:30 A.M.
Lunch: Mon.–Sat., 11:30 A.M.–2:30 P.M.
Dinner: Mon.–Sat., 5:30 P.M.–10:30 P.M.
             Sun., 4:30 P.M.–10 P.M.
Brunch: Sun., 11:30 A.M.–2:30 P.M.

BLACK FOREST INN ⓘ *German*

1 E. 26th St.
Minneapolis
(612) 872-0812
Maître d': Erich R. and Joanne B. Christ (owners)
Full Bar/Lot and Street Parking
AE, D, MC, V, CB
No dress restrictions

Owner Erich Christ suggests his menu is "ambitious." He includes schweinebraten, Gefuelte Krautrolle, Kalbnaxe Buergerlich and rouladen. Meals are prepared "from scratch" according to "recognized Old World recipes."

No reservations required
Lunch/Dinner: Mon.–Sat., 11 A.M.–1 A.M.
                Sun., Noon–Midnight

THE BLUE HORSE ㉓ *International*

1355 University Ave.
St. Paul
(612) 645d8101
Maître d': John M. Warling (manager)
Full Bar/Valet and Street Parking
AE, D, MC, V, CB
Jacket for men

If The Blue Horse can call seating for 125 people "intimate," you know they must be an establishment that tries harder than most. The international menu lists entrées from France, England, America and Italy. There is Puget Sound salmon, Filet of Beef Perigourdine, fettucine and linguine with clam sauce and Dungeness crab.

Reservations required
Lunch/Dinner: Mon.–Fri., 11 A.M.–1 A.M.
                Sat., 4 P.M.–1 A.M.
                Closed Sunday, Major Holidays

CAMELOT ㉑   *Continental*

5300 W. 78th St.
Bloomington, Minn.
(612) 835-2455
Maître d': John
Full Bar/Valet and Lot Parking
AE, D, MC, V, CB
No dress restrictions

The mythical abode of Arthur and Guinevere has been transported to this Minneapolis suburb, with tower, moat and drawbridge intact. This Medieval-style stone castle is divided into several small intimate dining areas. Specialties include prime rib, duckling, Steak Diane and a variety of fresh fish.

Reservations suggested
Lunch: Mon.–Sat., 11:30 A.M.–2:30 P.M.
Dinner: Mon.–Sat., 6 P.M.–11 P.M.
       Closed Sunday, Holidays

CHARLIE'S CAFE EXCEPTIONALE ⓯   *American*

701 Fourth Ave. South
Minneapolis
(612) 335-8851
Maître d': Henry Bathke
Full Bar/Valet Parking
AE, D, MC, V, CB
Jacket for men

Charlie's has been synonymous with Minneapolis dining for years and years. Of English Tudor design, with four dining rooms and three banquet rooms, it is a place for roast peppered rib eye of beef, Pompano en Papillote, Chicken Kiev and flaming desserts.

Reservations recommended
Lunch/Dinner: Mon.–Thurs., 11:15 A.M.–Midnight
              Fri., 11:15 A.M.–1 A.M.
              Sat., 5:30 P.M.–1 A.M.
              Closed Sunday

CHEZ COLETTE ⓴   *French*

L'hotel de France
5601 W. 78th St.
Bloomington, Minn.
(612) 835-1900
Full Bar/Valet and Street Parking
AE, D, MC, V
No dress restrictions

Named in honor of the French romantic novelist, Chez Colette proclaims itself "an authentic brasserie" and, as such, typical of the *joie de vivre* found in the Paris of the early 1900's. There are marble tables, beveled glass and brass trimmings. Specialties include bouillabaisse, pot-au-feu, charcuterie and, for breakfast, homemade croissants and café au lait.

No reservations required
Breakfast: Mon.–Fri., from 6:30 A.M.
             Sat.–Sun., from 7 A.M.
  Lunch: Daily, from 11:30 A.M.
  Dinner: Daily, from 5:30 P.M.

CHOUETTE ⓲   *French*

739 E. Lake St.
Wayzata, Minn.
(612) 473-4611
Maître d': John Day
Full Bar/Lot and Street Parking
AE, MC, V
Jacket, tie for men

Chouette brings "the exquisite charm of provincial France" to the shores of Lake Minnetonka, claims its owner, Jolley F. White. Look for such specialties as river trout in wine, crab and artichoke hearts and Veal Florentine. Desserts such as Grand Marnier Soufflé are presented on an antique five-tiered trolley.

Reservations required
Lunch: Mon.–Sat., 11:30 A.M.–2:30 P.M.
Dinner: Mon.–Sat., 6 P.M.–10 P.M.
Brunch: Sun., 11:30 A.M.–2:30 P.M. *(summer only)*

THE 510 HAUTE CUISINE ⓱   *Continental*

510 Groveland Ave.
Minneapolis
(612) 874-6440
Maître d': David Chamberlain
Beer and Wine/Valet, Lot and Street Parking
AE, V
No dress restrictions

The 510 offers a prix fixe, five-course dinner menu that changes daily and features at least four entrée selections. Some specialties are Veal Marsala, beef with capers and anchovies, rack of lamb, filet of sole and French-style pastries. There is a wine list of 100 labels.

Reservations required
Lunch: Mon.–Fri., 11:30 A.M.–2:30 P.M.
Dinner: Mon.–Sat., 6 P.M.–10 P.M.
Supper: Mon.–Sat., 10:30 P.M.–Midnight
        Closed Sunday

THE FLAME ROOM ⓮   *Continental*

Radisson Hotel
45 S. 7th St.
Minneapolis
(612) 333-2181
Maître d': Ken Gripp
Full Bar/Lot Parking
AE, D, MC, V, CB
No dress restrictions

Along with the food, the star attraction at The Flame Room is the Golden Strings, a group of eight violinists, two pianists and a bassist. Playing back-up are Veal Oskar, filet of sole and Filet à la Gustaf. The Strings play two shows every Friday and Saturday night.

Reservations required
Lunch/Dinner: Mon.–Fri., 11:30 A.M.–1 A.M.
              Sat., 6 P.M.–1 A.M.
              Closed Sunday

FOREPAUGH'S ㉕　　　　　　　　　　　　*Continental*

276 S. Exchange St.
St. Paul
(612) 224-5606
Maître d': Tor Aasheim (manager), Dale Beckerman
Full Bar/Valet and Lot Parking
AE, MC, V, CB
Jacket, tie for men

The Forepaugh mansion was built in 1870. In 1976, a restaurant group decided to restore the house, preserving much of the original woodwork. The result is a place where one can once again dine in style on such items as Stuffed Mushrooms Florentine, "Hotch Potch" seafood and a variety of steaks, salads and omelets.

Reservations required
Lunch: *Daily, 11 A.M.–2:30 P.M.*
Dinner: *Mon.–Thurs., 6 P.M.–10 P.M.*
　　　　Fri.–Sat., 5 P.M.–11 P.M.
　　　　Sun., 5 P.M.–9 P.M.

FUJI-YA ⑨　　　　　　　　　　　　*Japanese*

420 S. First St.
Minneapolis
(612) 339-2226
Full Bar/Lot Parking
AE
No dress restrictions

Fuji-Ya, which means "second to none" in Japanese, is said to be the city's first Japanese restaurant. Specialties are sukiyaki, tempura and teriyaki.

Reservations recommended
Lunch: *Mon.–Sat., 11 A.M.–2:30 P.M.*
Dinner: *Mon.–Thurs., 5 P.M.–9 P.M.*
　　　　Fri., 5 P.M.–9:30 P.M.
　　　　Sat., 5 P.M.–10 P.M.
　　　　Closed Sunday

GANNON'S ㉘　　　　　　　　　　　　*American*

2728 Gannon Rd.
St. Paul
(612) 699-2420
Full Bar/Lot Parking
Gannon charge only
No dress restrictions

Gannon's has a motto: "Where people come by choice, not by chance." An established restaurant in St. Paul for the past 30 years, Gannon's practically has trademark rights on their steaks, walleyed pike and thick beef liver steak smothered in onions.

Reservations required
Lunch: *Mon.–Sat., 11:30 A.M.–3 P.M.*
Dinner: *Mon.–Sat., 3 P.M.–11:30 P.M.*
　　　　Closed Sunday

JAX CAFE ❷   *Seafood/American*

1928 University Ave., N.E.
Minneapolis
(612) 789-7297
Maître d': Thea Stay
Full Bar/Lot and Street Parking
AE, D, MC, V, CB
No dress restrictions

Bring a hearty appetite to Jax Cafe. They haul in catch from their own pond (when it isn't frozen over), and they'll offer you pan-fried rainbow trout, lobster, chicken dumplings, stew and tenderloin tips, plus walleyed pike from the cold waters of the Bordern Lakes. If things get too robust for you, there are a few Weight Watchers selections.

Reservations recommended
Lunch/Dinner: Mon.–Sat., 11 A.M.–1 A.M.
          Closed Sunday

JAX OF GOLDEN VALLEY ❺   *American*

604 N. Lilac Dr.
Golden Valley, Minn.
(612) 521-8825
Full Bar/Valet Parking
AE, D, MC, V, CB
No dress restrictions

Another place for substantial fare, Jax of Golden Valley presents Long Island Duckling, Chicken Kiev, pheasant under glass, plus steaks and seafood. The staff is particularly proud of the appetizers, desserts and "beautiful" wine list.

Reservations suggested
Lunch: *Mon.–Sat., 11 A.M.–4 P.M.*
Dinner: Daily, 5 P.M.–11:30 P.M.

KOZLAK'S ROYAL OAK ㉒   *American*

4785 Hodgson
Shoreview, Minn.
(612) 484-8484
Full Bar/Lot Parking
AE, D, MC, V, CB
No jeans

The two-level dining room at Kozlak's features elegantly set tables, palms, ample space, soft lights and tall arched windows that overlook a garden. Specialties include Maine lobster, filet mignon, the ever-present walleyed pike and sole. Brunch is New Orleans-style.

Reservations advised
Lunch/Dinner: Tues.–Thurs., 11 A.M.–10:30 P.M.
               Fri.–Sat., 11 A.M.–11:30 P.M.
               Sun., 5 P.M.–9 P.M.
Brunch: *Sun., 11:30 A.M.–2:30 P.M.*

LA TERRASSE ⑳   *French*

L'hotel de France
5601 W. 78th St.
Bloomington, Minn.
(612) 835-1900
Full Bar/Valet and Lot Parking
AE, D, MC, V
No dress restrictions

Modeled after a Parisian sidewalk cafe, La Terrasse bills itself as "a sophisticated 'drop-in' restaurant where you would stop for a drink, a bowl of French onion soup, a pastry or the plat du jour." If your evening ends at dawn, this is the place to go.

No reservations required
Lunch/Dinner: Daily, 11 A.M. – 6:30 A.M.

LE CAFE ROYAL ⑳   *French*

L'hotel de France
5601 W. 78th St.
Bloomington, Minn.
(612) 835-1900
Full Bar/Valet and Lot Parking
AE, D, MC, V
No dress restrictions

Le Cafe Royal is a place of classic cuisine and service, of gold-mirrored walls and elegant glitter. Half of the menu changes weekly while the other half is composed of dishes from the French region currently being featured by L'hotel de France for the month. The wine list is reputed to be outstanding.

Reservations recommended
Lunch: Mon. – Fri., 11:30 A.M. – 2 P.M.
Dinner: Mon. – Sat., from 6 P.M.
        Closed Sunday

LE CARROUSEL ㉖   *Continental*

Radisson St. Paul
11 E. Kellogg Blvd.
St. Paul
(612) 292-1900
Full Bar/Valet Parking
AE, D, MC, V, CB
Good taste in dress required

You can see the mighty Mississippi from 22 stories up as you dine on the likes of Steak Diane, Chicken Oskar, walleyed pike and duckling. There is a buffet at lunch, plus lots of sandwiches and omelets. The restaurant *does* revolve, for those into that sort of thing.

Reservations recommended
Lunch: Mon. – Fri., 11:30 A.M. – 2:30 P.M.
Dinner: Sun. – Thurs., 5:30 P.M. – 10:30 P.M.
         Fri. – Sat., 5:30 P.M. – 11:30 P.M.
Brunch: Sun., 10:30 A.M. – 2 P.M.

LEEANN CHIN ⓰   *Chinese*

1571 Plymouth Rd.
Minnetonka, Minn.
(612) 545-3600
Maître d': John Banks
Beer and Wine/Lot Parking
AE, D, MC, V
No dress restrictions

There is no menu at Leeann Chin. You serve yourself from a buffet consisting of shrimp toast, hot and sour soup, lemon chicken, stir-fried beef tenderloin with vegetables, and seafood with vegetables. The restaurant is filled with museum-quality Chinese artifacts.

Reservations required (dinner)
Lunch: Mon.–Sat., 11 A.M.–2:30 P.M.
Dinner: Mon.–Thurs., 5 P.M.–10 P.M.
        Fri.–Sat., 5 P.M.–11 P.M.
        Sun., 5 P.M.–9 P.M.

LES QUATRE AMIS ❼   *French*

Hennepin and 5th St. South
Minneapolis
(612) 332-9008
Maître d': Jack Goettl
Full Bar/Lot and Street Parking
AE, MC, V
Jacket for men preferred (dinner)

Les Quatre Amis owner Harriet Goettl is proud of the restaurant's master chef, Roger Mallet, who was trained in France.

Reservations required
Lunch: Daily, 11:30 A.M.–2:30 P.M.
Dinner: Daily, 5:30 P.M.–10:30 P.M.

THE LEXINGTON ㉗   *American*

1096 Grand Ave.
St. Paul
(612) 222-5878
Maître d': Don Ryan (manager)
Full Bar/Lot Parking
Lexington charge only
Jacket for men
No jeans or shorts

The main bar at The Lexington might remind you of an English pub; the main dining room may remind you of an English palace. House specialties are shrimp scampi, pheasant, walleyed pike, Caesar salad, steaks and prime rib.

Reservations required
Lunch/Dinner: Mon.–Sat., 11 A.M.–1 A.M.
              Closed Sunday

LOWELL INN ㉔   American/Swiss

102 N. 2nd St.
Stillwater, Minn.
(612) 439-1100
Full Bar/Lot Parking
AE, MC, V
Jacket, tie for men preferred
No jeans or shorts

The Lowell Inn offers three dining rooms, three different moods. The George Washington Room may bring to mind Colonial Williamsburg. The Garden Room serves the same American fare, but in a garden setting, complete with trout pond. Fondue — shrimp or beef — is served in the Matterhorn Room.

Reservations required
Breakfast: Daily, 8 A.M. - 10:30 A.M.
Lunch: Mon. - Sat., Noon - 2 P.M.
Dinner: Mon. - Thurs., 6 P.M. - 8:30 P.M.
*   Fri. - Sat., 6 P.M. - 10 P.M.*
*   Sun., Noon - 8 P.M.*

MARQUIS ⑫   French

Marquette Hotel
Marquette Ave. at IDS Center
Minneapolis
(612) 332-2351
Full Bar/Street Parking
AE, D, MC, V, CB
Jacket for men

Classic French cuisine is served at Marquis. The service is reputed to be attentive and the harp music is said to be sweet.

No reservations required
Lunch: Mon -Fri., 11:30 A.M. - 2 P.M.
Dinner: Mon.-Sat., 6 P.M. - 10:30 P.M.
*   Closed Sunday*

MUFFULETTA ❹   Northern Italian/Creole

2260 Como Ave.
St. Paul
(404) 644-9116
Beer and Wine/Street Parking
No credit cards
No dress restrictions

Muffuletta's small, intimate dining rooms have a light and airy feeling about them. The pasta is homemade and includes fettuccine and linguine with white clam sauce. Plus, there are dressy sandwiches, Shrimp Creole, poached salmon and lots of salads.

Reservations recommended
Lunch/Dinner: Mon. - Sat., 11 A.M. - 11 P.M.
Brunch: Sun., 10 A.M. - 2:30 P.M.

MURRAY'S ❽   *Continental*

26 S. 6th St.
Minneapolis
(612) 339-0909
Full Bar/Lot and Street Parking
AE, D, MC, V, CB
No dress restrictions

Home of the Silver Butter Knife Steak for two (it's touted to be just that tender), Murray's is also known for its Cocktail Luncheon in the afternoon and its Queen's Dinner in the early evening. It's a Forties-era atmosphere with music of that time (and ours) playing in the background.

Reservations required
Lunch/Dinner: Mon.–Sat., 11 A.M.–Midnight
            Closed Sunday

THE NEW FRENCH CAFE ❿   *French*

128 N. 4th St.
Minneapolis
(612) 338-3790
Maître d': Pamela Sherman (owner/chef)
Full Bar/Lot and Street Parking
AE, D, MC, V
No dress restrictions

Chef and owner Pamela Sherman calls The New French Cafe an "atypical Midwestern French restaurant." For one thing, it is located in a renovated warehouse. For another, the chef serves Continental breakfast beginning at 8 A.M. The à la carte dinner menu features selections with a *nouvelle cuisine* emphasis.

Reservations required (lunch and dinner)
Continental Breakfast: Tues.–Sat., 8 A.M.–11 A.M.
Lunch: Tues.–Sat., 11:30 A.M.–2:30 P.M.
Dinner: Tues.–Thurs., 6 P.M.–9 P.M.
                    Fri.–Sat., 6 P.M.–10 P.M.
Brunch: Sun., 10:30 A.M.–2:30 P.M.

ORION ROOM ⓫   *Continental*

80 S. 8th St.
Minneapolis
(612) 372-3772
Maître d': James Polk
Full Bar/Lot Parking
AE, D, MC, V, CB
Jacket, tie for men preferred

Located 50 stories above the city, the Orion Room specializes in many things besides a view. There is pheasant, Veal Marsala, chateaubriand, flambé desserts and a variety of coffees.

Reservations required
Lunch: Mon.-Fri., 11:30 A.M.–2 P.M.
Dinner: Mon.-Thurs., 6 P.M.–10 P.M.
        Fri.–Sat., 6 P.M.–10:30 P.M.
        Closed Sunday

ROSEWOOD ROOM ⑬   *Continental*

Northstar Inn Hotel
618 Second Ave. South
Minnneapolis
(612) 338-2288
Full Bar/Valet Parking
AE, D, MC, V, CB
Jacket for men (evenings)

Definitely a "dress-up" place, the Rosewood Room has candlelight, white linen, dark paneled walls and brass trim. House specialty is Marmite Dieppoise, an assortment of fish and shellfish steamed in white wine and creamed cooking stock, served over rice.

Reservations required
Lunch: Mon.-Fri., 11:30 A.M.-2 P.M.
Dinner: Daily, 6 P.M.-10 P.M.

TAIGA ❸   *Chinese*

201 Main St. S.E.
Minneapolis
(612) 331-1138
Full Bar/Lot Parking
AE
No dress restrictions

Taiga, on the banks of the Mississippi, is noted for its Mandarin, Szechuan and Cantonese cuisine. The decor is "sophisticated contemporary," according to owner Reiko Weston.

Reservations recommended
Lunch: Mon.-Fri., 11:30 A.M.-2:30 P.M.
Dinner: Sun.-Thurs., 5 P.M.-9:30 P.M.
       Fri.-Sat., 5 P.M.-10:30 P.M.

THE WHITE HOUSE ❻   *International*

4900 Olson Memorial Highway
Minneapolis
(612) 588-0111
Maître d': Victor Levine, Jr.
Full Bar/Valet and Lot Parking
AE, MC, V
No dress restrictions

The combination is an unusual one, but it seems to work. There is American food in all its glory, including prime beef and fresh seafood. Then there are complete Cantonese and Polynesian dinners. To top it off, The White House also offers Northern Italian specialties — eight imaginative selections nightly.

Reservations suggested
Lunch/Dinner: Mon.-Fri., 11 A.M.-11 P.M.
              Sat., 5 P.M.-Midnight
              Closed Sunday

THE WINE CELLAR ⑬ *Continental*

Northstar Inn Hotel
618 Second Ave. South
Minneapolis
(612) 338-2288, Ext. 325
Full Bar/Lot Parking
AE, D, MC, V, CB
Jacket for men

The Wine Cellar presents a five-course meal in a very intimate setting. (You dine amid oak casks and brick archways.) There is a choice of five entrées that emphasize *nouvelle cuisine*. The wine list is the big thing, and the staff will help you make just the right selection.

Reservations required
Dinner: Mon.–Sat., 6 P.M.–10:30 P.M.
   Closed Sunday

NEW ORLEANS

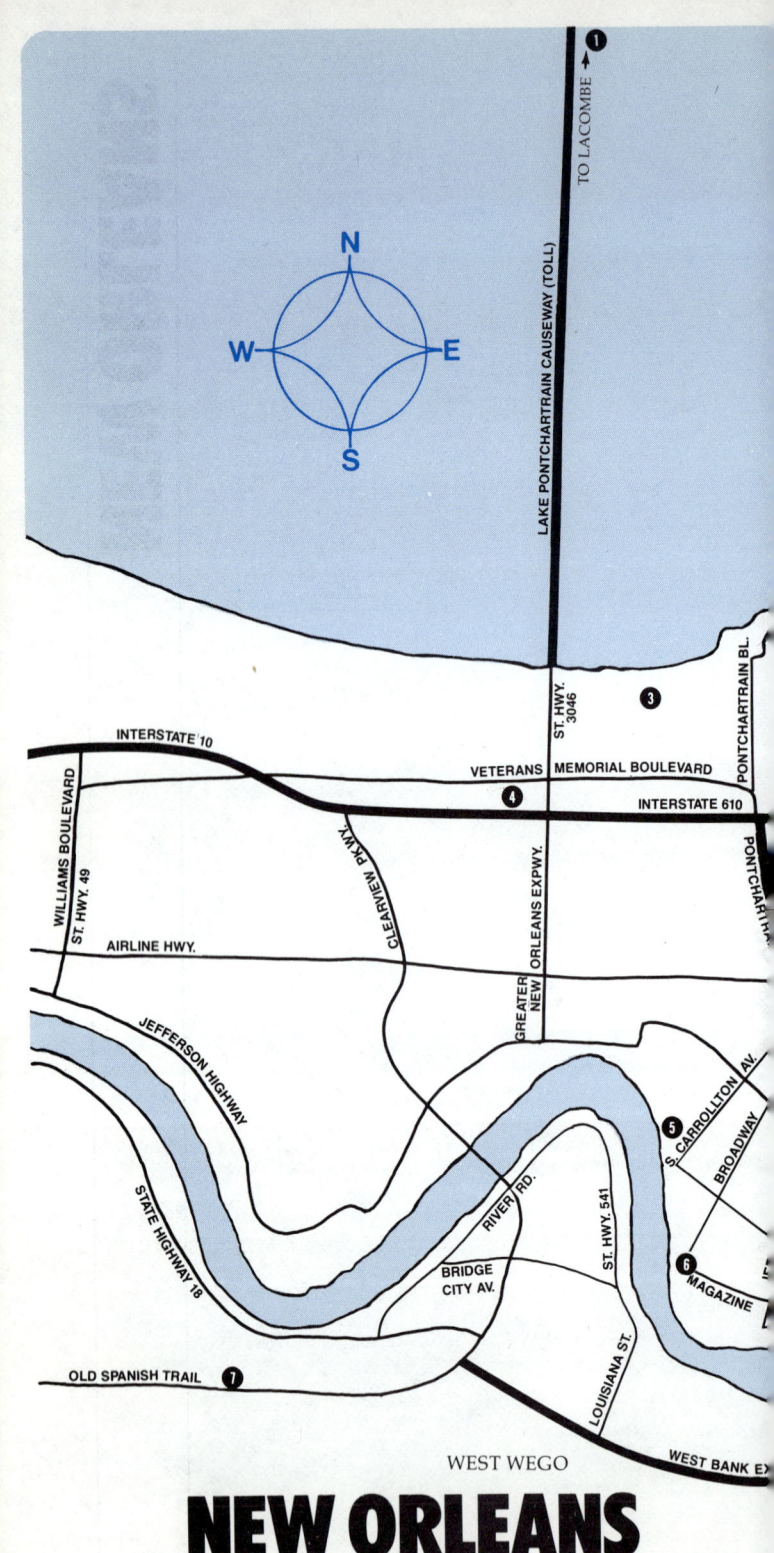

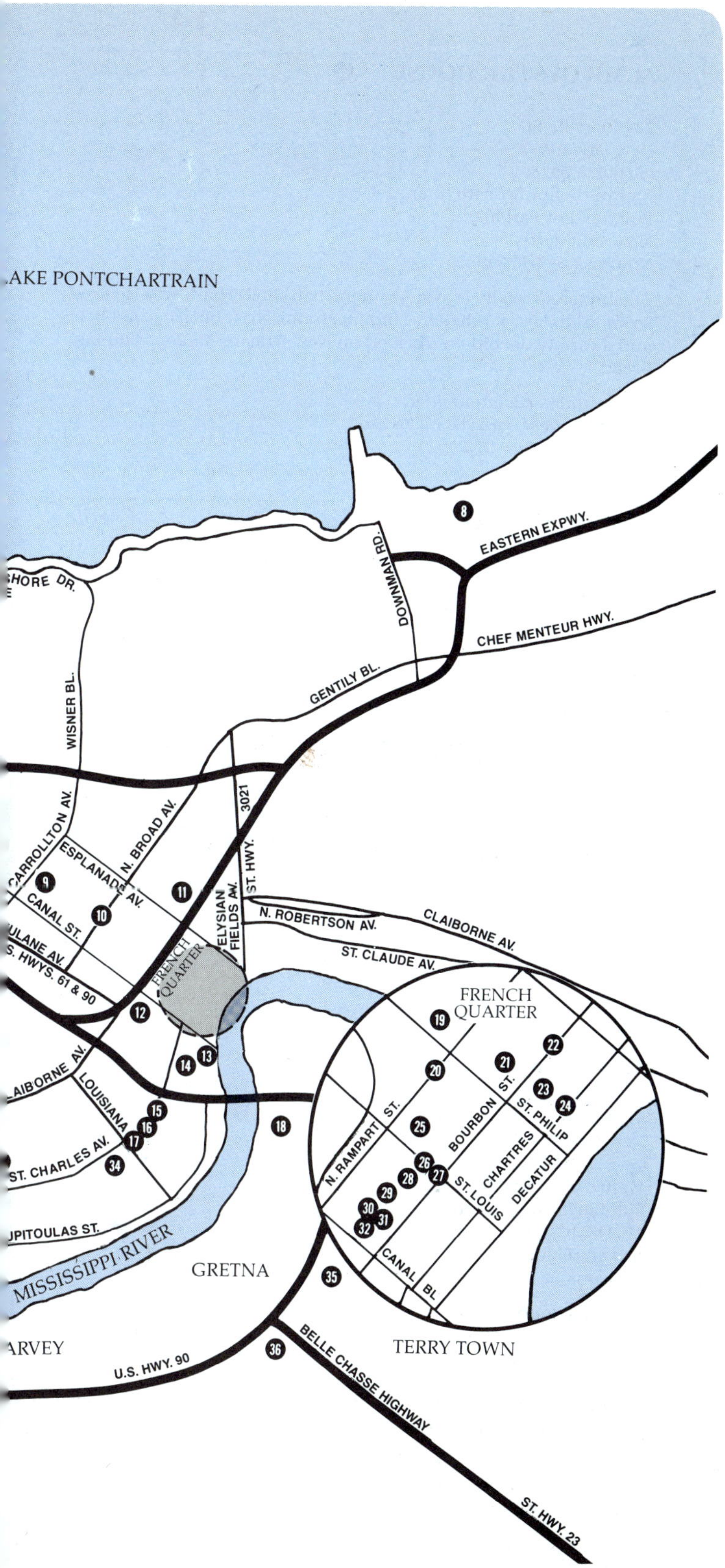
AKE PONTCHARTRAIN
8
EASTERN EXPWY.
SHORE DR.
DOWNMAN RD.
CHEF MENTEUR HWY.
GENTILY BL.
WISNER BL.
CARROLLTON AV.
N. BROAD AV.
3021
ST. HWY.
ESPLANADE AV.
9
10
11
CANAL ST.
ELYSIAN FIELDS AV.
N. ROBERTSON AV.
CLAIBORNE AV.
ST. CLAUDE AV.
ULANE AV.
S. HWYS. 61 & 90
FRENCH QUARTER
12
13
14
LAIBORNE AV.
LOUISIANA
15
16
17
ST. CHARLES AV.
34
18
UPITOULAS ST.
MISSISSIPPI RIVER
GRETNA
FRENCH QUARTER
19
20
21
22
23
24
25
26
27
28
29
30
31
32
N. RAMPART ST.
BOURBON ST.
ST. PHILIP
CHARTRES
DECATUR
ST. LOUIS
CANAL BL
35
36
ARVEY
TERRY TOWN
U.S. HWY. 90
BELLE CHASSE HIGHWAY
ST. HWY. 23

ACME OYSTER HOUSE ㉜   *Seafood*

724 Iberville St.
New Orleans
(504) 523-8928
Maître d': Jim Brocato (manager)
Full Bar/Lot Parking
No credit cards
No dress restrictions

The house specialty is oysters on the half shell. There are also fried seafood dishes, sandwiches, hot pastrami, roast beef, corned beef and a variety of cold cuts served on New Orleans' famous "po-boy" bread.

Reservations recommended
Lunch/Dinner: Daily, 11 A.M.–8 P.M.

ANTOINE'S ㉖   *Creole*

713-725 St. Louis St.
New Orleans
(504) 581-4422
Maître d': Henri Alciatore (manager)
Full Bar/Street Parking
AE, D
Jackets for men (evenings)

Antoine's is one of New Orleans' oldest and best-known restaurants. Established in 1840, it is presently in the hands of Roy Guste, Jr., a fifth-generation descendant of the original founding family. The French-Creole specialties include Oysters Rockefeller (invented here), Pompano en Papillote, Chicken Rochambeau and Lamb Noisettes Maison d'Or.

Reservations suggested
Lunch: Mon.–Sat., Noon–2 P.M.
Dinner: Mon.–Sat., 5:30 P.M.–9:30 P.M.
         Closed Sunday

ARNAUD'S ㉙   *Creole*

813 Rue Bienville
New Orleans
(504) 523-5433
Maître d': Louis Zalesjak
Full Bar/Street Parking
AE, D, MC, V, CB
Jacket, tie for men suggested
No jeans or shorts

Arnaud's, founded in 1918 by Count Arnaud Cazenave, has recently been restored to its original grandeur. Flickering gas lights illuminate the entry into the large Victorian-style main dining room. Smaller dining rooms surround it. Specialties include Shrimp Arnaud, Pompano en Croûte, Trout Meunière, Oysters Bienvielle and bread pudding for dessert.

Reservations requested
Lunch: Mon.–Fri., 11:30 A.M.–2:30 P.M.
Dinner: Daily, 6:30 P.M.–10:30 P.M.

BON TON CAFE ⓮   *Cajun*

401 Magazine St.
New Orleans
(504) 524-3386
Maître d': Wayne, Debbie and Alvin Pierce (owners)
Full Bar/Lot Parking
AE, V
No dress restrictions

Bon Ton is a restaurant "filled with the flavor of New Orleans in both its atmosphere and its food," state owners Wayne and Deborah Pierce. The simple elegance of old New Orleans brick walls and wrought iron chandeliers enhance the presentation of Cajun family recipes. Specialties include redfish, shrimp, crab meat and crawfish dishes.

Reservations required (evenings)
Lunch: Mon.–Fri., 11 A.M.–2 P.M.
Dinner: Mon.–Fri., 5 P.M.–9:30 P.M.
        Closed Saturday, Sunday

BRENNAN'S ㉓   *Creole*

417 Royal St.
New Orleans
(504) 525-9711
Maître d': David C. Wilson, Sr. (general manager)
Full Bar/Street Parking
AE, MC, V
Jacket, tie requested (evenings)

Brennan's is so well known for "Breakfast at Brennan's" (the Eggs Hussarde and Eggs Sardou, etc.) that manager David Wilson makes a point of emphasizing the dinner menu as well. There is a wide variety of local seafood entrées, plus dishes based upon veal, beef and fowl. Bananas Foster, a Brennan creation, is a popular dessert.

Reservations required
Breakfast/Lunch: Daily, 8 A.M.–2:30 P.M.
Dinner: *Daily, 6 P.M.–11 P.M.*
              Closed Christmas Eve, Christmas

BROUSSARD'S ㉘   *Creole*

819 Conti St.
New Orleans
(504) 581-3866
Maître d': Frank Manale
Full Bar/Street Parking
AE, D, MC, V, CB
Jacket for men

Located in the heart of the French Quarter, Broussard's, says co-owner S. Joseph Segreto, is "as much a delight to the eye as it is to the most discriminating palate." The chef's culinary art is revealed in such dishes as Pompano en Papillote, Duck Nouvelle Orleans and Veal Oskar.

Reservations suggested
Dinner: Daily, 5:30 P.M.– Midnight
        Closed Christmas, Mardi Gras (one day), Labor Day

CAMELLIA GRILL ❺   *American*

626 S. Carrollton Ave.
New Orleans
(504) 866-9573
No Wine or Spirits/Street Parking
No credit cards
No dress restrictions

The Camellia Grill is a "high quality, reasonably priced counter operation," says owner James Shwartz. There are a variety of sandwiches, fluffy omelets, freezes, pecan waffles, pecan pie, apple pie and cheesecake. Linen napkins are provided and waiters are in formal attire.

No reservations required
Breakfast/Lunch/Dinner: Daily, 9 A.M.–2 A.M.

CARIBBEAN ROOM ⓰   *Creole*

Pontchartain Hotel
2031 St. Charles Ave.
New Orleans
(504) 524-0581
Maître d': Douglas Lemar
Full Bar/Valet and Lot Parking
AE, D, MC, V, CB
Jacket for men

You might start with Crab Meat Remick or Biarritz for an appetizer, proceed to Trout Veronique or Eugene for a main course and finish with Strawberries Romanoff or Mile High Ice Cream Pie for dessert. You could also make stops along the way for Caesar salad or soft-shell Crabs Amandine. You'll find the Caribbean Room in the city's Garden District.

Reservations required
Lunch: Daily, Noon–2 P.M.
Dinner: Daily, 6 P.M.–10 P.M.

CASAMENTO'S ❻   *Creole*

4330 Magazine St.
New Orleans
(504) 895-9761
Beer and Wine/Street Parking
No credit cards
No dress restrictions

Noted not for its elegance but for its plentiful good food, Casamento's serves raw oysters on the half shell, a fried oyster loaf and oyster soup in an informal setting completely composed of tile — from counters to floors to walls.

No reservations required
Lunch: Tues.–Fri., 11:45 A.M.–1:30 P.M.
Dinner: Tues.–Sun., 5:30 P.M.–9 P.M.
    Closed Monday

CHEZ HELENE ⓫   *Soul/Creole*

1540 N. Robertson St.
New Orleans
(504) 947-9155
Maître d': Glenn Leslie
Full Bar/Street Parking
AE, MC, V
No dress restrictions

They say the chefs perform wide-ranging culinary miracles with old New Orleans family recipes in this small Soul and Creole restaurant. Owner Austin J. Leslie claims his Soul Gumbo has *the* authentic taste and texture. He also offers red beans and rice, fried chicken, stuffed bell peppers and bread pudding.

No reservations required
Lunch/Dinner: Tues.-Thurs., Sun., 11 A.M.-11 P.M.
            Mon., 11 A.M.-6 P.M.
            Fri.-Sat., 11 A.M.-1 A.M.

CHRISTIAN'S ⑨   *Creole*

3835 Iberville St.
New Orleans
(504) 482-4924
Maître d': Joe Carmouche
Full Bar/Lot Parking
AE, D, MC, V
Good taste in dress required
No jeans

Located inside a quaint old church just off Canal Street, Christian's specializes in local seafood prepared French and Creole style. There is bouillabaisse, stuffed trout, soft-shell crabs, Oysters Roland, Baby Veal Christian and steak. Owner Christian R. Ansel, Jr., says his excellent wines are reasonably priced.

Reservations required (evenings)
Lunch: Tues.-Sat., 11:30 A.M.-2 P.M.
Dinner: Tues.-Sat., 5:30 P.M.-10 P.M.
        Closed Sunday, Monday

COMMANDER'S PALACE ㉞   *Creole*

1403 Washington Ave.
New Orleans
(504) 899-8221
Maître d': George Rico
Full Bar/Valet Parking
AE, D, MC, V, CB
Jacket for men (evenings)

Founded in 1880 and located in the Garden District in a Victorian fantasy of a building, Commander's Palace claims to have originated the "Jazz Brunch." Their specialties are Crab Meat Imperial, Crêpe Kovacs and turtle soup, among many others.

Reservations required
Lunch: Mon.-Fri., 11:30 A.M.-2 P.M.
Dinner: Daily, 6:30 P.M.-10 P.M.
Brunch: Sat.-Sun., 11 A.M.-2 P.M.

CORINNE DUNBAR'S ⑮   *Creole*

1617 St. Charles Ave.
New Orleans
(504) 525-0689
Full Bar/Street Parking
No credit cards
Jacket, tie suggested

Owner/manager James J. Plauche, Jr., says Corinne Dunbar's "re-creates gracious dining" in an elegant antebellum mansion. Furnished in antiques of the period (1840), it is home for family Creole specialties such as Oysters Dunbar, banana puffs, gumbos and jambalaya.

Reservations required
Lunch: Tues.–Sat., Noon–2 P.M.
Dinner: Tues.–Sat., 6 P.M.–9:30 P.M.
    Closed Sunday, Monday

CROZIER'S ⑧   *French*

7033 Read Lane
New Orleans
(504) 241-8220
Maître d': Evelyn Crozier
Full Bar/Lot Parking
MC, V
Good taste in dress required

Crozier's is a classical French restaurant housed in a two-story balconied home. Walls are covered with posters and pictures from France. Specialties include Tournedos Gérard, Steak au Poivre, Coq au Vin and pâté maison. Desserts include caramel custard, chocolate mousse and fresh fruits in season.

Reservations required
Dinner: Tues.–Sat., 6 P.M.–9:30 P.M.
    Closed Sunday, Monday

FELIX'S ㉚   *Seafood*

739 Iberville St.
New Orleans
(504) 522-4440 or 522-0324
Full Bar/Lot Parking
AE, V
No dress restrictions

Located between Bourbon and Royal Streets in the French Quarter, Felix's specializes in raw oysters on the half shell, as well as a complete line of seafood. There is a large oyster bar on one side of the restaurant and a dining area on the other. Favorites include seafood gumbo, Shrimp Creole and Oysters Rockefeller and Bienville.

No reservations required
Lunch/Dinner: Daily, 11:30 A.M.–2 A.M.

GALATOIRE'S ㉒   *French*

209 Bourbon St.
New Orleans
(504) 525-2021
Maître d': Don Griffin, Leon Galatoire
Full Bar/Street Parking
No credit cards
Jacket, tie for men (evenings, Sunday)

Galatoire's is a fairly small place, done in the style of a French neighborhood café. It is well lighted, with mirrors on the walls and antique fans overhead. Specialties include Trout Meunière Amandine, pompano, bouillabaisse, Sweetbreads Financière and Shrimp Remoulade.

No reservations required
Lunch/Dinner: Tues.-Sat., 11:30 A.M.-9 P.M.
             Sun., Noon-9 P.M.
             Closed Monday

K-PAUL'S ㉔   *Creole/Cajun*

416 Chartres St.
New Orleans
(504) 524-7394
Beer and Wine/Street Parking
No credit cards
No dress restrictions

Paul Prudhomme runs this recently opened restaurant and he comes well recommended. Prior to opening his own place he was head chef at the Commander's Palace. K-Paul's is undoubtedly a restaurant to watch.

No reservations required
Lunch: Mon.-Fri., 11:30 A.M.-3 P.M.
Dinner: Mon.-Sat., 6 P.M.-10 P.M.
       Closed Sunday

LA LOUISIANE ㉛   *Creole*

725 Iberville St.
New Orleans
(504) 523-4664
Maître d': Nick Mosca, Joe Marcello (owners)
Full Bar/Street Parking
Major Credit Cards
Jacket for men

They like to call their specialties "masterpieces of authentic Louisiana cookery." There is also a wide-ranging wine collection. The service is meticulous.

Reservations required
Lunch/Dinner: Mon.-Fri., 11:30 A.M.-Midnight
             Sat., 5:30 P.M.-Midnight
             Sun., 5:30 P.M.-10:30 P.M.

LA PROVENCE ❶ — French

Highway 190
Lacombe, La.
(504) 626-7662
Maître d': Mauro Leiva
Full Bar/Lot Parking
MC, V
Good taste in dress required

Chef/owner Chris Kerageorgiou describes La Provence as "a small French country inn." There is a large patio for summer dining and a fireplace indoors for those chilly bayou nights. Specials are rack of lamb with herbs de Provence, quail, Duck à l'Orange and home-made pâté and sausages.

Reservations required
Dinner: Wed.–Sat., 5 P.M.–11 P.M.
    Sat., 1 P.M.–9 P.M.
        Closed Monday, Tuesday

LE RUTH'S ⑱ — Creole

636 Franklin St.
Gretna, La.
(504) 362-4914 (after 1:30 P.M.)
Maître d': "Larry T" Thibodeaux
Full Bar/Lot Parking
MC, V
Jacket for men

Le Ruth's offers substantial table d'hôte dinners served in the art-filled atmosphere of a 90-year-old Victorian home. Owner/chef Warren Le Ruth bakes his own French bread daily and serves such specialties as artichoke soup, Crab Meat St. Francis, crawfish, prime steak and lamb.

Reservations suggested
Dinner: Tues.–Sat., 5:45 P.M.–10 P.M.
    Closed Sunday, Monday

LOUIS XVI ㉕ — French

829 Rue Toulouse
New Orleans
(504) 581-7000
Maître d': Antoine Camenzuli
Full Bar/Valet Parking
AE, D, MC, V, CB
Jacket for men (evenings)

Located in the center of the French Quarter, Louis XVI French Restaurant likes to combine excellence of service with French-inspired international cuisine. Specialties include rack of spring lamb en croûte, Beef Wellington, Trout Louis XVI and Lobster Américaine.

Reservations required
Lunch: Mon.–Fri., 11:30 A.M.–2:30 P.M.
Dinner: Daily, 6:30 P.M.–11:30 P.M.

MAISON PIERRE   ㉑   Creole

430 Rue Dauphine
New Orleans
(504) 529-5521
Full Bar/Street Parking
Major Credit Cards
Good taste in dress required

There really is a Pierre behind Maison Pierre and he is a third-generation French Quarter restaurateur known for his finesse and creativity in the kitchen. He also takes special pride in his collection of fine wines.

Reservations required
Dinner: Wed.–Sun., 6:30 P.M.–Midnight
   Closed Monday, Tuesday

MARTI'S   ⑲   Creole

1041 Dumaine St.
New Orleans
(504) 524-6060
Full Bar/Lot and Street Parking
AE, D, V
No dress restrictions

Marti's, located across from the New Orleans Theater for the Performing Arts, has the ambience of a French neighborhood restaurant. Its specialty items include stuffed eggplant, Shrimp Remoulade, Trout Amandine, Redfish Pontchartrain and probably the best coffee and French bread in the world, according to owner Martin C. Shambra, Jr.

Reservations advised
Lunch: Mon.–Fri., 11:30 A.M.–2:30 P.M.
Dinner: Mon.–Sat., 6 P.M.–11 P.M.
   Closed Sunday

MASSON'S RESTAURANT FRANCAIS   ❷   French

7200 Pontchartrain Blvd.
New Orleans
(504) 283-2525
Maître d': Donald Chastain
Full Bar/Valet Parking
AE, D, MC, V, CB
Jacket for men

Masson's is unique among New Orleans restaurants in that its cuisine is French *Provincial* with certain Creole influences. Menu highlights include marinated rack of lamb, Poisson du Bayou Dubos and Les Mervielles de la Mer en Crêpes.

Reservations requested
Lunch: Mon.–Fri., 11:30 A.M.–2 P.M.
Dinner: Mon.–Sat., 5 P.M.–11 P.M.
   Sun., Noon–11 P.M.

MOSCA'S ❼ *Italian*

U.S. 90 West
Waggaman, La.
(504) 436-9942
Full Bar/Lot Parking
No credit cards
No dress restrictions

Mosca's is a family restaurant with a 15-item menu. Owner John Mosca says he specializes in shrimp, oysters and chicken "done our way." He also offers homemade spaghetti, ravioli and sausage, as well as fresh crab meat salads.

Reservations required
Dinner: Tues.-Sat., 5:30 P.M.-9:30 P.M.
    Closed Sunday, Monday

PASCAL'S MANALE ㉝ *Italian/Seafood*

1838 Napoleon Ave.
New Orleans
(504) 895-4877/78
Maître d': Martin H. Radosta,
    Gino S. Radosta, Robert Mullen
Full Bar/Street Parking
AE, D, MC, V, CB
No dress restrictions

In 1913 Frank Manale brought his treasured collection of Italian recipes and a bit of Old Italy to uptown New Orleans. Under the guidance of his nephew Pascal Radosta, the restaurant flourished by serving such specialties as barbecued shrimp, Brisket Marinara, stuffed tufoli, steaks and seafood.

Reservations required
Lunch/Dinner: Mon.-Fri., 11:45 A.M.-10 P.M.
        Sat., 4 P.M.-10:30 P.M.
        Closed Sunday

RED ONION ❹ *Continental*

2700 Edenborn Ave.
Metairie, La.
(504) 455-6677
Maître d': Frank Grimoskas, Frank Occhipinti, Jr.,
    Rosario Purpura, Sr. (owners)
Full Bar/Lot Parking
AE, D, MC, V, CB
No dress restrictions

Red Onion's three hosts offer the renowned New Orleans seafood dishes, plus live Maine lobster, rack of lamb and baby white veal. A battery of chefs and sous-chefs makes sure each dish is prepared "professionally and with consistency."

No reservations required
Lunch/Dinner: Mon.-Fri., 11 A.M.-11 P.M.
        Sat., 5 P.M.-Midnight
        Closed Sunday

RESTAURANT JONATHAN   *Creole/Seafood*

714 N. Rampart St.
New Orleans
(504) 586-1930
Maître d': Klein Stuart
Full Bar/Valet Parking
AE, D, MC, V
No dress restrictions

Restaurant Jonathan has received attention for its Art Déco interiors and the craftsmanship of chef Tom Cowman. House specialties include local fresh seafood, Bombay curries, roast duckling and Oysters and Crawfish Jonathan.

Reservations requested
Lunch: Mon.–Fri., 11:30 A.M.–2:30 P.M.
Dinner: Mon.–Thurs., 6 P.M.–10:30 P.M.
      Fri., 6 P.M.–11 P.M.
      Sat., 6 P.M.–Midnight
      Closed Sunday

THE RIB ROOM   *Continental*

Royal Orleans Hotel
621 St. Louis St.
New Orleans
(504) 529-5333
Maître d': Ernst Fisher
Full Bar/Lot Parking
AE, D, MC, V, CB
Jacket for men (evenings)

The Rib Room seems to take special pride in offering what they term America's favorite main course: prime rib. It is carved to order by the dining room chef. The menu also features classically prepared Tournedos Princesse and a wide selection of New Orleans seafood.

No reservations required
Lunch: Mon.–Sat., 11:30 A.M.–3 P.M.
Dinner: Daily, 6 P.M.–11:30 P.M.
Brunch: Sun., 10 A.M.–3 P.M.

RUTH CHRIS STEAKHOUSE   *American*

711 N. Broad
New Orleans (various locations)
(504) 821-4853
Full Bar/Lot Parking
AE, D, MC, V, CB
No dress restrictions

Owner Ruth Fertel serves only U.S. prime beef. The à la carte menu includes freshly sautéed mushrooms and broccoli with double cheese, buttery baked potatoes, broiled tomatoes and lots of beef.

No reservations required
Lunch/Dinner: Daily, 11:30 A.M.–11:30 P.M.

SAZERAC ⑫ — *French/Creole*

Fairmont Hotel
University Place
New Orleans
(504) 529-7111
Full Bar/Lot Parking
AE, D, MC, V
Jacket, tie for men

Sazerac envelops you in an atmosphere of sumptuous elegance. The staff is trained in the European tradition of service. Menu selections include seafood gumbo, lobster bisque, Speckled Trout Amandine, rack of lamb, Steak Diane and prawns baked with crab meat. A complimentary sorbet is served to cleanse the palate.

Reservations required
Lunch: Mon.-Fri., 11:30 A.M.-2:30 P.M.
Dinner: Daily, 6 P.M.-Midnight

TONY ANGELLO'S ③ — *Italian*

6262 Fleur de Lis
New Orleans
(504) 488-0888
Full Bar/Lot and Street Parking
AE, D, MC, V
No dress restrictions

This antique-filled home-turned-restaurant features a substantial sampling of traditional Italian "home-style" cuisine. It is a restaurant that is both family-run and "family-cooked"!

Reservations suggested
Dinner: Tues.-Sat., 6 P.M.-11 P.M.
   Closed Sunday, Monday

THE VERSAILLES ⑰ — *French*

2100 St. Charles Ave.
New Orleans
(504) 524-2535
Maître d': Keith Nelson
Full Bar/Valet Parking
AE, D, MC, V, CB
Jacket for men

Versailles chef/owner Gunter Preuss is particularly proud of his bouillabaisse, his escargots and his creative specialties such as Redfish Dore, Cream of Leek Soup Chantilly and Mignonette de Boeuf au Moelle. Preuss was trained in England, France, Switzerland, Sweden and Germany and is now proving what he has learned — in New Orleans.

Reservations required
Dinner: Mon.-Sat., 5:30 P.M.-10:30 P.M.
   Closed Sunday

VISKO'S ㊱   *Seafood*

516 Gretna Blvd.
Gretna, La.
(504) 368-4849
Full Bar/Lot Parking
AE, D, MC, V, CB
Good taste in dress required

Visko's interior is filled with numerous plants and tables that face an outdoor patio, creating the illusion of outdoor dining. There is a sit-down Oyster Bar. Specialties include shrimp and oysters, fried or sautéed, seafood salads, bread pudding and Oysters Meaux, fried and combined with Canadian bacon atop an English muffin.

No reservations required
Lunch/Dinner: Mon.–Thurs., 11 A.M.–10 P.M.
                Fri.–Sat., 11 A.M.–11 P.M.
                Closed Sunday

WILLY COLN'S ㉟   *Continental*

2505 Whitney Ave.
Gretna, La.
(504) 361-3860
Maître d': Erna Coln
Full Bar/Lot Parking
AE, MC, V
No jeans, sneakers, T-shirts

Chef Willy Coln combines everything that Europe has taught him about classic presentation with everything New Orleans has taught him about Creole preparation. He offers such specialties as Redfish Etouffe, Steak au Poivre with Louisiana hot peppers, wiener schnitzel and Bahamian seafood chowder.

Reservations required
Dinner: Tues.–Sat., 6 P.M.–10 P.M.
        Closed Sunday, Monday

WINSTON'S ⑬   *French*

New Orleans Hilton
2 Poydras St.
New Orleans
(504) 561-0500
Maître d': Fernando Barahona
Full Bar/Valet and Lot Parking
AE, D, MC, V, CB
Jacket, tie for men

Winston's features *la nouvelle cuisine* in the form of a verbal menu presented by "maid and butler" teams. The five-course meal is prix fixe. Some specialties include Frog Leg Mousse with saffron, Consommé au Canard, Rack of Lamb Mongolian, Tournedos Boursin au Poivre, Braised Rabbit au Vin Rouge and Poire Poche au Chocolat.

Reservations recommended
Dinner: Daily, 6 P.M.–11 P.M.

NEW YORK

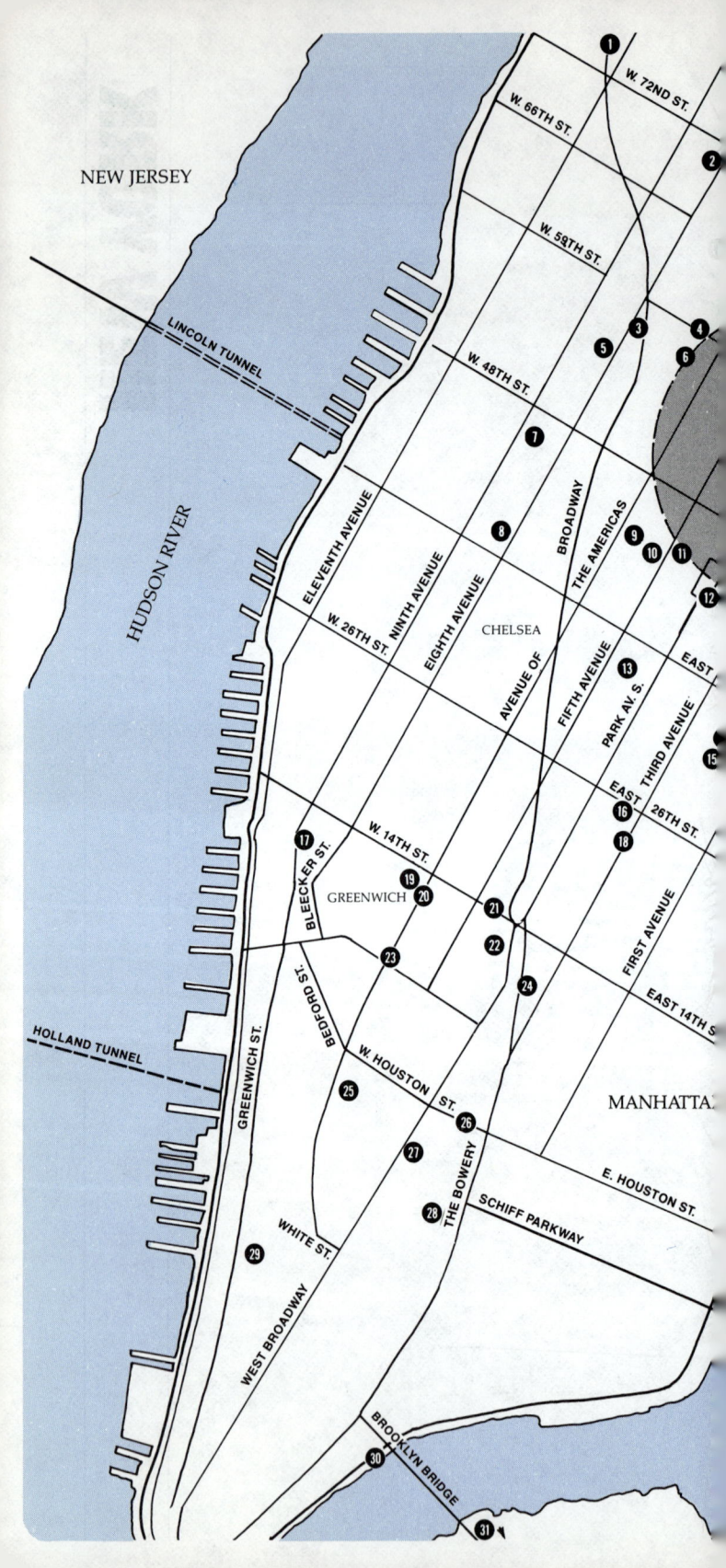

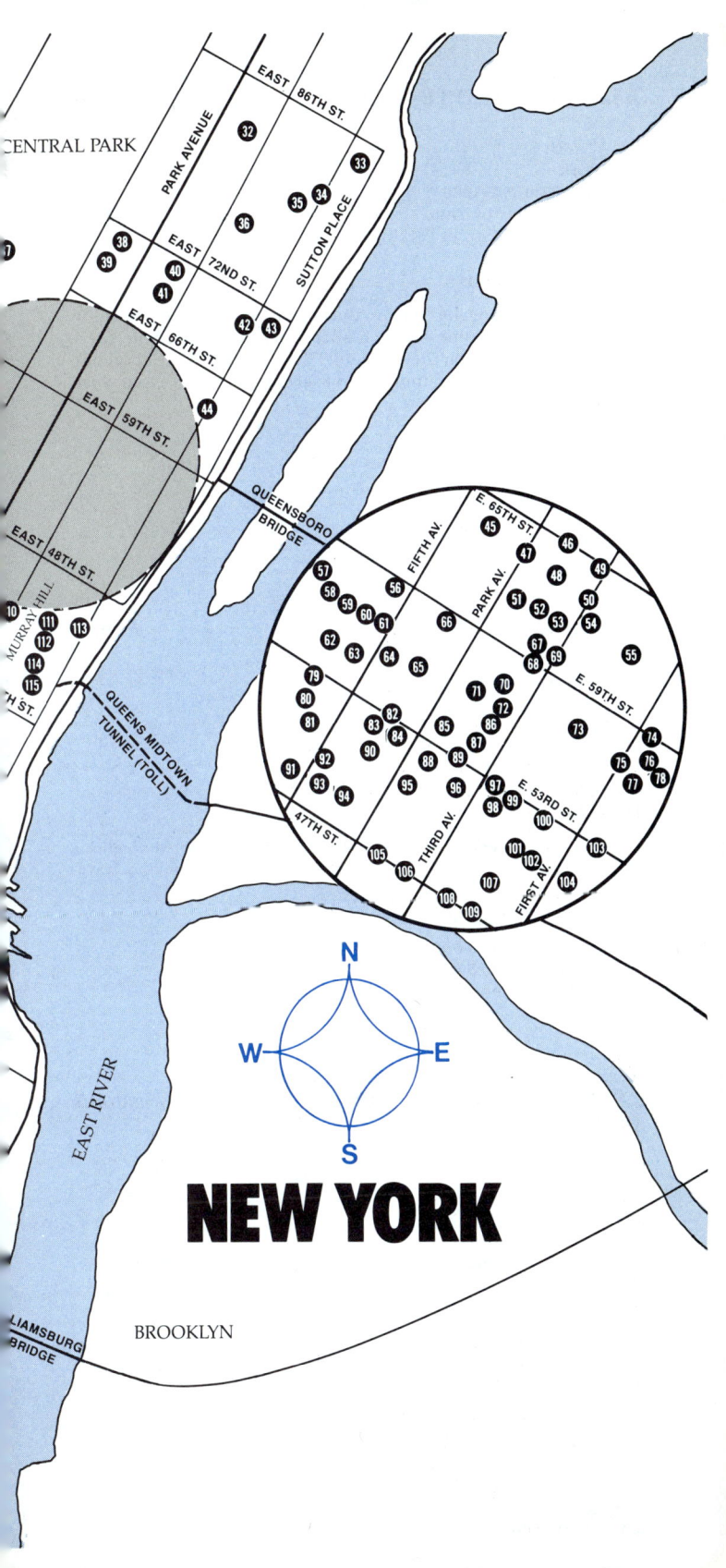

A LA FOURCHETTE ❽ *French*

342 W. 46th St.
New York
(212) 245-9744/246-1960
Maître d': James or Tina
Full Bar/Lot and Street Parking
House charge only
No dress restrictions

A La Fourchette envelops you in the cozy, carefree ambience of the Twenties. You can dine on such specialties as Filet of Sole Grenobloise, Duckling Bigarade, Cassoulet Toulousaine and Capon Barcelonette and still be on time for an 8:00 curtain. You are that close to most major theaters.

Reservations required
Lunch: Mon.-Fri., Noon-3 P.M.
Dinner: Mon.-Fri., 5 P.M.-11 P.M.
  Sat., 4:30 P.M.-11 P.M.
  Closed Sunday

ALFREDO'S ❹ *Italian*

240 Central Park South
New York
(212) 246-7050
Maître d': Luciano Gianella
Full Bar/Valet Parking
AE, D, MC, V
Jacket for men

Look for such specialties as Scallopini Mediterranean, Medaglioni di Blue Casino and Capelli d'Angelo Rene. The decor is extravagantly lavish.

Reservations required
Lunch: Mon.-Sat., Noon-3 P.M.
Dinner: Mon.-Sat., 5 P.M.-11 P.M.
  Closed Sunday

ASSEMBLY STEAK & FISH HOUSE ❽⓪ *American/Seafood*

16 W. 51st St.
New York
(212) 581-3580
Maître d': Bill Brodsky
Full Bar/Lot Parking
AE, D, MC, V, CB
Jacket for men

This steak and fish house features a "clublike" ambience and lots of the aforementioned. There are giant Maine lobsters, plus milk-fed veal and prime Porterhouse and sirloin steaks.

Reservations recommended
Lunch/Dinner: Mon.-Fri., 11:30 A.M.-11 P.M.
  Sat., 4:30 P.M.-11 P.M.
  Closed Sunday

AUBERGE SUISSE � *Swiss*

Citi-Corp Center
153 E. 53rd St.
New York
(212) 421-1420
Maître d': Robert Keller (owner/chef)
Full Bar/Street Parking
AE, D, MC, V, CB
No dress restrictions

"Whatever the Swiss dish, anticipate an original version," says owner and chef Robert Keller. He promises his Swiss dishes are unlike any you've ever tasted.

Reservations required
Lunch: Mon.-Sat., Noon-2:30 P.M.
Dinner: Mon.-Sat., 5 P.M.-10 P.M.
     Sun., Noon-6 P.M.

BALLATO'S ㉖ *Italian*

55 E. Houston St.
New York
(212) 226-9683
Maître d': John Ballato (owner)
Beer and Wine/Street Parking
No credit cards
No dress restrictions

Ballato's walls are covered with memorabilia documenting its illustrious clientele. There's a Warhol portrait, a Louise Nevelson print and photos of the powerful and the accomplished. House specialties include Boned Bass Livornese, Calf's Liver Veneziane and Vitello Valdostana.

Reservations required
Lunch: Mon.-Sat., Noon-2:30 P.M.
Dinner: Mon.-Sat., 5:30 P.M.-8:45 P.M.
     Closed Sunday

BARBETTA ❼ *Italian*

321 W. 46th St.
New York
(212) 226-9171
Maître d': Raul Nunez (manager)
Full Bar/Lot Parking
AE, D, MC, V, CB
Jacket, tie for men preferred

Opened in 1906 by Sebastian Maioglio, father of present owner Laura Maioglio, Barbetta is reportedly the oldest restaurant in New York continuously owned by the same family. Ms. Maioglio has redesigned the restaurant in an 18th-century style, complete with many authentic Northern Italian antiques. She serves the specialties of the Piedmont region.

Reservations required
Lunch: Mon.-Sat., Noon-2 P.M.
Dinner: Mon.-Sat., 5 P.M.-Midnight
     Closed Sunday

BENIHANA PALACE ❿ *Japanese*

15 W. 44th St. (and other locations)
New York
(212) 682-7120
Full Bar/Street Parking
AE, D, MC, V, CB
Good taste in dress required

The show goes on every day at Benihana. Stunning theatricality is combined with meticulous preparation. The chefs are well trained in the Benihana tradition. They present such specialties as steaks and seafood, onions and zucchini — all nimbly cut, sliced and tossed through the air.

Reservations required
Lunch: Mon.–Sat., Noon–2:30 P.M.
Dinner: Mon.–Thurs., 5:30 P.M.–11 P.M.
 Fri.–Sat., 5:30 P.M.–2 A.M.
 Closed Sunday

THE BOX TREE ⓴ *French*

242 E. 50th St.
New York
(212) 758-8320
Beer and Wine/Street Parking
No credit cards
Jacket for men

Three increasingly common but consistently prized elements are at work here: extreme intimacy (only eight tables), prix fixe dinners and specialties emphasizing *la nouvelle cuisine*. Rather uncommon is the frequent air delivery of vegetables from France. Look for such dishes as Lobster Mornay Box Tree, Saumon Mousseline and Vacherin Box Tree.

Reservations required
Lunch: Mon.–Fri., Noon–2:30 P.M.
Dinner: Daily, 6:30 P.M. and 9:30 P.M. seatings

BRASSERIE ⓹ *French*

100 E. 53rd St.
New York
(212) 751-4840
Full Bar/Street Parking
AE, D, MC, V, CB
No dress restrictions

The Brasserie is always there when you need it — and always open. From a croissant or brioche in the morning to quiches, omelets and sandwiches at noon to duckling, charcuterie or whatever at dinner and into the early-morning hours, the Brasserie can comfort and satisfy.

No reservations required
Breakfast/Lunch/Dinner: Daily, 24 hours

BRUSSELS RESTAURANT ⓼⓻   French

115 E. 54th St.
New York
(212) 758-0457
Maître d': Jean Ane
Full Bar/Street Parking
AE, D, MC, V, CB
Jacket, tie for men

Brussels is proud of its Belgian-accented French food and of its extensive wine cellar. Rooms are available for private parties.

Reservations required
Lunch/Dinner: Mon. – Fri., Noon – 10 P.M.
       Sat., Dinner Only

CAFE ARGENTEUIL ⓽⓼   French

253 E. 52nd St.
New York
(212) 753-9273/4
Maître d': Marcel Autret
Full Bar/Street Parking
AE, D, MC, V, CB
Jacket for men

An Art Nouveau decor and pleasant atmosphere describe Cafe Argenteuil, according to its proprietors, André Mailhan and Claude Uson. They present such dishes as Pompano en Croûte, cassoulet, Bass en Croûte and Medaillon de Veau Maintenon.

Reservations required
Lunch: Mon. – Fri., Noon – 3 P.M.
Dinner: Mon. – Fri., 6 P.M. – 10:30 P.M.
       Sat., 6 P.M. – 11 P.M.
       Closed Sunday

CAFE DES ARTISTES ❷   French

1 W. 67th St.
New York
(212) 877-3500
Maître d': Steve Gurgely, Jim Irving
Full Bar/Street Parking
AE, D, MC, V
No dress restrictions

Cafe des Artistes, in continuous operation for the past 74 years, has muraled walls depicting nubile nymphs cavorting in the woods (painted by Howard Chandler Christy), French regional specialties (smoked lamb, a Provençal fish stew, garlic chicken), an almost endless variety of desserts and baskets of wine brought to your table for selection.

Reservations required
Lunch: Mon. – Fri., Noon – 3 P.M.
Dinner: Mon. – Sat., 5:30 P.M. – 11 P.M.
       Sun., 7 P.M. – 11 P.M.
Brunch: Sat. – Sun., 11 A.M. – 3 P.M.

CAFE SAN MARTIN 43 *Continental*

1458 First Ave.
New York
(212) 288-0470
Maître d': Francisco San Martin
Full Bar/Street Parking
AE, D, MC, V
No dress restrictions

Cafe San Martin is a place of white brick walls, skylight, mirrors, cane-backed chairs and a profusion of flowers. It is also a place for such piquant specialties as Zarzuela de Mariscos (a mixture of fish and shellfish cooked to your order, in lobster sauce), Paella à la Valenciana, Fillet of Hake Madrilène and grain-fed chicken roasted on the spit.

Reservations required
Dinner: Daily, 5:30 P.M.-Midnight
Brunch: Sun., Noon-4 P.M.

CAPRICCIO 61 *Northern Italian*

11 W. 56th St.
New York
(212) 757-7795
Full Bar/Street Parking
AE, D, MC, CB
Jacket for men

Capriccio presents a full range of Northern Italian specialties. They include gnocchi, Costoletta Valdostana, Cozza Posillipo and, on Fridays only, a fish soup.

Reservations required
Lunch: Mon.-Fri., Noon-3 P.M.
Dinner: Mon.-Fri., 5 P.M.-11 P.M.
Sat., 4:30 P.M.-11:30 P.M.
Closed Sunday

CASA BRASIL 33 *Brazilian/Continental*

406 E. 85th St.
New York
(212) 288-5284
Maître d': Dona Helma (owner)
No Wine or Spirits/Street Parking
No credit cards
Jacket for men

Casa Brasil offers Continental cuisine most days, including roast duck, Beef Wellington, roast veal with mushrooms and rack of lamb. Wednesday is different. Then there's only Brazilian food and it's a special festive treat.

Reservations required
Dinner: Mon.-Thurs., 6:30 P.M.-9 P.M.
Fri.-Sat., 7 P.M. and 9:30 P.M. seatings
Closed Sunday

CELLAR IN THE SKY ㉙　　　　　　　　　*French*

1 World Trade Center
New York
(212) 938-1111
Maître d': Raymond Wellington (cellarmaster)
Full Bar/Lot Parking
AE, D, MC, V, CB
Jacket, tie for men

♕ ♕ ♕ ♕
🍴 🍴 🍴 🍴
⊘ ⊘ ⊘ ⊘
🍷 🍷 🍷 🍷
$ $ $ $

If you yearn to dine in an actual working wine cellar, here's your chance. The seven-course prix fixe dinners are accompanied by and designed around five different wines. Specialties include pheasant, duckling, a variety of hors d'oeuvre and petits fours.

Reservations required
Dinner: Mon.-Sat., 7:30 P.M. seating

CHALET SUISSE �94　　　　　　　　*Swiss/Continental*

6 E. 48th St.
New York
(212) 355-0855
Full Bar/Street Parking
AE, D, MC, V
Jacket, tie for men

♕ ♕ ♕
🍴 🍴 🍴
⊘ ⊘ ⊘
🍷 🍷 🍷
$ $ $

Chalet Suisse opened its doors in 1925, and, according to owner Konrad Egli, is the oldest Swiss restaurant in New York. Specialties include a variety of veal dishes and fondue.

Reservations required
Lunch: Mon.-Fri., Noon-2:30 P.M.
Dinner: Mon.-Fri., 5 P.M.-9:30 P.M.
　　Closed Saturday, Sunday

CHANTERELLE ㉘　　　　　　　　　*French*

89 Grand St.
New York
(212) 966-6960
Maître d': Karen Waltuck (co-owner)
Beer and Wine/Street Parking
AE, MC, V
No dress restrictions

♕ ♕ ♕ ♕
🍴 🍴 🍴 🍴
⊘ ⊘ ⊘ ⊘
🍷 🍷 🍷 🍷
$ $ $ $

A tiny place with a very limited number of selections, Chanterelle is big on creativity and innovation. Chef and owner (with wife Karen) David Waltuck offers such delicacies as lobster with cider and apples and bay scallops baked in pastry. The menus are hand-lettered, so you know interesting changes are in store every day.

Reservations required
Lunch: Tues.-Sat., 12:30 P.M.-2:30 P.M.
Dinner: Tues.-Sat., 6:30 P.M.-10 P.M.
　　Closed Sunday, Monday

NEW YORK　267

CHARLEY O'S ⓘ   *Irish/American*

33 W. 48th St.
New York
(212) 582-7141
Maître d': Ralph Ferrara
Full Bar/Lot Parking (dinner)
AE, D, MC, V, CB
No dress restrictions

Charley O's is an institution — a remarkably pleasant one. It's an Irish pub setting, with painted green walls and a "big long bar." No-nonsense specialties include corned beef and cabbage, Irish lamb stew, sirloin steak and prime rib.

Reservations required
Lunch: Mon.–Sat., 11:30 A.M.–3 P.M.
Dinner: Mon.–Sat., 5 P.M.–Midnight
   Closed Sunday

CHEZ PASCAL ⓘ   *French*

151 E. 82nd St.
New York
(212) 249-1334
Maître d': Marc Saccone
Full Bar/Street Parking
AE, D, MC, V
Jacket, tie for men

Candlelight dominates the scene at Chez Pascal, along with fresh flowers, brick walls and a fireplace. Look for such things as Salade d'Haricots Verts, Bass en Croûte, bouillabaisse and Canard au Poivre Vert.

Reservations required
Dinner: Mon.–Sat., 6:30 P.M.–11:30 P.M.
   Closed Sunday

CHRIST CELLA ⓘ   *American*

160 E. 46th St.
New York
(212) 697-2479
Maître d': John Vernazza
Full Bar/Street Parking
AE, D, MC, V, CB
Jacket, tie for men

"We are known across the country and even in Europe for our delicious steaks, filet mignon and seafood, including lobster," states the management. The description is straightforward and so is Christ Cella, with its simple decor and understated elegance.

Reservations required
Lunch: Mon.–Fri., Noon–3 P.M.
Dinner: Mon.–Sat., 5 P.M.–10:30 P.M.
   Closed Sunday

CLAUDE'S ㊱   *French*

205 E. 81st St.
New York
(212) 472-0487
Maître d': Richard Genova
Full Bar/Street Parking
AE, D, MC, V
Jacket for men

Claude's features a stunning contemporary interior of chrome, mirrors and burgundy hues. Diners have the option of selecting a seven-course prix fixe "gastronomique" dinner that changes daily. Other specialties might include Dover Sole and game in season.

Reservations required
Dinner: Mon.–Sat., 6 P.M.–10:45 P.M.
    Closed Sunday

CLOS NORMAND ㊴   *French*

42 E. 52nd St.
New York
(212) 753-3348/9
Maître d': Jean Jacques Mentz
Full Bar/Street Parking
AE, D, MC, V, CB
Jacket for men

Country French specialties are the order here, including selections from the cuisine of Normandy. The freshest available produce goes into the preparation of such dishes as Moules Normande, game terrine, rack of lamb in natural juice, garlic, shallots and herbs, and Crêpe Surprise, encasing a scoop of pecan ice cream in a caramel sauce.

Reservations required
Lunch: Mon.–Sat., Noon–3 P.M.
Dinner: Mon–Sat., 5:30 P.M.–11 P.M.
    Closed Sunday

THE COACH HOUSE ㉓   *American*

110 Waverly Pl.
New York
(212) 777-0303
Maître d': Paul Wilkins
Full Bar/Street Parking
AE, D, MC, V, CB
Jacket, tie for men

Once a turn-of-the-century carriage house, The Coach House is now a place of gentle lights, American antique brass chandeliers, original 18th-century paintings of the English Hunt, and all-around warmth. People keep asking for the black bean soup with Madeira, the prime beef selections, the rack of lamb and the whole striped bass.

Reservations required
Dinner: Tues.–Sun., 5:30 P.M.–10:30 P.M.
    Closed Monday

CZECH PAVILLION ⓻⑤   *Czech*

313 E. 58th St.
New York
(212) 752-9199
Maître d': Aya
Full Bar/Street Parking
AE, D, MC, V
No dress restrictions

The Czech Pavillion is an elegantly styled home for classic pre-war Czech cuisine. You dine surrounded by "antique" Czech costumes in frames and Czech crystal. The menu selections consist of roast goose, roast duck, Bohemian dumplings, Svickova (braised beef in sour cream with lingonberries), game in season and rich Czech pastries.

Reservations required
Dinner: Mon.–Sat., 6 P.M.–11:30 P.M.
      Sun., 5 P.M.–10 P.M.

DARDANELLES ㉒   *Armenian*

86 University Pl.
New York
(212) 242-8990
Maître d': Raymond and Louise
Full Bar/Street Parking
AE, D, MC, V, CB
Good taste in dress required

A comfortable spacing of tables sets Dardanelles apart from a number of New York restaurants. Armenian specialties include roast leg of lamb, fresh vegetable casserole, seafood prepared their special way, homemade pastry and yogurt. Standout features are the Yogurt Soup (Tahrana) and the Lemon Chicken Soup.

Reservations recommended
Lunch: Mon.–Fri., Noon–2:30 P.M.
Dinner: Daily, 4:30 P.M.–9:30 P.M.

DAVID K's ㊾   *Chinese*

1115 Third Ave.
New York
(212) 371-9090
Maître d': Steven Woo, Terry Don, Heyward Lee
Full Bar/Lot and Street Parking
AE, D
Jacket, tie for men

David K's is a two-tiered restaurant with a main dining room downstairs that features a glass-enclosed garden and a street-level lounge with a "free form" bar. Widely spaced tables are set with Rosenthal crystal, sterling silver place settings and fresh flowers. Specialties are Peking Duck, Orange Beef, broiled lobster (served out of the shell) and Walnut Chicken.

Reservations required
Lunch: Daily, Noon–3 P.M.
Dinner: Mon.–Thurs., 6 P.M.–Midnight
      Fri.–Sun., 6 P.M.–12:30 A.M.

DODIN-BOUFFANT 🌀 *French*

405 E. 58th St.
New York
(212) 751-2790
Full Bar/Street Parking
AE, D
Jacket, tie for men

Dodin-Bouffant, comfortably hidden away on two floors of a Manhattan townhouse, presents food with a "foundation in the traditions of France and a realization in the products of the United States." There are such dishes as Salade d'Agneau, Foie de Veau à la Graine de Moutarde and Saucisson de Legumes.

Reservations required
Dinner: Tues.–Sun., 6:30 P.M.–10 P.M.
   Closed Monday
   July and August, open Monday and closed Sunday

EL PARADOR CAFE 🌀 *Mexican*

325 E. 34th St.
New York
(212) 697-6812
Maître d': Carlos Jacott (manager)
Full Bar/Street Parking
No credit cards
No dress restrictions

Considered by some to be an ideal romantic hideaway, El Parador specializes in the grand cuisine of Mexico. There is plenty of Mexican beer, sangria and Margaritas to satisfy your thirst while you wait for a table. What follows includes shrimp in salsa verde, Chiles Rellenos and Chicken El Parador, plus a variety of substantial combination plates.

No reservations required
Dinner: Mon.–Sat., 5 P.M.–11 P.M.
   Closed Sunday

THE FOUR SEASONS 🌀 *International*

99 E. 52nd St.
New York
(212) 754-9494
Maître d': Oreste and Julian
Full Bar/Valet Parking (dinner)
AE, D, MC, V, CB
Jacket for men

What can one say about The Four Seasons that doesn't begin with "a legend in its own time"? As the seasons change, so do the menus and decor. There is the Pool Room, designed by Mies van der Rohe, the art exhibits — and the food. It is safe to say that everything is special. The wine list presented by owners Paul Kovi and Tom Margittai is said to be remarkable.

Reservations required
Lunch: Mon.–Sat., Noon–2:30 P.M.
Dinner: Mon.–Sat., 5 P.M.–11:30 P.M.
   Closed Sunday

GAGE & TOLLNER ③¹ *Seafood*

372 Fulton St.
Brooklyn, N.Y.
(212) 875-5181
Maître d': Edward Dewey, John Simmons (owners)
Full Bar/Street Parking
AE, D, MC, V, CB
No dress restrictions

This 100-year-old landmark is a Brooklyn tradition. It is known for its soft clam belly broil, lobster bisque, Crabmeat Virginia and Chicken Maryland with corn fritters, *and* for the original gas chandeliers that are lighted every night.

No reservations required
Lunch/Dinner: *Mon.-Fri., 11:30 A.M.-9 P.M.*
                Sat., 4 P.M.-11 P.M.
                Sun., 3 P.M.-9 P.M.

GAYLORD ⑥⁶ *North Indian*

50 E. 58th St.
New York
(212) 759-1710
Maître d': Husain (manager)
Full Bar/Lot Parking
AE, D, MC, V, CB
No dress restrictions

North Indian cuisine is prepared before your eyes in an unusual glass-enclosed kitchen. Marinated fish is roasted in a charcoal fire, tandoori is cooked in a clay oven, and the image of Lord Krishna, in the form of beaded murals, keeps a watchful eye over all.

Reservations required
Lunch: *Mon.-Fri., 11:30 A.M.-3 P.M.*
Dinner: *Daily, 5:30 P.M.-11 P.M.*
Brunch: *Sun., Noon-3 P.M.*

GIAMBELLI 50TH ⑨⁵ *Italian*

46 E. 50th St.
New York
(212) 688-2760
Maître d': John Camia, Virgilito Gatti (manager)
Full Bar/Valet Parking (dinner)
AE, D, MC, V, CB
No dress restrictions

Giambelli presents Northern Italian cuisine on three restaurant levels. There are such special dishes as shrimp crêpes, Scampi Raimondi, Costoletta di Vitello Milanese, Pollo Cacciatora, Fettuccine ala Giambelli, zabaglione and Fragole Portofino.

Reservations required
Lunch/Dinner: *Mon.-Thurs., Noon-Midnight*
                  Fri.-Sat., Noon-1 A.M.
                  Closed Sunday

GLOUCESTER HOUSE   ⑨⓪   *Seafood*

37 E. 50th St.
New York
(212) 755-7394
Maître d': L. Riley
Full Bar/Street Parking
AE, D, MC, V, CB
Jacket, tie for men

You'll know to expect seafood when you see the New England-style decor and the miniature boat display. There is fresh seafood *only*, including Maine lobster, shad roe, flounder, bluefish, snapper, halibut, clams and crabmeat. There is a variety of accompanying vegetables and potatoes.

Reservations required
Lunch: Daily, Noon – 2:30 P.M.
Dinner: Daily, 5:30 P.M. – 10 P.M.

GOLD COIN   ⑪⑪⑪   *Chinese*

835 Second Ave.
New York
(212) 697-1515
Maître d': Teddy Chang
Full Bar/Lot Parking (dinner)
AE, D, MC, V
Good taste in dress required

Gold Coin consists of three separate dining areas, each in an elegant and spacious setting. Featured are the regional cuisines from all the provinces of China. Specialties include Tangerine Beef, Velvet Shrimp, Lobster Delight, Peking Duck, steamed whole fish, Eight-Treasure Chicken and many vegetable dishes.

Reservations suggested
Lunch/Dinner: Mon. – Thurs., 11:30 A.M. – 10:30 P.M.
              Fri., 11:30 A.M. – 11:30 P.M.
              Sat., Noon – 11:30 P.M.
              Sun., Noon – 10:30 P.M.

THE GREENE STREET CAFE   ㉗   *Continental*

103 Greene St.
New York
(212) 925-2415
Full Bar/Street Parking
Major credit cards
No dress restrictions

A combination Soho nightclub and restaurant, The Greene Street Cafe was once a truck garage. It is now a place where New Yorkers come to see and be seen. The menu presents such down-to-earth specialties as breast of chicken in champagne sauce, steaks, pâtés and saucissons de fruits de mer.

Dinner: Sun. – Wed., 7 P.M. – 11:30 P.M.
        Thurs. – Sat., 7 P.M. – Midnight
Brunch: Sat. – Sun., Noon – 4 P.M.

HISAE'S PLACE ㉔   *Continental/Oriental*

35 Cooper Square
New York
(212) 228-6886
Maître d': Juan Villa (manager)
Full Bar/Street Parking
No credit cards
No dress restrictions

At Hisae's Place you'll dine in the reassuringly familiar setting of an old-fashioned neighborhood restaurant and bar. Freshly prepared vegetables, meat and seafood are prepared in Hisae's subtle style. Specialties include whole red snapper, sea bass, trout and Monk's fish tail.

Reservations required (four or more)
Dinner: Mon.–Thurs., 5 P.M.–Midnight
         Fri.–Sat., 5 P.M.–1 A.M.
         Sun., 5 P.M.–11 P.M.

HUNAM ⑫   *Chinese*

845 Second Ave.
New York
(212) 687-7471
Full Bar/Street Parking
AE, D, CB
No dress restrictions

Hunam is for those more serious about food than spacious surroundings. There are some unusual items for the adventurous to try: Turnip Cake, Hunam Preserved Duck, Crisp Chicken with Peanuts, Orange Flavor Beef and Shrimp Puff in Ginger Sauce.

Reservations suggested
Lunch/Dinner: Sun.–Thurs., 11:30 A.M.–11 P.M.
              Fri.–Sat., 11:30 A.M.–1 A.M.

HYOTAN NIPPON ㊻   *Japanese*

119 E. 59th St.
New York
(212) 751-7690
Maître d': K. Furuya
Full Bar/Street Parking
AE, D, MC, V
No dress restrictions

Food preparation is on display at Hyotan Nippon. The main kitchen is in the center of the large dining room so you can watch the skillful chefs prepare such special items as Jumbo Lobster Sashimi, tempura, sukiyaki and a variety of vegetable and "health-oriented" entrées.

Reservations recommended
Lunch: Mon.–Fri., Noon–2:30 P.M.
Dinner: Mon.–Thurs., 5:30 P.M.–10 P.M.
        Fri.–Sat., 5:30 P.M.–10:30 P.M.
        Closed Sunday

IL MONELLO ❶   *Italian*

1460 Broadway
New York
(212) 535-9310
Full Bar/Street Parking
AE, D, MC, V, CB
Jacket for men

The menu selections are made up of mostly Northern Italian specialties, including Muscoli Portofino, Zuppa di Pesce Livornese and Misto di Pesce fra Diavolo. Mr. Giovannetti, the owner, is known for his warm welcome and careful attention to detail.

Reservations required
Lunch: Mon.-Fri., Noon-3 P.M.
Dinner: Mon.-Thurs., 5 P.M.-11 P.M.
       Fri.-Sat., 5 P.M.-Midnight
       Closed Sunday

IL NIDO ❾❾   *Northern Italian*

251 E. 53rd St.
New York
(212) 753-8450
Maître d': Tony Rossini
Full Bar/Street Parking
AE, D, MC, V, CB
Jacket for men

Il Nido's à la carte menu features a number of scallopini and chicken dishes. Very special Italian cakes are served for dessert. All are homemade.

Reservations required
Lunch: Mon.-Sat., Noon-2:30 P.M.
Dinner: Mon.-Sat., 5:30 P.M.-10:30 P.M.
       Closed Sunday

IL VAGABONDO ❺❺   *Northern Italian*

351 E. 62nd St.
New York
(212) 832-9221
Full Bar/Street Parking
AE, D, MC, V, CB
No dress restrictions

A rustic atmosphere predominates — there's even a boccie court in one of the dining rooms! Guests must walk through the kitchen to get to their tables. Specials include osso bucco, homemade gnocchi, Veal Piccata, shrimp scampi, roast veal and Chicken Vagabondo.

No reservations required
Lunch: Mon.-Fri., Noon-3 P.M.
Dinner: Daily, 5:30 P.M.-Midnight

JOE & ROSE RESTAURANT ⓞ⁶   *Italian*

747 Third Ave.
New York
(212) 980-3985
Maître d': John Alzapiedi
Full Bar/Street Parking
AE, D
Jacket for men

In business since 1913, Joe & Rose's is still a family-run operation. Featured are prime steaks, veal, pasta and lobster. The manicotti is homemade and the vegetables are fresh. There is also roast beef and lamb chops.

Reservations required
Lunch: Mon.–Sat., Noon–3 P.M.
Dinner: Mon.–Sat., 5:30 P.M.–10:30 P.M.
        Closed Sunday

KITCHO ⑨   *Japanese*

22 W. 46th St.
New York
(212) 575-8880
Full Bar/Street Parking
AE, D
No dress restrictions

There is three-tiered dining at Kitcho: a modern ground-floor dining area and two floors of traditional tatami rooms where guests remove their shoes before entering. Special features are teriyaki, tempura, sushi and shitashi. There are interesting varieties of ice cream for dessert.

Reservations required
Lunch: Mon.–Fri., Noon–2:30 P.M.
Dinner: Mon.–Fri., 6 P.M.–10:30 P.M.
        Sun., 5 P.M.–10:30 P.M.
        Closed Saturday

LA BIBLIOTHEQUE ⓞ⁹   *French*

341 E. 43rd St.
New York
(212) 661-5757
Full Bar/Lot Parking
AE, D, MC, V, CB
No dress restrictions

Housed in a townhouse overlooking the United Nations Fountain, La Bibliothèque features such specialties as duck with hoisin sauce, Veal Paupiette and daily chef's specials. There is homemade linzer torte or pear and almond paste torte for dessert.

Reservations suggested
Lunch/Dinner: Mon.–Sat., Noon–Midnight
        Closed Sunday

LA CARAVELLE ⓖ *French*

33 W. 55th St.
New York
(212) 586-4252
Maître d': André
Full Bar/Street Parking
AE, D, MC, V, CB
Jacket, tie for men

The feeling of luxury and exclusivity is everywhere — from the impeccable good taste that goes into table appointments and decor to the care taken with each individual meal. Daily specialties might include Pain de Brochet Havriase or Poularde à l'Estragon. There are also regular features such as duckling, tournedos and fish.

Reservations required
Lunch: Mon. – Sat., Noon – 2:30 P.M.
Dinner: Mon. – Thurs., 6 P.M. – 10:30 P.M.
 Fri. – Sat., 6 P.M. – 11 P.M.
 Closed Sunday

LA COCOTTE ⓖ *French*

147 E. 60th St.
New York
(212) 832-8972
Maître d': Joseph
Full Bar/Street Parking
AE, D, MC, V, CB
Jacket for men

La Cocotte features a year-round garden and both *haute* and French Provincial cuisine. It's "the ideal atmosphere for business lunches, a shopping break from Bloomingdale's or a romantic tête-a-tête at dinner," says owner Ernest Guzmits. He offers Quenelles de Brochet avec Champagne, charcuterie Alsacienne, cassoulet and Veal Orloff.

Reservations required
Lunch: Mon. – Sat., Noon – 3 P.M.
Dinner: Mon. – Sat., 5:30 P.M. – 10:30 P.M.
 Closed Sunday

LA COLOMBE D'OR ⓰ *French Provincial*

134 E. 26th St.
New York
(212) 689-0666
Maître d': Leila Anichini
Full Bar/Street Parking
AE, MC, V
No dress restrictions

French country cooking is served in a cheerful setting of floral prints and banquettes. "The Golden Dove" specializes in bouillabaisse, cassoulet, pissaladière and Jambonnet à la Niçoise.

Reservations required on weekend
Lunch: Mon. – Fri., Noon – 2:30 P.M.
Dinner: Daily, 6 P.M. – 11 P.M.

LA COTE BASQUE 64   *French*

5 E. 55th St.
New York
(212) 688-6525
Full Bar/Street Parking
AE, D
Jacket, tie for men

A place for serious eating and, it seems, for serious people-watching, La Côte Basque offers classical cuisine served against a backdrop of lustrous murals. You are transported to the salon of a great mansion and count yourself lucky to be among the honored guests. A house specialty is Côte de Veau aux Morilles.

Reservations required
Lunch: Mon.–Sat., Noon–2:30 P.M.
Dinner: Mon.–Sat., 6 P.M.–10:30 P.M.
    Closed Sunday

LA GAULOISE 20   *French*

502 Avenue of the Americas
New York
(212) 691-1363
Full Bar/Street Parking
AE, D, MC, V
Jacket for men

If business or curiosity takes you to the lower part of Manhattan, you might want to keep La Gauloise in mind. Located at 13th Street, La Gauloise features daily specials for lunch and dinner, as well as a Sunday brunch.

Reservations required
Lunch: Mon.–Sat., Noon–3 P.M.
Dinner: Daily, 5:45 P.M.–11:30 P.M.
Brunch: Sun., Noon–4:30 P.M.

LA GOULUE 38   *French*

28 E. 70th St.
New York
(212) 988-8169
Full Bar/Street Parking
AE, D, MC, V
No dress restrictions

La Goulue is described as an Art Nouveau bistro-cafe, circa 1920. There is wood paneling, antique fixtures, a zinc bar, tin ceiling and lace curtains framing the windows. Look for Veau aux Morilles, cheese soufflé and Orange Napoleon.

Reservations required
Lunch: Mon.–Sat., Noon–3 P.M..
Dinner: Mon.–Sat., 6 P.M.–11:30 P.M.
    Closed Sunday

LA GRENOUILLE ❽❸ *French*

3 E. 52nd St.
New York
(212) 752-1495
Maître d': Jean Benjamin
Full Bar/No Parking
AE, D
Jacket for men

La Grenouille is full of Gallic élan, with its clusters of flowers, illuminated mirrors and general joie de vivre. They feature such items as Poularde au Champagne, Bass dans Son Fumet, quenelles, soufflés, Canard aux Fruits and, of course, *les grenouilles*.

Reservations required
Lunch: Mon.–Sat., 12:15 P.M.–3 P.M.
Dinner: Mon.–Sat., 6:15 P.M.–10:30 P.M.
    Closed Sunday

L'AIGLON ⓫ *French*

24 W. 55th St.
New York
(212) 753-7295
Maître d': Roger
Full Bar/Street Parking
AE, D, MC, V, CB
Jacket, tie for men

The Napoleonic decor is a suitable setting for the French cuisine with Italian overtones. Specialties include Steak l'Aiglon, prepared at your table, Veal Chop l'Aiglon and Duck à l'Orange.

Reservations required
Lunch/Dinner: Daily

LA PETITE FERME ⓴ *French*

973 Lexington Ave.
New York
(212) 249-3272
Maître d': Michael and Nan (manager)
Full Bar/Street Parking
AE, D, MC, V, CB
No dress restrictions

As its name suggests, La Petite Ferme brings a country garden atmosphere to the middle of Manhattan. House specialties include Moules Vinaigrette, poached trout in a sauce of butter, shallots and vinegar, poached lobster, Filet Sophie (filet mignon with truffles and wrapped in pastry), grilled swordfish and sautéed calf's liver.

Reservations recommended
Lunch: Mon.–Sat., Noon–2:30 P.M.
Dinner: Mon.–Sat., 6 P.M.–10:30 P.M.
    Closed Sunday

LA PETITE MARMITE ● French

5 Mitchell Pl.
New York
(212) 826-1084
Maître d': Gerard Butruille
Full Bar/Street Parking
AE, D, MC, V, CB
Jacket for men preferred

The expertise of the management and kitchen staff has gone into making La Petite Marmite something special, say many New Yorkers. It seems to be a favorite among U.N. diplomats, publishers and other celebrities. Specialties include poached bass, Moules Vinaigrette, Maquereau au Vin Blanc and *les petites marmites* (chunks of meat and vegetables served in a crock pot).

Reservations required
Lunch: Mon. – Fri., Noon – 3 P.M.
Dinner: Mon. – Sat., 6 P.M. – 10 P.M.
    Closed Sunday

LA RESIDENCE ● French

1568 First Ave.
New York
(212) 628-4100
Maître d': Primo Laurenti
Full Bar/Lot Parking
AE, D, V
Jacket for men

La Résidence is the result of owner George Colovic's years of experience at restaurants in New York and Washington (Lutèce, Rive Gauche, etc.). The food owes much to his creativity and to the changing seasons, which dictate the seafood selection and game specialties. Entrées include Bass Grenobloise and Côte de Veaux aux Raisins.

Reservations required
Dinner: Mon. – Sat., 6 P.M. – 11 P.M.
    Closed Sunday

LA TULIPE ● French

104 W. 13th St.
New York
(212) 691-8860
Maître d': John Darr (manager and co-owner)
Full Bar/Street Parking
AE, D, MC, V
No dress restrictions

Co-owner and chef Sally Darr (formerly food editor of *Gourmet*) and John Darr preside over this 14-table restaurant. Their specialties include Papillote de Red Snapper aux Legumes and homemade sherbets and ice cream "en tulipe."

Reservations required
Dinner: Tues. – Sun., 6:30 P.M. – 10 P.M.
    Closed Monday

LAURENT ㊼   *French*

111 E. 56th St.
New York
(212) 753-2729
Maître d': James
Full Bar/Street Parking
AE, D
Jacket, tie for men

"Superb French cuisine and attentive service amid distinguished surroundings" is how owner Laurent Losa likes to describe his restaurant. He offers seasonal specialties such as venison, shad roe and soft-shelled crabs. He is also proud of his selection of wines, maintained at their peak in air-conditioned cellars.

Reservations required
Lunch: Mon.-Sat., Noon-3 P.M.
Dinner Mon.-Sat., 6 P.M.-10:30 P.M.
    Sun., 5 P.M.-10:30 P.M.

LE CHANTILLY ㊼   *French*

106 E. 57th St.
New York
(212) 751-2931
Maître d': Paul Dessibourg
Full Bar/Street Parking
AE, MC, V
Jacket, tie for men

Le Chantilly is noted for true elegance without "foolish snobbery," says the management. They pride themselves on courteous, efficient service. Hors d'oeuvre are a special feature. Some entrées include Delice de Veau Franc-Comtois, Poularde Chantilly, Noisettes d'Agneau au Poivre Vert and Dolices de Sole Chantilly.

Reservations required
Lunch: Mon.-Sat., Noon-3 P.M.
Dinner: Mon.-Sat., 6 P.M.-11 P.M.
    Closed Sunday

LE CIRQUE ㊻   *French/Continental*

58 E. 65th St.
New York
(212) 794-9292
Maître d': Joe Garni
Full Bar/Lot Parking
AE, D
Jacket, tie for men

Le Cirque offers diners old-school elegance. The dining room is decorated with reproductions of murals from the Singerie in the Château de Versailles. Examples of the classic French and Continental cuisine include Pasta Primavera, duck with lemon, apples and raisins, Fettuccine al Prosciutto, lamb and pâté de campagne.

Reservations required
Lunch: Mon.-Sat., Noon-3 P.M.
Dinner: Mon.-Sat., 6 P.M.-10 P.M.
    Closed Sunday

LE COUP DE FUSIL ⑤⓪   *French*

160 E. 64th St.
New York
(212) 751-9110
Maître d': Pierre
Full Bar/Street Parking
AE, D, MC, V, CB
Jacket, tie for men

A small, intimate, cozy but elegant restaurant, Le Coup de Fusil specializes in *la nouvelle cuisine*. The menu changes according to ingredients available in season, but could include Le Poulet au Pot, Bass à la Julienne de Legumes or Navarin de Homard à la Truffe Noire.

Reservations required
Lunch: Mon.-Fri., Noon-2:30 P.M.
Dinner: Mon.-Fri., 5:30 P.M.-10:30 P.M.
  Sat., 5:30 P.M.-11 P.M.
  Closed Sunday

LE CYGNE ⑧⑤   *French*

53 E. 54th St.
New York
(212) 759-5941
Maître d': Robert LeLamer
Full Bar/Street Parking
AE, D
Jacket, tie for men

Elegant and small, with flowers on each table and maps of 18th-century Paris on the wall, Le Cygne serves classic French cuisine and some provincial specialties.

Reservations required
Lunch: Mon.-Fri., Noon-2 P.M.
Dinner: Mon.-Sat., 6 P.M.-10 P.M.
  Closed Sunday

LE LAVANDOU ⑤③   *French*

134 E. 61st St.
New York
(212) 838-7987
Maître d': Luc Chevalier
Full Bar/Street Parking
AE
Jacket, tie for men

Like so many New York French restaurants, Le Lavandou is comfortably intimate (or small and cozy). Its name comes from a province in the south of France. The special dishes also hail from that region, including Cassoulet Toulousaine, Striped Bass aux Aromates and Mignon de Boeuf Feuilletage.

Reservations required
Lunch: Mon.-Sat., Noon-2 P.M.
Dinner: Mon.-Sat., 6 P.M.-10:15 P.M.
  Closed Sunday

LE MADRIGAL ⓐ   *French*

216 E. 53rd St.
New York
(212) 355-0322
Maître d': Hubert
Full Bar/Lot Parking
AE, D, MC, V, CB
No dress restrictions

French Directoire paintings set the scene at Le Madrigal. The restaurant terrace overlooks a small garden. Classic French cuisine is served against this backdrop, including such specialties as Medaillon de Veau aux Morilles, Striped Bass Flambé Madrigal and Filet de Boeuf en Chemise au Poivre Vert.

Reservations required
Lunch: Mon.–Fri., Noon–3 P.M.
Dinner: Mon.–Sat., 6 P.M.–10:30 P.M.
 Closed Sunday

LE MANOIR ⓐ   *French*

120 E. 56th St.
New York
(212) 753-1447
Maître d': Robert
Full Bar/Street Parking
AE, D, MC, V, CB
No dress restrictions

A peaceful, serene atmosphere prevails at Le Manoir. It is an appropriate setting for such delicately subtle dishes as Bass Beurre Blanc, mussels in white wine, Poulet Vinaigre and Boeuf en Croûte.

No reservations required
Lunch: Mon.–Sat., Noon–3 P.M.
Dinner: Mon.–Sat., 5 P.M.–11 P.M.
 Closed Sunday

LE PERIGORD ⓐ   *French*

405 E. 52nd St.
New York
(212) 755-6244
Maître d': Georges Briguet
Full Bar/Street Parking
AE, D, MC, V
Jacket, tie for men

Located in fashionable Sutton Place, Le Perigord is proud of its extremely low noise level due to sound-absorbing matting supporting the wall fabric. The classical French specialties include Medaillon de Veau Archiduc, Grenadine de Veau Normande and Nage de Coquilles St. Jacques.

Reservations required
Lunch: Mon.–Fri., Noon–3 P.M.
Dinner: Mon.–Sat., 5:15 P.M.–10:30 P.M.
 Closed Sunday

LE PERIGORD-PARK ㊼ *French*

575 Park Ave.
New York
(212) 752-0050/1
Maître d': Louis Barlou
Full Bar/Street Parking
AE, D, MC, V
Jacket for men

Such specialties as Clams aux Fines Herbes et Vin Blanc and Truite Inspiration du Chef are served in an elegantly designed setting. There are crystal chandeliers, gold-colored banquettes and ivory tones in the main dining room and vaulted stucco ceilings, dark wood paneling and dim lighting in the second and third dining rooms.

Reservations required
Lunch: Mon.-Fri., Noon-3 P.M.
Dinner: Daily, 6 P.M.-11 P.M.

LE PLAISIR ㊶ *French/Eclectic*

969 Lexington Ave.
New York
(212) 734-9430
Full Bar/Street Parking
AE, D, MC, V
Jacket, tie for men

La nouvelle cuisine, prepared with both imagination and skill, is the order here. There are such specialties as game in season and pasta garnished with truffles. Artful presentation is as important as careful preparation.

Reservations required
Lunch: Tues.-Sat., Noon-2:30 P.M.
Dinner: Mon.-Sat., 7 P.M.-10:30 P.M.
      Closed Sunday

LE RELAIS ㊺ *French*

712 Madison Ave.
New York
(212) 751-5108
Maître d': François
Full Bar/Street Parking
AE
No dress restrictions

An elegant throwback to the orderly world of the 18th century, Le Relais features banquette seating as well as seating on a small terrace. Specialties include fresh fish, including cold salmon, liver, steak, lamb and roasted duck with a sauce of honey, raspberries and vinegar.

Reservations required
Lunch: Mon.-Sat., Noon-3 P.M.
Dinner: Mon.-Fri., 6:30 P.M.-11 P.M.
      Sat.-Sun., 7 P.M.-11 P.M.
Brunch: Sun., 12:30 P.M.-3:30 P.M.

L'ESCARGOT ⓖ   French

47 W. 55th St.
New York
(212) 245-4266/755-0968
Maître d': Frank Caselli (owner)
Full Bar/Street Parking
AE, D, MC, V, CB
No dress restrictions

Owner Frank Caselli calls L'Escargot "comfortable and warm," with its French Provincial decor in two maining dining rooms and a private party room. His specialties include Escargots aux Ricard, Steak au Poivre Vert, venison, Saumon Pochée au Vin Blanc and Salmis de Canard. There is a wide selection of international and domestic wines.

Reservations required
Lunch/Dinner: Mon.–Sat., Noon–Midnight
          Closed Sunday

LE STEAK ⓖ   French/American

1089 Second Ave.
New York
(212) 421-9072
Full Bar/Street Parking
AE, D
Jacket for men

You can easily understand the French-American connection at Le Steak. The "Le" stands for the French-style sauces served to enhance the steaks *and* for the accompanying *pommes frites*. The "Steak" part is very American — a good selection of prime steaks, carefully cooked to your order.

No reservations required
Dinner: Daily, 5:30 P.M.–11 P.M.

LE VEAU D'OR ⓖ   French

129 E. 60th St.
New York
(212) 838-8133
Maître d': Joseph Le Goff
Full Bar/Street Parking
AE
Jacket for men

This French-style bistro features typical bistro dishes such as cassoulet, onion soup and light entrées and appetizers.

Reservations suggested
Lunch: Mon.–Sat., Noon–2:30 P.M.
Dinner: Mon.–Sat., from 6 P.M.
          Closed Sunday

LUCHOW'S ㉑   *German*

110 E. 14th St.
New York
(212) 477-4860
Maître d': Heino Guelland
Full Bar/Street Parking
AE, D, MC, V, CB
No dress restrictions

This 99-year-old historical landmark specializes in such traditional German dishes as sauerbraten and Schnitzel à la Luchow. The restaurant is filled with numerous antiques and paintings.

Reservations required
Lunch: Mon.–Sat., 11:30 A.M.–2:30 P.M.
Dinner: Mon.–Sat., 5 P.M.–11 P.M.
      Sun., Noon–11 P.M.

LUTECE ⑩   *French*

249 E. 50th St.
New York
(212) 752-2225
Full Bar/Street Parking
AE
Jacket, tie for men

Lutèce is what seems to be the ultimate in thoroughly French food preparation and service. The daily specials are noted for their originality. Owner/chef André Soltner creates such pièces de résistance as Timbales d'Escargots à la Chablisienne, Cassolette de Crabe "Vieille France," Delice de Veau aux Girolles and Soufflé Glace aux Framboises.

Reservations required
Lunch: Tues.–Fri., Noon–1:45 P.M.
Dinner: Mon.–Sat., 6 P.M.–9:30 P.M.
      Closed Sunday

MADAME ROMAINE DE LYON ㉑   *French*

32 E. 61st St.
New York
(212) 758-2422
Maître d': Yvonne Fravola (owner)
Beer and Wine/Lot and Street Parking
No credit cards
No dress restrictions

Omelets reign supreme at Madame Romaine de Lyon. There are "around" 550 different varieties, according to owner Yvonne Fravola. They range from Rochambeau (spinach, sausage, mushrooms and cheese) to Jourdan (caviar, ham, bacon, onions, mushrooms and cheese) to Supreme (chestnuts and chocolate sauce).

No reservations required (except for four or more)
Lunch: Daily, 11 A.M.–3 P.M.

MAXWELL'S PLUM ㊹   *Continental*

64th St. and First Ave.
New York
(212) 628-2100
Full Bar/Street Parking
AE, D, MC, V, CB
No dress restrictions

Maxwell's Plum is known for its back-room dining area with its Tiffany glass ceiling, its casual sidewalk cafe and its singularly busy singles bar. The food is eclectic, the wine selection is varied and the scene is unforgettable.

Reservations required
Lunch/Dinner: Daily, Noon – 2 A.M.

MR. CHOW'S ⓱   *Chinese/Continental*

324 E. 57th St.
New York
(212) 751-9030
Maître d': Jean-Charles Pelluet
Full Bar/Street Parking
AE, D, MC, V
No dress restrictions

You might think you're on board a 1930's luxury liner. There's the lacquered walls, the marble and the whole Art Déco ambience. Specials include Peking Duck and drunken fish.

Reservations required
Lunch: Mon. – Fri., 12:30 P.M. – 2:30 P.M.
Dinner: Daily, 6:30 P.M. – Midnight

MR. LEE'S ⓲   *International*

337 Third Ave.
New York
(212) 689-6373
Full Bar/Street Parking
AE, D, MC, V
Jacket for men

The fare at Mr. Lee's has been described as a mélange of French and Mediterranean styles with Chinese overtones. The goal is to combine two of the world's great cuisines into an exciting new strain.

Reservations required
Lunch: Mon. – Fri., Noon – 3 P.M.
Dinner: Mon. – Sat., 6 P.M. – 11 P.M.
    Closed Sunday

MONSIGNORE II 86 *Italian*

61 E. 55th St.
New York
(212) 355-2070
Maître d': Baron DeTorok
Full Bar/Valet Parking
AE, D, MC, V, CB
Jacket, tie for men

A coral-colored interior with walls covered by glossy murals serves as backdrop for such specialties as Veal Fontina, Vitella Sorrentina, Bass Livornese and, for dessert, Zuppa Inglese. There are several pasta dishes, and if one you crave is not listed on the menu, just ask for it.

Reservations required
Lunch: Mon.–Fri., Noon–3 P.M.
Dinner: Mon.–Sat., 5:45 P.M.–Midnight
   Closed Sunday

NANNI 110 *Italian*

146 E. 46th St.
New York
(212) 697-4161
Maître d': Franco Bugoni
Full Bar/Lot Parking
AE, D, MC, V
No dress restrictions

The list of Italian specialties at Nanni is a long and tempting one: Risotto con Tartufi, Pollo Valdostana, Scampi Provinciale, Scaloppine Ortolana, Bass Marechiaro, etc. etc.

Reservations required
Lunch: Mon.–Fri., Noon–3 P.M.
Dinner: Mon.–Sat., 5:30 P.M.–11 P.M.
   Closed Sunday

NANNI AL VALLETTO 52 *Italian*

133 E. 61st St.
New York
(212) 838-3939
Maître d': Gianni Caravelli
Full Bar/Street Parking
AE, D, MC, V, CB
Jacket for men

Beauty and luxury envelop you at Nanni al Valletto, and the special dishes will no doubt add to your sense of well-being. There are such selections as Gnocchi alla Nanni, Snapper al Cartoccio, Calamari alla Luciana and Risotto alla Quaglie.

Reservations required
Lunch: Mon.–Fri., Noon–2:30 P.M.
Dinner: Mon.–Sat., 5:30 P.M.–11:30 P.M.
   Closed Sunday

NICOLA PAONE ⑮   *Italian*

207 E. 34th St.
New York
(212) 889-3239
Full Bar/Street Parking
AE, D
Jacket, tie for men

Service is given the same priority as food at Nicola Paone, states the owner of the same name. Dishes include Serenata (noodles mixed with cream and baked), Fish Malandrino, Chicken Baci Baci, Boom Boom and Nightgown. (Their true identity is for you to discover.)

Reservations required
Lunch: Mon.–Fri., Noon–1:30 P.M.
Dinner: Mon.–Sat., 5 P.M.–9:30 P.M.
   Closed Sunday

NIPPON ⑯   *Japanese*

145 E. 52nd St.
New York
(212) 688-5940
Maître d': Y. Makoshi
Full Bar/Street Parking
AE, D, MC, V, CB
No dress restrictions

You may not come upon too many dining rooms designed in a 7th-century Heian style. Nippon, with its tatami rooms equipped with foot wells for greater comfort, and its sushi bar made of prime hinoki wood, is such a place. Traditional Japanese dishes are prepared with cooking wine and refined vegetable oil. The cooking is termed "health-oriented."

Reservations required
Lunch: Mon.–Fri., Noon–2:30 P.M.
Dinner: Mon.–Thurs., 5:30 P.M.–10 P.M.
    Fri.–Sat., 5:30 P.M.–10:30 P.M.
   Closed Sunday

ORSINI'S ㊽   *Italian*

41 W. 56th St.
New York
(212) 757-1698
Maître d': Nino
Full Bar/Street Parking
AE, D, MC, V, CB
Jacket, tie for men

There is an Italian-garden feeling about Orsini's, with its tile tables and variety of plants. But that's only upstairs. Downstairs, the mood is romantic — all velvet walls, intimacy and Baroque decor. The cuisine is basically Roman, including Fettuccine Alfredo, Scampi alla Romano and Veal Piccata.

No reservations required
Lunch: Mon.–Sat., Noon–3 P.M.
Dinner: Mon.–Sat., 5:30 P.M.–1 A.M.
   Closed Sunday

THE OYSTER BAR & RESTAURANT ⑫ *Seafood*

Grand Central Station
Lower Level
New York
(212) 599-1000
Maître d': Marcel Kurzen (manager)
Full Bar/Lot Parking (garage)
AE, D, MC, V, CB
No dress restrictions

This premier seafood restaurant serves only the freshest available fish and shellfish. The menu changes daily, depending on market availability. On any given day there is a choice of over 100 different items. Fresh fish and shellfish are flown in from all parts of the U.S. and Europe.

Reservations required
Lunch/Dinner: Mon.–Fri., 11:30 A.M.–9:30 P.M.
    Closed Saturday, Sunday

THE PALACE ⑭ *French*

420 E. 59th St.
New York
(212) 355-5150
Maître d': Pierre Benjamin
Beer and Wine/Lot Parking
AE, D, MC, V, CB
Jacket, tie for men

The much-publicized Palace does offer guests a memorable dining experience. There are seven courses of *haute, haute cuisine* served by a corps of discreetly attentive waiters, sommeliers et al. The price is steep, but most Palace veterans say you are paying for more than a meal; you are paying for a carefully scripted theatrical presentation.

Reservations required
Dinner: Mon.–Sat., 7 P.M.–9:30 P.M.
    Closed Sunday

PALM ⑧ *American*

837 Second Ave.
New York
(212) 687-2953
Maître d': Bruno Molinari
Full Bar/Street Parking
AE, D, MC, V, CB
No dress restrictions

One of several Palms around the country, the New York flagship is famous for its sawdust floors, cartoons on the wall, giant lobsters and mammoth steaks. They say they have the creamiest cheesecake around — for those who can last until dessert.

Reservations required (lunch only)
Lunch/Dinner: Mon.–Sat., Noon–10:45 P.M.
    Closed Sunday

PANACHE   ⓘ④   *French*

359 E. 50th St.
New York
(212) 755-3552
Full Bar/Street Parking
AE, D, MC, V, CB
Good taste in dress required

Panache is a classic French restaurant with rosy-beige paneled fabric walls and contemporary lighting fixtures—it's called "the look of the 80's." Specialties include bouillabaisse, Canard au Poivre Vert and Crêpes Kiwi et Framboise. It is located near Beekman Place and the United Nations.

Reservations recommended
Lunch: Mon.–Fri., Noon–3 P.M.
Dinner: Daily, 6 P.M.–10:30 P.M.

PARIOLI ROMANISSIMO   ㊷   *Italian*

1466 First Ave.
New York
(212) 288-2391
Maître d': Adriano
Full Bar/Street Parking
AE, D
Jacket, tie for men

Bolognese and Northern Italian specialties are presented here in the form of Tortellini alla Arrabiata, Veal Scaloppine Capriccio, cannelloni and Pescatora Veneziana. It is all served in a romantic setting of flattering lights and Roman terraces.

Reservations required
Dinner: Tues.–Sat., 6 P.M.–11 P.M.
    Closed Sunday, Monday

PATSY'S   ❸   *Italian*

235 W. 56th St.
New York
(212) 247-3491/2
Full Bar/Street Parking
AE, D, V
Jacket for men

Patsy's has been serving hearty Neapolitan fare for the past 40 years. Some of the substantial specialties include Veal Marsala, Mussels alla Marinara, Cassuola di Pesce and heaping portions of pasta. There is also Chicken Contadina, Calf's Brains Arreganata, hot antipasto and Bass Marechiaro.

No reservations required
Lunch/Dinner: Sun., Tues.–Thurs., Noon–10:45 P.M.
    Fri.–Sat., Noon–11:45 P.M.
    Closed Monday

PEARL'S ⓽²   *Chinese*

38 W. 48th St.
New York
(212) 586-1060
Full Bar/Street Parking
No credit cards
Jacket, tie for men

Pearl's features the elegant *haute cuisine* of China and presents it in an equally elegant setting. The Lemon Chicken is often requested, along with a number of other painstakingly prepared dishes.

Reservations required
Lunch: Mon.–Fri., Noon–2:30 P.M.
Dinner: Sun.–Fri., 5 P.M.–10:30 P.M.
   Closed Saturday

PEN & PENCIL ⓷   *American*

205 E. 45th St.
New York
(212) 682-8660/1580
Maître d': Tullio and George
Full Bar/Valet Parking
AE, D, MC, V, CB
No dress restrictions

Considered by some to be America's finest steak house, Pen & Pencil is in its 44th year of operation. They specialize in the finest of prime aged beef. Owner John C. Bruno continues the family tradition by personally selecting all prime meats.

No reservations required
Lunch/Dinner: Mon.–Fri., 11:45 A.M.–11:30 P.M.
            Sat.–Sun., 4:30 P.M.–11:30 P.M.

THE QUILTED GIRAFFE ⓸   *French*

955 Second Ave.
New York
(212) 753-5355
Full Bar/Street Parking
AE, D, MC, V, CB
Jacket, tie for men

A rather recent addition to the New York *nouvelle cuisine* scene, The Quilted Giraffe has garnered raves. House specialties include Salmon Tartar, a strudel of crabmeat, and lamb chops with vegetables, prepared in a veil.

Reservations required
Lunch: Tues.–Fri., Noon–2 P.M.
Dinner: Mon.–Sat., 6 P.M.–10 P.M.
   Closed Sunday

QUO VADIS ㊽ *French*

26 E. 63rd St.
New York
(212) 838-0590
Maître d': Marcel Isnard
Full Bar/Street Parking
AE, D, MC, V, CB
Jacket, tie for men

Quo Vadis is an interesting combination of Roman decor and French cuisine. There are such specialties as Crêpes Quo Vadis, Carré d'Agneau and Soufflés Tous Parfums.

Reservations required
Lunch: Mon.-Sat., Noon-3:30 P.M.
Dinner: Mon.-Sat., 6 P.M.-11 P.M.
Closed Sunday
July and August, closed Saturday and Sunday

RAGA (91) *Indian*

57 W. 48th St.
New York
(212) 757-3450
Full Bar/Lot Parking
AE, D, MC, V, CB
No dress restrictions

Elegant and chic, with handcarved antique woodwork and brass trimmings, Raga specializes in Oysters Bombay, tandoori (clay oven barbecue), lamb and chicken dishes and a wide variety of Indian rices and breads. Indian music is featured each evening.

Reservations required
Lunch: Mon.-Fri., Noon-3 P.M.
Dinner: Daily, 5 P.M.-11 P.M.

THE RAINBOW ROOM & GRILL (81) *Continental*

30 Rockefeller Plaza
New York
(212) 757-9090/8970
Full Bar/Lot Parking
AE, D, MC, V, CB
Jacket, tie for men
Jacket for men (Grill)

Superb, unobstructed views of the city, Art Déco elegance, dancing cheek to cheek and loads of romance. All this has meant The Rainbow Room and Rainbow Grill to a lot of people for a very long time. There are French and Italian specialties, including Gulf Shrimp Maison.

Reservations recommended
Rainbow Room:
Dinner: Sun.-Mon., 5 P.M.-10 P.M.
Tues.-Sat., 5 P.M.-11:30 P.M.
Brunch: Sun., 11:30 A.M.-3 P.M.

Grill:
Dinner: Mon.-Thurs., 7:30 P.M.-11:30 P.M.
Fri.-Sat., 7:30 P.M.-12:30 A.M.
Closed Sunday

RAPHAEL ⓬   *French*

33 W. 54th St.
New York
(212) 582-8993/4
Maître d': Raphael Edery (owner)
Full Bar/Lot and Street Parking
AE, D
Jacket, tie for men

There's a French country aura about this small, sophisticated restaurant. The special dishes, focusing on *la nouvelle cuisine*, including Long Island Bay Scallops Marines à la Crème Fraîche, Steak de Saumon au Vinaigre de Framboise, Carré d'Agneau de Lait and Magret de Canard au Vinaigre de Miel.

Reservations required
Lunch: Mon.–Fri., Noon–2:15 P.M.
Dinner: Mon.–Sat., 6 P.M.–10 P.M.
   Closed Sunday

RENE PUJOL ⑤   *French*

321 W. 51st St.
New York
(212) 246-3023
Maître d': André Manoukian
Full Bar/Street Parking
AE, D, MC, V
No dress restrictions

René Pujol lists as his specialties Ballotine de Brochet en Croûte, Saumon à l'Oseille, Gratin de Homard au Whiskey, Dodine de Volaille aux Cèpes and Selle d'Agneau en Croûte. For dessert, there is Charlotte aux Poires and Mousse au Chocolat.

Reservations required
Lunch: Mon.–Sat., Noon–3 P.M.
Dinner: Mon.–Sat., 5 P.M.–11:30 P.M.
   Closed Sunday

RESTAURANT MAURICE ㊿   *French*

118 W. 57th St.
New York
(212) 245-7788
Full Bar/Lot Parking
AE, D, MC, V, CB
Jacket for men

This formal dining room features deep blue banquettes and beautiful murals. Recipes come from Alain Senderens of l'Archestrate in Paris. Meals begin with a sampling of hors d'oeuvre or Le Pigeon aux Endives Confite. Also offered are medallions of lobster on four different types of lettuce, with mangos and carrots.

Reservations required
Lunch: Daily, Noon–3 P.M.
Dinner: Daily, 6 P.M.–11:30 P.M.

THE RIGHT BANK ㊴

Continental

822 Madison Ave.
New York
(212) 737-2811
Full Bar/Street Parking
AE, D, MC, V, CB
No dress restrictions

At The Right Bank you dine in a casual, relaxed atmosphere, reminiscent of a small French cafe. There is an outdoor garden patio for cocktails and summer dining. The daily chef's specials include Duck aux Pommes, Beef Burgundy and Chicken Gismonde.

No reservations required
Lunch/Dinner: Daily, 11:30 A.M. - 1 A.M.

THE RIVER CAFE ㉚

Continental

1 Water St.
Brooklyn, N.Y.
(212) 522-5200
Full Bar/Street Parking
AE, D
Good taste in dress required

One of New York's "in" spots happens to be in Brooklyn—and on a barge beneath the Brooklyn Bridge! The River Cafe affords you a grand view of New York Harbor as well as such specialties as veal chops, calf's liver, fillet of sole and several different kinds of pasta.

Reservations required
Lunch: Daily, 11:30 A.M. - 2:30 P.M.
Dinner: Daily, 6 P.M. - 11 P.M.
Brunch: Sun., 11:30 A.M. - 3 P.M.

ROMEO SALTA (59)

Italian

30 W. 56th St.
New York
(212) 246-5772
Maître d': Salvatore Salta (owner)
Full Bar/Street Parking
AE, D, MC, V, CB
Jacket for men

Romeo Salta specializes in cuisine originating from the various provinces of Italy. Northern Italian specialties include swordfish steak in a tangy olive and caper sauce. From the central provinces comes Saltimbocca alla Romana, and from the deep south comes Pappardelle Giovanni—thick noodles in a hot spicy tomato sauce.

Reservations required
Lunch/Dinner: Mon. - Sat., Noon - 11:30 P.M.
Closed Sunday

RUSSIAN TEA ROOM   ❻   *Russian*

150 W. 57th St.
New York
(212) 265-0947
Full Bar/Lot and Street Parking
AE, D, MC, V, CB
Jacket for men

There are several legends surrounding the Russian Tea Room. One story goes that Nureyev gracefully slides into his private booth each night without great recognition or fanfare. Classic Russian cuisine is served amid samovars and original paintings. Look for Chicken Kiev, borscht, blinis, caviar and ice cold vodka.

Reservations requested
Lunch/Dinner: Sun. - Fri., 11:30 A.M. - 1 A.M.
              Sat., 11:30 A.M. - 2 A.M.

SALTA IN BOCCA   ⓭   *Northern Italian*

179 Madison Ave.
New York
(212) 684-1757
Full Bar/Street Parking
AE, D, MC, V, CB
No dress restrictions

"Just about everything listed merits superlatives," says Salta in Bocca co-owner Fulvio Tramontina just a bit immodestly. House specialties include Tortellini Gratinati, Spaghetti Carbonara, Pollo Scarpara, saltimbocca and Calamaretti Fritti "so light and delicious they jump into your mouth!"

Reservations required
Lunch/Dinner: Mon. - Thurs., Noon - 10:30 P.M.
              Fri. - Sat., Noon - 11 P.M.
              Closed Sunday

SEA FARE OF THE AEGEAN   ⓰⓿   *Seafood*

25 W. 56th St.
New York
(212) 581-0540
Maître d': Costa and Nick
Full Bar/Street Parking
AE, D, MC, V, CB
Jacket for men

Just the name of this restaurant gets you in a faraway frame of mind. Specialties such as Shrimps Santorini, striped bass en casserole (done in the Aegean style) and Mexican shrimp baked with Greek feta cheese and grilled with tomato and Santorini sauce are served in a setting filled with original art.

Reservations suggested
Lunch/Dinner: Mon. - Sat., Noon - 11 P.M.
              Sun., 1 P.M. - 11 P.M.
              Closed Major Holidays

SHEZAN 56 — North Indian

8 W. 58th St.
New York
(212) 371-1414
Maître d': Vinod Bhatia
Full Bar/Street Parking
AE, D, V
No dress restrictions

Shezan is a place for authentic Indo-Pakistani cuisine. They specialize in barbecued food cooked in a tandoor (clay oven). The curry is prepared with a special blend of herbs and spices. Freshly baked hot bread also comes from the unique clay ovens.

Reservations required
Lunch: Mon.–Fri., Noon–3 P.M.
Dinner: Mon.–Fri., 6 P.M.–11 P.M.
Sat., 6 P.M.–Midnight
Closed Sunday

SHUN LEE DYNASTY 107 — Chinese

900 Second Ave.
New York
(212) 755-3900
Maître d': Donald Mui (manager)
Full Bar/Lot Parking
AE, D, CB
No dress restrictions

A Chinese restaurant of modern design, Shun Lee Dynasty specializes in Szechuan, Hunan and classical Chinese cooking. There are several lobster and shrimp dishes, beef with orange-flavored sauce and Peking Duck.

Reservations suggested
Lunch/Dinner: Sun.–Thurs., 11:30 A.M.–11 P.M.
Fri.–Sat., 11:30 A.M.–1 A.M.

THE SIGN OF THE DOVE 54 — Continental

1110 Third Ave.
New York
(212) 861-8080
Maître d': Jean Fayet
Full Bar/Lot and Street Parking
AE, D, MC, V, CB
Jacket, tie for men

There is a French-Italian mix to the cuisine served at The Sign of the Dove. The elegant interior is set off by fresh flowers and beautiful plants. There is a strolling violinist on Friday and Saturday evenings.

Reservations recommended
Lunch: Tues.–Sat., Noon–3 P.M.
Dinner: Mon.–Thurs., 6 P.M.–Midnight
Fri.–Sun., 6 P.M.–1 A.M.
Brunch: Sun., Noon–4 P.M.

SOHO CHARCUTERIE & RESTAURANT ㉕ *French*

195 Spring St.
New York
(212) 226-3545
Full Bar/Street Parking
AE, MC, V
No dress restrictions

A combination retail gourmet shop and restaurant, Soho Charcuterie offers dishes described as "imaginative." There are such specialties as Ris de Veau Financière, Poulet à la Bière Noire and Croustade de Fruits de Mer. The decor reflects the simplicity of Soho design.

Reservations required
Lunch: Mon.–Fri., Noon–3 P.M.
        Sat., 11:30 A.M.–4 P.M.
Dinner: Tues.–Thurs., 6 P.M.–11 P.M.
        Fri., 6 P.M.–11:30 P.M.
        Sat., 6 P.M.–Midnight
Brunch: Sun., 11 A.M.–4:30 P.M.
        Closed Monday for dinner

TAVERN ON THE GREEN ㊲ *Continental*

67th St. and Central Park West
New York
(212) 873-3200
Maître d': Raymond Garcia, Paul Capocasale
Full Bar/Valet Parking
AE, D, MC, V, CB
No dress restrictions

Tavern on the Green is brass, oak and ancient brick, shimmering candles and crystal chandeliers imported from European palaces. The almost pastoral Central Park setting is unique among New York restaurants. Menu selections include rack of lamb, Dover Sole Connaught and Crêpes Jennifer.

Reservations suggested
Lunch/Dinner: Mon.–Fri., Noon–1 A.M.
              Sat., 11 A.M.–1 A.M.
              Sun., 10 A.M.–1 A.M.

TRATTORIA DA ALFREDO ⑰ *Italian*

90 Bank St.
New York
(212) 929-4400
Maître d': Charles Murdock
No Wine or Spirits/Street Parking
No credit cards
No dress restrictions

A tiny restaurant in humble surroundings, Trattoria da Alfredo features unusual and imaginative Italian food. Specialties include Veal Milanese, Carpaccio and the pasta of the day with a one-of-a-kind sauce. Wine is available at nearby stores.

Reservations required
Lunch: Mon., Wed.–Sat., Noon–2 P.M.
Dinner: Mon., Wed.–Sat., 6 P.M.–10:30 P.M.
        Sun., 5 P.M.–9:30 P.M.
        Closed Tuesday

"21" CLUB ⓻⓽ American

21 W. 52nd St.
New York
(212) 582-7200
Full Bar/Street Parking
AE, D, MC, V, CB
Jacket, tie for men
Dresses for women

Perhaps the best-known restaurant in New York, "21" puts you in league with the powerful and celebrated. The dining area downstairs looks like no other, with its Remington originals and "transportation collection" hanging from the ceiling. A variety of game birds and no-nonsense meat dishes are offered, plus Veal Charleroi, Lamb Terragon and Mushrooms Daum.

Reservations required
Lunch: Mon.-Sat., Noon-5:30 P.M.
Dinner: Mon.-Sat., 5:30 P.M.-1 A.M.
    Closed Sunday

UNCLE TAI'S HUNAN YUAN ⓵⓵⓹ Chinese

1059 Third Ave.
New York
(212) 838-0850
Maître d': Sandy Ching
Full Bar/Lot Parking (dinner)
AE, D
No dress restrictions

The management says Uncle Tai's was the first Hunan restaurant in New York. House specialties include Uncle Tai's Beef, shredded chicken with bean sprouts, vegetable pie, as well as an unusual venison in garlic sauce and sea bass and lobster in black bean sauce.

No reservations required
Lunch/Dinner: Sun.-Thurs., Noon-11 P.M.
    Fri.-Sat., Noon-11:30 P.M.

VIENNA '79 ⓷⓹ Austrian/Continental

320 E. 79th St.
New York
(212) 734-4700
Full Bar/Street Parking
AE, D, MC, V
Good taste in dress required

Young graduates of a Vienna hotel school run this new restaurant filled with Spanish Riding School engravings, flowers, friendliness and joie de vivre. Specialties include wiener schnitzel, filet mignon in a Roquefort sauce, creamy escargots, smoked fillet of trout and, of course, a full array of Vienna's famous desserts.

Reservations required
Dinner: Daily, 5:30 P.M.-11 P.M.

WINDOWS ON THE WORLD ㉙

American/International

1 World Trade Center
New York
(212) 938-1111
Maître d': Lee Harty, Alan Lewis (director)
Full Bar/Lot Parking
AE, D, MC, V, CB
Jacket, tie for men; no jeans

With its view to end all views, Windows on the World is incomparably dramatic. Every table has a clear view of the skyline, and of 50 miles beyond that. The menu represents the best of the world's cuisines as well as distinctly American cooking.

Reservations required
Lunch: Mon.–Fri., 1:40 P.M., 2 P.M., 2:15 P.M. seatings
 (non-members pay surcharge)
Dinner: Mon.–Sat., 5 P.M.–10 P.M.
Buffet: Sat., Noon–3 P.M.
 Sun., Noon–7 P.M.

ZAPATA'S ⑩③

Mexican

330 E. 53rd St.
New York
(212) 223-9408
Full Bar/Street Parking
AE, D, MC, V
No dress restrictions

"My restaurant is small. We can seat only 40 persons at one time. But if they leave happy, that is enough satisfaction for me." That is Zapata's owner Frank Ramos talking. He is proud of his sauces, his service and the authentic Mexican specialties he presents.

No reservations required
Lunch: Daily, Noon–3 P.M.
Dinner: Daily, 5 P.M.–11:30 P.M.

PHILADELPHIA

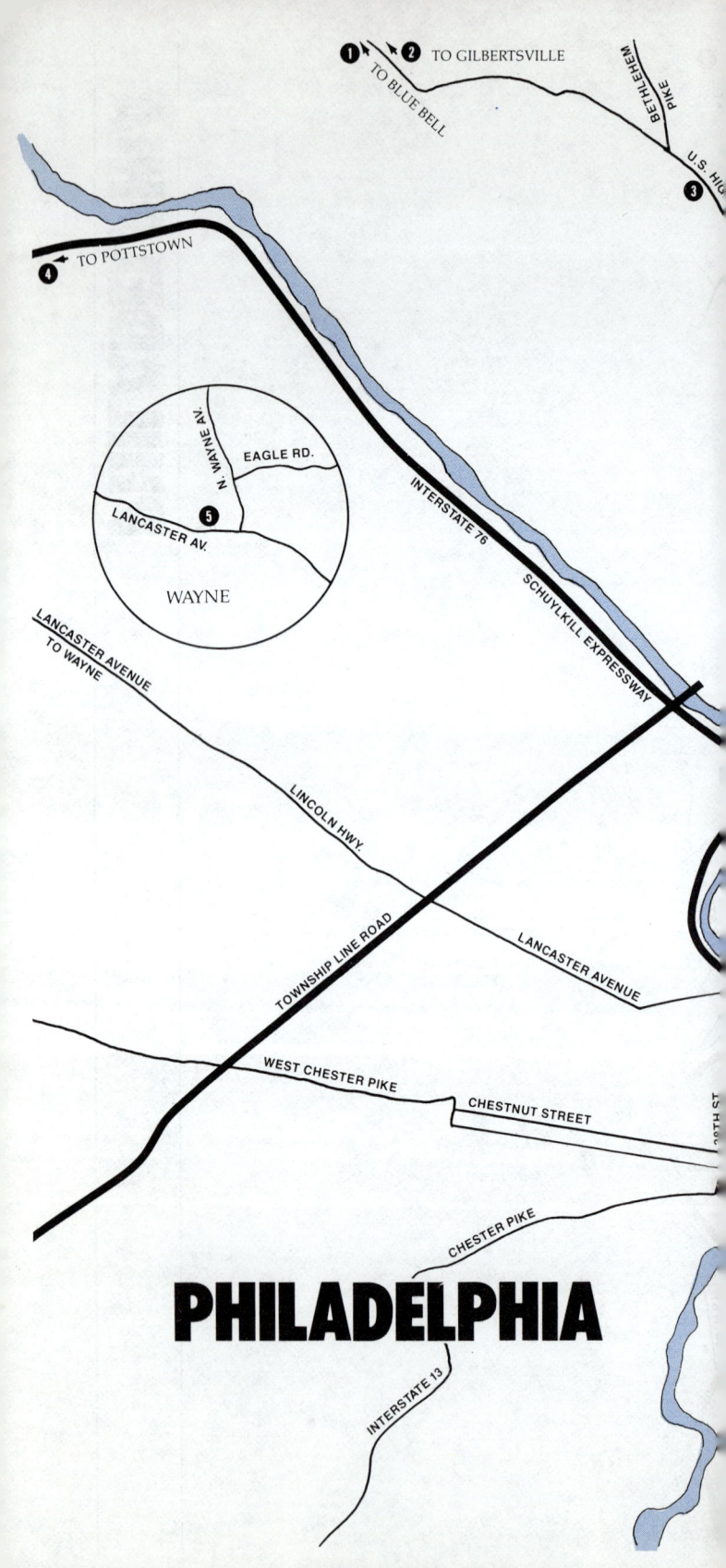

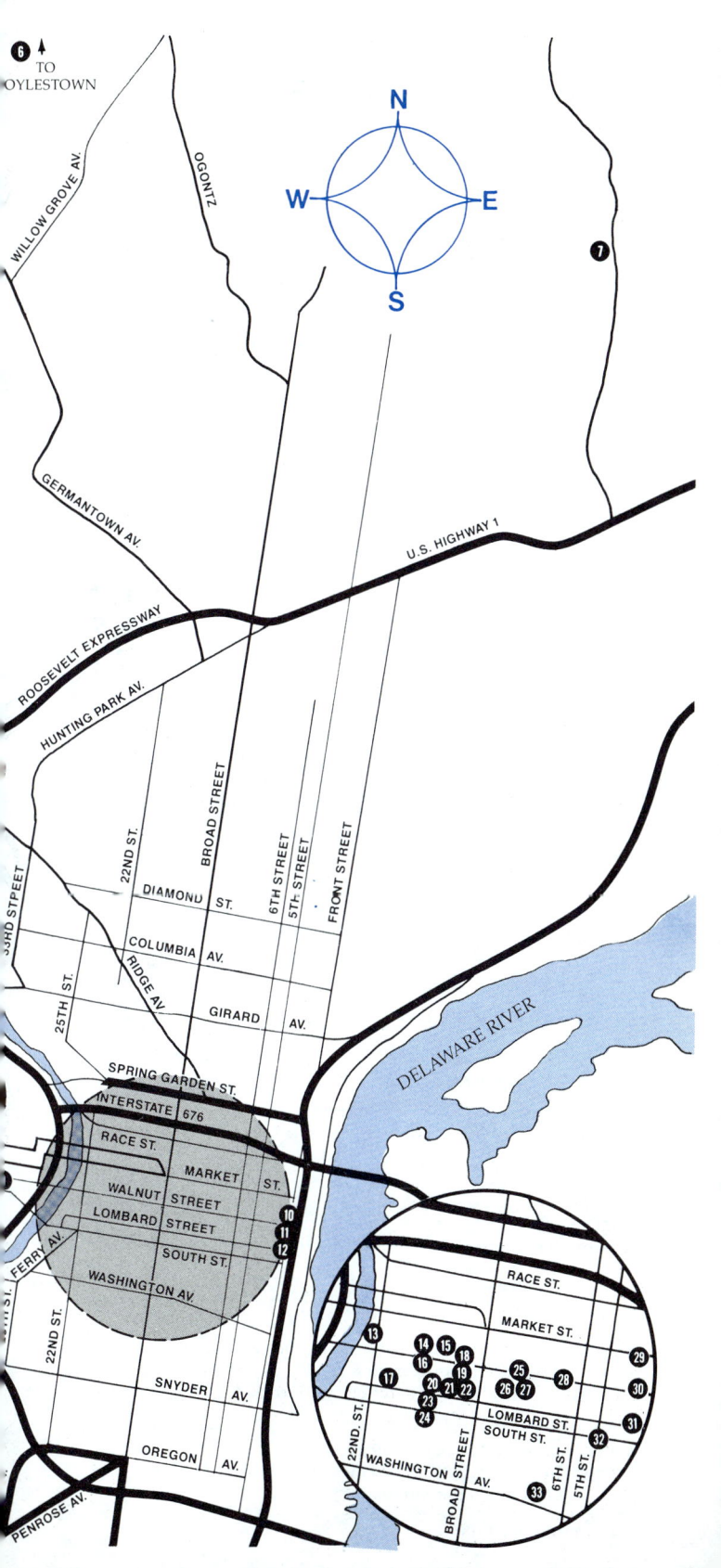

ARTHUR'S STEAK HOUSE ⑱   *American*

1512 Walnut St.
Philadelphia
(215) 735-2590
Maître d': Shirley and Herman Kahn (owners)
Full Bar/Lot Parking
AE, D, MC, V, CB
No dress restrictions

Richly appointed, with lots of oak and tapestry, Arthur's serves prime steaks, roast beef, veal, seafood and succulent duck.

Reservations required
Lunch/Dinner: Mon.–Fri., 11 A.M.–11 P.M.
              Sat., 4 P.M.–Midnight
              Closed Sunday

BLACK BANANA ㉙   *French*

201 N. 3rd St.
Philadelphia
(215) 925-4433
Maître d': Heinz
Full Bar/Lot and Street Parking
AE, D, MC, V
No dress restrictions

Although its name is usually associated with a fanciful ice cream dessert, this spacious restaurant features dishes on the lighter side of *haute cuisine*. Specialties change with the seasons. There is Spring's King Salmon, for instance, accompanied by a fresh sorrel and light cream sauce.

Reservations required on weekends
Dinner: Daily, 6 P.M.–2 A.M.

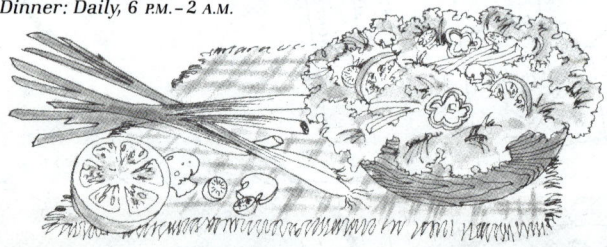

BLUE BELL INN ❶   *American*

601 Skippack Pike
Blue Bell, Pa.
(215) 646-2010
Maître d': Robert Savini
Full Bar/Lot Parking
AE, MC, V
Jacket for men

This 1743-vintage country inn retains many of the features of the original. Specials include broiled steaks, chateaubriand, fresh rainbow trout from a nearby hatchery, and frogs' legs from France.

Reservations required
Lunch: Tues.–Sat., Noon–2:30 P.M.
Dinner: Tues.–Sat., 5:30 P.M.–10 P.M.
        Closed Sunday, Monday

BOOKBINDER'S 15TH STREET ⑲ *Seafood*

215 S. 15th St.
Philadelphia
(215) 545-1137
Maître d': Sam and Richard Bookbinder (hosts)
Full Bar/Lot Parking
AE, D, MC, V, CB
No dress restrictions

Sam and Richard are fourth-generation Bookbinders in the process of continuing a Philadelphia seafood tradition. Their specialties include fresh lobster, snapper soup, Sole à la Booky's, Oysters Rockefeller, pepper pot soup, Mussels Fra Diablo and bouillabaisse.

No reservations required
Lunch: Mon.-Sat., 11:30 A.M.-4 P.M.
Dinner: Mon.-Fri. 4 P.M.-11 P.M.
　　　　Sat., 4 P.M.-Midnight
　　　　Sun., Noon-10 P.M.

THE COMMISSARY ⑮ *International*

1710 Sansom St.
Philadelphia
(215) 569-2240
Full Bar/Lot Parking
AE, D, MC, V, CB
No dress restrictions

The Commissary offers you a choice of three dining areas. Downstairs is a small, very uptown "self-service" restaurant featuring light meals and snacks. Upstairs is intimate and more formal, featuring Thai beef curry, roast duck, deep-fried Brie and fresh seafood. The Piano Bar features live music, of course, and exotic cognacs and coffees.

Reservations required for Upstairs
Lunch:　Mon.-Fri., 11:30 A.M.-2 P.M.
Dinner:　Mon.-Thurs., 5:30 P.M.-11 P.M.
　　　　 Fri.-Sat., 5:30 P.M.-Midnight
　　　　 Closed Sunday

CONTI CROSS KEYS INN ⑥ *American*

Route 611 and Route 313
Doylestown, Pa.
(215) 348-3539
Maître d': Walter J. Conti, Jr. (co-owner)
Full Bar/Valet and Lot Parking
AE, D, MC, V
Jacket for men

A historic landmark in Bucks County, the Conti Cross Keys Inn dates back to 1723. The Conti family has been specializing in fine food and careful service for over 40 years. There is an extensive menu of more than 250 items and, claims Walter Conti, Jr., the largest wine list in Pennsylvania.

Reservations required
Lunch/Dinner: Mon.-Fri., 11:30 A.M.-Midnight
　　　　　　　Sat., 5 P.M.-Midnight
　　　　　　　Closed Sunday, Holidays

COVENTRY FORGE INN ❹   *French*

Route 23, Coventry Rd.
Coventryville, Pa.
(215) 469-6222
Full Bar/Lot Parking
No credit cards
Jacket for men

Housed in a colonial building dating back to 1717, the Coventry Forge offers fresh local game in season and fresh available produce. You'll notice a number of reminders of the past, including an early Franklin stove made in the neighborhood forge and the original tools used to fashion it. Streams on the premises are stocked with trout.

Reservations required
Lunch: Tues.–Fri., 11:30 A.M.–2 P.M.
Dinner: Tues.–Fri., 5:30 P.M.–9 P.M.
        Sat., 5 P.M.–10 P.M.
        Closed Sunday, Monday

DEJA-VU ㉔   *French*

1609 Pine St.
Philadelphia
(215) 546-1190
Maître d': David Moore
Full Bar/Street Parking
AE, MC, V
No dress restrictions

"Possibly the smallest fine restaurant in the world," speculates owner and chef Salomon Montezinos about Déjà-Vu. He presents his original cuisine in a *very* intimate setting. The prix fixe dinner includes Cheveaux d'Anges, a surprise Déjà-Vu creation. The wine cellar is noted for its quality and variety.

Reservations required
Dinner: Tues.–Sat., 6 P.M.–9:30 P.M.
        Closed Sunday, Monday

DEUX CHEMINEES ㉗   *French*

251 S. Camac St.
Philadelphia
(215) 985-0367
Full Bar/Street Parking
AE, MC, V
No dress restrictions

Housed in a home dating back to 1824, Deux Cheminées does indeed have the required two fireplaces. Cuisine is described as "simply and deliciously French." The menu changes with the seasons, so that only strictly fresh ingredients may be used.

Reservations required
Lunch: Tues.–Fri., 11:30 A.M.–2 P.M.
Dinner: Tues.–Thurs., Sun., 5:30 P.M.–9:30 P.M.
        Fri.–Sat., 5:30 P.M.–10 P.M.
        Closed Monday

FAGLEYSVILLE COUNTRY HOTEL ❷ *International*

Route 1, Swamp Pike
Gilbertsville, Pa.
(215) 323-1425
Maître d': Jack Gleason (owner)
Full Bar/Lot Parking
AE, D, MC, V
No dress restrictions

You enter the world of the country hotel, circa 1865, when you step across the Fagleysville's threshold. Duck is the supreme specialty here. (Owner Jack Gleason says one customer freezes it and has it delivered to the Pope.) Different ethnic dinners are presented each month.

Reservations required
Dinner: Mon.-Sat., 5:30 P.M.-10 P.M.
Closed Sunday

THE FISH MARKET ⓴ *Seafood*

18th and Sansom Sts.
Philadelphia
(215) 567-3559
Full Bar/Street Parking
AE, D, MC, V, CB
No dress restrictions

True to its name, this restaurant doubles as a "gourmet" fish market. Restaurant *and* market specialties include shrimp, cheese and tomato pie, live lobster, bouillabaisse, poached salmon, Sole Oscar and crab bisque. Desserts are all made on the premises.

Reservations required (except Saturday evening)
Lunch: Mon.-Sat., 11:15 A.M.-3:45 P.M.
Dinner: Mon.-Sat., 4 P.M.-11 P.M.
Sun., 4 P.M.-10 P.M.

FROG ㉑ *International*

1524 Locust St.
Philadelphia
(215) 735-8882
Maître d': Gerard van de Loo (manager)
Full Bar/Street Parking
AE, D, MC, V, CB
No dress restrictions

An intimate and unpretentious restaurant, Frog is one of the renovated storefront-restaurants that kicked off the Philadelphia renaissance in downtown area dining. They offer an unusual and quixotic blend of French, Asian and American cuisines. The wine list is considered to be one of the finest on the East Coast and the desserts are decidely wicked.

Reservations suggested
Lunch: Mon.-Fri., Noon-2 P.M.
Dinner: Mon.-Thurs., 6 P.M.-10 P.M.
Fri.-Sat., 6 P.M.-11 P.M.
Sun., 5:30 P.M.-9:30 P.M.
Brunch: Sun., 11:30 A.M.-2 P.M.

THE GARDEN ㉓ — *Continental*

1617 Spruce St.
Philadelphia
(215) 546-4455
Maître d': Lynda Chase
Full Bar/Lot and Street Parking
AE, MC, V
Jacket for men in dining room

The candlelit dining room, the antique-filled Oyster Bar, the quaint small bar and the sun-splashed outdoor garden add up to the perfect setting for French country cooking. Owner Kathleen Mulhern has used an elegant old townshouse as the stage for entrées such as veal with leeks and celery and lobster in puff pastry. There is raspberry soufflé for dessert.

No reservations required
Lunch: Mon.–Sat., 11:30 A.M.–2:30 P.M.
Dinner: Mon.–Fri., 5:30 P.M.–9:30 P.M.
          Sat., 5:30 P.M.–10:30 P.M.
          Closed Sunday

IL GALLO NERO ㉒ — *Northern Italian*

254 S. 15th St.
Philadelphia
(215) 546-8065
Maître d': Giovanni Petri,
          Enzo and Carla Fusaro (owners)
Full Bar/Lot and Valet Parking
AE, D, MC, V, CB
No dress restrictions

Enzo Fusaro's favorite quotation states, "He lives doubly who also enjoys the past." It is reflected in his menu, which emphasizes the traditional dishes of his native Florence and the dishes of the Renaissance *haute cuisine*. He offers Vitello Gallo Nero, Cannelloni alla Angelo, Calamari al Verdicchio, and Risotto alla Aragosta.

Reservations required
Lunch: Mon.–Fri., 11 A.M.–3 P.M.
Dinner: Mon.–Fri., 5 P.M.–11 P.M.
          Sat., 5 P.M.–Midnight
          Sun., 3 P.M.–9 P.M.

LA CAMARGUE ㉕ — *French*

1119 Walnut St.
Philadelphia
(215) 922-3148
Maître d': Marcel Brossette
Full Bar/Lot and Street Parking
AE, MC, V
No dress restrictions

Stucco walls, beamed ceilings, sturdy oak dining tables and the season's fresh flowers add up to La Camargue. Drinks (called libations here) are poured from an antique armoire with numerous drawers that serve as liquor shelves. Featured are fillet of sole, red snapper, rack of lamb and lobster curry.

No reservations required
Lunch: Mon.–Fri., Noon–2 P.M.
Dinner: Mon.–Thurs., 6 P.M.–10 P.M.
          Fri.–Sat., 6 P.M.–11 P.M.
          Closed Sunday

LA FAMIGLIA ❿ *Italian*

8 S. Front St.
Philadelphia
(215) 922-2803
Maître d': Luca Sena (owner)
Full Bar/Lot and Street Parking
AE, D, MC, V, CB
Jacket for men

"La Famiglia is a gourmet delight!" states its owner, Luca Sena. What's more. Mama and Papa Sena prepare each meal! And, their recipes come directly from the Old Country! The service is unique in this day and age, say the Senas. It is a blend of European courtesy and graciousness. Wines are all imported and desserts are as Mama and Papa remember them to be.

Reservations required
Lunch: Tues.-Fri., Noon-2 P.M.
Dinner: Tues.-Sat., 5:30 P.M.-10 P.M.
       Sun., 4:30 P.M.-9 P.M.
       Closed Monday

LA PANETIERE ⓴ *French*

1602 Locust St.
Philadelphia
(215) 546-5452
Full Bar/Street Parking
AE, D
Jacket, tie for men

The setting for La Panetière is a gracious old townhouse, imbued with certain French accents here and there. Examples of the French *haute cuisine* include embellishments of lamb, lobster and pheasant. The wine list is notable.

Reservations required
Lunch: Mon.-Fri., Noon-2 P.M.
Dinner: Mon.-Sat., 6 P.M.-9:30 P.M.
       Closed Sunday

LA TERRASSE ❾ *French*

3432 Sansom St.
Philadelphia
(215) 387-3778
Maître d': Pamela Toy
Full Bar/Street Parking
AE, D, MC, V, CB
No dress restrictions

A relaxing, plant-filled terrace is the setting for such standbys as Veal Normande and Sea Bass Provençale. You'll hear the music of Mozart and Chopin played on the restaurant's Steinway and you'll be offered a selection from La Terrasse's list of rare and vintage wines.

Reservations suggested
Lunch: Mon.-Fri., 11:30 A.M.-2:30 P.M.
Dinner: Daily, 6 P.M.-11 P.M.
Brunch: Sun., 11:30 A.M.-3 P.M.

LA TRUFFE ⓫   *French*

10 S. Front St.
Philadelphia
(215) 627-8630/925-5062
Maître d': Marcel Pautrat
Full Bar/Lot and Street Parking
AE, D, MC, V, CB
Jacket for men

Located in the Society Hill section of the city, La Truffe makes maximum use of candlelight and fresh flowers to enhance its already elegant decor. Some offerings are Quenelles de Brochet, Faisan Carême, Homard aux Algues and Mousse au Chocolate Blanc.

Reservations required
Lunch: Tues.-Fri., Noon-2 P.M.
Dinner: Mon.-Sat., 6 P.M.-11 P.M.
  Closed Sunday

L'AUBERGE ❺   *French*

Spread Eagle Village
Strafford, Pa.
(215) 687-2840
Maître d': Jack Riley, Pamela R. Hill (manager)
Full Bar/Valet Parking
AE, D, MC, V
Jacket for men

Helen Sigel Wilson's L'Auberge has, appropriately enough, a French country inn atmosphere. There are multiple fireplaces, an atrium and two bars. House specialties include a number of soufflés, crêpes, quiches and mousses.

Reservations required
Lunch: Tues.-Sat., Noon-3 P.M.
Dinner: Tues.-Thurs., 6 P.M.-10 P.M.
  Fri.-Sat., 6 P.M.-11 P.M.
  Closed Sunday, Monday

LAUTREC ㉛   *French*

408 S. 2nd St.
Philadelphia
(215) 923-6660
Full Bar/Street Parking
AE
No dress restrictions

Located on historic Society Hill, this small, intimate restaurant presents an ever-changing menu of seasonal dishes. For instance, there are Escargots Lautrec, Mousseline de Coquilles with tomato sauce, Saumon en Croûte, Carré d'Agneau au Poivre Vert and some highly fanciful dessert "Spectaculars" such as Gateau Nuit et Jour.

Dinner: Tues-Sat., 6 P.M.-10 P.M.
Brunch: Sun., 11 A.M.-2:30 P.M.
  Closed Monday

LE BEAU LIEU ⓰   *Continental*

Barclay Hotel
18th St. and Rittenhouse Square East
Philadelphia
(215) 545-0300
Maître d': Elio Espinal
Full Bar/Valet Parking
AE, D, MC, V, CB
Jacket for men

The hotel name and the address are both Philadelphia famous. The restaurant is relatively new, but intent on earning its stripes. The menu lists such items as rack of lamb with plum sauce, Dover Sole, Veal Marsala, Scallops Provençal and Steak au Poivre.

No reservations required
Breakfast: Mon.–Sat., 7 A.M.–11 A.M.
Lunch: Mon.–Sat., Noon–3 P.M.
Dinner: Mon.–Sat., 5:30 P.M.–9 P.M.
            Sun., 5 P.M.–8:30 P.M.
Brunch: Sun., 11 A.M.–3 P.M.

LE BEC-FIN ㉖   *French*

1312 Spruce St.
Philadelphia
(215) 732-3000
Maître d': Michael McDonough
Full Bar/Lot Parking
No credit cards
Good taste in dress required

Georges Perrier, formerly of La Pyramide in Vienna and L'Osteau de Baumanière at Les Baux, is the "patron" of this intimate French restaurant. The decor is Louis XVI and the menu is seasonal, but always based upon *haute cuisine.* The prix fixe dinners include six courses.

Reservations required
Dinner: Mon.–Sat., 6 P.M. and 9 P.M. seatings
          Closed Sunday

MAUREEN ⓱   *French*

11 S. 21st St.
Philadelphia
(215) 561-3542
Maître d': Maureen Horn (co-owner)
Full Bar/Lot Parking
AE, MC, V
Jacket for men preferred

This unpretentious family-run restaurant (Maureen Horn is your host; husband Stephen is the chef) specializes in elegantly prepared cuisine. The Horns offer Lamb Wellington, veal served on a bed of lobster, shrimp and crab, and stuffed fish dishes in a pastry crust.

Reservations required
Dinner: Tues.–Sat., 5:30 P.M.–10 P.M.
          Closed Sunday, Monday

MORGAN'S   ⑬   *Mediterranean*

24th and Sansom Sts.
Philadelphia
(215) 567-6066
Maître d': Jon Devine
Full Bar/Street Parking
AE, D, MC, V
No dress restrictions

Owner Alphonse Pignataro calls Morgan's an "intimate and delightful sort of country inn tucked away in west center city Philadelphia." The cuisine is a blend of Mediterranean seasonings, with an emphasis on the cooking of France and Northern Italy. The menu, which changes every two months, may feature medallions of lamb in a nest of chestnut purée with Madeira sauce.

Reservations required
Lunch: Mon.–Fri., 11:45 A.M.–2 P.M.
Dinner: Mon.–Sat., 5:30 P.M.–11 P.M.
      Closed Sunday

OLD ORIGINAL BOOKBINDER'S   ㉚   *Seafood*

125 Walnut St.
Philadelphia
(215) 925-7027
Maître d': Anthony Pantalone
Full Bar/Valet and Lot Parking
AE, D, MC, V, CB
No dress restrictions

It's been on the Philadelphia dockside since 1865 and has been serving tourists and residents such specialties as live lobsters, fresh clams and oysters, snapper soup laced with sherry, fresh scrod and Kansas City prime steaks. It's a Philadelphia tradition.

No reservations required
Lunch/Dinner: Mon.–Fri., 11:45 A.M.–10 P.M.
              Sat., Noon–10 P.M.
              Sun., 1 P.M.–10 P.M.
              Sat.–Sun. (July and August), 3 P.M.–10 P.M.

RISTORANTE DA GAETANO   ㉘   *Northern Italian*

727 Walnut St.
Philadelphia
(215) 922-3771
Full Bar/Street Parking
AE, C
Jacket for men

You dine in a romantic cellar of terra cotta with red brick archways. The Northern Italian cuisine includes homemade pastas, cannelloni and a number of veal dishes such as osso bucco and Vitello Tonnato. Classic dishes from Genoa, Tuscany, Milan and Bologna are featured.

Reservations required
Lunch: Tues.–Fri., 11:30 A.M.–2 P.M.
Dinner: Tues.–Fri., 6 P.M.–10 P.M.
        Sat., 6 P.M.–11 P.M.
        Closed Sunday, Monday

RISTORANTE DI LULLO ❼   *Northern Italian*

7955 Oxford Ave.
Philadelphia
(215) 725-6000
Maître d': Antonio Schiavone
Full Bar/Lot Parking
AE, D, MC, V, CB
No dress restrictions

White tile, handmade wooden trimmings, green accents — such is the sophisticated setting for Ristorante Di Lullo. Filet of beef is served with a special sauce. There is also Paglia e Fieno alla Ghiotta, a dish consisting of contrasting egg and spinach noodles in cream sauce with tiny peas.

Reservations recommended
Dinner: Mon.-Thurs., 5 P.M.-11 P.M.
       Fri.-Sat., 5 P.M.-1 A.M.
       Sun., 4:30 P.M.-10:30 P.M.

THE SALOON ㉝   *Italian*

750 S. 7th St.
Philadelphia
(215) 922-3444
Maître d': Thomas Cross
Full Bar/Valet and Lot Parking
No credit cards
Good taste in dress required

The Saloon presents a vast collection of antiques, best described as "early Philadelphia," according to manager Frances Trani. The traditional Italian cuisine features some continental touches and is consistently good, Ms. Trani assures us.

Reservations required
Lunch: Mon.-Fri., 11:30 A.M.-2 P.M.
Dinner: Mon.-Sat., 5 P.M.-11:30 P.M.
        Closed Sunday

SIVA'S ⑫   *North Indian*

34 S. Front St.
Philadelphia
(215) 925-2700
Full Bar/Lot and Street Parking
AE, D, MC, V
Jacket for men

Authentic tandoori delicacies are offered here, which means the succulent meats are subtly spiced and baked alongside tantalizing breads in a traditional clay oven. The Delhi-born chefs can be seen at work behind the glass windows. Centuries-old recipes are used to prepare the vegetarian and meat dishes.

No reservations required
Lunch: Tues.-Fri., Noon-2 P.M.
Dinner: Tues.-Fri., 5:30 P.M.-10:30 P.M.
        Sat., 5:30 P.M.-11:30 P.M.
        Sun., 5 P.M.-9 P.M.
Brunch: Sun., 11:30 A.M.-3:30 P.M.

TELL ERHARDT'S ❸   *Continental*

Chestnut Hill Hotel
8229 Germantown Ave.
Philadelphia
(215) 247-2100
Maître d': Jeff Emmons
Full Bar/Lot Parking
AE, D, MC, V, CB
Good taste in dress required

The freshest ingredients available go into the preparation of such specialties as roast duck, Salmon en Croûte in champagne, poached bass in sorrel sauce and several veal dishes. The dessert list is extensive and includes fantasies focusing on kiwi, raspberries, strawberries and pineapple.

Reservations required
Lunch: Wed.–Sat., 11:30 A.M.–2 P.M.
Dinner: Wed.–Sun., 6 P.M.–10 P.M.
Brunch: Sun., Noon–3:30 P.M.
        Closed Monday, Tuesday

WILDFLOWERS ㉜   *Continental*

516 S. 5th St.
Philadelphia
(215) 923-6709
Full Bar/Street Parking
AE, MC, V, CB
No dress restrictions

There are two separate dining rooms at Wildflowers, each decorated with paintings and stained glass, and filled with plants. The menu changes as often as twice a week. The kitchen specializes in sautéed foods and brunch items.

No reservations required
Lunch/Dinner: From 11 A.M.

PHOENIX

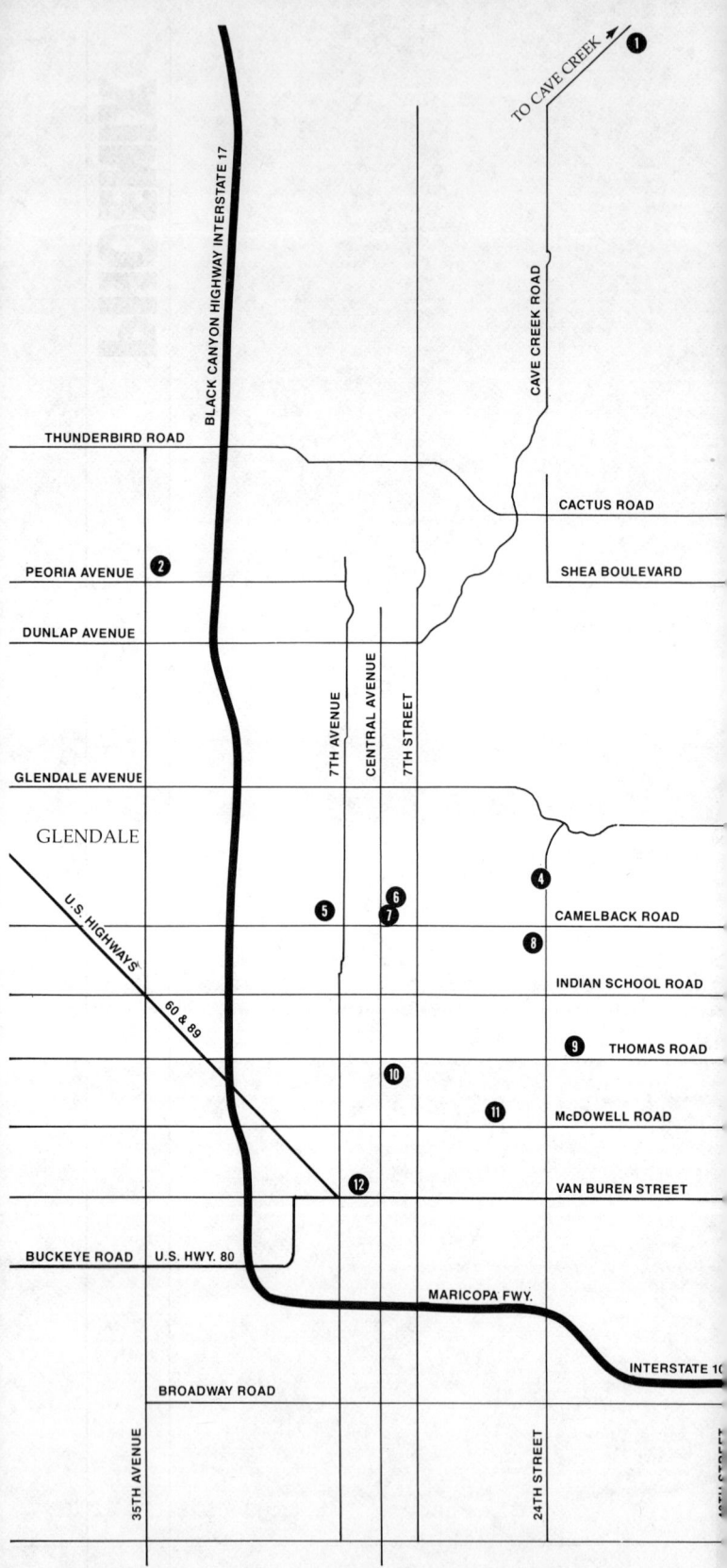

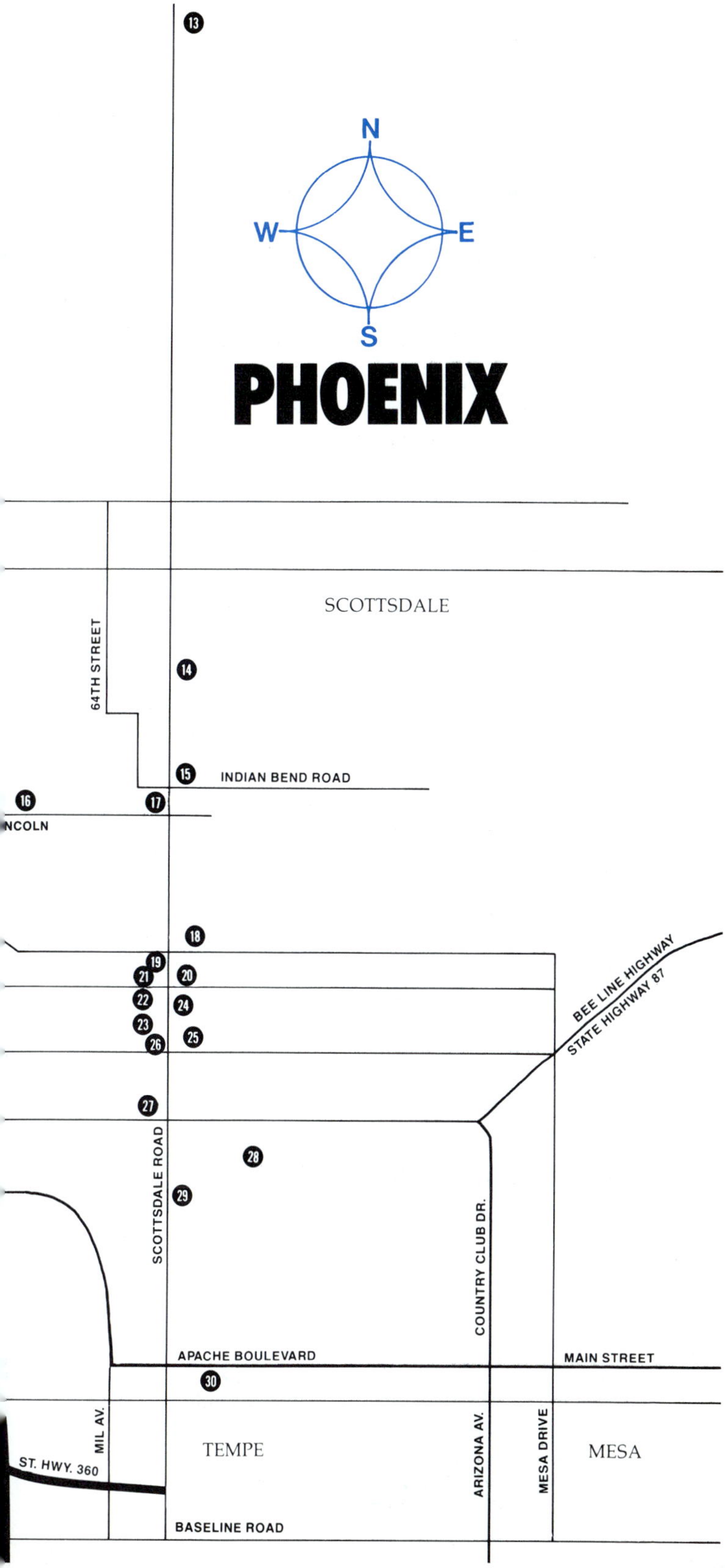

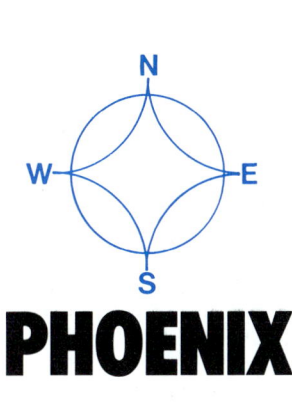

PHOENIX

SCOTTSDALE

64TH STREET

⓭

⓮

⓯ INDIAN BEND ROAD

⓰ ⓱

NCOLN

⓲

⓳ ⓴
㉑
㉒ ㉔
㉓ ㉕
㉖

BEE LINE HIGHWAY
STATE HIGHWAY 87

㉗

㉘

㉙

SCOTTSDALE ROAD

COUNTRY CLUB DR.

APACHE BOULEVARD   MAIN STREET

㉚

MIL AV.

ST. HWY. 360

TEMPE

ARIZONA AV.

MESA DRIVE

MESA

BASELINE ROAD

AVANTI ❾   *Italian*

2728 E. Thomas Rd.
Phoenix
(602) 956-0900
Maître d': Ramon, Franco, Benito, Angiolo (owners)
Full Bar/Valet Parking
AE, MC, V
Good taste in dress required

Avanti, also located in Scottsdale, at 3102 N. Scottsdale Rd., is known for its octopus salad, fresh mussels, striped sea bass (flown in twice weekly from Boston), paella, cioppino and zabaglione. As if all that weren't enough, a dedicated young crew of chefs from Italy, France and the U.S. will prepare just about anything else you might want.

Reservations required
Lunch: Mon.-Fri., 11 A.M.-3 P.M.
Dinner: Daily, 5 P.M.-11 P.M.

AVANTI, RESTAURANT ㉖   *Continental*
OF DISTINCTION

3102 N. Scottsdale Rd.
Scottsdale, Ariz.
(602) 949-8333
Maître d': Franco Ferrandi (owner)
Full Bar/Valet Parking
AE, MC, V
Good taste in dress required

Great food and interesting Arizona decor. That's owner Ferrandi's winning combination. He offers mussels, striped sea bass, octopus, East Coast lobster, Linguini Orlando, Beluga caviar and Osso Buco Milanese. The kitchen staff is European trained.

Reservations required
Dinner: Daily, 5:30 P.M.-11 P.M.

CAFE LA SERRE ㉙   *French*

1127 N. Scottsdale Rd.
Tempe, Ariz.
(602) 968-7411
Full Bar/Lot Parking
AE, MC, V
No dress restrictions

Here'a a romantic little restaurant that features classic French cuisine in a gardenlike setting. Specialties include bouillabaisse, rack of lamb and variations upon veal, duck and fresh fish.

Reservations required
Lunch/Dinner: Mon.-Fri., 11:30 A.M.-Midnight
*   Sat.-Sun., 5:30 P.M.-Midnight*

CHEZ LOUIS ㉔ *French*

7363 Scottsdale Mall
Scottsdale, Ariz.
(602) 945-3303
Full Bar/Lot Parking
AE, D, MC, V, CB
Good taste in dress required

Chez Louis offers both table d'hôte and à la carte selections. Special items include Coq au Vin, Frogs' Legs Provençales, Steak Diane and escargots. There is tableside presentation of some dishes. You can choose to dine either indoors or out.

Reservations required
Lunch/Dinner: Daily, 11:30 A.M. – 1 A.M.
  Closed Sunday, June – October
  Closed in August

DOUG LEE'S ASIA HOUSE ⑪ *Oriental*

2310 E. McDowell
Phoenix
(602) 267-7461
Maître d': Dorene Lee
Full Bar/Lot Parking
AE, D, MC, V, CB
No dress restrictions

At Asia House there are three separate dining areas for three different types of dinners. Choose from Cantonese, Japanese or Mongolian Barbecue. The prix fixe dinners consist of several courses, including dessert.

Reservations advised
Dinner: Tues. – Sun., 6 P.M. – 10 P.M.
  Closed Monday

DURANT'S FINE FOODS ⑩ *American*

2611 N. Central Ave.
Phoenix
(602) 264-5967
Maître d': Mike Mancuso
Full Bar/Valet Parking
AE, D, MC, V, CB
No dress restrictions

Durant's steaks are cooked over an open charcoal broiler exactly to your specifications. They claim their charcoal broiled salmon and prime rib are the best there is.

Reservations required
Lunch/Dinner: Daily

EL CHORRO LODGE ⓰   American

5550 E. Lincoln Dr.
Scottsdale, Ariz.
(602) 948-5170
Maître d': Katie Dow
Full Bar/Valet Parking
AE, D, MC, V, CB
No dress restrictions

A 44-year-old tradition in the Phoenix area, the El Choro Lodge is a converted adobe-style home near Camelback Mountain. There are three fireplaces, and Western art decorates the rustic walls. Chateaubriand and rack of lamb are specialties. Eggs Benedict is served all day.

Reservations required (lunch and dinner)
Breakfast: Daily, 9 A.M.–11:30 A.M.
Lunch: Daily, 11:30 A.M.–2:30 P.M.
Dinner: Daily, 6 P.M.–11 P.M.

ETIENNE'S ❸   French

Del Webb's La Posada Hotel
4949 E. Lincoln Dr.
Paradise Valley, Ariz.
(602) 959-8670
Maître d': Etienne (owner)
Full Bar/Valet Parking
AE, D, MC, V, CB
Jacket, tie for men preferred

The scene is classic French — from preparation to presentation to service. Specialties include Veal Madeira, Duck à l'Orange, Frogs' Legs Provençales and Filet Mignon Henri IV. There is a well-stocked wine cellar.

Reservations required
Lunch: Mon.–Sat., 11:30 A.M.–2:30 P.M.
Dinner: Mon.–Sat., 6 P.M.–10 P.M.
     Closed Sunday

FINCH'S ⓮   International

10305 N. Scottsdale Rd.
Scottsdale, Ariz.
(602) 948-0255
Maître d': Lee and Harriet Finch (owners)
Full Bar/Lot Parking
AE, MC, V
No dress restrictions

Finch's offers complete prix fixe dinners which include an appetizer pâté, soup, salad, dessert and entrées such as Beef Wellington, Roast Duck Rockefeller and Poached Red Snapper en Papillote. The owners say they have one of the largest selections of fine wines and liquors in the valley.

Reservations required
Dinner: Mon.–Sat., 5 P.M.–11 P.M.
     Closed Sunday

GARCIA'S DEL ESTE ❷⓿   *Mexican*

7633 E. Indian School Rd.
Scottsdale, Ariz.
(602) 945-1647
Full Bar/Lot Parking
AE, D, MC, V, CB
Good taste in dress required

Traditional Mexican foods are served in an atmosphere of warmth and friendliness, according to the management. Featured are Tostada Del Rey, crab enchiladas, chimichangas and chilled margaritas. There are strolling mariachis to put you in the proper mood.

No reservations required
Lunch/Dinner: Sun.–Thurs., 11 A.M.–11 P.M.
        Fri.–Sat., 11 A.M.–Midnight

THE GLASS DOOR ❷❷   *Continental*

6939 Main St.
Scottsdale, Ariz.
(602) 994-5303
Full Bar/Valet and Lot Parking
AE, MC, V
No dress restrictions

The Glass Door presents casual dining in a cozy atmosphere. The lengthy menu features Dover Sole, fresh salmon, Duck à l'Orange, Steak Diane, sliced tenderloin, Bananas Foster and Cherries Jubilee.

Reservations suggested
Lunch/Dinner: Mon.–Sat., 11:30 A.M.–10:30 P.M.
        Closed Sunday

GOLDEN EAGLE ❶❷   *Continental*

Valley Bank Center
201 N. Central
Phoenix
(602) 257-7700
Maître d': Adriano Braga
Full Bar/Lot Parking
AE, D, MC, V, CB
Jacket for men (evenings)

The Golden Eagle, often described as "plush," is on the 37th floor of the tallest building in Phoenix. Specialties include Shrimp Pernod, Steak Diane, Coquilles Saint-Jacques and Escargots Bourguignons. There is a banquet room one floor above that can accommodate 150 people.

Reservations required
Lunch: Mon.–Fri., 11:30 A.M.–2 P.M.
Dinner: Mon.–Sat., 6 P.M.–10 P.M.
        Closed Sunday

THE GOLD ROOM ❹ *Continental*

Arizona Biltmore
24th St. and Missouri
Phoenix
(602) 955-6600, Ext. 2700
Maître d': David Kilmer
Full Bar/Valet and Lot Parking
AE, D, MC, V, CB
Jacket, tie for men

The Gold Room has a quiet dignity all its own, says the management. It's a place to create romantic memories for years to come.

Reservations recommended (lunch and dinner)
Breakfast: Daily, 6:30 A.M.–10:30 A.M.
Lunch: Daily, Noon–2 P.M.
Dinner: Daily, 6:30 P.M.–10 P.M.

IANUZZI ⓲ *Italian*

7340 E. Shoeman
Scottsdale, Ariz.
(602) 949-0290
Full Bar/Valet Parking
AE, MC, V
Good taste in dress required

Ianuzzi offers a variety of traditional Italian dishes *and* a variety of Italian wines to accompany them. Specialties include Pollo Galeria, Fettuccine Carbonara and Vitello con Carciofi.

Reservations required
Dinner: Mon.–Sat., 5 P.M.–11 P.M.
   Closed Sunday

LA CHAMPAGNE ⓯ *French*

Registry Resort
7171 N. Scottsdale Rd.
Scottsdale, Ariz.
(602) 991-3800
Maître d': Jack Moore
Full Bar/Valet Parking
AE, D, MC, V, CB
Jacket required, tie requested

You enter an elegantly appointed dining room done in royal blue and burgundy hues. Your dinner could include spinach salad flamed with cognac, Supreme de Saumon Wellington, Coquilles Saint-Jacques Nantaise or filet mignon. A certain dramatic flair in service and presentation is in evidence here.

Reservations required
Dinner: Daily, 6:30 P.M.–11 P.M.

LA CHAUMIERE ㉑   *French*

6910 Main St.
Scottsdale, Ariz.
(602) 946-5115
Maître d': Thomas Foarde
Full Bar/Valet and Street Parking
AE, MC, V
Good taste in dress required

La Chaumière is a small place, designed in the quaint style of a country cottage in Brittany. Look for such specialties as Dover Sole, bouillabaisse, Rack of Lamb Bouquetière, Tournedos Rossini and Duck à l'Orange.

Reservations required
Dinner: Mon.–Sat., 5:30 P.M.–11 P.M.
    Closed Sunday, April–December

LOS OLIVOS MEXICAN PATIO ㉕ ㉘   *Mexican*

7328 2nd St.   1300 N. Hayden Rd.
Scottsdale, Ariz.   and   Tempe, Ariz.
(602) 946-2256   (602) 968-1161
Full Bar/Lot Parking
AE, D, MC, V, CB
No dress restrictions

Los Olivos is "exactly what you would expect in a family-owned restaurant," according to manager Ruby Quintana. House specialties include chimichangas, Carne Asada, Camarones Veracruzanos (shrimp) and Steak Picado.

No reservations required
Lunch/Dinner: Daily, from 11 A.M.

LUNT AVENUE MARBLE CLUB ❷ ❻ ㉗ ㉚   *American*

1212 E. Apache Blvd. (four other locations)
Tempe, Ariz.
(602) 968-9859
Full Bar/Street Parking
AE, MC, V
No dress restrictions

The Marble Club serves hamburgers almost every way you can imagine, plus pan pizza, lots of soups and salads, omelets, crêpes and quiche. The setting is a combination of antiques, leafy plants, stained glass and soft lighting. "It's the kind of place you could spend an eternity in," comments the management.

No reservations required
Lunch/Dinner: Daily, 11 A.M.–1 A.M.

MANCUSO'S ❺   *Northern Italian/French*

4622 N. 7th Ave.
Phoenix
(602) 266-9594
Maître d': Frank Mancuso (owner)
Full Bar/Lot Parking
AE, D, MC, V, CB
Jacket for men preferred

Owner Frank Mancuso offers selections from Northern Italy (Cannelloni Alfredo, Chicken Agnesi and veal specialties) and France (Beef Béarnaise, Duck à l'Orange, and frogs' legs). The interior is composed of royal blue crushed velvet furnishings and stark white pillars.

Reservations required
Dinner: Daily, 5:30 P.M.–10:30 P.M.

NAVARRE'S ❼   *Continental*

52 E. Camelback Rd.
Phoenix
(602) 264-5355
Maître d': Dennis Depron
Full Bar/Valet Parking
AE, D, MC, V, CB
Good taste in dress required

If the words candlelight, formal and intimate send you swooning, then Navarre's is for you. The extensive menu includes lobster and other fresh seafood, chateaubriand, veal, steaks, chicken and nightly chef's specials.

Reservations recommended
Lunch/Dinner: Mon.–Sat., 11:30 A.M.–1 A.M.
      Sun., 5 P.M.–Midnight

OAXACA ⓭   *Mexican*

8711 E. Pinnacle Rd.
Scottsdale, Ariz.
(602) 998-2222
Maître d': Luis Gay
Full Bar/Lot Parking
AE, D, MC, V
No dress restrictions

Styled after an old Mexican pueblo, Oaxaca overlooks the entire valley—Tempe, Scottsdale, Mesa and Phoenix. Specials include all the traditional Mexican dishes, plus a chef's creation of Sea Bass Vera Cruz, topped with a secret sauce.

Reservations required
Lunch: Tues.–Sat., 11:30 A.M.–2:30 P.M.
Dinner: Tues.–Sun., 5:30 P.M.–10 P.M.
    Closed Monday

ORANGERIE ❹   *Continental*

Arizona Biltmore Hotel
24th St. and Missouri
Phoenix
(602) 955-6600, Ext. 2800
Maître d': Demetrio Velasco
Full Bar/Valet and Lot Parking
AE, D, MC, V, CB
Jacket, tie for men

"Enjoy the grand elegance of yesteryear," the management advises. At Orangerie you can dine beneath crystal chandeliers, surrounded by a dizzying variety of plants. Specialties include Salmon Wellington, Duck à l'Orange and sinfully rich pastries. The added attraction is the hotel setting. It's an architectural delight.

Reservations recommended
Lunch: Daily, 11:30 A.M. – 2:30 P.M.
Dinner: Daily, 6:30 P.M. – 11 P.M.

OSCAR TAYLOR'S ❽   *American*

2420 E. Camelback Rd.
Phoenix
(602) 956-5705
Full Bar/Valet and Lot Parking
AE, MC, V
No dress restrictions

A black and white 1920's-era decor is the setting for smoked barbecued baby back ribs served with homemade apple sauce, prime aged meats cut to order and just-baked carrot cake. There is something called the "garbage salad" with everything in it — greens, artichokes, hearts of palm, cucumbers, tomatoes, etc.

No reservations required
Lunch/Dinner: Mon. – Sat., 11 A.M. – 11 P.M.
                Sun., 11 A.M. – 10 P.M.

THE OTHER PLACE ⓱   *American*

Smoke Tree Resort
7101 E. Lincoln Dr.
Scottsdale, Ariz.
(602) 948-7910
Full Bar/Valet Parking
AE, D, MC, V
Good taste in dress required

Pleasant relaxation seems to be the main feature here, along with such specialties as prime rib, gazpacho, fried chicken and a Sunday buffet brunch. The setting is reminiscent of an old Spanish home, with fireplaces, imported tile and spacious patios.

No reservations required
Lunch: Mon. – Sat., 11 A.M. – 3 P.M.
Dinner: Daily, 5 P.M. – Midnight
Brunch: Sun., 10 A.M. – 3 P.M.

PIERRE'S LE BISTRO ㉓ *French*

7131 Main St.
Scottsdale, Ariz.
(602) 947-6042
Full Bar/Street Parking
AE, D, MC, V, CB
Jacket for men (winter season)

Pierre's is a Parisian-style bistro. The dining is intimate and elegant. Pierre LeCoz does the cooking and claims that everything he prepares is a "specialty."

Reservations suggested
Dinner: Tues.–Sun., 5:30 P.M.–10:30 P.M.
    Closed July 20 to August 31

TRADER VIC'S ⑲ *Polynesian*

7111 Fifth Ave.
Scottsdale, Ariz.
(602) 945-6341
Full Bar/Valet and Street Parking
AE, D, MC, V, CB
Good taste in dress required

The trademark Trader Vic's Polynesian motif is featured, along with the exotic bar drinks. The Chinese-style oven turns out smoked chicken, Cornish hen, steaks and a special Indonesian Lamb Roast.

Reservations recommended
Lunch: Mon.–Sat., 11:30 A.M.–2:30 P.M.
Dinner: Daily, from 5 P.M.

TROIS AMIS ❶ *French*

37645 N. Cave Creek Rd.
Cave Creek, Ariz.
(602) 488-3740
Maître d': Linda DuBois
Full Bar/Lot Parking
AE, MC, V, CB
No dress restrictions

Trois Amis is patterned after a French country inn. Its two cozy rooms are filled with antiques. House specialties include sweetbreads, chateaubriand and the Chef's Special, which consists of thin slices of filet mignon embellished with Béarnaise sauce and mushrooms.

No reservations required
Lunch: Mon.–Sat., 11:30 A.M.–3 P.M.
Dinner: Daily, 5:30 P.M.–10 P.M.
Brunch: Sun., 11:30 A.M.–3:30 P.M.

PITTSBURGH

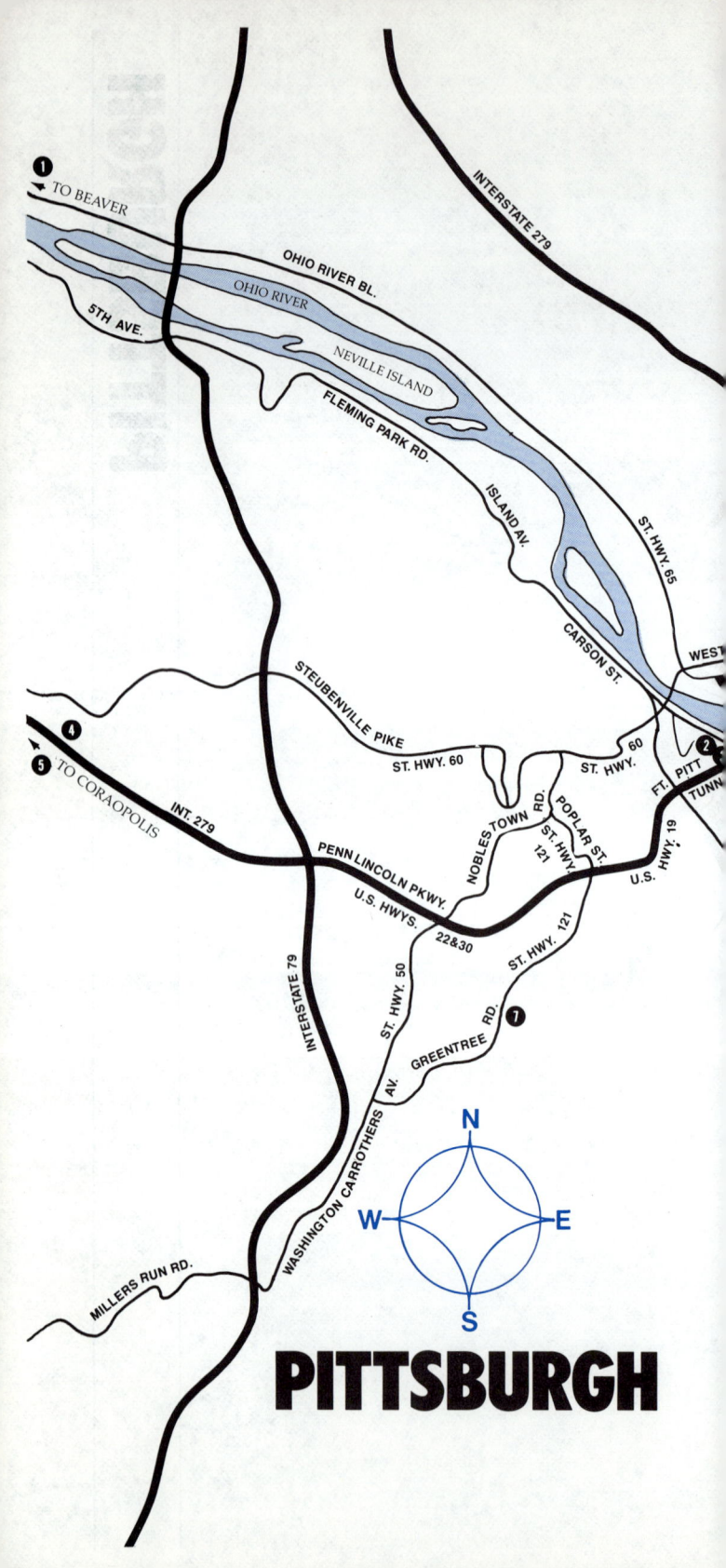

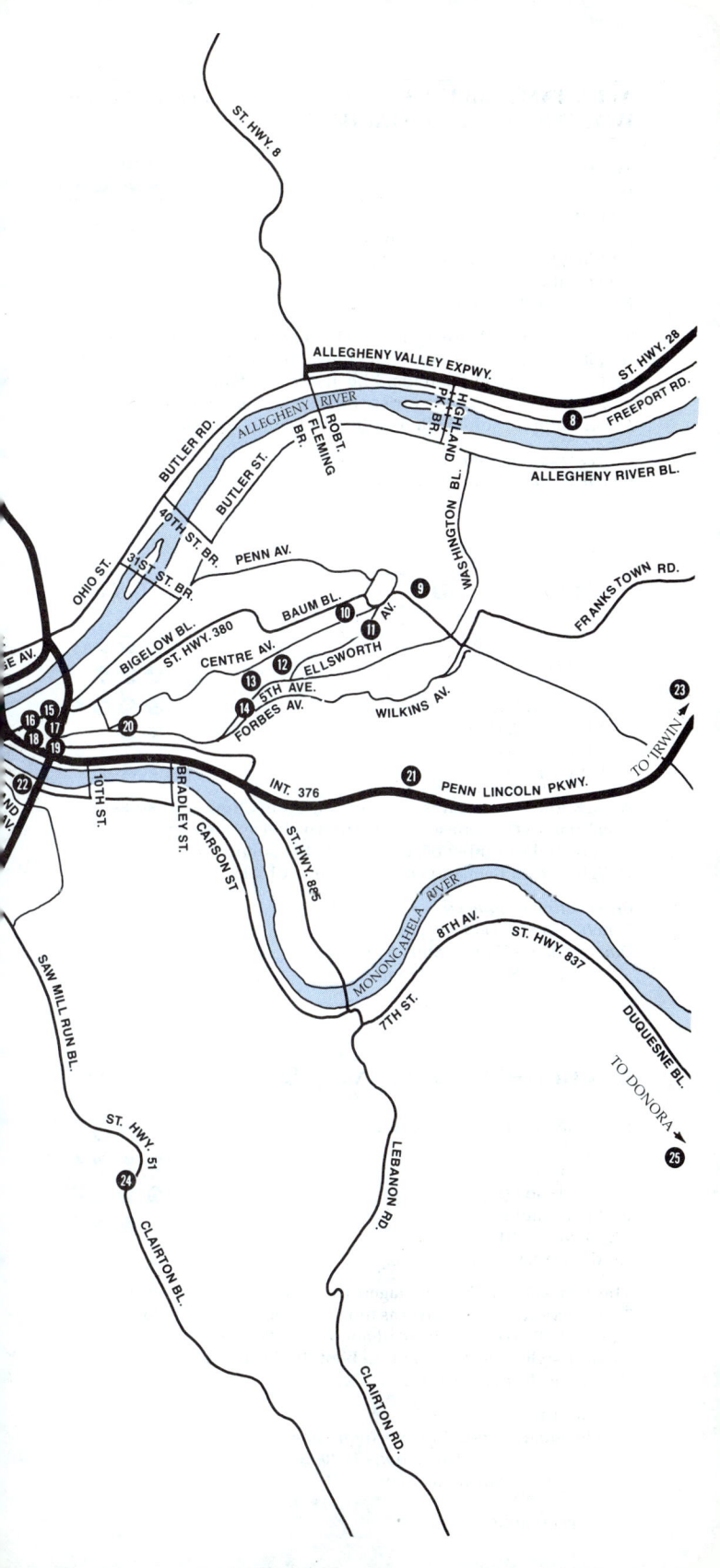

ALEX TAMBELLINI'S   *American/Italian*
WOOD STREET RESTAURANT

213 Wood St.
Pittsburgh
(412) 281-9956
Maître d': Alex Tambellini (manager)
Full Bar/Lot and Street Parking
No credit cards
No dress restrictions

Tambellini's Wood Street strives to be comforting. Its wood-paneled denlike dining room and large, fully stocked bar give the hungry and weary reason for hope. Zhe Tambellini family specializes in good service and a wide variety of fresh seafood, including Boston scrod, salmon, soft-shelled crabs and Lemon Sole Italian Style.

No reservations required
Lunch/Dinner: Mon. – Sat., 11 A.M. – Midnight
           Closed Sunday

ANNA KAO'S   *Chinese*

1034-38 Freeport Rd.
Pittsburgh
(412) 782-3010
Maître d': Bill Sy
Full Bar/Lot Parking
No credit cards
Jacket for men

Anna Kao's concentrates on a wide variety of Chinese cuisines, from Szechuan to Cantonese. A well-known chef and teacher, Anna Kao has created a number of signature dishes such as Imperial Seafood Delight, Ko Ta Beef and Orange Sesame Chicken.

Reservations required
Lunch: Tues. – Fri., 11:30 A.M. – 2 P.M.
Dinner: Tues. – Thurs., Sun., 5 P.M. – 10 P.M.
       Fri. – Sat., 5 P.M. – 11 P.M.

BEN GROSS RESTAURANT   *Continental*

Route 30 (822 Lincoln Highway W.)
Irwin, Pa.
(412) 863-7450
Maître d': Joe Cepicka
Full Bar/Valet Parking
AE, D, MC, V, CB
No dress restrictions

The Gross family has managed this restaurant for over 40 years. They serve such specialties as tournedos of beef, prime rib, Chicken Sauté à la Pierre, Caesar salad and Grand Marnier Soufflé *and* offer cabaret-style entertainment, to boot. It's located 4½ miles west of the Pennsylvania Turnpike.

No reservations required
Lunch/Dinner: Mon. – Thurs., Noon – 10 P.M.
               Fri. – Sat., Noon – 11:30 P.M.
               Closed Sunday

CAFE CAPPUCCINO ⓲   *Continental*

The Bank Center
414 Wood St.
Pittsburgh
(412) 261-1008
Full Bar/Lot and Street Parking
AE, MC, V
No dress restrictions

Co-owner Thomas McMahon calls Cafe Cappuccino "a charming European-style sidewalk cafe set under live ficus trees." This little bit of Europe is located in the center of an inner-city mall created out of an old bank building. The menu features crêpes, salads, fondues, beautiful desserts and exotic European coffees.

No reservations required
Lunch/Dinner: Mon. – Thurs., 11 A.M. – 10 P.M.
              Fri. – Sat., 11 A.M. – 11:30 P.M.
              Closed Sunday

CAFE STEPHEN B'S ⓫   *Eclectic*

5847 Ellsworth Ave.
Pittsburgh
(412) 361-0188
Maître d': Stephen Balaban (owner)
Full Bar/Lot Parking
AE, D, MC, V, CB
No dress restrictions

Cafe Stephen B's bright contemporary interior is the setting for healthful salads, open-faced sandwiches, "add-on" hamburgers and homemade desserts. But that's just lunch. For dinner, there is beef in pastry with prosciutto and Béarnaise sauce, sole with Hollandaise and stuffed boneless breast of chicken.

No reservations required
Lunch/Dinner: Mon., 11:30 A.M. – 11 P.M.
              Tues. – Thurs., 11:30 A.M. – Midnight
              Fri. – Sat., 11:30 A.M. – 1 A.M.
              Sun., 5 P.M. – 9:30 P.M.
Brunch: *Sun., 11 A.M. – 3 P.M.*

CHRISTOPHER'S ❷   *Continental*

1411 Grandview Ave.
Pittsburgh
(412) 381-4500
Maître d': Mario Angheloni, George Mahramas
Full Bar/Valet Parking
AE, D, MC, V, CB
Jacket for men

Christopher's basic components are industrial, functional, yet somehow beautiful. One wall is made entirely of coal — 20 tons of it! Steel, glass and aluminum complete the look. You'll overlook the Steel City itself as you dine on Escargots Bourguignonne, Caesar salad, roast rack of lamb, rainbow trout stuffed with crab meat and Shrimp Barzac.

Reservations required
Dinner: Mon. – Sat., 5 P.M. – 2 A.M.
        Closed Sunday

THE COLONY ❼   American

Greentree and Cochran Rds.
Scott Township, Pa.
(412) 561-2060
Full Bar/Street Parking
AE, D, MC, V, CB
Jacket, tie for men

The Colony has smart and sophisticated written all over it. A limited menu, an open-hearth grill, the essence of modern decor—all are restaurant features. Steak is *the* specialty. It seems that the salad bar, brought to your table, is to others of its genre what a boutique is to a department store.

Reservations required
Dinner: Mon.–Thurs., 5:30 P.M.–11 P.M.
Fri.–Sat., 5:30 P.M.–11:30 P.M.
Closed Sunday

THE COMMON PLEA ⓱   Continental

308 Ross St.
Pittsburgh
(412) 281-5140
Full Bar/Lot Parking
No credit cards
Jacket, tie for men preferred

A restaurant specializing in comfort, personal attention and prompt service, The Common Plea does have a clientele of lawyers and politicians, but anyone can step up to the bar. Specialties include bouillabaisse, Shrimp Romano, Veal Marsala and Chicken Scallopini.

Reservations required
Lunch: Mon.–Fri., 11:30 A.M.–2:30 P.M.
Dinner: Mon.–Sat., 4:30 P.M.–10 P.M.
Closed Sunday

DE FORO ⓮   French/Italian

428 Forbes Ave.
Lawyer's Building
Pittsburgh
(412) 391-8873
Maître d': Antonio Settembre (co-owner)
Full Bar/Lot Parking
AE, D, MC, V, CB
No dress restrictions

A French-trained kitchen staff supplies the magic that goes into such specialties as Sea Bass Pernod, chateaubriand, Tournedos Rossini or Bordelaise, Bahamian lobster and rack of lamb. The out-of-the-ordinary cuisine borrows from several cultures.

No reservations required
Lunch: Mon.–Fri., 11:30 A.M.–2:30 P.M.
Dinner: Tues.–Sat., 6 P.M.–10 P.M.
Closed Sunday, Monday evening

GRAND CONCOURSE ㉒ *Seafood*

1 Station Square
Pittsburgh
(412) 261-6363
Maître d': James Cavasina (manager)
Full Bar/Lot Parking
AE, D, MC, V, CB
No dress restrictions

Grand Concourse receives a shipment of fresh seafood daily from Boston. It is located in a former railroad depot and is a fine example of well-preserved Edwardian splendor.

Reservations required
Lunch: Mon.-Fri., 11:30 A.M.-2:30 P.M.
Dinner: Mon.-Sat., 5 P.M.-11 P.M.
Sun., 5 P.M.-9 P.M.
Brunch: Sun., 10:30 A.M.-3 P.M.

HUGO'S ROTISSERIE ⑳ *Continental*

Pittsburgh Hyatt House
Chatham Center
112 Washington Pl.
Pittsburgh
(412) 288-9326
Maître d': David D. DiBenedetto
Full Bar/Lot Parking
AE, D, MC, V, CB
Jacket for men suggested

Hugo's Rotisserie cultivates an atmosphere that is rich with romance. There is tableside preparation and a rotisserie — in full display. You can watch your very own duck, cut of beef or chicken roast and revolve on the spit. There is a salad and hors d'oeuvre bar of ample magnitude.

Reservations required
Lunch: Mon.-Fri., 11:30 A.M.-2:30 P.M.
Dinner: Mon.-Fri., 5:30 P.M.-11:30 P.M.
Sat., 5 P.M.-Midnight
Sun., 5 P.M.-10 P.M.
Brunch: Sun., 11 A.M.-2 P.M.

HYEHOLDE ⑤ *Continental*

190 Hyeholde Dr.
Coraopolis, Pa.
(412) 264-3116
Full Bar/Valet Parking
AE, D, MC, V
No dress restrictions

Hyeholde bills itself as "a refuge for those who yearn for things as they once were." A country inn with a grand and gracious reputation, Hyeholde serves a variety of seafood dishes, filet mignon, a mixed grill and Roast Rack of Lamb Persille. They use only fresh in-season vegetables and they bake their own bread and rolls.

Reservations required
Lunch: Mon.-Fri., 11:30 A.M.-2 P.M.
Dinner: Mon.-Sat., 5 P.M.-10 P.M.
Closed Sunday

KLEIN'S ⓰   *Hungarian*

330 Fourth Ave.
Pittsburgh
(412) 232-3311
Maître d': Ned Fine (co-owner)
Full Bar/Lot Parking
AE, D, MC, V, CB
No dress restrictions

Klein's has been in business for more than 80 years and is now run by the fourth generation of restaurateurs. In addition to the Hungarian fare, there are such seafood specialties as lobster, Crab Imperial and shrimp. Co-owner Ned Fine says Klein's is famous for its Caesar salad and garlic puffs.

Reservations suggested (three or more)
Lunch/Dinner: Mon.–Fri., 11 A.M.–10 P.M.
                Sat., 4:30 P.M.–10 P.M.
                Closed Sunday

LA NORMANDE ⓾   *French*

5030 Centre Ave.
Pittsburgh
(412) 621-0744
Full Bar/Valet Parking
AE, D, MC, V, CB
Jacket for men

Nouvelle French specialties are served here with a discernible measure of pride and finesse. There is steak with bone marrow, for instance, and fresh roast Mallard duck, plus rack of lamb, various terrine appetizers, veal with morelles and tarragon and, for dessert, a Grand Marnier Soufflé. The wine list is fully French and vintage ports and cognacs are available.

Reservations required
Dinner: Mon.–Thurs., 6 P.M.–10 P.M.
         Fri.–Sat., 6 P.M.–11 P.M.
         Closed Sunday

LE MONT ❸   *Continental*

1114 Grandview Ave.
Pittsburgh
(412) 431-3100
Maître d': Alex F. Colaizzi
Full Bar/Valet Parking
AE, D, MC, V, CB
No jeans

Le Mont has worked out a mathematically devised mirror arrangement so that every guest can see the city from every table. The work of the kitchen is more subjective, and consists of offerings such as prime rib, Red Snapper Le Mont and Rack of Lamb Persille.

Reservations required
Dinner: Mon.–Sat., 5 P.M.–2 A.M.
         Sun., 4 P.M.–11 P.M.

LOUIS TAMBELLINI'S ❻   *American/Italian/Seafood*

160 Southern Ave. (moving to
Pittsburgh Saw Mill Run Blvd.
(412) 481-1118 in November, 1981)
Maître d': Giancarlo (John) Tambellini (manager)
Full Bar/Valet Parking
No credit cards
Good taste in dress required

While serving a full range of Italian and American specialties, manager John Tambellini points to his seafood selections before mentioning anything else. He lists fresh Scrod Polignac, Stuffed Lemon Sole, lobster bisque, Oysters Bienville and poached salmon. He also offers many veal dishes: Cordon Bleu, Romano, saltimbocca.

No reservations required
Lunch/Dinner: Mon.-Sat., 11:30 A.M.-11 P.M.
  Closed Sunday

NEW MEADOW GRILL ❾   *Seafood/Italian*

420 Larimer Ave.
Pittsburgh
(412) 362-8622
Maître d': Alex Napolitano (owner)
Full Bar/Lot Parking
No credit cards
No dress restrictions

"Nothing frozen here," states New Meadow Grill owner Alex Napolitano quite emphatically. Instead, he serves freshly prepared versions of Spaghetti Tetrazzini, Caruso and Marinara, Chicken Cacciatore, Veal Parmigiana and Eggplant Parmigiana. Of course, there's also seafood — lots of it — including clams, lobster, shrimp, soft-shelled crab and lump crab meat.

No reservations required
Dinner: Wed.-Sun., 5 P.M.-10 P.M.
  Closed Monday, Tuesday

NINO'S ⓬   *Continental*

214 N. Craig St.
Pittsburgh
(412) 621-2700
Full Bar/Lot Parking
AE, D, MC, V, CB
Good taste in dress required

Nino's is a Mediterranean-style restaurant, with an ample seating capacity and formal dining. The 30-entrée menu covers such categories as fresh fish, lobster and steak. The chef prepares four special items daily. Dessert incudes homemade chocolate cheesecake and cannoli.

Reservations required
Lunch: Mon.-Sat., 11:30 A.M.-3 P.M.
Dinner: Mon.-Fri., 5 P.M.-11 P.M.
  Sat., 5 P.M.-Midnight
  Closed Sunday

NORMAN'S ㉔   American

3600 Saw Mill Run Blvd.
Pittsburgh
(412) 884-4899
Full Bar/Lot Parking
MC, V
No dress restrictions

If you're hungry in Pittsburgh in the wee hours of the morning, this is the place to go. Norman's serves hearty American food — steaks, hamburgers, omelets, sandwiches — plus Italian and seafood specialties. You can choose to eat a lot or to nibble on a few things — it's that kind of menu and that kind of casual restaurant.

No reservations required
Breakfast/Lunch/Dinner: Mon.-Fri., 11 A.M.-4 A.M.
             Sat., 8 A.M.-5 A.M.
             Sun., 8 A.M.-4 A.M.

PARK SCHENLEY ⑬   Continental

3955 Bigelow Blvd.
Pittsburgh
(412) 681-0800
Maître d': Louis A. Perla
Full Bar/Valet Parking
AE, D, MC, V, CB
Jacket for men

Owner Frank Blandi pinpoints his restaurant's decor to a five-year period (1930 to 1935). He has been serving his French-influenced specialties for more than 25 years. There are such menu selections as Fillet of Sole Véronique, Poulet Côte d'Azur, Chateaubriand Bouquetière and Les Manicottis Farcis au Ricotta.

Reservations required
Lunch/Dinner: Tues.-Thurs., 11 A.M.-11:30 P.M.
             Fri., 11 A.M.-12:30 A.M.
             Sat., 11 A.M.-1:30 A.M.
             Sun., 3 P.M.-10 P.M.
             Closed Monday

POLI'S ㉑   Seafood

2607 Murray Ave.
Pittsburgh
(412) 521-6400
Maître d': Joseph and Larry Poli (owners)
Full Bar/Valet Parking
AE, D, MC, V, CB
No dress restrictions

Poli's bar is completely nautical, with a rowboat hanging before your eyes and portholes for tables. Numerous cappuccinos and espressos are served. Dining room specialties include stone and soft shell crabs in season, plus assorted fish platters, lobster, and the daily catch.

No reservations required
Lunch/Dinner: Tues.-Fri., 11:30 A.M.-11 P.M.
             Sat., 11:30 A.M.-Midnight
             Sun., 1 P.M.-10 P.M.

THE REDWOOD ㉕   *French/Italian*

87 Castner Ave.
Donora, Pa.
(412) 379-6540
Maître d': Francis Roncacé (chef)
Full Bar/Street Parking
No credit cards
Jacket for men

The Redwood offers large doses of romance and intimacy in a candlelit Victorian setting. You can stroll through the *two* wine cellars or have a cocktail in the garden before dining. There are such specialties as filet mignon broiled on the sword, with a rosemary and wine sauce, and lobster stuffed with Crab Imperial.

Reservations required
Dinner: Tues. – Sat., 6:30 P.M. – 9:30 P.M.
        Closed Tuesday – Thursday, January and February
        Closed Sunday, Monday, year-round

SGRO'S ❹   *American*

4400 Campbell's Run Rd.
Pittsburgh
(412) 787-1234
Full Bar/Street Parking
AE, D, MC, V, CB
Jacket for men

Owned by a family steeped in the tradition of running restaurants, Sgro's has a reputation for uncompromising quality. You can find such things as cream of broccoli soup, Continental Breast of Chicken and Vegetable Risi Bisi on the menu, as well as the innovative daily whims of the chef.

Reservations required (Saturday)
Lunch: Mon. – Sat., 11:30 A.M. – 2:30 P.M.
Dinner: Mon. – Fri., 5 P.M. – 10 P.M.
      Sat., 5 P.M. – 11 P.M.
      Closed Sunday

TOP OF THE TRIANGLE ⓯   *American*

U.S. Steel Building
600 Grant St.
Pittsburgh
(412) 471-4100
Maître d': David Johnson
Full Bar/Lot Parking
AE, D, MC, V
Good taste in dress required

If you went to a "Top of" restaurant and didn't see for miles around a city, you'd be disappointed, right? No need for tears here. The Top of the Triangle affords you a view of the Golden Triangle, the three rivers and a good piece of western Pennsylvania. Their specialty is a steak dinner. And, there's Sky High Pie for dessert!

Reservations required
Lunch: Mon. – Fri., 11:30 A.M. – 3 P.M.
      Sat., Noon – 3 P.M.
Dinner: Mon. – Fri., 5:30 P.M. – 10 P.M.
      Sat., 5:30 P.M. – Midnight
      Closed Sunday

THE WOODEN ANGEL ❶   *American*

W. Bridgewater St.
Beaver, Pa.
(412) 774-7880
Maître d': Alex Sebastian (owner/chef)
Full Bar/Lot Parking
AE, D, MC, V
Jacket for men

Host Alex Sebastian offers some unusual fresh seafood appetizers (Angels on Horseback, Oysters Casino and baked Maryland crab), followed by the freshest vegetables around and well-prepared American favorites. Select from a menu that includes rack of lamb, steaks, baked shrimp, lobster tail and Fisherman's Stew. There are more than 200 wines — American only — to choose from.

Reservations required
Dinner: Tues.–Sat., 5 P.M.–11 P.M.
    Closed Sunday, Monday

ST. LOUIS

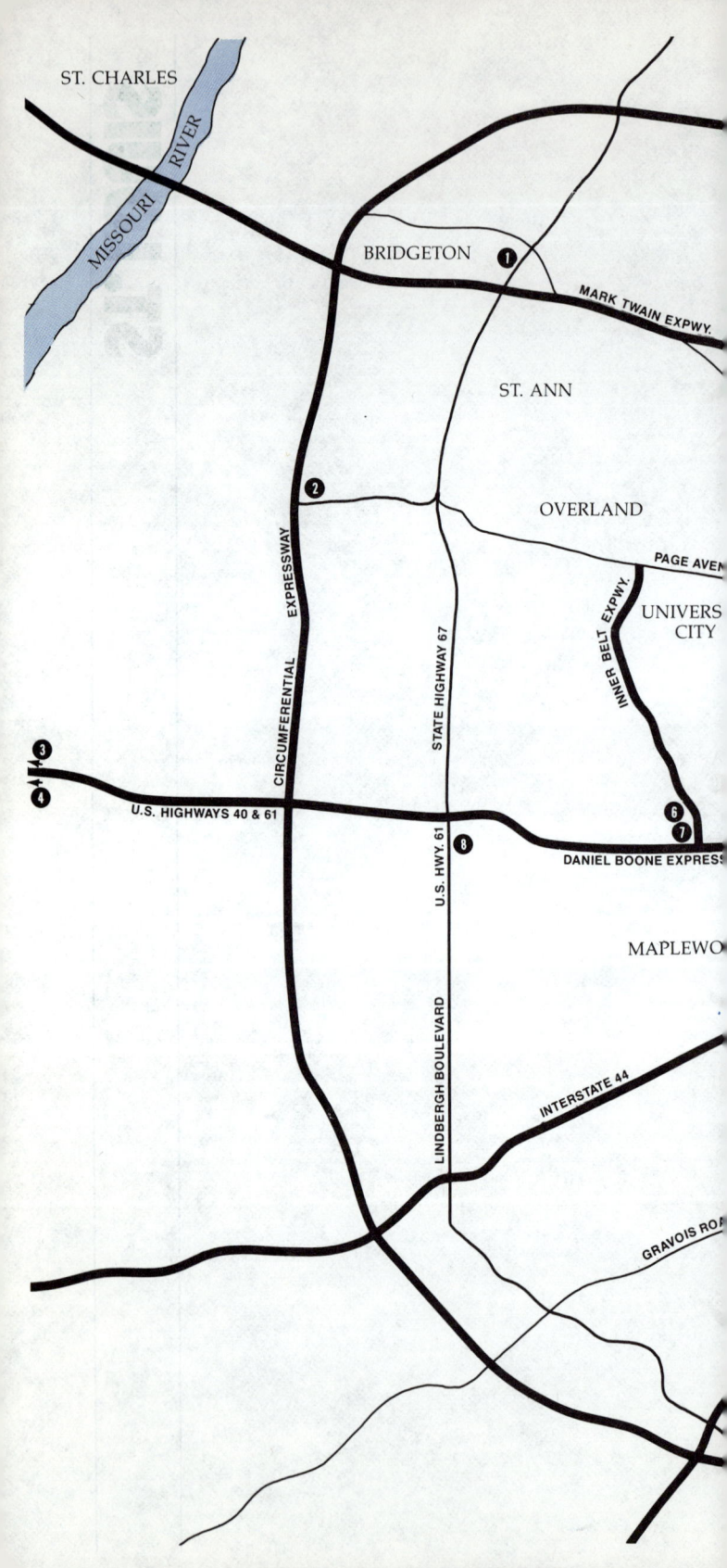

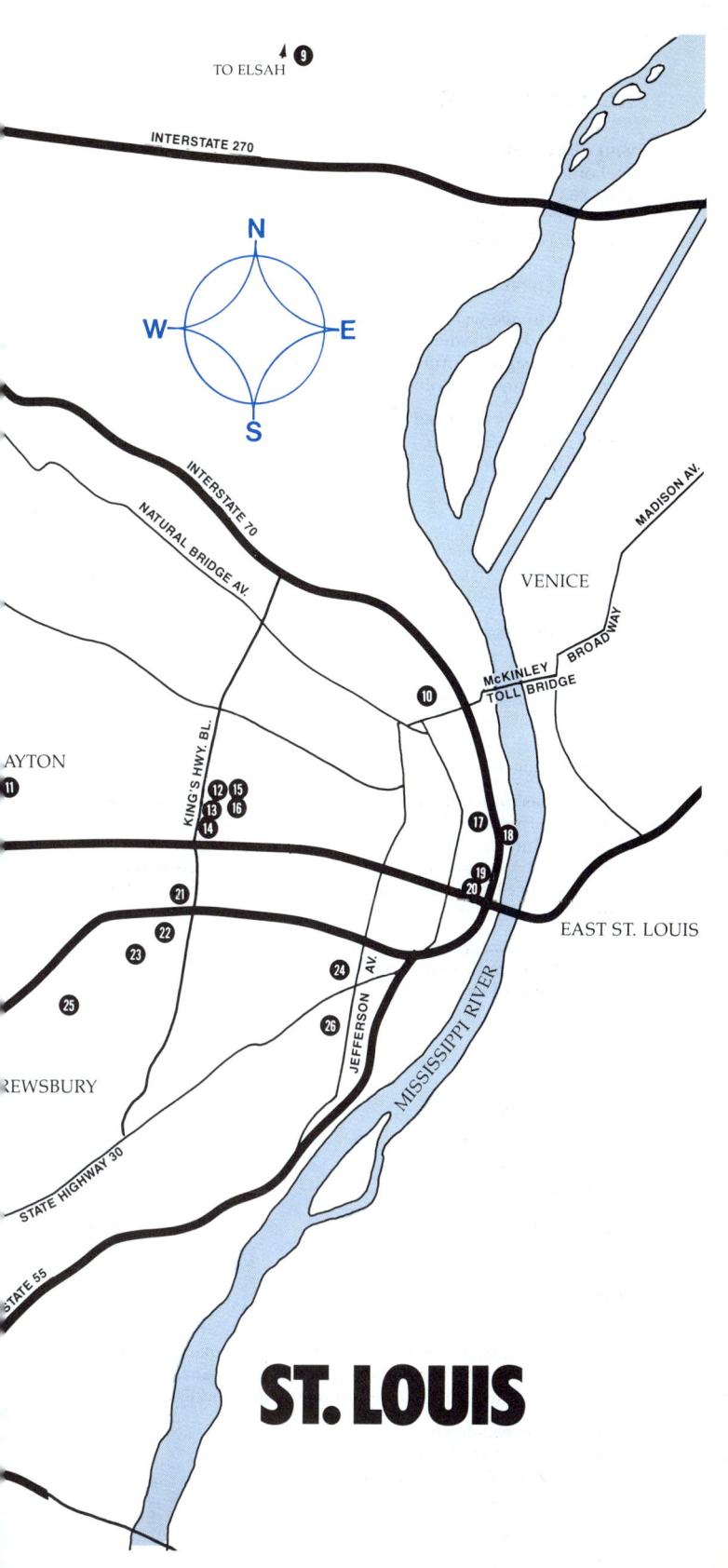

AL BAKER'S ❻ *Italian/Continental*

8101 Clayton Rd.
St. Louis
(314) 863-8878
Maître d': Geary David
Full Bar/Valet Parking
AE, D, MC, V
Jacket for men

"Benvenuto, we welcome you to our restaurant as we would welcome you to our home," exults owner Al Baker. He features Rack of Lamb Monasteraki, stuffed tenderloin and fresh fish. He also boasts the largest, most complete wine cellar in St. Louis.

No reservations required
Dinner: Mon.–Sat., 4 P.M.–1 A.M.
       Closed Sunday

AL'S ⓲ *Italian*

1200 N. Main St.
St. Louis
(314) 421-6399
Maître d': David Young
Full Bar/Valet Parking
MC, V
Jacket, tie for men

Al's provides mid-19th-century elegance in decor and a wide selection of international favorites in cuisine. Most specialties are given an Italian interpretation, however. There is no printed menu. Instead, the day's available meats and seafood are presented to you upon a silver platter while an amiable table captain describes each entrée.

No reservations required
Dinner: Mon.–Sat., 5 P.M.–Midnight
       Closed Sunday, Major Holidays, first two weeks of July

ANTHONY'S ⓴ *Continental*

10 S. Broadway
St. Louis
(314) 231-2434
Maître d': David Kledge
Full Bar/Valet Parking
MC, V
Jacket, tie for men

A restaurant of contemporary design, Anthony's offers food that is prepared simply, but *elegantly*. You dine overlooking a garden in a quiet, almost hushed atmosphere. You can choose from selections that inlclude rack of lamb, sweetbreads, veal and fish.

Reservations required
Lunch: Mon.–Sat., 11:30 A.M.–2 P.M.
Dinner: Mon.–Sat., 5:30 P.M.–10 P.M.
       Closed Sunday

BALABAN'S ⑮ — *Continental*

(Main Dining Room)
405 N. Euclid Ave.
St. Louis
(314) 361-9071
Maître d': Dennis Potter
Full Bar/Valet Parking
MC, V
No dress restrictions

Balaban's prides itself on serving fine food in a relaxed atmosphere. There are four dining rooms and a sidewalk cafe that is glass enclosed in winter. Specialties include Beef Wellington, tenderloin of beef baked in a pastry shell, whole live Maine lobster prepared to order and various "off-the-menu" seafood items: scrod, red snapper and swordfish.

No reservations required
Dinner: Mon.–Sat., 5 P.M.–1:30 A.M.
Brunch: Sat., 11:30 A.M.–2:30 P.M.
 Closed Sunday

CAFE DE FRANCE ⑲ — *French*

410 Olive St.
St. Louis
(314) 231-2204
Full Bar/Street Parking
AE, D, MC, V
Good taste in dress required

A recent addition to the restaurant scene in St. Louis, Cafe de France offers classically oriented *haute cuisine*.

Reservations required
Lunch: Mon.–Fri., 11:30 A.M.–2 P.M.
Dinner: Mon.–Thurs., 5:30 P.M.–10:30 P.M.
 Fri.–Sat., 5:30 P.M.–11:30 P.M.
 Closed Sunday

CHEZ LOUIS ⑪ — *French*

26 N. Meramec Ave.
St. Louis
(314) 863-8400
Maître d': Michael Polzin
Full Bar/Lot and Street Parking
AE, MC, V
No dress restrictions

Chez Louis is modeled after a contemporary Parisian bistro. Numerous posters line the walls and a heavy French influence is felt throughout. Examples of both *nouvelle* and classical French cuisine are featured. Look for preparations of duckling, fresh fish, veal and escargots.

Reservations recommended
Lunch: Mon.–Fri., 11:30 A.M.–2 P.M.
Dinner: Mon.–Sat., 6 P.M.–10 P.M.
 Closed Sunday

CUNETTO HOUSE OF PASTA   ㉓   Italian

5453 Magnolia
St. Louis
(314) 781-1135
Maître d': Vincent J. Cunetto,
Joseph Cunetto (owners)
Full Bar/Lot and Street Parking
AE, D, MC, V
No dress restrictions

A relaxed "family" atmosphere prevails at Cunetto's. The bar sports an apothecary motif (the original building owners were pharmacists). Menu specialties include linguini, seafood, and canneloni with red or white sauce. The portions are generous, say the owners.

No reservations required
Lunch: Mon.–Fri., 11 A.M.–2 P.M.
Dinner: Mon.–Thurs., 5 P.M.–10:30 P.M.
        Fri.–Sat., 5 P.M.–Midnight
        Closed Sunday

DE BERGERAC   ❷   French

342 West Port Plaza
St. Louis
(314) 878-0001
Maître d': Rick Thaller
Full Bar/Valet Parking
AE, D, MC, V, CB
Jacket, tie for men

Haute cuisine and classic Parisian-style red velvet banquettes are what you'll find at de Bergerac. Oriental rugs and gleaming silver enhance the experience. Dinner selections include Filet of Sole à la Normande, Filet Mignon en Croûte Duxelles, Ris de Veau Meunière and Grand Marnier Soufflé.

Reservations required
Dinner: Mon.–Sat., 6 P.M.–Midnight
        Closed Sunday

DOMINIC'S   ㉑   Italian

5101 Wilson Ave.
St. Louis
(314) 771-1632
Maître d': Jackie Galati
Full Bar/Valet Parking
AE, D, MC, V
Jacket, tie for men

Intimate and precisely appointed, with oil paintings lining the walls and crystal chandeliers hanging from the ceiling, Dominic's is "very Continental" Italian-style. Owner/chef Dominic Galati offers such selections as Fettuccine alla Panna, linguine, saltimbocca, Tournedos Rossini and homemade desserts.

Reservations required (except Saturday)
Dinner: Tues.–Thurs., 5 P.M.–11 P.M.
        Fri.–Sat., 5 P.M.–Midnight
        Closed Sunday, Monday, Major Holidays

DUFF'S ❶⓰   *International*

392 N. Euclid
St. Louis
(314) 361-0522
Maître d': Ginger Carlson Mostov, Karen Duffy,
    Timothy Kirby (owners)
Full Bar/Street Parking
MC, V
No dress restrictions

"Duff's has a comfortable and informal atmosphere with a serious eye toward food," comments Ginger Mostov, one of three owners. There is an international selection of entrées, including Steak au Poivre Moutarde, Scallops de Jonghe, S'chee and Matambre. The menu changes bimonthly. There is an extensive selection of wines.

No reservations required
Lunch/Dinner: Tues.–Sat., 11 A.M.–Midnight
              Sun., 5:30 P.M.–Midnight
              Closed Monday

THE ELSAH LANDING ❾   *American*

118 La Salle St.
Elsah, Ill.
(314) 374-1607
No Wine or Spirits/Street Parking
No credit cards
No dress restrictions

The Elsah Landing is a country inn 12 miles north of Alton, Illinois, but in the St. Louis area. It's located in a restored 19th-century village along the Mississippi. The fare includes many unusual homemade breads, soups, sandwiches and desserts.

No reservations required
Lunch/Dinner: Tues.–Sun., 11:30 A.M.–7:30 P.M.
              Closed Monday

GIOVANNI'S ON THE HILL ㉒   *Italian*

5201 Shaw Ave.
St. Louis
(314) 772-5958
Maître d': Giovanni Gabriele (owner)
Full Bar/Valet Parking
AE, D, MC, V
Jacket for men

Haute cuisine with an Italian flair is served in a subtly intimate setting. The kitchen seems to excel in pasta preparations, veal and "spur-of-the-moment" inventiveness. Saltimbocca is a Giovanni's specialty, as is the Trenette al Pesto (fresh basil and pine nut sauce over noodles). The desserts are described as "unusual."

No reservations required
Dinner: Tues.–Sat., 5 P.M.–Midnight
          Closed Sunday, Monday

HENRY VIII ❶ *Continental*

Henry VIII Inn and Lodge
4690 N. Lindberg
St. Louis
(314) 731-4888
Maître d': Mark Hanon (co-owner)
Full Bar/Valet and Lot Parking
AE, D, MC, V, CB
Good taste in dress required

A warm, family operation, Henry VIII offers French-style service and hearty American and Continental cuisine. Specialties are roast prime rib of beef, Duck à l'Orange, baby Maine lobster, Steak au Poivre and scampi. There are home-baked breads and a wine cart to help you make selections from the cellar.

Reservations required
Breakfast/Lunch/Dinner: Daily, 7 A.M. – Midnight

JEFFERSON AVENUE BOARDING HOUSE ㉖ *American*

3265 S. Jefferson Ave.
St. Louis
(314) 771-4100
Maître d': Gregg
Full Bar/Street Parking
AE, D, MC, V, CB
No dress restrictions

A very small, elegant restaurant located in a restored turn-of-the-century building, the Jefferson Avenue Boarding House features the fine food of St. Louis as it was prepared at the time of the 1904 World's Fair. There are continually changing menu selections.

Reservations required
Lunch/Dinner: Mon. – Thurs., 11 A.M. – 10 P.M.
             Fri., 11 A.M. – Midnight
             Sat., 6 P.M. – Midnight
             Sun., 6 P.M. – 10 P.M.
Brunch: Sun., 10 A.M. – 2 P.M.

KEMOLL'S ❿ *Italian*

4201 N. Grand Blvd.
St. Louis
(314) 534-2705
Maître d': Mark and Ellen Cusumano
Full Bar/Lot Parking
AE, D, MC, V
Good taste in dress required

"Many people refer to Kemoll's as an institution rather than a restaurant," comments the management. And people mean that in the kindest possible way. Kemoll's has been serving Italian fare to the people of St. Louis for the past 54 years. There are such specialties as Veal Saltimbocca, cannelloni, Paglia e Fieno and Calzone Romano.

No reservations required
Lunch/Dinner: Mon. – Thurs., 11 A.M. – 10 P.M.
             Fri. – Sat., 11 A.M. – Midnight
             Closed Sunday

L'AUBERGE BRETONNE ❹   *French*

13419 Olive Street Rd.
Chesterfield, Mo.
(314) 878-7706
Full Bar/Lot Parking
AE, D, MC, V
Good taste in dress required

Classic French cuisine is served here, rather than just the regional fare of Brittany. Featured are Quenelles de Saumon, lobster bisque, red snapper in lobster sauce, roast duck and Foie de Veau Lyonnais.

Reservations suggested
Dinner: Mon.–Thurs., 6 P.M.–10:30 P.M.
    Fri.–Sat., 5:30 P.M.–11:30 P.M.
    Closed Sunday

LE BISTRO ❸   *French*

14430 S. Outer Rd.
Chesterfield, Mo.
(314) 434-3133
Maître d': Mme. and M. Gilbert Andujar
Full Bar/Lot Parking
AE, MC, V
Jacket for men

Dine in either of two ways at Le Bistro: cafe style on the ground level and formally and elegantly one level up. Feast on such delights as homemade pâté, baby squid, sweetbreads, duck, veal, frogs' legs and rack of lamb. Dessert means chocolate and banana mousse or Strawberries Le Bistro — with lots of cream and liqueurs.

Reservations required
Dinner: Mon.–Sat., 5 P.M.–11 P.M.
    Closed Sunday

MIKADO ⓮   *Japanese*

18 S. Kingshighway Blvd.
St. Louis
(314) 367-1266
Full Bar/Lot Parking
AE, D, MC, V
No dress restrictions

Mikado features a Japanese-style dining room with the traditional cushion seating. (There is booth seating, if you prefer.) Specialties include sushi, sashimi, tempura, sukiyaki and some Chinese selections. There are also "American-style" steaks.

Reservations required
Dinner: Tues.–Thurs., Sun., 5 P.M.–11 P.M.
    Fri.–Sat., 5 P.M.–Midnight
    Closed Monday

NANTUCKET COVE ⑬   *Seafood*

40 N. Kingshighway Blvd.
St. Louis
(314) 361-0625
Full Bar/Valet Parking
AE, MC, V
No dress restrictions

This New England-style seafood restaurant specializes in live Maine lobster, Boston flounder, Florida red snapper and charcoal-broiled swordfish. There is also freshwater catfish and rainbow trout. Fresh oysters are shucked at the bar.

No reservations required
Dinner: Mon.–Sat., 5 P.M.–11 P.M.
        Closed Sunday

PORT ST. LOUIS ⑤   *Seafood*

15 N. Central
Clayton, Mo.
(314) 727-1142
Maître d': Wade DeWoskin (owner)
Full Bar/Valet Parking
AE, D, MC, V, CB
Jacket for men

Port St. Louis doesn't discriminate in terms of its fine fish and seafood. Delicacies from the ocean, river *and* bay are flown in daily. Prime steaks and a variety of "exquisite" desserts are also offered. You dine in an opulent Victorian setting filled with carefully selected antiques.

Reservations suggested
Dinner: Daily, 5 P.M.–11:30 P.M.

RAFFAELE'S ㉔   *Italian*

3161 S. Grand Blvd.
St. Louis
(314) 776-5313
Full Bar/Street Parking
AE, D, MC, V
Good taste in dress required

Called "one of the most inventive Italian restaurants in St. Louis," Raffaele's serves a variety of pasta dishes (Paglia e Fieno is notable), and unusual entrées (for an Italian restaurant) such as sweet and sour chicken.

Reservations recommended
Lunch: Tues.–Fri., 11 A.M.–2 P.M.
Dinner: Tues.–Sat., 5 P.M.–11 P.M.
        Sun., 4 P.M.–9 P.M.
        Closed Monday

SCHNEITHORST'S HOFAMBERG INN ❽ — German/American

1600 S. Lindbergh
St. Louis
(314) 993-5600
Full Bar/Street Parking
AE, D, MC, V, CB
No dress restrictions

Schneithorst's has been serving sauerbraten to St. Louis residents since 1917. Modeled after an old Bavarian inn, it presents a number of German specialties, along with prime rib, choice steaks and fresh fish from Boston and New Orleans.

No reservations required
Lunch/Dinner: Mon.-Sat., 11 A.M.-1 A.M.
         Sun., 10 A.M.-8 P.M.

SPIRO'S ㉕ — Greek

3122 Watson Rd.
St. Louis
(314) 645-8383
Full Bar/Street Parking
MC, V
No dress restrictions

Considered by many to be the best Greek restaurant in St. Louis. The traditional Greek entrées are featured (shish kabob, broiled rack of lamb and pastichio) and a variety of salads. Retsina, the piquant Greek red wine, is a good complement to the savory food.

Reservations required (weekends)
Lunch: Mon.-Fri., 11 A.M.-2 P.M.
Dinner: Mon.-Thurs., 4:30 P.M.-11 P.M.
         Fri.-Sat., 4:30 P.M.-11:30 P.M.
         Closed Sunday

TENDERLOIN ROOM ⓬ — American

Chase-Park Plaza Hotel
212 N. Kingshighway Blvd.
St. Louis
(314) 361-2500
Maître d': Hack Ulrich
Full Bar/Valet, Lot and Street Parking
AE, D, MC, V, CB
Jacket, tie for men

The decor is plush Victorian and the atmosphere is warm and cozy. The Tenderloin Room offers prime steaks broiled over an open fire. The wines are described as "choice" and the desserts are termed "irresistible."

No reservations required
Lunch: Mon.-Fri., 11:30 A.M.-2 P.M.
Dinner: Sun.-Fri., 5:30 P.M.-10:30 P.M.
         Sat, 5:30 P.M.-Midnight

TONY'S ❼   *Italian*

826 N. Broadway
St. Louis
(314) 231-7007
Maître d': Herb Cray
Full Bar/Street Parking
AE, D, MC, V
Jacket, tie for men

You can visit Tony's wine cellar before dining on such specialties as Veal Piedmontese, prime steaks, homemade pasta, Lobster Albanello and zabaglione. The service has earned a reputation for being especially attentive.

No reservations required
Dinner: Tues.–Sat., 5 P.M.–Midnight
       Closed Sunday, Monday, Major Holidays

YEN CHING ❼   *Chinese*

1012 S. Brentwood
Richmond Heights, Mo.
(314) 721-7507
Maître d': Virginia Pei (co-owner)
Full Bar/Lot Parking
AE, MC, V
Good taste in dress required

John and Virginia Pei offer such specialties as Peking Duck, Yen Ching Beef, Hot Braised Whole Fish, a Hot 'n' Cold Plate and a Happy Family entrée.

No reservations required
Lunch/Dinner: Tues.–Sun.
           Closed Monday

SAN DIEGO

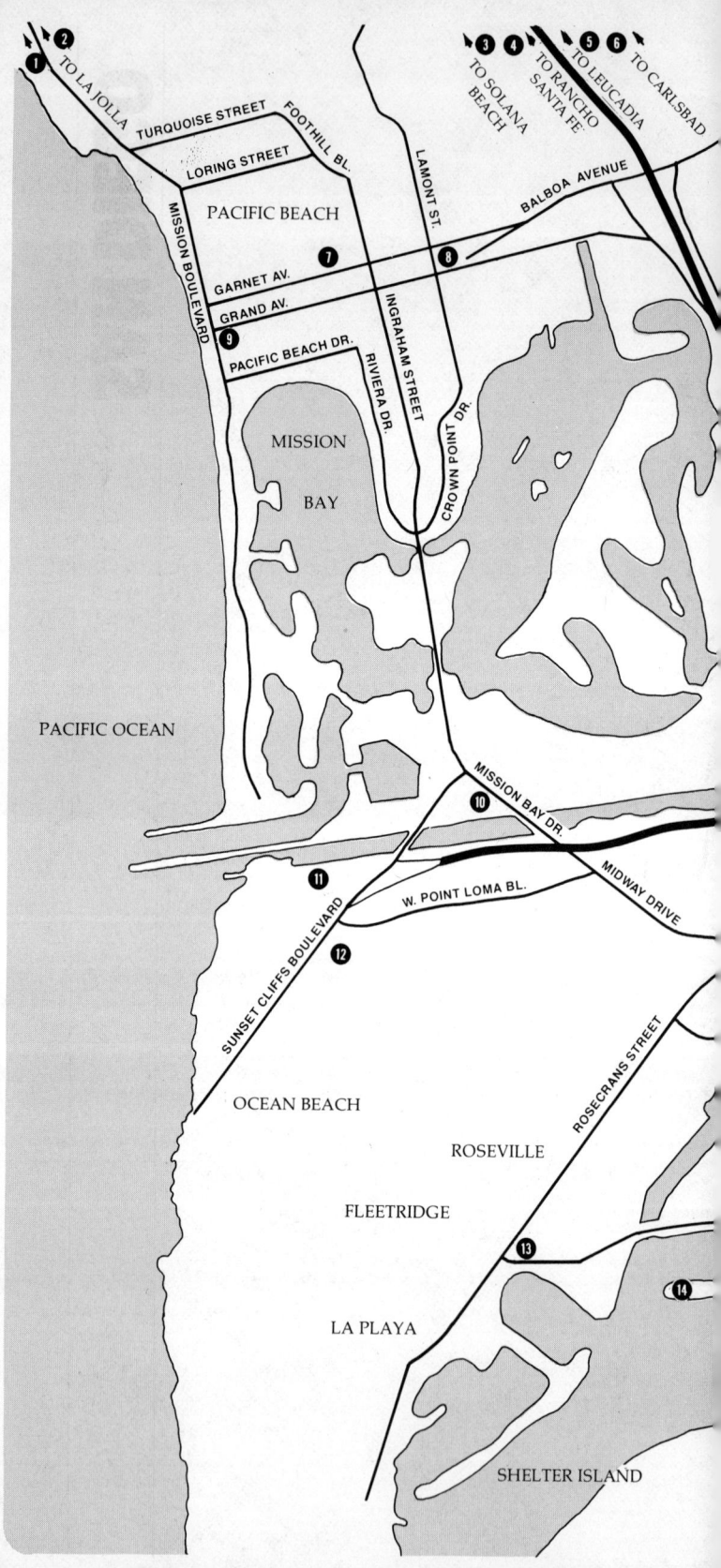

ANTHONY'S HARBORSIDE ㉖   *Seafood*

1355 "A" N. Harbor Dr.
San Diego
(714) 232-6358
Maître d': Mario Valerio
Full Bar/Lot and Street Parking
MC, V
Good taste in dress required

Anthony's Harborside features more than 30 different seafood entrées, prepared in a variety of ways—broiled, charcoal cooked, fried or sautéed. Manager Michael Ghio describes the salad bar as "about the best in the West." It stars crab, marinated octopus, several chowders and many, many types of vegetables and condiments.

No reservations required
Lunch: Mon.–Fri., 11:30 A.M.–4 P.M.
Dinner: Daily, 4:30 P.M.–10:30 P.M.

ANTHONY'S STAR OF THE SEA ROOM ㉕   *Seafood*

1360 Harbor Dr.
San Diego
(714) 232-7408
Maître d': George Pietsch
Full Bar/Street Parking
MC, V
Jacket, tie for men

Well known in the San Diego area and elsewhere, Anthony's offers most of the local fruits of the sea as well as signature dishes such as Sole à l'Admiral and Cioppino ala Catherine.

Reservations required
Dinner: Daily, 5:30 P.M.–10:30 P.M.

BERTRAND'S ❺   *French*

1950 Highway 101
Leucadia, Calif.
(714) 753-0434
Maître d': Bertrand Hugh
Full Bar/Valet Parking
MC, V
Jacket for men preferred

Located on a bluff overlooking the Pacific, near the La Costa resort, Bertrand's focuses on *la nouvelle cuisine.* The view is beautiful and so, promises owner Sam Rosen, is the food.

Reservations required
Dinner: Tues.–Sun.; 6 P.M.–10 P.M.
    Closed Monday

CAFE EUROPA ㉚ *Continental*

1733 S. Hill
Oceanside, Calif.
(714) 433-5811
Full Bar/Lot Parking
MC, V
No dress restrictions

Cafe Europa sports a European look both inside and out. Chef Siegfried Heil's specialties include Orange Duckling and Duckling Cumberland. Viennese hazelnut torte awaits for dessert.

Reservations required
Lunch: Tues.–Fri., 11:30 A.M.–2 P.M.
Dinner: Tues.–Sun., 6 P.M.–10 P.M.
    Closed Monday

CASINA VALADIER ❽ *Italian/Continental*

4445 Lamont St.
San Diego
(714) 270-8650
Maître d': Giuseppe Ferrari (owner)
Full Bar/Street Parking
AE, D, MC, V, CB
Jacket for men

Homemade pasta and veal dishes are served in two "elegantly appointed" intimate dining rooms. There is also rabbit in mustard sauce, Scampi Italiano or Provençal, shrimp bisque and Amaretto Mousse.

Reservations required
Dinner: Tues.–Sat., 5:30 P.M.–10 P.M.
    Closed Sunday, Monday

CHRISTIAN'S DANISH INN ⓱ *Scandinavian*

8235 University Ave.
Le Mesa, Calif.
(714) 462-4800
Maître d': Dorothy Hansen (co-owner)
Beer and Wine/Lot Parking
MC, V
Good taste in dress required

The prix fixe dinner menu changes daily but always emphasizes fresh, seasonal foods. Pastries are made daily on the premises. More than 275 different wines are stored in the underground wine cellar! A cozy, intimate "homelike" ambience prevails.

Reservations required
Dinner: Tues.–Sat., 6 P.M.–9 P.M.
    Closed Sunday, Monday

EL TORITO ㉔   Mexican

1590 Harbor Island Dr.
San Diego   (various locations)
(714) 299-3464
Full Bar/Lot Parking
AE, MC, V
Good taste in dress required

El Torito invites you on a Mexican "adventure" in both food and atmosphere. All restaurants are styled as south-of-the-border haciendas, complete with imported Mexican tile. All the standard Mexican dishes are featured, plus such specials as Camerones Flores (shrimp wrapped in bacon) and Tacos Mexicanos.

No reservations required
Lunch/Dinner: Mon.–Thurs., 11:30 A.M.–10:30 P.M.
              Fri.–Sun., 11:30 A.M.–11:30 P.M.
Brunch: Sun., 9:30 A.M.–2 P.M.

GIULIO'S ⑨   Northern Italian

809 Thomas St.
San Diego
(714) 488-9126
Maître d': Jack Peveri (manager)
Full Bar/Valet Parking
AE, MC, V
Good taste in dress required

Giulio's features traditional Northern Italian specialties such as Valdostana di Vitello, Scampi Giulio and Sea Bass Oreganato. Homemade pastas include Torteloni Verdi and Tortelli Piancentina. There are four dining areas and a patio for al fresco dining during the summer months.

No reservations required
Lunch: Mon.–Fri., 11:30 A.M.–2 P.M.
Dinner: Mon.–Thurs., 5 P.M.–10 P.M.
        Fri.–Sat., 5 P.M.–11 P.M.
        Sun., 5 P.M.–10 P.M.

GRANT GRILL ㉗   American

U. S. Grant Hotel
326 Broadway
San Diego
(714) 232-3121
Maître d': Gommarus "Mac" Schouten
Full Bar/Valet Parking
AE, D, MC, V, CB
No dress restrictions

Located in the heart of the city, the U.S. Grant Grill serves a variety of seafood dishes, grill specialties and international selections. Everything from mock turtle soup to flaming Cherries Jubilee is featured.

No reservations required
Lunch/Dinner: Mon.–Fri., 11:30 A.M.–12:30 A.M.
              Sat.–Sun., 5 P.M.–12:30 A.M.

HOB NOB HILL ㉒   *American*

2271 First Ave.
San Diego
(714) 239-8176
Beer and Wine/Street Parking
AE, D, MC, V, CB
No dress restrictions

A family restaurant in business for more than 35 years, Hob Nob Hill boasts a versatile menu as well as San Diego's finest in-house bakery.

No reservations required
Breakfast/Lunch/Dinner: Sun.–Fri., 7 A.M.–9 P.M.
            Closed Saturday

JOHN TARANTINO'S ⓭   *Italian/Seafood*

5150 N. Harbor Dr.
San Diego
(714) 224-3555
Full Bar/Lot Parking
AE, MC, V
No dress restrictions

This wharfside restaurant emphasizes style and lively Italian cuisine. You dine overlooking San Diego's bustling sport fishing marina. The fare ranges from rich soups to fresh seafood to beef and chicken entrées. You might choose King Neptune's Delight, a combination of crabs' legs, scallops, shrimp and lobster, sautéed with mushrooms, butter and wine.

No reservations required
Lunch/Dinner: Mon.–Thurs., 11:30 A.M.–10 P.M.
            Fri.–Sat., 11:30 A.M.–11 P.M.
            Sun., 4 P.M.–10 P.M.

LA CHAUMINE ❼   *French*

1466 Garnet Ave.
San Diego
(714) 272-8540
Maître d': Roland Chassang
Full Bar/Lot Parking
AE, D, MC, V, CB
Good taste in dress required

The management's job is to make you feel as comfortable and contented as possible. The kitchen vies with the serving staff for top honors. Specialties include Veal Marsala, Duck à l'Orange and frogs' legs, all accompanied by soup, salad and fresh vegetables.

No reservations required
Dinner: Tues.–Sun., 6 P.M.–11 P.M.
        Closed Monday

LA MAISON DES PESCADOUX ⑪   *French/Seafood*

2265 Bacon St.
San Diego
(714) 225-9579
Full Bar/Lot and Street Parking
MC, V
No dress restrictions

Chef Marcel Perrin (formerly of La Bourgogne in San Francisco) creates seafood masterpieces in the classic French manner. Many believe his sauces cannot be equaled. Specialties include Quenelles Kermor, Salmon or Lobster en Croûte, Lobster à l'Américaine and Dover Sole Duman.

Reservations required
Dinner: Tues.–Sat., 6 P.M.–11 P.M.
   Closed Sunday, Monday

LA MEDITERRANEE ③   *French*

635 S. Highway 101
Solana Beach, Calif.
(714) 755-3615
Maître d': Louis Zalesjak (manager)
Full Bar/Valet Parking
D, MC, V
Jacket for men

If seaside dining spells romance for you, La Méditerranée is a good place to begin an evening. You dine by candlelight as a harpist plays in the background. There are such specialties as Sea Bass en Croûte, Salmon Seattle, Beef Wellington, Steak au Poivre, Entrecôte Forestière, Grand Marnier Soufflé and Cafe Diablo Flambé.

Reservations required
Dinner: Daily, 6 P.M.–10 P.M.

LE FONTAINEBLEAU ㉘   *Continental*

Westgate Hotel
1055 Second Ave.
San Diego
(714) 238-1818
Maître d': Bernard
Full Bar/Valet Parking
AE, D, MC, V, CB
Good taste in dress required

In this casual city, Le Fontainebleau is a place of exceptional elegance. Waiters wear white gloves and tails. Many items are prepared tableside. Some specialties are Medallions of Veal Vieux Carré, Crevettes au Pernod and Crêpes Maxim. There is an extensive list of European and California wines.

Reservations required
Lunch: Mon.–Fri., 11:45 A.M.–2 P.M.
Dinner: Daily, 6:30 P.M.–10 P.M.

L'ESCARGOT ❷   *French*

5662 La Jolla Blvd.
La Jolla, Calif.
(714) 459-6066
Maître d': Curt Genter
Full Bar/Street Parking
AE, MC, V
Good taste in dress required

Chef and owner Pierre Lustrat prides himself on creativity in the kitchen. This translates into such delicacies as Escargots au Poivre Vert, Saumon Saint Jean-de-Luz, Caneton St. Vigneronne and Tarte Tatin. He terms the restaurant's ambience "attractive and classic."

Reservations required
Dinner: Daily, 6 P.M. – 11 P.M.

LUBACH'S ㉓   *Continental*

2101 Harbor Dr.
San Diego
(714) 232-5129
Maître d': David Wolff
Full Bar/Valet Parking
MC, V
Jacket for men

This family-owned waterfront restaurant focuses on seafood specialties (Coquilles au Gratin, Shad Roe Amandine) as well as Roast Duck Montmorency and calf's sweetbreads.

Reservations suggested
Lunch/Dinner: Mon. – Fri., Noon – Midnight
                    Sat., 4 P.M. – Midnight
                    Closed Sunday, Holidays

MANDARIN GARDEN ⓯   *Chinese*

8242 Mira Mesa Blvd.
San Diego
(714) 566-4720
Maître d': Johnson Sia (owner)
Full Bar/Lot Parking
AE, D, MC, V
No dress restrictions

Owner Johnson Sia combines authentic Chinese cuisine with friendly service. He makes particular mention of his Kung Poa Shrimp, Peking Duck, Mongolian Beef, Moo-Shi Pork and assortment of cold appetizers.

Reservations required
Lunch/Dinner: Sun. – Thurs., 11:30 A.M. – 9:30 P.M.
                    Fri. – Sat., 11:30 A.M. – 10:30 P.M.

MANDARIN HOUSE ❶ ⑳   *Chinese*

6765 La Jolla Blvd.   2604 Fifth Ave.
San Diego   and   San Diego
(714) 454-2555   (714) 232-1101
Full Bar/Lot Parking
AE, MC, V
No dress restrictions

The interior is done in cool beige tones and a quiet, formal style. You may choose either Peking or Szechuan selections. There is Peking Duck and Crispy Beef among many other entrées.

Reservations suggested
Lunch/Dinner: Mon.–Thurs., 11:30 A.M.–10 P.M.
              Fri., 11:30 A.M.–11 P.M.
              Sat., Noon–11 P.M.
              Sun., 2:30 P.M.–10 P.M.

MILLE FLEURS ❹   *French*

Country Squire Courtyard
Paseo Delicias
Rancho Santa Fe, Calif.
(714) 756-3085
Maître d': Dirk Delfortrie
Full Bar/Valet and Street Parking
AE, D, MC, V
No dress restrictions

Mille Fleurs offers intimate candlelight dining in a charming, off-the-beaten-track planned community. Specialties include mustard soup, home-smoked salmon, salmon baked in mustard sauce and veal sautéed in a watercress and cream sauce. Homemade pastries vary daily.

Reservations required
Lunch: *Daily, Noon–3 P.M.*
Dinner: Wed.–Sun., 6 P.M.–10 P.M.
Brunch: Sun., 10:30 A.M.–3 P.M.
         Closed Monday, Tuesday evenings
         and for lunch, October 1–May 1

MING'S GARDEN ❷   *Chinese*

5771 La Jolla Blvd.
La Jolla, Calif.
(714) 495-9043
Full Bar/Lot Parking
AE, C, MC, V
Good taste in dress required

Ming's Garden features a touch of European ambience due, in part, to the Parisian training of owner David Tse. Tse also studied his craft in Barcelona and Majorca. His father, She Chan Tse, is a chef of some renown, and has cooked for heads-of-state, royalty and "world-famous" celebrities.

No reservations required
Lunch/Dinner: Sun.–Thurs., 11:30 A.M.–9:30 P.M.
              Fri.–Sat., 11:30 A.M.–10:30 P.M.

MISTER A'S ㉑   *Continental*

Fifth Avenue Financial Center
2550 Fifth Ave.
San Diego
(714) 239-1377
Maître d': Giuseppe Villani
Full Bar/Valet and Street Parking
AE, D, MC, V, CB
Jacket for men

Mister A's features a Renaissance-inspired decor and a panoramic view of San Diego, the harbor and even Mexico. Specialties include Mister A's Beef Wellington, Flaming Sword du Roi and Veal Oskar.

Reservations required
Lunch/Dinner: Mon.-Fri., 11 A.M.-2 A.M.
               Sat.-Sun., 5 P.M.-2 A.M.

MON AMI ❸   *French*

731 S. Highway 101
Solana Beach, Calif.
(714) 755-6955
Maître d': Gary Parker
Full Bar/Lot and Street Parking
AE, D, MC, V
No dress restrictions

Chef Guy Lafontaine's cuisine ranges in style from Paul Bocuse to Michel Guérard (from traditional to *nouvelle*). Co-owner June Berridge says the most frequently touted entrées are the chef's 16 different preparations of fork-tender veal, the daily fresh fish special and rack of lamb.

No reservations required
Dinner: Daily, 6 P.M.-10 P.M.

NINO'S ❿   *Northern Italian*

4501 Mission Bay Dr.
San Diego
(714) 274-3141
Full Bar/Lot Parking
AE, MC, V
No dress restrictions

This small, family-owned beach area restaurant presents a calm quiet face to the world. Owner Nino prepares the food himself, including Veal Marsala, Veal Parmesan, filet mignon and fresh fish in wine and butter. His masterwork is a combination of filet mignon, veal, chicken livers, eggplant and cheese.

Reservations recommended
Lunch: Wed.-Fri., Noon-2 P.M.
Dinner: Wed.-Sun., 5 P.M.-10:30 P.M.
       Closed Monday, Tuesday

OAK TREE ❷   American

7811 Herschel
La Jolla, Calif.
(714) 454-1315
Full Bar/Street Parking
MC, V
Good taste in dress required

Housed in an old cottage just off La Jolla's main shopping strip, the Oak Tree features a brick patio with wooden tables "around an old oak tree." Featured are Chicken Cordon Bleu (and veal), Caesar salad, prime beef and jumbo shrimp. Homemade popovers are served with the meals.

Reservations suggested
Lunch/Dinner: Mon.–Thurs., 11:30 A.M.–9 P.M.
            Fri.–Sat., 11:30 A.M.–10 P.M.
            Closed Sunday

OLD TRIESTE ⓰   Italian

2335 Morena Blvd.
San Diego
(714) 276-1841
Maître d': Tommy
Full Bar/Lot Parking
AE, D, MC, V, CB
Jacket for men

Old Trieste presents itself as a sharp, well-run restaurant with a full range of Italian specialties. Featured are milk-fed veal, homemade cannelloni, chicken livers with mushrooms, filet mignon, fried zucchini and minestrone soup.

Reservations requested
Lunch: Tues.–Fri., Noon–2 P.M.
Dinner: Tues.–Sat., 5:30 P.M.–10:30 P.M.
        Closed Sunday, Monday

PERNICANO'S CASA DI BAFFI ⓳ *Italian/Continental*

3840 Sixth Ave.
San Diego
(714) 296-2048
Maître d': Mr. Baffi
Full Bar/Lot and Street Parking
AE, MC, V
No dress restrictions

Get ready for a few changes in procedure at Casa di Baffi. Your entrée will arrive *first*, followed by all the other goodies that usually come *before*. There is a pasta of the day, plus deep-fried vegetables, steaks, broiled pork chops, Pepper Chicken, veal and seafood. Owner George J. Pernicano advises guests to "come hungry."

Reservations required
Dinner: Daily, from 6 P.M.

PIRET'S CHARCUTERIE ❷ ⓴   *French*

902 W. Washington St.   La Jolla Village Square
San Diego   and   8657 Villa La Jolla Dr.
(714) 297-2993   La Jolla, Calif.
                               (714) 455-7955
Maître d': Jack Monaco (manager)
Beer and Wine/Street Parking
MC, V
No dress restrictions

Piret's is a complete French restaurant and deli, with elaborate pâtés, pastries, imported cheeses, California and imported wines and other delicacies. You may also dine on such specialties as white veal sausage, cabbage pie, onion and tomato tarts and unusual quiches. The menu features a different country French entrée daily.

No reservations required
Lunch/Dinner: Daily, 11:30 A.M. – 9:30 P.M.

PISCES ❻   *Seafood*

7640 El Camino Real
Carlsbad, Calif.
(714) 436-9362
Maître d': Marny de Vries (manager)
Full Bar/Lot Parking
AE, MC, V
Jacket for men

Delicacies of the sea are featured, including a flaming seafood brochette, crab, Scallops Florentine and desserts such as chocolate and Grand Marnier soufflés.

Reservations required
Dinner: Daily (except Wednesday), from 6 P.M.

RHEINLANDER HAUS ❷   *German*

2182 Avenida de la Playa
La Jolla, Calif.
(714) 454-6770
Maître d': Alfred Williams (co-owner)
Full Bar/Street Parking
AE, D, MC, V, CB
No dress restrictions

Á European atmosphere prevails at Rheinlander Haus. There is dining either on the patio or in the richly decorated dining room. A strolling accordion player gets you in an oom pah pah mood. Featured are sauerbraten, roast pork, German sausages, oxtail soup and a huge German Farm Brunch.

No reservations required
Lunch: Mon. – Sat., 11:30 A.M. – 4 P.M.
Dinner: Daily, 5 P.M. – 10 P.M.
Brunch: Sun., 10 A.M. – 3 P.M.

SKY ROOM ❷   *Continental*

La Valencia Hotel
1132 Prospect St.
La Jolla, Calif.
(714) 454-0771
Maître d': Salvador
Full Bar/Valet Parking
AE, MC, V
Jacket for men

As you might expect, the Sky Room is located at the top of this gracious old hotel. It is tiny, with only a handful of tables, but with a menu of grand design. Offered are salmon with champagne sauce, Veal Piccata, Sole Nantua, Tournedos Stanley and Chicken Chanterelle.

Reservations required
Lunch: Mon.-Fri., 11:30 A.M.-2 P.M.
Dinner: Daily, 6 P.M.-9 P.M.

SU CASA ❷   *Mexican*

6738 La Jolla Blvd.
La Jolla, Calif.
(714) 454-0369
Full Bar/Lot Parking
AE, D, MC, V, CB
No dress restrictions

This 16th-century-style Spanish hacienda is filled with lush plants, oak tables, a central fountain and a sense of fun. Specialties include King Crab Verde Enchilada and abalone. Owner Marshall Pellar calls his margaritas "world famous."

No reservations required
Lunch: Daily, 11:30 A.M.-3 P.M.
Dinner: Sun.-Thurs., 5 P.M.-9:30 P.M.
        Fri.-Sat., 5 P.M.-10:30 P.M.

TEN DOWNING ㉙   *Continental*

1250 Sixth Ave.
San Diego
(714) 235-6566
Maître d': Joe Gauci (owner)
Full Bar/Street Parking
AE, MC, V
No dress restrictions

There's something of the English pub about Ten Downing. They serve prime rib, Beef Wellington, fish, duckling and Cornish hen. There is homemade English Trifle for dessert.

No reservations required
Lunch: Mon.-Fri., 11 A.M.-3 P.M.
Dinner: Mon.-Sat., 5 P.M.-11:30 P.M.
        Closed Sunday

THEE BUNGALOW ⓬   *Continental*

4996 W. Point Loma Blvd.
San Diego
(714) 224-2884
Beer and Wine/Lot Parking
MC, V
Good taste in dress required

The duck dishes are considered very special here, including Duck à l'Orange and à la Cumberland with bing cherries and black currants. There is also rack of lamb, poached salmon stuffed with crab meat and veal entrées. There's a "countrified" feel to Thee Bungalow, even though it's in the heart of the city's Ocean Beach section.

Reservations required
Dinner: Tues.–Sat., 6 P.M.–11 P.M.
        Sun., 5 P.M.–10 P.M.
        Closed Monday

TOM HAM'S LIGHTHOUSE ⓮   *Seafood*

2150 Harbor Island Dr.
San Diego
(714) 291-9110
Maître d': Jim Bergen
Full Bar/Lot Parking
AE, D, MC, V, CB
Good taste in dress required

Tom Ham's offers you a spectacular view of San Diego Bay and the city skyline. It is supposedly the only restaurant in the U.S. that houses an authentic lighthouse. Specialties include a variety of seafood, steaks and Mexican entrees.

Reservations suggested
Lunch: Mon.–Fri., 11:30 A.M.–3:30 P.M.
Dinner: Mon.–Sat., 5 P.M.–11:30 P.M.
         Sun., 4 P.M.–10:30 P.M.
Brunch: Sun., 10 A.M.–2 P.M.

TOP O' THE COVE ❷   *Continental*

1216 Prospect St.
La Jolla, Calif.
(714) 454-7779
Maître d': John Salas
Full Bar/Street Parking
AE, MC, V
Jacket, tie for men

This 19th-century English cottage overlooking La Jolla Cove specializes in Filet Walter, Sweetbreads en Brochette, curry dishes and some Mexican-style entrées. There is a terraced garden and Victorian gazebo to explore when dinner is done.

Reservations required
Dinner: Daily, 6 P.M.–11 P.M.

SAN FRANCISCO

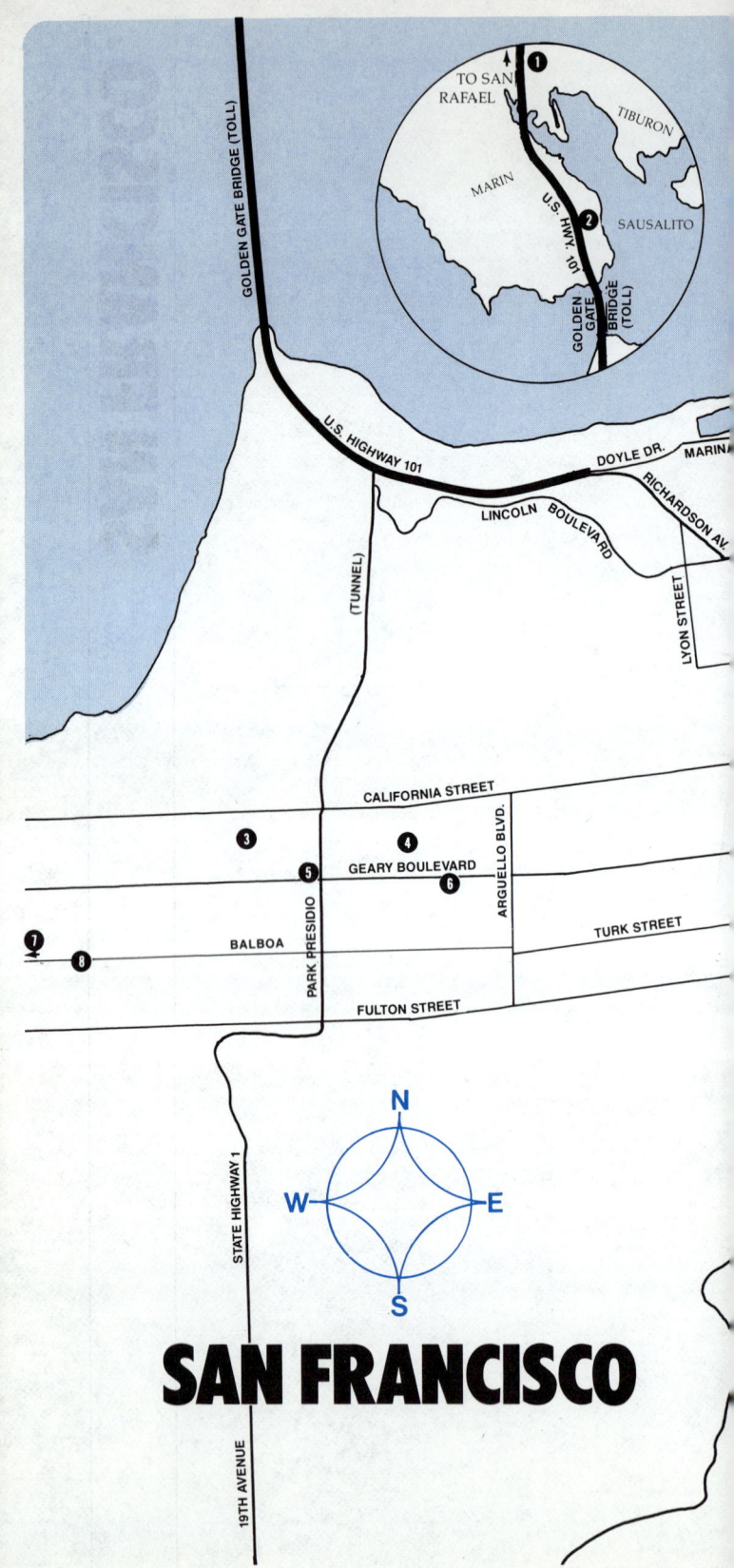

SAN FRANCISCO

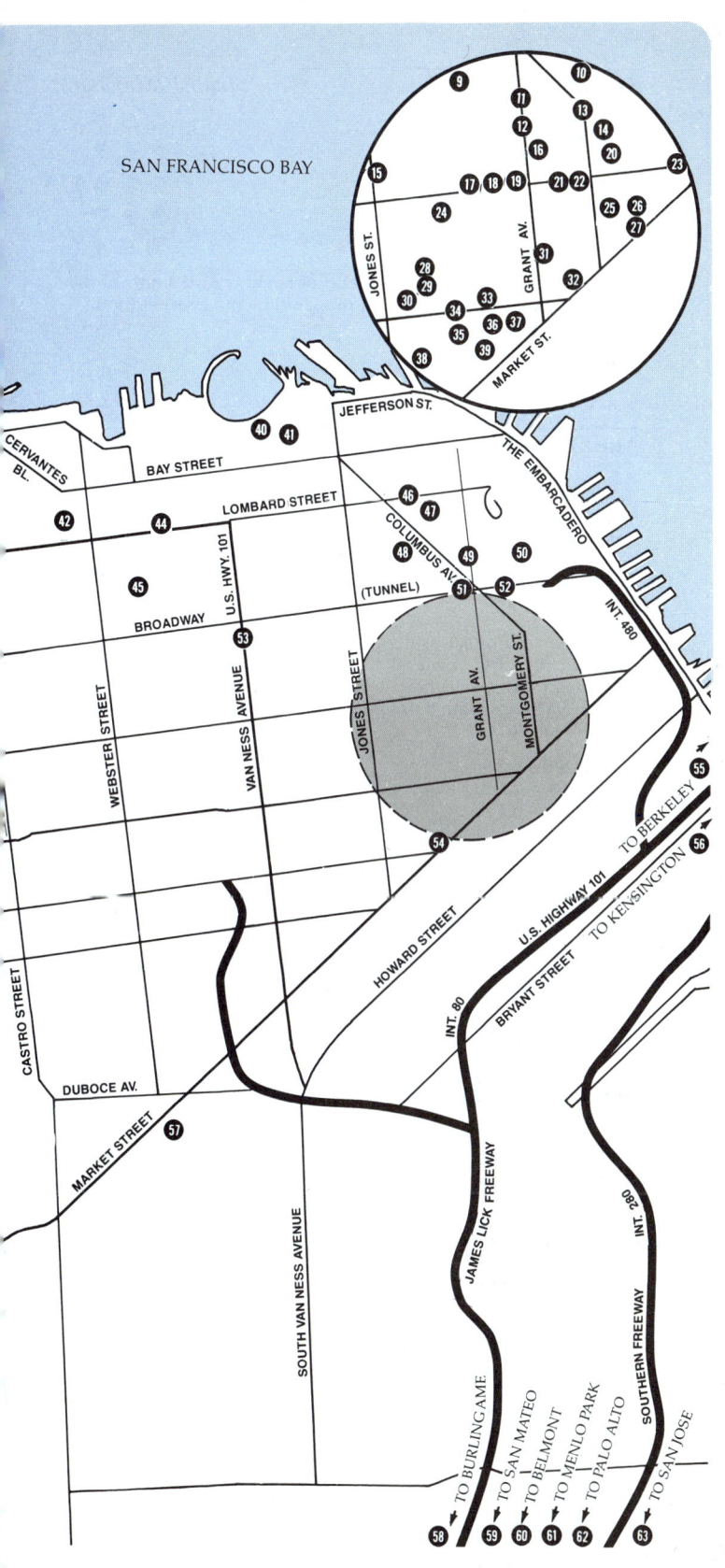

ALEJANDRO'S ❸   *Spanish/Mexican*

1840 Clement St.
San Francisco
(415) 668-1184
Full Bar/Street Parking
MC, V
No dress restrictions

Alejandro's presents a happy blend of Spanish and south-of-the-border cooking. Care is taken in preparation and presentation.

Reservations suggested
Dinner: Daily, 5 P.M.–11 P.M.

ALEXIS ⓘ   *Continental*

1001 California St.
San Francisco
(415) 885-6400
Full Bar/Valet Parking
AE, D, MC, V, CB
Jacket, tie for men

Alexis offers nothing less than "the ornate splendor of the ancient Byzantine Empire." Owner R. E. Lee calls his menu "cosmopolitan" in concept. Most selections favor the cuisine of the Middle East, however. There are such things as blini, Squab Byzantine and Rack of Lamb Karski.

Reservations required
Dinner: Mon.–Sat., 5 P.M.–2 A.M.
       Closed Sunday

ALFRED'S ㊿   *Italian*

886 Broadway
San Francisco
(415) 781-7058
Maître d': Armando "Mac" Mariano
Full Bar/Valet and Lot Parking
AE, D, MC, V, CB
No dress restrictions

"Alfred's has served San Franciscans and other people of the world since 1928," explains co-owner Albert Petri. The concentration is on steaks, charcoal broiled over Mexican mesquite, *and* on fine Italian cuisine. Every week Alfred's receives a shipment of prime Eastern corn-fed beef and milk-fed veal.

Reservations suggested
Lunch: Mon.–Fri., from 11:30 A.M.
Dinner: Daily, from 5:30 P.M.

AMELIO'S ㊻ *Italian*

1630 Powell St.
San Francisco
(415) 397-4339
Maître d': Christopher Shearman (owner)
Full Bar/Lot Parking
AE, D, MC, V, CB
Jacket for men

Amelio's is a place to soak up the atmosphere of an old speakeasy. Warm and romantic, with pink tablecloths, candlelight, rosewood walls and deep red draperies, it is one of this city's most durable restaurants. Offered are such selections as Veal all'Amelio, Costotta Papagalio and Quail Boann.

Reservations required
Dinner: Daily, 5:30 P.M.–11 P.M.

BASTA PASTA ㊾ *Italian*

1268 Grant Ave.
San Francisco
(415) 434-2248
Beer and Wine/Valet and Lot Parking
MC, V
No dress restrictions

Lots of you-know-what is served in a comfortably casual atmosphere. Along with the pasta al dente are entrées of broiled fish and veal. It's nice to know it will still be open to welcome you when the midnight hungries strike.

No reservations required
Lunch/Dinner: Daily, 11:30 A.M.–2 A.M.

THE BIG FOUR ⑰ *Continental*

Huntington Hotel
1075 California St.
San Francisco
(415) 771-1140
Maître d': Peter Seely
Full Bar/Valet Parking
AE, MC, V
Jacket, tie for men

The Big Four refers to 19th-century railroad and mining tycoons — the likes of C. P. Huntington, Charles Crocker, Mark Hopkins and Leland Stanford. With such a heritage behind it, it is perhaps surprising to discover menu selections that are reasonably priced. There are such items as rack of lamb, fresh salmon and Filet of Buffalo.

Reservations required
Lunch: Mon.–Sat., 11:30 A.M.–2:30 P.M.
Dinner: Mon.–Sat., 5:30 P.M.–11 P.M.
       Closed Sunday

BLUE BOAR INN   ④④   *French*

1713 Lombard St.
San Francisco
(415) 567-8424
Maître d': Georg Isaak, Cindie Jansen
Full Bar/Valet Parking
AE, D, MC, V, CB
No dress restrictions

Manager André Jansen calls the Blue Boar "an unusual mix of informality and elegance." Modeled after an English inn—all intimate and cozy—it offers comfortable seating on two levels. Specialties include potted shrimp, Oysters Rockefeller, Beef Wellington, rack of lamb, suckling pig, Petrale Sole Bonne Femme or Véronique and, of course, wild boar.

Reservations required
Dinner: Mon.–Sat., 6 P.M.–1 A.M.
         Sun., 5 P.M.–11 P.M.

BLUE FOX   ⑭   *Continental*

659 Merchant St.
San Francisco
(415) 981-1177
Maître d': Bernie Auer
Full Bar/Valet Parking
AE, D, MC, V, CB
Jacket, tie for men

The Blue Fox consists of three elegant dining rooms *and* three private rooms of considerable splendor. It has been under the watchful eye of owner Mario Mondin for almost 40 years. Some specialties are Noisettes of Lamb Antoinette, Tortellini alla Veneziana and Vitello Tonnato.

Reservations requested
Dinner: Mon.–Sat., 5:30 P.M.–10:45 P.M.
         Closed Sunday

CANLIS   ㉔   *American*

Fairmont Hotel
950 Mason St.
San Francisco
(415) 392-0113
Maître d': Bruce S. Stream
Full Bar/Valet and Street Parking
AE, D, MC, V, CB
Jacket for men

They seem to do everything right here. Beef and lamb are prepared over an open-hearth broiler; fresh seafood is flown in from around the country; wines from around the world are featured, along with a collection of California wines that is considered noteworthy.

Reservations suggested
Dinner: Daily, 6 P.M.–Midnight

CARAVANSARY ③¹ ④²   *Middle Eastern*

2263 Chestnut St.   310 Sutter St.
San Francisco   and   San Francisco
(415) 921-3466   (415) 362-4640
Maître d': Khajag Sarkissian (owner)
Full Bar (Sutter)/Street Parking
AE, D, MC, V
No dress restrictions

Both Caravansarys combine retail shops with full-service restaurants. You can browse through a wide selection of special-duty cookware, freshly roasted coffee beans, fine wines and cheeses before sitting down to lunch or dinner. Favorites include lamb dishes, roast duck, quiches and The Aram Sandwich.

Reservations required
Lunch: Mon. – Sat., 11 A.M. – 3 P.M.
Dinner: Mon. – Sat., 5 P.M. – 10 P.M.
Brunch: Sun., 11 A.M. – 3 P.M. (Chestnut)
          Closed Sunday (Sutter)

CARNELIAN ROOM   ②²   *Continental*

Bank of America Center
555 California St.
San Francisco
(415) 433-7500
Full Bar/Lot Parking
AE, D, MC, V, CB
Jacket, tie for men

You can't get more into the heart of this city's financial district than at the Carnelian Room. (It becomes the private and exclusive Bankers Club during the day.) Dinner specialties include Rex Sole Cardinale (poached and filled with crab), Scampi Chablisienne, medallions of venison with chanterelles and a potpourri of other delicacies.

Reservations required
Dinner: Daily, 6 P.M. – 11 P.M.
Brunch: Sun., 10 A.M. – 3 P.M.

CHEZ LEON   ③⁹   *French*

124 Ellis St.
San Francisco
(415) 982-1093
Maître d': Louis
Full Bar/Valet Parking
AE, D, MC, V, CB
Jacket for men

One of San Francisco's several small, intimate French restaurants, Chez Leon specializes in fresh baked salmon in a pastry shell, Veal Jeanette and daily innovations from the chef.

Reservations required
Lunch: Tues. – Sat., 11:30 A.M. – 2:30 P.M.
Dinner: Tues. – Fri., 5:30 P.M. – 10 P.M.
          Sat., 5:30 P.M. – 11 P.M.
          Closed Sunday, Monday

CHEZ MICHEL ㊶   *French*

804 North Point
San Francisco
(415) 771-6077
Maître d': Michel Elkaim (owner)
Full Bar/Street Parking
MC, V
Jacket for men

Perhaps the only French restaurant in the Fisherman's Wharf area, Chez Michel features an Art Déco interior, with beveled mirrors, canopied ceilings and lots of brass and wood. Specialties include Beef Wellington, roast duck, pepper steak, rack of lamb and fresh seafood.

Reservations required
Dinner: Tues. – Sun., 5:30 P.M. – 1 A.M.
    Closed Monday

CHEZ PANISSE ㊾   *French/Californian*

1517 Shattuck Ave.
Berkeley, Calif.
(415) 548-5525
Maître d': Alice Waters (chef and co-owner)
Beer and Wine/Street Parking
No credit cards
No dress restrictions

This French-inspired cafe and restaurant serves à la carte Provençal dishes in the cafe *and* complete dinners in the restaurant. The menu changes daily, but could include such specialties as oysters, spring lamb, various salads and local goat cheese.

Reservations required
Cafe:
Lunch/Dinner: Mon. – Sat., 11:30 A.M. – Midnight
    Closed Sunday
Restaurant:
Dinner: Tues. – Sat., 6 P.M. – 9:15 P.M.
    Closed Sunday, Monday

THE COACHMAN ⑨   *Continental*

1057 Powell St.
San Francisco
(415) 362-1696
Maître d': Cliff Saunders
Full Bar/Street Parking
AE, D, MC, V, CB
No dress restrictions

The Coachman will remind you of a charming British-style pub, with its oak-paneled bar, fireplace and list of British brews. You'll be surrounded by Toby jugs, hunting horns and old English prints. In the same tradition are the menu specialties: Cock-a-Leekie Soup, steak and kidney pie, prime rib and trifle.

No reservations required
Dinner: Daily, 6 P.M. – 11 P.M.

DELICES DE FRANCE 54   French

320 Mason St.
San Francisco
(415) 433-7560
Beer and Wine/Street Parking
AE, D, MC, V, CB
No dress restrictions

A combination charcuterie, patisserie and brasserie, Delices de France also offers its guests a pleasantly decorated dining room. There are countless pâtés to choose from, as well as cassoulet, soups, salads and pastries. The dinner menu varies daily, but "one always finds a nice selection of seafood, meats and other examples of fine French cooking," says owner Jean Lapuyade.

No reservations required
Lunch/Dinner: Mon. – Sat., 10 A.M. – 9 P.M.
Closed Sunday

DOROS 13   Continental

714 Montgomery St.
San Francisco
(415) 397-6822
Maître d': Harald Weber
Full Bar/Valet Parking
AE, D, MC, V, CB
Jacket, tie for men

Owner Don Dianda is especially proud of Doros' wine cellar featuring a wide selection of California and European wines. On the menu you'll find such specialties as Veal à la Doros, Veal Parmigiana, Breast of Chicken Archduke and Tornedos Rossini.

Reservations required
Lunch: Mon. – Fri., 11:30 A.M. – 2:30 P.M.
Dinner: Mon. – Sat., 6 P.M. – 10 P.M.
Closed Sunday, Holidays

EMILE'S SWISS AFFAIR 63   French/Swiss

545 S. 2nd St.
San Jose, Calif.
(408) 289-1960
Maître d': Stephanie Wright
Beer and Wine/Street Parking
AE, D, MC, V
No dress restrictions

"An evening at Emile's is reminiscent of Europe's fine countryside inns," claims owner Dee Ann Mooser. The French-Swiss background of husband and chef Emile is reflected in the innovative cuisine and in the selection of imported and domestic wines.

Reservations required
Dinner: Tues. – Sun., 5:30 P.M. – 9:30 P.M.
Closed Monday

EMPRESS OF CHINA ⑫   *Chinese*

838 Grant Ave.
San Francisco
(415) 434-1345
Maître d': Stanley Toy (manager)
Full Bar/Street Parking
AE, D, MC, V
Jacket for men

In the heart of San Francisco's Chinatown, the Empress of China features North China Sizzling Rice Soup, Barbecued Young Quail, Szechaun Spiced Beef, Peking Duck, Empress Lobster Prawns, Hundred Blossom Lamb and Lichee or Lemon Chicken.

Reservations required
Lunch: Daily, 11:30 A.M.–3 P.M.
Dinner: Daily, 5 P.M.–11 P.M.

ERNIE'S ⑩   *French*

847 Montgomery St.
San Francisco
(415) 397-5969
Maître d': Jean Rusterholtz
Full Bar/Valet Parking
AE, D, MC, V, CB
Jacket, tie for men

The congenial turn-of-the-century ambience found at Ernie's extends to three separate dining rooms. The walls are all covered with a heavy silk brocade and floors are carpeted in matching burgundy hues. Some of Ernie's offerings include Faison Souvaroff, Selle d'Agneau Farci aux Aromates, Coquilles Saint-Jacques and Poulet à la Crême de Poire et Endives.

Reservations required
Dinner: Daily, 5:30 P.M.–11 P.M.

FLEUR DE LYS ㉘   *French*

777 Sutter St.
San Francisco
(415) 673-7779
Maître d': Maurice Rouas (owner)
Full Bar/Valet Parking
AE, D, MC, V, CB
Good taste in dress required

Maurice Rouas' gaily decorated restaurant is home for such specialties as Filet d'Agneau en Chemis, Tournedos de Boeuf Brigitte (in a truffle and almond sauce with pâté de foie gras) and Escalope de Veau en Champagne.

Reservations required
Dinner: Tues.–Sun., 6 P.M.–11 P.M.
    Closed Monday

FOURNOU'S OVENS ⓳ *Continental*

Stanford Court Hotel
905 California St.
San Francisco
(415) 989-1910
Maître d': Joseph De Martino
Full Bar/Lot Parking
AE, D, MC, V
Jacket for men

Located in the gracious Stanford Court, Fournou's Ovens is a restaurant of tiles and terraces, including some large tiled ovens. The savory meats which cook in those ovens include roast duckling, rack of lamb and filet of pork. The roasting seals in the juices to perfection.

Reservations required
Dinner: Daily, 5:30 P.M.–11 P.M.

THE FRENCH ROOM ㉞ *Continental*

Four Seasons Clift Hotel
495 Geary St.
San Francisco
(415) 775-4700
Maître d': Hans Behringer
Full Bar/Valet Parking
AE, D, MC, V, CB
Jacket, tie for men (dinner)

The management calls The French Room "distinctively elegant, traditional and luxurious." Cart service is featured. Choose from such specialties as prime rib, and fresh fish cooked to order. The wine list has been cited as being of "collector's caliber."

Reservations recommended
Lunch: Daily, 11 A.M.–2 P.M.
Dinner: Daily, 6 P.M.–11 P.M.
Brunch: Sun., 11 A.M.–2:30 P.M.

GAYLORD INDIA RESTAURANT ㊵ *Indian*

Ghirardelli Square
San Francisco
(415) 771-8822
Full Bar/Lot Parking
AE, D, MC, V, CB
No dress restrictions

Gaylord is elegantly furnished, and offers excellent views of the bay, Alcatraz and the Marin County headlands. Manager/chef Kishore Kripalani also offers the specialties of tandoori cooking, including roasted and skewered chicken, lamb, shrimp and fish. There are also vegetarian entrées.

Reservations recommended
Lunch: Daily, 11:30 A.M.–3 P.M.
Dinner: Daily, 5 P.M.–11 P.M.

GEORGE'S SPECIALTIES ❽   *Russian*

3420 Balboa
San Francisco
(415) 752-4009
No Wine or Spirits/Street Parking
Major credit cards
No dress restrictions

A Russian food lover's haven, George's is tiny but lovable. The hearty home cooking includes pickled cucumbers, beets and mushrooms, kidney soup, chicken breast in a sauce of sour cream and mushrooms, Chicken Stroganoff, cabbage rolls and stuffed zucchini.

No reservations required
Lunch/Dinner: Tues. – Sat., 11 A.M. – 8 P.M.
    Closed Sunday, Monday

GRISON'S STEAK HOUSE ㊾   *American*

2100 Van Ness Ave.
San Francisco
(415) 673-1888
Maître d': Frank Beke, Eduardo Armendizo
Full Bar/Lot Parking
No credit cards
No dress restrictions

Prime rib is served from a carving cart. There is also Maine lobster—just arrived — and cheesecake made on the premises.

No reservations required
Dinner: Mon. – Sat., 5 P.M. – 10:30 P.M.
    Sun., 3 P.M. – 10:30 P.M.

HONG KONG ㊼   *Chinese*

245 Church St.
San Francisco
(415) 621-3020
No Wine or Spirits/Street Parking
MC, V
No dress restrictions

Hong Kong boasts the widest variety of dim sum in San Francisco. If you're eager to sample this unusual Oriental delicacy, this is the place to go.

No reservations required
Lunch/Dinner: Mon. – Sat., 11:30 A.M. – 9 P.M.
    Closed Sunday

HUNAN ⑤⓪   *Chinese*

924 Sansome St.
San Francisco
(415) 956-7727
Full Bar/Street Parking
AE, MC, V
No dress restrictions

A locally popular restaurant, Hunan features the cuisine of that particular Chinese province. Specialties include spicy bean curd with meat sauce, chicken salad, smoked ham, chicken or duck and steamed spareribs. There are sweet rice dumplings for dessert.

No reservations required
Lunch/Dinner: Mon.–Fri., 11:30 A.M.–9 P.M.
Closed Saturday, Sunday

IMPERIAL PALACE ⑪   *Chinese*

919 Grant Ave.
San Francisco
(415) 982-4440
Maître d': Tommy Toy (manager)
Full Bar/Lot Parking
AE, D, MC, V, CB
Jacket, tie for men

Serving both the exotic and the familiar, the Imperial Palace will show you what San Francisco's Chinatown is all about. There are such dishes as Minced Squab Salad, Peking Duck, Lobster Imperial and barbecued lamb.

Reservations recommended
Lunch/Dinner: Sun.–Thurs., 11 A.M.–1 A.M.
Fri.–Sat., 11 A.M.–2 A.M.

THE IRON HORSE ㉜   *Continental*

19 Maiden Lane
San Francisco
(415) 362-8133
Maître d': Lou Finess
Full Bar/Street Parking
AE, D, MC, V, CB
Jacket for men

Situated on Maiden Lane, whose gaudy, bawdy history is a colorful part of San Francisco's heritage, The Iron Horse features intimate dining and impeccable service. The cuisine is a skillful blending of Old San Francisco and continental Italian.

Reservations required
Lunch/Dinner: Mon.–Sat., from 11:30 A.M.
Closed Sunday

JACK'S ❷⓿ *French*

615 Sacramento St.
San Francisco
(415) 421-7355
Maître d': Alphonse and Norman
Full Bar/Lot and Street Parking
No credit cards
Jacket, tie for men

Jack's was established in 1864 and rebuilt on the same site following the 1906 earthquake and fire. The "Old San Francisco" atmosphere here is the real thing. Specialties include Sole Marguery, broiled English mutton, sautéed sweetbreads, Honeycomb Tripe and sautéed chicken.

Reservations advised
Lunch/Dinner: Mon.–Sat., 11:30 A.M.–9:30 P.M.
             Sun., 4 P.M.–9:30 P.M.

KAN'S ⓰ *Chinese*

708 Grant Ave.
San Francisco
(415) 982-2388
Maître d': Josephine Jue
Full Bar/Street Parking
AE, D, MC, V, CB
Jacket suggested for men

Owner Guy Wong simply terms Kan's "the ultimate in authentic Chinese cuisine." Special care is taken in the preparation of each individual dish. Some of those dishes include Peking Duck, lemon chicken, crab curry, melon cup soup and Rock Cod à la Caen.

Reservations required
Lunch/Dinner: Mon.–Fri., Noon–10 P.M.
             Sat., 4:30 P.M.–11 P.M.
             Sun., 4:30 P.M.–10 P.M.

KEE JOON'S CUISINE OF CHINA ❺❽ *Chinese*

433 Airport Blvd.
Burlingame, Calif.
(415) 348-1122
Full Bar/Lot Parking
AE, MC, V
Jacket for men

This penthouse restaurant overlooks San Francisco Bay. The interior features a marble fountain and an aviary and the hand-carved paneling represents a motif from the Sun Dynasty. Special dishes include Mongolian Lamb, barbecued young quail flambé and Manchurian Beef.

Reservations required for more than three
Lunch: Mon.–Fri., 11:30 A.M.–2 P.M.
Dinner: Sun.–Thurs., 5 P.M.–10 P.M.
       Fri.–Sat., 5 P.M.–10:30 P.M.

KIRIN ❺ *Chinese/Korean*

6135 Geary Blvd.
San Francisco
(415) 752-2412
Beer and Wine/Street Parking
Major credit cards
No dress restrictions

Kirin offers you tastes of the cuisines of Szechuan, Peking and Hunan, with a slightly Korean accent. Entrées are imaginative — such as whole rock cod in ginger sauce, cherry pork, shark-fin soup with crab and lobster, and Hunan-style lamb.

Reservations suggested
Lunch/Dinner: Daily, 11:30 A.M. - 10 P.M.

LA BONNE AUBERGE (59) *French*

2075 S. El Camino
San Mateo, Calif.
(415) 341-2525
Maître d': Huguette del Perugia (co-owner)
Beer and Wine/Street Parking
MC, V
No dress restrictions

Styled after a French country inn, La Bonne Auberge specializes in seafood. Chef and owner (with wife Huguette) Philippe del Perugia was trained at l'Ecole Hotelière in Paris. His preparations include bouillabaisse, trout in a crust, and mussels.

Reservations required
Dinner: Wed. - Sat., 5:30 P.M. - 10 P.M.
Sun., 5 P.M. - 9 P.M.
Closed Monday, Tuesday

LA BOURGOGNE ㉟ *French*

330 Mason St.
San Francisco
(415) 362-7352
Full Bar/Valet Parking
AE, D, MC, V, CB
Jacket, tie for men

La Bourgogne is quiet and elegant with formal French decor in shades of gold and royal blue. Fresh-cut roses grace the tables. Specialties include Dover Sole Chambertin, Filet de Boeuf en Croûte à la Mode du Nivernais and Carré d'Agneau.

Reservations advised
Dinner: Mon. - Sat., 5:30 P.M. - 12:45 A.M.
Closed Sunday

LA MERE DUQUESNE ㉚   *French*

101 Shannon Alley
San Francisco
(415) 776-7600
Maître d': Christopher Stellman
Full Bar/Lot Parking
AE, MC, V
No dress restrictions

Owner Gilbert D. V. Duquesne says his restaurant "re-creates the Old World charm of a French country manor." The interior has provincial print wallpaper, beamed ceilings and gleaming copper accoutrements. The house specialty is Le Veau du Pecheur — Provimi veal sautéed over a bed of creamed spinach, topped with scallops, shrimp and prawns.

Reservations required
Lunch: Mon.–Sat., 11:30 A.M.–2:30 P.M.
Dinner: Daily, 5:30 P.M.–10 P.M.

LA MIRABELLE ㊽   *French*

1326 Powell St.
San Francisco
(415) 421-3374
Maître d': Fritz Frankel, Gilbert Barosi (co-owner)
Full Bar/Valet Parking
AE, D, MC, V, CB
Jacket for men

The rich sensuality of La Belle Epoque comes alive again at La Mirabelle. You'll dine in a setting of plush red draperies, high ceilings and candlelight. Special dishes include Cervelle au Beurre Noir (calf's brain), Moules Farcies (mussels), Veal Murat with artichokes, Poached Salmon Bocuse and Filet de Truite au Poivre Vert.

Reservations required
Dinner: Tues.–Sat., 5:30 P.M.–10:30 P.M.
       Closed Sunday, Monday

LA TERRASSE ❹   *French*

3740 El Camino Real
Palo Alto, Calif.
(415) 494-0700
Maître d': Abi Maghamfar (manager)
Full Bar/Valet and Lot Parking
MC, V
No dress restrictions

"La Terrasse exudes the romance and reverie of a Renoir painting," says the management. The dining rooms are candlelit and intimate, and the outdoor dining terrace may be one of the loveliest in the bay area. Featured are such specialties as Escalope de Veau Orloff, Carré d'Agneau, Le Lapin Marchand and home-baked pastries.

Reservations required
Lunch: Mon.–Fri., 11:30 A.M.–2 P.M.
Dinner: Mon.–Sat., 5:30 P.M.–10 P.M.
       Closed Sunday

LE CENTRAL ㉕ *French*

453 Bush St.
San Francisco
(415) 391-2233
Maître d': Michel Bonnet
Full Bar/Street Parking
MC, V
No dress restrictions

Well located, between Union Square and the financial district, Le Central may remind you of a chic Parisian bistro. The unusual menu lists such items as Celery Remoulade, Saumon Beurre Nantais and Cassoulet Central. Brothers Pierre and Claude Cappelle are in firm control of the precise service and presentation.

Reservations advised
Lunch/Dinner: Mon.–Fri., 11:45 A.M.–10:30 P.M.
Sat., 6 P.M.–10:30 P.M.
Closed Sunday

LE CLUB ⓯ *French*

1250 Jones St.
San Francisco
(415) 771-5400
Maître d': Brian Griffin (manager)
Full Bar/Valet Parking
AE, D, MC, V
Jacket, tie for men

Located in San Francisco's historic Nob Hill section, Le Club consists of two dining rooms: one is French provincial, the other Victorian in ambience. House specialties include saddle of lamb with chestnut purée, Beef Cendrillion Béarnaise and duckling in Cointreau.

Reservations required
Dinner: Mon.–Sat., 5 P.M.–Midnight
Closed Sunday

LE CYRANO ⓺ *French*

4134 Geary Blvd.
San Francsico
(415) 287-1090
Maître d': Janine Bovigny (co-owner)
Full Bar/Street Parking
No credit cards
No dress restrictions

Le Cyrano concentrates on the cooking of the French countryside. There are such special dishes as roast young duckling in orange sauce, Coquilles St. Jacques Normande and Medaillons de Veau du Chef.

Reservations required
Dinner: Mon.–Sat., 5 P.M.–10:30 P.M.
Closed Sunday

LE POT AU FEU ⓺⓵   French

1149 El Camino Real
Menlo Park, Calif.
(415) 322-4343
Maître d': Jean and Nina Cornil (owners)
Beer and Wine/Lot and Street Parking
MC, V
No dress restrictions

A bistro-type restaurant with an indoor terrace, Le Pot au Feu features umbrellas from France, copper on the walls and an intimate atmosphere. The food is French provincial. Only the freshest ingredients are used, say the owners.

No reservations required
Dinner: Tues.–Sat., 6 P.M.–10 P.M.
       Closed Sunday, Monday

L'ETOILE ⓵⓻   French

1075 California St.
San Francisco
(415) 771-1529
Maître d': Jacques Rusterholtz
Full Bar/Valet Parking
AE, D, MC, V, CB
Jacket, tie for men

Perched atop Nob Hill, L'Etoile is a model of elegant sophistication. There is a small, romantic bar and a stylish, romantic dining room. You'll sit on curved banquettes, surrounded by great urns of fresh flowers. Specialties are such items as Quenelles Maison Cardinal, Noisettes d'Agneau Grand Veneur and Poularde Etuvée Champenoise.

Reservations required
Dinner: Mon.–Sat., 6 P.M.–10:30 P.M.
       Closed Sunday

LE TRIANON ⓷⓻   French

242 O'Farrell St.
San Francisco
(415) 982-9353
Maître d': Yvette Marie Verdon (co-owner)
Full Bar/Valet Parking
AE, D, MC, V, CB
Jacket, tie for men

Rene Verdon, French Master Chef and former White House chef to the Kennedys, presides at Le Trianon. Featured are the great classical dishes of French *haute cuisine* as well as M. Verdon's own creations. Specialties include Mousseline de Saumon St. Jacques, l'Escalope de Saumon à l'Imperiale, l'Estoufée de Canard aux Olives and Mousse Chocolat.

Reservations required
Dinner: Mon.–Sat., 6 P.M.–10:30 P.M.
       Closed Sunday, Holidays

LE VIVOIR ❷   *French*

Casa Madrona Hotel
156 Bulkley Ave.
Sausalito, Calif.
(415) 332-1850
Beer and Wine/Lot Parking
AE, D, MC, V, CB
Good taste in dress required

Hidden among the trees and flowers, overlooking Sausalito's yacht harbor, is this little French-style inn. Besides the spectacular view of the bay, there are such specialties as Les Pigeons de Berville.

Reservations required
Dinner: Daily, 6 P.M. – 10:30 P.M.

LIAISON ❻❷   *French/Italian*

4101 El Camino Way
Palo Alto, Calif.
(415) 494-8848
Maître d': Franco Siccardi (owner)
Full Bar/Lot Parking
AE, MC, V
No dress restrictions

Liaison features a rustic provincial setting and an extensive wine list, including California, French and Italian selections. Specialties include Vitello Tonato, Veal Piccata, Saddle of Lamb Florentine, Sweetbreads Sauté and Northern Italian pasta dishes.

Reservations required
Lunch: Mon. – Fri., 11:30 A.M. – 2.30 P.M.
Dinner: Mon. – Sat., 5:30 P.M. – 10:30 P.M.
          Sun., 4:30 P.M. – 10 P.M.

L'ORANGERIE ❸❻   *French*

419 O'Farrell St.
San Francisco
(415) 776-3600
Maître d': Hans Brandt
Full Bar/Valet Parking
AE, MC, V, CB
Jacket, tie suggested for men

Intimate and luxurious, with an atmosphere as peaceful as a country greenhouse, L'Orangerie is French dining without compromise, according to its owner, Roselyne Dupart. Specialties include veal with white grapes, Porc à L'Orangerie and Grand Marnier Soufflé. Your memories of L'Orangerie will always be wistful, promises Mme. Dupart.

Reservations suggested
Dinner: Mon. – Sat., 5:30 P.M. – 1:30 A.M.
          Closed Sunday

MAMOUNIA ❼ *Moroccan*

4411 Balboa St.
San Francisco
(415) 472-1372
Beer and Wine/Street Parking
MC, V
No dress restrictions

You'll relax on low, luxuriously covered banquettes, in the tradition of Morocco. Embroidered pillows help you do it in style. You eat with your fingers, as is the Moroccan custom.

Reservations required
Dinner: Tues.–Sat.
Closed Sunday, Monday

THE MANDARIN ㊵ *Chinese*

Ghirardelli Square
900 North Point
San Francisco
(415) 673-8812
Maître d': Lin Chien
Full Bar/Street Parking
AE, D, MC, V, CB
No dress restrictions

Owner Mme. Cecilia Chiang says The Mandarin was the first restaurant in the U.S. to feature the spicy and unusual dishes of Northern China, especially those from the provinces of Szechuan and Hunan. Her specialties include Diced Minced Squab, Crispy Chicken Salad, Beggar's Chicken and Prawns à la Szechuan.

No reservations required
Lunch/Dinner: Daily, Noon–Midnight
Closed Thanksgiving, Christmas

MAURICE ET CHARLES BISTROT ❶ *French*

901 Lincoln Ave.
San Rafael, Calif.
(415) 456-2010
Maître d': Maurice Amzallag, Marcel Cathala (owners)
Beer and Wine/Lot Parking
AE, MC, V
No dress restrictions

Swift service and a comfortably relaxed atmosphere complement the innovative French selections at Maurice et Charles. There are such items as Endive Sauce Anchoiade (embellished with a light anchovy sauce), Quennelles Truffée du Bistrot (highlighted with mushrooms and shrimp) and young wild boar from Northern California.

Reservations required
Dinner: Mon.–Sat., 6:30 P.M.–10:30 P.M.
Closed Sunday

MODESTO LANZONE'S ㊵   *Italian*

Ghirardelli Square
900 North Point
San Francisco
(415) 771-2880
Maître d': Alexander Gailas
Full Bar/Lot Parking
AE, D, MC, V, CB
No dress restrictions

A place known for its friendliness and warmth, Modesto Lanzone's is also famous for its pasta. Choose from Fettuccine al Pesto, Linguine alla Vongole (with clam sauce), Ravioli Genovese or Gnocchi Verdi al Sugo. There is also saltimbocca, Chicken Cacciatora, Veal Scaloppine and Calamari Genovese.

Reservations required
Lunch/Dinner: Tues.-Fri., 11:45 A.M.-11 P.M.
                Sat.-Sun., 4 P.M.-Midnight
                Closed Monday

NARSAI'S ㊶   *French/Mediterranean*

385 Colusa Ave.
Kensington, Calif.
(415) 527-7900
Maître d': Samuel David
Full Bar/Lot and Street Parking
AE, D, MC, V, CB
Good taste in dress required

Located just north of Berkeley, Narsai's features "highly imaginative" French and Mediterranean cuisine in an "elegantly different" setting. Specialties include Rack of Lamb Assyrian, Chateaubriand Farci and Le Faisan Rôti aux Truffes. The wine cellar stocks over 2,000 wines. Different cuisines from around the world are presented every Monday evening.

Reservations required
Dinner: Sun.-Thurs., 5 P.M.-10 P.M.
          Fri.-Sat., 5 P.M.-11:30 P.M.

NORTH BEACH RESTAURANT ㊼   *Italian*

1512 Stockton St.
San Francisco
(415) 392-1700
Maître d': Flavio Lombella
Full Bar/Valet Parking
AE, D, MC, V, CB
No dress restrictions

"North Beach is no ordinary Italian restaurant," say the owners. Fresh fish comes directly from their own fishing boat. Pasta is made daily in their own kitchen. The prosciutto is home-cured and salami is prepared the old-fashioned way at their North Beach factory. The dining rooms are traditional in feeling and the waiters seasoned.

Reservations required
Lunch/Dinner: Daily, 11:30 A.M.-11:30 P.M.

ONDINE ❷ *French*

558 Bridgeway
Sausalito, Calif.
(415) 332-0791/982-1740
Maître d': Rene
Full Bar/Valet and Lot Parking
AE, D, MC, V, CB
Jacket for men, no jeans

Co-owner Alfred Roblin is also master chef at Ondine. His kitchen presents such classic French offerings as Duck à l'Orange, Grand Marnier Soufflé, Squab Montmorency, Saumon Champagne and Pheasant Rôti en Plumage.

Reservations recommended
Dinner: Daily, 5:30 P.M.–11 P.M.

PAPRIKAS FONO ❹⓪ *Hungarian*

Ghirardelli Square
San Francisco
(415) 441-1223
Full Bar/Lot Parking
MC, V
Good taste in dress required

Close your eyes and you're in Old Budapest rather than Old San Francisco. Paprikas Fono presents gulyas, a beef and vegetable soup of considerable substance, plus paprikas of chicken or veal, homemade strudel and an array of other desserts guaranteed to foil any diet.

Reservations advised
Lunch: Daily, 11 A.M.–4:30 P.M.
Dinner: Mon.–Thurs., 4:30 P.M.–11 P.M.
          Fri.–Sun., 4:30 P.M.–10:30 P.M.

PERRY'S ❹⑤ *American*

1944 Union St.
San Francisco
(415) 922-9022
Full Bar/Street Parking
AE, MC, V
No dress restrictions

Perry's is an undisputed San Francisco institution. The bar area is lively, to say the least, and the quality and quantity of the drinks are remarkable. Hamburgers are popular, as are the homemade potato chips. Eggs Benedict and Eggs Blackstone (with crumbled bacon and sliced tomato) are featured at brunch.

No reservations required
Breakfast/Lunch/Dinner: Daily, 9 A.M.–2 A.M.

PHIL LEHR'S STEAKERY ⓷⓼   *American*

Hilton Hotel Tower
Ellis and Taylor Streets
San Francisco
(415) 673-6800
Maître d': Charles Guerra
Full Bar/Lot and Street Parking
AE, D, MC, V
Jacket for men

This steakhouse is famous for originating the "pay by the ounce" method of serving choice beef. Popular specialties include Beef Wellington, rack of lamb, breast of chicken stuffed with wild rice, Salmon Wellington (in season) and desserts flamed at your table.

Reservations required
Dinner: Daily, 5 P.M. – Midnight

PINE BROOK INN ⓺⓪   *Continental*

1015 Alameda de las Pulgas
Belmont, Calif.
(415) 591-1735
Maître d': Klaus Zander
Full Bar/Lot Parking
MC, V
No dress restrictions

The Pine Brook Inn is Pennsylvania Dutch in concept. Thus there are many German/American dishes served for lunch, dinner and brunch. You dine overlooking gardens and a gently flowing brook.

Reservations required
Lunch: Mon. – Fri., 11:30 A.M. – 2:30 P.M.
Dinner: Tues. – Sat., 6 P.M. – 10:30 P.M.
            Sun., 5 P.M. – 9 P.M.
Brunch: Sun., 11 A.M. – 2 P.M.

RISTORANTE ORSI ⓶⓺   *Italian*

375 Bush St.
San Francisco
(415) 981-6535
Maître d': Adriano Orsi
Full Bar/Valet Parking (evenings)
AE, D, MC, V, CB
Jacket, tie for men

As owner Joe Orsini always says, "Una cena da Orsi e reminiscente a una serta a Firenze." Or, as we might understand it, "A dinner at Orsi is reminiscent of an evening in Florence." His specialties include Beef alla Orsi, Veal alla Valdostana, Lamb di Medici, Chicken all'Entrusca and Capon alla Valdostana.

Reservations required
Lunch/Dinner: Mon. – Fri., 11:30 A.M. – 11:30 P.M.
                      Sat., 5:30 P.M. – 11:30 P.M.
                      Closed Sunday

ROLF'S SINCE 1960   ㊶   *Austrian*

757 Beach St.
San Francisco
(415) 673-8881
Maître d': Armin Weber (co-owner)
Full Bar/Valet Parking
AE, D, MC, V, CB
Jacket for men

If you're looking for romance...in a formal setting...with a fabulous view, look into Rolf's. Chandeliers, tall tapered candles, gleaming silver, sparkling crystal — all create the required mood. Co-owner Armin Weber says even the food is romantic: tender veal in a delicate cream sauce with mushrooms, luscious desserts, stimulating coffees.

Reservations recommended
Lunch: Tues.–Sun., 11:30 A.M.–3 P.M.
Dinner: Tues.–Sun., 5 P.M.–11 P.M.
   Closed Monday

SAM'S GRILL   ㉗   *Seafood*

374 Bush St.
San Francisco
(415) 421-0594
Maître d': Gary Seput (owner)
Full Bar/Street Parking
MC, V
No dress restrictions

This "old time" San Francisco restaurant features waiters in black tuxedoes, white linen tablecloths starched within an inch of their lives and *13 curtained private dining booths!* Specialties include charcoal-broiled Petrale Clams Elizabeth, Deviled Crab à la Sam and Sam's Special Seafood Plate.

No reservations required
Lunch/Dinner: Mon.–Fri., 11 A.M.–8:30 P.M.
   Closed Saturday, Sunday

SCOTT'S SEAFOOD GRILL & BAR   ㊸   *Seafood*

2400 Lombard St.
San Francisco
(415) 563-8988
Full Bar/Street Parking
AE, MC, V
No dress restrictions

Locally popular for a wide variety of fresh seafood, Scott's may not be big on elegant ambience, but it is big on quality food. Owner Martin Newman explains, "We endeavor to serve fresh, top quality food prepared to order, with honesty and simplicity." Special items include Petrale Sole, Fisherman's Stew, sautéed seafood dishes and the catch of the day.

No reservations required
Lunch/Dinner: Daily, 11 A.M.–11 P.M.

TADICH GRILL ㉓   *Seafood*

240 California St.
San Francisco
(415) 391-2373
Maître d': Chris Sentovich
Full Bar/Street Parking
No credit cards
No dress restrictions

It seems there has been a Tadich Grill as long as there has been a San Francisco. Established in 1849, it offers table or counter service. *The* specialty is local seafood — all kinds of it — from fresh salmon to Rex Sole to sea bass. It always seems to be crowded.

No reservations required
Lunch/Dinner: Mon.-Sat., 11:30 A.M.-8:30 P.M.
             Closed Sunday

TRADER VIC'S ㉙   *Polynesian*

20 Cosmo Place
San Francisco
(415) 776-2232
Maître d': Michael Gutierrez
Full Bar/Valet and Lot Parking
AE, D, MC, V, CB
Jacket, tie for men

Trader Vic's is famous — all over the country. Even those who've never been have some idea of what to expect. There is really a variety of cuisines offered here — Oriental, Continental and American. Most have at least a hint of the South Seas. The atmosphere is exclusively Polynesian.

Reservations required
Lunch: Mon.-Fri., 11:30 A.M.-2:30 P.M.
Dinner: Mon.-Fri., 5 P.M.-1 A.M.
        Sat., 4:30 P.M.-1 A.M.
        Sun., 4:30 P.M.-Midnight

VANESSI'S ㊾   *Italian*

498 Broadway
San Francisco
(415) 421-0891
Maître d': Dragamir, Jack, Robert
Full Bar/Street Parking
AE, D, MC, V, CB
No dress restrictions

Vanessi's has been serving Italian regional dishes for more than 40 years. You'll find such specialties as minestrone soup, beef, chicken and crab cannelloni, baked lasagne and *15 veal entrées.*

Reservations required
Lunch/Dinner: Mon.-Sat., 11:30 A.M.-1:30 A.M.
             Sun., 4:30 P.M.-12:30 A.M.

VICTOR'S ㉝ *French*

St. Francis Hotel
Powell and Geary Sts.
San Francisco
(415) 956-7777
Maître d': Claude de Leon
Full Bar/Valet Parking
AE, D, MC, V, CB
Jacket for men

Victor's, a restaurant with a considerable past, now features *la nouvelle cuisine*. Specialties include Lobster à la Nage, Medallion of Lamb en Croûte, Veal Jerez, quenelles in lobster sauce, rack of lamb and sweet bay shrimp. It is dining in the grand manner. Of particular note is a 30,000-bottle wine cellar of California and European labels.

Reservations required
Dinner: Daily, 6 P.M.–11 P.M.

YAMATO SUKIYAKI HOUSE ㉑ *Japanese*

717 California St.
San Francisco
(415) 397-3456
Maître d': Raymond Tamori
Full Bar/Street Parking
AE, D, MC, V, CB
Good taste in dress required

Yamato specializes in sukiyaki, prepared at the table, steak teriyaki and seafood tempura. There is also a sushi bar *and* Japanese floor seating at low tables (with back rests and leg wells). Service is by kimono-clad waitresses.

Reservations suggested
Lunch: Tues.–Fri., 11:45 A.M.–2 P.M.
Dinner: Tues.–Sun., 5 P.M.–10 P.M.
    Closed Monday

SEATTLE

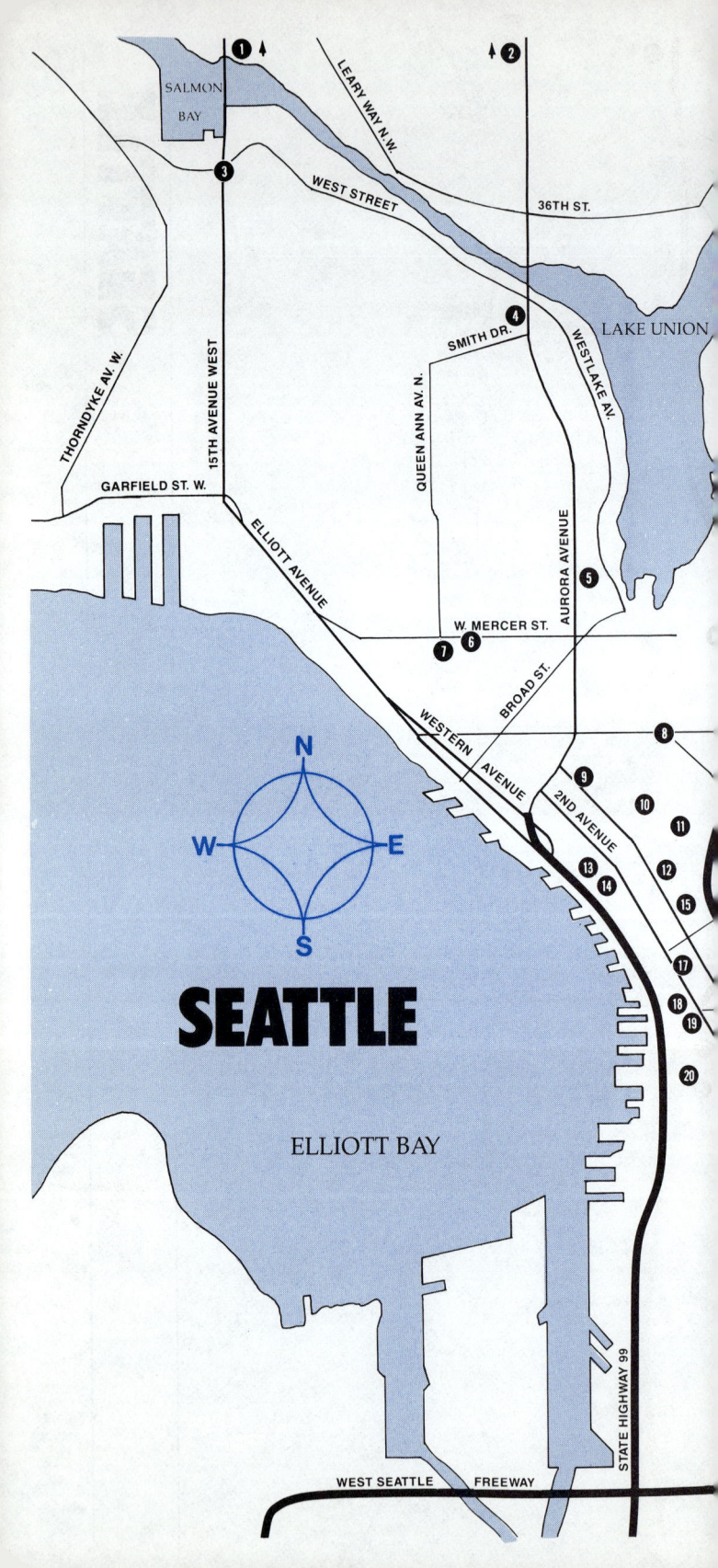

ADRIATICA ❺   *Mediterranean*

1107 Dexter North
Seattle
(206) 285-5000
Full Bar/Street Parking
AE, D, MC, V, CB
No dress restrictions

Housed in an old Victorian mansion near downtown, Adriatica features charcoal-grilled fresh seafoods, fresh pasta and Italian roast chicken. You dine overlooking sailboat-crowded Lake Union.

Reservations required
Dinner: Tues.-Sat., 5 P.M.-Midnight
      Closed Sunday, Monday

ATLAS CHINESE RESTAURANT ㉗   *Chinese*

424 Maynard Ave. South
Seattle
(206) 623-0913
No Wine or Spirits/Street Parking
No credit cards
No dress restrictions

Owner/manager M. Faye Hong says, "Our restaurant serves family dinners catering to customers who enjoy authentic Cantonese dishes." There are daily specials to choose from, in addition to a regular menu. You may have to wait for a table, but it seems to be worth it.

No reservations required
Dinner: Daily, 4 P.M.-11 P.M.

BRASSERIE PITTSBOURG ⑱   *French*

602 First Ave.
Seattle
(206) 623-4167
Full Bar/Lot and Street Parking
AE, MC, V
No dress restrictions

Classic French cuisine is featured in what is Seattle's oldest restaurant (since 1893). Owners François and Julia Kissel offer a buffet-style lunch and a dinner choice of 20 entrées — depending upon what is fresh and available in season. The original tin ceiling has been preserved and the dining room is filled with 18th-century furnishings.

Reservations suggested
Lunch: Mon.-Sat., 11:30 A.M.-2:30 P.M.
Dinner: Mon.-Thurs., 5:30 P.M.-10 P.M.
       Fri.-Sat., 5:30 P.M.-11 P.M.
       Closed Sunday

BUSH GARDEN ㉙   *Japanese*

614 Maynard Ave. South
Seattle
(206) 682-6830
Maître d': Pentson Sugamura
Full Bar/Lot Parking
AE, MC, V
No dress restrictions

Both picturesque and atmospheric in character, Bush Garden features dining in private tatami rooms, or at tables if you prefer. The chefs are from Tokyo and specialize in preparing each dish to perfection.

Reservations required
Lunch/Dinner: Mon.-Fri., 11:30 A.M.-2 A.M.
              Sat., 5 P.M.-2 A.M.
              Sun., 4 P.M.-8:30 P.M.

CANLIS ❹   *American*

2576 Aurora Ave. North
Seattle
(206) 283-3313
Maître d': Douglas Guiberson
Full Bar/Valet Parking
AE, D, MC, V
Jacket for men

Canlis is definitely a "dress-up" place. Tables are set with heavy linen, fine china and sterling. The menu lists such items as prime steaks and fresh seafood. Co-owner Gloria Canlis Hoedemaker says both are "impeccably prepared on an open-hearth charcoal broiler."

Reservations required
Dinner: Mon.-Sat., 5:30 P.M.-12:30 A.M.
       Closed Sunday

CHEZ CLAUDE ❷   *French*

419 Main St.
Edmonds, Wash.
(206) 778-9888
Full Bar/Street Parking
AE, D, MC, V
Good taste in dress required

A small-town restaurant with a big-city menu, Chez Claude presents such specialties as rack of lamb, scampi, Veal Murat and steamed vegetables. The setting is French Provincial casual.

Reservations required
Dinner: Tues.-Sun., 5 P.M.-11 P.M.
       Closed Monday

CITY LOAN PAVILLON ⑲   *French*

206 First Ave. South
Seattle
(206) 624-9970
Full Bar/Street Parking
AE, MC, V
No dress restrictions

Owned by the same couple that gave Seattle Brasserie Pittsbourg, the City Loan Pavillon is "romantic, French and original," according to co-owner Julia Kissel. There is glass-enclosed terrace dining beneath sparkling chandeliers and leafy trees. Classic French favorites are featured as well as "imaginative" offerings that lean toward *la nouvelle cuisine.*

Reservations suggested
Lunch/Dinner: Mon.–Fri., 11 A.M.–10 P.M.
              Sat., 5 P.M.–Midnight
              Sun., 5 P.M.–10 P.M.

CREPE DE PARIS ⑮ ㉓   *French*

1333 5th Ave.		1927 43rd Ave. East
Seattle	and	Seattle
(206) 623-4111		(206) 329-6620

Full Bar/Valet Parking
AE, D, MC, V
No dress restrictions

The specialty here is crêpes, of course. They are large and filled with a variety of tempting ingredients. Also served is pâté, fresh fish and rack of lamb.

Reservations recommended for dinner
Lunch/Dinner: Mon.–Thurs., 11 A.M.–11 P.M.
              Fri.–Sat., 11 A.M.–Midnight
Brunch: Sun., 11 A.M.–11 P.M.

DEVILLE'S ON BROADWAY ㉔   *French*

1833 Broadway Ave.
Seattle
(206) 325-5392
Full Bar/Lot Parking
AE, MC, V
No dress restrictions

This may be Seattle's answer to the French boulevard cafe. The difference is that fresh fish from Puget Sound is served, plus Duck à l'Orange, Salade Niçoise and rich, rich desserts.

Reservations recommended
Lunch: Mon.–Fri., 11:30 A.M.–2:30 P.M.
Dinner: Sun.–Thurs., 5 P.M.–Midnight
          Fri.–Sat., 5 P.M.–2 A.M.
Brunch: Sun., 10:30 A.M.–2:30 P.M.

EL GAUCHO ⓫   American

624 Olive Way
Seattle
(206) 682-3202
Maître d': Bentley Main (manager)
Full Bar/Lot and Street Parking
AE, D, MC, V
Good taste in dress required

El Gaucho's house specialty is choice aged beef broiled over a charcoal fire. If that doesn't tempt you, there is plenty of fresh seafood, as well as rack of lamb, Cornish game hen, chateaubriand and barbecued spareribs. You dine by candlelight in booths covered in mink. If *that* isn't romantic, nothing is.

Reservations advised
Lunch/Dinner/Hunt Breakfast: Mon.–Thurs., 11 A.M.–2:30 A.M.
                              Fri., 11 A.M.–4 A.M.
                              Sat., 5 P.M.–4 A.M.
                              Closed Sunday

F. X. McRORY'S STEAK, ⓴   American
CHOP & OYSTER HOUSE

419 Occidental St.
Seattle
(206) 623-2424
Full Bar/Street Parking
AE, MC, V
No dress restrictions

Co-owner Michael M. McHugh claims F. X. McRory's has Seattle's largest stand-up oyster bar *and* the world's largest collection of bourbons. Plus, he has over 100 imported and domestic beers! McRory's is across the street from the Kingdome sports complex, so all this may come in handy. There are also 21-day-old steaks and chops.

No reservations required
Dinner: Daily, from 5 P.M.

GERARD'S RELAIS DE LYON ㉑   French

17121 Bothell Way N.E.
Bothel, Wash.
(206) 485-7600
Full Bar/Lot Parking
D, MC, V
Good taste in dress required

Relais means a rest stop while traveling and, according to Gerard Parrat's liberal interpretation, it also means a place for classic French cuisine. His specialties include Saumon en Croûte, Côté de Boeuf à la Facon Maison, Veal Ciboulette and home-baked pastries.

Reservations required
Dinner: Tues.–Sun., 5 P.M.–11 P.M.
         Closed Monday

SEATTLE   399

HENRY'S OFF BROADWAY ㉖ *Continental*

1705 E. Olive Way
Seattle
(206) 329-8063
Maître d': Lucho de la Combe
Full Bar/Valet and Street Parking
AE, MC, V
No dress restrictions

"Henry's has flair," says co-owner William Schwartz. "From the terrace entrance to the glamorous oyster bar and dining rooms, it is a place elaborately furnished in a style reminiscent of the 1930's." Menu specialties include broiled fresh fillet of salmon, Marchand de Vin, Oysters Rockefeller, Veal Armagnac and Rack of Lamb Dijon.

No reservations required
Lunch: Mon.-Fri., 11:30 A.M.-2:30 P.M.
Dinner: Mon.-Thurs., 5:30 P.M.-10:30 P.M.
         Fri.-Sat., 5:30 P.M.-11:30 P.M.
         Sun., 5 P.M.-10 P.M.
Brunch: Sun., 10 A.M.-2 P.M.

JAKE O'SHAUGHNESSEY'S ❻ *American*

100 Mercer St.
Seattle
(206) 285-1897
Full Bar/Lot Parking
AE, MC, V
No dress restrictions

How's this for a matter-of-fact claim: "Jake O'Shaughnessey's features the world's largest collection of bar liquor." That's co-owner Michael M. McHugh talking. He adds that you'll also find food at his restaurant, such as alderwood-roasted fresh salmon, Puget Sound Sea Stew and Saloon Beef (aged prime rib roasted in pure grain roasting salt).

No reservations required
Dinner: Daily, 5 P.M.-11 P.M.

JONAH AND THE WHALE ㉕ *Continental*

11211 Main St.
Bellevue, Wash.
(206) 455-5240
Maître d': Steven K. Burnell
Full Bar/Lot Parking
AE, D, MC, V, CB
No dress restrictions

Out-of-the-ordinary dishes are offered at Jonah and the Whale (no whale, though). There are such things as Saddle of Venison à la Forestière and Poached Fillet of Halibut en Casserole Norvégienne. A strolling violinist helps create the proper mood for quiet, elegant dining.

Reservations required
Lunch: Mon.-Fri., 11:30 A.M.-2 P.M.
Dinner: Mon.-Thurs., 6 P.M.-10:30 P.M.
         Fri.-Sat., 6 P.M.-11 P.M.
         Closed Sunday

LABUZNIK ⓭ *Central European*

1924 1st Ave.
Seattle
(206) 682-1624
Full Bar/Street Parking
AE, MC, V
Good taste in dress required

At Labuznik you can dine either cafe style — on soups, hors d'oeuvre, pasta or Steak Tartare — or in a more formal dining room. There you are offered such entrées as Bohemian roast duck, roast pork with dumplings and weiner schnitzel.

Reservations required
Dinner: Tues. – Thurs., 4:30 P.M. – 10 P.M.
Fri. – Sat., 4:30 P.M. – 11 P.M.
Closed Sunday, Monday

LE PROVENCAL ㉒ *French*

212 Central Way
Kirkland, Wash.
(206) 827-3300
Maître d': Philippe Gayte (owner)
Full Bar/Lot and Street Parking
AE, D, MC, V
No dress restrictions

You are offered a taste of the French countryside at Le Provençal. Its warm and rustic atmosphere is the setting for such specialties as Huîtres du Corsaire, Tournedos en Feuilleté, Carré d'Agneau and Daube Avignonnaise. There is an extensive selection of wines.

Reservations required
Dinner: Mon. – Sat., 5:30 P.M. – 9:30 P.M.
Closed Sunday

LE TASTEVIN ❼ *French*

501 Queen Anne Ave. North
Seattle
(206) 283-0991
Maître d': Emile Ninaud
Full Bar/Lot Parking
MC, V
No dress restrictions

At Le Tastevin, fresh local salmon joins a group of classic French specialties such as Ris de Veau, Canard Normandie and Pigeonneau Rôti à la Diable. The interior is reminiscent of a French country inn.

Reservations required
Lunch: Tues. – Fri., 11:30 A.M. – 2:30 P.M.
Dinner: Mon. – Sat., 5 P.M. – 11 P.M.
Closed Sunday

MAXIMILIEN IN THE MARKET ⑭   *French*

85 A Pike St.
Seattle
(206) 682-7860
Full Bar/Street Parking
AE, MC, V
No dress restrictions

Owner Julia Fissel calls her restaurant "a real French market cafe in the heart of Seattle's historic renovated Pike Place Farmers' Market." You dine overlooking the bay and the Olympic Mountains. There are hot buttery croissants, a breakfast soufflé, market-fresh Northwest produce and tempting desserts.

No reservations required
Breakfast/Lunch/Dinner: Mon. – Wed., 7:30 A.M. – 5:30 P.M.
Thurs. – Sat., 7:30 A.M. – 10 P.M.
(longer summer hours)
Closed Sunday

THE MIKADO ㉘   *Japanese*

514 S. Jackson St.
Seattle
(206) 622-5206
Maître d': Irwin and Bruce Yoshimura (owners)
Full Bar/Lot Parking
AE, MC, V
No dress restrictions

Authenticity reigns supreme here. The Mikado features an elaborate sushi and sashimi menu and private tatami rooms for Japanese seating. Specialties include Mikado Beef, King Crab Batayaki, Salmon Teriyaki and Chicken Shioyaki (boneless, seasoned with salt and broiled).

Reservations recommended
Dinner: Mon. – Sat., 5:30 P.M. – 10 P.M.
Closed Sunday

MIRABEAU ⑯   *French*

First National Bank Bldg.
Fourth and Madison
Seattle
(206) 624-4550
Maître d': Angelo Papas
Full Bar/Lot Parking
AE, MC, V
Good taste in dress required

Your first impression of the Mirabeau might be that it's afloat on a sea of scenic views. There is Mount Rainier in the distance and the Olympic range, and there is downtown Seattle 729 feet below you. Special dishes served in this heady atmosphere include fresh quail with sour cream, Salmon Westport, prawns with Pernod and duck with turnips.

Reservations suggested
Lunch: Mon. – Fri., 11:30 A.M. – 2:30 P.M.
Dinner: Mon. – Thurs., 5:30 P.M. – 10:30 P.M.
Fri. – Sat., 5:30 P.M. – 11 P.M.
Closed Sunday

MRS. MALIA'S ❼   *American*

820 Second Ave.
Seattle
(206) 624-3287
Maître d': William Kraut
Full Bar/Lot and Street Parking
MC, V
No dress restrictions

Mrs. Malia's was once a bank, but oh how the dividends have changed. You can now withdraw fresh local seafood plus entrées of chicken, veal and lamb. Owner Richard Malia contracts with local farmers for the freshest of local produce, spices and herbs. Wines of the Pacific Northwest are featured.

Reservations available
Lunch: Mon.–Fri., 11 A.M.–3 P.M.
Dinner: Mon.–Thurs., 5:30 P.M.–10 P.M.
   Fri.–Sat., 5:30 P.M.–11 P.M.
   Closed Sunday

RAY'S BOATHOUSE ❶   *Seafood*

6049 Seaview Ave. N.W.
Seattle
(206) 789-3770
Maître d': Stein (manager, co-owner)
Full Bar/Lot Parking
AE, D, MC, V
No dress restrictions

Ray's Boathouse is located on Puget Sound, at the mouth of the ship's canal — all the better to snare the freshest fish available and serve them to you. The catch is prepared simply but sumptuously. There is a variety of appetizers on any given day and a complete wine list.

Reservations recommended
Lunch/Dinner: Mon.–Fri., 11:30 A.M.–2 A.M.
   Sat., Noon–2 A.M.
   Sun., 4 P.M.–2 A.M.

ROSELLINI'S FOUR-10 ❾   *Continental*

Fourth and Wall Sts.
Seattle
(206) 624-5464
Maître d': John Kevo
Full Bar/Valet Parking
AE, D, MC, V
Jacket, tie for men preferred

The atmosphere and personality of the Four-10 is one of "easy elegance," says the management. This means there's little pretension embellishing the tapestried walls, crisp table linens and gleaming silver serving pieces. Entrées focus on the finest meats, fish and poultry available.

Reservations required
Lunch/Dinner: Mon.–Fri., 11 A.M.–Midnight
   Sat., 5 P.M.–Midnight
   Closed Sunday, except special holidays

ROSELLINI'S OTHER PLACE ⑫ *French*

319 Union St.
Seattle
(206) 623-7340
Maître d': Tony Kischner (manager)
Full Bar/Lot Parking
AE, D, MC, V
No dress restrictions

This Rosellini's has a stated mission in life: to utilize the finest products of the region and apply to those products the care in preparation that one would expect to find in the best restaurants of Europe. The constantly changing menu can include fresh game, poultry, veal, lamb, beef and fish. The wine list covers 800 labels.

No reservations required
Lunch: Mon.–Fri., 11 A.M.–5 P.M.
Dinner: Mon.–Sat., 5 P.M.–Midnight
   Closed Sunday

SIMON'S ㉛ *Continental*

17401 S. Center Parkway
Tukwila, Wash.
(206) 575-3500
Full Bar/Lot Parking
AE, MC, V
No dress restrictions

Simon's is all open space and skylights. You're meant to feel like you're dining in an open courtyard. Specialties include rack of lamb, veal, fresh fish, chicken and steak. The mocha mousse is the dessert specialty.

Reservations required
Lunch: Mon.–Fri., 11 A.M.–2:30 P.M.
Dinner: Mon.–Thurs., 5:30 P.M.–10:30 P.M.
   Fri.–Sat., 5:30 P.M.–11:30 P.M.
   Sun., 5 P.M.–10 P.M.

SNOQUALMIE FALLS LODGE ㉚ *American*

Snoqualmie Falls City Rd.
Snoqualmie, Wash.
(206) 888-2451
Full Bar/Lot Parking
AE, MC, V
No dress restrictions

A bit off the beaten track, but most say it's well worth it. The Snoqualmie Falls Lodge prepares food the way you wish your mother had. There are old-fashioned country-style farm breakfasts (fritters, plump biscuits, rich preserves and sweet mountain honey), immediately followed by hearty country dinners.

Reservations required
Breakfast: Daily, 8 A.M.–1:30 P.M.
Dinner: Daily, 2:30 P.M.–10 P.M.

THIRTEEN COINS ❽ *Italian/American*

125 Boren Ave. North
Seattle
(206) 682-2513
Maître d': James L. Donovan (manager)
Full Bar/Lot and Street Parking
AE, D, MC, V
No dress restrictions

Here's a place to satisfy the hungries and quench the thirst at any hour of the day, night or early morning. There is a variety of American, Italian and seafood dishes. With all cuisines, the specialty is the way Thirteen Coins sautés its preparations. The wine list is extensive.

No reservations required
Breakfast/Lunch/Dinner: Daily, 24 hours

TRADER VIC'S ❿ *Polynesian*

Washington Plaza Hotel
Fifth and Westlake
Seattle
(206) 624-8520
Maître d': Sam Schneider
Full Bar/Street Parking
AE, D, MC, V, CB
Good taste in dress required
Jacket for men (dining room)

A scion of a venerable family, Seattle's Trader Vic's has all the cheerful exotica of its siblings, plus the access to Puget Sound seafood that only this city can provide. There are also succulent curries, steaks and barbecued meats.

Reservations recommended
Lunch: Mon.-Sat., 11:45 A.M.-2:30 P.M.
Dinner: Mon.-Sat., 5:30 P.M.-10:30 P.M.
    Sun., 5:30 P.M.-9 P.M.

THE WHARF ❸ *Seafood*

Fisherman's Terminal
1735 W. Thurman
Seattle
(206) 283-6600
Full Bar/Lot Parking
AE, MC, V
No dress restrictions

At The Wharf, you'll dine overlooking the West Coast's largest fishing fleet. If that doesn't inspire you to sample some of the local seafood, nothing will.

No reservations required
Breakfast/Lunch/Dinner: Mon.-Sat., 6:30 A.M.-12:30 A.M.
    Sun., 6:30 A.M.-8 P.M.

WASHINGTON D.C.

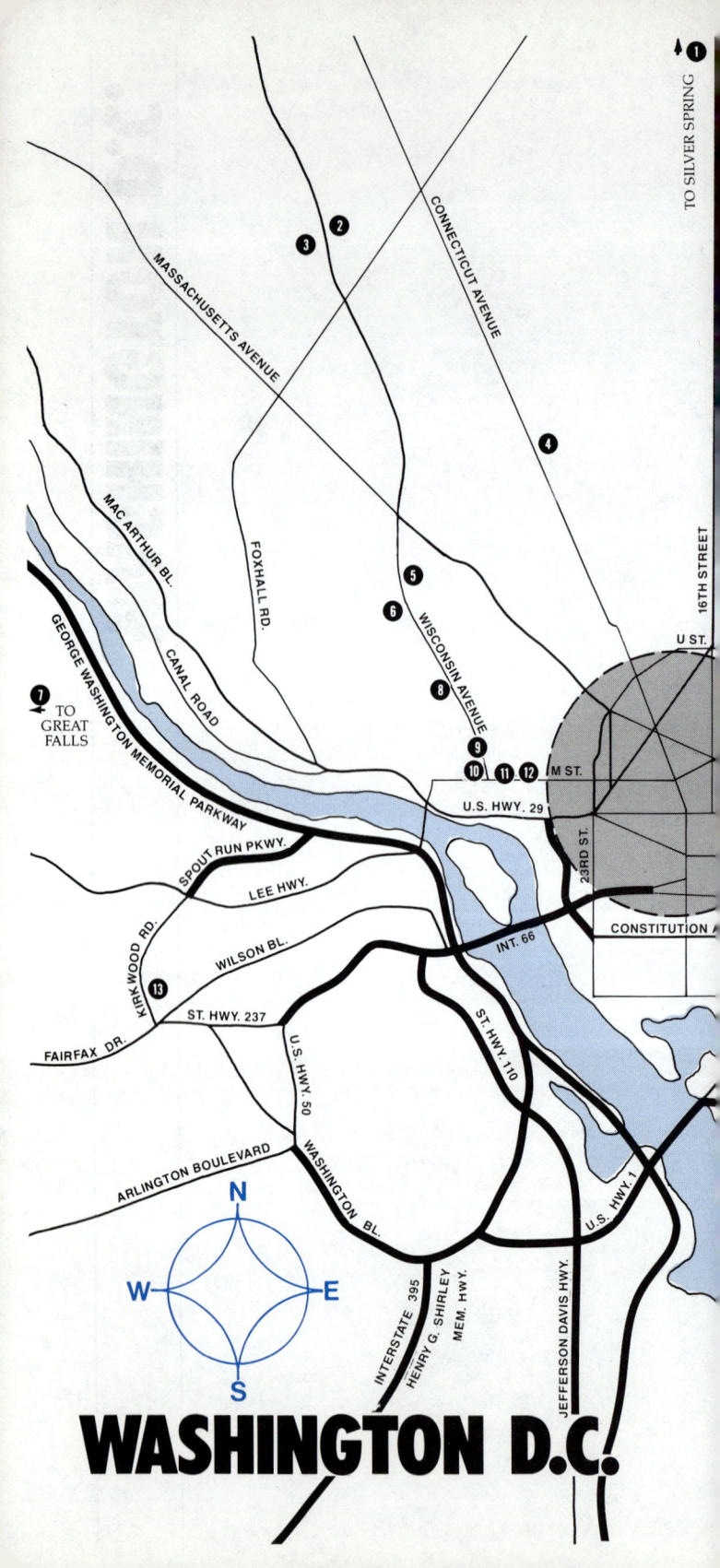

THE AMERICAN CAFE ❿ ㉒   *American*

1211 Wisconsin Ave. N.W.
Washington, D.C.
(202) 337-3600
and
227 Massachusetts Ave. N.E.
Washington, D.C.
(202) 547-8500
Maître d': Robert Giaimo, Mark Caracuzzi,
        James Sullivan (owners)
Full Bar/Street Parking
MC, V
Good taste in dress required

The emphasis at The American Cafe is on fresh natural ingredients presented with imagination and style. The menu was developed with the help of some of the nation's foremost food authorities, say the owners. There are eight entrées, luxurious dessert crêpes and a variety of soups, salads and sandwiches.

No reservations required
Lunch/Dinner: Sun.–Thurs., 11 A.M.–2 A.M. (3 A.M. Wisconsin Ave.)
               Fri.–Sat., 11 A.M.–3 A.M. (4 A.M. Wisconsin Ave.)

APANA ⓫   *Indian*

3066 M St. N.W.
Washington, D.C.
(202) 965-3040
Maître d': Amarjeet Singh
Full Bar/Street Parking
AE, D, MC, V, CB
No dress restrictions

Apana's menu includes meat, seafood and vegetarian dishes from various regions of India, served in an elegant atmosphere with great attention to detail.

Reservations recommended
Dinner: Sun.–Thurs., 6 P.M.–11:30 P.M.
       Fri.–Sat., 6 P.M.–Midnight

A. V. RISTORANTE ITALIANO ㉟   *Italian*

607 New York Ave. N.W.
Washington, D.C.
(202) 737-0550
Full Bar/Lot Parking
AE, D, MC, V, CB
No dress restrictions

This is a "family type" restaurant featuring "all types of Italian foods." The daily specials range from shad roe to whole roasted suckling pigs. The menu lists over 200 items, including Veal Marsala, rabbit in white wine and timballo (stuffed shells).

No reservations required
Lunch/Dinner: Daily

CANTINA D'ITALIA ⑲   Northern Italian

1214-A 18th St. N.W.
Washington, D.C.
(202) 659-1830
Maître d: Joseph and Marilyn (owners)
Full Bar/Street Parking
AE, D, MC, V, CB
Good taste in dress required

Cantina d'Italia, not surprisingly, offers diners a sampling of the regional cuisines of Italy. Areas covered include the Piedmont and Val d'Aosta. Look for such special dishes as Vitello con Salsa di Formaggio, Coniglio al Limone, Anitra in Umido and a variety of pastas.

Reservations required
Lunch: Mon.–Fri., 11:30 A.M.–2:30 P.M.
Dinner: Mon.–Fri., 6 P.M.–11 P.M.
    Closed Saturday, Sunday

CARVERY ㉑   French

Mayflower Hotel
1127 Connecticut Ave. N.W.
Washington, D.C.
(202) 347-3000
Maître d': Zina Silo
Full Bar/Lot Parking
AE, D, MC, V, CB
No dress restrictions

If you're into 16th-century Spanish decor combined with that of old Georgetown, the Carvery is for you. There's also wood paneling from aged barns to add that special touch. On the menu you'll find Beef Wellington, prime rib and fresh seafood. The management promises you'll get the VIP treatment, no matter who you are.

No reservations required
Breakfast/Lunch/Dinner: Daily, 6:30 A.M.–11:30 P.M.

THE COMPANY INKWELL ⑬   French

4109 Wilson Blvd.
Arlington, Va.
(703) 525-4243
Full Bar/Valet Parking
Major credit cards
Good taste in dress required

Romance is given every chance to blossom at The Company Inkwell. The soft lights, deferential service and quiet intimacy of the place see to that. There are several fresh seafood and veal entrées, game in season and flaming Coffee Inkwell.

Reservations required
Lunch: Mon.–Fri., 11:30 A.M.–2:30 P.M.
Dinner: Mon.–Sat., 6 P.M.–10:30 P.M.
    Closed Sunday

CRISFIELD'S ❶ — *Seafood*

8012 Georgia Ave.
Silver Spring, Md.
(301) 589-1306
Beer and Wine/Lot Parking
No credit cards
Good taste in dress required

"Simplified and old-fashioned" is how owner Lillian Landis describes Crisfield's. "We strive to prepare prime seafood products to perfection," she continues. In other words, there are no cover-up sauces or spices to spoil the simplicity.

No reservations required
Lunch/Dinner: Tues.-Thurs., 11 A.M.-9:30 P.M.
  Fri.-Sat., 11 A.M.-10:30 P.M.
  Sun., Noon-9 P.M.
  Closed Monday

CSIKO'S ❹ — *Hungarian*

3601 Connecticut Ave. N.W.
Washington, D.C.
(202) 362-5624
Maître d': Erzsebet Thuleweit (owner)
Full Bar/Lot Parking
AE, D, MC, V, CB
Jacket for men

Csiko's Hungarian specialties include the venerable stuffed cabbage, Veal Paprikash (or chicken), a hearty goulash soup and plump little noodles. The setting is European dramatic — with large mirrors, chandeliers and dark red carpeting.

Reservations required (weekends)
Dinner: Mon.-Sat., 6 P.M.-10:30 P.M.
  Closed Sunday

DOMINIQUE'S ㉜ — *French*

1900 Pennsylvania Ave. N.W.
Washington, D.C.
(202) 452-1126
Full Bar/Valet Parking
AE, MC, V, CB
Good taste in dress required

A place of considerable charm, according to most, Dominique's is a warm and caring French restaurant close to the Kennedy Center. The cuisine is decidedly innovative and includes simply prepared variations upon smoked fish, trout, venison, wild boar and roasted petite quail. The wine list is equally imaginative.

Reservations required
Lunch: Mon.-Fri., 11:30 A.M.-2:30 P.M.
Dinner: Mon.-Sat., 6 P.M.-1 A.M.
  Closed Sunday

EL TIO PEPE

Spanish

2809 M St. N.W.
Washington, D.C.
(202) 337-0730
Full Bar/Street Parking
AE, D, MC, V
Jacket, tie for men

If you're tempted by whitewashed walls, Moorish tiles, flamenco and paella, then you'll be tempted by El Tio Pepe. Besides the Latin ambience and the paella, there is Conchitas Tio Pepe, zarzuela, Calamares Rellenos and a large selection of Spanish wines.

Reservations required
Lunch: Mon.-Fri., Noon-2:30 P.M.
Dinner: Mon.-Sat., 5:30 P.M.-11 P.M.
Closed Sunday

GERMAINE'S

Oriental

2400 Wisconsin Ave. N.W.
Washington, D.C.
(202) 965-1185
Maître d': Hugh Fanning
Full Bar/Lot and Street Parking
AE, D, MC, V
Jacket for men

The cuisine is truly "Pan-Asian," with selections from Vietnam, Indonesia, the Philippines and India represented. Specialties include various pâtés, a multitude of seafood dishes and "anything from the charcoal grill," according to co-owner (with wife Germaine) Dick Swanson.

Reservations required
Lunch: Mon.-Fri., Noon-2:30 P.M.
Dinner: Mon.-Thurs., 6 P.M.-10 P.M.
Fri.-Sat., 6 P.M.-11 P.M.
Sun., 5 P.M.-9 P.M.

GOLDEN PALACE

Chinese

726 7th St. N.W.
Washington, D.C.
(202) 783-1225
Full Bar/Lot and Street Parking
AE, D, MC, V
No dress restrictions

All Golden Palace chefs come directly from Hong Kong, assures manager William Chow. Authentic Cantonese cuisine is the order of the day.

No reservations required
Lunch: Daily, 11 A.M.-3 P.M.
Dinner: Daily, 5 P.M.-Midnight

HARVEY'S ㉔   *Seafood*

1001 18th St. N.W.
Washington, D.C.
(202) 833-1858
Maître d': Robert and Rene
Full Bar/Valet Parking (dinner)
AE, D, MC, V, CB
Good taste in dress required

Owner Alex Stuart claims Harvey's is one of the oldest restaurants in Washington. Founded in 1858, it specializes in seafood. Harvey's is credited with the creation of Crab Imperial. You can still order it, along with sautéed crabmeat with Smithfield ham, veal cutlet with Crab Meat Jacoulet, red snapper, she-crab soup and Chesapeake Bay striped bass.

Reservations required
Lunch: Mon.-Fri., 11:30 A.M.-3 P.M.
Dinner: Sun.-Fri., 5 P.M.-10:30 P.M.
       Sat., 5 P.M.-11 P.M.
       Closed Sunday in July and August

IL GIARDINO ㉓   *Northern Italian*

1110 21st St. N.W.
Washington, D.C.
(202) 223-4555
Maître d': Mario Fazio
Full Bar/Valet Parking
AE, D, MC, V, CB
Jacket, tie for men

Located close to the White House, Il Giardino features mostly Northern Italian cusine, including fresh homemade pastas, Lombatina di Terri, Red Snapper Mavechiaro and Carre Valdostana.

Reservations required
Lunch: Mon.-Fri., Noon-3 P.M.
Dinner: Mon.-Sat., 6 P.M.-11 P.M.
       Closed Sunday

JACQUELINE'S ⓱   *French*

1990 M St. N.W.
Washington, D.C.
(202) 785-8877
Full Bar/Street Parking
AE, D, MC, V, CB
Good taste in dress required

Jacqueline's is the product of owner Jacqueline Rodier's energy and imagination. A below-ground hideaway, it features an intimate, tasteful setting and specialties such as Carré d'Agneau aux Herbes de Provence, Truite Cleopatra, Canard Montmorency Fricasse d'Escargots au Cognac and Saumon au Champagne.

Reservations required
Lunch: Mon.-Fri., 11:30 A.M.-2:30 P.M.
Dinner: Mon.-Sat., 6 P.M.-10:45 P.M.
       Closed Sunday

JAPAN INN ❽   *Japanese*

1715 Wisconsin Ave. N.W.
Washington, D.C.
(202) 377-3400
Maître d': Yoshio Tanabe, Hitoshi Yoshikawa
Full Bar/Lot Parking
AE, D, V
No dress restrictions

The Japan Inn is divided into three dining rooms, each specializing in a different style of Japanese food. There is a tempura corner, a traditional Japanese dining room featuring sukiyaki and shabu-shabu and a Teppan-yaki room, where diners can watch chefs prepare steak, chicken or shrimp.

Reservations required
Lunch: Mon.–Fri., Noon–2 P.M.
Dinner: Mon.–Thurs., 6 P.M.–10 P.M.
*   Fri.–Sat., 6 P.M.–10:30 P.M.*
*   Closed Sunday*

JEAN PIERRE ㉗   *French*

1835 K St. N.W.
Washington, D.C.
(202) 466-2022
Maître d': Jean-Michel Farret (owner)
Full Bar/Lot Parking
AE, D, MC, V, CB
Jacket, tie for men

Because it's under the watchful eye of owner Jean-Michel Farret, Jean Pierre is considered one of Washington's most respected French restaurants. Specialties include trout soufflé with lobster sauce, Feuillete de St. Jacques, beef with Roquefort sauce and fresh fruit soufflés.

Reservations required
Lunch: Mon.–Fri., Noon–2 P.M.
Dinner: Mon.–Sat., 6 P.M.–10 P.M.
*   Closed Sunday*

THE JOCKEY CLUB ⓮   *Continental*

Fairfax Hotel
2100 Massachusetts Ave. N.W.
Washington, D.C.
(202) 293-2749
Maître d': Paul Delisle
Full Bar/Valet Parking
AE, D, MC, V, CB
Jacket, tie for men

Managed by the same group that runs New York's "21" Club, The Jockey Club resembles its illustrious parent in a number of ways. Sedate and refined, it offers guests a "civilized" dining experience. You can choose roast duck, Crab Imperial, chicken hash or Steak Diane.

Reservations required
Dinner: Mon.–Sat., 6 P.M.–11 P.M.
*   Sun., 6 P.M.–10 P.M.*
Brunch: Sat.–Sun., Noon–2:30 P.M.

L'AUBERGE CHEZ FRANCOIS ❼ *French*

332 Springvale Rd.
Great Falls, Va.
(703) 759-3800
Maître d': Freida Bene and Paul Haeringer
Full Bar/Lot Parking
AE, MC, V
Jacket for men

This restaurant may remind you of a French country inn transplanted to the rolling hills of Virginia. Features include Choucroute Garnie à l'Alsacienne, Saumon Soufflé de l'Auberge and Poulet Sauté au Riesling et Truffes des Pauvres.

Reservations required
Dinner: Tues.-Sat., 6 P.M.-9:30 P.M.
         Sun., 2:30 P.M.-8:30 P.M.
         Closed Monday

LE BAGATELLE ㉕ *French*

2000 K St. N.W.
Washington, D.C.
(202) 872-8677
Maître d': Jacques Scarella
Full Bar/Valet Parking (dinner)
AE, D, MC, V, CB
Jacket, tie for men

Le Bagatelle is an outdoor-indoor restaurant, filled as it is with fresh flowers and plants. A latticed gazebo is the appropriate backdrop. Specialties include Crab Imperial à la Robert Greault (the chef and owner), Escalope de Veau à l'Armagnac, fresh seasonal seafood and homemade pastries and ice cream.

Reservations required
Lunch: Mon.-Fri., Noon-3 P.M.
Dinner: Mon.-Sat., 6 P.M.-11 P.M.
         Closed Sunday

LE GAULOIS ㉙ *French*

2133 Pennsylvania Ave. N.W.
Washington, D.C.
(202) 466-3232
Full Bar/Lot and Street Parking
AE, MC, V
No dress restrictions

Small and informal, with the accent on food, Le Gaulois presents a limited menu consisting of quiche, stuffed eggs, baked zucchini and pâté. However, there is a long list of daily specials, such as a casserole of garden vegetables, veal scallopini, roast lamb, venison, lobster and roast duck. *The* specialty is pot-au-feu.

Reservations required
Lunch: Mon.-Fri., 11 A.M.-2:30 P.M.
Dinner: Mon.-Thurs., 5:30 P.M.-11 P.M.
         Fri.-Sat., 5:30 P.M.-Midnight
         Closed Sunday

LE LION D'OR ⓯   *French*

1150 Connecticut Ave. N.W.
Washington, D.C.
(202) 296-7972
Maître d': Paul
Full Bar/Lot Parking
AE, D, MC, V, CB
Jacket, tie for men; no jeans

Another of Washington's chef-owned French restaurants, Le Lion d'Or offers both contemporary creations and examples of classic cuisine. Dishes are all imaginative and vary according to the seasons. Chef/owner Jean Pierre Goyenvalle terms his wine selection "very impressive."

Reservations required
Lunch: Mon.–Fri., Noon–2 P.M.
Dinner: Mon.–Sat., 6 P.M.–10 P.M.
   Closed Sunday

LE PAVILLON ㉛   *French*

1820 K St. N.W.
Washington, D.C.
(202) 833-3846
Maître d': Janet Wong (manager)
Full Bar/Valet and Street Parking
AE, MC, V, CB
Jacket, tie for men

There's a warm, residential feeling to this restaurant of *nouvelle cuisine* and formal decor. Specialties include Navarin of Lobster (baked and removed from the shell, then served with vintage white wine sauce and vegetables) and white chocolate mousse, served in a cookie tulip.

Reservations required
Lunch: Mon.–Fri., 11:45 A.M.–1:30 P.M.
Dinner: Mon.–Sat., 6:45 P.M.–9:30 P.M.
   Closed Sunday

LE PROVENCAL ⓰   *French*

1234 20th St. N.W.
Washington, D.C.
(202) 223-2420
Maître d': Christian Mattei
Full Bar/Valet Parking
AE, D, MC, V, CB
Jacket, tie for men

Some of Le Provençal's robust south-of-France offerings include Bouillabaisse Marseillaise, Terrine de Fruits de Mer, stuffed trout, Carré d'Agneaux aux Herbes, Shrimps Farcis, Escalope de Veau au Ricard, Tarte aux Epinards and Gateau au Pastis.

Reservations required
Lunch: Mon.–Sat., 11:30 A.M.–3 P.M.
Dinner: Mon.–Sat., 6 P.M.–11 P.M.
   Closed Sunday, Major Holidays

MIKADO ❷ *Japanese*

4707 Wisconsin Ave. N.W.
Washington, D.C.
(202) 244-1740
No Wines or Spirits/Street Parking
MC, V
No dress restrictions

There is a full range of Japanese dishes offered at Mikado, including sukiyaki, shabu-shabu and sushi.

Reservations required
Lunch: Tues.–Fri., 11:30 A.M.–2:30 P.M.
Dinner: Tues.–Sun., 5:30 P.M.–10 P.M.
Closed Monday

THE MONTPELIER ⓴ *International*

Madison Hotel
1177 15th St. N.W.
Washington, D.C.
(202) 862-1600
Maître d': Marco Gherardi
Full Bar/Valet Parking
AE, D, MC, V, CB
Jacket, tie for men

French classic cuisine meets a variety of international specialties at The Montpelier. The elegant setting is one of crystal chandeliers, velvet dining chairs and rosewood paneling. There is live lobster, barbecued entrées such as spareribs and chicken (done in the restaurant's hickory pit) and other seafood items.

Reservations required
Lunch: Mon.–Fri., Noon–2:30 P.M.
Dinner: Mon.–Sat., 6 P.M.–10:30 P.M.
Sun., 6 P.M.–10 P.M.
Brunch: Sun., 11 A.M.–3 P.M.

OLD EUROPE ❻ *Continental*

2434 Wisconsin Ave. N.W.
Washington, D.C.
(202) 333-7600
Maître d': Glenda McWhorter
Full Bar/Valet Parking
AE, D, MC, V, CB
Jacket, tie for men (dining room)

One of Old Europe's unique features is its seasonal festivals — Mayfest, Octoberfest and those celebrating the hunting season and growing season. House specialties include schnitzel, sauerbraten, Zwiebel Rostbraten, rainbow trout and sausages galore. The German wine list is extensive.

No reservations required
Lunch/Dinner: Mon.–Thurs., 11:30 A.M.–Midnight
Fri.–Sat., 11:30 A.M.–1 A.M.
Sun., Noon–Midnight

THE PINES OF ROME ❸   *Italian*

4709 Hampden Lane
Bethesda, Md.
(301) 657-8775
Maître d': Marco Troiano (owner)
Beer and Wine/Street Parking
AE, D, MC, V, CB
No dress restrictions

Here you'll find all types of fresh fish and seafood, plus veal and pasta dishes. As an added attraction, there are hard-to-find specialties such as octopus and stuffed goose.

No reservations required
Lunch/Dinner: Tues. – Sun., 11:30 A.M. – 11 P.M.
  Closed Monday

THE PRIME RIB ㉚   *American*

2020 K St. N.W.
Washington, D.C.
(202) 466-8811
Maître d': Garth (manager)
Full Bar/Lot and Valet Parking (dinner)
AE, D, MC, V
Jacket for men

The Prime Rib states its case very simply. "We feature well-aged beef in an elegant Art Déco setting," says manager Garth Weldon. Other specialties include Crab Imperial, rack of lamb and fried potato skins. There is live music at lunch and dinner.

Reservations recommended
Lunch: Mon. – Fri., 11:30 A.M. – 2:30 P.M.
Dinner: Mon. – Sat., 5 P.M. – 11 P.M.
  Closed Sunday

RIVE GAUCHE ❾   *French*

Georgetown Inn
1310 Wisconsin Ave. N.W.
Washington, D.C.
(202) 333-6440
Maître d': Michel (chef)
Full Bar/Valet Parking
AE, D, MC, V, CB
Jacket, tie for men

One of Washington's most established French restaurants, Rive Gauche features a cuisine that is both classic and light. Specialties include Coquilles Saint-Jacques Vapeur, Côte de Veau aux Morilles, Soufflé de Homard Plaza-Athénée and homemade fresh fruit sherbet.

Reservations required
Lunch: Mon. – Sat., Noon – 2:30 P.M.
Dinner: Daily, 6 P.M. – 10:30 P.M.

SANS SOUCI ③③ *French*

726 17th St. N.W.
Washington, D.C.
(202) 298-7424
Maître d': Pierre Sosnitsky (manager)
Full Bar/Lot Parking
AE, D, MC, V, CB
Jacket, tie for men

A restaurant renowned as much for its clientele as for its cuisine, Sans Souci has catered to political and journalistic types for quite some time. The food is in the classic *haute cuisine* tradition.

Reservations required
Lunch: Mon.–Sat., Noon–2:30 P.M. (members only)
Dinner: Mon.–Sat., 6 P.M.–10:30 P.M.
    Closed Sunday

TIBERIO ㉖ *Northern Italian*

1915 K St. N.W.
Washington, D.C.
(202) 425-1915
Full Bar/Valet Parking
AE, D, MC, V, CB
Jacket for men

A locally popular Northern Italian restaurant, Tiberio features such delicacies as milk-fed veal, freshly made pastas and home-baked breads and pastries. The attitude is subtle and discreet, the setting, stylish and chic.

Reservations required
Lunch: Mon.–Fri., Noon–3 P.M.
Dinner: Mon.–Sat., 6 P.M.–11 P.M.
    Closed Sunday

TRUDIE BALL'S EMPRESS ㉘ *Chinese*

1018 Vermont Ave. N.W.
Washington, D.C.
(202) 737-2324
Maître d': P. J. Hsu
Full Bar/Lot Parking
AE, D, MC, V, CB
Jacket for men

The house specialty here is Peking Duck—and it's available without the usual advance notice! There are three floors of dining, plus banquet facilities for as many as 200 people. The Hunan specialties include whole fish with hot bean sauce, lamb sautéed with scallions and steamed rainbow trout stuffed with black mushrooms.

Reservations required
Lunch: Mon.–Sat., 11:30 A.M.–3 P.M.
Dinner: Mon.–Sat., 5 P.M.–11 P.M.
    Sun., Noon–11 P.M.

THE TWO CONTINENTS ㉞ *Continental*

Hotel Washington
1420 F St. N.W.
Washington, D.C.
(202) 347-4499
Maître d': Gus Jiminez
Full Bar/Lot and Street Parking
AE, D, MC, V, CB
No dress restrictions

A physically handsome dining spot, The Two Continents serves Continental specialties to the powerful and beautiful. Look for bouillabaisse, Quiche Lorraine, Sea Trout St. Tropez and Tournedos Rossini.

Reservations suggested (lunch)
Lunch: Mon.–Fri., *11:30 A.M.–3 P.M.*
Dinner: Mon.–Fri., *6 P.M.–10:30 P.M.*
　　　　Sat.–Sun., *5 P.M.–11 P.M.*

WASHINGTON PALM ⑱ *American*

1225 19th St. N.W.
Washington, D.C.
(202) 293-9091
Full Bar/Valet Parking
AE, D, MC, V, CB
Good taste in dress required

The usual hearty array of steaks and seafood is offered at this Palm branch. The lobster is renowned. The portions are enormous.

Reservations required
Lunch: Mon.–Fri., *11:45 A.M.–3 P.M.*
Dinner: Mon.–Fri., *3 P.M.–10:45 P.M.*
　　　　Sat., *6 P.M.–10:45 P.M.*
　　　　Closed Sunday

DINER'S DICTIONARY

DINER'S DICTIONARY

The following special-information sections can make dining out even more enjoyable for you. The Vintage Guide and Glossary of Wine Tasting Terms can come in handy when discussing the merits of a particular wine with the waiter or sommelier.

The Diner's Dictionary can help you order the selections you *really* want from a menu written in either French, Spanish, Italian or German. Terms such as *à la paysanne* (French for country style), *frutti di mare* (Italian for shellfish), *huevos* (Spanish for eggs) and *Starke Getränke* (German for spirits) are explained clearly and briefly.

Pronunciation:
a = a as in cat
ah = a as in almond

BASIC MENU	French	German
Appetizers	hors d'oeuvres	Vorspeisen
Beverages	boissons	Getränke
Beef	boeuf	Rindfleisch
Chicken	poulet	Hahn
Desserts	desserts	Nachspeisen
Duck	canard	Ente
Fish	poissons	Fische
Goose	oie	Gans
Lamb	agneau	Lamm
Meat	viande	Fleisch
Pork	porc	Schweinefleisch
Salad	salade	Salat
Seafood	fruits de mer	Meeresfrüchte
Soup	soupe, potage	Suppe
Veal	veau	Kalbfleisch
Vegetables	légumes	Gemüse
Venison	venaison	Wildbret
Alcoholic Beverages	boissons alcooliques	alkoholische Getränke
Hamburgers	bifteck haché	Frikadelle mit belegte Brötchen
Sandwiches	sandwiches	belegte Brote
Spirits	spiriteux	starke Getränke

ay = a as in may
ee = e as in equal
eh = e as in end
ey = i as in iron
oh = o as in go
n = nasal sound in some French words
kh = German ch
uh = the short sound of u in undo
u = u as in up
eu = sound of u as in rue; some French and German words; almost ew
eo = German sound of ö; stretch your mouth as though you were going to say ee, but say o or u (ö or ü) for umlauted words and some French words.
zh = soft j as in barrage
ai = as in air for Italian e

Italian	Spanish	BASIC MENU
antipasti principii	entradas	**Appetizers**
bevande	bebidas	**Beverages**
bue, manzo	carne	**Beef**
pollo	pollo	**Chicken**
dolci o frutta	postres	**Desserts**
anitra	pato	**Duck**
pesce	pescados	**Fish**
oca	ganco	**Goose**
agnello	cordero	**Lamb**
carne	carne	**Meat**
porco	carne de cerdo	**Pork**
insalata	ensalada	**Salad**
frutti di mare	mariscos	**Seafood**
ministre, zuppe	sopa	**Soup**
vitello	ternera	**Veal**
legumi	legumbres	**Vegetables**
cacciogione	carne de venado	**Venison**
bevande alcooliche	bebidas alcohólicas	**Alcoholic Beverages**
polpetta di carne tra due fette di pane	carne picada de vaca	**Hamburgers**
tartine	entremeses	**Sandwiches**
bevande con alto contenuto alcoolico	bebidas alcohólicas fuertes	**Spirits**

A

Aalsuppe (Ger.) eel soup; esp Hamburg
abbacchio (It.) lamb, as *Abbacchio con Piselli*, lamb stew with peas; esp. Piedmont
à blanc (Fr.) meat boiled until it just turns color, before cooking
abricots (Fr.) apricots
aceitunas (Sp.) olives
affumicato (It.) smoked
aglio (It.) garlic
agneau (Fr.) lamb, as *Agneau en Daube*, potted lamb
agnello (It.) spring lamb, as *Agnello alla Parmigiana*, breaded lamb steaks with Parmesan cheese
agnellotti (It.) meat-stuffed dumplings
agua (Sp.) water
ai ferri (It.) grilled, broiled, as *Bistecca ai Ferri*, grilled steak
aigre (Fr.) sour
ail (Fr.) garlic, as *Gigot à l'Ail*, leg of mutton in garlic sauce
aioli (Fr.) garlic-flavored mayonnaise
ajo (Sp.) garlic
à l', à la, au, aux (Fr.) in the style of, as *Boeuf à la Flamande*, beef Flemish style
a la, al (Sp.) in the style of, as *Jamón al Jerez*, ham in sherry
al, al', alla (It.) in the style of, as *Animelle al Prosciutto*, sweetbreads and ham
à la broche (Fr.) on skewers
à la carte (Fr.) priced by the dish; opp. *table d'hôte*
à la king (Am.) with rich cream sauce, usually on chicken or fish
à la mode (Fr.) in the particular style; refers to meat, larded, braised, simmered with vegetables, as *Boeuf à la Mode*, pot roast
à la paysanne (Fr.) country style, as *Rôti de Porc à la Paysanne*, roast pork loin, country style
à la vapeur (Fr.) steamed
albicocca (It.) apricot
al burro (It.) with butter, as *Fettuccine al Burro e Parmigiana*, pasta with butter and grated Parmesan cheese — no sauce
alcachofes (Sp.) artichokes
al dente (It.) not overcooked, just right, as *Spaghetti al Dente*, spaghetti cooked to order and just a little chewy
al doppio burro (It.) with twice as much butter, as *Spaghetti al Doppio Burro*, with plenty of butter and cream; esp. Rome
al forno (It.) baked, as *Agnello al Forno*, baked lamb
al horno (Sp.) baked
à l'huile (Fr.) in oil, as *à l'huile d'olive*, in olive oil
alla cacciatore (It.) hunter's style, refers to two different sauces: tomato or rosemary and vinegar sauce, as *Bistecca alla Cacciatore* — tomato — and *Abbacchio alla Cacciatore* — rosemary and vinegar
alla casalinga (It.) homestyle
alla marinara (It.) seaman's style, as *Scampi alla Marinara*, shrimps in a no-meat sauce: tomatoes, olives, garlic, herbs
alla matriciana (It.) country style, as *Spaghetti alla Matriciana*
allemand (Fr.) German, as *à l'Allemand*, German style
allumettes (Fr.) like matchsticks, food cut in strips, as *Allumettes*, pastry strips spread with garnishes
almejas (Sp.) clams
amande (Fr.) almond, as *Amandine*, sauce with blanched almonds used with fish or vegetables
ananasso (It.) pineapple
anatra (It.) duck
andouille (Fr.) pork sausage; esp. northern France
anguila (Sp.) eel
anguilla (It.) eel

anguille (Fr.) eel, as *Anguilles à la Bordelaise,* Bordeaux-style eels, in butter and wine
animelle (It.) sweetbreads, as *Animelle al Prosciutto,* sweetbreads and ham
antipasto (It.) hors d'oeuvre
Apfel (Ger.) apple as *Apfel mit Leberfulle,* liver-stuffed apples
Apfelkuchen (Ger.) sliced apples baked in thin cake dough
Apfelsinen (Ger.) oranges, as *Apfelsinensaft,* orange juice
apio (Sp.) celery
aragosta (It.) lobster
aranci (It.) oranges
arrosto (It.) roast, as *Arrosto Semplice di Vitello,* pot roast of veal
arroz (Sp.) rice, as *Arroz con Pollo,* stewed chicken with saffron rice
artichauts (Fr.) artichokes
Artischoken (Ger.) artichokes
asparago (It.) asparagus
asperge (Fr.) asparagus
aspic (Fr.) jellied meat or fish
aubergine (Fr.) eggplant
au beurre noir (Fr.) browned butter, as *Cervelles au Beurre Noir,* brains in browned butter
auf...Art (Ger.) in the style of, as *auf deutsche Art,* German style
au gratin (Fr.) sprinkled with breadcrumbs before baking, often with cheese
au jus (Fr.) in natural juices, as *Rosbif au Jus,* roast beef in its own juices
au naturel (Fr.) plain, simply cooked
au sec (Fr.) cooked "dry," tightly covered without added water
aux champignons (Fr.) with mushrooms

B

baba (Fr.) round yeast cake soaked in syrup, as *Baba au Rhum,* rum cake
babeurre (Fr.) buttermilk
bacalao (Sp.) dried codfish, as *Bacalao a la Vizcaíno,* codfish stewed in oil, onions, peppers, tomatoes; esp. Basque
baccalà (It.) dried, salted codfish
Backen (Ger.) bake; *gebackt,* baked
baguette (Fr.) long loaf of bread
ballotine (Fr.) boned meat roll
bavaroise (Fr.) Bavarian custard, a rich cream
beignet (Fr.) a puffed pastry fritter, as *Beignets au Fromage,* cheese fritters
Bel Paese (It.) mild, semisoft cheese
berenjenas (Sp.) eggplants
beurre (Fr.) butter
bien hecho (Sp.) well done
Bier (Ger.) beer
bière (Fr.) beer
Bierkäse (Ger.) white, strong cheese
bifteck (Fr.) steak, as *Bifteck au Pommes Frites,* steak with fried potatoes
birra (It.) beer
bisque (Fr.) fish, shellfish, chicken or game soup, as *Bisque de Homard,* lobster soup
bistecca (It.) steak, as *Bistecca alla Pizzaiola,* Neapolitan steak
blancmange (Fr.) a milky pudding
Blumenkohl (Ger.) cauliflower
Blutwurst (Ger.) sausage with bacon and pork's blood
boeuf (Fr.) beef, as *Boeuf à la Mode en Gelée,* beef in aspic

Boeuf Bourguignon (Fr.) beef stew, vegetables, in Burgundy wine
boliche (Sp.) pot roast
bolitto (It.) boiled beef, as *Bollito Misto*, boiled mixed meats
bombe (Fr.) dessert of ices, whipped cream, fruits
bouillabaisse (Fr.) fish and shellfish chowder
bouilli (Fr.) boiled; boiled beef — *bouilli* is a French national dish
Braten (Ger.) roast, grill, fry, as *Hackbraten*, meat loaf
Bratwurst (Ger.) pork sausage
Brust (Ger.) breast, as *Gefullte Kalbsbrust*, stuffed breast of veal
bue (It.) beef, as *Bue alla Lombardia*, Lombard pot roast
Butter (Ger.) butter, as *Buttermilch*, buttermilk

C

cacciucco (It.) seafood stew
calamares (Sp.) small squid, as *Calamares en Su Tinta*, squid cooked in a sauce including its own ink and served with rice
caldo (Sp.) broth, gravy, as *Caldo Gallego*, thick soup of beef, pork, pork feet, ham, turnips, greens and potatoes
callos (Sp.) tripe
camerón (Sp.) shrimp
campesina (Sp.) farmer, country, *a la campesina*, country style
canard (Fr.) duck
cannelloni (It.) stuffed macaroni with meat filling
cappalletti (It.) stuffed squares of dough, used for soups
capretto (It.) kid, as *Capretto al Forno*, baked kid; esp. Rome
caracoles (Sp.) snails
carbonnade (Fr.) meat grilled over charcoal
carciofi (It.) artichokes, as *Carciofi con Parmigiana*, artichokes with Parmesan cheese
carne (Sp.) meat, as *Carne Estofado*, meat stew
casseruola (It.) casserole
cassoulet (Fr.) a stew with white beans, pork, bacon, mutton; esp. south of France
castaña (Sp.) chestnut
cebolla (Sp.) onion
ceci (It.) chick peas or garbanzo beans
cèpes (Fr.) large mushrooms, as *Cèpes à la Bordelaise*, mushrooms, Bordeaux style
cervelles (Fr.) brains, as *Cervelles au Beurre Noir*, brains in browned butter
champignons (Fr.) mushrooms
charcuteries (Fr.) cold cuts
chasseur, à la (Fr.) hunter's style, as *Sauce à la Chasseur*
chiles (Sp.) peppers
chorizos (Sp.) sausages
chou (Fr.) cabbage
choucroute (Fr.) sauerkraut
chou-fleur (Fr.) cauliflower
chuletas (Sp.) chops, cutlets, as *Chuletas de Cordero a la Navarra*, lamb chops with ham, tomatoes, onion, sausage; esp. Navarre, northern Spain
civet (Fr.) wine stew, as *Civet de Lièvre*, jugged hare
cochino (Sp.) pig, as *Cochino Asado*, roast pork
cochon (Fr.) pig, as *Cochon de Lait*, suckling pig
cocido (Sp.) stew of beef, pork, ham, bacon, cabbage, chick peas, etc.
coniglio (It.) rabbit, as *Coniglio in Casseruola*, rabbit casserole
coquille (Fr.) seafood in the shell
costato (It.) ribs, as *Costato di Manzo alla Pizzaiola*, rib steaks with tomato and oregano

costillas (Sp.) ribs, as *Costillas de Cerdo*, pork spareribs
costole (It.) ribs, as *Costole di Maiale con Fagiolini*, braised spareribs with green beans
costoletta, cotoletta (It.) chop, cutlet, as *Costoletta di Vitello*, veal cutlet
côte (Fr.) rib, as *Côtes de Porc*, pork spareribs
côtelette de veau (Fr.) veal chop, as *Côtelettes de Veau à la Bonne Femme*, veal chops, homestyle
coulis (Fr.) thick, shellfish soup
cozza (It.) mussel
crème (Fr.) cream, whipped cream, custard, as *Crème Fraîche*, a heavy French cream
crêpe (Fr.) thin pancake rolled around various fillings, as *Crêpes Suzette*, dessert crêpes
cresson, cresson de fontaine (Fr.) watercress
crochette (It.) croquettes, as *Crochette di Pesce*, fish croquettes
croûte (Fr.) crust

D

Dampfnudeln (Ger.) sweet dessert dumplings
deutsches Beefsteak (Ger.) hamburgers, German style
diable, sauce (Fr.) deviled sauce, as *Pieds de Cochon Diable*, deviled pigs' feet
dieppoise (Fr.) shrimp, mussels, shrimp with white sauce
dolci (It.) sweets

E

éclair (Fr.) pastry, puffed, with whipped cream or custard filling
écrevisse (Fr.) crayfish
Ei (Ger.) egg
Eierpflanze (Ger.) eggplant
Eisbein (Ger.) pig's knuckles
en gelée (Fr.) in aspic
ensalada (Sp.) salad, as *Ensalada de Pollo*, chicken salad
entrecôte (Fr.) steak cut from "between the ribs," as *Entrecôte Bordelaise*, steak with spicy wine sauce
entrée (Fr.) usually, main course
entremeses (Sp.) hors d'oeuvre
entremets (Fr.) side dishes
épaule (Fr.) shoulder, as *Epaule d'Agneau à la Niçoise*, lamb shoulder, Nice style
épice (Fr.) spice
épinard (Fr.) spinach, as *Epinards aux Poires*, spinach greens and pear purée
Erbse (Ger.) pea, as *Erbsensuppe*, pea soup, often served with sausage
Erdbeere (Ger.) strawberry, as *Erdbeerentorte*, strawberry cake
escalope (Fr.) thinly sliced meat, as *Escalopes de Veau à la Crème*, veal cutlets in cream
escargot (Fr.) snail, as *Escargots au Champagne*, snails marinated in champagne, in this dish stuffing for mushrooms
espárrago (Sp.) asparagus, as *Espárragos en Salsa*, in an egg and pepper sauce
espinaca (Sp.) spinach, as *Espinacas Espárragos*, spinach in an asparagus sauce
estofado (Sp.) meat stew, as *Estofado a la Campesino*, country-style stew
Estouffat Catalán (not quite Sp., not quite Fr.) beef pot roast with white beans, Catalonian style

estragon (Fr.) tarragon
étuvée (Fr.) stew, as *Etuvée de Veau*, veal stew (in red wine); esp. Provence

F

fabada (Sp.) stew, as *Fabada Asturiana*, pork stew with white beans; esp. Asturia
fagiano (It.) pheasant
fagioli (It.) dried white beans
faisan (Fr.) pheasant, *faisandé*, gamy
farci (Fr.) stuffed, as *Moules Farcies*, stuffed mussels
Fasan (Ger.) pheasant
fava (It.) bean
fedelini (It.) fine pasta
fegato (It.) liver
fettuccine (It.) thin, flat pasta, as *Fettuccine al Sugo*, with meat sauce
filet (Fr.) fillet of meat, chicken, fish, as *Filet de Boeuf Braisé*, *Filet de Sole*, braised fillet of beef, fillet of fish
Filet de Boeuf Wellington (Fr.) beef fillet in pastry
filete (Sp.) fillet
filetto (It.) fillet, as *Filetto Ripieno*, stuffed beef fillets
fines herbes (Fr.) mixed fresh herbs, as *Omelettes aux Fines Herbes*
finocchio (It.) fennel, as *Finocchio al Formaggio*, sautéed fennel with cheese
flageolet (Fr.) small green kidney bean
flambé (Fr.) set afire, as any dish set afire after spirits have been poured over it
flan (Fr., Sp.) custard, as *Flan Fourrée de Fruits*, fruit-filled custard; *Flan de Naranja*, orange carmelized custard
Fleisch (Ger.) meat, as *Fleischklösse mit Pilzen*, meatballs with mushrooms
Fleischsalat (Ger.) salad of cold meats
florentine (Fr.) dish includes spinach
flûte (Fr.) crusty bread
foie (Fr.) liver, as *Foie de Canard au Raisins*, duck liver with grapes
foie d'oie (Fr.) goose liver
foie gras (Fr.) goose liver (literally, fat liver) as *Pâté de Foie Gras*, puréed goose liver
fondua (It.) casserole of cheese and truffles; esp. Piedmont
fondue (Fr.) melted cheese and wine, as *Fondue Neuchâteloise*, Swiss fondue
Forelle (Ger.) trout, as *Forellen*, river trout with melted butter and lemon
formaggio (It.) cheese
four, fourné (Fr.) oven, baked
fourré (Fr.) filled, as *Flan Fourée de Fruits*, custard filled with fruits
Fra Diavolo (It.) tomato and herb sauce, as *Aragosta Fra Diavolo*, lobster with tomato-herb sauce
fragola (It.) strawberry
fraise (Fr.) strawberry
framboise (Fr.) raspberry
frappé (Fr.) iced
fresa (Sp.) strawberry
friandises (Fr.) variety of small cakes
fricandelles (Fr.) chopped meat in patties or balls, fried and braised

fricasé (Sp.) fricassee, as *Fricasé de Pollo*
fricassée (Fr.) stew of poultry or other meats in a light gravy
frijoles (Sp.) beans, as *Frijoles Refritos*, "refried beans," with onions, tomatoes, garlic
frite (Fr.) fried, as *Pommes de Terre Frites*, fried potatoes
frito, fritas (Sp.) fried, as *Patatas Fritas a la Francesca*, French fries
frittata (It.) omelet
fritto (It.) fried, as *Fritto Misto di Pesce*, deep-fried mixture of fish in batter
fritto misto (It.) meat, fish, vegetables, cut small and deep-fried in batter
froid (Fr.) cold
fromage (Fr.) cheese
fruits de mer (Fr.) seafood
frutti di mare (It.) shellfish
funghi (It.) mushrooms

G

galantine (Fr.) reshaped and boned game, poultry or meat, as *Galantine de Veau*, stuffed veal breast, rolled
galette (Fr.) broad, flat cake, seabiscuit, as *Galette de Sarrasin*, buckwheat pancake
gallina (Sp.) hen, as *Gallina en Pepitoria*, chicken in spicy tomato sauce
gamberetto di mare (It.) shrimp
Gans (Ger.) goose, as *Gänsebraten*, roast goose
ganso (Sp.) goose
garbure (Fr.) bacon and vegetable soup; esp. Pyrenees
gâteau (Fr.) cake, as *Gâteau Saint-Honoré*, rich cake with caramel-glazed cream puffs
gaufre (Fr.) waffle, as *Gaufre Fourré*, stuffed waffle
gazpacho (Sp.) cold vegetable soup of raw vegetables; esp. Andalusia
Gebacken (Ger.) fried, as *Gebackener Karpfen*, fresh, panfried carp
Gedämpft (Ger.) stewed
Gefüllt (Ger.) stuffed, as *Gefüllter Kohl*, stuffed cabbage
Gekocht (Ger.) boiled, as *Gekochtes Rindfleisch*, boiled beef
gelato (It.) ice cream
gelée (Fr.) jellied, as *Boeuf Froid en Gelée*, cold, jellied beef
Gemüse (Ger.) vegetables
Gerstensuppe (Ger.) thick barley soup
Gervais (Fr.) cream cheese
Geschmort (Ger.) stewed
gibelotte (Fr.) rabbit stew
gibier (Fr.) game
gigot (Fr.) leg of mutton as *Gigot d'Agneau*, leg of lamb
glacé (Fr.) iced, frozen, candied, glazed
glorias (Sp.) small sweet-potato pies
gnocchi (It.) dumplings, as *Gnocci al Sugo*, dumplings with meat sauce
Gorgonzola (It.) blue-veined, Roquefort-type cheese
granita (It.) ices, variety of ice cream
grissini (It.) breadsticks
guayaba (Sp.) guava, as *Guayaba con Queso*, guava with cheese
guisado (Sp.) stew, as *Guisado Español*, Spanish stew
Gugelhupf (Ger.) yeast cake in a ring mold
Gulasch (Ger.) beef, pork or veal cubes, stewed with paprika and onions, esp. Hungarian

H

habas (Sp.) broad bean, as *Habas en Cazuela*, bean casserole with eggs
Hackbraten (Ger.) meatloaf
Hamburger Kümmelfleisch (Ger.) lamb, with onions, cabbage, potatoes and caraway seeds
hareng (Fr.) herring
haricots (Fr.) beans, as *Haricot de Mouton*, lamb stew with white beans
haricots verts (Fr.) green beans
Hase (Ger.) hare, rabbit, as *Hasenbraten*, roasted whole rabbit or hare
Hasenpfeffer (Ger.) hare or rabbit braised in red wine and spices
helado (Sp.) ice cream
hielo (Sp.) ice
hochepot (Fr.) beef, pig's ear, sausage, cabbage and other vegetables
Holsteiner Schnitzel (Ger.) breaded veal cutlets with fried eggs and anchovies
homard (Fr.) lobster, as *Homard à l'Armoricaine*, lobster in the Armorican style (Brittany)
Honig (Ger.) honey, as *Honigkuchen*, spicy honey cake
Hörnchen (Ger.) crescent-shaped rolls
hors d'oeuvre (Fr.) appetizer or canape served before meal
huevos (Sp.) eggs, as *Huevos a la Flamenca*, fried eggs, smoked pork sausage, tomatoes, wine; esp. Andalusia
Huevos a la Malagueña (Sp.) eggs fried in individual casseroles with tomatoes, onions, etc.; esp. Málaga, southern Spain
Huevos Revueltos (Sp.) scrambled eggs
huile (Fr.) oil, as *huile d'olive*, olive oil
huîtres (Fr.) oysters
Hummer (Ger.) lobster
hussarde (Fr.) garnish of tomato with onion, potato, horseradish filling

I

île flottante (Fr.) floating island, custard dessert with meringue
in bianco (It.) plain, as *Bianco Pesce*, plain boiled fish
in carrozza (It.) literally, in a carriage, as *Mozzarella in Carrozza*, mozzarella cheese baked between two bread slices
insalata (It.) salad, as *Insalata Verdi*, green salad
involto (It.) "bundle," as *Involto di Vitello alla Milanese*, rolled veal, veal birds, Milan style
irlandaise, à l' (Fr.) Irish style, usually with potatoes

J

jambe (Fr.) leg, as *Jambe de Porc*, leg of pork of fresh ham
jambon (Fr.) ham, as *Jambon à la Montmorency*, ham steaks with cherry sauce
jardin (Fr.) garden, as *Salade du Jardin*, raw, fresh vegetable salad
jardinière (Fr.) mixed vegetables
jarret (Fr.) knuckle, as *Jarret de Veau Ossu Buco*, veal shank osso-buco style
Johannisbeere (Ger.) currants, as *Johannisbeerküchen*, currant tarts
Jorbküse (Ger.) white cheese
julienne (Fr.) food cut in strips
jus (Fr.) juice, as *au jus*, in its own juices; *jus d'herbes*, herb juices

K

Kaffee (Ger.) coffee, as *Kaffee mit Sahne*, coffee with whipped cream; Germany
Kaffee mit Schalagobers (Ger.) Viennese coffee with heavy whipped cream topping
Kaiserschmarren (Ger.) sweet dessert omelet
Kalb (Ger.) calf, as *Kalbsnierenbraten*, roast loin of veal
Kalbshaxe (Ger.) veal shanks
Kartoffel (Ger.) potato, as *Kartoffelklösse*, potato dumplings
Kipfel (Ger.) crescent-shaped rolls
Kirsche (Ger.) cherry, as *Kirschwasser*, brandy from cherries
Klops (Ger.) meatballs, as *Königsberger Klops*, veal meatballs served in sour cream
Knockwurst (Ger.) large frankfurterlike sausage
Knödel (Ger.) dumpling
Kohl (Ger.) cabbage, as *Kohlsuppe*, cabbage soup
Kotelett (Ger.) chop, cutlet, as *Schweinkoteletten*, pork chops
Krabben (Ger.) shrimp
Kraut (Ger.) herb, cabbage, as *Krautrouladen*, ground meat, rice or crumbs wrapped in cabbage leaf
Kuchen (Ger.) cake, as *Lebkuchen*, honey cake
Kümmel (Ger.) caraway, as *Kümmelsuppe*, caraway-seed soup; esp. northern Germany

L

Lachs (Ger.) salmon
lait (Fr.) milk
laitue (Fr.) lettuce, as *Laitues Farcies à la Flamande*, lettuce, boiled and stuffed with pork and calf's liver, Flemish style
Lamm (Ger.) lamb, as *Lamm Balkinsches Art*, Balkan lamb stew
Lammauflauf (Ger.) Austrian lamb and veal loaf
langosta (Sp.) lobster
langostinos (Sp.) shrimp or crayfish
langoustine (Fr.) prawn
langue (Fr.) tongue, as *Langue de Boeuf Provençale*, beef tongue with a nut-raisin-sauce, style of Provence
lapereau (Fr.) young rabbit, as *Lapereau à la Normand*
lapin (Fr.) rabbit, as *Lapin en Blanquette*, stewed rabbit in mushroom cream sauce
lasagne (It.) broad noodles, layered with chopped meat, mozzarella and ricotta cheeses, tomatoes and sausage
latte (It.) milk
lattuga (It.) lettuce
Lausch (Ger.) leek, as *Lauschgraten*, leeks au gratin (with cheese)
Leber (Ger.) liver, as *Leber mit Apfeln und Zwiebeln*, calf's liver with apples and onions
Leberknödel (Ger.) liver dumpling, as *Leberknödelsuppe*, a liver-dumpling soup
Leberwurst (Ger.) liverwurst
leche (Sp.) milk
lechuga (Sp.) lettuce
legumbre (Sp.) vegetable
légume (Fr.) vegetable, as *Légumes Verts*, green vegetables
legumi (It.) vegetables
Lende (Ger.) loin, as *Lendenbraten*, roast beef
lengua (Sp.) tongue, as *Lengua a la Madrileña*, Madrid-style baked tongue
lenguado (Sp.) sole
lenticchie (It.) lentils
lepre (It.) hare

lièvre (Fr.) hare
limande (Fr.) flounder, sand dab
lomo (Sp.) loin, as *Lomo a la Cádiz*, pork loin in sherry

M

macaron (Fr.) macaroon, as *Macarons de Nancy*, almond macaroons
macarrón (Sp.) macaroon
maccheroni (It.) macaroni
macédoine (Fr.) cut-up fruit or vegetables
macedonia (It.) fruit salad, as *Macedonia di Frutta*, fruit compote
madeleine (Fr.) small, buttery cakes
madrilène (Fr.) tomato-flavored clear soup, sometimes jellied
maiale (It.) pork, as *Maialino di Latte*, suckling pig
maionese (It.) mayonnaise
maïs (Fr.) corn
maître d'hôtel beurre (Fr.) seasoned butter
maíz (Sp.) corn
Makrele (Ger.) mackerel
mandarine (Fr.) tangerine
mandarino (It.) tangerine
mandeln (Ger.) almonds
manicotti (It.) large, hollow tubes of delicate dough stuffed with ricotta cheese
manzana (Sp.) apple
manzo (It.) beef, as *Manzo al Forno*, baked beef pot roast
maquereau (Fr.) mackerel
mariné (Fr.) pickled
marinère, à la (Fr.) seaman's style, as *Moules à la Marinière*, mussels in onion and garlic sauce
Markklösse (Ger.) beef-marrow balls in broth
marron (Fr.) chestnut
Maultasche (Ger.) similar to ravioli, with meat filling
Mehl (Ger.) flour, as *Mehlspeise*, dessert pudding
mejillón (Sp.) mussel
melanzana (It.) eggplant, as *Melanzana alla Parmigiana*, eggplant with mozzaarella and tomato sauce
melocotón (Sp.) peach
melón (Sp.) melon
melone (It.) melon, as *Melone e Prosciutto*, ham and melon, an hors d'oeuvre
merluza (Sp.) codfish, as *Merluza a la Vinagreta*, codfish in vinegar sauce
Milch (Ger.) milk
mille-feuille (Fr.) Genoese pastry
minceur (Fr.) slenderness, as *cuisine minceur*
minestra (It.) soup
minestrone (It.) vegetable soup, as *Minestrone in Stagione*, vegetable soup according to the season
mirepoix (Fr.) diced mixture of carrots, onions, celery with herbs, sometimes bacon
moletas (Sp.) sweetbreads, as *Moletas de Vitela con Porto*, veal sweetbreads with port wine
mollejas (Sp.) sweetbreads, as *Mollejas a la Española*, sweetbreads, Spanish style
moule (Fr.) mussel, as *Moules Farcies au Currie*, stuffed, curried mussels
mousse (Fr.) custardlike dessert; *Mousse au Jambon*, ham mousse, molded, with mayonnaise, ham, onions, cream, gelatine
mousseron (Fr.) mushroom, as *Mousseron à la Crème*, small mushrooms with a rich cream sauce

mousseux (Fr.) sparkling
moutarde (Fr.) mustard
mouton (Fr.) mutton (sheep)
mozzarella (It.) fresh, sweet Neapolitan cheese
Muscheln (Ger.) mussels, shellfish
Müsli (Ger.) cereal or cereals with nuts and fruits; literally, mixture

N

Nachspeise (Ger.) dessert
nasello (It.) whiting
nature (Fr.) plain, natural, as *Pommes de Terre Nature*, plain cutlet fried in butter
navarin (Fr.) lamb or mutton stew, as *Navarin d'Agneau*, lamb stew
navet (Fr.) turnip, as *Navets Glacés*, glazed turnips
negroni (It.) apéritif of sweet vermouth, gin, Campari bitter, over ice
neroli (Fr.) orange-blossom extract and almond pastries flavored with it
neufchâtel (Fr.) cream cheese
niçoise, à la (Fr.) in the style of Nice, as *Salade Niçoise*, with anchovies, tomatoes, olives, capers, etc.
nids (Fr.) nests
Nieren (Ger.) kidneys, as *Nieren Lelia*, kidneys with mustard sauce; Salzburg style
nivernaise, à la (Fr.) in the style of Nevers, garnished with small glazed onions and carrots
noce (It.) walnut
Nockerl (Ger.) dumplings, as *Wiener Nockerln*, Viennese dumplings used in soups
noisette (Fr.) hazelnut, shaped like hazelnuts, as potatoes or meat rounds
noques (Fr.) Alsatian dumplings, as *Noques à la Viennoise*, small balls of sweets
normande (Fr.) sauce with cider, wine, as *Sole à la Normande*, sole with sauce Normande and truffles, shellfish, mushrooms
Nudel (Ger.) noodle, as *Nudelsuppe*, noodle soup
Nuss (Ger.) nut, as *Nusstorte*, nut cake

O

Oblaten (Ger.) thin, wafflelike wafers, slightly sweetened
Obst (Ger.) fruit, as *Obsttorte*, fruit tart
Ochse (Ger.) ox, as *Ochsenfleisch*, beef
Ochsenbraten (Ger.) beefsteak
oeuf (Fr.) egg, as *oeufs durs*, hard-boiled eggs
Oeufs à la Neige (Fr.) a meringue custard and strawberry dessert
Oeufs Brouillés (Fr.) scrambled eggs
oie (Fr.) goose, as *Oie Farcie*, stuffed goose
oignon (Fr.) onion, as *Oignons Farcis*, onions with a meat stuffing
oiseau (Fr.) bird, as *Oiseaux de Veau sans Tête*, veal cutlets, stuffed and rolled to make "veal birds"
Olla Podrida (Sp.) literally, rotten pot; beef, ham, bacon, cabbage, etc., stew
omelette (Fr.) omelet, as *Omelette à l'Ail*, garlic omelet; esp. Pyrenees
os (Fr.) bone

osso (It.) bone, as *Osso Buco* (literally, bone with a hole) *alla Milanes*, Milanese style, braised veal shanks with marrow
Österreichisches (Ger.) Austrian, as *Osterreichisches Ei*, stuffed hard-boiled egg
ostras (Sp.) oysters

P

paella (Sp.) a rice and chicken, vegetables, sausage, meat, seafood dish — and/or *Paella Valenciana*, seafood variety containing clams, lobster, chicken, sausage, peas, garlic and saffron rice
pain (Fr.) bread, as *Pain à l'Anis*, anise-seed bread; esp. Alsace-Lorraine
palourde (Fr.) clam
Pampelmuse (Ger.) grapefruit
pamplemousse (Fr.) grapefruit
pan (Sp.) bread, as *Pan Rápido*, cakelike bread
panaché (Fr.) mixed
panade (Fr.) soup of bread soaked in milk, stock, egg, butter
pancetta affumicata (It.) bacon, as *Uova con Panecetta*, eggs and bacon
pane (It.) bread, also appears in names of cakes and pastries, as *Panettone*, spiced yeast cake with raisins and citron
panino (It.) bread roll
panna (It.) whipped cream
pannequets (Fr.) thin pancakes filled with jam, meat, seafood, mushrooms
papas (Sp.) potatoes, as *Papas en Ajo Pollo*, potatoes with beaten egg, vegetables, stewed with saffron seasoning; esp. Andalusia
papillote, en (Fr.) baked in parchment, aluminum foil or paper
Paprikahuhn (Ger.) braised paprika chicken and sour cream; esp. Austria
parfait (Fr.) ice cream
parmigiana, alla (It.) Parma style, with mozzarella and tomato
parmigiano (It.) Parmesan cheese
pasta (It.) generic name for noodles and macaronis, as *Pasta e Fagioli*, pasta and beans
pasticceria (It.) pastry
patata (Sp.) potato, as *Patatas Asada a la Cabaña*, roast potatoes, cabin style
pâté (Fr.) paste or purée, as *Pâté de Foie Gras*, goose-liver purée
pato (Sp.) duck, as *Pato con Arroz*, duck with rice
paupiette (Fr.) stuffed slice of meat, as *Paupiette de Veau à la Bonne Femme*, thin slices of beef, stuffed and rolled, country style
pavo (Sp.) turkey, as *Pavo Asado*, roast turkey
pecorino (It.) sheep's milk cheese, for grating; Roman
pepe (It.) pepper
peperone (It.) pepper, as *Peperoni Ripieni*, stuffed pepper
pepino (Sp.) cucumber
pepitas (Sp.) pumpkin seeds
pepitoria (Sp.) fricassee, as *Pepitoria de Gallina*, fricassee of fowl
perdiz (Sp.) partridge, as *Perdiz en Escabeche*, baked and braised marinated partridge
perdreau (Fr.) young partridge
perigourdine, à la (Fr.) dishes or sauces with pâté de foie gras and truffles
Perlhuhn (Ger.) guinea hen
pernice (It.) partridge, as *Pernici allo Zabaione*, partridges roasted with zabaione sauce
pèsca (It.) peach, as *Pesche Rigalo*, peaches stuffed with macaroons

pescado (Sp.) fish, as *Pescado con Arroz*, fish and rice
persil (Fr.) parsley, as *Persillade de Boeuf*, beef sautéed with chopped parsley
pesce (It.) fish, as *Pesci Arrosti*, baked fish
pesto (It.) green sauce made for pasta and potatoes, made with oil, garlic, herbs, anchovies; esp. Genoa
petite marmite (Fr.) clear, strong soup served with meat, vegetables, croûte, in individual pot
Pfannkuchen (Ger.) thin dessert pancake filled with jam
Pflaume (Ger.) plum, as *Pflaumenkuchen*, halved, pitted plums baked in thin cake dough
picadillo (Sp.) minced meat
picante (Sp.) spicy
piccata (It.) thinly sliced meat, as *Piccata al Marsala*, veal scallops with Marsala wine
pieds de cochon (Fr.) pig's feet, as *Pieds de Cochon Diable*, deviled pig's feet
pikant (Ger.) spicy, as *Pikantes Schweinefleisch*, marinated slices of pork, roasted
Pilze (Ger.) mushrooms
pimiento (Sp.) green or red pepper
pizza (It.) flat, baked, pielike dishes, as *Pizza di Polenta*, cornmeal pie
plátanos (Sp.) bananas
poire (Fr.) pear
poireau (Fr.) leek
pois (Fr.) pea
poisson (Fr.) fish
poitrine (Fr.) breast, as *Poitrine de Veau à l'Etuvée*, braised breast of veal
poivrade (Fr.) peppery sauce
poivre (Fr.) pepper
polenta (It.) cornmeal mush, as *Polenta cogli Osei*, "cornmeal mush with little birds"
polipi (It.) squid
pollitos (Sp.) squabs or young chickens
pollo (It., Sp.) chicken, as *Polla alla Cacciatora* (It.), *Arroz con Pollo* (Sp.), rice and chicken
polpette (It.) meatballs, as *Polpette di Vitello*, veal meatballs in tomato sauce
polpettone (It.) meat loaf
pomme (Fr.) apple
pomme de terre (Fr.) potato, as *Pommes de Terre Lyonnaises aux Oignons*, fried with onions
pomodoro (It.) tomato, as *Salsa de Pomodoro*, tomato sauce
Pont l'Eveque (Fr.) table cheese
porc (Fr.) pork, as *Côtelette de Porc*, pork chop
potage (Fr.) soup, as *Potage aux Légumes*, vegetable soup
pot-au-feu (Fr.) soup and main course in one: meat and vegetables
pots de crème (Fr.) chilled dessert of flavored cream, very rich
pouillard (Fr.) partridge
poularde (Fr.) roasting chicken, as *Poularde Truffée et Cuite au Bouillon*, chicken cooked with truffles in its own juice
poule (Fr.) chicken, as *Poule au Pot*, stuffed chicken, vegetables
poulet (Fr.) young chicken, as *Poulet Farci*, stuffed spring chicken
Preisselbeere (Ger.) cranberry or other tart berry
printanier (Fr.) literally, springlike, as *Soupe Printanière*, soup made of spring vegetables
profiterole (Fr.) cream puff with chocolate frosting
prosciutto (It.) ham, sliced very thin, salted, spiced and pressed; usually served with melon or in antipasti

provençal (Fr.) of Provence, as *à la provençal*, with tomatoes, garlic, oil
provola (It.) soft cheese, like mozzarella, as *Provola Affumicata*, smoked provola
provolone (It.) hard cheese, often used for grating
pruneaux (Fr.) prunes
puchero (Sp.) meat and vegetable stew
puerco (Sp.) pork, as *Puerco Horneado*, spiced roast loin of pork
purée (Fr.) mashed, as *Purée de Pommes de Terre*, mashed potatoes

Q

quadrucci (It.) pasta squares
quagliata (It.) cheese from goat's milk
quark (Ger.) cottage cheese, as *Quarkauflauf*, cottage cheese soufflé
quatre-épices (Fr.) four spices, used for meats
quenelle (Fr.) finely chopped and seasoned meat or fish, often with eggs, etc., served alone or with soup, as *Quenelles de Foie Gras*, balls of minced goose liver, as dumplings for soup
quesillo (Sp.) custard
queso (Sp.) cheese, as *Queso Suizo*, Swiss cheese
queue (Fr.) tail, as *Queue de Boeuf*, oxtail, *de Homard*, lobster tail
quiche (Fr.) filled, unsweetened tart or pie, as *Quiche Lorraine*, bacon and cheese tart
quignon (Fr.) pie-shaped piece of bread
quinquina (Fr.) apéritif wine
quisquilla (Sp.) shrimp

R

rábano fuerte (Sp.) horseradish
rafano (It.) horseradish
ragoût (Fr.) stew, as *Ragoût de Mouton Irlandais*, Irish stew
ragú (Sp.) stew, as *Ragú de Cordero*, pork stew
Rahm (Ger.) cream, as *Rahmsuppe*, creamed pea soup, with macaroni and smoked meats
raifort (Fr.) horseradish, as *Sauce au Raifort*, horseradish sauce
raisin (Fr.) grape; *raisins secs*, raisins
rana (Sp.) frog, as *Ranas en Pepitoria*, frog's leg stew
ratatouille (Fr.) eggplant mixture with marrows, tomatoes, olive oil, Niçoise
ravigote (Fr.) spicy dish, as *Moules Ravigote*, highly seasoned mussels
ravioli (It.) square of dough stuffed with spinach, chopped meat and cheese or with ricotta and boiled or fried and topped with sugar and cinnamon
Reis (Ger.) rice, as *Reisauflauf*, rice soufflé, dessert
relleno (Sp.) stuffed
remoulade (Fr.) braised or sautéed roll of beef, with or without filling
ribes (It.) currants
ricotta (It.) white fresh cheese
Rind, Rindfleisch (Ger.) beef, as *Rinderrouladen*, rolled, stuffed slices of beef
riñones (Sp.) kidneys, as *Riñones al Jerez*, kidneys in sherry
ripieno (It.) stuffed
ris (Fr.) sweetbreads, as *Ris de Veau au Gratin*, sweetbreads in cheese sauce

riso (It.) rice, as *Risotto*, boiled or steamed rice with sauce and Parmesan cheese; rice-based dishes, *Risotto con le Costagne*, with chestnuts

riz (Fr.) rice, as *Riz au Lait*, rice pudding; *à l'Imperatice*, rice cream with crystallized fruits

rognon (Fr.) kidney, as *Rognons de Veau au Cognac*, veal kidneys in cognac

rognone (It.) kidney, as *Rognoni al Vino Bianco*, kidneys in white wine

roh (Ger.) raw, rare

Rosinen (Ger.) raisins

Rostbraten (Ger.) roast beef

rôti (Fr.) roast, as *Rôti de Porc au Cidre*, roast pork in cider

rotoli (It.) rolled fillets of beef, stuffed, as *Rotoli di Manzo*, rolled, stuffed beef fillets

Rotkraut (Ger.) red cabbage

rouille (Fr.) sauce of pimiento and garlic

Rouladen (Ger.) rolled fillets, as *Rinderrouladen*, rolled beef fillets

Rührei (Ger.) scrambled egg

S

Sacher Torte (Ger.) chocolate cake with apricot jam filling

Saft (Ger.) juice, as *Orangensaft*, orange juice

Sahne (Ger.) cream, as *sauer Sahne*, sour crem

saison, en (Fr.) in season

sal (Sp.) salt, as *sal y pimienta*, salt and pepper; *salado*, salty

salade (Fr.) salad, as *Salade de Pommes de Terre*, potato salad

Salat (Ger.) salad

salchicha (Sp.) sausage

salé (Fr.) salted

salmón (Sp.) salmon, as *Salmón Ahumado*, smoked salmon

salmone (It.) salmon, as *Salmone Affumicato*, smoked salmon

salsa (It., Sp.) sauce, gravy, as *Salsa de Pomodoro*, tomato sauce

salsiccia (It.) sausage, as *Salsiccia alla Mozzarella*, sausage with cheese

saltimbocca (It.) little rolls of thinly sliced veal stuffed with prosciutto, cheese, etc.

Salz (Ger.) salt, as *Salz und Pfeffer*, salt and pepper; *salzig*, salty

sauce (Fr.) sauce, gravy, as *Sauce Citron*, lemon sauce; *Sauce Anglaise*, ketchup

saucisse (Fr.) sausage, as *Saucisson de Lyon*, delicate salami

sauer (Ger.) sour, as *Saure Nieren*, kidneys in a sour wine sauce

Sauerbraten (Ger.) spiced pot roast

Sauerkraut (Ger.) sauerkraut, as *Eisbein mit Sauerkraut*, pig's knuckles and sauerkraut

saumon (Fr.) salmon, as *Saumon Fumé*, smoked salmon

sauté (Fr.) fried lightly in butter, as *Ris de Veau Sauté à la Crème*, sweetbreads sautéed in cream

scaloppa (It.) breaded slice of meat, as *Scaloppa di Vitelli Impannata*, breaded veal cutlet

scaloppine (It.) thinly sliced meat, usually veal, breaded and fried or stewed, as *Scaloppine al Carciofi*, veal cutlets with artichoke hearts

scarola (It.) escarole, as *Scarola in Brodo*, escarole in broth

Schichttorte (Ger.) layercake

Schinken (Ger.) ham, as *Schinken in Wein*, fresh marinated ham in wine

Schnapps (Ger.) various strong, distilled liquors

Schnitz (Ger.) sliced, dried fruit, as *Schnitz und Knepp*, boiled apples and dumplings, sometimes with ham

Schnitzel (Ger.) veal cutlet, literally, small slice, as *Wiener Schnitzel*, breaded veal cutlets, fried
Schwein (Ger.) pork, as *Schweinebraten*, roast pork
scungilli (It.) a seafood extracted from a conch and served with a hot sauce
sedano (It.) celery
Seezunge (Ger.) sole
sel (Fr.) salt, as *du sel et du poivre*, salt and pepper; *sel blanc*, table salt
selle (Fr.) saddle, as *Selle d'Agneau au Four*, oven-roast saddle of lamb
Semmel (Ger.) roll
Senf (Ger.) mustard
sformato (It.) cooked in a mold, as *Sformato di Carne alla Siciliana*
sogliola (It.) sole or flounder, *Filetto di Sogliola*, fillet of sole
sole (Fr.) sole, as *Filet de Sole à la Bonne Femme*, "plain" fillet of sole
Sosse (Ger.) sauce, gravy
soufflé (Fr.) light, fluffy mixture of foods with beaten egg whites, dessert or main course, as *Soufflé au Jambon*, ham soufflé
soupe (Fr.) soup, as *Soupe à l'Oignon aux Halles*, onion soup with Gruyère cheese over toast; esp. Paris
Spargel (Ger.) asparagus, as *Spargelsuppe*, asparagus soup
Spätzle (Ger.) egg and flour dumplings dipped into boiling water or soup
Speck (Ger.) bacon
spiedini (It.) mozzarella between slices of bread with anchovies, baked
spinace (It.) spinach
Spinat (Ger.) spinach
spumone (It.) a variety of Italian ice cream
starke Getränke (Ger.) spirits
stracchino (It.) Milanese soft cheese
stracciatella (It). Roman egg-drop soup
Streuselkuchen (Ger.) crumb cake
Strudel (Ger.) sheet of thin dough rolled up with various fillings and baked, as *Apfelstrudel*, apple strudel; dessert
stufatino (It.) stew, as *Stufatino Firenze*, Florentine veal stew
stufato (It.) stewed meat, pot roast, as *Stufato di Manzo*, beef pot roast
succo (It.) juice, as *succo di pomodoro*, tomato juice
sucra, sucré (Fr.) sugared, sweet, as *sucreries*, sweets
susina (It.) plum
süss (Ger.) sweet, as *Süsser Wein*, sweet wine

T

tacchino (It.) turkey
tagliatelle (It.) noodles, as *Tagliatelle in Brodo*, noodles in broth
tarte (Fr.) tart, as *Tarte aux Cerises*, cherry tart
tartina (It.) sandwich
tartufi (It.) truffles
Taschenkrebs (Ger.) crabs
taureau (Fr.) steer, as *Taureau de Camargue, Cuit une Nuit et une Matin*, very slowly cooked beef ("night and day") with black olives and wine; esp. Provence
té (Sp.) tea, as *té débil*, weak tea; *té forte*, strong tea; *té helado*, iced tea
tè (It.) tea, as *tè debole*, weak tea; *tè forte*, strong tea; *té in ghiaccio*, iced tea

Tee (Ger.) tea, as *schwacher Tee*, weak tea; *starker Tee*, strong tea; *Eistee*, iced tea
ternera (Sp.) veal, as *Ternera con Berenjenas*, baked veal with eggplant
terrine (Fr.) potted meat, named for the earthenware pot in which it's cooked
tétras (Fr.) grouse
thé (Fr.) tea, as *thé faible*, weak tea; *thé fort*, strong tea; *thé glacé*, iced tea
Thunfisch (Ger.) tuna
timbale (Fr.) steamed, molded custard
tisane (Fr.) infusion of herbs, herb tea
tomate (Fr.) tomato, as *Tomates Farcies à la Provençale*, tomato stuffed with ground beef, onions, anchovies
tomate (Sp.) tomato
Tomaten (Ger.) tomatoes, as *Tomatensosse*, tomato sauce
tonno (It.) tuna
torrijas (Sp.) bread slices soaked in milk or wine, fried and covered with sugar and cinnamon, like American French toast
torrone (It.) nougat
torta (It.) pie, as *Torta di Prosciutto*, ham pie; also cake, *Torta di Crema*, layer cake
Torte (Ger.) cake, as *Schwarzwälder Kirschtorte*, a chocolate cake with sherry and whipped cream filling; esp. Black Forest
tortellini (It.) shell of dough filled with meat
torticas (Sp.) small rum cakes; esp. Seville
tortilla (Sp.) a round, thin cake of unleavened cornmeal bread
tournedos (Fr.) fillet steak, as *Tournedos à la Sauce Blanche à la Crème avec Truffes*, filet mignon with cream sauce and truffles
tourte (Fr.) raised pie with fish, meat or fruit inside, as *Tourte Lorraine*, veal-pork pie
tourtière (Fr.) pie dish; French Canadian, pork pie
tranche (Fr.) slice, as *Tranche de Veau et Cocombres*, veal slices with cucumbers
triglia (It.) red mullet, as *Triglia alla Livornese*, mullet, Leghorn style
tripaux (Fr.) stuffed mutton feet
tripe (Fr.) tripe, as *Tripe à la Mode Caen*, stuffed mutton tripe; esp. Provence
trippa (It.) tripe, as *Trippa alla Fiorentina*, tripe in meat sauce
trota (It.) trout
trucha (Sp.) trout
trufas (Sp.) truffles
truite (Fr.) trout, as *Truite en Bleu*, trout in vinegar
Truthuhn (Ger.) turkey

U

uccelletti (It.) strips of rolled, stuffed veal
uovo (It.) egg, as *Uova Fritte*, fried eggs

V

vaca (Sp.) cow
Valencienne (Fr.) dish served with rice
veau (Fr.) veal, as *Veau au Noix d'Acajou*, veal with cashew nuts
velouté (Fr.) smooth white sauce, based on chicken or veal stock
venaison (Fr.) venison
verdura (It., Sp.) vegetables
vert-pré (Fr.) grilled meat served with potatoes and watercress
viandes (Fr.) meats
vichyssoise (Fr.) leak and potato soup, served cold

vin (Fr.) wine, as *vin blanc, vin rouge*, white wine, red wine
vinaigre (Fr.) vinegar, as *vinaigrette* dressing, for salad, cooked vegetables, grilled meats
vitello (It.) veal, as *Vitello Tonnato*, leg of veal with tuna sauce
volailles (Fr.) poultry, as *Volailles à la Crème*, poultry in a cream sauce, butter and cognac
vongole (It.) clams of the small Mediterranean variety
Vorspeisen (Ger.) appetizers

W

Wacholderbranntwein (Ger.) gin
Wein (Ger.) wine, as *Weisswein, Rotwein*, white wine, red wine
Weinbergschnecken (Ger.) snails
Weinsuppe (Ger.) name for soups with wine as ingredient
Weintrauben (Ger.) grapes
Weiss (Ger.) white, as *Weisskohl*, white cabbage
Westfälischer Schinken (Ger.) Westphalian ham, cured and sliced thin, served cold
Wiener Schnitzel (Ger.) Viennese-style breaded veal cutlets

Z

zabaione, zabaglione (It.) dessert eggnog, solid or liquid, with wine
zanahoria (Sp.) carrot
Zitrone (Ger.) lemon, as *Tee mit einer Scheibe Zitrone*, tea with a slice of lemon
zucchero (It.) sugar
zucchino (It.) zucchini squash, as *Zucchini Ripieni*, stuffed zucchini
zumo (Sp.) juice
Zunge (Ger.) tongue, as *Zunge mit Meerrettich*, tongue with horseradish sauce
zuppa (It.) soup, as *Zuppa alla Cacciatora*, creamed meat soup
zuppa inglese (It.) not a soup; soft, rich, Roman cake
Zwetschgenknödel (Ger.) broiled or steamed dumplings with a plum in the center, a dessert

VINTAGE GUIDE

FRANCE

	Red Bordeaux	Sauternes	Red Burgundy	White Burgundy	Loire	Red Rhone	Champagne
1962	5	6	6			5	
1963	1	0	1			2	
1964	4	2	6			6	
1965	0	0	0			0	
1966	7	5	5			6	
1967	4	7	4			5	
1968	1	0	1			2	
1969	2	4	6	5	5	6	7
1970	7	7*	5	4	5	6	5
1971	6	6*	7	7	6	5	7
1972	3	3	5*	4	3	6	
1973	4	3	3	5	5	5	6
1974	3	1	3	5	6	4*	5
1975	7*	7*	2	5	5	4*	
1976	6*	4*	7*	6*	6	6*	6
1977	3	3	4	4	3	5*	
1978	7*	5*	7*	6	6	6*	4
1979	6*	5*	4*	5*	5*	5*	6

7=the Best   0=no good   *=recommended for laying down

	GERMANY		ITALY			PORTUGAL	CALIFORNIA	
	Rhine	Moselle	Barolo	Chianti Classico Riserva	Soave	Porto	Red	White
	3	3	6	6			5	
	2	2	3	1		7	5	
	5	5	7	6			5/6	
	0	0	6	4			4	
	4	4	1	4		6*	6	
	3	3	6	4		6*	5	
	2	2	4	6			6	
	5	5	5	6		3	3	3
	5	4	6	6		7*	7	5
	7	7	7	7			5	4/5
	3	3	1	2/3	4	4*	5/6	6
	5	5	4	3	5		6/7	6/7
	3	2	6/7	6/7	5		6/7	6/7
	5	7	6	6	6	7*	5	6
	7	6	4*	5	6		6/7	4/5
	4	4	4*	7*	6	7*	5	6
	5	5/6	7*	7*	5		5/6	6
	5	5	6*	6*	6*		5*	6*

WINE TASTING TERMS

Acetic or acescence: The smell or taste of vinegar (acetic acid).

Acid: Wine contains various acids. *Tartaric* gives freshness and zestiness; if too little the wine is dull, too much it is too tart. *Acetic* is the acid of vinegar and its presence indicates the wine is spoiling. *Malic* gives appley smells and tastes. *Citric* is often present and smells of lemons.

Aftertaste: The sensation in the mouth and nose remaining after the wine has been swallowed.

Alcohol: Grape sugar is converted by the yeast to alcohol, mainly ethyl alcohol. Alcohol is what gives the wine much of its body, its substance. Table wines range from 7%-14%; sherries and ports from 15%-20%.

Amabile: Italian designation for sweetness; the Spanish use DULCE and the French DOUX.

Aroma: The smell of young wines coming from the grape as opposed to the odors that develop in a wine after aging that are known as BOUQUET.

Astringent: The drying, mouth-puckering effect from a high tannin content. Not bitterness. Astringency usually softens and mellows with age.

Baked: A smell coming from very ripe grapes when the juice in the slightly shriveled grapes is caramelized.

Big: Full of flavor, body, alcohol, acidity. The opposite of THIN.

Bottle age: Unlike other beverages, wine changes after bottling and improves for a period, then declines. Those wines whose charm is freshness and fruitiness, such as Beaujolais and French Colombard, deteriorate from aging.

Brut: A champagne term meaning dry. It is without strict definition and is no guarantee of quality.

Character: The opposite of dullness. Used for wines with definite qualities.

Clean: Sound wine without any "off, foreign or unpleasant smells or tastes."

Corky: The smell of a bad cork. A term often used but the condition occurs very rarely.

Depth: Having levels of quality, the opposite of superficial.

Dry: The absence of sweetness, does not mean sour. Is a relative term. What is too sweet to some may be very dry to others.

Dumb: Undeveloped, often a wine in an "adolescent stage."

Extract: The essence of the grape which adds to the wine's body.

Fat: Fullness of body, usually full of glycerine and alcohol.

Finesse: Gracefulness, delicacy, distinguished character.

Firm: Positive in its characteristics, the opposite of FLABBY.

Flinty: An inexact term meaning steely. Often used with fine Chablis.

Fruity: Attractive, generalized smell of fruit, not necessarily of grapiness.

Grassy: The smell of grass or new-mown hay.

Hard: Severe tastes from high tannin and/or acid. Often mellows with time.

Limpid: Clear appearance.

Luscious: The balance of sweetness, fruitiness, ripeness.

Mellow: Mature, without rough edges, associated with age.

Musty: Due to poor barrels and often disappears within a few minutes after the wine is poured into the glass.

Oaky: Smell coming from oak barrels that is found in good white Burgundies (or Chardonnays) and in Red Bordeaux (also Cabernet Sauvignon).

Oxidized: Flat, stale, off-tastes or odors due to overexposure to air.

Round: Well-balanced, mature wine without raw edges of immaturity, without harshness.

Soft: Mellow, without roughness or hotness to the throat.

Sour: Excess acidity.
Strong: Powerful, alcoholic.
Supple: A combination of vigor and drinkability.
Sweet: High residual sugar content. Some wines without any sugar remaining have a sweetness coming from glycerol and nonfermentable sugars.
Tannin: Extract of the skin and stem of the grapes which causes puckering and drying of the mouth. Mainly in red wines.
Tart: Sharpness caused by high acidity. A relative term.
Taut: Severe tastes and mouth feels.
Thin: Lacking body, watery feel.
Vanillin: An extract from exposure to oak, smells like vanilla extract.
Vinosity: Having positive, winey character.
Volatile acidity: Present, to some extent, in most wines, but the excess indicates the first step in the production of vinegar.
Watery: Lacking fruit, extract, alcohol and acidity. After swallowing it leaves no aftertaste.
Woody: Undesirable tastes coming from too long contact with wood.

INDEX

BEST OF THE BEST

After our readers completed their ratings of America's Best Restaurants, we found a select group of restaurants that had high marks in all categories. In terms of ambience, food, service and wine, these restaurants are truly the "Best of the Best."

Ambria, Chicago
Ambrosia, Los Angeles
Anthony's, St. Louis
Anthony's Star of the Sea Room, San Diego
Bacchanal Room, Las Vegas
Benno's, Detroit
Bernard's, Los Angeles
Bertrand's, San Diego
Brenner's, Houston
Cafe Budapest, Boston
Cafe de France, St. Louis
Cafe Giovanni, Denver
Cafe Pacific, Dallas
Cafe Royal, Dallas
Casa Vecchia, Miami
Chanterelle, New York
Charlie's Cafe Exceptionale, Minneapolis
Chez Cary, Los Angeles
Chez Louis, St. Louis
Chez Michel, Honolulu
Chouette, Minneapolis
Claude's, New York
The Coach House, Denver
The Colony, Pittsburgh
Crabtree's, Baltimore
Crozier's, New Orleans
The Dinner Horn Country Inn, Kansas City
Ernie's, San Francisco
Footers, Denver
The Four Seasons, New York
The French Room, San Francisco
The Garland, Cleveland
Gerard's Relais de Lyon, Seattle
Giovanni's, Cleveland
Hyeholde, Pittsburgh
Jasper's, Kansas City
Jean-Claude, Dallas
John Dominis, Honolulu
La Caravelle, New York
La Côte Basque, New York
La Grenouille, New York
La Serre, Los Angeles
L'Auberge du Port, Cleveland
La Vieille Maison, Miami
Le Bec Fin, Philadelphia
Le Bistro, St. Louis

Le Cygne, New York
Le Français, Chicago
Le Lavandou, New York
Le Pavillon, Washington, D.C.
Le Restaurant, Los Angeles
L'Ermitage, Los Angeles
Le St. Germain, Los Angeles
L'Escoffier, Los Angeles
L'Etoile, San Francisco
Le Vallauris, Palm Springs
London Chop House, Detroit
L'Orangerie, Los Angeles
Lutèce, New York
Ma Maison, Los Angeles
Mansion on Turtle Creek, Dallas
Michael's, Los Angeles
Michel's at the Colony Surf, Honolulu
Nikolai's Roof, Atlanta
Oaxaca, Phoenix
The Palace, New York
Palace Court, Las Vegas
Pano's & Paul's, Atlanta
Peppercorn Duck Club, Kansas City
Perino's, Los Angeles
The Plum Room, Miami
The Prime Rib, Baltimore
The Quilted Giraffe, New York
Restaurant Duglass, Detroit
Simon's, Seattle
Stall 1043, Baltimore
Third Floor, Honolulu
Tio Pepe, Baltimore
Tony's, Houston
Tony's, St. Louis
Trader Vic's, Phoenix
"21" Club, New York

A

The Abacus, Chicago, *Chinese,* 50
The Abbey, Atlanta, *Continental,* 4
Acme Oyster House, New Orleans, *Seafood,* 246
Adriano's, Los Angeles, *Northern Italian,* 176
Adriatica, Seattle, *Mediterranean,* 396
Ah Wok, Detroit, *Chinese,* 112
A La Fourchette, New York, *French,* 262
Alameda Plaza Roof, Kansas City, *Continental,* 152
Al Baker's, St. Louis, *Italian/Continental,* 342
Albion's, Los Angeles, *French,* 176
Aldo's, Detroit, *Italian,* 112
Alejandro's, San Francisco, *Spanish/Mexican,* 370
Alexis, San Francisco, *Continental,* 370
Alex Tambellini's Wood Street Restaurant, Pittsburgh, *American/Italian,* 330
Alfredo's, New York, *Italian,* 262
Alfred's, San Francisco, *Italian,* 370
Alfred's European Restaurant, Honolulu, *Continental,* 126
Aliette's Bakery, Detroit, *French,* 112
Alouette, Chicago, *French,* 150
Alpine Village Inn, Las Vegas, *Swiss/German,* 166
Al's, St. Louis, *Italian,* 342
Ambria, Chicago, *French,* 50
Ambrosia, Los Angeles, *Continental,* 176
Amelia's, Los Angeles, *Italian,* 177
Amelio's, San Francisco, *Italian,* 371
The American, Kansas City, *American,* 152
The American Cafe, Washington, D.C., *American,* 410
The Anchorage, Minneapolis/St. Paul, *Seafood,* 232
Andre's Swiss Candies, Pastries & Tea Room, Kansas City, *Swiss,* 152
Angelo's, Dallas/Fort Worth, *Barbecue,* 86
Anna Kao's, Pittsburgh, *Chinese,* 330
Annie's Santa Fe, Kansas City, *Mexican,* 153
Another Season, Boston, *Continental,* 32
Anthony's, Atlanta, *Continental,* 4
Anthony's, St. Louis, *Continental,* 342
Anthony's Harborside, San Diego, *Seafood,* 342
Anthony's Pier 4, Boston, *Seafood,* 32
Anthony's Star of the Sea Room, San Diego, *Seafood,* 354
Antoine's, New Orleans, *Creole,* 246
Antonio's, Los Angeles, *Mexican,* 177
Apana, Washington, *Indian,* 410
Arnaud's, New Orleans, *Creole,* 246
Arnie's, Chicago, *Continental,* 51
Arnie's North, Chicago, *Continental,* 51
Arno's, Houston, *Northern Italian,* 140
Arthur's, Dallas/Fort Worth, *American,* 86
Arthur's Steak House, Philadelphia, *American,* 304
Assembly Steak & Fish, New York, *American/Seafood,* 262
The Athenian, Baltimore, *Greek,* 18
Athens Olympia, Boston, *Greek,* 32
Atlas Chinese Restaurant, Seattle, *Chinese,* 396
Auberge Suisse, New York, *Swiss,* 263
Aunt Fanny's Cabin, Atlanta, *Southern,* 4
Au Pere Jacques, Cleveland, *French,* 72
Au Petit Cafe, Los Angeles, *French,* 177
Au Provence, Cleveland, *French/Creole,* 72
Aux Delices, Los Angeles, *French,* 178
Avanti, Phoenix, *Italian,* 318
Avanti, Restaurant of Distinction, Phoenix, *Continental,* 318

Avenue One, Chicago, *American*, 51
A.V. Ristorante Italiano, Washington, D.C., *Italian*, 410

B

Bacchanal Room, Las Vegas, *Continental*, 166
Bagatelle, Dallas/Fort Worth, *Continental*, 86
Bagatelle, Los Angeles, *French*, 178
Bagwells 2424, Honolulu, *Continental*, 126
The Bakery, Chicago, *Continental*, 52
Balaban's, St. Louis, *Continental*, 343
Balaton, Cleveland, *Hungarian*, 72
Ballato's, New York, *Italian*, 263
Bamboo House, Baltimore, *Chinese*, 18
Barbetta, New York, *Italian*, 263
The Barn of Barrington, Chicago, *Continental*, 52
Basta Pasta, San Francisco, *Italian*, 371
Battista's Hole in the Wall, Las Vegas, *Italian*, 166
Bay Tower Room, Boston, *Continental*, 33
Beaudry's, Los Angeles, *Continental*, 178
Bel-Air Hotel, Los Angeles, *Continental*, 179
Belmont Pier, Los Angeles, *Seafood/Mediterranean*, 179
Ben Gross Restaurant, Pittsburgh, *Continental*, 330
Benihana Palace, New York, *Japanese*, 264
Benno's, Detroit, *Continental*, 113
Berardi & Son's, Denver, *Italian*, 100
The Berghoff, Chicago, *German*, 52
Bernard's, Los Angeles, *French*, 179
Bertrand's, San Diego, *French*, 354
The Big Four, San Francisco, *Continental*, 371
The Bijou, Detroit, *Continental*, 113
Binyons, Chicago, *American*, 53
The Bistro, Los Angeles, *Continental*, 180
Bistro Garden, Los Angeles, *Continental*, 180
Black Banana, Philadelphia, *French*, 304
Black Forest Inn, Minneapolis/St. Paul, *German*, 232
The Blackhawk, Chicago, *American*, 53
Blue Bell Inn, Philadelphia, *American*, 304
Blue Boar Inn, San Francisco, *French*, 372
Blue Fox, San Francisco, *Continental*, 372
Blue Hawaii, Honolulu, *Continental*, 126
The Blue Horse, Minneapolis/St. Paul, *International*, 232
Bon Ton Cafe, New Orleans, *Cajun*, 247
Bookbinder's 15th Street, Philadelphia, *Seafood*, 305
The Box Tree, New York, *French*, 264
The Brass Elephant, Baltimore, *Northern Italian*, 18
Brasserie, Dallas/Fort Worth, *Continental*, 87
Brasserie, New York, *French*, 264
Brasserie Pittsbourg, Seattle, *French*, 396
The Brass Key, Atlanta, *International*, 5
Brennan's, Dallas/Fort Worth, *Creole*, 87
Brennan's, Houston, *Creole*, 140
Brennan's, New Orleans, *Creole*, 247
Brennan's of Buckhead, Atlanta, *Creole*, 5
Brenner's, Houston, *American*, 140
Bristol Bar & Grill, Kansas City, *Seafood*, 153
The Broker Restaurant, Denver, *Continental*, 100
Broussard's, New Orleans, *Creole*, 247
Brussels Restaurant, New York, *French*, 265
Buckhorn Exchange, Denver, *American*, 100
Bud Bigelow's, Houston, *American*, 141
Bugatti, Atlanta, *Northern Italian*, 5

Bush Garden, Seattle, *Japanese,* 397
Buttonwood Tree Inn & Pub, Kansas City, *Continental,* 153

C

Cafe Argenteuil, New York, *French,* 265
Cafe Bohemia, Chicago, *American,* 53
Cafe Budapest, Boston, *Hungarian,* 33
Cafe Cappuccino, Pittsburgh, *Continental,* 331
Cafe Chauveron, Miami, *French,* 220
Cade de France, St. Louis, *French,* 343
Cafe des Artistes, Baltimore, *French,* 19
Cafe des Artistes, New York, *French,* 265
Cafe Europa, San Diego, *Continental,* 355
Cafe Four Oaks, Los Angeles, *American,* 180
Cafe Giovanni, Denver, *Italian/French,* 101
Cafe La Serre, Phoenix, *French,* 318
Cafe Pacific, Dallas/Fort Worth, *Seafood,* 87
Cafe Plaza, Boston, *Continental,* 33
Cafe Promenade, Boston, *Continental,* 34
Cafe Promenade, Denver, *Continental,* 101
Cafe Provençal, Chicago, *Country French,* 54
Cafe Royal, Dallas/Fort Worth, *French,* 88
Cafe San Martin, New York, *Continental,* 266
Cafe Stephen B's, Pittsburgh, *Eclectic,* 331
Calluad Restaurant, Dallas/Fort Worth, *French,* 88
Camellia Grill, New Orleans, *American,* 248
Camelot, Minneapolis/St. Paul, *Continental,* 233
Canlis, Honolulu, *American,* 127
Canlis, San Francisco, *American,* 372
Canlis, Seattle, *American,* 397
Cantina d'Italia, Washington, D.C., *Northern Italian,* 411
Cape Cod Room, Chicago, *Seafood,* 54
Capriccio, Baltimore, *Northern Italian,* 19
Capriccio, New York, *Northern Italian,* 266
Caravansary, San Francisco, *Middle Eastern,* 373
Caribbean Room, New Orleans, *Creole,* 248
Carl's Chop House, Detroit, *American,* 113
Carnelian Room, San Francisco, *Continental,* 373
The Carriage House, Dallas/Fort Worth, *Continental,* 88
Carson's — The Place for Ribs, Chicago, *Barbecue,* 54
Carvery, Washington, D.C., *French,* 411
Casa Brasil, New York, *Brazilian/Continental,* 266
Casamento's, New Orleans, *Creole,* 248
Casa Romero, Boston, *Mexican,* 34
Casa Vecchia, Miami, *Northern Italian,* 220
Casina Valadier, San Diego, *Italian/Continental,* 355
Cattlemen's Steak House, Dallas/Fort Worth, *American,* 89
Caucus Club, Detroit, *American,* 114
Cavalier, Honolulu, *Continental,* 127
Cellar in the Sky, New York, *French,* 267
Chalet Suisse, New York, *Swiss/Continental,* 267
Chambord, Los Angeles, *French,* 181
Champeau's Top of the "I," Honolulu, *French,* 127
Chanteclair, Los Angeles, *Continental,* 187
Chanterelle, New York, *French,* 267
Charley Brown's, Los Angeles, *American,* 181
Charley O's, New York, *Irish/American,* 268
Charley's Crab, Detroit, *Seafood,* 114
Charley's Eating & Drinking Saloon, Boston, *American,* 34
Charley's 517, Houston, *Continental,* 141
Charlie's Cafe Exceptionale, Minneapolis/St. Paul, *American,* 233

Chasen's, Los Angeles, *Continental,* 182
Chateaubriand, Dallas/Fort Worth, *Continental,* 89
Chateau Pyrenees, Denver, *Continental,* 101
The Chesapeake, Baltimore, *American,* 19
Chez Cary, Los Angeles, *Continental,* 182
Chez Claude, Seattle, *French,* 397
Chez Colette, Minneapolis/St. Paul, *French,* 233
Chez Helene, Los Angeles, *French Canadian,* 182
Chez Helene, New Orleans, *Soul/Creole,* 249
Chez Jay, Los Angeles, *French,* 183
Chez Leon, San Francisco, *French,* 373
Chez Louis, Phoenix, *French,* 319
Chez Louis, St. Louis, *French,* 343
Chez Michael, San Francisco, *French,* 374
Chez Michel, Honolulu, *French,* 128
Chez Panisse, San Francisco, *French/Californian,* 374
Chez Pascal, New York, *French,* 268
Chez Paul, Chicago, *French,* 55
Chez Vendôme, Miami, *French,* 220
Chianti, Los Angeles, *Northern Italian,* 183
Chiapparelli's, Baltimore, *Italian,* 20
The Chimney, Dallas/Fort Worth, *Austrian/Swiss,* 89
Chiquita's, Dallas/Fort Worth, *Mexican,* 90
Chouette, Minneapolis/St. Paul, *French,* 234
Christ Cella, New York, *American,* 268
Christian's, New Orleans, *Creole,* 249
Christian's Danish Inn, San Diego, *Scandinavian,* 355
Christine Lee's Gaslight, Miami, *Chinese,* 221
Christopher's, Pittsburgh, *Continental,* 331
The Chronicle, Los Angeles, *American,* 183
City Loan Pavillon, Seattle, *French,* 398
Claude's, New York, *French,* 269
Clos Normand, New York, *French,* 269
Club 41, Miami, *French,* 221
Coach & Six, Atlanta, *American,* 6
The Coach House, Denver, *Continental,* 102
The Coach House, New York, *American,* 269
The Coachman, San Francisco, *Continental,* 374
The Colony, Pittsburgh, *American,* 332
Colony Steak House, Kansas City, *American,* 154
Colorado Mine Company, Denver, *American,* 102
Commander's Palace, New Orleans, *Creole,* 249
The Commissary, Philadelphia, *International,* 305
The Common Plea, Pittsburgh, *Continental,* 332
The Company Inkwell, Washington, D.C., *French,* 411
The Consort, Chicago, *Continental,* 55
Conti Cross Keys Inn, Philadelphia, *American,* 305
Copley's, Boston, *Continental,* 35
Corinne Dunbar's, New Orleans, *Creole,* 250
The Cottage, Chicago, *Continental,* 55
The Country Fare Inn, Baltimore, *Continental,* 20
The Country Place, Atlanta, *French,* 6
Courtlandt's, Houston, *Continental,* 141
The Courtyard, Dallas/Fort Worth, *Continental,* 90
The Cove, Los Angeles, *Continental,* 184
Coventry Forge Inn, Philadelphia, *French,* 306
Crabtree's, Baltimore, *Continental,* 20
Crêpe de Paris, Seattle, *French,* 398
Cricket's, Chicago, *Continental,* 56
Crisfield's, Washington, D.C., *Seafood,* 412
Crozier's, New Orleans, *French,* 250
Csiko's, Washington, D.C., *Hungarian,* 412
Cunetto House of Pasta, St. Louis, *Italian,* 344

Cye's Rivergate, Miami, *American*, 221
Czech Pavillion, New York, *Czech*, 270

D

Danny's, Baltimore, *Continental*, 21
Dan Tana's, Los Angeles, *Northern Italian*, 184
Dante, Los Angeles, *Northern Italian*, 184
Dardanelles, New York, *American*, 270
Dar Maghreb, Los Angeles, *Moroccan*, 185
David K's, New York, *Chinese*, 270
Davio's, Boston, *Italian*, 35
De Bergerac, St. Louis, *French*, 344
De Foro, Pittsburgh, *French/Italian*, 332
Déjà-Vu, Philadelphia, *French*, 306
Delices de France, San Francisco, *French*, 375
The Depot, Miami, *American*, 222
Dertad's, Boston, *Continental*, 35
Deux Cheminées, Philadelphia, *French*, 306
Deville's on Broadway, Seattle, *French*, 398
Diamond Lil's, Las Vegas, *American*, 167
Dining Pavillon, Honolulu, *International*, 128
Dini's Sea Grill, Boston, *Seafood*, 36
The Dinner Horn Country Inn, Kansas City, *American*, 154
Diplomat, Atlanta, *Continental*, 6
Dodin-Bouffant, New York, *French*, 271
Dome of the Sea, Las Vegas, *Seafood*, 167
Dominic's, St. Louis, *Italian*, 344
Dominique's, Washington, D.C., *French*, 412
Don's Seafood Restaurant & Steakhouse, Houston, *Seafood/Cajun*, 142
Doro's, Chicago, *Northern Italian*, 56
Doros, San Francisco, *Continental*, 375
Doug Lee's Asia House, Phoenix, *Oriental*, 319
The Down Under, Miami, *Continental*, 222
Dudley's, Denver, *French*, 102
Duff's, St. Louis, *International*, 345
Durant's Fine Foods, Phoenix, *American*, 319
Durgin Park, Boston, *American*, 36

E

The Early American Room, Detroit, *American*, 114
Earth by April, Cleveland, *Seafood/Vegetarian*, 73
The Egg and the Eye, Los Angeles, *Continental*, 185
El Cholo, Los Angeles, *Mexican*, 185
El Chorro Lodge, Phoenix, *American*, 320
El Gaucho, Seattle, *American*, 399
Eli's The Place for Steak, Chicago, *American*, 56
El Padrino, Los Angeles, *Continental*, 156
El Parador Cafe, New York, *Mexican*, 271
The Elsah Landing, St. Louis, *American*, 345
El Tio Pepe, Washington, D.C., *Spanish*, 413
El Torito, San Diego, *Mexican*, 356
Embers, Miami, *American*, 222
Emerson St. East, Denver, *American*, 103
Emile's Swiss Affair, San Francisco, *French/Swiss*, 375
Emilios, Los Angeles, *Italian*, 186
Emil-Lene's Sirloin House, Denver, *American*, 103
Empress of China, San Francisco, *Chinese*, 376
En Brochette, Los Angeles, *International*, 186

Entourage, Los Angeles, *French,* 187
Enzio's, Chicago, *Northern Italian,* 57
Ernie's, San Francisco, *French,* 376
Etienne's, Phoenix, *French,* 320
Eugene's, Chicago, *Continental,* 57
Ewald's, Dallas/Fort Worth, *Continental,* 90

F

Fagleysville Country Hotel, Philadelphia, *International,* 307
Fanny's World Famous Restaurant, Chicago, *American/Italian,* 57
Farmer's Daughter, Chicago, *International,* 58
Felix's, New Orleans, *Seafood,* 250
Fiasco, Los Angeles, *Continental,* 187
The 57 Restaurant, Boston, *American/Continental,* 36
Finch's, Phoenix, *International,* 320
The Fine Affair, Los Angeles, *Continental,* 187
Fiori, Baltimore, *Italian/Continental,* 21
The Fish Market, Philadelphia, *Seafood,* 307
Five Crowns, Los Angeles, *Continental,* 188
The 510 Haute Cuisine, Minneapolis/St. Paul, *Continental,* 234
Flagstaff House, Denver, *Continental,* 103
The Flame Room, Minneapolis/St. Paul, *Continental,* 234
Fleur de Lys, San Francisco, *French,* 376
Florentine Room, Chicago, *Northern Italian,* 58
Fond de la Tour, Chicago, *French,* 58
Food Among the Flowers, Miami, *Continental,* 223
Footers, Denver, *Northern Italian,* 104
Forepaugh's, Minneapolis/St. Paul, *Continental,* 235
The Forge, Miami, *American,* 223
Foulard's, Houston, *French,* 142
Fournou's Ovens, San Francisco, *Continental,* 377
The Four Seasons, New York, *International,* 271
Fox and Hounds, Detroit, *American,* 115
Francesca's, Boston, *Italian,* 37
François, Los Angeles, *Continental,* 188
French Connection, Cleveland, *French,* 73
The French Restaurant, Atlanta, *French,* 7
The French Room, San Francisco, *Continental,* 377
Frog, Philadelphia, *International,* 307
Fuji-Ya, Minneapolis/St. Paul, *Japanese,* 234
F.X. McRory's Steak, Chop & Oyster House, Seattle, *American,* 399

G

Gage & Tollner, New York, *Seafood,* 272
Gaido's, Houston, *Seafood,* 142
Galatoire's, New Orleans, *French,* 251
Gallagher, Boston, *French/American,* 37
The Gandy Dancer, Detroit, *Seafood,* 115
Gannon's, Minneapolis/St. Paul, *American,* 234
Garcia's del Este, Phoenix, *Mexican,* 321
The Garden, Philadelphia, *Continental,* 308
The Garland, Cleveland, *French/Italian,* 73
Gatti, Miami, *Northern Italian/Continental,* 223
Gaylord, New York, *North Indian,* 272
Gaylord India Restaurant, San Francisco, *Indian,* 377
Gene & Gabe's, Atlanta, *Northern Italian,* 7
George's Specialties, San Francisco, *Russian,* 378

Gerard's Relais de Lyon, Seattle, *French,* 399
Germaine's, Washington, D.C., *Oriental,* 413
Giambelli 50th, New York, *Italian,* 272
Gianotti's, Chicago, *Italian,* 59
The Ginger Man, Los Angeles, *American,* 188
Giovanni's, Cleveland, *Continental,* 74
Giovanni's on the Hill, St. Louis, *Italian,* 345
Giulio's, San Diego, *Northern Italian,* 356
Giuseppe!, Los Angeles, *Italian,* 189
Gladstone's 4 Fish, Los Angeles, *Seafood,* 189
The Glass Door, Phoenix, *Continental,* 321
Gloucester House, New York, *Seafood,* 273
Gold Coin, New York, *Chinese,* 273
The Golden Bowl, Cleveland, *Italian,* 74
Golden Eagle, Phoenix, *Continental,* 321
The Golden Mushroom, Detroit, *Continental,* 115
The Golden Ox, Kansas City, *American,* 154
Golden Palace, Washington, D.C., *Chinese,* 413
Golden Steer Steakhouse, Las Vegas, *American,* 167
The Gold Room, Phoenix, *Continental,* 322
Gordon, Chicago, *Continental,* 59
Grand Concourse, Pittsburgh, *Seafood,* 333
Grant Grill, San Diego, *American,* 356
Grape, Dallas/Fort Worth, *Continental,* 91
Greek Islands, Chicago, *Greek,* 59
The Greenhouse, Los Angeles, *Continental,* 189
The Green Street Cafe, New York, *Continental,* 273
Grison's Steak House, San Francisco, *American,* 378
Guadalajara, Dallas, *Mexican,* 91
Guarino's, Cleveland, *Italian,* 74
Guido's, Los Angeles, *Northern Italian,* 190

H

Hala Terrace, Honolulu, *International,* 128
Hal's Mid-Mediterranean, Atlanta, *Hungarian,* 7
Hampton's, Los Angeles, *American,* 190
Hanohano Room, Honolulu, *Continental,* 129
Harry's Bar & American Grill, Los Angeles, *Northern Italian/American,* 190
Harry Starker's, Kansas City, *American,* 155
Harvey House, Baltimore, *American,* 21
Harvey's, Washington, D.C., *Seafood,* 414
Haussner's, Baltimore, *German/Seafood,* 22
Heck's Cafe, Cleveland, *Continental,* 75
Henry VIII, St. Louis, *Continental,* 346
Henry's Off Broadway, Seattle, *Continental,* 400
Hereford House, Kansas City, *American,* 155
The Hermitage, Boston, *Continental,* 37
Hersh's Orchard Inn, Baltimore, *Continental,* 22
Hisae's Place, New York, *Continental/Oriental,* 274
Hobbit Hole, Houston, *Vegetarian,* 143
Hob Nob Hill, San Diego, *American,* 357
Hollenden Tavern, Cleveland, *American,* 75
Hong Kong, San Francisco, *Chinese,* 378
The Houndstooth, Boston, *Continental,* 38
House of Lords, Las Vegas, *Continental,* 168
Hugo's, Atlanta, *Continental,* 8
Hugo's Rotisserie, Pittsburgh, *Continental,* 333
Hugo's Window Box, Houston, *Continental,* 143
Hunam, New York, *Chinese,* 274
Hunan, San Francisco, *Chinese,* 379

The Hungry Farmer, Denver, *American,* 104
Hunter's Hollow Taverne, Cleveland, *Continental,* 75
Hyeholde, Pittsburgh, *Continental,* 333
Hyotan Nippon, New York, *Japanese,* 274
Hy's Steak House, Honolulu, *Continental,* 129

I

Ianuzzi, Phoenix, *Italian,* 322
Il Gallo Nero, Philadelphia, *Northern Italian,* 308
Il Giardino, Washington, D.C., *Northern Italian,* 414
Il Monello, New York, *Italian,* 275
Il Nido, New York, *Northern Italian,* 275
Il Vagabondo, New York, *Northern Italian,* 275
Imperial Palace, Kansas City, *Chinese,* 155
Imperial Palace, San Francisco, *Chinese,* 379
The Inn at Fowler's Mill, Cleveland, *Continental,* 76
Iron Gate, Cleveland, *Continental,* 76
The Iron Horse, San Francisco, *Continental,* 379
Italian Gardens, Kansas City, *Italian,* 156

J

Jack's, San Francisco, *French,* 380
Jacqueline's, Washington, D.C., *French,* 414
Jacques Seafood, Detroit, *Seafood/Continental,* 116
Jake O'Shaughnessey's, Seattle, *American,* 400
James Tavern, Cleveland, *American,* 76
Japan Inn, Washington, D.C., *Japanese,* 415
Jasper's, Kansas City, *Continental,* 156
Javier's, Dallas/Fort Worth, *Mexican,* 91
Jax Cafe, Minneapolis/St. Paul, *Seafood/American,* 236
Jax of Golden Valley, Minneapolis/St. Paul, *American,* 236
Jean-Claude, Dallas/Fort Worth, *French,* 92
Jean Claude's Cafe, Baltimore, *French,* 22
Jean Pierre, Washington, D.C., *French,* 415
Jefferson Avenue Boarding House, St. Louis, *American,* 346
Jess & Jim's, Kansas City, *American,* 156
Jimmy's, Los Angeles, *French,* 191
Jimmy's Harborside, Boston, *Seafood,* 38
Jimmy's Place, Chicago, *Continental,* 60
Jim's Garage, Detroit, *Continental,* 116
Jim's Steak House, Cleveland, *American,* 77
The Jockey Club, Washington, D.C., *Continental,* 415
Joe & Rose Restaurant, New York, *Italian,* 276
Joe Dale's Cajun House, Atlanta, *Cajun,* 8
Joe Muer's, Detroit, *Seafood,* 116
Joe's Stone Crab, Miami, *Seafood,* 224
Joe T. Garcia's, Dallas/Fort Worth, *Mexican,* 92
John Dominis, Honolulu, *Seafood,* 129
John Eager Howard Room, Baltimore, *American,* 23
John Tarantino's, San Diego, *Italian/Seafood,* 357
Jonah and the Whale, Seattle, *Continental,* 400
Jovan, Chicago, *French,* 60
Joyce Chen Restaurant, Boston, *Chinese,* 38
Jozef's, Dallas/Fort Worth, *Seafood,* 92

K

Kaleidoscope, Miami, *Continental,* 224
Kan's, San Francisco, *Chinese,* 380

Kaphan's, Houston, *American*, 143
Karson's Inn, Baltimore, *American*, 23
Kee Joon's Cuisine of China, San Francisco, *Chinese*, 380
Keg & Quarter, Cleveland, *Continental*, 77
Kemoll's, St. Louis, *Italian*, 346
The King's Contrivance, Baltimore, *French*, 23
Kirby's Charcoal Steaks, Dallas/Fort Worth, *American*, 93
Kirin, San Francisco, *Chinese/Korean*, 381
Kitcho, New York, *Japanese*, 276
Klein's, Pittsburgh, *Hungarian*, 334
Knoll's Black Forest Inn, Los Angeles, *German*, 191
Kobe Japanese Steak House, Honolulu, *Japanese*, 130
Kozlak's Royal Oak, Minneapolis/St. Paul, *American*, 236
K-Paul's, New Orleans, *Creole/Cajun*, 251

L

La Bella Fontana, Los Angeles, *Continental*, 191
La Bibliothèque, New York, *French*, 276
La Bonne Auberge, Kansas City, *French*, 157
La Bonne Auberge, San Francisco, *French*, 381
La Bourgogne, San Francisco, *French*, 381
Labuznik, Seattle, *Central European*, 401
La Camargue, Philadelphia, *French*, 308
La Caravelle, New York, *French*, 277
La Cave, Palm Springs, *French*, 214
La Champagne, Phoenix, *French*, 322
La Chaumière, Phoenix, *French*, 323
La Chaumine, San Diego, *French*, 357
La Cheminée, Chicago, *French*, 60
La Cocotte, New York, *French*, 277
La Colombe d'Or, New York, *French Provincial*, 277
La Côte Basque, New York, *French*, 278
La Dolce Vita, Los Angeles, *Italian*, 192
La Famiglia, Los Angeles, *Northern Italian*, 192
La Famiglia, Philadelphia, *Italian*, 309
La Fontaine, Chicago, *French*, 61
La Fontanella, Denver, *Italian*, 104
La Gauloise, New York, *French*, 278
La Goulue, New York, *French*, 278
La Grange, Los Angeles, *French*, 192
La Grenouille, New York, *French*, 279
La Grotta, Atlanta, *Northern Italian*, 8
La Hacienda de los Morales, Houston, *Continental*, 144
L'Aiglon, New York, *French*, 279
La Louisiane, New Orleans, *Creole*, 251
La Maison des Pescadoux, San Diego, *French/Seafood*, 358
La Masia, Los Angeles, *Spanish*, 193
La Méditerranée, Kansas City, *French*, 157
La Méditerranée, San Diego, *French*, 358
La Mère Duquesne, San Francisco, *French*, 382
La Mirabelle, San Francisco, *French*, 382
Land's End, Los Angeles, *Seafood/French*, 193
La Normande, Pittsburgh, *French*, 334
La Panetière, Philadelphia, *French*, 309
La Petite Ferme, New York, *French*, 279
La Petite Marmite, New York, *French*, 280
La Polonaise, Los Angeles, *Basque/French*, 193
La Provence, New Orleans, *French*, 252
La Résidence, New York, *French*, 280
La Rotisserie, Detroit, *International*, 117
La Scala, Los Angeles, *Italian*, 194
Las Casuelas Nuevas, Palm Springs, *Mexican*, 214

La Serre, Los Angeles, *French,* 194
La Terrasse, Philadelphia, *French,* 309
La Terrasse, Minneapolis/St. Paul, *French,* 237
La Terrasse, San Francisco, *French,* 382
La Toque, Los Angeles, *French,* 194
La Truffe, Philadelphia, *French,* 310
La Tulipe, New York, *French,* 280
L'Auberge Bretonne, St. Louis, *French,* 347
L'Auberge Chez François, Washington, D.C., *French,* 416
L'Auberge du Port, Cleveland, *French,* 77
L'Aubergue, Philadelphia, *French,* 310
Laurent, New York, *French,* 281
Lautrec, Philadelphia, *French,* 310
La Vieille Maison, Miami, *French,* 224
Lawry's The Prime Rib, Chicago, *American,* 61
Lawry's The Prime Rib, Los Angeles, *American,* 195
Le Bagatelle, Washington, D.C., *French,* 416
Le Bastille, Chicago, *French,* 61
Le Beau Lieu, Philadelphia, *Continental,* 311
Le Bec Fin, Philadelphia, *French,* 311
Le Bistro, St. Louis, *French,* 347
Le Bocage, Boston, *French,* 39
Le Bon, Honolulu, *French,* 130
Le Cafe de Paris, Honolulu, *French,* 131
Le Cafe Royal, Minneapolis/St. Paul, *French,* 237
Le Carrousel, Kansas City, *Continental,* 156
Le Carrousel, Minneapolis/St. Paul, *Continental,* 237
Le Cellier, Los Angeles, *French,* 195
Le Central, San Francisco, *French,* 383
Le Chantilly, New York, *French,* 281
Lechner's Gourmet Restaurant, Boston, *German,* 39
Le Cirque, New York, *French/Continental,* 287
Le Club, San Francisco, *French,* 383
Le Cordon Bleu, Miami, *French,* 225
Le Coup de Fusil, New York, *French,* 282
Le Cygne, New York, *French,* 282
Le Cyrano, San Francisco, *French,* 383
Le Dôme, Los Angeles, *French,* 195
Le Dôme of the Four Seasons, Miami, *Continental,* 225
Leeann Chin, Minneapolis/St. Paul, *Chinese,* 238
Le Festival, Chicago, *French,* 62
Le Festival, Miami, *French,* 225
Le Fontainebleau, San Diego, *Continental,* 358
Le Français, Chicago, *French,* 62
Legal Seafoods, Boston, *Seafood,* 39
Le Gaulois, Washington. D.C., *French,* 416
Le Lavandou, New York, *French,* 282
Le Lion d'Or, Washington, D.C., *French,* 417
Lelli's Inn, Detroit, *Northern Italian,* 117
Le Madrigal, New York, *French,* 283
Le Manoir, New York, *French,* 283
Le Mignon, Chicago, *Continental,* 62
Le Mont, Pittsburgh, *Continental,* 334
Leonello's, Cleveland, *Continental,* 78
Le Parisien, Miami, *French,* 226
Le Pavillon, Washington, D.C., *French,* 417
Le Perigord, New York, *French,* 283
Le Perigord-Park, New York, *French,* 284
Le Perroquet, Chicago, *French,* 63
Le Petit Moulin, Los Angeles, *French,* 196
Le Plaisir, New York, *French/Eclectic,* 284
Le Pot au Feu, San Francisco, *French,* 384
Le Profile (T. Michael's), Denver, *French,* 105

Le Provençal, Seattle, *French,* 401
Le Provençal, Washington, D.C., *French,* 417
Le Relais, New York, *French,* 284
Le Restaurant, Los Angeles, *French,* 196
L'Ermitage, Los Angeles, *French,* 196
Le Ruth's, New Orleans, *Creole,* 252
Le St. Germain, Los Angeles, *French,* 197
Le Saint-Michel, Los Angeles, *French,* 197
Le Sanglier, Los Angeles, *French,* 197
L'Escargot, Chicago, *French,* 63
L'Escargot, New York, *French,* 285
L'Escargot, San Diego, *French,* 359
L'Escoffier, Los Angeles, *French,* 198
L'Espalier, Boston, *French,* 40
Les Pyrénées, Los Angeles, *French,* 198
Les Quatre Amis, Minneapolis/St. Paul, *French,* 238
Les Saisons, Dallas/Fort Worth, *French,* 93
Le Steak, New York, *French/American,* 285
Les Trois Mousquetaires, Miami, *French,* 226
Le Tastevin, Seattle, *French,* 401
Le Titi de Paris, Chicago, *French,* 63
L'Etoile, Los Angeles, *French,* 198
L'Etoile, San Francisco, *French,* 384
Le Trianon, San Francisco, *French,* 384
Le Vallauris, Palm Springs, *French,* 215
Le Veau d'Or, New York, *French,* 285
Le Vivoir, San Francisco, *French,* 385
Lew Mitchell's Orient Express, Los Angeles, *Chinese/American,* 199
The Lexington, Minneapolis/St. Paul, *American,* 238
Liaison, San Francisco, *French/Italian,* 385
Library, Buttery & Pub, Las Vegas, *Continental,* 168
Lillie Langtry, Las Vegas, *Chinese,* 168
Lily's of Boston, Boston, *French,* 40
Lobster Pot, Kansas City, *Seafood,* 158
Locke-Ober Cafe, Boston, *Continental,* 40
London Chop House, Detroit, *American,* 117
L'Orangerie, Los Angeles, *French,* 199
L'Orangerie, San Francisco, *French,* 385
Lord Fletcher Inn, Palm Springs, *English,* 215
Los Feliz Inn, Los Angeles, *Continental,* 199
Los Olivos Mexican Patio, Phoenix, *Mexican,* 323
Louis XVI, New Orleans, *French,* 252
Louis Tambellini's, Pittsburgh, *American/Italian/Seafood,* 335
Lowell Inn, Minneapolis/St. Paul, *American/Swiss,* 239
Lubach's, San Diego, *Continental,* 359
Luchow's, New York, *German,* 286
Lunt Avenue Marble Club, Phoenix, *American,* 323
Lutèce, New York, *French,* 286

M

Madame Romaine de Lyon, New York, *French,* 286
Madame Wu's Garden, Los Angeles, *Chinese,* 200
Maile, Honolulu, *Continental,* 131
Maison Marconi, Baltimore, *Italian,* 24
Maison Pierre, New Orleans, *Creole,* 253
Maison Robert, Boston, *French,* 41
Maldonado's, Los Angeles, *Continental,* 200
Ma Maison, Los Angeles, *French,* 200
Mamounia, San Francisco, *Moroccan,* 386
Mancuso's, Phoenix, *Northern Italian/French,* 324
The Mandarin, Los Angeles, *Chinese,* 201

The Mandarin, San Francisco, *Chinese,* 386
Mandarin Garden, San Diego, *Chinese,* 359
Mandarin House, San Diego, *Chinese,* 360
Mandarin Palace, Honolulu, *Chinese,* 131
Mansion on Turtle Creek, Dallas/Fort Worth, *American,* 93
Mario's, Dallas/Fort Worth, *Italian,* 94
Mario's, Detroit, *Italian,* 118
Market Street Exhange, Cleveland, *International,* 78
Marquis Room, Minneapolis/St. Paul, *French,* 239
Marrakesh, Los Angeles, *Moroccan,* 201
Marti's, New Orleans, *Creole,* 253
Masson's Restaurant Français, New Orleans, *French,* 253
Mataam Fez, Denver, *Moroccan,* 105
Matteo's, Honolulu, *Italian,* 132
Maureen, Philadelphia, *French,* 311
Maurice et Charles Bistrot, San Francico, *French,* 386
Mauro's, Los Angeles, *Italian,* 201
Maximilien in the Market, Seattle, *French,* 402
Maxim's, Houston, *French,* 144
Maxim's de Paris, Chicago, *French,* 64
Maxwell's Plum, New York, *Continental,* 287
McKinnon's Louisiane, Atlanta, *Creole,* 9
McNally Doyle Red Fox Inn, Cleveland, *Continental,* 78
Medium Rare, Palm Springs, *American,* 215
Mekong, Honolulu, *Thai,* 132
Melvyn's, Palm Springs, *Continental,* 216
Michael's, Los Angeles, *French,* 202
Michel Richard, Los Angeles, *French,* 202
Michel's at the Colony Surf, Honolulu, *French,* 132
The Midnight Sun, Atlanta, *Scandinavian,* 9
Mikado, St. Louis, *Japanese,* 347
The Mikado, Seattle, *Japanese,* 402
Mikado, Washington, D.C., *Japanese,* 418
Mille Fleurs, San Diego, *French,* 360
Milton Inn, Baltimore, *Continental,* 24
Ming's Garden, San Diego, *Chinese,* 360
Mirabeau, Seattle, *French,* 402
Mrs. Malia's, Seattle, *American,* 403
Mister A's, San Diego, *Continental,* 361
Mr. Chow, Los Angeles, *Chinese/Continental,* 202
Mr. Chow's, New York, *Chinese/Continental,* 287
Mr. Lee's, New York, *International,* 287
Mr. Peppe, Dallas, *French,* 94
Modern Gourmet, Boston, *French,* 41
Modesto Lanzone's, San Francisco, *Italian,* 387
Mon Ami, San Diego, *French,* 361
The Money Tree, Detroit, *Continental,* 118
Mon Grenier, Los Angeles, *French,* 203
Mon Petit, Denver, *French,* 105
Monsignore II, New York, *Italian,* 288
The Montpelier, Washington, D.C., *International,* 418
Morgan's, Philadelphia, *Mediterranean,* 312
Morton's, Los Angeles, *Continental,* 203
Mosca's, New Orleans, *Italian,* 254
Moustache Cafe, Los Angeles, *Continental,* 203
Muffuletta, Minneapolis/St. Paul, *Northern Italian/Creole,* 239
Murray's, Minneapolis/St. Paul, *Continental,* 240
Musso & Frank Grill, Los Angeles, *Continental,* 204

N

Nakato, Atlanta, *Japanese,* 9
Nanni, New York, *Italian,* 288

Nanni al Valletto, New York, *Italian,* 288
Nantucket Cove, St. Louis, *Seafood,* 348
Narsai's, San Francisco, *French/Mediterranean,* 387
Navarre's, Phoenix, *Continental,* 324
The New French Cafe, Minneapolis/St. Paul, *French,* 240
New Hellas Cafe, Detroit, *Greek,* 118
New Meadow Grill, Pittsburgh, *Seafood/Italian,* 335
New River Storehouse, Miami, *Caribbean,* 226
New York Spaghetti House, Cleveland, *Italian,* 79
Nick's Fishmarket, Chicago, *Seafood,* 64
Nick's Fishmarket, Honolulu, *Seafood,* 133
Nick's Fishmarket, Los Angeles, *Seafood,* 204
Nick's Supper Club, Las Vegas, *Continental,* 169
Nicola Paone, New York, *Italian,* 289
Nikolai's, Roof, Atlanta, *French/Russian,* 10
9 Knox Street, Boston, *English,* 41
The Ninety-Fifth, Chicago, *Continental,* 64
Nino's, Pittsburgh, *Continental,* 335
Nino's, San Diego, *Northern Italian,* 361
Nino's Place at Maître Jacques, Boston, *Continental,* 42
Nippon, New York, *Japanese,* 289
No Name Restaurant, Boston, *Seafood,* 42
Normandy French Restaurant, Denver, *French,* 106
Norman's, Pittsburgh, *American,* 336
North Beach Restaurant, San Francisco, *Italian,* 387

O

Oak Tree, San Diego, *American,* 362
Oaxaca, Phoenix, *Mexican,* 324
Olde Obrycki's Crab House, Baltimore, *Seafood,* 24
Old Europe, Washington, D.C., *Continental,* 418
Old Original Bookbinder's, Philadelphia, *Seafood,* 312
Old Swiss House, Dallas, *Continental,* 94
Old Trieste, San Diego, *Italian,* 362
Old Vinings Inn, Atlanta, *Continental,* 10
The Old Warsaw (La Vieille Varsovie), Dallas/Fort Worth,
    French, 95
The Olive Tree, Kansas City, *Mediterranean,* 158
Ondine, San Francisco, *French,* 388
Orangerie, Phoenix, *Continental,* 325
Orion Room, Minneapolis/St. Paul, *Continental,* 240
Orlando-Orsini, Los Angeles, *Italian,* 204
Orsini's, New York, *Italian,* 289
Oscar Taylor's, Phoenix, *American,* 325
The Other Place, Phoenix, *American,* 325
The Oyster Bar & Restaurant, New York, *Seafood,* 290

P

Pacific Dining Car, Los Angeles, *American,* 205
The Palace, New York, *French,* 290
Palace Arms, Denver, *American,* 106
Palace Court, Las Vegas, *French,* 169
The Palm, Los Angeles, *American,* 205
Palm, New York, *American,* 290
Panache, New York, *French,* 291
Pan Asia, Cleveland, *Chinese,* 79
Pano's & Paul's, Atlanta, *Continental,* 10
Papadakis Taverna, Los Angeles, *Greek,* 205
Papillon, Dallas/Fort Worth, *Continental,* 95
Paprikas Fono, San Francisco, *Hungarian,* 388
The Paradise Cafe, Chicago, *Continental,* 65

Parioli Romanissimo, New York, *Italian,* 291
Parker's Dining Room, Boston, *Continental,* 42
Park Schenley, Pittsburgh, *Continental,* 336
Parthenon, Cleveland, *Greek,* 79
Pascal's Manale, New Orleans, *Italian/Seafood,* 254
Pasquinel's, Denver, *Continental,* 106
Patrico's, Kansas City, *Mexican,* 158
Patry's, Dallas/Fort Worth, *French,* 95
Patsy's, New York, *Italian,* 291
Paul Bhalla's Cuisine of India, Los Angeles, *Indian,* 206
Pearl of the Orient, Cleveland, *Chinese,* 80
Pearl's, New York, *Chinese,* 292
The Peasant Uptown, Atlanta, *French,* 11
Peerce's Downtown, Baltimore, *Continental,* 25
Peerce's Plantation, Baltimore, *Continental,* 25
Pen & Pencil, New York, *American,* 292
Peppercorn Duck Club, Kansas City, *Continental,* 159
Peppone, Los Angeles, *Italian,* 206
Perino's, Los Angeles, *Continental,* 206
Pernicano's Casa di Baffi, San Diego, *Italian/Continental,* 362
Perry's, San Francisco, *American,* 388
Petite Auberge, Atlanta, *French,* 11
Philips Supper House, Las Vegas, *Continental,* 169
Phil Lehr's Steakery, San Francisco, *American,* 389
Pierre's Le Bistro, Phoenix, *French,* 326
Pierre's Quorum, Denver, *French,* 107
Pier W, Cleveland, *Seafood,* 80
Pillar House, Boston, *American,* 43
The Pimlico Hotel, Baltimore, *International,* 25
Pine Brook Inn, San Francisco, *Continental,* 389
The Pines of Rome, Washington, D.C., *Italian,* 419
Piret's Charcuterie, San Diego, *French,* 363
Pisces, San Diego, *Seafood,* 363
Pittypat's Porch, Atlanta, *Southern,* 11
Plaza III, Kansas City, *American,* 159
Pleasant Peasant, Atlanta, *French,* 12
The Plum Room, Miami, *French,* 227
Poli's, Pittsburgh, *Seafood,* 336
Polo Lounge, Los Angeles, *Continental,* 207
Pontchartrain Wine Cellars, Detroit, *Continental,* 119
Port St. Louis, St. Louis, *Seafood,* 348
Port Tack, Las Vegas, *Seafood,* 170
Pottery Steakhouse, Honolulu, *American,* 133
The Prime Rib, Baltimore, *American,* 26
The Prime Rib, Washington, D.C., *American,* 419
Prince Hamlet, Miami, *Danish,* 226
Princess Garden, Kansas City, *Chinese,* 159
Proud Peacock, Honolulu, *Coantinental,* 133
The Pump Room, Chicago, *Continental,* 65
Pyramid Room, Dallas/Fort Worth, *French,* 96

Q

The Quilted Giraffe, New York, *French,* 292
Quo Vadis, New York, *French,* 293

R

Raffaele's, St. Louis, *Italian,* 348
Raga, New York, *Indian,* 293
Raimondo's, Miami, *Italian,* 226
The Rainbow Room & Grill, New York, *Continental,* 293
Raintree, Cleveland, *Continental,* 80

Rangoon Racquet Club, Los Angeles, *Continental,* 207
The Raphael, Kansas City, *American/Seafood,* 160
Raphael, New York, *French,* 294
Ray's Boathouse, Seattle, *Seafood,* 403
The Red Lion, Houston, *British,* 144
Red Onion, New Orleans, *Continental,* 254
The Redwood, Pittsburgh, *French/Italian,* 337
Regency Room, Las Vegas, *French,* 170
René Pujol, New York, *French,* 294
Restaurant Duglass, Detroit, *French,* 119
Restaurant Jonathan, New Orleans, *Creole/Seafood,* 255
Restaurant Maurice, New York, *French,* 294
Rheinlander Haus, San Diego, *German,* 363
The Rib Room, New Orleans, *Continental,* 255
The Right Bank, New York, *Continental,* 295
Ristorante da Gaetano, Philadelphia, *Northern Italian,* 312
Ristorante di Lullo, Philadelphia, *Northern Italian,* 313
Ristorante Orsi, San Francisco, *Italian,* 389
Ritz-Carlton Dining Room, Boston, *Continental,* 43
Rive Gauche, Washington, D.C., *French,* 419
The River Cafe, New York, *Continental,* 295
The Rivioli, Houston, *Continental,* 145
Rolf's Since 1960, San Francisco, *Austrian,* 390
Romeo Salta, New York, *Italian,* 295
Rosellini's Four-10, Seattle, *Continental,* 403
Rosellini's Other Place, Seattle, *French,* 404
Rosewood Room, Minneapolis/St. Paul, *Continental,* 241
The Royal Eagle, Detroit, *Polish,* 119
Rudi's, Houston, *Continental,* 145
Rue de Paris, Atlanta, *French,* 12
Ruggles, Houston, *Continental,* 145
Russian Tea Room, New York, *Russian,* 296
Ruth Chris Steakhouse, New Orleans, *American,* 255

S

Sage's on State, Chicago, *Seafood,* 65
Saigon Flavor, Los Angeles, *Vietnamese,* 207
St. Botolph, Boston, *Continental,* 43
St. Moritz, Los Angeles, *Continental,* 208
The Saloon, Los Angeles, *American,* 208
The Saloon, Philadelphia, *Italian,* 313
Salta in Bocca, New York, *Northern Italian,* 296
Sam's Grill, San Francisco, *Seafood,* 390
Sam Wilson's, Kansas City, *American,* 160
S & D Oyster Company, Dallas/Fort Worth, *Seafood,* 96
San Jacinto Inn, Houston, *Seafood,* 146
Sans Souci, Washington, D.C., *French,* 420
Savoy Grill, Kansas City, *Seafood,* 160
Sazerac, New Orleans, *French/Creole,* 256
Scandia, Los Angeles, *Scandinavian,* 208
Schneithorst's Hofamberg Inn, St Louis, *German/American,* 349
Scott's Seafood Grill & Bar, San Francisco, *Seafood,* 390
Sea Fare of the Aegean, New York, *Seafood,* 296
The Seashell, Los Angeles, *French/Seafood,* 209
Sgro's, Pittsburgh, *American,* 337
Shanghai Winter Garden, Los Angeles, *Chinese,* 209
Sheik Restaurant, Detroit, *Lebanese,* 120
Shezan, New York, *North Indian,* 297
Ships Tavern, Honolulu, *Seafood,* 134
Shun Lee Dynasty, New York, *Chinese,* 297
Sign of the Dove, New York, *Continental,* 297

Silvana's, Los Angeles, *Continental/Northern Italian,* 209
Simon's, Seattle, *Continental,* 404
Siva's, Philadelphia, *North Indian,* 313
Sky Room, San Diego, *Continental,* 364
Snoqualmie Falls Lodge, Seattle, *American,* 404
Soho Charcuterie & Restaurant, New York, *French,* 298
Sonny Byran's Smokehouse, Dallas/Fort Worth, *Barbecue,* 96
The Spanish Steps, Las Vegas, *American/Spanish,* 170
Sperte's Laffite, Denver, *Seafood,* 107
Spiro's, St. Louis, *Greek,* 349
Stall 1043, Baltimore, *French,* 26
Stanford & Sons, Kansas City, *American,* 161
Steffon's Gourmet Wizardry, Cleveland, *Continental,* 81
Stella of Boston, Boston, *Italian,* 44
Stephenson's Old Apple Farm, Kansas City, *American,* 161
Stratton's, Los Angeles, *Continental,* 210
Studio Grill, Los Angeles, *Continental,* 210
Su Casa, Chicago, *Mexican,* 66
Su Casa, San Diego, *Mexican,* 364
Sultan's Table, Las Vegas, *Continental,* 171
Sun Dial, Atlanta, *Continental,* 12
Sweetwater, Chicago, *American,* 66
Swiss Chalet, Houston, *Swiss/German,* 146
Swiss Echo, Los Angeles, *Swiss,* 210

T

Tadich Grill, San Francisco, *Seafood,* 391
Taiga, Minneapolis/St. Paul, *Chinese,* 241
Tango, Chicago, *Seafood,* 66
Tante Louise, Denver, *Continental,* 107
The Tavern of Richfield, Cleveland, *American,* 81
Tavern on the Green, New York, *Continental,* 298
Tell Erhardt's, Philadelphia, *Continental,* 314
Tenderloin Room, St. Louis, *American,* 349
Ten Downing, San Diego, *Continental,* 364
That Place on Bellflower, Cleveland, *French,* 81
Theatrical Restaurant, Cleveland, *American,* 82
Thee Bungalow, San Diego, *Continental,* 365
Third Floor, Honolulu, *Continental,* 134
Thirteen Coins, Seattle, *Italian/American,* 405
Thompson's Sea Girt House, Baltimore, *Seafood,* 26
A Thousand Cranes, Los Angeles, *Japanese,* 211
Tiberio, Washington, D.C., *Northern Italian,* 420
Tio Pepe, Baltimore, *Spanish,* 27
Tokyo Gardens, Houston, *Japanese,* 146
Tom Ham's Lighthouse, San Diego, *Seafood,* 365
Tom Jones, Baltimore, *Continental,* 27
Tony Angello's, New Orleans, *Italian,* 256
Tony's, Houston, *Continental,* 147
Tony's, St. Louis, *Italian,* 350
Top of the Crown, Kansas City, *Continental,* 161
Top of the Triangle, Pittsburgh, *American,* 337
Top o' the Cove, San Diego, *Continental,* 365
Toulouse, Atlanta, *French,* 13
The Tower, Los Angeles, *French,* 211
Tower Garden & Restaurant, Chicago, *French,* 67
Trader Vic's, Los Angeles, *Polynesian,* 211
Trader Vic's, Phoenix, *Polynesian,* 326
Trader Vic's, San Francisco, *Polynesian,* 391
Trader Vic's, Seattle, *Polynesian,* 405
Trattoria, Honolulu, *Italian,* 134
Trattoria da Alfredo, New York, *Italian,* 298

Trois Amis, Phoenix, *French,* 326
Trudie Ball's Empress, Washington, D.C., *Chinese,* 420
Truffles, Chicago, *Continental,* 67
Trumps, Los Angeles, *International/Eclectic,* 212
Turn of the Century, Denver, *American,* 108
Tweeny's Cafe, Detroit, *International,* 120
"21" Club, New York, *American,* 299
The Two Continents, Washington, D.C., *Continental,* 421

U

Uncle Tai's Hunan Yuan, Houston, *Chinese,* 147
Uncle Tai's Hunan Yuan, New York, *Chinese,* 299
The Union Oyster House, Boston, *Seafood,* 44

V

Valentino, Los Angeles, *Italian,* 212
Vanessi's, San Francisco, *Italian,* 391
Verita's La Cantina, Los Angeles, *Mexican,* 212
The Versailles, New Orleans, *French,* 256
Victor's, San Francisco, *French,* 392
Vienna '79, New York, *Austrian/Continental,* 299
Vineyard, Las Vegas, *Italian,* 171
Vineyards, Detroit, *Continental/Seafood,* 120
Vinton's, Miami, *Continental,* 228
Visko's, New Orleans, *Seafood,* 257
Vittorio's, Atlanta, *Italian/American,* 13
The Voyagers, Boston, *Continental,* 44

W

Wagon Wheel, Cleveland, *French,* 82
Wally's Desert Turtle, Palm Springs, *Continental,* 216
Washington Palm, Washington, D.C., *American,* 421
Wellshire Inn, Denver, *International,* 108
The Wharf, Seattle, *Seafood,* 405
Whiffenpoof, Miami, *Continental,* 228
The White House, Minneapolis/St. Paul, *International,* 241
Wildflowers, Philadelphia, *Continental,* 314
The Willows, Honolulu, *International,* 135
Willy Coln's, New Orleans, *Continental,* 257
Windows on the World, New York, *American/International,* 300
The Windsor, Los Angeles, *Continental,* 213
The Wine Cellar, Minneapolis/St. Paul, *Continental,* 242
Win Schuler's, Detroit, *American,* 121
Winston's, New Orleans, *French,* 257
Wo Fat, Honolulu, *Chinese,* 135
The Wooden Angel, Pittsburgh, *American,* 338

Y

Yamashiro, Los Angeles, *Japanese,* 213
Yamato, Los Angeles, *Japanese,* 213
Yamato Sukiyaki House, San Francisco, *Japanese,* 392
Yellow Fingers, Los Angeles, *French,* 214
Yen Ching, St. Louis, *Chinese,* 350

Z

Zachary's, Boston, *Continental,* 45
Zapata's, New York, *Mexican,* 300

Bon Appétit Magazine's Guide to AMERICA'S BEST RESTAURANTS

What a Great Gift Idea!

How many times have you heard your friends or associates say that they needed to find the perfect restaurant for that special occasion? With BON APPETIT'S Guide to America's Best Restaurants, everything they need to know is at their fingertips. This handy guide to the nation's best restaurants is perfect for anyone who eats out, whether for business or pleasure. And with the readers of BON APPETIT making the restaurant selections, your friends can be sure of finding unique and excellent restaurants in every city included in the guide.

So, don't you think your friends deserve the best too! Why not give the gift that is sure to please—the BON APPETIT Restaurant Guide. This guide is available to you at just $7.95 each, plus $1 shipping and handling. (California residents add 6% sales tax.) (#00187). Or—if you order 10 or more Restaurant Guides, the price is just $6.25 each (over 20% discount), plus $1 shipping and handling. (California residents add 6% sales tax.) (#00198)

Please send all orders to: BON APPETIT Restaurant Guide, Dept. MG91 c/o Wilshire Marketing Corporation, 8460 Higuera St., Culver City, CA 90230. Credit Card Holders CALL TOLL FREE 800-421-4448 Mon-Fri 7am to 7pm, Sat 7am to 1pm, Pacific Time. In Calif. call 800-252-2071.

Bon Appétit
Restaurant Reviewer

Be Your Own Restaurant Critic!

Every time you discover a new favorite restaurant—take note for future reference in the BON APPETIT Restaurant Reviewer.

You're the critic as you create your own personal book of dining experiences. Keep it handy and you'll never have to wonder where to eat again!

The BON APPETIT Restaurant Reviewer includes an index by cuisine to categorize every restaurant according to its specialty. Plus there's a personal evaluation section, a phone/address section and a diner's dictionary with complete ordering information in four languages.

Compact enough to fit into briefcase, pocket, purse or glove compartment so that you may write anywhere, anytime. It's the perfect travel companion and a unique gift for the gourmet and those who entertain out.

The BON APPETIT Restaurant Reviewer is the perfect companion for your BON APPETIT Restaurant Guide—so why not order it today and be prepared for your next dining experience. The Restaurant Reviewer is available for only $12.95, plus $1.25 shipping and handling. (California residents add 6% sales tax.) (#04105)

Please send all orders to: BON APPETIT Restaurant Reviewer, Dept. MJ91 c/o Wilshire Marketing Corporation, 8460 Higuera St., Culver City, CA 90230. Credit Card Holders CALL TOLL FREE 800-421-4448 Mon-Fri 7am to 7pm, Sat 7am to 1pm, Pacific Time. In Calif. call 800-252-2071.